MW01490842

THE EDWARDS COMMENTARY
on the
DOCTRINE AND COVENANTS

THE EDWARDS COMMENTARY
ON THE
DOCTRINE AND COVENANTS

By F. Henry Edwards

An introduction to the Book of
Doctrine and Covenants (Reorganized Church)
plus a brief historical treatment of each
section, stating the conditions under which
it was given, its import for the time it was
given, and its applications to the problems
and needs of the church today.

HERALD PUBLISHING HOUSE

Independence, Missouri

1986

COPYRIGHT © 1986
Herald Publishing House
Independence, Missouri

All rights in this book are reserved. No part of the text may be reproduced in any form without written permission of the publishers, except brief quotations used in connection with reviews in magazines or newspapers.

Library of Congress Cataloging in Publication Data

Edwards, Francis Henry, 1897 -
  The Edwards Commentary on the Doctrine and Covenants.

  "An introduction to the Book of Doctrine and Covenants (Reorganized Church) plus a brief historical treatment of each section, stating the conditions under which it was given, its import for the time it was given, and its application to the problems and needs of the church today."
  1. Reorganized Church of Jesus Christ of Latter Day Saints. Book of Doctrine and Covenants.   2. Smith, Joseph, 1805–1844. Doctrine and Covenants.   I. Title.
BX8628.E33   230'.9'3   77-7385
ISBN   0-8309-0187-6

Printed in the United States of America

FOREWORD

When my first *Commentary* was published in 1938 it was felt that a study of the historical background of the revelations in the book of Doctrine and Covenants was needed. In the six printings of the *Commentary* it was revised at a number of points, generally to bring it up-to-date, but the passage of time, the receipt of further guidance, and the development of emphases not covered hitherto have combined to advise the preparation and publication of this book.

Nearly a hundred and fifty years separate us from the times in which the earliest sections of the Doctrine and Covenants were given. We have forgotten, if we have ever known, many small but important details of church history which provide light for understanding the words of the prophets. This book attempts to provide some of the desired background, and to do so as faithfully as possible.

Assistance in the preparation of the original edition of this book (1938) was received from many sources, so many that individual mention of those contributing is impossible. But I am happy to acknowledge with my best thanks the informed and discerning criticism of the late Elder S. A. Burgess.

My thanks are also due my daughter-in-law, Nancy (Mrs. Lyman F.), whose review of the introductory section of the *Commentary* has been most helpful.

This edition differs from the earlier printings in three major respects: some biographical notes formerly included have been eliminated since they are now available in Church History Volumes 5, 6, 7, and 8; a considerable number of comments on the text have been added; and the book has been brought up-to-date.

F. Henry Edwards

DIVINE REVELATION

— I —

God seeks to make himself known to men. Indeed, we would never truly know him if he had not taken the initiative to reveal himself to us. Between "In the beginning God" with which the Bible begins, and "I am Alpha and Omega, the first and the last, the beginning and the end" with which it concludes a long history of God's dealings with men, the initiative is always with him. Nowhere in the Scriptures do we find men arriving at the fullness of the truth about God by themselves. On the contrary, all the spiritual giants we come to know in the Scriptures have a sense of having been guided into understanding. Man after man comes before us with an unshakable inner conviction that he has been sought out and found by God. Everywhere it is God who is the great Doer. Men are but receivers.[1] There is deep significance in the wording of the ancient covenant which says: "I am the Lord thy God, which brought thee out of the land of Egypt, out of the house of bondage."[2]

God seeks to make himself known throughout all creation. As the Psalmist says, "The heavens declare the glory of God; and the firmament showeth his handiwork."[3] The Hebrews felt the wonder of creation so deeply that with them the call to proclaim God as Creator was often a call to worship.[4] Moreover, creation is not something accomplished long ago by a single word or act of Divinity. Creation is still going forward, and all life depends on the sustaining grace of God. By that fact it reveals his present concern.[5] Emil Brunner has put it this way:

The created world is not simply the world, but the world-from-God, the world in which God is present and operating.... There is no divine creation which is not as such also a divine manifestation and a divine presence at work.[6]

Our heavenly Father has also taken the initiative to make himself known to us in the nature of our own creation.

7

He has so fashioned us that it is instinctive for us to feel after him. This need to know God, and our capacity for knowing him, lie at the very core of personality. We may not recognize this need. Yet we are restless until it is satisfied. This is a mark of our greatness and the key to integrity. We find inner unity and peace and power as we fulfill the purpose of our creation under God.

— II —

That God has taken the initiative in making himself known is seen in the work of the prophets. According to their own uniform testimony, these men of God were called to their work. They did not call themselves. Indeed they could not. No human psychology can provide or explain their insight into the nature of God and what this demands of men in terms of mercy and justice and love. The truth declared by them is not something dreamed up or manufactured out of their prior understanding. It carries its own credentials, making its appeal from heart to heart, from soul to soul, and carrying conviction. The testimony of Jeremiah in this connection is typical:

I said, I will not make mention of him, nor speak anymore in his name. But his word was in mine heart as a burning fire shut up in my bones, and I was weary with forebearing, and I could not stay.[7]

We are apt to think of prophets as lonely men, living apart from their fellows, solitary and austere. There is some truth in this. Men of clear and high vision tend to be set apart by that vision. But this is not the complete picture. Behind the prophet, those with eyes to see can generally discern others who have not bowed to Baal.[8] The word of God came to John in the wilderness, but there were others "just and devout, waiting for the consolation of Israel."[9] There is the direct inspiration of the prophets,[10] and there is this pervasive and supporting inspiration which prepares the way and builds up understanding. Both are evidences of divine concern.

8

Prophecy is a constant element in the biblical idea of revelation. In the second half of Isaiah, for example, strong emphasis is laid on the fact that prophecy is an indication and example of God's revealing and redeeming activity. Moreover, since Israel had been chosen as a means of blessing to all the nations of the earth,[11] the outreach of the message of the prophets is an indication of divine approach to every man. "Prophets were to Israel what, in God's purpose, Israel was to be to the whole world."[12]

— III —

Beyond any revelation of Divinity in creation or in the ministry of the prophets, is the further revelation in the life of our Lord Jesus Christ. This revelation is final in the sense that it can never be superseded. Jesus himself said, "He that hath seen me hath seen the Father."[13] We may come to understand the revelation of God in Christ more fully through the guidance of the Holy Spirit, but our growing understanding will always center in the Lord Jesus.

The incarnation was not an afterthought to meet an unforeseen emergency which developed in the course of human history. The coming of Jesus was planned before the beginning of time. "God so loved the world that he gave his Only Begotten Son."[14] Jesus came, by the will of the Father, to show beyond all question what is the breadth and length and depth and height of the love that sent him.[15] It was out of the grace and mercy of God that the whole scheme of redemption grew. God did not have to be perrsuaded or placated and he does not now have to be persuaded or placated. The initiative for our understanding and redemption has always been with God.

A few years ago, the Jewish scholar, Dr. Claude Montefiore, set himself to see whether there was anything quite new in the teaching of Jesus, anything which no prophet or rabbi had said before him. The one thing that Dr. Montefiore singled out as absolutely distinctive was the picture of the divine Shepherd going out into the wilderness to seek the lost sheep; the New Testament picture of God is not one of receiving those who return to him but of going out after those who have not sought him. That, says Dr. Montefiore, "is a new figure" and "one of the excellencies of the gospel."[16] This distinctively Christian emphasis on the divine initiative in revelation and redemption is experienced in many forms and particularly in stories like that of the woman seeking the lost coin,[17] and incidents like that concerning Zaccheus.[18] "Ye have not chosen me, but I have chosen you," said the Master.[19] It is not the sheep that find the shepherd but the shepherd that finds the sheep. His journey toward us is begun long before ours is begun toward him.

— IV —

All that has been said so far about the divine initiative in revelation and redemption now needs to be qualified. Most strictly speaking, the revelation of God is not in creation, nor in the words of the prophets, nor even in the life and teachings of the Lord Jesus Christ. Rather, it is in our perception of God at work in these events. There is no revelation in deeds or facts themselves, but only in understanding. But here, too, God has taken the initiative. Indeed, he does for us something that we could not possibly do for ourselves. He quickens knowledge within us. Elihu, the son of Barachel, expressed this for us long ago, "There is a spirit in man; and the inspiration of the Almighty giveth them understanding."[20]

If he is to reveal himself to us, our heavenly Father must persuade us to let him work within us, as well as around us. Thus though the evidences of his love and power may be all about, the ability to understand these evidences is reserved for men of goodwill; men in whose lives the Spirit of God causes them to recognize the work of God and the testimony of truth wherever these occur. Greater revelations of Divinity await our greater growth. Our Father has many things to say to us, but we cannot bear them until the time is ripe.

We should also take careful note that the ability to see and to understand the things of God is not an extraordinary faculty communicated to a man apart from what he is. This ability is related to man's entire self—his mind, his heart, his life—and is the finest fruitage of a personality reconciled to God. Jesus saves us and reconciles us to God in order that he may reveal God to us; and he reveals God to us as fully as we can now understand him, in order that we might be saved and reconciled in preparation for a greater revelation.

This progressive adaptation of the revelation of God to our capacity and experience is made necessary by our nature. We must proceed from where we are to where we want to go, and from what we already know to what we wish to understand. The immigrant coming to the United States does not see the full meaning of the American way of life all at once, but must grow in understanding. The truth which he learns soon after his arrival is not contradicted by the truths which he learns after many years; yet the significance of the first truth he perceives is modified as his experience is broadened. In like manner, it is not possible for God immediately to make known the secrets of his will to us when our lives have hitherto been shaped by sordid and uninspiring daily contacts. The first big change that God makes in revealing himself to us is to bring us from among aliens into the fellowship of his people. Then he gradually discloses the truth about himself and about his way of life for us; and as the revelation all around us is met by the growing understanding within, so we come to realize the truth, which has been awaiting our growth, but which we have not yet been ready to receive.

This spirit of enlightenment and truth is active, not passive. Holman Hunt has given us a moving picture of the Christ who stands without the door, knocking, and waiting for the door to be opened from within. But,

11

moving as the picture is, Jesus is likely to stay outside the door until his Spirit penetrates the soul of the householder. The full glory of God is not only that he knocks from without but that he also enlightens and persuades from within.

This persuasion precedes all our responses, and persists with unabated invitation:

Whither shall I go from thy Spirit? or whither shall I flee from thy presence? If I ascend up into heaven, thou art there; if I make my bed in hell, behold, thou art there. If I take the wings of the morning, and dwell in the uttermost parts of the sea; even there shall thy hand lead me, and thy right hand shall hold me. If I say, Surely the darkness shall cover me; even the night shall be light about me. Yea, the darkness hideth not from thee; but the night shineth as the day; the darkness and the light are both alike to thee.[21]

The New Testament Christians had a deep sense of indebtedness for the revelation of God without and within. "It pleased God to reveal his Son in me," writes the apostle Paul.[22] John says, "Of his fullness have we all received."[23] Peter says, "Grace and peace be multiplied unto you through the knowledge of God, and of Jesus our Lord, according as his divine power hath given unto us all things that pertain into life and godliness, through the knowledge of him that hath called us to glory and virtue."[24]

— V —

God takes the initiative in revealing himself, but he takes his own time and awaits his own occasions. The revelation which came to Isaiah in the year that King Uzziah died was not given to him until the loss of his king had opened his eyes to his need for God.[25] Peter, James, and John were not given the transfiguration experience until the appropriate time arrived.[26] Jesus had many things to say to the Twelve, but they must wait for the ministry of the Spirit which would guide them into all truth.[27]

The revelation of the Father is never complete. Always it is geared to our capacity and concern, and always it promises more than it gives. Even though a man who has had experience with God should use the same words to express that experience as he did ten years ago, nevertheless—if he has lived with his experience—he now puts more meaning into the words he uses than ever he did before. The explanation which Peter gave the elders at Jerusalem after baptizing Cornelius will serve to illustrate this. Peter told the brethren of his vision, of the welcome given him by Cornelius, of his preaching, and of the endowment received by the household of Cornelius. Then he said: "Then remembered I the word of the Lord."[28] That was true. But Peter "remembered" in light of his intervening experience. The words of the Lord had new meaning for him now that he had grown to the point of better understanding.[29]

We are sometimes impatient and rebellious when it seems that God is hiding himself.[30] Instead, we should be deeply grateful, for if the full splendor of his glory should break in on us, who could stand? Would we not all be like the priests at the dedication of the temple of Solomon?[31] Instead of rebellion and denial, our failure to see should cause us to review the quality of our seeking. He cannot be known with the intellect alone, nor in joy alone, nor by the man who seeks by himself. The search demands heart, soul, mind, and strength.[32] There is revelation in the darkness as well as in the light.[33] And here, possibly more than anywhere else, every man needs the help of his brother, of the present age and of ages long past.

— VI —

The responsive element in revelation is clearly stated in the preface to the Doctrine and Covenants: ". . . he that repents not, from him shall be taken even the light which he has received, for my Spirit shall not always strive with man. . . ."[34] This response is not only the attempt to understand but the eagerness to be transformed by what we come to understand. It is failure to repent, not just failure to think, which leads to loss of light previously enjoyed.

13

Men of God in every age have taken very seriously the failure to live by light already received. Paul makes his own concern very clear in the statement which emphasizes the love of the Father for us and the responsibility which ensues therefrom. In his letter to the saints in Galatia, he said: "But now, after that ye have known God, or rather are known of God, how turn ye again to the weak and beggarly elements, whereunto ye desire again to be in bondage?. . . I am afraid for you."[35]

It is this response to the overtures of Divinity which gives individual significance to what God has done for every man, and at the same time joins together those who are called into the fellowship of believers. Every man needs to know God for himself. This knowledge grows in him as he diligently seeks God.[36] He needs the companionship which assures him that he is not following "cunningly devised fables."[37] This he finds in the testimony of men of like devotion and parallel experience.

[1]H. R. Mackintosh, *The Divine Initiative,* Student Christian Movement, London, p. 45. [2]Exodus 20:2. [3]Psalm 19:1. [4]Psalms 95:1-7; 104. [5]Psalm 104:30. [6]*Man in Revolt,* p. 91. [7]Jeremiah 20:9. [8]I Kings 19:18; Romans 11:1-5. [9]Luke 3:2; 2:25. [10]Amos 3:7. [11]Genesis 22:23; 26:4. [12]John Baillie, *The Christian Apprehension of God,* Scribners. [13]John 14:9. [14]John 3:16. [15]Ephesians 3:18. [16]See D.M. Baillie, *God in Christ,* Faber and Faber, London, p. 63. [17]Luke 15:8. [18]Luke 19:5. [19]John 15:16. [20]Job 32:8. [21]Psalm 139:7-12. [22]Galatians 1:15. [23]John 1:16. [24]II Peter 1:2, 3. [25]Isaiah 6:1. [26]Matthew 17:1-8. [27]John 16:12, 13. [28]Acts 11:16. [29]Acts 15:6-11. [30]Isaiah 45:15. [31]I Kings 8:11; Malachi 3:2. [32]Mark 12:35. [33]Psalm 139:12; Micah 7:8; II Corinthians 4:16; Isaiah 29:18. [34]D. and C. 1:5g. [35]Galatians 4:9, 11. [36]Hebrews 11:6. [37]II Peter 1:16.

REVELATION AND ITS RECORD

— I —

Revelation is a spiritual experience. It involves perception of what was not seen before and this perception is possible only because of the spiritual endowment of the perceiver.

What we see with our eyes, or hear with our ears, or feel with our hands may provide the material for new understanding. Understanding arises from within, but our hearts, our minds, our conscience are in all of these together.

In the ordinary affairs of daily life we interpret as we go along what comes to us by way of our five senses, and we do this without undue difficulty. But on the professional level the doctor, for example, studies for years to learn the meaning of what his special instruments enable him to see. When the doctor tries to explain what his examination has disclosed he finds that when he is pushing into new areas of understanding he can do this successfully only in conversation with another doctor. He must explain as they look together.

On the spiritual level revelation is even more demanding and more personal. Here understanding cannot be conveyed in words but is gained only in experience guided by the Spirit of God. It is not reserved for the wise and prudent, but is granted to dedicated disciples. Jesus prayed: "I thank thee, O Father, Lord of heaven and earth, because thou hast hid these things from the wise and prudent, and hast revealed them unto babes."[1] The apostle Paul wrote:

Eye hath not seen, nor ear heard, neither have entered into the heart of man, the things which God hath prepared for them that love him. But God hath revealed them unto us by his Spirit.[2]

— II —

In light of the foregoing we might say that revelation cannot be recorded but can only be experienced—and in one sense this is entirely true. What is revealed can never be fully expressed in words for it loses something in the telling. When we say, for example, that God is holy, we may convey something which is of major importance, but we have not conveyed all that we would like to impart. The fullness of divine holiness extends beyond

15

the realms language can reach.

Thus, when we think of what is involved in making a record of revelation it becomes evident that something more is involved than we can supply. This does not mean that no record of revelation should be made. It does mean that any such record must be made under the guidance of light and truth greater than our own: the light and truth of the Spirit of God. It means, moreover, that what is recorded will not transmit in its fullness the experience with which it deals except as the record is read under the enlightment and guidance of the Spirit which prompted it.

Men must work with God, guided by his Spirit, to open the windows of life, to perfect the record of truth, and to clear the channels of revelation in order that God may show new values in the word already written and may write more clearly than ever those new things which he now wishes to say to us. John Robinson was true to the very genius of Christianity when he declared to the Pilgrim Fathers that "the Lord hath yet more light and truth to break forth from his Word."

The attempt to find a static finality in religion has never succeeded. The "faith which was once delivered unto the saints"[3] has actually grown and developed, even while always remaining consistent with itself, as any faith must develop when it is directly related to growing experience in a changing world.

The Bible is "the word of God." But it is not the "last word." It is rather the "seminal word" out of which new apprehensions of truth spring up in the minds of men. Anyone who has tried to picture the beauty of the sunset, either in words or in color, and has realized how little this attempt can convey to one who has not himself seen the sunset, must know also how inadequate the mere record of revelation is to convey to men the spiritual essence of the presence of God. Paul had this in mind when he wrote that Christ

hath made us ministers of the new testament; not of the letter, but of the Spirit; for the letter killeth, but the Spirit giveth life. But if the ministration of death, written and engraven in stones, was glorious, so that the children of Israel could not steadfastly behold the face of Moses for the glory of his countenance; which glory was to be done away; how shall not the ministration of the Spirit be rather glorious?[4]

Revelation is one thing, and the record of revelation is another. The revelation of God has come to men by dreams, visions, meditation, and by unusual happenings in the quiet ongoing of daily life. But to record the truth thus received has involved the almost insurmountable problem of injecting spiritual significance into words which have become heavy and soiled in the commerce of human experience. The Scriptures fully recognize this peculiar difficulty of putting spiritual truths into earthly language. Thus Paul reminded the saints in Corinth,

What man knoweth the things of a man, save the spirit of man which is in him? even so the things of God knoweth no man, except he has the Spirit of God. Now we have received, not the spirit of the world, but the Spirit which is of God; that we might know the things that are freely given to us of God. Which things also we speak, not in the words which man's wisdom teacheth, but which the Holy Ghost teacheth; comparing spiritual things with spiritual. . . . We have the mind of Christ.[5]

— III —

The high point of revelation is that God is love; he is also the cause and center of all truth and goodness. In him resides all power. His thoughts are immeasurably higher than our thoughts. His righteousness is of a richer quality than our righteousness. No human imagination can plumb the depths or scale the heights of the provision which our Father has made for our good. Our ideas of what may be good for us may be mistakes, but nothing which is truly for our benefit is beyond his will or his power to provide.

It is difficult for us truly to believe what has just been stated. We have dwelt so long in the kingdoms of this world that we tend to think in minimums rather than in maximums. Slavery is in our blood. Yet in the kingdom of God it is a fundamental law that the Lord has decreed that the earth shall provide for his saints,[6] that it is the work and the glory of God to bring to pass the immortality and eternal life of man[7] and that "he that hath eternal life is rich."[8] We are most truly godlike as we expect great things of him, for we are no longer servants but friends. "Every good gift and every perfect gift is from above, and cometh down from the Father of lights, with whom is no variableness, neither shadow of turning."[9]

It is not "too good to believe" that our heavenly Father should speak to his children in these last days or that the record of his self-disclosures to men in this dispensation should be compiled for our instruction and guidance.

Revelation is one thing, and its record is another. But the record of the revelation of God becomes alive again as that record is studied by disciples in whom dwells the enlightening Spirit of God. We shall not be unduly concerned about the exact phrasing in which revelation is recorded, nor even when further light makes it possible to enrich this phrasing in the attempt to convey this further light. What is important is that the record shall prove the gateway to understanding, as it has to many thousands who have studied it under the guidance of the Holy Spirit.

— IV —

The Old Testament is a collection of legal, historical, and prophetic narratives, poems, sermons, etc., forming the cream of the religious literature of the children of Israel. The New Testament is a collection of missionary tracts, pastoral letters, prophetic writings, etc., written primarily for the early Christian church. The Book of Mormon is a collection of historical narratives and prophetic and sermonic writings designed primarily for the ancient inhabitants of America, but partly also for the instruction of those who should succeed them in this land.

The Doctrine and Covenants is a different type of book

18

from either the Bible or the Book of Mormon. It is a compilation of revelations, minutes, etc. Its problems are the problems of the modern world and modern Saints. It is therefore a valuable and instructive modern commentary on the other standard books and sheds light on the many problems which had not arisen or were not important in an earlier day, and are either passed by or hinted vaguely in the other standard books. It gives light, moreover, on matters which must have engaged the attention of New Testament and Book of Mormon Christians, but which were not discussed at length in their religious literature. Thus we find in the Doctrine and Covenants important instruction regarding the practice of stewardship in an industrial world, detailed instruction regarding the organic structure of the church, highly ethical teachings on slavery, war, and peace, etc.

The narrative form of the Bible and of the Book of Mormon gives these books an interest and a human appeal which the Doctrine and Covenants can never have. Yet the Doctrine and Covenants has the tremendous advantage of dealing with specific spiritual problems of our time, and behind each of the revelations there is a situation in the life of some person or of the church. By studying each section against its appropriate background we will find that these have an interest rivaling their importance, and that the Doctrine and Covenants is not merely a set of precepts but a compilation of living documents having to do with living needs.

The Doctrine and Covenants is avowedly an unfinished book. Members of the committee first appointed to compile the revelations were ordained "to be stewards over the revelations and the commandments which I have given unto them, and which I shall hereafter give unto them."[10] It was in harmony with this that the general conference passed a resolution September 13, 1878, stating:

This body...recognizes...the revelations of God contained in the book of Doctrine and Covenants and all other revelations which have been or shall be revealed through God's appointed prophet, which have been or may be hereafter accepted by the church as the standard of authority on all matters and church government and doctrine....

The church expects that instruction will continue to be received from Divinity and will be embodied in the Doctrine and Covenants.

— V —

All the revelations included in the Doctrine and Covenants were given through the men who have occupied in the prophetic office in this dispensation, as follows:

Joseph Smith, Jr., (D and C. 1-98, 100-106, 108)	106
Joseph Smith III (D. and C. 114-122, 124-131)	17
Frederick M. Smith (D. and C. 132-138)	7
Israel A. Smith (D. and C. 139-144)	6
W. Wallace Smith (D. and C. 145-152)	9

This is not to say that all the inspired communications received through the presidents of the church are included in the Doctrine and Covenants. The prophecy on the Civil War, for example, has the same claim to be included as many other revelations received through the first president of the church, but for some reason it did not find a place in the 1835 edition and the Reorganized Church has never felt free to insert it. It has been included in editions issued by the Mormon church from 1876 onward.

The inclusion of the revelations received through the prophet-presidents of the church and approved by the church is in accord with the practice of the body, and this is based on the law given to the church in an early day:

"No one shall be appointed to receive commandments and revelations in this church excepting my servant Joseph Smith, Jr., for he receiveth them even as Moses; and thou shalt be obedient unto the things which I shall give unto him, even as Aaron, to declare faithfully the commandments and revelations, with power and authority unto the church."[11]

Other instruction has come to various individuals or groups within the church, and even to the church itself, through members of the priesthood, including members of the presidency, but no such instruction has been printed in the Doctrine and Covenants.[12]

Under special circumstances instruction received through men other than the president of the church has been extremely important, especially that given during the period of reorganization, 1852-60. For example a revelation received by Jason W. Briggs November 18, 1851, (Church History, Volume 3, pages 200, 201), was of outstanding importance to the Saints who had been scattered in the "dark and cloudy day." Its instructions were followed, and many of its promises have been fulfilled.

Another inspired communication which was important in determining the course of development of the Reorganization was received just prior to the conference of April, 1853. In accordance with this communication a majority of the Quorum of Twelve were chosen and ordained and initial steps were taken toward the reorganization of the church and priesthood.[13]

— VI —

The 1976 edition of the Doctrine and Covenants now contains:

One hundred and forty-five revelations.

Minutes of the organization of the Standing High Council of the church (99).

Our statement of belief regarding marriage (111).

Our statement of belief regarding governments and laws in general (112).

Former Section 107 (A).

Former Sections 109, 110 (B, C).

The statement concerning the deaths of Joseph and Hyrum Smith (D).

The minutes of the Lamoni Council of 1894 (E).

It has been noted that two out of three of these communications were received through the first president of the church. In this connection it may be noted that ninety-nine revelations received prior to 1834 have found place in the Doctrine and Covenants as compared with eight received during the period 1834-1844. The point of division between the period of frequent revelation and the period of infrequent revelation therefore falls about 1834. The reason is probably that the organization of the church was practically completed about this time since the High Council was organized in August 1834 and the Twelve and Seventy in February 1835. A further reason for this change in the frequency of the revelations is that the idea of modern revelation was new to the early Saints. It was one of the distinguishing marks of the church, and because of it the members of the church were constantly persecuted. These facts tended to make the Saints almost overeager to secure the mind of God on every problem. This tendency made it necessary for the Lord to remind them:

It is not meet that I should command in all things, for he that is compelled in all things, the same is a slothful and not a wise servant; wherefore he receiveth no reward. Verily I say, Men should be anxiously engaged in a good cause, and do many things of their own free will, and bring to pass much righteousness; for the power is in them, wherein they are agents unto themselves. And inasmuch as men do good, they shall in nowise lose their reward. But he that doeth not anything until he is commanded, and receiveth a commandment with doubtful heart, and keepeth it with slothfulness, the same is damned.[14]

There appear to be three outstanding reasons for the greater number of revelations received during earlier years. They are:

(1) One half of the revelations given through our first president are directed to individuals and contain more or less definite personal instruction. No communications addressed to individuals through any of the later prophets are included in the Doctrine and Covenants, although such communications have been received and have been recognized as inspired by the persons to whom they were addressed.

(2) A large number of the remaining revelations to the church are concerned with details of church government and organization. The early Saints had few precedents

to guide them in these matters, and such instruction was necessary at the beginning of the movement but did not need to be repeated. Having once been given, such communications as Sections 17, 42, 68, and 104 are available for all time.

(3) Practically all the other revelations are concerned with the enunciation and clarification of fundamental gospel principles, such as the laws and principles relating to Zion, stewardships, rewards and punishments. These were needed, but these, too, were given once for all and are available today even as they were in earlier years.

In spite of this explanation it will be obvious to those who think deeply regarding this problem that we need light on the solution of many important spiritual problems, and that such light is likely to be forthcoming only as the Saints move forward in unity to the accomplishment of the purposes entrusted to them by Divinity. It is to be expected that as we enter more fully into the practice of stewardship and the establishment of Zion the very fact of our progress will bring us to points along the way where we must have divine direction.

Without exception the communications given to the Reorganization are dated near to the times at which conferences have been held. This is due to the fact that our practice provides for the approval of all communications by the general conferences before they are accepted as law to the church. It is of interest to reflect on the effect of expecting revelation at conference time only, and on the changes which might result from a church-wide eagerness and preparation to receive the word of God at other times and under other circumstances. Practically every revelation received and accepted by the Reorganization has been given in answer to specific prayer and for the solution of specific problems.

— VII —

We need such a book as the Doctrine and Covenants to enrich our understanding of the Scriptures.

The New Testament does not give us a complete picture of the church in action. Nowhere is the structure of church government presented in clear outline, nor are the duties and mutual relations of the officers of the church clearly defined. Many hints are given; references are made from which it is possible to reconstruct a fairly complete picture of the apostolic church with its ministry, its basic teachings, its gifts and blessings, and something of the ethical standards of its people. There is need, however, for current inspiration to correct and to confirm and broaden our interpretation of the record and to fill in omitted parts whose presence is vital to an understanding of the whole. Again, there is need for inspired guidance in piloting the church through the uncharted seas of our modern industrial life, and for illumination regarding problems which have arisen in our attempt to apply the principles of the gospel in circumstances which are different from any which have previously existed.

The need of the world is the kingdom of God. This kingdom, however, is not merely the perfection of the kingdoms of this world. It is a new creation, born from above. It is inspired with the life of the Spirit and moves toward the accomplishment of its eternal destiny under the guidance of its heavenly king. If this is true—and the truth of the fact is becoming more apparent every day—then our imperative need for the kingdom of God is directly paralleled by an equally imperative need for spiritual enlightenment. Without this there is no hope that the kingdom can be built. Certainly such a book as the Doctrine and Covenants, which is so fully concerned with the coming of the kingdom, is needed at a time when men are becoming acutely conscious of the necessity for the kingdom but are at a loss to know how it shall be brought into being.

The doctrinal teachings of the book of Doctrine and Covenants are in full and rich accord with those of the other Standard Books of the church. The instructions on baptism,[15] eternal judgment,[16] life after death,[17] priesthood duties and responsibilities,[18] tithing,[19] and similar important matters are all sound and enlightening. Understanding of the doctrines elucidated in these revelations will not degrade men. Life lived in accord with them will make man Christian in the best sense.

The revelations contained in this book set a high moral standard. Consider, for example, the revelation on the basic law of the church received before the church was one year old, and before the young prophet was twenty-six years old.[20] Its teachings on such matters as integrity, marital fidelity, gossip, property rights and responsibilities, pride, cleanliness, and industry have not been excelled.

The Doctrine and Covenants makes an important contribution to our understanding by its emphasis on proper preparation and education. It is itself a witness to the necessity for inspired guidance, yet nowhere does the book put any premium on ignorance or prejudice or superstition. It affirms that "the glory of God is intelligence[21] and incites men to "seek learning by study, and also by faith."[22] Its emphases are on light and growth and progress, and it is admittedly best appreciated by people who are anxiously engaged in building the kingdom.

Most of all, the picture of Divinity presented in the book of Doctrine and Covenants is in accord with our best understanding of our heavenly Father. He is depicted at all times as a God of love and wisdom and power, passionately concerned that justice and equity and fraternity shall reign among men and that his people shall recognize their responsibility to him for using their gifts and talents in promoting righteousness. Every mention of the Father and of the Son shows them to be concerned in the building of the kingdom and in the salvation of the obedient. Moreover the Doctrine and Covenants definitely states that further understanding of the nature and purpose of God and his work among men is directly dependent on further spiritual progress on the part of the people. Teachings such as these do not come from any source other than Divinity. The forces of evil never prompted a would-be prophet to tell his disciples that "no one can assist in this work, except he shall be humble and full of love, having faith, hope, and charity, being temperate in all things whatsoever shall be intrusted to his care."[23]

Bishop Charles Gore, an outstanding Anglican prelate, said:

> It is impossible not to feel that men who exhibit a new power in life are thereby proved to have come into closer touch with reality, and if this new power appears as a direct consequence of theological beliefs the new power so far accredits the beliefs.

In the Restoration movement such a power was actually let loose on the world, and the early Saints attributed the presence of this power in their midst to the fact of divine guidance in their endeavors to build the kingdom of God. In matters of such public concern as slavery, war, education, and industrial relations the ethical standards of the Saints were far in advance of the standards of their times. When the ministers of those days were asked why they set such a high standard, they pointed to the book of Doctrine and Covenants and read therefrom the word of God. According to the test proposed by Dr. Gore, the facts of their lives accredit their belief.

A book which insists upon the necessity for divine endowment in order to do the work of the world effectively, which affirms the possibility of that endowment, and which bases the gift of the endowment upon the observance of fundamental physical and mental and spiritual principles of such a high quality is the kind of book which men ought to trust to influence their lives creatively. Such a book is the book of Doctrine and Covenants.

---

[1]Matthew 11:27. [2]I Corinthians 2:9, 10. [3]Jude 3. [4]II Corinthians 3:6-8. [5]I Corinthians 2:11-13, 16. [6]D. and C. 101:2. [7]Ibid. 22:23. [8]Ibid. 6:3c. [9]James 1:17. [10]D. and C. 70:1b. [11]Ibid. 27:2. [12]Ibid. 107:29d; 104:17; 46:1; 16:5g. [13]Church History 3:217, 218. [14]D. and C. 58:6. [15]D. and C. 16:6d; 17:7. [16]Ibid. 18:1, 2. [17]Ibid. 76. [18]Ibid. 104, 120-122. [19]Ibid. 106. [20]Ibid. 42. [21]Ibid. 90:6a. [22]Ibid. 85:36a. [23]Ibid. 11:4b.

PUBLISHING THE REVELATIONS*

— I —

The revelations given through Joseph Smith, Jr., both before the organization of the church and during the early months of its existence, were preserved and then Joseph Smith, Oliver Cowdery, and John Whitmer arranged and copied them. Further copies of the revelations were circulated to some extent, but it appears that this circulation was confined to a few members of the church. David Whitmer says that the revelations were kept secret, but this probably means that they were not made available to unbelievers.

In the revelation given July 1831,[1] Elder W. W. Phelps was called to act as printer to the church, and was instructed to set up his establishment at Independence, Missouri. On the way back to Kirtland after the dedication of the land of Zion, Joseph Smith, Sidney Rigdon, and Oliver Cowdery possibly called at Cincinnati and there made tentative gestures toward the purchase of a press and type. Soon after this, in September 1831, a conference was held in Ohio, and W. W. Phelps was instructed to go to Cincinnati and there purchase a press and type before proceeding to Independence, Missouri. On arrival in Independence he was to establish and publish *The Evening and the Morning Star*. This Elder Phelps did, and the first number of the *Star* was issued at Independence, Missouri, in June 1832. On the front page it carried what became Section 17 of the later editions of the Doctrine and Covenants under the title "Articles and Covenants of the Church of Christ."[2] The publication of the revelations continued in the

---

*The contents of this chapter are not greatly different from the first edition of this *Commentary* (1938). Details are as accurate as my information has permitted. However, the field is covered from a somewhat different angle in Richard Howard's very able *Restoration Scriptures* (1969) to which the student may wish to refer.

Star until the printing office was destroyed and the papers scattered July 20, 1833.

— II —

THE BOOK OF COMMANDMENTS

The first action taken by the church looking toward the printing of the revelations in book form was at a conference held at Hiram, Ohio, beginning November 1, 1831. Those present were Joseph Smith, Jr., Oliver Cowdery, David Whitmer, John Whitmer, Peter Whitmer, Jr., Sidney Rigdon, William E. McLellin, Orson Hyde, Luke Johnson, and Lyman E. Johnson.[3] At this conference the revelation known as the "Preface" was received. Certain items in addition to the covenants and commandments were also received at this time,[4] and instructions were given that Joseph Smith, Jr., Martin Harris, Oliver Cowdery, John Whitmer, Sidney Rigdon, and William W. Phelps should be appointed "stewards over the revelations and commandments which I have given unto them, and which I shall hereafter give unto them."

Oliver Cowdery and John Whitmer left almost immediately for Independence, carrying written copies of the revelations given to that date, but the originals remained at Kirtland with Joseph Smith. These copies had been made by John Whitmer and either Joseph Smith or Oliver Cowdery. The compilation of revelations was to be known as the Book of Commandments.

At a conference held May 1, 1832, at Independence, Missouri, the brethren decided to limit the first edition of the Book of Commandments to three thousand copies, and designated W. W. Phelps, Oliver Cowdery, and John Whitmer to supervise this publication. It was intended that the Book of Commandments should be a vest-pocket edition of the revelations of God to the church, and such a book was being printed in 32-mo, brevier type, when a mob destroyed the press, pied the type, and scattered

28

the printed material on the streets of Independence.

It is not likely that the mob was primarily concerned with the Book of Commandments, but came together in reaction to a front page editorial which had appeared in *The Evening and the Morning Star* and which was interpreted by some as inviting the free Negroes of the United States to gather at Independence.[5]

The following item from the May issue of *The Evening and Morning Star* for 1833 indicates the progress of the work of publishing the Book of Commandments at that time.

REVELATIONS

Having given, in a previous number, the Preface to the Book of Commandments now in press, we give below, the close, or as it has been called, the Appendix. It affords us joy to lay before the saints, an article frought with so much heavenly intelligence, having previously published many from the same book for their instruction.

We hope that while they read it, they will remember, that it is a voice from him who spake as never man spake. We hope that while they are blessed with revelation upon revelation, with commandment upon commandment, and with precept upon precept, they will remember to do them. We hope that while they are thus blessed with the precious word of their Lord from heaven, in these last days, to fulfill that which was spoken in days of old, they will hearken to his counsels and lend an ear to all his precepts.

Indeed it is a source of joy to us, to know, that all the prophecies and promises which are contained in them, which have not been fulfilled, will come to pass. The saints may lift up their heads and rejoice, for their redemption will soon be perfected. Soon the curtain of heaven will be unfolded, as a scroll is unfolded after it is rolled up, and they will see their Lord face to face. In view of these coming scenes, they may lift up their heads and rejoice, and praise his holy name, that they are permitted to live in the days when he returns to his people his everlasting covenant, to prepare them for his presence.

The book from which this important revelation is taken, will be published in the course of the present year, at from 25 to 50 cents a copy. We regret that in consequence of circumstances not within our control, this book will not be offered to our brethren as soon as was anticipated. We beg their forbearance, and solicit an interest in their prayers, promising to use our exertions with all our means to accomplish the work.

No later work was done on the Book of Commandments, but some of the sheets which had been printed were preserved and were subsequently bound by private individuals. It is also possible that a box of printed sheets had been previously dispatched to Kirtland for cloth binding since there was no bookbinder and no materials for binding on the frontier in Independence. Some of these may have been bound.

It is not now possible to determine the precise number of copies of the unfinished *Book of Commandments* which were put together and bound. Richard Howard estimates the number at "several hundred at least" and in support of this he mentions that a number of church leaders seemed to have them in their possession. If this was so, it is likely that they were assembled from the printed sheets sent to Kirtland. On the other hand William E. Berrett suggests that perhaps there were twenty copies preserved.[6] Dr. Berrett probably has reference to the number preserved in Independence.

Five forms of the book (160 pages) had been set and printed at the time of the catastrophe. The last words set were "the blood of Ephraim" in paragraph 47 of chapter (section) 65.

A portion of the copy used by Oliver Cowdery and W. W. Phelps from which the Book of Commandments was being set up, including the very sheet from which the last page was set, was preserved by Oliver Cowdery and passed from him at his death in 1850 into the custody of David Whitmer, his brother-in-law, and from the Whitmer heirs to Joseph Smith III in 1903, together with the manuscript of the Book of Mormon and the John Whitmer manuscript "History of the Church," and other papers.

When the Book of Commandments was printed, a federal act of February 3, 1831, required the filing of title with the clerk of the United States District Court and then after publication and within a limited number of months copies had to be filed. The title page of the Book of Commandments was accordingly filed for copyright

February 13, 1833, and it was expected that the book would be filed later as in the case of the Book of Mormon.

The title page of the Book of Commandments was like this:

A
BOOK
of
COMMANDMENTS,
FOR THE GOVERNMENT OF THE
CHURCH OF CHRIST,
Organized According to Law, on the
6th of April, 1830

ZION:
Published by W. W. Phelps & Co.

* * * * * *

1833

The last chapter of the Book of Commandments is dated September, 1831. Some of the revelations given between this date and the time when the press was destroyed had already been published in *The Evening and the Morning Star* but were not in the Book of Commandments. If these had been added the Book of Commandments would have included up to Section 93 of the Doctrine and Covenants plus the appendix. The appendix had appeared in the May 1833 issue of *The Evening and the Morning Star* but was not printed in the Book of Commandments.

After the expulsion of the Saints from Jackson County, the publishing plant of the church was moved to Kirtland, Ohio, and there the incomplete volume of *The Evening and the Morning Star* was continued. The last number of the *Star* was issued in September 1834 and contained a prospectus for reprinting the first and second volumes. From this the following is quoted:

There are many typographical errors in both volumes, and especially

31

in the last, which we shall endeavor carefully to correct, as well as principles if we discover any. It is also proper for us to say that in the first 14 numbers, in the revelations, are many errors, typographical and others, occasioned by transcribing the manuscript, and as we shall have access to originals we shall endeavor to make proper corrections.[7]

The reissue of the *Star* commenced in January 1835. In an editorial in this issue, Oliver Cowdery, who had helped prepare the earlier issues, expressed his surprise at the many errors which had crept into the original:

On the revelations we merely say, that we were not a little surprised to find the previous print so different from the original. We have given them a careful comparison, assisted by individuals whose known integrity and ability is uncensurable. Thus saying we cast no reflections upon those who were intrusted with the responsibility of publishing them in Missouri, as our own labors were included in that important service to the church, and it was our unceasing endeavor to have them correspond with the copy furnished us. We believe they are now correct. If not in every word, at least in principle. For the special good of the church we have also added a few items from other revelations.[8]

There have been persons who have preferred to give credence to the Book of Commandments as against the book of Doctrine and Covenants. To do this is to deny the testimony of the various quorums of the church as presented in Doctrine and Covenants 108A, and this despite the testimony of the very men who had prepared and taken a leading part in publishing both books, Joseph Smith, Oliver Cowdery, and W. W. Phelps.

Reprints of the Book of Commandments were made in Salt Lake City, Utah, by the *Salt Lake Tribune* in 1884 and 1903. Reprints were also made by C. A. Wickes in Lamoni, Iowa, in 1903 and by Charles Putnam and Daniel MacGregor in Independence in 1926.

— III —

The second attempt to publish the revelations in book form was initiated at a conference held at Kirtland, Ohio, September 24, 1834. During this conference a meeting

of the high council was held with the First Presidency
of the church in charge, and the following action was
taken and was later approved by the conference:

The council then proceeded to appoint a committee to arrange
the items of the doctrine of Jesus Christ, for the government of the
Church of Latter Day Saints which church was organized on the
sixth of April, 1830. These items are to be taken from the Bible,
Book of Mormon, and the revelations which have been given to
the church up to this date, or shall be until such arrangements
are made.

The committee appointed consisted of Joseph Smith, Jr.,
through whom the revelations were given; Oliver Cowdery, a
member of the committee appointed by revelation in 1831
and intimately connected with the copying and earlier
publication of the revelations; Sidney Rigdon, who was also
a member of the early committee; and Frederick G.
Williams of the First Presidency. When the work of this
committee had been completed, a general assembly was
called at Kirtland August 17, 1835, to approve their
work. The minutes of this meeting are printed in the
Doctrine and Covenants as Section 108A.

At the time of the general assembly Joseph Smith and
Frederick G. Williams of the First Presidency were away
from Kirtland on a mission. They were fully informed of
what was happening, however, and joined with the other
two members of the committee of compilation in signing
the following testimony:[9]

To the members of the church of the Latter Day Saints:

Dear Brethren: We deem it to be unnecessary to entertain you
with a lengthy preface to the following volume, but merely to say that
it contains in short, the leading items of the religion which we have
professed to believe.

The first part of the book will be found to contain a series of
Lectures as delivered before a Theological class in this place, and in
consequence of their embracing the important doctrine of salvation,
we have arranged them into the following work.

The second part contains items or principles for the regulation of
the church, as taken from the revelations which have been given since
its organization, as well as from former ones.

There may be an aversion in the minds of some against receiving
anything purporting to be articles of religious faith, in consequence of

there being so many now extant; but if men believe a system, and profess that it as given by inspiration, certainly, the more intelligibly they can present it, the better. It does not make a principle untrue to print it, neither does it make it true not to print it.

The church viewing this subject to be of importance, appointed, through their servants and delegates the High Council, your servants to select and compile this work. Several reasons might be adduced in favor of this move of the Council, but we only add a few words. They knew that the church was evil spoken of in many places—its faith and belief misrepresented, and the way of truth thus subverted. By some it was represented as disbelieving the Bible, by others as being an enemy to all good order and uprightness, and by others as being injurious to the peace of all governments civil and political.

We have, therefore, endeavored to present, though in few words, our belief, and when we say this, humbly trust, the faith and principles of this society as a body.

We do not present this little volume with any other expectation than that we are to be called to answer to every principle advanced, in that day when the secrets of all hearts will be revealed, and the reward of every man's labor be given him.

With sentiments of esteem and sincere respect, we subscribe ourselves,
Your brethren in the bonds of the gospel of our Lord Jesus Christ,

> Joseph Smith, Jr.,
> Oliver Cowdery,
> Sidney Rigdon,
> F. G. Williams.

Kirtland, Ohio, February 17, 1835.

The members of the Twelve also were away from Kirtland at this time, but they, too, were informed of what was being done. Their written testimony appears in Doctrine and Covenants 108A:5. The names of the members of the Twelve were not appended. All of these apostles had been selected the preceding February and it was customary to list them, where necessary, in the order of their seniority. They were

Thomas B. Marsh	Parley P. Pratt
David W. Patten	Luke S. Johnson
Brigham Young	William Smith
Heber C. Kimball	Orson Pratt
Orson Hyde	John F. Boynton
William E. McLellin	Lyman E. Johnson

A further testimony giving light on the attitude of the early men toward the revelations is that of John Whitmer, historian of the church and intimately connected with both the Book of Commandments and the Doctrine and Covenants. In his "Address when leaving the editorial chair of the *Messenger and Advocate,*" in March, 1836, after bearing testimony to the Book of Mormon he adds:

I would do injustice to my own feeling if I did not here notice still further the work of the Lord in these last days: The revelations and commandments given to us are, in my estimation, equally true with the *Book of Mormon,* and equally necessary for salvation. It is necessary to live by every word that proceedeth from the mouth of God: and I know that the Bible, *Book of Mormon,* and book of *Doctrine and Covenants* of the Church of Christ of Latter Day Saints, contain the revealed will of heaven. I further know that God will continue to reveal himself to his church and people, until he has gathered his elect into his fold, and prepared them to dwell in his presence.[10]

— IV —

The first (1835) edition of the book of Doctrine and Covenants was divided into two sections: "Seven Lectures on Faith," delivered before the Kirtland class in theology during the winter of 1834, and the Covenants and Commandments. The section on Covenants and Commandments contained the Preface, ninety-eight other sections, the Appendix (it was Section 100, but now is Section 108), articles on "Marriage," and on "Governments and Laws in General," and the minutes of the general assembly at which the book was accepted.

The stated purpose of the committee was to arrange "items of doctrine of Jesus Christ for the government of his church." This led them to arrange the revelations following the "Preface" so that those related to church order and government came first:

1. On Church Government (17)
2. Priesthood—Quorums (104)
3. Lineal Priesthood (83)
4. The Standing High Council (99)
5. Priesthood, etc. (84)

The title page of the 1835 edition of the Doctrine and Covenants was as below:

Doctrine and Covenants
of
The Church of the
LATTER DAY SAINTS
Carefully Selected
FROM THE REVELATIONS OF GOD,
And Compiled By
JOSEPH SMITH Junior
OLIVER COWDERY,
SIDNEY RIGDON,
FREDERICK G. WILLIAMS
Presiding Elders of said Church
PROPRIETORS.

KIRTLAND, OHIO
Printed by F. G. W   iams & Co.
For the
Proprietors
*   *   *   *   *   *

1835

The second edition of the Doctrine and Covenants was issued about September 1844 from Nauvoo, Illinois, by John Taylor, a member of the Quorum of Twelve who was editor of the *Times and Seasons*. It was published under the copyright of Joseph Smith, Jr., 1835. Here is the title page:

THE
DOCTRINE AND COVENANTS
of
THE CHURCH OF JESUS CHRIST
of
LATTER DAY SAINTS:
Carefully selected from the Revelations of God.
BY JOSEPH SMITH,
PRESIDENT OF SAID CHURCH.

SECOND EDITION.
Nauvoo, Ill.

Printed by John Taylor

1844

This edition of the Doctrine and Covenants included the same material as the 1835 edition plus the following:

Revelation received following the persecutions in Zion, February 1834 (100); revelation on the redemption of Zion given June 1834 (102); revelation to T. B. Marsh, president of the Twelve, concerning the calling of the Twelve, given at Kirtland, Ohio, July, 1837 (105); revelation on tithing given at Far West, Missouri, July 1838 (106); revelation concerning the temple at Nauvoo, the ministry of leading offices, etc., given at Nauvoo, Illinois, January 1841 (now Appendix A); two letters written by Joseph Smith, September 1 and 6, 1842 (now Appendices B and C); statement on "the martyrdom of Joseph and Hyrum Smith" (113).

The minutes of the general assembly of 1835 and the alphabetical index were omitted from this edition. The third and fourth American editions were issued in 1845 and 1846 respectively and were practically identical to the second edition.

The first European edition was published in Liverpool, England, under the authority of Wilford Woodruff. It appeared in 1845 and followed the second American edition closely. Many other English language editions have appeared down the years and have been supplemented by translations into other languages, mostly by the Church of Jesus Christ in Salt Lake City. These include the Welsh, Danish, Swedish, Dutch, Hawaiian, Maori, Armenian, Spanish, Portuguese, Finnish, Japanese, Norwegian, Kongan, Samoan, Italian, Tahitian, and Korean.[11] In 1944 translations, but not publications, were available in Bulgarian, Chinese, Icelandic, Russian and Hungarian.

The *Utah edition* of the Doctrine and Covenants published in 1876 is noteworthy in that it included the revelation on the Civil War, but not the section on marriage which had been adopted in 1835. It also included a number of other sections among which was the document on celestial marriage[12] dated July 12, 1843. The later versions of the Doctrine and Covenants published by the Utah church followed this format until 1921. An edition of the Doctrine and Covenants issued by the Mormon church in 1921 included "The Manifesto" issued in 1890 by Wilford Woodruff prohibiting the practice of polygamy. The document is not numbered as one of the sections of the book, nor is it divided into verses or defined as the will of the Lord. This edition omits the Lectures on Faith.

The first edition of the Doctrine and Covenants issued under the authority of the Reorganized Church was published in 1864 from Cincinnati, Ohio. The revelations were arranged in chronological order with the exception of the Preface and Appendix. Sections 22 and 36 appeared for the first time as part of the Book of Doctrine and

Covenants, although they had been printed during the lifetime of the Martyr.

Title page of the 1864 edition:

BOOK

of

DOCTRINE AND COVENANTS

of

The Church of Jesus Christ

of

LATTER - DAY SAINTS.

Carefully selected from the revelations of God, and given in the order of their dates.

CINCINNATI:

Printed By The Publishing Committee of The Reorganized Church of Jesus Christ of Latter-Day Saints.

1864.

The edition of 1880 was identical with that of 1864 except that it included also the revelations of 1861, 1863, and 1865. Their inclusion had been authorized at the semiannual general conference of the Reorganized Church held September 13, 1878, at which the following resolution was adopted:

Resolved, That this body, representing the Reorganized Church of Jesus Christ of Latter Day Saints, recognize the Holy Scriptures, the Book of Mormon, the revelations of God contained in the Book of Doctrine and Covenants, and all other revelations which have been or shall be revealed through God's appointed prophet, which have been or may be hereafter accepted by the Church as the standard of authority on all matters of church government and doctrine, and the final standard of reference on appeal in all controversies arising, or which may arise in this Church of Christ.[13]

Announcement of the publication of a "New Revised Edition" of the Doctrine and Covenants was made by the Board of Publication of the Reorganized Church in the *Saints' Herald* in 1897. The announcement stated:

The manuscript of this edition was carefully compared with the Authorized Edition of 1835, which was adopted by a General Assembly of the church at Kirtland, and known as the Kirtland edition. Some typographical errors that crept into and passed through later editions have been corrected, and some omissions supplied.

The revelation of the late Civil War, "minutes of the General Assembly of 1835," the minutes of the "Joint Council" 1894, and revelation given to the Reorganized Church, are all included in the volume. The "Lectures on Faith" are omitted, but may be published later in pamphlet form, for those who may want them.

The concordance has been revised and enlarged, greatly aiding study and general use of the book. The concordance, and lists of names, persons and places mentioned in the revelations, are included in the volume.

Ready reference to the books is greatly facilitated by the substitution of figures for the old style Roman letter in section and page heading. Figures can be read at a glance.

The 1952 "Enlarged and Improved edition of the Doctrine and Covenants," published by the Reorganized Church, is noteworthy in that its long paragraphs were divided, the subdivisions being marked a, b, c, etc., and its typographical errors had been corrected.

An "enlarged and improved edition" of the Doctrine and Covenants was published in 1970 from Independence, Missouri. This too was corrected as to typographical errors, etc. It contained an introduction which began with two paragraphs of historical material. This was followed by what had hitherto appeared as Section 108A. Following this came three concluding paragraphs as follows:

This present edition is so arranged that the items of uncertain

40

authority are included in a historical appendix and prefaced with
introductions explaining the circumstances of publication and the
reasons for placement in the appendix.

Those sections which make up the body of the book include only
those which were approved by the 1835 General Assembly or by a
General or World Conference of the church. The approval of the
format of this edition by 1970 World Conference specifically authorized
the retention of Sections 22, 36, 100, 102, 105, and 106 which had
appeared in earlier editions without Conference approval.

As a record of the revelations of God and statements of basic
doctrine based upon them, we present to the Saints and to the world
the Book of Doctrine and Covenants. May the Holy Spirit enlighten
all who study its content.

This was signed by the three members of the First
Presidency—W. Wallace Smith, Maurice L. Draper, and
Duane E. Couey.

The sections affected by the action of 1970 were Section
107 (Appendix A), 109 (B), 110 (C), 113 (D), and the
Joint Council minutes of 1894 which had been published
as Section 123 and now became Section E.

---

[1]D. and C. 57:5. [2]*Journal of History* 1:137. [3]*Ibid.* 68:2. [4]*Ibid.* 70:1. [5]*Ibid.*
64:7b. [6]William E. Berrett, *Teachings of the Doctrine and Covenants*, Deseret
Book Co. (1956), p. 74. [7]*The Evening and the Morning Star*, 2:384. [8]*Ibid.*
(reprint) 1:16. [9]Church History 1:578-9.[10]*Messenger and Advocate*, 2:287. [11]*Church
Almanac*, 1976:44, Deseret News. [12]Utah Doctrine and Covenants 132. [13]*Saints
Herald* 25:295-296.

— V —

THE LECTURES ON FAITH

The 1835 edition of the Doctrine and Covenants contains
seven lectures the first being headed:

THEOLOGY.

Lecture First

On the Doctrine of the Church of the

Latter Day Saints.

OF FAITH.

The preface to this edition stated:

The first part of the book will be found to contain a series of Lectures as delivered before a Theological class in this place [Kirtland, Ohio], and in consequence of their embracing the doctrine of salvation, we have arranged them into the following work.

The first five lectures were followed by questions which sought to call attention to the emphases made in the lectures. It was felt that no such questions were needed for the sixth and last lectures and they were omitted.

The lectures occupied pages 5 to 74, and the later section, containing the revelation, occupied pages 75 to 257.

The revelation of December 27, 1832, gave instructions for the establishment of the School of the Prophets which was evidently to be under the direction of the First Presidency.[1] Further instruction was given March 8, 1833.[2] This educational ministry was so important that it was to be available at the two major centers of church activity, Independence and Kirtland. The school at Independence was under the direction of Parley P. Pratt. About sixty of the elders met for instruction once a week, the place of meeting being under some tall trees in a retired place. Here the elders were greatly blessed. The revelation of August 2, 1833, commends Parley for his role in connection with this school.[3]

In Kirtland the School of the Prophets was organized in February 1833 and was continued until April. The expulsion of the Saints from Missouri in the fall of 1833 and the consequent burdens laid on the leaders and members of the church in Kirtland apparently prevented continuance of the school in Kirtland until November 1834. At that time Joseph Smith wrote:

It now being the last of the month, and the elders beginning to come in, it was necessary to make preparations for the school for the elders, wherein they might be more perfectly instructed in the great things of God, during the coming winter. A building for a printing office was nearly finished, and the lower story of this building was set apart for that purpose [the school] when it was completed.[4]

The *Millennial Star* reported for December 1, 1834:

Our school for the elders was now well attended, and with the lectures

42

on theology, which were regularly delivered, absorbed for the time being everything else of a temporal nature. The classes being mostly elders, gave the most studious attention to the all-important object of qualifying themselves, as messengers of Jesus Christ, to be ready to do his will in carrying glad tidings to all that would open their eyes, ears, and hearts.[5]

Concerning his further connection with preparation of the Lectures on Faith Joseph wrote:

During the month of January, I was engaged in the school of the elders, and in preparing the Lectures on theology for publication in the Book of Doctrine and Covenants, which the committee appointed last September were now compiling.[6]

The school closed the last week in March 1835.

There has been some concern regarding the omission of the Lectures on Faith from the Doctrine and Covenants since 1897.[7] The reason for this omission seems to be fairly clear. Some, and possibly all, of the lectures were delivered by Joseph Smith, and they were prepared for publication by him, so that it appears they received his approval or endorsement. But they were not held to be on the same level as the revelations. As John Smith said in the General Assembly at which the 1835 edition was approved, "the lectures were judiciously arranged and compiled, and were profitable for doctrine."[8] Their major value today is historical.

---

[1]D. and C. 85:39-44. [2]*Ibid.* 87:3, 5. [3]*Ibid.* 97:2b, c. [4]Church History 1:524, 525. [5]*Ibid.* 1:530. [6]*Ibid.* 1:539. [7]See Israel A. Smith in this connection, S. H. 100:579. [8]D. and C. 108:4d-e.

INTRODUCTION TO THE 1970 EDITION

Changes in the format of the Doctrine and Covenants led the First Presidency to insert an explanatory introduction to the edition of 1970. After the first paragraph of this introduction, which is covered in this *Commentary* as part of the story of the publication of the revelations, the Presidency included the text of what had previously appeared as Section 108A. This is concerned with the minutes of the General Assembly at which the 1835 edition of the Doctrine and Covenants was accepted.

To the foregoing was added a paragraph concerning the authority for the inclusion of the revelations subsequent to those appearing in the 1835 edition. The introduction also states the reasons for the transfer to appendices of what had previously appeared as Sections 107, 109, 110, 113, and 123.

SECTION 1

This revelation was given at the home of Father John Johnson in Hiram, Portage County, Ohio, November 1, 1831, during a conference at which the elders were considering the publication of the revelations in book form. If it appeared in its chronological position it would immediately precede Section 67.

Hiram is a small village situated about thirty miles from Kirtland, Ohio. It is of importance in church history because here a number of revelations were received, and here Joseph spent considerable time in the preparation of the Inspired Version of the Holy Scriptures. Here, also, several conferences were held, including one at which it was decided to issue the Book of Commandments.

No believer who has studied the Preface carefully as a whole and in relation to the other revelations ever thinks of changing it for a more suitable modern preface. It rightfully belongs at the beginning of any compilation of the revelations. Accordingly, although it was originally intended as a preface to the Book of Commandments, it has been published as the first section of every edition of the Doctrine and Covenants.

The opening paragraph is largely introductory and is addressed primarily to the members of the church, which was about nineteen months old at that time. This salutation is immediately broadened to include all men. The predominating note of this revelation, and, indeed, of many of the revelations through the Martyr, is one of warning.

"This is mine authority" (2a)*. The revelations contained in the book of Doctrine and Covenants are authoritative for the following reasons:

They were given of God.

They are true, and carry within themselves the evidence of their divinity.

They have been approved by the church.

The Lord has commanded their publication and commended them to the attention of the people.

"The wrath of God shall be poured out upon the wicked" (2d). Down the ages the prophets sent of God have all felt and proclaimed the deep reality of the wrath of God. "Wrath" as it is to be understood in this connection is vastly different from ill-temper. It means, rather, divine opposition to all that seeks to thwart the purpose of God in the creation of mankind. It exists always as a counterpart of the love of God, and if we are to understand either we must take the other into account. God hates iniquity just because he loves righteousness. His anger is controlled by his love, but is not dissipated by it as long as a cause for anger remains.

Consider the reasons given for the anger of the Lord, and note how natural is the sequence of apostasy here portrayed:

Men will not hear the voice of the Lord nor of his servants.

They have strayed from the ordinances of God.

They have broken his everlasting covenant.

They seek not the Lord to establish his righteousness.

Every man walketh in his own way and after the image of his own God.

"His sword is bathed in heaven" (3b). This is an expression from Isaiah 34:5, where "bathed in heaven" has been interpreted as "annointed in love." Consider in this connection, "behold therefore the goodness and severity of God" (Romans 11:22).

---

*The numbers in parentheses refer to the paragraph so numbered in the section being discussed.

"The image of his own god... whose substance is that of an idol" (3e). Men have built-in need to worship, but prefer to worship lesser gods fashioned according to their own desires. So we come to worship beauty or understanding or the country of our nativity, or wealth, or power, or prestige, and in giving them our heart's love we fall into the sin of idolatry. This is not to say that these are unimportant. They may well be means to the fulfillment of the purpose of God in us. But they should never be in command. "Thou shalt have no other gods before me" was spoken for all time.

"Proclaim these things unto the world" (4a). Here the missionary note is sounded again. Christianity refuses to be circumscribed. It reaches out, defying all bounds. Our faith does not need protection but proclamation. It was not devised that it might be hidden under a bushel but that it should be proclaimed from the housetops.

The reasons given in this paragraph for the coming forth of the Restoration movement are worthy of careful consideration. Note them:

To fulfill the prophecies
To vindicate the wisdom of God
To increase faith in the earth
To establish the everlasting covenant
To preach the gospel to the ends of the earth

"These commandments... were given unto my servants in their weakness, after the manner of their language" (5a). Even at this early date the young prophet was conscious of the limitations of language, for he had seen many things which could not be fully expressed in the words which he wrote down. This should be kept well in mind as we study the revelations in this book, for we shall find repeatedly that we cannot understand fully unless we enter into the spirit in which the revelations were received. Any attempt to interpret these revelations which does not give full weight to the boundless love of God and to his infinite concern for our well-being is certain to fall short of reality.

Here the Lord states that the purposes of the revelations were

To increase understanding

To correct errors

To instruct those seeking wisdom

To stimulate repentance

To strengthen the humble

To give power to translate the Book of Mormon

To authorize and inspire the foundation of the church and its development from obscurity toward its God-given destiny

"Bring it forth out of obscurity and out of darkness" (5e). This is a possible reference to the spiritual darkness which preceded the coming forth of the light of the gospel. It may also be regarded as a reference to the prophecy of John the Revelator[1] and a fulfillment of his further prophecy that an angel should fly "in the midst of heaven, having the everlasting gospel to preach unto them that dwell on the earth."[2]

"The only true and living church upon the face of the whole earth" (5e). There is direct connection between truth and life. Revelations which appear later in the volume, but which were given prior to this one, describe the word of God as being "quick and powerful, sharper than a two-edged sword." The church of Jesus Christ must preach a message of living truth. We may therefore say that a dead church cannot be the church of God. The church of Jesus Christ must live and do the work of the kingdom.

"My spirit shall not always strive with man" (5g). He who persistently refuses to exercise his spiritual powers soon discovers that his own neglect or his own willfullness has robbed him of these powers. An athlete who neglects training loses his standing, and in a similar way the man who neglects his spiritual training loses his spiritual health. Sometimes parasites look beautiful, but they are on the way to extinction.

"The day speedily cometh . . . when peace shall be taken

from the earth" (6b). This prophecy has been literally fulfilled in a way which Joseph Smith could not have anticipated, except by inspiration. The armed conflicts of this century have been the most terrible in history. The new industrial order which was beginning to come in a century ago has been accompanied by strikes, lockouts, industrial disasters, and many other disturbances. Race riots have been numerous. Destructions of nature are frequent and terrible. Quite literally, peace has been taken from the earth.

---

[1]Revelation 12:6. [2]*Ibid.* 14:6.

SECTION 2

Martin Harris acted as scribe for Joseph at Harmony, Pennsylvania, from April 12, 1828, to June 14, 1828, during which period one hundred and sixteen foolscap pages of the Book of Mormon manuscript were translated. His wife and others were opposed to his giving Joseph this help, and to quiet their ridicule he arranged with Joseph to show the manuscript to his father and mother, his brother, his wife, and a Mrs. Cobb, his wife's sister. In his zeal he showed the writings to more than these, and somehow the manuscript was taken from him and was never recovered.[1]

Joseph himself had exceeded instructions in permitting Martin to take the manuscript and to show it to others. Therefore, in the revelation given in Harmony, Susquehanna County, Pennsylvania, July 1828, both he and Martin were severely rebuked. The Urim and Thummim and the plates were taken from the young prophet, and were restored only after he had greatly humbled himself. The lesson learned at this time was nevertheless extremely valuable. Henceforth Joseph knew from experience that it is better to obey God than man.

48

"The works, and the designs, and the purposes of God, can not be frustrated" (1a). The difficulty referred to in the preceding paragraph had been anticipated, and the loss of the manuscript had been compensated in advance.[2] But the principle here stated is much more far-reaching than any specific application of it. Let us keep it well in mind. We have our agency, but our heavenly Father has his agency also, and he is much wiser than we are. It is hardly surprising, therefore, that he can bring his eternal purposes to pass no matter how we rebel individually or even as groups. The secret is not that our agency is overruled but that we are so fashioned that we turn to God naturally as a child turns to his parents.

"Although a man may have many revelations, and have power to do many mighty works, yet, if he boast in his own strength, and sets at naught the counsels of God, . . . he must fall" (2b). The truth of this statement has been repeatedly attested in the history of the church, both ancient and modern. Lucifer, the Son of the Morning, once dwelt in the majestic presence of Divinity, yet he fell and became the chief of the sons of perdition.[3] Judas Iscariot was once possessed of fine spiritual possibilities, yet he betrayed his Master. No man is safe except as he is humble and faithful.

"Thou art Joseph" (4a). The names of outstanding servants of God are sometimes quite significant. Abraham means "father of a multitude." Israel means "prince with God." John means "the gift of God." Peter means "a rock." Joseph means "he shall add."

A more significant interpretation of this statement is that Joseph is the prophet referred to in II Nephi 2:29. According to this prophecy, a descendant of the Joseph who was sold into Egyptian captivity would bring forth the word of God in the latter days, and this seer would be named Joseph, which would also be the name of his father.

"Thou wast chosen to do the work of the Lord" (4a). This may refer to the earlier vision of Joseph in which he was called to usher in this dispensation, but more probably it refers to his choice in the preexistent state; Isaiah,

49

Jeremiah, John,[4] and others were thus chosen.

"Thou shalt be delivered up and become as other men, and have no more gift" (4c). This seems to indicate that through Joseph's choice for this particular work he received additional gifts, not merely the supplementing of the gifts which were already his.

"For this very purpose are these plates preserved" (6c). This statement of the purpose of the Book of Mormon, which gives emphases to the salvation of the various tribal groups in America, should be considered in connection with the statement of Moroni found in the introduction of the Book of Mormon.

"Rely upon the merits of Jesus Christ" (6a). This phrase relates to an important aspect of the Atonement made possible through the sacrifice of the Lord Jesus Christ. The word "merits" was in frequent use in this connection among Christians of various denominations at the time this revelation was received and for many years afterward. It has not been abandoned by Christians of more recent decades as much as it has been superseded by other terms. The word does not appear in the New Testament.

BIOGRAPHICAL NOTE

Martin Harris (see also Doctrine and Covenants 3:15, 18; 52; 58; 70; 99) was born May 18, 1783, at East Town, Saratoga County, New York. He became one of the three witnesses of the Book of Mormon plates; paid for the printing of five thousand copies of the first edition; gave his services as proofreader, and paid his own expenses while traveling many hundreds of miles in the interests of the book. Brother Harris was baptized shortly after the organization of the church, was ordained a priest almost immediately, and a high priest on June 13, 1831. He served as a member of the first High Council at Kirtland from its organization in February 17, 1834, until September, 1837. He was one of the committee of three who selected the members of the first Quorum of Twelve and assisted in the ordination of those chosen. He lived in Kirtland until he was in his eighty-seventh year, when he was induced to go to Utah. Here he lived until his death in July 1875. He reaffirmed his testimony concerning the Book of Mormon whenever opportunity occurred.

[1]Church History, Volume 1, page 23. [2]Section 3:8, 9, 10. [3]Section 76:3. [4]Isaiah 49:5; Jeremiah 1:5; Section 83:4. [5]Jacob 1:10-14.

SECTION 3

When the hundred and sixteen pages of Book of Mormon manuscript were lost through the vacillation of Joseph and the carelessness of Martin Harris, the Urim and Thummim was taken away from Joseph. The revelation given during July or August 1828 in Harmony, Pennsylvania, records the conditions under which this sacred instrument was returned to him and the gift of translation recommitted to his care. It also explains the provision which had been made before time for meeting this emergency.

There are times when the Lord grants the unwise requests of his children in order that they may learn through their experiences that they are dependent on him for guidance in all things. For example, Israel demanded a king and, after warning the people of the consequences of their demand, the prophet of God consented.

Whatever may have been the purpose in permitting the theft of the manuscript of the early pages of the Book of Mormon it is not without its parallel in the Bible. A prophecy given by Jeremiah was burned by King Jehoiakim, and it was not only restored but was made more full. Here is the account:

Then took Jeremiah another 'roll, and gave it to Baruch the scribe, the son of Neriah; who wrote therein from the mouth of Jeremiah all the words of the book which Jehoiakim king of Judah had burned in the fire; and there were added besides unto them many like words.[1]

"By the means of the Urim and Thummim" (1a). This

51

phrase did not occur in the Book of Commandments version of this revelation, but was interpolated in the 1835 edition of the Doctrine and Covenants. The possible reason for this interpolation is ably discussed by Richard Howard[2] but leaves some uncertainty as to why the means used in the "translation" was now designated "Urim and Thummim" instead of its earlier designations as "spectacles," "interpreters," or "seer," and was sufficiently important for the interpolations to be made at all. If there was no sound reason for adding this information one wonders why it was made.

"You also lost your gift" (1b). Regarding this catastrophe Joseph later wrote:

> I commenced humbling myself in mighty prayer before the Lord, and, as I was pouring out my soul in supplication to God, that if possible, I might obtain mercy at his hands, and be forgiven of all that I had done contrary to his will, an angel stood before me, and answered me, saying, that I had sinned in delivering the manuscript into the hands of a wicked man, and, as I had ventured to become responsible for his faithfulness I would of necessity have to suffer the consequences of his indiscretion, and I must now give up the Urim and Thummim into his [the angel's] hands.
>
> This I did as I was directed, and as I handed them to him, he remarked, "If you are very humble and penitent, it may be you will receive them again; if so, it will be on the twenty-second of next September."
>
> After the angel left me, I continued my supplications to God, without cessation, and on the twenty-second of September I had the joy and satisfaction of again receiving the Urim and Thummim, with which I have again commenced translating, and Emma writes for me, but the angel said that the Lord would send me a scribe, and I trust his promise will be verified. The angel seemed pleased with me when he gave me back the Urim and Thummim, and he told me that the Lord loved me, for my faithfulness and humility.[3]

"Do not run faster, or labor more than you have strength and means. . . but be diligent unto the end" (1d). Even in so important a work as this the Lord required only a reasonable service of Joseph. This principle is basic and is reiterated many times in the course of the revelations.[4] The Lord is attempting to do a great work *in* his ministry as well as *through* his ministry, and the man who serves him with

diligence and with reasonable care for the Father's investment of health and understanding in him will serve far
more effectually than the man who works himself too hard
at spasmodic intervals but at other times forgets his
diligence.

The remainder of paragraph 1, the whole of paragraph 2,
and part of paragraph 3, together with the whole of
paragraphs 5 and 6, are given over to an explanation of the
device by which the enemies of Joseph expected to entrap
him. Briefly the position was this: The enemies of the Book
of Mormon had in their possession the original manuscript
of the first one hundred and sixteen pages of the translation,
and they were determined to overthrow the work which
Joseph was doing. If Joseph published an exact duplicate
of the first translation, these enemies would change the
manuscript in their hands and then claim that the dis-
crepancies showed fraud. If, on the other hand, the second
translation expressed the same thought as the first but in
slightly different language, the situation would be even
worse. In either case, the maze of explanations into which
Joseph would be plunged would submerge him and accomplish the designs of his enemies in spite of his innocence.
In such a dilemma the procedure followed by Joseph was
the only one which would relieve him of embarrassment
and yet preserve the record. He was told not to translate
the lost portion again, but to explain to those interested
that the content of the stolen manuscript is covered in
greater detail on the plates of Nephi. This he did.

Nephi left two records:

The larger plates of Nephi were made by Nephi shortly after
they left Jerusalem, and were handed down from one ruler (or Nephi)
to another, down to the days of Mosiah II, who delivered them to
Alma, and from him they were handed down the prophetic line,
and were finally deposited in the Hill Cumorah about A.D. 384. They
contained the civil history of the nation, from the time they left
Jerusalem until the Battle of Cumorah. Upon them Nephi inscribed the
history kept at first by his father Lehi. After the smaller plates were
full, about 160 B.C., in addition to the civil history, the ecclesiastical
history of the nation was also kept on these plates. It was from these

plates that Mormon made his abridged history.

The smaller plates of Nephi were made at the command of God by Nephi, thirty years after they left Jerusalem, and were handed down from one generation to another through the line of prophets, being last in the hands of Amaleki, who filled them and delivered them into the possession of King Benjamin, about 160 B.C.[5]

Mormon made his abridged history from the larger set of plates, and it was the forepart of this abridged history which was lost. In continuing the translation, Joseph substituted the extended account of the same transactions found on the smaller plates of Nephi which had been deposited by Mormon and Moroni with the other sacred records.

"They love darkness rather than light, because their deeds are evil" (3a). This is an application of John 3:19 to a specific situation, and emphasizes the fact that the doubts with which Joseph was being received were not always due to an honest examination of his testimony but, rather, to a stubborn refusal to see what they did not want to see. "Many," said Fenlon, "exaggerate their doubts to excuse themselves from action."[6]

"Their faith, that my gospel. . .might come unto their brethren, the Lamanites" (10). (See Enos 1:12-27.)

"If this generation harden not their hearts" (13a). Compare this with the following:

This Moses plainly taught to the children of Israel in the wilderness, and sought diligently to sanctify his people that they might behold the face of God; but they hardened their hearts, and could not endure his presence, therefore, the Lord, in his wrath (for his anger was kindled against them), swore that they should not enter into his rest.[7]

"Whosoever belongeth to my church need not fear, for such shall inherit the kingdom of heaven" (13b). Evidently "belongeth" has a stronger meaning than "has membership in." The thought here appears to be that salvation is to be found by the people of God among the people of God. It is not to be found by good men in isolation from their fellows, nor by bad men who have given merely formal obedience to the ordinances and sacraments involved in

54

membership. Salvation is for the saints—the doers of the word—within the kingdom.

"Other sheep have I which are not of this fold" (14c). This statement is illuminated in the words of the Master to his disciples of the Nephite Christian era on this land:

Verily, I say unto you, that ye are they of whom I said, "Other sheep I have which are not of this fold; them also I must bring, and they shall hear my voice, and there shall be one fold, and one shepherd."... And verily, verily I say to you, that I have other sheep which are not of this land; neither of the land of Jerusalem; neither in any parts of that land round about where I have been to minister.... They shall hear my voice and shall be numbered among my sheep, that there may be one fold and one shepherd; therefore I go to show myself to them.[8]

"Whosoever repenteth and cometh unto me, the same is my church" (16a). At this time the church was not yet organized, but Joseph was receiving instruction regarding its organization, nature, and purpose. This simple definition of the meaning of church membership is therefore very important. As will be seen, it makes repentance and disciple-ship basic to real membership.

THE URIM AND THUMMIM

The Urim and Thummim were believed by some to have been in the possession of Abraham about 1921 B.C. They became a part of the sacred vestments of the high priests in the time of Moses, about 1491 B.C., and were used in obtaining revelations from God. Those who had used the Urim and Thummim were called seers. The prophet Samuel was a seer and had the Urim and Thummim. From him King Saul sought light about 1056 B.C. Iddo was a seer and kept the genealogies about 971 B.C. Amos, the prophet, was mentioned as a seer as late as 787 B.C. This is the last mention of seers among the Israelites. After the captivity, the lineage of certain claimants to the priest's office could not be determined because no one among them had the Urim and Thummim.[9]

a. The Book of Mormon does not mention the Urim and

Thummim. The divinely provided means of interpretation were called "interpreters" and were given to the Brother of Jared in the "mount," on the Eastern Hemisphere about 2200 B.C. for the purpose of translating languages and revealing to the children of men the secrets of the Lord. No further mention is made of them till 124 B.C., when King Mosiah had them. We are not told where he obtained them, but he used them to translate an unknown language and gave them to Alma the younger. From Alma they were handed down from generation to generation with the sacred records and things and were deposited, with the abridged record and a breastplate, by Moroni, A.D. 421, in the stone box in the manner in which they were discovered by Joseph Smith, Jr., A.D. 1827.[10]

b. They consisted of two transparent stones set in the rims of a silver bow, somewhat like spectacles. When light was sought, the seer prayed earnestly and looked into the Urim. There the answer appeared. For example: languages were translated in this manner. It is hard to believe that the procedure was entirely automatic. On the contrary, the fact that they could be used only by "seers," and not by anyone else, seems to indicate the importance of moral excellence in using this means of revelation.[11]

THE BOOK OF MORMON MANUSCRIPT

After the translation of the Book of Mormon was completed, Oliver Cowdery transcribed the whole manuscript so that before the work of printing began there were two copies in existence. One of these copies is now in the hands of the Reorganized Church. The other was placed in the cornerstone of the Nauvoo House at Nauvoo, Illinois, but when it was subsequently removed little of it was legible. There has been some controversy as to which was the original. It is most likely that the pages of the two manuscripts were mixed somewhat. About one third of the one owned by the Reorganized Church shows marks of having been in the hands of the printer. It was evidently not used by the printer as a whole, but the part bearing printer's marks is composed of the actual pages from which this part of the 1830 edition of the Book of Mormon was printed. The remainder is either the original as dictated by Joseph Smith, or it is Oliver Cowdery's copy of this original. No other complete "original manuscript" of the Book of Mormon exists.

¹Jeremiah 36:32. ²*Restoration Scriptures*, p. 207ff. ³*Joseph Smith the Prophet and His Progenitors*, pages 146-149. ⁴Section 119:9, etc. ⁵*Outline Studies of the Book of Mormon*, pages 12 and 13. ⁶*Spiritual Letters to Men*, "To One Irresolute in His Conversion, Letter III." ⁷Section 83:4. ⁸III Nephi 7:20-26. ⁹Exodus 28:30; Leviticus 8:8; Numbers 27:21; I Samuel 9:18, 19; 28:6; II Chronicles 12:15; Ezra 2:63; Nehemiah 7:65; Amos 7:12; Mosiah 5:72-81. ¹⁰Section 15:1. ¹¹Mosiah 5:64-81; 12:18-21; 13:1, 2; Alma 17:55, 56; Mormon 4:100; Ether 1:87-89, 93, 99; Sections 3:1; 15:1; Church History, Volume 1, chapters 2 to 6; Oliver Cowdery's Letters; Lucy Smith's History (from W. W. Smith's *Outline Studies of the Book of Mormon*); Numbers 27:21; I Samuel 28:6.

SECTION 4

This revelation was given in Harmony, Pennsylvania, February 1829, and is addressed to Joseph Smith, Sr. Joseph Smith, Jr., had purchased a small farm from his wife's father, and his own father came to visit him. Joseph, Sr., had given his son consistent support from the time of the initial steps toward the coming forth of the Book of Mormon. He continued to be deeply interested, and it is altogether likely that the revelation addressed to him was received in answer to his inquiries.

"*A marvelous work is about to come forth*" (1a). The opening paragraph of this revelation is a salutation which is repeated in the revelations to Oliver Cowdery,¹ Hyrum Smith,² Joseph Knight,³ and David Whitmer.⁴ It emphasizes the fact that "a great and marvelous work is about to come forth"⁵ and stresses the supreme power and divinity of the Father. It is interesting to note the vital concept of God and of his word and work expressed in this revelation and continued throughout the book. A hundred years ago people thought of the word of God as the lifeless record of a once vital experience, but the Saints were welcomed into "the true and living church" and were ministered to by the living Word of God.

This marvelous work may refer either to the publication of the Book of Mormon, which was now in process of translation, or to the establishment of the church, which was to occur about fourteen months after this date.

The Book of Mormon is a "marvelous work' in the following respects:

> That Joseph, with limited education and hampered by lack of means, should be the instrument of its discovery and publication.
>
> That its existence should be unsuspected prior to its publication, but that it fulfilled many biblical prophecies so minutely.
>
> In the high standard of its teachings and prophecies.
>
> In the effect which it has produced in the world.
>
> In the evidences which have come forth to confirm it since its publication.

The church may be properly regarded as "a marvelous work and a wonder" for the following reasons:

> Its organization marked the opening of a new dispensation under the authority of heaven.
>
> It is directed by a divinely commissioned priesthood.
>
> It lives for and responds to divine revelation.
>
> It reaffirms the fundamental principles of the gospel.
>
> It is a gospel of power, the signs following the believer.
>
> It is organized after the New Testament pattern.
>
> It is the harbinger of Zion.

"Ye that embark in the service of God" (1b). Note the clear discernment with which the twenty-three-year-old prophet set before his father the basic elements of discipleship and ministry. Note, too, the similar counsel of the apostle Peter:

And besides this, giving all diligence, add to your faith virtue; and to virtue knowledge; and to knowledge temperance; and to temperance patience; and to patience godliness; and to godliness brotherly kindness; and to brotherly kindness charity.[5]

BIOGRAPHICAL NOTES

Joseph Smith, Sr., father of the Martyr[6] was born in Topsfield, Essex County, Massachusetts, July 12, 1771. Joseph, Sr., was the first person to receive the message of his son Joseph after the angel appeared to the young man, and he was closely associated with every important movement of the church until the time of his death. On April 6, 1830, Joseph, Sr., was baptized and shortly afterward was ordained a priest. He was set apart as patriarch December 18, 1833,[7] and as Presiding Patriarch January 21, 1836.[8] He died September 14, 1840, from tuberculosis brought on by hardships suffered in escaping from the mob in Missouri.

[1]Section 6:1a. [2]*Ibid.* 10:1a. [3]*Ibid.* 11:1a. [4]*Ibid.* 12:1a. [5]II Peter 1:5-7. [6]Section 21; 87:6; 99:2. [7]Church History 1:631. [8]Church History 2:16.

SECTION 5

The translation of the Book of Mormon from plates which he had never seen, even though he had acted as scribe for Joseph, was a great strain upon the credulity of Martin Harris. At times and particularly when he was under the influence of his wife and some of his friends, he became doubtful of the whole proceeding and begged Joseph for some indubitable proof that he was not being imposed upon.

Joseph's earlier experience with Martin had so deeply impressed the prophet that there was small likelihood that he would transgress the strict commandment that the plates should not be shown to anyone. Yet Joseph either recognized the difficulty of Martin's position or was pushed to extremities by the latter's persistence, for he evidently inquired of the Lord what he could do in the dilemma. The answer was received while Joseph was still in Harmony, Pennsylvania, in March 1829 and is self-explanatory.

The instruction received by Joseph for Martin Harris is as follows:

Joseph is to "stand as a witness of these things" (the plates, etc.) (1b).

He is to show them only to the persons to whom he is commanded to show them (1c).

He has only such power over them as God grants to him (1c).

He is blessed with the gift of translation, which is the first gift bestowed upon him (1d).

The plates of the Book of Mormon have been preserved for a wise purpose (3a).

This purpose will be known to future generations, but Joseph's generation is to believe on his testimony and that of three additional witnesses (3e).

Martin is not yet sufficiently humble, but if he will be faithful and prayerful he will be one of these witnesses (5b).

"You should not show them except to those persons to whom I command you" (1c). These include the eight witnesses whose testimony is published with that of the three witnesses at the beginning of every copy of the Book of Mormon. Their names were Christian Whitmer, Jacob Whitmer, Peter Whitmer, Jr., John Whitmer, Hiram Page, Joseph Smith, Sr., Hyrum Smith, Samuel H. Smith. Herman C. Smith has this to say about their testimony.

The testimony of these witnesses is plain, and of a nature to preclude the possibility of their having been deceived. They could not have been mistaken, hence their testimony is true, or they are liars. What inducement could have been offered them to lie? The cause was unpopular; yes, bitterly and violently persecuted. They had every reason to believe that contumely, persecution, and ostracism would be their portion if they thus publicly espoused this cause. Joseph Smith had neither wealth, emolument, nor positions of honor to offer them.[1]

Not one of these witnesses ever renounced his testimony, and John Whitmer, the last survivor of the eight, wrote

60

Heman C. Smith from Far West under date of December 11, 1876, as follows:

From what you have written I conclude you have read the *Book of Mormon*, together with the testimonies that are thereto attached, in which testimonies you read my name subscribed as one of the eight witnesses to said book. That testimony was, is, and will be true, henceforth and forever.

"*Hereafter you shall be ordained and go forth*" (2b). One of the evidences of the divinity of the calling and work of Joseph Smith is the patience which he exhibited during these years of preparation. Other reformers have been eager to organize according to their understanding, but Joseph waited patiently until the time was fulfilled and he was properly commissioned.

"*The testimony of three of my servants*" (3b). (See the Book of Mormon, II Nephi 11:133-135, and Ether, Chapter 2.)

"*Clear as the moon and fair as the sun, and terrible as an army with banners*" (3d). This is a quotation from the Song of Solomon (6:4, 10), and is applied to the church both here and in Doctrine and Covenants 102:9. Since the Song of Solomon is not included in the Inspired Version of the Holy Scriptures it would seem that it ranks on a par with the Apocrypha.

"*My word shall be verified at this time as it hath hitherto been verified*" (3h). The "signs of the times" which are enumerated here and elsewhere in the revelations to the church have been multiplied since this revelation was given. It is well to note that although our increasing understanding of natural phenomena has made plain to us something of the way in which natural forces work, our understanding does not yet pierce to final causes.

"*Yield to the persuasions of men no more*" (4a). Joseph depended on his friends for secretarial and other help, so that their requests for reassurance concerning the plates came with considerable force. Communication of this message to them probably did much to promote their understanding and continued cooperation.

"Then will I grant unto him a view of the things which he desires to see" (5b). Such a promise as this is inconceivable if Joseph was endeavoring to defraud Martin Harris. If Joseph had been a fraud, he would have shown Harris some plates outright or would have offered some permanent excuse for withholding them. As it was, directed of God, Joseph required certain spiritual preparation on the part of Martin but guaranteed that if he would make this preparation he should actually see the plates. The issue was thus in Martin's hands.

"He shall say no more unto them concerning these things, except. . . I have seen them, and they have been shown unto me by the power of God" (5c). Note the emphasis on simple testimony. Martin Harris was a good man and a sincere man, but he was not brilliant. In the hands of shrewd and antagonistic questioners he might easily have been confused. Here, therefore, he is instructed to give a simple and unadorned testimony of the basic facts in the case. This instruction was elaborated in a later revelation.[2] Martin remained faithful to his testimony until his death.

---

[1]Church History 1:48. [2]Section 18:2-6.

SECTION 6

Oliver Cowdery first met Joseph on or about April 5, 1829, at Harmony, Pennsylvania, and this revelation was given in that place shortly afterward when he was already writing for Joseph. This seems to indicate an intimate trust for so short an acquaintance, but each claims that he had prior spiritual instruction regarding the work in which they were to be jointly engaged.

During the month of April, the translation continued with little delay. Of this experience Oliver Cowdery says:

These were days never to be forgotten—to sit under the sound of a voice dictated by the inspiration of heaven, awakened the utmost gratitude of this bosom! Day after day I continued uninterrupted, to write from his mouth, as he translated, with the Urim and Thummim, or, as the Nephites would have said "Interpreters," the history, or record, called *The Book of Mormon.*[1]

"Whoso desireth to reap, let him thrust in his sickle with his might, and reap while the day lasts" (2a). Here is a characteristic note of urgency. It is found in the book of Acts, and is echoed in the life of every real missionary who has felt the hunger of God for the harvest of souls.

"Whosoever will is called" (2b). This affirmation had been made to Joseph Smith, Sr., and later was made to Hyrum Smith,[2] to Joseph Knight,[3] and was then broadened to include still others.[4] Quite evidently it represents a basic conviction confirmed to Joseph by the Holy Spirit. Whosoever desires to serve God is called to that service, for no man really desires to minister to men in the stead of Jesus unless he has first been moved upon by the Spirit of the Master. Desire to serve is the beginning, but not the end. Only those can serve God effectively who have been born of him and are willing to learn his ways so that they can teach these ways to their fellows. That is why this paragraph continues: "If you will ask of me, you shall receive, if you will knock it will be opened unto you."

Paragraph two of this section is identical with paragraphs two of Sections 10, 11, and 12.

"Seek to bring forth and establish the cause of Zion" (3a). This is the first specific mention of Zion in the revelations. Think of the challenge it must have brought to Joseph and Oliver, just beginning to be conscious of the great events which were taking shape around them. Zion is not merely a social or industrial experiment. It is a "Cause," having moral and spiritual significance as well as social and industrial resultants. Joseph wrote later:

The Church of Jesus Christ was founded upon direct revelation, as the true church of God has ever been, according to the Scriptures. And through the will and blessings of God I have been the instrument in his hands, thus far, to move forward THE CAUSE OF ZION.[5]

G. A. Studdert Kennedy, one of the best loved of England's younger ministers, wrote in one of his most popular books:

It is of the very being of Christianity that it is a social life. Perfection and redemption alike come through the body. If you take out of the New Testament the idea of the kingdom of God, and the Beloved Community, which is the seed from which it grows in time, there is nothing intelligible left. It is in the Beloved Community that the gift of eternal life, and therefore the power of man's redemption and completion, is to be found.[6]

"Seek not for riches, but for wisdom" (3b). Only truly wise persons can manage temporal riches soundly. Others are often defeated by the temptations to pride and selfishness which accompany great possessions. Paul told Timothy that "they that will be rich fall into temptation and a snare and into many foolish and hurtful lusts."[7] *The Emphasized New Testament* renders this "they that are determined to be rich."

"He that hath eternal life is rich" (3c). Eternal life can be experienced in time and beyond. It has duration, but first of all it must have quality. It is the life of God which is shared with men on the terms set forth in the gospel.[8]

"The mysteries of God shall be unfolded to you" (3b). The mysteries of the kingdom of God can be understood only by those who are willing to make a venture of faith under the guidance of the Holy Spirit. The mysteries of godliness must be approached with such intelligence as we can command, but also by way of faith and love and service. Note Doctrine and Covenants 76:2, 8; 83:3; 87:5 in this connection, together with the many New Testament references.

Paragraphs three and four were also directed to Hyrum Smith a month later.

"If you desire, you shall be the means of doing much good in this generation" (4a). This promise was fully vindicated in the subsequent life of Oliver. He did do much good in his generation, and the mysteries of God were unfolded to him. The commandments here given to

64

Oliver are such as would be given to the "second elder," so that this title which was later bestowed upon him was not an empty one. While reading this revelation, it is instructive to keep in mind the commandments to Sidney Rigdon and Frederick G. Williams, counselors to Joseph. Although the Presidency was not organized at this early date, the germs of the presidential function were there.

"Say nothing but repentance unto this generation" (4b). True repentance is motivated by the Spirit of God in response to the love of God[9] and it is related to every other aspect of discipleship. It has no acceptable substitutes, so that the call to repentance reoccurs again and again throughout the Scriptures.[10] The truly repentant sinner joins with other repentant ones who are seeking to kill evil in the world by establishing the kingdom of God. That is why Peter told the Jews at Pentecost to "repent" and also to be baptized, every one of you." Repentance is a vital part of the gospel.

"Exercise thy gift" (5c). Many of us tend to think of a gift as something received. It is. But the best gifts, those which we are admonished to "covet earnestly,"[11] must also be exercised. They enable us to achieve what we could not otherwise achieve, but their exercise is a necessary factor in that achievement. Perhaps the most outstanding artists—musicians, painters, poets, sculptors—are most aware of this. Apparently Oliver was not so aware, and his failure at this point was costly to him and to the church.[12]

"There is no gift greater than the gift of salvation" (5e). Members of the church sometimes regard the lesser spiritual gifts as guarantees of divine favor. This is not so. The lesser gifts of the gospel are means given of God for our salvation, but the greatest gift of all is the gift of salvation itself.

"Admonish him in his faults and also receive admonition of him" (8b). This principle of mutual aid is mentioned in each of the standard books, but requires both humility and wisdom of a high order to be effective. It must operate

both ways. Paul indicates the need for goodness and knowledge and advises the use of hymns and psalms in this connection.[13] The Book of Mormon records of Alma and his associates that "they did admonish their brethren; and they were also admonished, every one, by the word of God. . . ."[14]

"I am the light which shineth in darkness, and the darkness comprehendeth it not" (10). This phrase is familiar to all students of the Gospel of John. In the Inspired Version it is rendered, "The light shineth in the world, and the world perceiveth it not." The light "shineth." The present tense used here has no exact parallel in our language. It means that the light is always shining. It shines more brightly in the darkness than at any other time. It shines and is not overcome.

"I grant unto you a gift—to translate even as my servant Joseph" (11b). This promise is difficult to understand since it was apparently never fulfilled. Even if it had been fulfilled it is difficult to understand what would then have been the revelation between Joseph and Oliver. But the fact that such a promise was given indicates Joseph's willingness to accept the ministry of Oliver if circumstances justified this. His attitude was hardly that of a dictator, although Joseph was clearly in charge.[15]

BIOGRAPHICAL NOTES

Oliver Cowdery was born October 3, 1806, in Wells, Rutland County, Vermont. He taught school in Manchester, New York, in the winter of 1828-29 and boarded in the home of Joseph Smith, Sr. Here he became acquainted with the story of the Book of Mormon. In April 1829 he joined Joseph at Harmony, Pennsylvania, and from that time forward acted as his scribe in the translation of the Book of Mormon. Thereafter, Oliver was closely associated with Joseph in the work of the church.

Oliver is frequently mentioned in the early revelations.[16] He was baptized by Joseph Smith on May 15, 1829, under the instruction and commission of John the Baptist

66

and, after baptizing Joseph, was ordained by Joseph to the Aaronic priesthood.[17] During the month of June 1829, Oliver Cowdery, David Whitmer, and Martin Harris—the three witnesses—were shown the plates of the Book of Mormon. No one of these three ever denied the testimony which he gave at this time.

When the church was organized on April 6, 1830, Oliver was one of the six charter members; at this time he was ordained an elder by Joseph Smith, and then he ordained Joseph. Five days later Oliver preached the first sermon delivered in the new church organization. This was at Father Whitmer's house at Fayette, New York. The following October, Oliver was sent with Parley P. Pratt, Peter Whitmer, and Ziba Peterson on a mission to the Lamanites. On their way west these brethren stopped at Kirtland, Ohio, and planted the work there. Oliver was one of those present in August 1831 at the dedication of the temple site in Independence, at the dedication of the land of Zion, and at the laying of the cornerstone of the temple. Immediately after these ceremonies, he returned with Joseph Smith to Kirtland. The following November, he and John Whitmer were sent back to Missouri with the revelations received to that date, which had been ordered to be published. He later acted on the committee which prepared the 1835 edition of the Doctrine and Covenants. He was a member of the first high council of the church organized in Kirtland, February 7, 1834, and was clerk for a considerable period. Later he became one of the presidents of the council. With Sidney Rigdon he was left in charge of the church at Kirtland when Joseph Smith departed for Missouri in May 1834 at the head of Zion's Camp. In February 1835 he and the other two Book of Mormon witnesses chose the first members of the Quorum of Twelve in this dispensation. On April 3, 1836, he was joined with Joseph Smith in a very remarkable vision.[18]

At a conference of the church in Kirtland September 3, 1837, Oliver was made one of the assistant counselors to the president of the church, but after his removal to

Missouri, he fell into disfavor with the church. At the meeting of the high council and the bishopric at Far West, February 10, 1838, action was taken against him, and on the following April 12 he was cut off from the church. Oliver's removal from the church was extremely unfortunate and seems to have been dictated, in part at least, by prejudice, although he had probably lost some of his early zeal. He died March 3, 1850, at Richmond, Missouri. His last words were "Brother David [Whitmer], be true to your testimony to the Book of Mormon."

---

[1]*Messenger and Advocate*, Volume 1, page 14. [2]Section 4:1c. [3]Section 10:2b. [4]Section 11:2b. [5]Joseph Smith in *Ruff's History of the Denominations*, 1844. [6]*The Wicket Gate*. [7]I Timothy 6:9. [8]Section 18:2. [9]Romans 2:4. [10]Sections 10:4; 12:4; 13:3; 16:3; 18:2; 424:2; 152:4c. [11]I Corinthians 12:31. [12]Section 9:3. [13]Romans 5:14; II Thessalonians 3:15; Colossians 3:16. [14]Mosiah 11:149. [15]Section 27:2d. [16]Sections 6, 7, 8, 9, 17, 18, 23, 27, 110. [17]Church History, Volume 1, page 36. [18]Church History, Volume 1, pages 46, 47.

SECTION 7

While engaged in translation of the Book of Mormon Joseph and Oliver found they could not agree as to whether John the Beloved died toward the end of the first century or whether his life had been miraculously extended in order that he might continue his ministry on earth. They prayed for enlightenment and Joseph received the revelation which is recorded in Section 7. It was given at Harmony, Pennsylvania, in April 1829.

This section should be studied against a background of John 21:20-23 and the parallel situation recorded in III Nephi 13:12-24 and IV Nephi 1:15.[1]

The information contained in this revelation runs counter to the generally accepted interpretation of John 21 referred to, it being held by many that the statement of Jesus concerning John's survival was misunderstood and that John himself, in an endeavor to correct this, wrote: ". . . Jesus said not unto him, He shall not die, but, If I will that he tarry till I come, what is that to thee?"[2] It had been suggested that this explanatory statement was added to the gospel after the death of John.[3]

No fundamental doctrine appears to be involved in this section, but it should be noted that it fits naturally into the concept of dispensational ministry which is basic to the Restoration faith as illustrated in the ministry of Moroni, John the Baptist, Peter, James, and John, and others at the opening of the present age.

Comparison of this section with its parallel in the Book of Commandments shows that the Doctrine and Covenants version contains material which does not appear in the earlier publication. The additions apparently are elaborations of the text by Joseph as he prepared it for the 1835 publication.

Study of the two versions in parallel columns makes clear what additions were made.

Book of Commandments	Doctrine and Covenants
1. And the Lord said unto me, John, my beloved, what desirest thou?	And the Lord said unto me: John, my beloved, what desirest thou? For if you shall ask what you will, it shall be granted unto you.
2. And I said, Lord give unto me power that I may bring souls unto thee.	And I said unto him: Lord, give unto me power over death, that I may live and bring souls unto thee.
3. And the Lord said unto me: Verily, verily I say unto thee, because thou desirest this, thou shalt tarry till I come in my glory.	And the Lord said unto me: Verily, verily, I say unto thee, because thou desirest this thou shall tarry until I come in my glory, and shalt prophesy

before nations, kindreds, tongues and people.

4. And for this cause, the Lord said unto Peter:—If I will that he tarry till I come, what is that to thee? for he desirest of me that he might bring souls unto me: but thou desirest that thou might speedily come unto me in my kingdom.

And for this cause the Lord said unto Peter: If I will that he tarry till I come, what is that to thee? For he desired of me that he might bring souls unto me, but thou desirest that thou mightest speedily come unto me in my kingdom.

5. I say unto thee, Peter, this was a good desire, but my beloved has undertaken a greater work.

I say unto thee, Peter, this was a good desire; but my beloved has desired that he might do more, or a greater work yet among men than what he has before done.

6.

Yea, he has undertaken a greater work; therefore I will make him as flaming fire and a ministering angel; he shall minister for those who shall be heirs of salvation who dwell on the earth.

7.

And I will make thee to minister for him and for thy brother James; and unto you three I will give this power and the keys of this ministry until I come.

8. Verily, I say unto you, ye shall both have according to your desires, for ye both joy in that which ye have desired.

Verily I say unto you, ye shall both have according to your desires, for ye both joy in that which ye have desired.

"He shall minister for those who shall be heirs of salvation" (2). Evidently John is one of those ministers referred to in Doctrine and Covenants 76:7: "The telestial receive it [the Holy Spirit] of the administering of angels, who are appointed to minister for them, or who are appointed to be ministering spirits for them, for they shall be heirs of salvation." In this connection, study also the following from the writer of the Hebrew letter: "Are they not all ministering spirits, sent forth to minister for them who shall be heirs of salvation?"[4]

---

[1]Matthew 16:28; Mark 9:1; Luke 9:27. [2]John 21:23. [3]See *Interpreter's One Volume Commentary*, p. 728. [4]Hebrews 1:14. For a parallel passage in the Book of Mormon, see III Nephi 13:12-24 and IV Nephi 1:15.

SECTION 8

The revelation in Doctrine and Covenants 8 was given through Joseph Smith at Harmony, Pennsylvania, April 1829 during the period when Oliver Cowdery was acting as his scribe in the translation of the Book of Mormon.

"Shall you receive a knowledge of whatsoever things you shall ask in faith" (1b). Joseph must have felt considerable assurance in making this inspired promise to Oliver, for it accorded fully with his own experience. As Oliver later learned, such faith as is here required is not mere blind credulity nor is it an effortless waiting for God to demonstrate his power. It includes action based on a deep conviction of the love of God for his obedient children.

"Concerning the engraving of old records" (1b). It was

71

quite natural that Oliver, who had a fine and inquiring mind, should become interested in the engravings on the plates as well as in the contents of these plates. He is here promised that he can receive knowledge regarding these engravings in the same way that Joseph is receiving knowledge regarding the translation. Fulfillment of this promise is attested in the testimony of the Three Witnesses where the engravings are specifically mentioned.

"I will tell you in your mind and in your heart" (1c). This is evident from many testimonies. Note, for example, that it is written concerning the testimony of the apostle Peter of the Messiahship of Jesus. Undoubtedly Peter had given honest consideration to this matter in the months prior to his confession, but when he made this confession the Lord could say to him with truth, "Flesh and blood hath not revealed it unto thee, but my father which is in heaven."[1]

"This is the spirit of revelation" (2a). In many manifestations of the spirit of revelation the mind is enlightened and the heart is warmed. Although what is revealed may be set forth in words, these alone cannot embody the total experience. For this to happen the inquirer must enjoy the Spirit as does the revelator. As we approach the scriptures alertly and with humble expectancy of new understanding, our best efforts are crowned by insights which are the further gift of God.

"It shall deliver you . . ." (2b). The Spirit of God brings deliverance. Many times the source of this deliverance is quite evident.[2] At other times it is only after the event, looking backward, that the part of the Spirit in this deliverance is clearly seen. In telling the other disciples of the guidance given him concerning the baptism of the household of Cornelius, Peter said, "Then remembered I the word of the Lord. . . ."[3] But this remembering was not of words only, for these words had lain quiescent in the mind of Peter for many years. His remembering it was an inspired recall in which Peter saw meanings which had

72

escaped him until they were now quickened by the Spirit of God.

"You have another gift, which is the gift of Aaron" (3b). I do not know that the meaning of "the gift of Aaron" has ever been satisfactorily explained. The problem is made a little more difficult than it would otherwise be by the fact that Oliver is clearly stated to have other gifts, so that when he was specially blessed we can never be finally sure whether he was exercising the "gift of Aaron" or one of these additional gifts.

The fact that Oliver was closely associated with Joseph in many of the major events of these early years has inclined some to interpret the "gift of Aaron" as akin to the gift of speech exercised by Aaron on behalf of Moses:

The Lord said unto Moses, See, I have made thee a god to pharaoh: and Aaron thy brother shall be thy prophet. Thou shalt speak all that I command thee: and Aaron thy brother shall speak unto pharaoh, that he send the children of Israel out of his land.[4]

In further connection with the "gift of Aaron" Dr. Sidney B. Sperry of Brigham Young University has called attention to the rather marked differences between the version of this section in the Book of Commandments and that in the Doctrine and Covenants.[5] For easy comparison I include the pertinent paragraphs in parallel columns.

Book of Commandments

Now this is not all, for you have another gift, which is the gift of working with the rod: Behold it has told you things; behold there is no other power save God, that can cause this rod of nature, to work in your hands, for it is the work of God; and

Doctrine and Covenants

You have another gift, which is the gift of Aaron, behold it has told you many things; behold, there is no other power save the power of God that can cause the gifts of Aaron to be with you; therefore doubt not, for it is the work of God, and you shall therefore whatsoever you shall ask me to tell you by that means, that will I grant unto you, that you shall know.

hold it in your hands, and do marvelous works; and no power shall be able to take it away out of your hands, for it is the work of God.

And, therefore, whatsoever you shall ask me to tell you by that means, that will I grant unto you, and you shall have knowledge concerning it; remember, that without faith you can do nothing.

It may be that what is called "the gift of working with the rod," also called the "rod of nature" in the same sentence, is refined rather than contradicted when the later version calls it "the gift of Aaron." But the fact that Oliver could hold it in his hands makes it difficult to think of his gift as eloquence or persuasiveness.

In 1886 someone addressed this question to the *Saints' Herald*: "Why did the church change some of the revelations in this Book of Commandments when they compiled the Book of Doctrine and Covenants and then put them in the Doctrine and Covenants as the correct ones?" The answer given by the *Herald* editors (Joseph Smith and W. W. Blair) is fairly extensive but includes the following:[6]

God has the same right to authorize his appointed Seer to add to any of the revelations certain words and facts, that he has to give him any revelations at all. And the people of God have no proper grounds for rejecting such additions, or what purports to be revelation, given by and through God's authorized and accredited Seer, unless they perceive that it contradicts and contravenes the word of God already received and endorsed—which thing very, very rarely occurs, and when it does it proves speedily fatal to that Seer, as a protection to God's people against deception and as a punishment, a sign, and a warning.—See Deut. 18:20; Jer. 28:1-17; Ezek. 14:3-11. Add to this Helaman 3:13,— "thou shalt not ask what is contrary to my will;" and Doc. & Cov. 7:3—"do not ask for that for which you ought not"; and the teachings of Joseph the Seer,—"We never inquire at the hand of God for special revelation only in case of there being *no previous revelation* to suit the case." ". . . It is a great thing to enquire at the hand of God, or come into His presence; and we feel fearful to approach Him with subjects that are of little or no importance, to satisfy the queries of individuals, especially about things, the knowledge of which men ought to obtain, in all sincerity before God, for themselves, in humility, by the prayer of faith."

[1]Matthew 16:17. [2]Psalm 34:4. [3]Acts 11:16. [4]Exodus 7:1-2. [5]See also *Saints' Herald* 112:311. [6]*Times and Seasons* 5:753; *Millennial Star,* 14:413; *Saints' Herald* 33:802, 803.

SECTION 9

The revelation concerning translation which was given through Joseph Smith to Oliver Cowdery in Harmony, Pennsylvania, in April 1829 was directly related to the one which precedes it. It is of great importance in helping us to understand the process of divine revelation.

"Because you did not translate" (1a). It is unfortunate that we have so little information concerning this experience. Apparently it was not of such moment as to cause either Joseph or Oliver to dwell on it in later years. What transpired was that Oliver, who had not yet seen the plates but was acting as "scribe" to Joseph, became exceedingly anxious to have the power to translate bestowed upon him.[1] It was against this background that the revelations were given. It seems that Oliver did make some attempt to translate, but approached his task fearfully and, perhaps, doubtingly, and was unable to continue.

"Other records have I, that I will give unto you power that you may assist to translate" (1b). We have no evidence that this promise to Oliver was ever fulfilled. Nor can we say with assurance why this is so. From the fact that no additional translation like this has yet been made with the assistance of Oliver or of anyone else, it appears that in this matter the purpose of God has been frustrated up to the present time. We wonder why. It may be that Oliver

was not sufficiently diligent. If so, this is a sobering thought for us. How many times is the divine purpose frustrated because those chosen to do his work fail to measure up to the task?

"It is not expedient that you should" (2a, 4a). Note the recurrence of the word *expedient*. There are two kinds of expediency, the expediency which is rightful adjustment to changing circumstances and which violates no principle and the expediency which has a sinister tone and which is rooted in personal ambition rather than in the good of the Cause. In reading through the revelations we find that the former type of expediency is mentioned on several occasions.[2]

"You have not understood; you have supposed that I would give it unto you, when you took no thought" (3a). This is one of the most revealing statements in the early revelations. In the light of this principle it appears that Joseph did not translate without effort, but that he "studied it out in his mind" under divine guidance. Oliver, on the other hand, sought inspiration which made no demands on him and for this very reason was denied. I do not mean that Oliver was lazy. That is not true. But he did not fully understand the nature of revelation. Our heavenly Father was not concerned merely to convey certain words to this generation. He wanted Joseph and Oliver to grow in understanding as they made the records available. He wanted the words to become flesh. In harmony with this principle he later instructed the Saints to "seek learning even by study, and also by faith."[3] We grow spiritually as we are diligent in spiritual things. We are blessed as we serve the Lord with heart and might and mind. Revelation is very rarely the mere conveyance of information. It is most frequently the inspiration of heart and mind with light and understanding after man has done his utmost to understand the purpose and will of God.

---

[1]Joseph Smith, *Times and Seasons*, III:853. [2]Sections 42:15; 47:1; 71:1; 73:2; 117:2, 11, 14; 118:2; 127:2. [3]Section 85:36.

76

SECTION 10

This revelation was given through Joseph Smith to his oldest living brother, Hyrum, in May 1829. When Hyrum learned that Joseph was translating the Book of Mormon at Harmony, he went there and sought personal light regarding the divinity of the work. This revelation was given in response to his petition.

The first four paragraphs of this section are identical with the first four paragraphs of Section 6.

"Put your trust in that Spirit which leadeth to do good; yea, to do justly, to walk humbly, to judge righteously, and this is my Spirit" (6). Instruction such as this bears its own credentials. Deceivers do not advise their close associates this way. This was the word of God a hundred years ago, and no matter what progress we make, it will still carry its own evidences of Divinity.

"You need not suppose that you are called to preach until you are called" (8a). When Hyrum became convinced of the truth, he was eager to commence proclaiming it immediately, but he was not adequately prepared and had not yet been ordained. We need to keep the divinely imposed order of things well in mind today—first the knowledge of the truth, then power according to our desires based on faith.

"Cleave unto me with all your heart, that you may assist in bringing to light. . .the translation of my work" (9b). This was partially fulfilled when Hyrum became one of the eight witnesses to the Book of Mormon. It was more completely fulfilled when he became one of the leading officers of the church which gave this book to the world.

"First seek to obtain my word, and then shall your tongue be loosed" (10a). When they were translating the Book of Mormon, Joseph and Oliver underwent a rigorous preparation for their later ministry. The arduous task of dictating this book word by word, and of writing it out in longhand, could not fail to familiarize them with its

contents. We also know that they frequently discussed the principles which they discovered during the translation, and this must have been a liberal education in itself. Hyrum was intimately connected with this work. He had read the Bible many times, but he had not had this discipline. There is, therefore, wisdom in this instruction that Hyrum should become better acquainted with the message of the Restoration before he should seek to proclaim it.

"Deny not the spirit of revelation nor the spirit of prophecy" (11b). Hyrum knew that Joseph was a good man. He knew, moreover, that the work about which Joseph had told him was in harmony with the Bible. But it was difficult for him to believe that God would actually reveal himself to righteous men as he had done in earlier dispensations. Nowadays we are more familiar with the idea of prophecy and revelation and very few of us have had to completely rearrange our thinking as Hyrum did in order to make place therein for a self-revealing Divinity. Once Hyrum was convinced of revelation and of prophecy, he held to these gospel truths with a tenacity which never weakened.

The whole of this section will repay careful study. When the relative situations of Joseph and Hyrum are realized and the spiritual quality of the instruction here contained is appreciated, it will be recognized that this revelation alone marks Joseph as a prophet of God.

BIOGRAPHICAL NOTES

Hyrum Smith[1] was the second son of Patriarch Joseph Smith and elder brother of the prophet, having been born February 9, 1800, at Tunbridge, Vermont. He was baptized in Seneca Lake, New York, in June 1829, and became one of the eight witnesses to the Book of Mormon. At a conference held in Far West, Missouri, November 7, 1837, Frederick G. Williams was rejected as counselor to the president of the church and Hyrum Smith was chosen

78

to succeed him. He continued in this office until called by revelation to succeed his father as presiding patriarch of the church in 1841. Hyrum was devoted to his brother and served with him to the end. They were assassinated together at Carthage, Illinois, June 27, 1844.

---

[1]Sections 21, 52:3, 75:5; Appendices A, 107:5; D.

SECTION 11

Joseph Smith had to provide for his physical needs in addition to devoting himself to his spiritual concerns. Despite charges made by his enemies, he was not lazy, but he and Oliver were both eager to discharge their more important responsibilities. He therefore welcomed the splendid help of Joseph Knight, about whom he says:

> About the same time came an old gentleman to visit us, of whose name I would make honorable mention; Mr. Joseph Knight, Sr., of Colesville, Broome County, New York, who, having heard of the manner in which we were occupying our time, very kindly and considerately brought a quantity of provisions, in order that we might not be interrupted in the work of translation by want of such necessaries to life; and I would just mention here (as in duty bound) that he several times brought us supplies (a distance of at least thirty miles) which enabled us to continue the work which otherwise we must have relinquished for a season. Being very anxious to know his duty as to this work, I inquired of the Lord for him.[1]

The revelation given in response to these prayers was received in Harmony, Pennsylvania, May 1829.

Paragraphs one, two, and three are identical with the first two and one-half paragraphs of the revelation given to Oliver Cowdery[2] and with the first two and one-half paragraphs of the revelation to Hyrum Smith.[3] There is nothing strange in this repetition of fundamentally important instruction to the men who were inquiring about essentially the same thing. Each of these men wanted to be assured of the divinity of the work that Joseph was doing and to know what his own relation to this work should be. The revelations therefore mention certain things which are necessary for all to know, and then they go on with specific instruction related to the individual needs of the inquirers

"No one can assist in this work, except he shall be humble" (4b). The dictionary defines humble as "claiming little as one's desert; not proud or assertive in spirit, manner, or seeming; lowly; meek." The basic idea of this sentence therefore seems to be that anyone who desires to assist in this work must recognize its importance and the comparative unimportance of his personal interests. Anyone who is humble in this way will not think of himself more highly than he ought but will find his place in the movement and then will give all that he can give. He will "make himself of no reputation," and will not seek reasons for giving a partial devotion. He will abase himself beside the greatness of the task in which he is engaged.

"And full of love" (4b). The work of God must be carried forward in the Spirit of God. Zion cannot be built unless it is "by the principles of the law of the celestial kingdom"[4] and the most fundamental of these principles is the principle of love. The would-be church worker must be full of love for the work. No academic interest will suffice; a passionate emotional concern is imperative.

"Having faith" (4b). Effective church workers have a basic conviction that this work must succeed because God is in it. They know the Lord and are assured of his power, and out of this assurance comes the strength for continuance in every difficulty. Faith is "vision plus valor." It is the insight to see God in his work and courage to act accordingly.

"Hope" (4b). The apostle Paul repeatedly emphasized three major aspects of stable Christian life: faith, hope, and charity. These, he said, must abide.[5] We have tended to emphasize faith and charity but to overlook the importance of the Christian hope. We do well to remember that life

80

without hope is utterly desolate and that Paul was quite right when he said that "we are saved by hope."[6] But reasonable men cannot hope without good reason for doing so. All this is behind Paul's deep joy in the gospel which breaks out in such statements as

The Lord Jesus Christ . . . is our hope.[7]
I know whom I have believed, and am persuaded that he is able to keep that which I have committed unto him.[8]
The God of hope fill you with all joy and peace in believing that ye may abound in hope, through the power of the Holy Ghost.[9]
If in this life only we have hope in Christ, we are of all men most miserable.[10]
Sorrow not, even as others which have no hope. For if we believe that Jesus died and rose again, even so them also which sleep in Jesus will God bring with him.[11]

Both Peter and John join Paul in their appreciation of the hope which the gospel imparts. Peter says:

His divine power hath given unto us all things that pertain unto life and godliness, through the knowledge of him that hath called us unto glory and virtue; whereby are given unto us exceeding great and precious promises; that by these ye might be partakers of the divine nature, having escaped the corruption that is in the world through lust.[12]

And John says:

Beloved, now are we the sons of God, and it doth not yet appear what we shall be; but we know that, when he shall appear, we shall be like him; for we shall see him as he is. And every man that hath this hope in him purifieth himself, even as he is pure.[13]

"And charity" (4b). Moroni writes: "Cleave unto charity which is the greatest of all, for all things must fail; but charity is the pure love of Christ, and it endureth forever; and whoso is found possessed of it in the last day, it shall be well with him."[14] When we add this to Paul's matchless discussion of charity,[15] we realize that here is an absolutely vital attribute of sainthood. How many branches have been torn asunder because some of their members could not suffer long and still be kind or were too easily provoked or thought evil too readily?

BIOGRAPHICAL NOTES

Joseph Knight (see also Doctrine and Covenants 21) was a Universalist. He was interested in the truth, and after a time invited Joseph to visit with him and to preach among his friends. In April 1830 Joseph accepted this invitation and held several meetings in the neighborhood of the Knight home. A remarkable spiritual experience served to convince Newell Knight, son of Joseph Knight, that God was in the work, and Newell was baptized almost immediately. This broke down the barriers which had hindered Joseph Knight. He, his wife, Emma Smith, and others were baptized in June 1830 by Oliver Cowdery.

The last paragraph of Section 21 was addressed to Joseph Knight shortly before his baptism and was undoubtedly instrumental in helping to convince him of the divinity of the work. He later became quite active according to his strength and ability.

---

[1]*Times and Seasons* 3:884. [2]Section 6. [3]Section 10. [4]Section 102:2. [5]I Corinthians 13:13. [6]Romans 8:24. [7]I Timothy 1:1. [8]II Timothy 1:12. [9]Romans 15:13. [10]I Corinthians 15:19. [11]I Thessalonians 4:13, 14. [12]II Peter 1:3, 4. [13]I John 3:2, 3. [14]Moroni 7:52. [15]I Corinthians 13.

SECTION 12

The revelation addressed to David Whitmer in June 1829 was received at Fayette, Seneca County, New York. Of his early experience with this family Joseph wrote later:

Shortly after commencing to translate, I became acquainted with Mr. Peter Whitmer, of Fayette, Seneca County, New York, and also with some of his family. In the beginning of the month of June his son David Whitmer came to the place where we were residing, and brought with him a two horse wagon, for the purpose of having us accompany him to his father's place and there remain until we should finish the work. He proposed that we should have our board free of charge, and also the assistance of one of his brothers to write for me, as also his own assistance when convenient.

Having much need of such timely aid in an undertaking so arduous, and being informed that the people of the neighborhood were anxiously awaiting the opportunity to inquire into these things, we accepted the invitation, and accompanied Mr. Whitmer to his father's house, and there resided until the translation was finished, and the copyright secured. Upon our arrival, we found Mr. Whitmer's family very anxious concerning the work, and very friendly toward ourselves. They continued so, boarded and lodged us according to proposal, and John Whitmer, in particular, assisted us very much in writing during the remainder of the work.

In the meantime, David, John, and Peter Whitmer, Jr., became our zealous friends, and assistants in the work.[1]

Paragraphs one and two are identical with paragraphs one and two of Sections 6, 10, and 11.

"Seek to bring forth and establish my Zion" (3a). The *cause* of . Zion had already been mentioned in earlier revelations[2]; now the reason for proclaiming and establishing this cause, which is implied in all that has gone before, is given its fundamental justification. Zion is not a merely human enterprise; God himself is involved. This inspired work says, "my Zion."[3]

Diverse but related meanings of the term "Zion" become apparent as one studies the revelations. We note that Zion is referred to as a people,[4] the pure in heart,[5] a land,[6] a place,[7] a city,[8] a new Jerusalem,[9] a kingdom.[10] Sometimes Zion may well refer to the church, since Zion was referred to as being built up[11] and contended with.[12] But, always, behind the specific references, Zion refers to the kingdom of God.

"If you keep my commandments and endure to the end, you shall have eternal life; which gift is the greatest of all the gifts of God" (3b). It is interesting to note that David is here told that eternal life is the greatest of all gifts, while his brother-in-law, Oliver Cowdery, had been previously assured that salvation is the greatest of all gifts. Evidently the term "eternal life" and "salvation" are used interchangeably.

"You may stand as a witness of the things of which you

83

both shall hear and see" (4). This was fulfilled when David became one of the three witnesses to the Book of Mormon.

"A light which cannot be hid in darkness" (5). The conflict between light and darkness results in one or the other being extinguished. The two cannot exist side by side. Yet the light which centers in Jesus Christ refuses to be quenched. If men prefer darkness rather than light, they lose their great opportunity. But before long someone else responds to the light, and the work of God is again moving forward with strength and power.

BIOGRAPHICAL NOTES

David Whitmer (see also Doctrine and Covenants 15, 16, 29, 52) was born near Harrisburg, Pennsylvania. He was baptized in June 1829 and was one of the charter members of the church and one of the "three witnesses" of the Book of Mormon plates. Ordained an elder at the organization of the church and a high priest October 25, 1831, he was chosen president of the high council in Clay County in July 1834 and served there faithfully for the next four years. In some unfortunate church dissension in the spring of 1838 David Whitmer and other prominent men of the church were cut off. David protested that the action was illegal. When it was confirmed, he removed to Clay County, Missouri, and later to Richmond, Ray County, Missouri. Here he died January 25, 1888, having borne faithful testimony to the divine authenticity of the Book of Mormon until his death.

---

[1]*Times and Seasons* 3:384-5. [2]Section 6:3, 10:3, 11:3. [3]*Ibid.* 12:3a, 58:3, 77:3. [4]*Ibid.* 36:2h. [5]*Ibid.* 94:5c. [6]*Ibid.* 57:5c, 58:11a. [7]*Ibid.* 58:10, 83:12, 105:14. [8]*Ibid.* 36:a, 12g; 45:12c; 94:5b. [9]*Ibid.* 36:12g, 45:12b. [10]*Ibid.* 102:9b. [11]*Ibid.* 102:2b. [12]*Ibid.* 87:8.

SECTION 13

John Whitmer was the third son of Peter Whitmer, Sr.,
and became very much interested in the message of Joseph
and Oliver when they came to stay in his father's house in
June 1829. Like his father and the other members of his
family, he became quite eager to know for himself regarding
the work which Joseph was doing and this revelation was
given in response to his prayer for light.

"With sharpness and with power" (1b). The reference
here seems to go back to the phrase already used in the
introduction of the revelations to Oliver Cowdery, Hyrum
Smith, Joseph Knight, and David Whitmer: "Give heed
to my word, which is quick and powerful, sharper than a
two-edged sword." Brief consideration will show how
apt this characterization was, particularly among the
people who had been schooled to think of the word of
God as a dead thing, issuing from him two thousand
years previously and enshrined since that time in a closed
book. The word of God is alive, dividing swiftly and surely
between truth and error.

*"The thing which will be of the most worth to you, will
be to declare repentance unto this people, that you may
bring souls unto me"* (3). John was about twenty-six
years of age at this time, ambitious and eager for success.
His query which is answered in this paragraph is therefore
a perfectly natural one, and the reply is entirely in harmony
with the word of God in every age. Young, vigorous, and
eager men who wish to know what will be of greatest
worth to them need to listen once more to the voice of
God: "Declare repentance unto this people, that you may
bring souls unto me."

BIOGRAPHICAL NOTES

John Whitmer is mentioned in this revelation and in
Sections 25, 29, 47, 69, 70, and 108A. He was born

85

August 27, 1802; was baptized June 1829; and became one of the eight witnesses of the Book of Mormon. He was ordained an elder soon after the organization of the church and a high priest June 3, 1831. In November 1831 he was selected by revelation to accompany Oliver Cowdery to Jackson County with the copies of the revelations. These he had previously assisted Joseph in copying and preparing for publication in the Book of Commandments. Later John Whitmer was chosen as one of the seven high priests in charge of the church in Jackson County. He became disaffected in the troubles of 1837 and 1838 and was excommunicated March 10, 1838. He died at Far West, Missouri, July 11, 1878.

JOHN WHITMER'S HISTORY

In March 1831 John Whitmer was appointed church historian. This was less than a year after the organization of the church. Although he was repeatedly urged to keep a minute account of the happenings of those early days, and the wisdom of this instruction has since been abundantly vindicated, the history which he compiled consisted of only about one hundred and thirty-eight pages in long hand. This came into the possession of the church in 1903 and was published in the first volume of the *Journal of History* in 1908. There it covers about forty-eight pages.

SECTION 14

Peter Whitmer, Jr., was the fifth son of Peter Whitmer, Sr. This revelation was probably addressed to him at the same time the previous one was addressed to his brother, and they are identical in content. He was baptized in June 1829 and became one of the charter members of the church in the following April. In October 1830 he accompanied Elders Parley P. Pratt, Oliver Cowdery, and Ziba Peterson on the first mission to the Lamanites and gave excellent service on that important mission. He was active in the work in Jackson County and Clay County until his death on September 22, 1836. In common with the other witnesses to the Book of Mormon he was true to his testimony to the end of his life.

SECTION 15

This revelation was given in Fayette, Seneca County, New York, June 1829, and shortly afterward Oliver Cowdery, David Whitmer, and Martin Harris were shown the Book of Mormon plates by the angel Moroni. Joseph Smith tells of these events in the following language:

In the course of the work of translation we ascertained that three special witnesses were to be provided by the Lord, to whom he would grant that they should see the plates from which this work [the Book of Mormon] should be translated, and that these witnesses should bear record of the same. . . .

Almost immediately after we had made this discovery, it occurred to Oliver Cowdery, David Whitmer, and the aforementioned Martin Harris (who had come to inquire after our progress in the work) that they would have me inquire of the Lord, to know if they might not obtain of him to be these three special witnesses; and finally they became so very solicitous, and teased me so much, that at length I complied, and through the Urim and Thummim, I obtained of the Lord for them the following revelation:[1]

"*The plates*" (1b). The records of the ancient inhabitants of this continent were engraved on metallic plates. Of these, six come prominently before us: (1) the brass plates secured from Laban at the time of Lehi's departure from Jerusalem; (2) the larger plates of Nephi started by him very shortly after the departure from Jerusalem; (3) the smaller plates of Nephi, made by Nephi at the command of God thirty years after the departure from Jerusalem; (4) the record of Zeniff; (5) the twenty-four gold plates of Ether; and (6) the plates of Mormon's abridgment. These plates were about seven by eight inches in size and a little thinner than common tin. The whole volume was about six inches in thickness and was held together like a book by three rings running through the edge of the plates. Part of this loose-leaf book was sealed.

"The breastplate" (1b). A breastplate was found with the plates and the Urim and Thummim and is described as being large enough to cover the vital parts of a man of extra large size, having four straps of the same material, by which it was fastened to the wearer: two to fasten over the shoulders and two about the hips. The whole breastplate was shaped so as to conveniently fit the wearer.[2]

"The sword of Laban" (1b). This sword was taken from Laban by Nephi when he obtained the brass plates. The blade was of steel and the hilt of gold, both skillfully made. It was carried by Nephi to America, and was used by him as a pattern for other swords to defend the Nephites against the Lamanites.

"The Urim and Thummim" (1b). See notes on Section 3.

"The miraculous directors" (1b). This was a round ball of curious workmanship made of brass with two spindles or pointers which worked according to the faith of the operator. It was used in directing the Nephites when they traveled. Revelations were received through it also, appearing in the form of writing upon the ball. It was given to Lehi in the wilderness, along the Red Sea in Arabia, while on the journey to the promised land.

"That my servant, Joseph Smith, Jr., may not be destroyed" (2b). The pressure under which Joseph labored when he was the sole witness of the Book of Mormon plates is reflected in the following quotation from his mother's narrative:

Joseph was no longer to be the sole witness of the existence of the plates and the correctness of their translation. How joyful must have been his feelings as he realized that the burden which before he had borne alone was now to be shared by others. No wonder that he exclaimed when the wonderful vision had been concluded, "Father, Mother, you do not know how happy I am; the Lord has now caused the plates to be shown to three more besides myself. They have seen an angel, who has testified to them, and they will have to bear witness to the truth of what I have said, for now they know for themselves that I do not go about to deceive the people, and I feel as though I was relieved of a burden which was almost too heavy for me to bear, and it rejoices my soul that I am not any longer to be entirely alone in the world."[3]

Of the vision of the plates, Joseph wrote:

Not many days after the above commandment was given, we four, viz.: Martin Harris, David Whitmer, Oliver Cowdery, and myself, agreed to retire into the woods, and try to obtain by fervent and humble prayer, the fulfillment of the promises given in the revelation; that they should have a view of the plates, etc. We accordingly made choice of a piece of woods convenient to Mr. Whitmer's house, to which we retired, and having knelt down we began to pray in much faith, to Almighty God, to bestow upon us a realization of these promises. According to previous arrangements I commenced, by vocal prayer to our heavenly Father, and was followed by each of the rest in succession. We did not yet, however, obtain any answer, or manifestation of the divine favor in our behalf. We again observed the same order of prayer, each calling on and praying fervently to God in rotation; but with the same result as before. Upon this our second failure, Martin Harris proposed that he would withdraw himself from us, believing as he expressed himself that his presence was the cause of our not obtaining what we wished for. He accordingly withdrew from us, and we knelt down again, and had not been many minutes engaged in prayer, when presently we beheld a light above us in the air of exceeding brightness, and behold, an angel stood before us. In his hands he held the plates which we had been praying for these to have a view of. He turned over the leaves one by one so that we could see them, and discover the engravings thereon distinctly. He addressed himself to David Whitmer, and said, "David, blessed is the Lord, and he that keeps his commandments." When immediately afterwards, we heard a voice from out of the bright light above us, saying, "These plates have been revealed by the power of God, and they have been translated by the power of God; the translation of them which you have seen is correct, and I command you to bear record of what you now see and hear."

I now left David and Oliver, and went in pursuit of Martin Harris, whom I found at a considerable distance, fervently engaged in prayer. He soon told me, however, that he had not yet prevailed with the Lord, and earnestly requested me to join him in prayer, that he also might realize the same blessings which we had just received. We accordingly joined in prayer, and ultimately obtained our desires, for before we had yet finished, the same vision was opened to our view; at least it was again to me, and I once more beheld, and heard the same things; whilst at the same moment Martin Harris cried out, apparently in ecstacy of joy, "'Tis enough; mine eyes have beheld," and jumping up he shouted, "Hosanna," blessing God, and otherwise rejoiced exceedingly.[4]

The testimony of these witnesses is plain and of a nature to preclude the possibility of their having been deceived. They could not have been mistaken, hence their testimony is true or they are liars. What inducement could have been offered them to lie? The cause was bitterly and violently persecuted. They had every reason to believe that contumely, persecution, and ostracism would be their portion if they thus publicly espoused this cause. Joseph Smith had neither wealth, emolument, nor positions of honor to offer them.

Some of these witnesses have left on record no further testimony than that found in the document to which they subscribed in 1829. The three witnesses, whose testimony is most important, have reaffirmed it, however; so also has John Whitmer, the last survivor of the eight witnesses.[5]

As far as we know, this was the last revelation which Joseph Smith received by the aid of the Urim and Thummim. Section 1 of the Doctrine and Covenants was given at Hiram, Ohio, November 1, 1831, long after the Urim and Thummim was given up. It is perhaps safe to say that the Urim and Thummim was used in connection with fourteen revelations—Sections 2 to 15, inclusive.[6]

---

[1]*Times and Seasons,* Volume 3, pages 897-899; Church History, Volume 1, page 45. [2]Mosiah 5:65. [3]*Joseph Smith and His Progenitors,* page 147. [4]*Times and Seasons,* Volume 3, pages 897, 898. [5]Church History, Volume 1, pages 48, 49. [6]*Times and Seasons,* Volume 3, pages 897, 916.

SECTION 16

Shortly after the three witnesses had received satisfying evidence regarding the plates, Joseph and Oliver met in the upper chamber of Father Whitmer's house at Fayette, New York, and prayed earnestly regarding the bestowal of the Melchisedec priesthood which had been promised them when they were ordained to the Aaronic priesthood. In answer to their petitions, they were told that their ordination to the eldership should take place at a time when it would be opportune for the church to vote upon their selection as spiritual teachers. It was on this occasion, in June 1829, that the revelation in Section 16 was received.

"Rely upon the things which are written" (1c). It will be noted that this instruction is preceded by the assertion, "You know that they are true." The written word is doubly enlightening to those who are assured of its divinity. This assurance makes further revelation an unfolding of that which has gone before, and continuous revelation a never ending process of divine disclosure.

"The foundation of my church" (1c). Joseph and Oliver had prayed about the formal initiation of the marvelous work which had been prophesied. Since this is clearly the case, the patience of these impetuous young men, who waited for nearly a year before the church organization was perfected, supports their claim that they were acting under strict commandments from God.

"Marvel not that I have called him unto mine own purpose" (2c). There were times when it was difficult for Oliver to understand why Joseph had been chosen. Joseph was admittedly of limited education, while Oliver had enough education to teach; yet Joseph possessed intrinsic qualifications which Oliver did not possess. These had undoubtedly been accruing through many generations according to God's unerring purpose. It was required of Oliver that he should be "humble and full of love" if he was to assist in the work to which God had called him—to second place and not to first place.

"You are called even with that same calling with which he [Paul] was called" (3b). Neither Oliver nor David was ever a member of the Quorum of Twelve. That they were likened to Paul, an apostle, is partly explained by the revelation of September 22 and 23, 1832, wherein the Lord addresses himself to his "servant Joseph Smith, Jr., and six elders" and says: "You are mine apostles, even God's

high priests."[1] In the Bible it is recorded that James, the Lord's brother,[2] and Paul and Barnabas[3] and Silvanus and Timotheus[4] were all apostles. Some of these may have belonged to the Quorum of Twelve, but evidently there are apostles in the church who are not necessarily numbered with the Twelve.

"Remember the worth of souls is great in the sight of God" (3c). It is significant that in the first revelation dealing specifically with the organization of the church and the call of the Twelve, strong emphasis is placed on repentance and salvation. This is as it should be in view of the preeminently missionary character of the church.

"Contend against no church, save it be the church of the Devil" (4d). The Lord proposes that the church shall grow by an affirmative proclamation of the truth rather than through an attempt to discredit the work of other organizations. There are times when it is imperative that we shall draw a clear distinction between the doctrine of Christ and the proclamations which are not in harmony therewith, but our major emphases should never lie in this direction. In this connection read III Nephi 5:29-31.

"The twelve are they who shall desire to take upon them my name, with full purpose of heart" (5b). This is clearly in harmony with the spirit of the apostles. In this connection note I Corinthians 9:1 and Section 104:12. This revelation made it clear that when the church was organized it should be after the pattern of the New Testament church. This teaching was revolutionary at that time, for the idea of a continuing apostolic Council of Twelve had long since been abandoned in favor of the various other ministerial theories held by the several churches.

"Baptize in my name" (5c). From this early mention of baptism, as well as from the more complete subsequent discussions of the doctrine, it is clear that while baptism has real social and psychological values, its essential value is in the fact that through it men are allied with Christ and his church. Baptism must be more than an empty form. It must be an actual self-dedication in the name of Christ.

Membership in the body of Christ—his church—is also vital. We are made whole through Christ among our fellows. The salvation to which our Lord calls us is not an individual matter. Its richness is experienced in the fellowship of the kingdom. And while this may never be fully achieved in this life it should be more fully enjoyed in the church than anywhere else on earth.

"*You are they who are ordained of me to ordain priests and teachers to declare my gospel*" (5e). Earlier in the revelation the twelve have been designated as those who are "called to go into all the world to preach my gospel unto every creature." Here they are instructed to ordain priests and teachers, who, with other standing ministers, will be able to take care of the branches built up through missionary activity. This is in harmony with Sections 120:1, 2 and 122:7.

"*You shall search out the twelve*" (6a). The "twelve traveling counselors," who "are called to be the twelve apostles or special witnesses of the name of Christ in all the world,"[5] are not always called by revelations given to the prophet and approved by the appropriate priesthood groups and conferences. When a successor was chosen to fill the office from which Judas had fallen, the necessity of making a choice was explained to a hundred and twenty of the saints by the apostle Peter. The record is not clear as to who took the initiative in determining that the new member of the twelve should be either "Joseph called Barsabas, who was surnamed Justus," or Matthias. But it is quite clear that the actual choice was sought in earnest prayer and that the casting of lots was the means by which they sought to discover and to obey the will of God.

In this revelation Oliver Cowdery and David Whitmer were commanded to "search out the twelve." Martin Harris, the third Book of Mormon witness, was associated with them as was President Joseph Smith. To guide them in their choice was their knowledge of the elders who had been members of Zion's Camp. While those who were to choose the twelve were acquainted with this responsibility from June 1829, the twelve were not chosen until February 1835. Evidently they awaited the conversion of those who were to be selected, for at this time none of the yet-to-be members of the twelve had been baptized.

"*Children who have arrived to the years of accountability*" (6d). Agency is vital to an effective contract, and baptism is essentially a contract between God and his children who know what they are about. In this connection the student can read Moroni 8 with profit.

"*Unto the convincing of many of their sins, that they may come unto repentance*" (7b). Note this clear statement of the necessity for a "conviction of sin" as a prelude to effective repentance. Much of our repentance is too superficial. It does not pierce to the deeper recesses of our being. Apostolic work of this convincing character is as necessary today as it was a century ago.

-----

¹Section 83:1, 10. ²Galatians 1:19. ³Acts 14:14. ⁴I Thessalonians 1:1, 2, 6. ⁵Acts 1:15-26.

SECTION 17

In the Book of Commandments this section was designated "The Articles and Covenants of the Church of Christ." It was probably prepared by Joseph Smith with the assistance of Oliver Cowdery (note the "we" in paragraphs 3d, 4a, 6a, 6b, 6c, 6f) to incorporate instruction received in "the spirit of prophecy and revelation" and was adopted at the first conference of the church, June 1, 1830. The first three paragraphs appear to be historical and descriptive narratives giving both information and testimony concerning the divine guidance leading to "the rise of the church of Christ."

Paragraphs two and three contain history and testimony rather than revelation. Paragraphs four, five, and six, while not complete, give as near a basic statement of belief as is to be found in any one place in the book. It is not suggested that these were consciously modeled on the historic creeds or that they lacked a revelatory foundation, but comparison suggests that they were written by one or more persons who were familiar with the structure of the ancient statements of faith. The "spirit of prophecy and revelation" confirmed to Joseph and Oliver the truths which they now expressed in phrases familiar to them and others of their company.

"The church of Christ" (1). On May 3, 1834, a conference was held in Kirtland and, among other transactions, action was taken on the name of the church. Prior to this time the church had been called "The Church of Christ," "The Church of Jesus Christ," "The Church of God," "The Church of the Firstborn," or whatever appellation best suited the writer or speaker. Obviously, uniformity was desirable. "Latter Day Saints" was agreed upon, but "The Church of Christ" was still used also. In 1838 the approved title of the church became "The Church of Jesus Christ of Latter Day Saints." The essence of the name chosen is "The Church of Jesus Christ." The addition of "Latter Day Saints" was made to avoid confusion with "The Church of Christ" ("Christians") and similarly named groups.

The 1972 report of a World Conference committee on the name of the church stated that the word "Reorganized" "crept in" as an official appendage to the name of the church on the title page of the Doctrine and Covenants published in 1864.[1] It further states that

the first official action on the Reorganization took place on October 21, 1872, when the Articles of Incorporation were adopted by the Conference. Article one states "the name of this association and organization shall be "The Reorganized Church of Jesus Christ of Latter Day Saints...."

In the body of this report there is also the following, a formative statement from an editorial by President Elbert A. Smith:

First, the church on earth having at one or more times during the history of the world lapsed into a disorganized condition, as prophets predicted, it is perfectly proper and logical to speak of the church today as having been "reorganized." Second, the members of the church are recognized by the Lord in his inspired record as saints, and the era in which we live being the last days, and the approach of our Lord and Savior drawing near, it is perfectly proper and logical to speak of the members of the church as "Latter Day Saints." Third, the church having been built upon the rock of Jesus Christ, and having been purchased by him with his own blood, it is perfectly proper and logical to call it "The Church of Jesus Christ." Hence we must conclude that the name in its entirety is logical and scriptural.

The report then continued:

We should point out that the word "reorganized," as argued by Elbert A. Smith, is used because at one or more times during the history of the world the church on earth has lapsed into a disorganized condition. Attention is called to this because most often the argument today is that this is needed to distinguish the church from the church of Jesus Christ of Latter Day Saints with headquarters in Salt Lake City, Utah. Brother Smith did not use this last argument, but rather he did point out that the church has lapsed into a disorganized condition at one or more times during the history of the world.

During the past quarter of a century a number of attempts were made to change the name of the church or else to secure General Conference agreement on a contraction which could be used when the formal designation of the church is not necessary. Action favoring the use of the term "Saints" was approved in 1972, but did not find ready acceptance throughout the church. In 1976, on recommendation of the First Presidency, all prior resolutions pertaining to the name of the church were rescinded and it was resolved,

that the church be identified locally by such terms as may be responsive to time and place and circumstances. . . that the English language name of the church wherever it is used officially and legally be "The Reorganized Church of Jesus Christ of Latter Day Saints."[2]

"Organized and established agreeably to the laws of our country" (1a). The church was organized April 6, 1830. It is possible that John Whitmer and one or two others who were not present at the meeting had already been baptized; but Joseph, Sr., Lucy, and Emma of the Smith family and Martin Harris, Christian Whitmer, Jacob

96

Whitmer, and Hyrum Page of the Book of Mormon witnesses were baptized on or soon after April 6, 1830.

The prophet's account of the organization is as follows:

Whilst the *Book of Mormon* was in the hands of the printer, we still continued to bear testimony and give information, as far as we had opportunity; and also made known to our brethren that we had received commandment to organize the church, and accordingly we met together for that purpose, at the house of the above-mentioned Mr. Whitmer (being six in number) on Tuesday, the sixth day of April, A.D. one thousand eight hundred and thirty.

Having opened the meeting by solemn prayer to our heavenly Father we proceeded (according to previous commandment) to call on our brethren to know whether they accepted us as their teachers in the things of the kingdom of God and whether they were satisfied that we should proceed and be organized as a church according to the said commandment which we had received. To these they consented by an unanimous vote. I then laid my hands upon Oliver Cowdery and ordained him an elder of the "Church of Jesus Christ of Latter Day Saints," after which he ordained me also to the office of an elder of said church. We then took bread, and brake it with them, also wine, blessed it, and drank it with them. We then laid our hands on each individual member of the church present that they might receive the gift of the Holy Ghost, and be confirmed members of the church of Christ. The Holy Ghost was poured out upon us to a very great degree. Some prophesied, whilst we all praised the Lord and rejoiced exceedingly.[3]

The standing of Joseph Smith as "first elder" (1b) is clear. That of Oliver Cowdery as "second elder" is not quite so clear. Both are called apostles[4] although the apostolic quorum had not yet been organized. In 1835 the members of the Quorum of Twelve were called through the three Book of Mormon witnesses, with Joseph Smith also participating. Oliver was one of these witnesses. But his designation as "second elder" apparently had less significance after this time. He was never a member of the First Presidency or of the Twelve although in September 1837 he and Joseph Smith, Sr., Hyrum Smith, and John Smith, were sustained as "assistant counselors" and (with the members of the First Presidency) were "considered the heads of the church."[5]

"God ministered unto him by an holy angel" (2b).

This was Moroni,[6] the messenger sent from the presence of God to instruct Joseph regarding the Book of Mormon plates.[7]

"Confirmed to others by the ministering of angels" (2e). Notably to the three witnesses; see their testimony at the forefront of the Book of Mormon.

"Proving to the world that the Holy Scriptures are true" (2e). This refers directly to the Book of Mormon, which vindicates the prophetic foresight recorded in Isaiah 29:1-14, in Ezekiel 37:15-28, etc. It refers in part, also, to the vindication of other prophecies.[8]

"By them shall the world be judged" (3a). It is a little difficult to be sure what is the antecedent of "them," but a little study makes it fairly clear that both the Book of Mormon and the Holy Scriptures are referred to. The thought is that the combined testimony of these two witnesses together with that of angels and of an inspired priesthood leaves men without excuse.

"It shall turn to their own condemnation" (3c). When men reject the counsel of God, such rejection condemns them in their own selves, just as failure to respond to an impulse of kindliness turns that impulse into a malignant thing. It is related of Jesus that at one time he came into a Samaritan village and when the Samaritans refused him their hospitality, his disciples urged him to punish the villagers by calling down fire from heaven. Instead of doing so, Jesus merely passed on, and in his passing by there came to those villagers the greatest possible condemnation. That village might have become famous throughout the world as the place of some great deed of salvation, or one of its sons might have brought it glory in the service of the Master. Instead it is lost in obscurity, its name unknown.

In paragraph 4 of this section is a *fundamental statement of the Latter Day Saint idea of God*. It should be closely studied in connection with the statements of the Bible and Book of Mormon and the other statements of the revelations, for our contribution to the development of the idea of

God is an important indicator of our spiritual stature.

The following tabulation of Doctrine and Covenants references concerning the nature and attributes of Divinity is taken from some notes prepared by Elder Walter W. Smith.

The attributes of Divinity, sections 85:2, 10; 90:1.
    Self-existence, sections 17:4; 18:2; 22:1; 39:1; 61:1; 76:1.
    Unchangeability, sections 2:1; 17:2, 4.
    Eternity, sections 2:1; 34:1, etc.
The Godhead are one in all things, sections 10:1-12; 17:4; 90:1.
    Three persons, sections 17:5; 22:17; 36:1; 90:1.
    The Father, sections 36:1; 42:15; 45:11; 90:4.
    The Son, sections 16:7; 17:2, 4, 5; 59:1; 90:1.
    The Holy Ghost, sections 34:5; 46:1; 85:1; 97:2.
God is the Creator, sections 22:23; 76:3; 90:1.
God is the Lawgiver, sections 42:22, 23; 85:31.
God is to be seen of the Saints, sections 67:3; 83:3; 85:12; 91:2; 94:5.

"After his own image and in his own likeness" (4b). With such a statement as this written into modern revelation, Latter Day Saints think of man as being essentially in the same image as God. This point of view is confirmed by many scriptural citations,[9] but much more important than any possible resemblance of form is our spiritual kinship with Divinity. We are made in his likeness in all our yearnings for truth, beauty, and goodness. As Bernard Iddings Bell has said: "While it may be true that in the functions of our physical bodies we are akin to the animals, it is also true that in our yearnings and strivings we are akin to God himself. The former may be important, but the latter is all important."

"And gave unto them commandments" (4b). Those who accept this statement at its face value must believe in an original revelation from God to man which was given prior to the time when "by the transgression of these holy laws, man became sensual and devilish, and became fallen man."

"He suffered temptations, but gave no heed unto them" (5b). This cannot mean that these temptations were not real, but that the Master was not overcome by them. The writer to the Hebrews says that Jesus "was in all points

tempted like as are we, yet without sin."[10]

"*That as many as would believe and be baptized, in his holy name, and endure in faith to the end, should be saved*" (5d). This is a concise enumeration of some of the basic conditions of salvation. The initial word *that* ties the believing and being baptized to the gift of the Son of God, his temptations, crucifixion, resurrection, and reigning power which are mentioned previously. Baptism, furthermore, must be "in his holy name" to be effective. This is but another way of saying that it must be done by his authority and for the achievement of his purposes. Yet again, salvation is not guaranteed to those who are just immersed, but only to those who are baptized and "endure in faith to the end." The Book of Mormon is particularly clear in regard to the points mentioned in this paragraph.[11]

"*All those from the beginning*" (5e). One of the distinctive beliefs of the church is that the gospel has been preached among men from the beginning. This is fully attested by the scriptures.[12]

"*Which Father, Son, and Holy Ghost are one God, infinite and eternal, without end*" (5h). See notes on paragraph 4.

"*Justification through the grace of our Lord and Savior Jesus Christ, is just and true*" (6b). Justification means the act of God in receiving a man who has been a sinner, but who now seeks to do the will of God, as though he is righteous. It is the forgiveness which God graciously extends to all who truly repent. Paul discusses justification at length in his letters to the Galatians and the Romans.

"*Sanctification through the grace of our Lord and Savior Jesus Christ, is just and true*" (6c). Sanctification means setting apart to the service of God. This may be in formal ordination for special service, or in confirmation for the high calling of sainthood, or in other ways. The evidence of sanctification is not such a setting apart but a complete devotion to the cause of truth.

"*There is a possibility that man may fall from grace*" (6d). Some Bible students doubt this. It will be remembered, however, that Lucifer, Son of the Morning, fell from the

100

very presence of God.[13] Judas fell from the apostleship.[14] The writer to the Hebrews discusses this question at some length, and renders his decision in harmony with this statement of the revelation.

Note the conditions of effective baptism (7). Sinners must

Humble themselves before God.

Recognize their need of God and enter into his church by the same door as others.

Come forth with broken hearts and contrite spirits.

Recognize their partial responsibility for the presence of sin in the world.

Witness before the church that they have truly repented of all their sins.

Show willingness to take upon them the name of Jesus Christ.

Have "a determination to serve him to the end."

Manifest by their works evidence of fitness for baptism.[15]

Receive of the Spirit of Christ unto the remission of their sins.[16]

"An apostle is an elder" (8b). This is in harmony with I Peter 5:1, and with the later revelation which indicates that all those who hold the Melchisedec priesthood may officiate in the office of elder or in the Aaronic priesthood as occasion may require. Webster gives the following definitions for some of the words used here and in the succeeding paragraphs:

Preach: To proclaim by public discourse, to deliver or pronounce, to proclaim tidings, to give serious advice, especially on morals or religion.

Teach: To show how, to train, or accustom to some action, to direct as an instructor, to impart the knowledge of (Syn.—instruct, inform, inculcate, tell, guide, counsel).

Expound: To set forth, state, present, to interpret (Syn.— explain).

Exhort: To incite by words or advice; to animate or urge by arguments, to urge strongly, hence to incite and encourage; advise, counsel.

Invite: To request, to offer allurements to; to attract (Syn.—bid, call, ask, summon, implore, beg, entreat, persuade, allure, entice).

Warn: To put on guard; to give notice, information, or intimation beforehand; to caution, to inform, to give notice to, to notify, to bid; command, to admonish, advise (Syn.—forewarn, caution).

Watch over: To tend, guard; to have in keeping, to give heed to, to observe actions or motions for any purpose; vigil, to be vigilant.

"Administer bread and wine—the emblems of the flesh and blood of Christ" (8b). In the Book of Commandments this reads, "administer the flesh and blood of Christ, according to the scriptures." The rephrasing was an important clarification.

"The elders are to conduct the meetings. . . according to the commandments and revelations of God" (9). Evidently, those whose duty it is to preside should prepare themselves by careful study of the commandments and revelations so that, when called upon to act, they will have a basic understanding of their responsibilities and limitations. This must be reinforced by lives which merit the indwelling of the Holy Ghost. Neither is sufficient by itself. Even an elder who is living well needs to study what has been revealed for his guidance, and certainly every student needs to live for the endowment of the Spirit.

"The priest's duty is. . . to visit the house of each member, and exhort them to pray vocally and in secret, and attend to all family duties" (10b). This is one of the most important duties falling to the lot of the priest—to move among the members from house to house, meeting them in the privacy of their homelife, strengthening them with wise counsel, exhorting them to attend to all their duties, and in all this representing the interest of the church in their welfare. The priests go into these homes representing God and the church.[17]

"He is to take the lead of meetings when there is no elder present" (10d). In practice it has been our custom to

use the Aaronic priesthood to take charge of meetings occasionally. While there may be some argument for such a practice, the strict interpretation of the law is that, when elders are available, the Aaronic priesthood are not to take the lead of meetings. The point appears to be that meetings shall be directed by experienced ministers.

"*If occasion requires*" (10e). Endless controversy has been waged over the exact meaning of this and parallel sentences, yet in the nature of things there can be no final definition of the exact occasion which will require the priest to assist the elder or the deacon to assist the teacher. Quite evidently, however, where an elder and a priest are both available for the exercise of these various functions, the elder will take the lead and will be assisted by his brother of the Aaronic priesthood. Certainly, also, no occasion will so require the priest to assist the elder as the occasion when the elder cannot be present but the priest is available.

When the duties of the elders, priests, teachers, and deacons are compared with each other, it will be seen that the most distinctive task of the teacher is to "*see that the church meet together often*" (11b). This would seem to indicate that he is to perform his other functions in common with the other brethren of the priesthood, but that this is his outstanding task and that his other work is to be achieved through seeing that the Saints meet together frequently and that they meet in the Spirit of the Master, having no hard feeling toward each other nor gossiping nor speaking evilly of each other. If the teachers of the church would devote themselves to the constructive task of bringing the Saints together in frequent services with fully prepared hearts and minds, the negative aspects of their task would be almost eliminated and their constructive power in the work of the church would be multiplied.

There is no complete statement of the duties of the deacon in the Doctrine and Covenants. The statement prepared by President Joseph Smith in 1900 was adopted by the

General Conference and has become the guide to the duties of the deacon.[18]

"Ordained according to the gifts and callings of God unto him" (12a). Priesthood is a stewardship in which men are set apart to use their divinely given talents in the service of God and of their fellows. Men are not called to perform tasks for which they have no qualifications but "according to" their qualifications. Sometimes the gifts upon which a man's call is based have not yet been developed sufficiently to be easily recognized. Always talents which are used in divine service become enriched and developed by such use.

Functions which were at first discharged by the elders in the absence of higher officers were quite properly restricted to certain other councils and quorums as the men became available for the organization. Joseph Smith, for example, presided over the infant church as an elder. But later revelation provided that the president of the church must be a high priest.[19]

"From time to time, as said conferences shall direct or appoint" (13). While special conferences may be called from time to time by those having general or regional jurisdiction, the normal assemblies of conferences will be governed by rules laid down by those conferences.

"The several elders composing this church of Christ are to meet in conference. . . to do whatever church business is necessary to be done at the time" (13). At this time there were no local conferences. These grew as the necessity for them arose. The elders constitute the basic membership of conferences, their responsibilities in this connection being legislative rather than administrative or judicial.

The elders were not necessarily the only members of the conferences, even at the beginning. For example, the conference or council authorizing the formation of the Standing High Council of the church included high priests, elders, priests, and members all of whom apparently "voted in the name and for the church."[20] The early conferences of the Reorganization were not restricted to elders. By their

104

own action, mission conferences in the early Reorganization were sometimes restricted to elders or to elders and priests.

With the growth of the church some restriction had to be placed on the number of conference participants, since the participation of more than a relatively small number makes for confusion rather than for clarity. This limitation on conference membership becomes most apparent and urgent in relation to world conferences, and the earlier rule that elders are ex-officio members of the World Conference was revised by the conference of 1964 to provide that only such elders as are members of the general quorums, the church secretary, general conference appointees, superannuated appointees, and presidents of districts, branches, and stake congregations, have ex-officio rights in the world assemblies.[21]

Many have supposed that paragraphs 16 and 17 of this section show that provision was made prior to April 6, 1830, for the various officers here mentioned. This is not necessarily true. These two paragraphs may have been received after the organization of the church and included in this section as the most fitting place for their publication. They are not to be found in *The Evening and the Morning Star* of June 1832, nor in the reprint of June 1833. The first publication of the two paragraphs, as far as I have been able to discover, was in the Kirtland reprint of *The Evening and the Morning Star* of January 1835.

In further explanation it may be stated that none of the revelations were officially approved by the church in book form until the Doctrine and Covenants was received in 1835. Section 17, which was Section 2 of that edition, was approved with the inclusion of the two paragraphs in question. Paragraphs 16 and 17 do not violate any other instruction received. They merely go into greater detail regarding necessary phases of administration.

"*No person is to be ordained to any office in this church. . . without the vote of that church*" (16a). In this connection the following General Conference resolution adopted April 15, 1910, is important:

Resolved, that no ordination to any office in the priesthood shall obtain until the "call" has been approved by those holding the Melchisedec priesthood and in authority, whether it be in stakes, districts, or branches.

It will be noted that it is not sufficient for the call to be approved by men holding the Melchisedec priesthood, but these elders must also be the regularly appointed officers of branch or district or General Church.[22]

"Every president of the high priesthood" (17). The president of the high priesthood is the president of the church.[23] Joseph was ordained president of the high priesthood of the church at Amherst, Ohio.

I called a general council of the church, and was acknowledged as the president of the high priesthood, according to a previous ordination at a conference of high priests, elders, and members, held at Amherst, Ohio, on the twenty-fifth of January, 1832. The right hand of fellowship was given to me by the bishop, Edward Partridge, in behalf of the church. The scene was solemn, impressive, and delightful.[24]

"Sufficient time to expound all things. . . previous to their partaking of the sacrament and being confirmed" (18b). In actual practice we instruct prospective church members in the duties of church membership prior to their baptism, so that it has been quite legitimate for their confirmation to follow almost immediately. Those who join the church from the church school might well be baptized when they are ready to affirm their allegiance to God and the church, and then continue their study until they are prepared for full membership. The advantage of delaying confirmation until prospective members understand "all things concerning the church of Christ" is that they thus gain the advantage of obedience to the ordinance of baptism in their preparation for the full church membership.

The ordinance of the blessing of children (19) should not be administered to children who are old enough to be baptized.[25]

"Capable of repentance" (20). Young children are not eligible for baptism, since they are not "capable of repentance," in the sense of this instruction, nor are mental incompetents. These are not allowed to make legal

106

contracts.[26] The minister officating in the ordinance of baptism should be careful to use the words specified here. They differ slightly from the Book of Commandments which uses "authority" rather than "commissioned," as does III Nephi 5:25.

"Bless and sanctify this bread [wine] to the souls of all those who partake [drink] of it" (22, 23). It is to be noted here that the bread and wine used in the sacrament are simply blessed for the use of those who partake of them on that occasion and with an understanding of their purpose. The bread and wine are emblems only, and are to be partaken in remembrance of the body and blood of Jesus. They become efficacious to our salvation if they are partaken of worthily. Unworthy participation in so sacred an ordinance must necessarily bring its condemnation. Any of the bread or wine which is unused is merely bread and wine and has no sacramental properties.

"Any member of the church of Christ transgressing, or being overtaken in a fault, shall be dealt with as the Scriptures direct" (24). (See Matthew 5:23, 24; Doctrine and Covenants 42:20-23.)

"The several conferences" (25a). The following from the pen of President Joseph Smith is well worth remembering:

The holding of local and general conferences we believe to have been, and still to be, one of the surest, safest, and best means that could have been or that can be used to the accomplishment of a proper assimilation of thought and spirit among brethren, and the right understanding of doctrine among the teachers and those taught. These local and general conferences we believe to be authorized by the general laws of the church under which the promulgation of the gospel was to be carried on; and they are not therefore the creatures of local organizations called churches or branches. They are natural and necessary assemblings of the church officers for the transaction of necessary business connected with the carrying out of the great program of salvation, and for the free interchange of thought, expression of opinion, and the preaching of the word. We trust that such assemblings will be more largely attended than heretofore.

The range of business which may be done at these conferences is very wide, and comprises all "things necessary to be done"; the necessity for the doing of any particular business being the law governing the case, "according to the Bible, *Book of Mormon*, and the *Doctrine and Covenants.*"[27]

"*A list of the names of the several members*" (25a). Here is provision for the church statistician, and for a careful record of the church membership. A careful analysis of the baptisms of the various branches is a splendid indication of the vitality of the work in these branches.

At the conclusion of this analysis of Section 17, the following comment by Herman C. Smith is particularly apropos:

> Was Joseph Smith making provision for all this stupendous organization and its practical workings by his own wisdom and cunning? If so, he was taking desperate chances on being able to find the requisite material—the men to fill the places provided for them. Yet as time moved on, men who had not known of the existence of Joseph Smith when the provision was made, came forward one by one, dropped into line, took the positions provided for them, subscribed to the fraud, if fraud it was, and cheerfully suffered persecution, violence, and death for the cause.[28]

---

[1]See notes on paragraphs 16 and 17. [2]*Journal of History* 17:291. [3]*Times and Seasons*, Volume 3, pages 944, 945. [4]Section 19:1a, 3b. [5]Church History, Volume 2, page 107. [6]Section 26:2; 110:20. [7]Church History, Volume 1, pages 12-15. [8]Zechariah 2:1-4; Revelation 14:6. [9]Hebrews 1:3; Genesis 1:26; 32:30; Exodus 33:11; John 5:37. [10]Hebrews 4:15. [11]Nephi 12:10-35; Moroni 6:3. [12]Galatians 3:8, 9; I Corinthians 10:2-4; Hebrews 4:2. [13]Isaiah 14:12-15. [14]Acts 1:25. [15]Matthew 3:7-9. [16]Acts 2:38. [17]Elbert A. Smith in *Duties of Branch Officers*, page 39. [18]See *General Conference Resolution* 449. [19]Section 104:11b. [20]Section 99:3. [21]*General Conference Bulletin*, 1964:214-217. [22]Section 125:14; see also *Daily Herald* 1932:102. [23]Section 104:11. [24]*Times and Seasons*, Volume 5, pages 611, 612, 624. [25]General Conference Resolutions, April 9, 1913. [26]Moroni 8:11-28. [27]*Saints' Herald*, Volume 18, page 743. [28]Church History, Volume 1, pages 77, 78.

SECTION 18

Martin Harris was greatly concerned regarding the teachings of Joseph and Oliver and his own relation to the new religious movement. His relatives were afraid that he was being victimized in being asked to finance the publication of the Book of Mormon, and he himself was greatly concerned about the question of eternal damnation. He talked with the prophet about these matters and the important revelation, now Section 18 of the Doctrine and Covenants, was given in answer to his petition. It was received by Joseph at Manchester, New York, March, 1830, about a month prior to the organization of the church.

The words *"alpha and omega"*(1) are the first and last letters of the Greek alphabet. In the New Testament the two are always used together and apply to God or to Jesus Christ.[1] In Jewish thought the whole extent of a process or a period is indicated by reference to its beginning and its end. The basic use of the expression, which appears in Isaiah 44:6; 48:12, accents the uniqueness of the one God as creator and redeemer, as the ultimate source and ground of existence. When applied to Jesus it expresses his unique sovereignty.[2]

"Surely every man must repent or suffer" (1d). Those who do not repent continue in sin and so fail to set in motion the processes of righteousness which alone can bring immortality and eternal life. The unrepentant sinner suffers because he lives in spiritual darkness and because as long as he does so his life lacks the creative forces of forgiveness.

"It is not written that there shall be no end to this torment; but it is written endless torment" (1e). Much of the current preaching a hundred years ago was an endeavor to frighten people into the kingdom of heaven by preaching the terrors of hell. It was important that men and women should realize the awfulness of sin and its terrible consequences. It still is important. But it was important also that men should not be given a revolting idea of God. It was here that current religion was especially weak. Martin Harris is assured that "endless torment" and "endless punishment" are both "endless" in the sense that they proceed from him who is eternal, without beginning of days or end of years. In this connection read carefully Section 76:4.

"Endless punishment is God's punishment" (2e). Divine punishment is not something added because the majesty

and dignity of the Almighty have been flouted; it is the natural flowering of an ungodly way of living, an inevitable resultant against which the messengers of God have been warning men from the beginning of time. Jesus taught us that the righteous life, although apparently costly at times, cannot be separated from its legitimate rewards even by death. Similarly the unrighteous life, even though sometimes desirable and happy, cannot be separated from its own tainted fruitage. Eternal punishment has been written into the very nature of things by the Creator.

"I command you to repent" (2f). Despite his weakness, Martin Harris was truly consecrated. If he had failed to do his part in publishing the Book of Mormon, he would never have escaped remorse. Something of this is indicated where he is reminded of his feelings when the Spirit of the Lord was withdrawn from him. Darkness is more devastating than ever to those who have known the light.

"Confess your sins" (2e). Read Section 42:23 in this connection. The mere fact of making a statement of sinning has no spiritual significance. Adequate confession demands (a) that we shall learn the mind of Christ, (b) that we shall see our sinning as he sees it, (c) that we shall loathe it as he loathes it, (d) that in this spirit we shall acknowledge our responsibility, and (e) that we shall make whatever restitution is possible and so show our sincere repentance. The ordinances of the gospel should be powerful factors in helping sinners to see themselves as they really are, and in persuading them to make the restitution which the gospel requires. John wrote, "If we confess our sins, he is faithful and just to forgive us our sins, and to cleanse us from all unrighteousness."[3]

"Preach naught but repentance" (2l). This instruction is still timely. Many of us have lost any deep awareness of the awfulness of sin. We need to be stirred again regarding our own shortcomings, many of which are not mere mistakes but are treason against the Lord who bought us. Any "gospel" which omits the call to repentance is false.

"Thou shalt not covet thine own property" (3b). Here is

a revolutionary statement of the very essence of stewardship. Stewardship is the management of the divine investment in us for the achievement of the purposes of God. We have no right to manage his investment in us for any purpose which the Lord does not approve. Martin Harris is here warned against coveting his own property through desiring to spend it for his own ends when it was required for the work of God.

"Thou shalt pray vocally. . . before the world. . . and thou shalt declare glad tidings" (4a, b). Martin Harris's trouble seems to have been that he wanted to stand on the sidelines and yet feel the thrill of the game. The Lord here tells him to commit himself irrevocably to the Restoration movement. Conviction would come to him in defending the church even more quickly than it would come in meditating by himself. This is true today, too. Many a man has been converted himself in converting others.

"Of tenets thou shalt not talk, but thou shalt declare repentance and faith on the Savior, and remission of sins by baptism and by fire; yea, even the Holy Ghost" (4d). This is personal evangelism of the simplest and most effective kind. Knowledge of the gospel follows the word of testimony and the enlightenment of the Spirit.

"Pay the debt thou hast contracted with the printer" (5d). In agreement with Joseph, Martin Harris had contracted to pay for five thousand copies of the Book of Mormon to be printed for $3,000. Pressure was being brought to bear upon him not to fulfill this contract, but he did so. He testified to David B. Dillee that this money was repaid to him, the inference being that this was from the income from the sale of the book.

Revelation 1:8; 22:13. [2]*Interpreter's Dictionary of the Bible,* A/D, 88. [3]I John 1:9.

SECTION 19

On Tuesday, the sixth of April, 1830, six of those who had

been baptized met to organize the church. After opening the meeting by solemn prayer Joseph and Oliver called on their brethren to know whether these accepted them as teachers in the things of the kingdom of God, and whether they were satisfied that the church should be organized according to the commandments received. To these things those present consented by unanimous vote. Accordingly Joseph ordained Oliver an elder, after which Oliver ordained Joseph to the office of elder. The brethren then partook of the Communion and were later confirmed by the two elders for the receipt of the Holy Ghost. Revelation had already been given providing for the more complete organization of the church, and although a partial organization was all that was possible at this time, each of those present was ordained to the priesthood. The charter members of the church, in the order of their baptism, were Oliver Cowdery, Joseph Smith, Samuel H. Smith, Hyrum Smith, David Whitmer, and Peter Whitmer.[1]

Before separating, further instruction was received from the Lord and this is contained in Section 19.

There shall be a record kept among you" (1a). Evidently one of the things which had been impressed upon the mind of Joseph during his years of preparation for the prophetic office was the extreme importance of keeping a proper record of important events. This instruction was repeated to him and to the infant church at this time, and was reaffirmed quite frequently in the early days. If it had been followed faithfully, we would by this time have a mass of material from which to draw conclusions of great value in our work.

"Inspired of the Holy Ghost to lay the foundation thereof" (1b). The church is not a man-made organization. While we admire and respect Joseph Smith, the church is not his church. The church is *the* church only so far as it is *of* Jesus Christ.

"Thou shalt give heed unto all his words and commandments" (2a). He who receives the servants of God receives also the Master who sends them. It is in this sense that the

church is here instructed to pay diligent heed to the words and commandments given through Joseph. We expect that the Father will reveal himself through the one who has been chosen and ordained as the mouthpiece of God to the church. This does not mean that we must receive the word of the prophet blindly but that we shall so live that our diligent heed to this word shall be accompanied by the testimony of the Spirit of God in our own souls.

"Him have I inspired to move the cause of Zion in mighty power for good" (2d). "The cause of Zion" is very dear to the heart of the Lord, and has found a prominent place in the purpose and work of the church from the very beginning. It is not something added to our gospel endeavor. It is a vital element in the gospel and the goal of our inspired endeavors.

"I will cause that he shall mourn for her no longer" (2e). It is difficult to understand the meaning of this phrase in the light of after events, for certainly Joseph was only just beginning to enter into the series of difficulties which descended upon him because of his diligence in the cause of Zion. The solution seems to be in the future tense, "I *will* cause," etc. The work of Zion is not to be accomplished without bitter pain and anguish.

"I will bless all those who labor in my vineyard, with a mighty blessing" (3a). Every one of the six who were present at this meeting suffered great hardships for the cause of Zion. Two of them were assassinated. Yet the testimony of those who labor earnestly in the vineyard of the Lord is that this promise is repeatedly fulfilled. In spite of the cost of effective church service, its rewards are sure.

"Jesus was crucified by sinful men for the sins of the world" (3a). Note the importance of this concise statement of the atonement made to the charter members of the church on the very day it was organized.

"He should be ordained" (3b). There is one point in the ordination commanded in this revelation which may trouble some students, and this is that Joseph ordained Oliver to

the eldership prior to his own ordination. A similar occurrence is recorded at the June Conference of 1831 when those holding the office of elder ordained their brethren to the high priesthood. In this connection it should be noted that when Joseph was ordained to the presidency of high priesthood, he also was ordained by those who held a lesser office than he. The explanation is that those in whom the rights of priesthood exist may officiate in any ordination where *emergencies* demand and where a clear *command of God is known*, although where the church is perfectly organized, the general rule is for the greater to ordain the lesser. Certainly the command of God is sufficient warrant for the performance of any act, and we can conceive of no better means of conferring authority in this dispensation than the means employed.

"*The first preacher of this church*" (3c). Oliver Cowdery delivered the first public discourse in the church in the home of Peter Whitmer, Sr., at Fayette, New York, on the Sunday following the organization of the church.

---

¹*Journal of History* 14:254.

SECTION 20

Even prior to April 6, 1830, many persons were interested in the work that Joseph was doing, and as soon as the church was organized some of these wished to become members if they could do so without severing the church connections they already had. The situation was closely akin to that in the apostolic church when interested Jews wanted to help as long as they could do so and still remain Jews. This question had to be solved before the apostolic church could go forward. It had to be solved before the Restoration movement could make progress. The revelation covering this point was given at Manchester, New York, in April 1830.

When we remember the clear instruction given Joseph in 1820 that he should join none of the other churches, it will be seen that the course indicated in this revelation is the only consistent and harmonious one. If the organization was to be just one more movement, men could transfer to it from any other without again going through the form of baptism. But if the new church was to be spiritually distinctive it was entirely fitting that all members should enter through the door of baptism.

An important aspect of baptism is the authority of the person officiating. To have admitted new members by transfer from other churches would have been equivalent to recognizing the authority of other ministers to baptize. This would have been fatal to our beliefs regarding a distinctive priesthood.

SECTION 21

One of the characteristics of the revival services frequently held in the vicinity where the church came into being was an intense conviction of sin. Careful students of our early church history have noted that this feeling carried over into the church, and one of the spiritual phenomena of those early days was the deep concern of those converted regarding their spiritual standing. It will be seen from reading this revelation that the group of men to whom it is addressed had all been eager for assurance that their sins were forgiven. Indeed, the main purpose of the revelation seems to be encouragement and reassurance in this regard.

This section is a composite of inspired counsel given at Manchester, New York, April 6, 1830. The five paragraphs are addressed to Oliver Cowdery, Hyrum Smith, Samuel Smith, Joseph Smith, Sr., and Joseph Knight and in the

Book of Commandments appeared as separate chapters. They were combined in the 1835 edition of the Doctrine and Covenants.

"Beware of pride" (1a). Oliver was a schoolteacher and was probably better educated than the members of the Smith family and the Saints gathered in from the neighborhood. He seems to have been aware of this and to have had difficulty in reconciling himself to the leadership of Joseph.

"Thy heart is open, and thy tongue loosed" (2a). In May 1829, nearly a year prior to the giving of this revelation, Hyrum had been warned, "You need not suppose that you are called to preach until you are called."[1] Now he has matured in experience, and he is called to minister in the priesthood.

"Thy calling is to exhortation and to strengthen the church continually." This is addressed to Hyrum (2a) and also to Samuel (3). The duties of Hyrum Smith as outlined here anticipate his call to be presiding patriarch of the church. This is emphasized in the phrase "this because of thy family."[2] While the major task of the church at this time and for a number of years was along missionary lines, Hyrum is nevertheless specifically instructed that his task is "to strengthen the church continually." Winning souls to Christ and strengthening those who have been won are both fundamental ministerial tasks. Neglect either of them and the whole church suffers.

"Thou art not as yet called to preach before the world" (3). Samuel Smith was ordained on the day this revelation was given. Within a short time after this he became actively engaged in the work of the ministry.

"This is thy duty from henceforth and for ever" (4). Joseph Smith, Sr., father of the Martyr, to whom these words are addressed, was naturally regarded as the father or counselor of the little group. His ministry for the ten remaining years of his life was in entire harmony with the instruction contained in this paragraph.

"It is your duty to unite with the true church" (5b). Mr.

116

Knight had been investigating for a considerable period.[3] He continued to investigate for about two months after receiving this revelation and was then baptized, probably in June 1830.

BIOGRAPHICAL NOTES

Oliver Cowdery (see Section 6).

Hyrum Smith (see Section 10).

Samuel Harrison Smith (see Doctrine and Covenants 52:6; 75:3) was born March 13, 1808, in Vermont, and was the fourth son of Joseph and Lucy Smith and a younger brother of the Martyr. He was the third person baptized into the church and was one of its six charter members and one of the eight witnesses to the Book of Mormon. He was ordained to the priesthood immediately after the organization of the church; a high priest June 3, 1831; and a member of the High Council February 17, 1834. His brothers attained greater prominence in the church than Samuel did, but none of them was more fully devoted. He died at Nauvoo, Illinois, July 30, 1844, slightly over one month after his brothers Joseph and Hyrum had been assassinated.

---

[1]Section 10:8. [2]Appendix A, Section 107:29. [3]Joseph Knight (see Section 11).

SECTION 22

Section 22 is a revelation received by Joseph Smith in June 1830 which was first published in the *Times and Seasons.*[1] It was first included in the Cincinnati edition of the Doctrine and Covenants in 1864. Apparently this was done by the personal decision of the compiler, Elder Isaac Sheen. Later it was found that the text of this section differed at a few points from that of the Inspired Version and by action of General Conference of 1909 these differences were corrected.[2] Its inclusion in the Doctrine and Covenants was not given specific official approval until the General Conference of 1970, although it had appeared in the forepart of the Inspired Version.

"*He saw God face to face, and he talked with him*" (1).[3] The position of Moses is differentiated from that of succeeding prophets in that, while the Lord made himself known to those in dark speeches, he knew Moses face-to-face, and spoke to him mouth to mouth. There was an immediacy, freedom, and unveiled character in the intercourse of Moses with God which suited the place of honor he occupied, and the work he had to do in the economy of revelation.

"*The glory of God was upon Moses; therefore Moses could endure his presence*" (1). Something of the spirit and power of God, which gives light and understanding, was upon Moses.[4] Compare this experience with those of the brother of Jared, Peter, James, and John, and Joseph.

"*My works are without end*" (3b). When we think of the nature of God, we recognize that his works must be without end. He is still active in the work of creation. In this connection read paragraph 23 and remember that the idea of progress, which is the keynote of modern thought, was not approved widely until after the time of Darwin. In 1830 most people believed that the work of God had been completed long ago.

"*My works. . . never cease*" (3b). How like our heavenly Father this is, and how like the teachings of the Bible. Yet how revolutionary the idea of continuous revelation was when Joseph began his ministry!

"*No man can behold all my works except he behold all my glory*" (3c). Beholding the work of God is not just a matter of eyesight. It involves appreciation, and this is impossible without the Spirit of God. Many men looked on Jesus in the days of his flesh but failed to "see" his divinity. Similarly, many men look today on the works of God but fail to see the Creator. No man can really *see* the works of God unless he is endowed with the glory of God and his understanding is enlarged through this endowment.

118

"No man can behold all my glory, and afterwards remain in the flesh, on the earth" (3a). Consider what a partial revelation of the glory of God meant in the lives of Peter, James, and John.[5] Many years after the transfiguration, this and the resurrection remained the two major experiences in the life of the apostle Peter,[6] and gave him assurance amid all the doubts and difficulties of those cruel years. Note, also, the testimony of Joseph Smith and Sidney Rigdon in this connection.[7] If a partial enlightenment meant so much, what would a fullness mean?

"Thou art in the similitude of mine Only Begotten" (4a). Moses was a prophet and high priest and as such he led his people in seeking the kingdom of God. He was like Jesus also in the fact of his transfiguration and of his temptation. In all these ways, and in many others, Moses was the prototype of the Master.

"He is full of grace and truth" (4a). Compare this with Section 90:2.

> He received not of the fullness at the first, but received grace for grace; and he received not of the fullness at first, but continued from grace to grace, until he received a fullness; and thus he was called the Son of God, because he received not of the fullness at the first.

When this revelation was addressed to Moses the things which were to happen were so certain because of the very nature of Jesus our Savior that they were taken for granted as though they had already happened.

"I am a son of God, in the similitude of his Only Begotten" (8b). Moses reverted to this assurance continually with a new and exalted sense of destiny. In essence his position was this: Since I am fashioned after the likeness of the Son of God, then I must not be traitor to the great destiny which this implies.

"I could not look upon God except his glory should come upon me" (8c). All of us are humbled in the presence of a truly great man. This is a faint clue to the situation of Moses. No man can stand unashamed in the presence of God, except as he shares the life of divinity.

"Call upon God in the name of mine Only Begotten, and

119

worship me" (10). This is in harmony with the statement of Peter, "Neither is there salvation in any other; for there is none other name under heaven, given among men, whereby we must be saved."[8] Jesus himself has said also: "I am the way, the truth and the life: no man cometh unto the Father but by me."[9] Whoever, therefore, was saved before Christ came in the flesh was saved by and through him. Christ is "the Savior of all men, especially those that believe."[10] He "tasted death for every man."[11] It must be, therefore, that the atonement of Christ reaches back to Adam and forward to the last man who shall live on earth and shall need salvation. He was, is, and will be the same Redeemer and Savior to all who believe on his name.

"Tell me, I pray thee, why these things are so, and by what thou madest them?" (20). The insatiable thirst for understanding, which is the drive behind modern science at its best, has characterized the men of God in every age. It is the divine purpose to share this understanding with men. Note that the glory of God continued with Moses as Moses sought an answer to his question.

"Worlds without number have I created" (21c). This statement was made long before the discoveries of modern astronomy. There is in this sentence a wealth of meaning which was undreamed of at the time of Joseph Smith.

"This is my work and my glory, to bring to pass the immortality, and eternal life of man" (23b). After pointing out the universal scope of divine creation, the Father says that his work and his glory nevertheless center in man. Immortality is only desirable when it is wedded to spiritual quality. We do not want to spend much time here or in the hereafter with mean and despicable people. We do want to spend all the time we can with persons of genuine and durable quality. The work of God is crowned with glory when we who were created for eternal life enter into that life freely and happily and in response to his guidance.

"They shall be had again among the children of men" (24b). Joseph Smith, with Sidney Rigdon as scribe, diligently

continued his task of revising and correcting the scriptures, and on July 2, 1833, Sidney Rigdon, Joseph Smith, and Frederick G. Williams wrote to "the brethren in Zion," saying, "We this day finished the translation of the Scriptures, for which we returned gratitude to our Heavenly Father, and sat down immediately to answer your letters."

The version of the Scriptures made by Joseph Smith was not published in his lifetime. At his death in June 1844 the manuscripts were left in the hands of his widow, Mrs. Emma Smith, who retained them until 1866. At that time she delivered them into the hands of William Marks, Israel L. Rodgers, and William W. Blair, who had been appointed by the General Conference of the Reorganized Church of Jesus Christ of Latter Day Saints of that year to procure them for publication. This committee delivered them into the hands of the Committee of Publication, consisting of Joseph Smith, Israel L. Rodgers, and Ebenezer Robinson. The book was placed on sale in the closing days of 1867.[12] In this connection read also I Nephi 3:169-172, 192-194; II Nephi 2:19-23; Doctrine and Covenants 42:15. In view of the history of the Inspired Version the latter is particularly interesting with its promise that the scriptures "will be preserved in safety."

[1]*Times and Seasons* 4:71. [2]GCM 1909:1226. [3]See Genesis 17:6; Exodus 24:9-12; Ether 1:69-85. [4]Section 90:4. [5]Matthew 17:1-9. [6]II Peter 1:16-18. [7]Section 76:3. [8]Acts 4:12. [9]John 14:6. [10]I Timothy 4:10. [11]Hebrews 2:9. [12]See *Joseph Smith's "New Translation" of the Bible*, Introduction.

SECTION 23

This revelation was received in July 1830 at Harmony, Susquehanna County, Pennsylvania. It is addressed to Joseph and Oliver.

"Thou hast been delivered from all thine enemies" (1b). The entire countryside was stirred by the news that the work in which Joseph Smith and Oliver Cowdery were col-

laborating had resulted in the organization of the church. Many of the citizens took sides, those who joined the church becoming ardent Latter Day Saints and those who were not baptized becoming active antagonists of the new organization. Joseph found it difficult to secure money in order to support his family while he was engaged in his religious work.

"*Thou art not excusable in thy transgressions*" (1c). This was a difficult time for Joseph, and he needed the reassurance which came with the inspired reminder of his calling and his deliverance from persecution. But he also needed to be reminded that his strength was in his obedience. Such reminders came to him here and on other occasions.[1] That this was freely confessed by the fact that these revelations were made public attests the sincerity of the prophet. Note the importance of forgiveness to the ministry of such other leaders of the early church as Thomas B. Marsh, who was to be the first president of the Twelve;[2] Edward Partridge,[3] who was to be the first bishop of the church; the leading elders in Zion;[4] William E. McLellin, who was to be another of the charter members of the Twelve.[5]

"*They shall support thee*" (2a). One of the earliest problems of the church was that of supporting the ministry. Joseph was a poor man. He could not afford to give his time to church work without making some provision for supplying his temporal needs. Here he is assured that the churches to which he ministers will care for him. This principle has since become part of our financial policy. The call to expound the Scriptures was given to all members of the priesthood,[6] and to Emma Smith,[7] but was a special responsibility of Joseph.

"*Writing the things which shall be given thee by the Comforter*" (3a). During these early years of organization and explanation many revelations were received, and these had to be copied and made known to the Saints.

"*In temporal labors thou shalt not have strength, for this is not thy calling*" (4c). Joseph was an industrious man, and like others he probably wished to accumulate sufficient property to keep himself and his family in comfort. Here, however, he is warned that his peculiar gifts are such as fit him to direct the spiritual activities of the church, but that he must rely upon his ministry to supply his temporal wants.

"He [Oliver] shall not suppose that he can say enough in my cause" (5a). The note of urgency which we have already observed in the revelations is again sounded here. The work of the church was so important that Oliver must not take time for other activities. His life must be centered in the proclamation of the gospel. He must depend on his ministry, not only for his temporal necessities but also for the satisfaction of his own spiritual hunger.

Looking back, we can see that there was a special reason for this note of urgency. The need for proclamation of the gospel is always urgent, but at the beginning of the Restoration the times were uniquely propitious for the coming forth of the "great and marvelous work" and for making the testimony of the gospel part of the burgeoning experience of the American people.

"Require not miracles, except I shall command you" (6a). Miraculous powers are resident in the gospel, but miraculous intervention is properly a result of right-doing rather than an incentive to right-doing. Because of this the Saints were instructed from the first to concentrate on the basic matters of spiritual life and not to expend their spiritual energies in running after miraculous manifestations. If such manifestations are given first place, matters of even greater spiritual significance are relegated to second place.

"Casting off the dust of your feet against them as a testimony" (6b).[8] This instruction was followed closely by some of the early elders of the church.

"Whosoever shall go to law with thee shall be cursed by the law" (7b). This is of course predicated upon the righteousness of those who are attacked. The Saints cannot claim protection under this statement unless they are careful

to deal righteously with all men, so that any legal action undertaken against them is actual persecution.

"The church shall give unto thee in the very hour what thou needest for food" (7c). The Lord here puts the task of financing the ministry upon those to whom his servants minister. This principle was emphasized repeatedly in the early church, and was in harmony with the teachings of the Book of Mormon with which the Saints were already familiar.

---

[1]Section 2:3, 4. [2]*Ibid.* 30:2. [3]*Ibid.* 35:1a. [4]*Ibid.* 60:2f; 81:1a. [5]*Ibid.* 75:2b. [6]*Ibid.* 17:8d, 10d, 11f. [7]*Ibid.* 24:2c. [8]Matthew 10:14; Acts 13:51.

SECTION 24

This revelation is addressed to Emma Smith, the wife of Joseph. It was received while the prophet was still at Harmony, Susquehanna County, Pennsylvania, in July 1830. Its assurances were particularly comforting, as Emma's family turned against her shortly afterward and she was henceforth to be isolated from her own people and thrown into the very center of the life of the church.

"Thou shalt receive an inheritance in Zion" (1b). Emma was of good pioneer stock and was concerned with building a home and providing for the family which she and Joseph hoped to rear. It was a great venture of faith to throw in her lot with her prophet-husband and so to jeopardize her opportunities for building the home her heart desired.

"Thou art an elect lady" (1c). This title, with its indefinite article, might well have been shared by others. But Emma Smith came to have such a unique place in the life of the church that by common consent the title has been changed from *"an* elect lady" to *"the* elect lady."

Emma Smith was regarded as an "elect" lady in another sense. When the "female relief society of Nauvoo" was organized March 17, 1842, Emma was elected as president. In telling of this event her husband wrote:

I gave much instruction, read in the New Testament, and Book of Doctrine and Covenants, concerning the Elect Lady and showed that the elect meant to be elected to a certain work, etc., and that the revelation was then fulfilled by sister Emma's election to the presidency of the society, she having previously been ordained to expound the Scriptures.[1]

"Murmur not because of the things which thou hast not seen" (1d). Undoubtedly this refers to the plates of the Book of Mormon. There is no record that Emma ever saw the plates, and quite naturally her curiosity was aroused with regard to them. Nevertheless she had great faith in the prophetic mission of her husband and accepted his testimony. This was attested in many ways, one of them being her careful preservation of the manuscript of the Inspired Version of the Scriptures. Her situation reminds us of that of the apostle Thomas whose doubt and later conviction led the Lord to say, "Because thou hast seen me, thou hast believed; blessed are they that have not seen, and yet have believed."[2]

"Thou shalt be ordained under his hand to expound Scriptures, and to exhort the church" (2c). Emma was not ordained to any office in the priesthood. Although she was set apart to expound Scriptures and to exhort the church, there is little evidence that she did so in any formal way, except perhaps in the Relief Society meetings. In later years other women of the church have given notable service in the related fields of exposition and exhortation, although not ordained to this work. Marietta Walker, for example, was associated with Elder Henry A. Stebbins in compiling *A Compendium of the Faith and Doctrine of the Reorganized Church of Jesus Christ* which was prepared for the use of the ministry and of sabbath schools.[3] For fifty years Christiana Salyards wrote and edited quarterlies which were widely used among the ministry

in their preaching as well as being the official texts for Sunday school classes.

"Make a selection of sacred hymns" (3b). Until the time of James I no hymnbooks were known. There were metrical versions of the songs and isolated hymns in considerable numbers, but until George Withers published his *Hymns and Songs of the Church* in 1623 no hymnbooks in our sense of the word were obtainable.

Despite the pressures of home duties, Emma Smith apparently entered immediately into the important work assigned to her. Hymns selected by her were published in the *Evening and Morning Star* 1832 and 1833, and *A Collection of Sacred Hymns* selected by Emma was issued from the press of F. G. Williams and Company at Kirtland in 1835. This hymnal was probably used at the dedication of the Kirtland Temple. It contained ninety hymns and was a book of 120 pages exclusive of the title page, the preface, and the index. It was of pocket size, and contained such present favorites as "Arise, My Soul, Arise," "Come, All Ye Sons of Zion," "Glorious Things of Thee Are Spoken," "Guide Us, O Thou Great Jehovah," "How Firm a Foundation," "How Pleased and Blessed Was I," "Jesus, Mighty King in Zion," "Joy to the World! The Lord Is Come," "Let Us Pray, Gladly Pray," "Now, Let Us Rejoice in the Day of Salvation," "Redeemer of Israel," and "The Spirit of God Like a Fire Is Burning."

The following remarks were made in the preface to this collection:

In order to sing by the Spirit, and with the understanding, it is necessary that the *Church of the Latter Day Saints* should have a collection of "SACRED HYMNS," adapted to their faith and belief in the gospel, and as far as can be, holding forth the promises made to the fathers who died in the precious faith of a glorious resurrection, and a thousand years' reign on earth with the Son of Man in his glory. Notwithstanding the church, as it were, is still in its infancy, yet, as the song of the righteous is a prayer unto God, it is sincerely hoped that the following collection, selected with an eye single to his glory, may answer every purpose till more are composed, or till we are blessed with a copious variety of the songs of Zion.

A collection of sacred hymns for the Church of Christ of Latter Day Saints was selected and published by Benjamin C. Elsworth in 1839. It had a preface almost identical with that in Emma Smith's collection of 1835, and contained most of the hymns she had chosen plus a few others—a hundred and fourteen hymns altogether. A larger collection of two hundred and ninety-six hymns was published in England in 1840 or early 1841 by authority of Brigham Young, Parley P. Pratt, and John Taylor of the Twelve. In 1843 there was *A Collection of Sacred Hymns Adapted to the Faith and Views of the Church of Jesus Christ of Latter Day Saints*, compiled by John Hardy, Boston, Dow and Jackson Press. This small book contained one hundred and sixty pages with index and included one hundred and fifty-five hymns.

BIOGRAPHICAL NOTE

Emma Hale Smith was born in Harmony, Pennsylvania, in 1804. She was married to Joseph Smith in 1827, and acted as his scribe while he was translating the early part of the Book of Mormon. She shared the fortunes of her husband in Kirtland, Far West, and Nauvoo, and became the mother of eight children, four dying in infancy and four reaching manhood. These were Joseph (1832-1914), Frederick (1836-1862), Alexander (1838-1909), and David (1844-1904). After the assassination of Joseph, she refused to go west with the Twelve and remained in the vicinity of Nauvoo. Here, in 1847, she married Major Lewis C. Bidamon. During the "dark and cloudy day" Sister Bidamon retained the manuscript of the Inspired Version of the Holy Scriptures but later made this available to the Reorganization, by whom it was published. She became identified with the Reorganization when her son, Joseph, became its president, and remained faithful until her death at Nauvoo, Illinois, April 30, 1879.

Because of her refusal to go to Utah, few early Mormon writers reported kindly on Emma. More recently, however, this attitude has changed and she is recognized as a person of distinction, not merely as the wife of Joseph Smith but also in her own right. The *Deseret News* of Salt Lake City for Friday, October 4, 1935, contained an article entitled "One Hundred Years of Mormon Hymnology." Concerning Emma it said:

> She was a gracious hostess and friend of her husband's friends. She was cultured—the innate culture of birth, augmented by self-training and the refinement of experiences that came into her life as a helpmate of God's prophet.
>
> She possessed a charm of superior womanhood. Her dress, her demeanor, her features, all bespoke the "Elect Lady." The brilliant, kindly eye, alight with the intellect of womanly soul; the brow, the lips, the chin and curve of the neck. Dressed in tastes that bespeaks the patrician. Where would one find a higher type?...
>
> She was the companion and helpmate of the Prophet; she shared with him his joys and sorrows, and with him passed through the persecutions of New York, Ohio, Missouri and Illinois. God knew her; knew her heart, her mind, her inmost soul. God trained her for her calling, as he trained her husband for his; and God called her an "Elect Lady."

---

[1]History of the Church (Mormon) IV:552-553. [2]John 20:29. [3]Published in Lamoni, Iowa, September 1888.

SECTION 25

This revelation is addressed to Joseph Smith, Oliver Cowdery, and John Whitmer and was given at Harmony, Pennsylvania, in July 1830. John Whitmer was at this time residing with Joseph and was giving considerable help in writing.

The conference referred to is the second conference of the church. It was held at Fayette, New York, September 1830.

In looking forward to this conference the brethren named became concerned regarding procedure in church government. In response to prayer they were here instructed in the principle of common consent, which is basic to church life. (See notes on Section 27:4.)

SECTION 26

Concerning this revelation Joseph wrote:

Early in the month of August [1830], Newel Knight and his wife paid us a visit, at my place, at Harmony, Pennsylvania, and as neither his wife nor himself had been confirmed as yet, it was proposed that we should confirm them, and partake together of the sacrament, before he and his wife should leave us. In order to prepare for this, I set out to go to procure some wine for the occasion, but had gone only a short distance when I was met by a heavenly messenger, and received the following revelation; the first paragraph of which was written at this time.

Then follows the revelation known as Section 26. The Book of Commandments dates this revelation September 4, 1830. This was probably the date when the later paragraphs were added.

In obedience to the above commandment we prepared some wine of our own make, and held our meeting, consisting only of five; viz., Newel Knight and his wife, myself and my wife, and John Whitmer. We partook together of the sacrament after which we confirmed these two sisters (persons) into the church, and spent the evening in a glorious manner.[1]

"It mattereth not what ye shall eat, or what ye shall drink, when ye partake of the sacrament" (1b). The practice of the church is to use unfermented wine or water.[2] In Polynesia the milk of the green coconut is substituted for the wine.

"Ye shall partake of none, except it is made new among you" (1a). The Communion service should be surrounded with every dignity and with all fitting symbolism, and the special preparation of the wine for this service is entirely in harmony with the spirit of the occasion.

". . .with Moroni, whom I have sent unto you to reveal the Book of Mormon. . .to whom I have committed the *keys of the record of the stick of Ephraim"* (2a-b). This should be read in connection with Ezekiel 37:15-20 which biblical commentators have generally held to refer to the reunion of the tribes of Israel, but which Latter Day Saints have held to refer to the uniting of the Bible and the Book of Mormon to the confounding of false doctrine.[3]

"Elias, to whom I have committed the keys of bringing to pass the restoration of all things" (2b). Many of the reformers expected that such a work of restoration as is here mentioned would mark the work of God in the latter days. Martin Luther said: "I cannot tell what to say of myself. Perhaps I am Phillip's [Melancthon's] forerunner. I am preparing the way for him, like Elias, in spirit and in power."[4] Roger Williams, John Wesley, Alexander Campbell, and others expressed themselves similarly.

"Elijah, unto whom I have committed the keys of the power of turning the hearts of the fathers to the children and the hearts of the children to the fathers" (2e). Of a meeting held in the temple on April 3, 1836, Joseph wrote in part,

> After this vision had closed, (a vision of Jesus and Moses and Elias), another great and glorious vision burst upon us, for Elijah the prophet who was taken to heaven without tasting death, stood before us and said: "Behold the time has fully come which was spoken of by the mouth of Malachi, testifying that he [Elijah] should be sent before the great and dreadful day of the Lord come, to turn the hearts of the fathers to the children, and the children to the fathers, lest the whole earth be smitten with a curse. Therefore the keys of this dispensation are committed into your hands, and by this ye may know that the great and dreadful day of the Lord is here, even at the doors."[5]

"By whom I have ordained you and confirmed you to be apostles and especial witnesses of my name" (3a). The historical evidence concerning this ordination is not as full as we might desire. Elder Heman C. Smith wrote his conclusion as follows:

> Some have concluded from this language...that Peter, James, and John literally laid their own hands on the heads of Joseph and Oliver. But this commandment was to the effect that they should ordain

130

each other. This they afterwards did, as Joseph Smith relates in his history.[6]

Some have supposed that they received two ordinations; one, under the hands of Peter, James, and John, and one by each other; but it is scarcely supposable that they would fail to mention so important an item. There is no historical evidence of such an event. Nor is there any evidence that Peter, James, and John were present, either when the instruction was given to ordain them or when the ordination actually took place. The only historical account of their appearance is in the epistle quoted from above, and the place of that appearance is definitely given as between Harmony, Susquehanna County (Pennsylvania), and Colesville, Broome County (New York), while the place of instruction concerning ordination, as also the ordination itself, was at Fayette, Seneca County (New York). It is not safe then to write historically that Joseph Smith and Oliver Cowdery were ever ordained literally under the hands of Peter, James, and John. He who does so writes recklessly and without sufficient evidence upon which to base his conclusion.[7]

"A dispensation of the gospel for the last times; and for the fullness of times, in the which I will gather together in one all things" (3b, c). The church believes that the work of God in the various dispensations of time is moving rapidly toward culmination in these latter days. In this "hastening time," the authority of these other ages is recommitted to men, the keys of this authority being held by the First Presidency who are to lead in building the kingdom of God among men and thus put the capstone on the work of every other dispensation. Those who share this feeling of the slow but purposeful working out of the plan of the ages gain a sense of the tremendous sweep of the divine purpose.

---

[1]Times and Seasons 4:117-119. [2]General Conference Resolution 702. [3]II Nephi 2:17-23. [4]D'Aubique's History of the Reformation 2:105; see, also, Acts 3:21; Isaiah 40:1-5; 62:10-12; Revelation 14:6, 7. [5]Church History, Volume 2, page 46. [6]Times and Seasons, 3:945. [7]Church History, Volume 1, Pages 64, 65.

SECTION 27

This revelation is addressed to Oliver Cowdery and was

given at Fayette, New York, shortly after Joseph had removed there from Harmony, Pennsylvania. This removal was primarily occasioned by persecution in Harmony. When Joseph reached Fayette, he found that the Saints were considerably disturbed by certain spurious revelations received through a "peep-stone" by Hiram Page, who was a brother-in-law of Oliver Cowdery and of David Whitmer and one of the eight witnesses of the Book of Mormon. These revelations referred in the main to the building of the new Jerusalem, about which the Saints were very eager, but they did not agree with the revelations already received through Joseph. The situation soon became quite critical. The problem was twofold: (a) to settle the immediate difficulty and (b) to determine a procedure which would eliminate possible repetitions of the trouble. The first of these problems was provided for in the instructions of paragraphs 4 and 5. The second was provided for in paragraphs 2 and 3 and in subsequent revelation.

"He receiveth them even as Moses" (2a). The parallel drawn here between Joseph and Oliver on the one hand and Moses and Aaron on the other saved a great deal of explanation, for the early Saints were always willing to follow a scriptural precedent. In effect this instruction says that just as former-day Israel had one great prophetic leader with associate and subordinate officers, so must modern Israel be led by a modern prophet with associates and counselors. Note how clearly this principle is stated:

No one shall be appointed to receive commandments and revelations in the church except Joseph.

Oliver, the second elder, is to be obedient to the things given through Joseph, even as Aaron was obedient to those given through Moses.

Oliver, like Aaron, is to declare these commandments and revelations faithfully and with power and authority to the church.

Oliver may speak or teach by way of commandment as he shall be led by the spirit of wisdom.

Specifically, Oliver, who is the second elder, must not command Joseph, the first elder.

Joseph holds the keys of the mysteries and the revelations until another is appointed in his stead.

"Until I shall appoint unto them another in his stead" (2d). This appointment must be in harmony with the law of succession in the prophetic office. This instruction was elaborated in later revelations.[1]

"Thou shalt go unto the Lamanites" (3a). Oliver was more intimately connected with the coming forth of the Book of Mormon than anyone other than Joseph Smith himself. Since the days when he first sat under the inspiration of heaven in performing this wonderful work, Oliver had been eager to carry the gospel to the Indian peoples. Though acceptance of this call entailed many hardships, Oliver welcomed it and was happy to go.

It is interesting to note that the revelation which required Oliver to make amends for his mistake in listening to Hiram Page also entrusted him with this important mission. The confidence thus shown in Oliver must have done a great deal to prepare the way for repentance in the matter of the peep-stone revelations. Many times in the history of the church the Lord has helped good men overcome their mistakes by calling them to difficult tasks for him. Orson Hyde is an illustration of this. He had been in open rebellion against the administration of the church prior to June 1837, but during that month he attended the meeting in the temple where Heber C. Kimball was being set apart to preside over the British Mission. In the spirit of the occasion he acknowledged his faults and asked forgiveness and offered to accompany Brother Kimball on his mission. The offer was accepted and Orson Hyde did good work in England and in the United States for several years thereafter.

Although Oliver was the first elder to be appointed on this mission to the Lamanites, Peter Whitmer, Jr., was associated with him almost immediately,[2] and soon thereafter Parley P. Pratt and Ziba Peterson were also added to the number. In the course of their journey, these missionaries visited Ohio, where Parley P. Pratt was well known. They stayed in the vicinity of Kirtland for about three weeks and baptized over one hundred people, including Sidney Rigdon, Isaac

Morley, Lyman Wight, and John Murdock. Within a short time the membership of the church in and around Kirtland increased to over one thousand.

Doctor F. G. Williams, later to become counselor to President Joseph Smith, was baptized at Kirtland and joined the missionary party. Together the five men continued their journey west until they reached Independence, Missouri, early in 1831. Four of them had been four months on their journey, and at times their only food had been frozen cornbread and raw pork. Independence was a trading post established in 1827.

"No man knoweth where the city shall be built" (3c). Evidently the Saints were very curious to know the location of Zion. This had been one of the themes of the spurious revelations received through Hiram Page. The Saints were assured in this sentence that such instruction as had come to Hiram Page was not of God.

"It shall be on the borders by the Lamanites" (3d). This promise immediately invested the mission to the West with even more importance than it would otherwise have had. Oliver now went willingly across fifteen hundred miles of frontier country to the place which the Lord had selected for the center place of Zion.

The church had its beginning in a frontier environment, and the frontier was extremely important in the formation of our early church life. This frontier was more than the line of furthermost settlement. It was the natural home of men of restless pioneer spirit, the place of individual opportunity, the line whereon was being generated a new type of civilization in which New England and European ideals of education and character and political institutions were being tested and transformed.

"Thou shalt not leave this place until after the conference" (4a). This was the second conference of the church, held September 1, 1830. At this time the church had about seventy members.

"Between him and thee alone" (4b). Joseph was naturally considered as opposed to the revelations coming through

134

Hiram Page, but it was well known that Oliver had given some heed to them. Oliver therefore made an excellent ambassador to win Hiram to repentance. This practical demonstration of the working of the law of repentance and reconciliation was of great value to the infant church. Consider in this connection the basic law of the church given in the revelation of February 9, 1831.[3]

"Neither shall anything be appointed unto any of this church contrary to the church covenants" (4c). These covenants have been ordained by God and accepted by his people. Note the parallel here with the establishment of the covenant with Israel at Sinai.[4]

"All things must be done in order and by common consent in the church, by the prayer of faith" (4c). The establishment and maintenance of orderly procedures is vital to the life and growth of the church. The Hiram Page incident, the manner in which it was handled, and the fact that the settlement was concurred in by Hiram and the other participants in the conference illustrated this.[5]

Earlier in this paragraph, the Saints were instructed to appoint Joseph to preside over the conference "by the voice of the conference." The Lord had appointed Joseph to preside over his church, and the Saints were instructed to approve this. Since several of them had been disturbed by Hiram Page, the task of making this choice a sincere one was a significant exercise in self-discipline. The common consent required a common willingness to seek the will of the Lord and a common consent to do it in fellowship and mutual understanding.

"Thou shalt assist to settle all these things, according to the covenants of the church, before thou shalt take thy journey among the Lamanites" (5a). Note the excellent harmony between this provision for immediate settlement of difficulties and the instruction of Jesus in a similar situation.[6]

BIOGRAPHICAL NOTES

Hiram Page joined the church on the first Sunday after its organization, April 11, 1830, when about thirty years of age. Prior to this time he had given his testimony to the world as one of the eight witnesses to the Book of Mormon. Despite the apparent ease with which he had been deceived, Brother Page was sincerely eager for right to prevail, and Joseph writes, "The stone was discussed, and after considerable investigation, Brother Page, as well as the whole church, who were present renounced the said stone, and all things connected therewith, much to our mutual satisfaction and happiness." Brother Page moved to Independence with the body of the Saints and later to Far West. He was never very prominent in church affairs but was highly respected. He became involved in the difficulties of 1837 and 1838 and this led to the severance of his church connections, but he nevertheless remained true to his testimony to the Book of Mormon. He died in August 1852.

---

[1]Section 43:2; 152. [2]Section 29:2. [3]Section 42:23. [4]Exodus 19:3-5. [5]Church History 1:124-125. [6]Matthew 5:23, 24, 28.

SECTION 28

This revelation was given through the Prophet Joseph at Fayette, New York, shortly before the second conference of the church held in September 1830. It was given in the presence of six elders.

"Whose arm of mercy hath atoned for your sins" (1a). It is apparent from this paragraph that the elders had been praying for the forgiveness of their sins. No man ever finds himself in the presence of Divinity without a sense of his sinfulness, but every man who is truly forgiven rises from his knees endowed with new power. G. Studdert-Kennedy says:

When the miracle of forgiveness has actually taken place, and the man or woman has seen God in his glory, as the forgiven sinner always does, and has risen out of the depths of shame and darkness and of guilt into which this vision always plunges him—the next state is to love much, because much has been forgiven. Guilt must pour itself out in gratitude; and unless that gratitude is to waste away in emotion and evaporate into sentiment, it must take form in practical service, in the positive attack upon the forces of evil; and so the forgiven sinner is always a soldier in Christ's church militant here on earth.

"*Ye are chosen out of the world to declare my gospel with the sound of rejoicing. . . . Lift up your hearts and be glad, for I am in your midst, and am your advocate with the Father; and it is his good will to give you the kingdom*" (2a, b). Those who are called to minister among men in the name of God share the heritage of other men with its resources and limitations, but they are not as other men since they have been chosen to share in the "marvelous work and a wonder." Those chosen are to declare the gospel with the sound of rejoicing. This does not call for a mere recital of facts, but for testimony that in the gospel its advocates find the most worthy purpose and challenges of life.

"*Ye are called to bring to pass the gathering of mine elect*" (2c). Here is another statement of the fact and purpose of the gathering. It had been preceded by references to "the cause of Zion" and by the appointment of the mission to the West and was soon followed by the designation of the place of Zion and the gathering of the Saints to that place.

Note the clear sequence of events[1] as stated in paragraphs 2 to 8:

Prior to the coming of Christ there will be many desolations and signs in heaven and in the earth (4 and 5).

Christ will come again (2):

With power and great glory (2g).
With all the hosts of heaven (2g).

To dwell in righteousness with men on earth a thousand years (2g).

At this time the wicked shall not stand (2g).

The twelve who were with Christ in his ministry at Jerusalem will stand on his right hand (3b):

Clothed with robes of righteousness (3b).

In glory akin to that of Christ (3b).

To judge the whole house of Israel who have loved the Lord (3b).

At this first resurrection the dead in Christ shall arise to be with him (3c).

Following the Millennial Reign:

Men will again begin to deny their God (6a).

The earth will be spared for a little season (6a).

Before the earth shall pass away:

All the dead shall awake and come forth (7a).

The righteous will be gathered to eternal life (7a).

Christ will be ashamed to own the wicked before his father (7b).

"Depart from me ye cursed into everlasting fire, prepared for the Devil and his angels" (7c).

The details of their punishment have not been declared, nor do we have basis for understanding to the full the judgments of God (8).

When heaven and earth shall be consumed and pass away (6b), there shall be a new heaven and a new earth (6b).

Nothing shall be lost (6a).

"Then shall all the dead awake" (7a). Note the following in this connection:

It is the belief of the church that the doctrine of the resurrection provides for the raising from the dead of all men, each in his own order, through the atonement wrought by Jesus. (See Sections 28:7; 43:5; 45:10; 63:13; 76:3, 4, 7; 85:6, 29.)[2]

"All things unto me are spiritual" (9a). This is a fundamental truth clearly set forth. Its meaning does not

138

become clear, however, except as it is considered against a background of the eternal purpose of God which is the basic theme of this revelation. This purpose finds fulfillment in the immortality and eternal life of man, and the means which our heavenly Father uses in pursuing this purpose are so caught up into this spiritual purpose as to become part of the purpose itself.

In the measure that things become spiritual to us, they take on significance above and beyond that which we usually attribute to them. The ordinary bread and wine which are consecrated for use in the Communion service illustrate this, for they become emblems of the broken body and the spilled blood of the Lord Jesus Christ. It is not difficult for us to see this, since the Lord's Supper is provided for us by the grace of God, and we know that participation in it is one of the highest privileges that life can offer. But we need to see the sacramental principle which is involved in a larger context. Any temporal things which we use in daily life can become spiritual when they are directed toward divinely approved ends. Tithing, for example, when contributed in the spirit of thanksgiving, becomes a means of expressing our devotion and at the same time of liberating the church to perform its spiritual tasks.

"*The Devil. . . rebelled against me*" (10a). The right of agency is inherent in men and angels. It is inconceivable that we shall ever become so good that evil will cease to tempt us. Certain lower temptations lose their power as we become more like God, but our very progress leads us to other planes which have their peculiar temptations also. Thus it was that the Nephites, after nearly two hundred years of righteousness, found that their honesty and thrift and industry had led to such prosperity that they became proud and lifted up in the joy of their own achievements. This lack of humility caused their fall. Lucifer, a son of the morning, highly placed in the councils of heaven, was not free from the temptations of pride and arrogance.

"It must needs be that the Devil should tempt the children of men" (10d). Conflict seems to be a principle of life. On a low plane we fight with each other for properties and comforts and opportunities. On a higher plane we fight with ourselves, seeking to overcome unrighteousness by conquering our own carnal desires. In this conflict with self, we are always conscious of temptation downward. Agency centers in recognizing alternatives and choosing freely between them.

"Because of his transgression [Adam] became spiritually dead" (11b, c). Adam was cast from the presence of God because of his disobedience. There is a sense in which this may be regarded as a punishment, but it is also an inevitable consequence. To be truly in the presence of God involves sharing the spirit of the Father. Transgression occurs when we flout the love of God and "every man walketh in his own way, and after the image of his own god, whose image is in the likeness of the world. . . ."[3]

"Thus did I, the Lord God, appoint unto man the days of his probation; that by his natural death, he might be raised in immortality unto eternal life, even as many as would believe" (12b, c). The Inspired Version of the Holy Scriptures teaches that Adam and his seed received the ministry of angels declaring the opportunities of the gospel. Despite the disobedience of our father Adam, and of the inevitable loss which this entailed upon him and upon his children, the way of salvation has been made possible through faith on the Lord Jesus Christ, repentance from the works of death, and union with him in the building of his kingdom. The fact that men are endowed with agency means that a fall was possible always. Indeed, the fall was foreseen before the foundation of the world. The wonderful love of God toward us is shown, first, in his glorious purpose for us, that we are created to become like him; second, in the infinite courage which started us toward the achievement of our destiny in spite of knowledge of its cost; and third, in the inexpressible love which made God dedicate his own Son to our salvation even before the beginning of time.

Because of that love Jesus became the "Lamb slain before the foundation of the world," winning for us the redemption which we could not win for ourselves. "Behold what manner of love the Father has bestowed upon us that we shall be called the sons of God."

"They that believed not . . . can not be redeemed from their spiritual fall, because they repent not, for they love darkness rather than light, and their deeds are evil, and they receive their wages of whom they list to obey" (12c, d). Men have their agency. If agency should be taken away, we would be less than men. The very fact that men have been endowed with agency therefore means that if they are disobedient willfully, and will not repent, they must pay the price of their own wickedness.

"Little children . . . can not sin . . . until they begin to become accountable" (13a). This statement is now taken for granted, yet a century ago infant damnation was one of the popular doctrines of the major churches. Since agency is vital to responsibility, children who cannot choose intelligently cannot be held responsible.

---

[1]Cf. Malachi 4:1. [2]*General Conference Resolutions*, page 391. [3]Section 1:3e.

SECTION 29

This revelation was given at Fayette, New York, in September 1830. The background of this revelation is similar to that of Section 27.

Paragraph 1 is directed to David Whitmer, who had been involved in the seer-stone difficulty with his brother-in-law, Hiram Page. He is here chided for the instability of heart and mind which made it possible for him to be deceived.

"Those who were set over you" (1b). At this time Joseph and Oliver were known as the first and second elders of the church, although they had been designated also

as apostles,[1] and David had himself been called "with that same calling with which he [Paul] was called."[2] Evidently those "set over" David were Joseph and Oliver. These constituted the Presidency over the small group of Saints. Note paragraph 2d in this connection.

"*Wherefore, you are left to inquire for yourself*" (1c). Since David had in some measure lost confidence in Joseph, it was impossible for the Lord to use Joseph freely as his minister to David. Those who lose faith in the ministry of the church thereby lose something valuable as well as robbing the ministry of the support which is essential to their effective functioning.

"*You shall take your journey with your brother Oliver*" (2a). Here Peter Whitmer, Jr., is joined with Oliver Cowdery, in the mission to the Lamanites.[3] Peter was also a brother-in-law of Oliver.

"*None have I appointed to be his counselor, over him, in the church*" (2d). Here is a further indication of the preeminence of Joseph by right of his office as prophet, seer, and revelator.

"*Your whole labor shall be in Zion, with all your soul, from henceforth*" (3c). Although somewhat overshadowed by his brother, David, John Whitmer gave important service as Church Historian and as one of the seven presiding high priests in Jackson County.[4]

---

[1]Section 17:1. [2]Section 16:3. [3]See notes on Section 27. [4]See notes on Section 13.

SECTION 30

This revelation was given at Fayette, New York, at the time of the second conference of the church which convened September 26, 1830. It is addressed to Thomas B. Marsh who had been baptized recently and ordained an elder. On reading the revelation one gets an impression of a composite awareness in the mind and heart of the prophet which pushed into somewhat disorganized verbiage, moving backward and forward between personal and ministerial concerns.

"*They will believe and know the truth and be one with you in my church*" (1b). Elder Marsh's wife had been convinced of the divinity of the work when the church had not yet been organized, but the frequent references scattered throughout the revelation indicate that there were family difficulties, probably sickness. Nevertheless Thomas was given important missionary responsibility.

"*You shall strengthen them and prepare them against the time when they shall be gathered*" (3b). From the beginning, the early Saints were concerned about the gathering. It soon became apparent, however, that any successful gathering must include personal, social, and spiritual adjustments which would require both spiritual guidance and earnest self-discipline. Mere change of location would not be enough. Those who gathered must add to their faith the virtues which pertain to the fellowship of the people of God.[1] In the fall of 1832 Elder Marsh led a company of Saints to Jackson County, Missouri.

"*You shall be a physician unto the church*" (4a). Evidently Joseph saw no inconsistency between the practice of administration to the sick and the healing ministry of a church physician. Little has been recorded of Elder Marsh's ministry in this office. The office of church physician was revised in 1906, but was subsequently merged with the chairmanship of the Medical Council.[2]

BIOGRAPHICAL SKETCH

Thomas B. Marsh was born in Acton, Middlesex County, Massachusetts, November 1, 1799. He visited the printing office of E. B. Grandin at Palmyra, New York, while the Book of Mormon was in process of being printed and obtained some loose sheets. Soon afterward he visited Joseph Smith, Sr., where he met Oliver Cowdery and from him received an account of the plates and of their translation. Brother Marsh returned home, taking the sheets with him, and presented them to his wife with an account of their history. She received them as genuine. He entered at once into correspondence with Oliver Cowdery and Joseph Smith and, in September 1830, moved to Palmyra and soon afterward was baptized by David Whitmer. In a short time he was ordained an elder and at the conference of 1831 was ordained a high priest. On July 7, 1834, he became a member of the high council in Zion.

Elder Marsh was chosen one of the charter members of the Quorum of Twelve in this dispensation, although he was not present at the time. He arrived in Kirtland in April 1835 and was then ordained. He was the senior member of the quorum and was selected as its first president. Later, Section 105 was addressed to him in this capacity.

On February 10, 1838, Apostles T. B. Marsh and David W. Patten were presidents pro tem of the church in Missouri. The following October, however, Brother Marsh became involved in some difficulties with his brethren and he was inactive for nearly twenty years. He went to Salt Lake City in 1857, confessed his faults, and was forgiven and received into the Mormon church. He died in January 1866 and is buried in Ogden, Utah.[3]

---

[1]II Peter 1:5-11. [2]Section 127:1-2, 129:2. [3]*Saints Herald* 42:470.

SECTION 31

The appointment of Oliver Cowdery and Peter Whitmer on a mission to the Lamanites aroused great interest among the Saints and caused a number of the brethren to seek permission to accompany the missionaries. Accordingly Joseph inquired of the Lord, and this revelation was received at Fayette, New York, in October 1830. It is concerned almost entirely with designating Parley P. Pratt and Ziba Peterson as members of the missionary company.

144

Oliver Cowdery, who was probably regarded as the leader of the little group, was but twenty-five years old at the time of this mission. Parley P. Pratt was twenty-three. Peter Whitmer, Jr., had just attained his majority. Ziba Peterson, while not as young as these other three, was also a young man. They had little money to use upon their journey but nevertheless set out in faith and accomplished their purpose.

The influence of the recent Hiram Page difficulty was still felt, as reflected in the words *"They shall give heed to that which is written and pretend to no other revelation"* (1d).

BIOGRAPHICAL NOTES

Parley P. Pratt (see also Sections 49; 50:8; 94:2; 100:7; 107:40) was born April 12, 1807, in New York, and was converted through reading the Book of Mormon. He was baptized and ordained an elder in September 1830. After the successful termination of the mission to the West, he rejoined the body of the church in Ohio and was ordained a high priest in June 1831. He was the twelfth man chosen for membership in the first Quorum of Twelve and was ordained at that time.

The Kirtland Temple was dedicated March 27, 1836. Many of those who had been employed in its construction could find no other work in the vicinity and the financial disruptions being felt throughout the remainder of the country reached them and contributed to their uncertainty and challenged their faith. Elder Pratt was affected by the spirit which was prevalent, but he recovered and made confession of his error. Before the close of the year he published the third edition of *The Voice of Warning*, which has been one of the most influential tracts ever published by the church. He was an eloquent and persuasive preacher. Some of his hymns have enriched the worship of the Saints through the succeeding years.

Parley P. Pratt went to Utah and accepted the leadership of Brigham Young. While on a mission for them he was killed in Arkansas, May 14, 1857.

Ziba Peterson was baptized by Oliver Cowdery, April 18, 1830. He, too, was a young man. He went on a mission west and is reported to have established a school at Lone Jack, Missouri. He became involved in some unspecified difficulties and was placed under official silence in August 1831.[1]

---

[1]Section 58:14b.

SECTION 32

This revelation is addressed to Ezra Thayer and Northrop Sweet, and was received through Joseph Smith at Fayette, New York, October 30, 1830.

"A crooked and a perverse generation" (1c). Shortly after descending from the Mount of Transfiguration, Jesus described the unbelieving Jews as a "faithless and perverse generation."[1] Paul admonished the Philippian saints to live without blame "in the midst of a crooked and a perverse nation." The basic idea here is that often the rebelliousness of unbelievers was not due primarily to ignorance or misunderstanding but to perversity. They were willfully persistent in living according to their own standards and purposes.

"It is the eleventh hour, and for the last time I shall call laborers into my vineyard" (1d). This note of urgency is characteristic of the revelations in the Doctrine and Covenants. In recognition of this and similar revelations the Saints have referred to the gospel as "the latter-day glory" and "the dispensation of the fullness of times."[2]

They *"err in many instances, because of priestcrafts, all having corrupt minds"* (1e). This is not merely a denunciation, but a warning. Sin does not arise solely from unsound teaching, but also from the self-centeredness

146

which blinds many to perception of the truth.

"Even so will I gather mine elect from the four quarters of the earth" (2b). Note the growing emphasis in the gathering and the worldwide scope of the gospel proclamation. There was nothing insular about the attitude and expectations of the early Saints. It is significant, also, that the paragraph which sets forth the gathering also sets out the basic doctrines which will make that gathering effective.

"Mine elect. . . , even as many as will believe in me, and hearken unto my voice" (2b). God has prepared men to serve him according to his will and in diverse capacities. This election has to be consumated by the choice of the elect before it can become effective. "The elect" are those who hear and respond to the voice of God, accepting the responsibilities which go with his call. As Israel Zangwill wrote of his own people many years ago, "a chosen people must first of all be a choosing people. God chooses those whom he persuades to do his will."

"Open your mouths and they shall be filled" (2f). The setting shows the mouths of the witnesses will be filled with the message of repentance. This phrase has been sadly misunderstood. It is not a license for spiritual idleness and irresponsibility, but a guarantee of spiritual support to those who thrust in their sickles and reap with all their might, mind, and strength. There is no promise here to those who expect the Lord to provide the message without any effort on their part. The promise is to those who study the word of God and prepare both heart and mind, who are diligent in service and humble before the Lord. These know that without divine aid their ministry will be entirely ineffective, but they know also that God can and does vitalize both the study and the experience of the faithful minister for the benefit of the Saints.

"This is my gospel" (3a). Here is the basic declaration of the early missionaries: faith in God, repentance, baptism for remission of sins, the baptism of fire and of the Holy Ghost, patient continuance in preparation for the gathering.

"The Book of Mormon, and the Holy Scriptures, are given of me for your instruction" (3d). This instruction is so familiar as to be commonplace, but it is nevertheless still vital. Nothing will be so effective in building the spiritual quality of the church as church attendance, prayer, study of the standard books, and observance of the law of stewardship. Give us these basic activities on the part of the Saints and our growth in the other activities of the gospel is assured.

BIOGRAPHICAL NOTES

Ezra Thayer was a bridge, dam, and mill builder in and around Palmyra and had many times employed Father Smith and his sons, including Joseph. He joined the church after hearing Joseph tell the story of the Book of Mormon. Later, he was called to go on a mission with Thomas B. Marsh but failed to go. His place was taken by Selah Griffin.[3] He was ordained a high priest and represented the church in the purchase of the Peter French farm and the Arnold Mason cannery at Kirtland. He found it difficult to comply with the law of consecration[4] but retained his basic faith. In 1860 he heard Elder W. W. Blair tell of the Reorganization and renewed his association with the church at that time.

Northrop Sweet was active for a time, but later became prominent in an organization called "The Pure Church of Christ."[5]

---

[1]Matthew 17:17, Luke 9:31. [2]Ephesians 1:10. [3] Section 56:2. [4]*Ibid.* 56:3 [5]Davis, *The Story of the Church*, pages 83, 467.

SECTION 33

Early in November 1830 a young man who afterwards became a leading minister of the church came to Joseph to inquire concerning his duty. This young man was Orson Pratt, who had been recently baptized by his brother, Parley P. Pratt. Joseph inquired of the Lord at his request and received the instructions contained in this revelation, which was probably given November 4, 1830, at Fayette, New York.

Note the central place of Jesus, the Lord, in this revelation. Young ministers will do well to study the redemptive work of Jesus and to include in their preaching a strong testimony of his power to save.

This communication was a disclosure of the divine mind to Orson Pratt, and a warrant for his ordination and commissioning, but it announces no new doctrine. Every phrase not directed to Orson personally can be duplicated elsewhere. Much of the revelation has to do with such reiteration for the sake of emphasis, to point out the pertinence of that which has been announced elsewhere and in other situations.

"Cry repentance unto a crooked and perverse generation" (1d). This instruction concerning repentance is often repeated in the revelations and is basic to the evangelistic message of the church. Orson Pratt was won with the only declaration appropriate to the times for his was truly "a crooked and perverse generation," as is ours. Sober-minded men and women of every generation know this, but for many "the cares of this world, and the deceitfulness of riches, and the lusts of other things entering in, choke the word"[1] and their momentary insight becomes unfruitful. To be effective, testimony must issue in commitment. The good seeds must be received into fruitful ground.

"Preparing the way of the Lord for his second coming" (1d). The apostle Peter wrote that the Lord has given us "exceeding great and precious promises; that by these [we] might be partakers of the divine nature."[2] One of the most precious of these promises is that those who love the Lord Jesus may look forward with confidence to his return and to close association with him.

149

BIOGRAPHICAL NOTES

Orson Pratt (see Sections 75:3; 100:7; 107:40) was born September 19, 1811, and was a younger brother of Parley P. Pratt. He was baptized on his nineteenth birthday and immediately entered into missionary work, traveling on foot from New York to Kirtland early in 1831 and preaching and baptizing by the way. For many years he was among the most able missionaries of the church. On February 2, 1832, he was ordained a high priest, and in 1834 he was a member of Zion's Camp on its memorable march to Zion. On July 7, 1834, he was ordained one of the Standing High Council of Zion. Orson Pratt was the ninth apostle chosen and the third youngest of the first Quorum of Twelve in this dispensation. He was not in Kirtland at the time of his selection but arrived on April 26, 1835, and was ordained that day.

In the spring of 1840 Apostle Pratt and others of his quorum went to Europe where he labored faithfully in England and Scotland, returning to America in the spring of 1841. In 1844 he stood with the majority of the Twelve and in 1847 participated in the proceedings which helped to elevate Brigham Young to the presidency. Although he had little formal education in early life, he was a brilliant student and became the most outstanding scholar among the early Utah Mormon leaders. He died at his home in Salt Lake City, Utah, October 3, 1881.

---

¹Mark 4:16. ²II Peter 1:4.

SECTION 34

The mission to the West was one of the most important steps in the early development of the church. One of the immediate results was the establishment of the church in

150

Kirtland, Ohio, where some of the most thrilling events of the age transpired, and where the temple yet stands as a monument to the faithfulness and patient endurance of the early Saints. Here the leading quorums of the church were organized, and here and in the vicinity were found some of the men who were destined to become prominent in the church and her councils. These included such leaders as Sidney Rigdon, Frederick G. Williams, Orson Hyde, Lyman Wight, Luke S. Johnson, Lyman E. Johnson, Edward Partridge, and Newel K. Whitney.

This revelation is the first addressed to Sidney Rigdon, who had journeyed with Edward Partridge from Ohio to New York for the purpose of visiting the prophet and learning more of the work of the church. It was received in Fayette, New York, in December 1830.

"Listen to the voice of the Lord your God" (1a). The opening sentence of this revelation must have come to Sidney Rigdon as a very welcome message. He had participated in considerable spiritual pioneering, but always his purpose had been to discover the will of God "whose course is one eternal round, the same today as yesterday and forever."

"They may become the sons of God" (1b). Compare this with the following: "Behold what manner of love the Father hath bestowed upon us, that we should be called the sons of God. . . beloved, now are we the sons of God."[1] "He came unto his own, and his own received him not. But as many as received him, to them gave he power to become the sons of God, even to them that believe on his name: which were born, not of blood, nor of the will of the flesh, nor of the will of man, but of God."[2] "As many as are led by the Spirit of God, they are the sons of God."[3]

"I have looked upon thee and thy works" (2a). Sidney had ministered to many of the people of the vicinity, some of whom later joined him in the Restoration. In recent years he had been prominently connected with the efforts of Thomas and Alexander Campbell, Walter Scott,

151

and others to promote a return to primitive Christianity.

"Thou wast sent forth even as John, to prepare the way before me" (2b). Try to consider the history of the church with Kirtland omitted, and then try to consider Kirtland without the preparatory work of Sidney Rigdon there. Certainly the Lord used Rigdon a long time before he came into the church in preparing the ground for a major center of early church activity.

"They received not the Holy Ghost" (2c). For a parallel situation read Acts 19:1-7.

"There shall be a great work in the land" (3a). Note the courage of this prediction. Joseph and Sidney lived to see the membership of the church multiplied many times. The work which had just been planted in Kirtland they saw go on to Independence and to Far West and to Nauvoo. At that time the Book of Mormon was the only publication of the church. In less than fifteen years the church published many hundreds of books and pamphlets and tracts. The Saints built cities, established a university, laid down printing presses, proclaimed the gospel of Christ. The work of God through the church surely was "a great work in the land." It still is.

The Saints have been instructed that "they are not to boast themselves of these things."[4] A humble restatement of great spiritual experience is nevertheless truly inspiring. Men and women of honor and of intelligence and of controlled emotions have testified in every decade since 1830 of the healing, revealing, and saving power of the gospel of Christ. The gospel is truly both a marvelous work and a wonder.

"There are none that doeth good except those who are ready to receive the fullness of my gospel" (3e). At first sight this statement may be a little startling. Joseph surely did not mean that no good whatever will be done by those who—like Sidney prior to this time—have not accepted the fullness of the gospel. Rather, it would seem that any good done by anyone falls short of its richest possibilities except as it is done in the name of Christ and points

beyond itself to the kingdom. This passage prompts re-membrance of the cup of cold water mentioned by Jesus,[5] which was obviously of value in itself in a hot and dry land, but which falls short of its fullest value unless given "in the name of a disciple." The purpose of this statement is not to condemn the earlier ministry of Sidney but to encourage him to enter fully into the greater work which now beckoned him.

"I have called upon the weak things of the world" (4a). Compare this with the words of Paul.[6] Note also "your faith should not stand in the wisdom of men but in the power of God."[7]

"Watch over him that his faith fail not" (5a). This is a common duty of the brethren. Jesus prayed that Peter's faith should not fail.[8] It was after this date that Peter denied his Lord, but Jesus continued to uphold him so that finally the faith of Peter was equal to his task. If widely practiced in the church today, such mutual support would quickly multiply the effectiveness of the priesthood.

"Thou shalt write for him" (5a). Oliver Cowdery had been secretary to Joseph before leaving on the mission to the West. His place was now taken by Sidney Rigdon, who from this time on was associated very intimately with the prophet and was later ordained as his counselor. They collaborated in producing the Inspired Version of the Holy Scriptures which fulfilled the prophecy contained in this paragraph, and which has been copyrighted and published by the Reorganized Church.

"It shall be given unto him to prophesy; and thou shalt preach my gospel; and call on the holy prophets to prove his words, as they shall be given him" (5d). Elder Rigdon was an able preacher and was extremely well versed in the scriptures. He was already qualified in many ways for the commission which was given him, and his power in ministry increased steadily. Note the close parallel between the instruction here given to Sidney Rigdon and that previously given to Oliver Cowdery, whose relations with Joseph had been very similar to those now developing

between Joseph and Sidney.

"Keep all the commandments and covenants by which ye are bound" (6a). Safety lies in the word *all*. No man is spiritually safe who ignores any of the commandments from the least to the greatest.

"By the keys which I have given shall they be led" (6b). A keynote of the early church was authority. Effective leadership in spiritual things is directly determined by real authority.

BIOGRAPHICAL NOTES

Sidney Rigdon (see also Sections 58:13; 63:14; 73; 76; 97; 107:32) was born in St. Clair township, Allegheny County, state of Pennsylvania, February 19, 1793. In his youth he worked as a farmer and later became a Baptist minister, but separated from that denomination when he became convinced that their teachings were not in harmony with those of the scriptures. For two years he supported himself by working as a tanner, and then he reentered the ministry. This time he was not connected with any denomination. He continued to preach in various places, laying special emphasis on repentance and baptism for the remission of sins and the gift of the Holy Ghost. In this way he built up several churches, and he was thus engaged in the fall of 1830 when he was visited by his friend, Elder Parley P. Pratt. After some delay, Sidney was converted through reading the Book of Mormon and was baptized and ordained an elder. He began to preach immediately. After December 1830 Sidney acted as scribe for Joseph Smith in the translation of the Holy Scriptures and was a participant in the glorious vision recorded in Section 76. It was while engaged in this work that he and Joseph were severely maltreated by a mob at Hiram, Ohio, on March 25, 1832. Soon after this he visited Missouri and assisted in dedicating the land of Zion and the Temple Lot.

Sidney Rigdon was ordained first counselor to President

Joseph Smith on March 18, 1833, and as such took active oversight of the church in the absence of President Smith from Kirtland, so that he is entitled to much of the credit for the erection of Kirtland Temple. In October 1838 he was one of those taken prisoner at Far West by General Lucas, and was sentenced to be shot, but was saved by the heroic conduct of General Alexander Doniphan. With others he was then taken to Independence and again to Richmond where he was again under sentence of death, but he obtained a release and went to Illinois.

After the death of the Martyr, Elder Rigdon differed from the Twelve on the question of presiding authority; he claimed superior rank as the only surviving member of the First Presidency. At a meeting held in Nauvoo, August 8, 1844, a vote was taken to "sustain the Twelve in their office and calling," and this has always been interpreted by the Utah church as a rejection of Elder Rigdon's claims, despite the fact that he was not heard and no vote was taken on the specific question of his function in the existing circumstances. Elder Rigdon died at Friendship, New York, July 14, 1876.

---

[1] I John 3:1, 2. [2] John 1:11-13. [3] Romans 8:14. [4] Section 83:11. [5] Matthew 10:38. [6] I Corinthians 1:18-29. [7] I Corinthians 2:5. [8] Luke 22:32.

SECTION 35

When Sidney Rigdon went to Western New York to visit Joseph Smith, he was accompanied by Edward Partridge, a businessman of Painesville, Ohio. Partridge had not been willing to join the church until he had met the young prophet, but the light he received on this visit was sufficient to convince him, and he was baptized by Joseph in the Seneca River on December 11, 1830. The addition of Sidney Rigdon and Edward Partridge to the ranks was a tremendous gain to the church at this time.

"As many as shall come before my servants" (2a). In the early days of the church there was a persistent demand for spiritual leadership. The men who were baptized joined the new movement with every intention of extending it to the ends of the earth. Men of this caliber could invariably render some service in one of the grades of the priesthood and most of them were therefore ordained.

In this connection the following quotation from Professor W. B. Selbie is of interest:

> Preaching has been called the imparting of truth through personality. It is therefore a great business and demands the finest qualities of head and heart, real powers of expression, and a living acquaintance with the moral and spiritual needs of men. It involves teaching, no doubt, but it is far more than teaching. When we teach we simply impart information, but when we preach we are out to get a verdict, to persuade men and bring them to the point of assent and decision. We inevitably raise the question, "What, then, are you going to do about it?" And until that question is answered preaching cannot have its perfect work.

"Sidney Rigdon and Joseph Smith, Jr." (2a). Oliver Cowdery had been designated "second elder"[1] and prior to this time had been the closest ministerial associate of Joseph. In September, however, he was called to the mission to the West[2] which culminated in the designation of the land of Zion. Sidney now stepped into his place as Joseph's scribe and closest official associate. The instruction linking Sidney with Joseph at this time was particularly important since Sidney had been so prominently associated with those who were now joining the church in and around Kirtland. He was personally acquainted with a number of those who were ordained and sent on missions.

BIOGRAPHICAL NOTES

Edward Partridge (see Sections 41:3; 50:8; 51:1; 58:15) was born August 27, 1793, at East Pittsfield, Massachusetts. He was baptized in December 1830 and ordained to the eldership at that time or shortly thereafter. In the latter

156

part of January he was called to be bishop of the church. He was ordained at Kirtland in 1831 and in harmony with instructions received through revelation located in Independence. For a time he was in charge of both spiritual and temporal concerns in Jackson County. He shared the trials of the Saints at the time of their expulsion and was imprisoned at Richmond, Missouri, during the winter of 1838 and 1839. He died of pleurisy, in Nauvoo, May 27, 1840. Bishop Partridge was described in a later revelation as "like unto Nathaniel of old in whom there is no guile," and his services in the church were of this character.[3]

---

[1]Sections 17:1, 19:1. [2]*Ibid.* 27:3, 5a. [3]*Ibid.* 41:3.

SECTION 36

In June 1830 Joseph began an inspired correction of the Holy Scriptures.[1] It was while engaged in this work in December 1830 that Joseph and his helper, Sidney Rigdon, received an extract from the prophecy of Enoch.

The circumstances attending the receipt of this revelation are described by Joseph as follows:

It may be well to observe here that the Lord greatly encouraged and strengthened the faith of his little flock which had embraced the fullness of the everlasting gospel, as revealed to them in the *Book of Mormon,* by giving some more extended information on the Scriptures, the translation of which had already commenced. Much conjecture and conversation frequently occurred among the Saints concerning the books mentioned, and referred to in various places in the Old and New Testaments, which were now nowhere to be found. The common remark was, that they were lost books; but it seems the apostolic church had some of these writings as Jude mentions or quotes the prophecy of Enoch, the seventh from Adam. To the joy of the flock, which in all, from Colesville to Canandaigua, New York, numbered about seventy members, did the Lord reveal the following doings of olden times from the prophecy of Enoch.[2]

157

This section first appeared in the 1864 edition of the Doctrine and Covenants which was compiled by Isaac Sheen in compliance with an action of the semiannual conference of 1863. For reasons not now known Elder Sheen added Sections 22 and 36 which had appeared in the *Times and Seasons.* Since these two sections now form part of the Inspired Version of the Holy Scriptures it would appear that there is no commanding reason for their continued inclusion in the Doctrine and Covenants. The action authorizing this inclusion was probably taken in deference to the precedent set by Elder Sheen and followed in subsequent editions.

"Our father Adam taught these things" (1a). "These things" evidently refers to the preaching of the gospel, as will be understood after reading Genesis 6:26 to 71 in the Inspired Version of the Holy Scriptures. The antiquity of the gospel which is here affirmed was one of the treasured beliefs of early Latter Day Saints.[3]

"Many have believed and become the sons of God" (1a). See notes on Section 34:1.

"I saw the Lord" (1c). Compare this experience with the experiences of Moses,[4] of Jacob,[5] of Abram,[6] of Moses and Aaron, and of the elders of Israel.[7] Note particularly the experience of the brother of Jared.[8]

"The Holy Spirit, which bears record of the Father and the Son" (1c). This is the function of the Holy Spirit. If this is kept in mind, many of our theological difficulties in defining the place and work of the Holy Spirit will vanish.

"So powerful was the word of Enoch, and so great was the power of language that God had given him" (2c). With the possible exception of Moses, the leaders of the people of God in the various dispensations seem to have been men of "great power of language," and it will be remembered that Moses might have been blessed with this gift if he had had greater faith. The keynote to this power seems to be absolute conviction of authority from God.

The wonders recorded in this paragraph are most readily

believable if we have faith in the kind of God who will thus respond to the great faith of his people. The tendency to disparage these great wonders arises in large measure from lack of faith in our own experience which causes us to lack parallel instances of divine intervention.

"The Lord called his people Zion, because they were of one heart and one mind, and dwelt in righteousness" (2h). "The kingdom of God is...righteousness [that is, right doing], and peace, and joy in the Holy Ghost."[9] Reflecting on this Bishop J. A. Koehler has said:

> Zion-building is kingdom of God building. The call of the church is to build Zion, and the devotion of the church to this task is the price of divine favor. There are reasons why this is so. The prosperity of human souls is conditioned in the prosperity of Zion, the redemption of which is through the operation of every agency of salvation known to the church—missionary, pastoral, and all the rest.

"The city of holiness, even Zion" (3a). This name is important. It is from the spiritual quality of the city that its other attributes spring. Note the relation between this quotation and the statement of the Psalmist, "Out of Zion, the perfection of beauty, God hath shined."[10]

"How is it that you can weep" (6c). Enoch here enumerates some of the attributes of Divinity and then expresses wonder that God can be touched by sorrow. Yet, as Enoch perceives later, it is the very greatness of God which causes him to weep. Great love means great capacity for happiness, but it also means great capacity for sorrow. The more a person does wrong the more intensely do good people who love him suffer because of his wrongdoing. When God contemplated the wickedness of humanity he wept because he loved men so much.

"A prison have I prepared for them" (7h). In this connection note the following: "Christ also hath once suffered for sins, the just for the unjust, that he might bring us to God, being put to death in the flesh, but quickened by the Spirit: by which also he went and preached unto the spirits in prison; which sometime were disobedient, when once the long-suffering of God waited in the days

159

of Noah, while the ark was preparing, wherein few, that is, eight souls were saved by water."[11]

"His heart swelled wide as eternity" (8b). The prophetic vision of Enoch was not a matter of foresight merely, but also of deep feeling. He saw what was going to happen, and as he looked over the earth, he felt something of the yearning after men which had made God himself weep.

"When will my Creator sanctify me?" (10b). In this connection the following quotation will be of considerable interest:

> There are in the last resort only two doctrines possible as to the nature of the universe—one holding it to be dead, lifeless, a mechanism going by a kind of clockwork, and the other holding it to be essentially alive—and that not as a cabbage is alive, but as we are, conscious of itself as a unitary whole, and knowing what it is about. This is the doctrine which I find myself forced to accept as by far the better alternative of the two. The sayings of the gospel—"God is not a God of the dead but of the living"—I take as covering everything in space and time, all that the astronomers tell us that is going on in the unimaginable depths of space, all that the historians can tell us of what has gone on in the unimaginable depths of time. All is alive, and it is one life, frankly an immortal life, that animates the whole....If then, there is anything in which I am one with that universe, anything in which I am the sharer in its life, then, too, I become a sharer in its immortality. Life and immortality, not death and mechanism, are the key-words of the real universe, and so far as you and I are true sons of the universe, so far as we reproduce its nature in ourselves, life and immortality are the key-words to our reality, also....
>
> When the universe is thought of in this manner (as living in itself)—and it is only the accident of our times and the peculiar mental habits and stock notions we have developed, which make it difficult for us to think of it—when the universe is thought of in this manner, it ceases to be the mere scene or theatre on which our life is transacted—which is all a dead universe can ever amount to. It becomes essentially a Companion, a living Companion—no new idea, but one which was perfectly familiar to the Stoics and may be found running through all the writings of Marcus Aurelius. That being so, there is now room for raising the question whether you and your Great Companion are not fellow-workers, out for the same thing, whether your purpose and your business are not one with the purpose and business on which the Soul of the World is also intent.[12]

"A remnant of his seed should always be found among all

nations" (10b). This almost seems to indicate that some who were not the seed of Noah survived the flood, for otherwise all those living after the flood—and not just a "remnant"—were the seed of Enoch. However, it may be that the seed of Enoch refers particularly to those who followed in his footsteps and became his seed through righteousness.

"Shall the earth rest?" (11a). In this connection consider the following: "The Lord. . . swore that they should not enter into his rest, while in the wilderness, which rest is the fullness of his glory."[13] The question of Enoch was therefore equivalent to saying, "When the Son of Man comes in the flesh, shall the earth enter into the fullness of his glory?"

"The day shall come that the earth shall rest" (12d). "Rest" used here does not mean stagnation, but harmonious activity which will be possible when the earth shall have entered into the fullness of the glory of God.

"Great tribulations shall be among the children of men" (12e). Many of these tribulations were yet future when this revelation was given.

"Righteousness will I send down out of heaven" (12e). This may have reference to angelic administration promised in the last days, or it may have a wider application to the revelations subsequently received.

"Truth will I send forth out of the earth" (12e). This is specifically fulfilled in the coming forth of the Book of Mormon, but it is also fulfilled in the numerous archaeological evidences supporting both the Bible and the Book of Mormon and, in fact, in all those discoveries from the earth which confirm to men the goodness of God and his creative handiwork through the ages.

"Righteousness and truth will I cause to sweep the earth as with a flood" (12f). As righteousness and truth work in the hearts of men, those of like precious faith will of necessity be swept together. They will be divided from those in whose hearts these have no place.

"Then shall you and all your city meet them there" (13a). Jude says, "And Enoch also, the seventh from Adam, prophesied of these, saying, Behold, the Lord cometh

with ten thousand of his saints."[14]

[1]The historical background of this section is ably discussed in *Restoration Scriptures* by Church Historian Richard Howard, pages 223, 228, 232. [2]*Times and Seasons* 4:336. [3]See Galatians 3:8, 9; I Corinthians 10:2-4. [4]Exodus 19:20, 21; Numbers 12:4, 5. [5]Genesis 32:29, 30. [6]Genesis 17:1-6. [7]Exodus 24:9-12. [8]Ether 1:69-85. [9]Romans 14:17. [10]Psalm 50:2. [11]I Peter 3:18-20; see also Section 76:6. [12]L. P. Jacks in *A Living Universe*, pages 101, 102, 104. [13]Section 83:4. [14]Jude 14.

SECTION 37

This revelation to Joseph Smith, Jr., and Sidney Rigdon was the last received in the opening year of our church history and bears the date of December 1830. At this time the prophet was still staying in Fayette, New York.

"It is not expedient in me that ye should translate any more until ye shall go to the Ohio" (1a). Joseph Smith had commenced the translation of the Holy Scriptures ("the Inspired Version") some months prior to this time, with Sidney Rigdon as his "scribe" (secretary). The work proceeded intermittently.[1]

"Ye shall go to the Ohio" (1a). The doctrine of the gathering had been revealed to the Saints before this time,[2] but this was the first intimation of any particular place of gathering. In his book *The Frontier in American History*, Dr. F. J. Turner has this to say:

From the beginning the Ohio Valley seems to have been a highway for migration, and the home of a culture of its own. Its population showed a mixture of nationalities and religions. Less English than the colonial coast, it was built on a basis of religious feeling different from that of Puritan New England. The Scotch-Irish Presbyterians with the glow of the covenanters; German sectaries with serious-minded devotion to one or another of a multiplicity of sects, but withal deeply responsive to the call of the religious spirit, and the English Quakers all furnish a foundation of emotional responsiveness to religion and a readiness to find a new heaven and a new earth in politics as well as in religion. Mr. Bryce has well characterized the South as a region of "high religious voltage," but this characterization is especially applicable to the Upland South, and its colonies in the Ohio Valley.

"Ye shall not go until ye have preached my gospel in those parts, and have strengthened up the church" (1b). From the beginning the Lord had instructed the Saints both to be active in missionary labor and to safeguard their missionary gains.

"Assemble together at the Ohio" (2a). It was in response to this instruction that the first great migration of the church took place. From Fayette, New York, to Kirtland, Ohio, is about two hundred miles, a much more difficult journey in those days than it is today.

"Let every man choose for himself until I come" (2b). This seems to refer to the means of conveyance between Fayette and Kirtland. The early Saints were so happy in their belief in divine revelation that they were inclined to expect inspired instruction regarding the details of their daily lives. Here and elsewhere the Lord encourages them to exercise their own good sense in the ordinary concerns of each day.

---

[1]Church History 1:159, 165, 215, 220, 231, 233, 235, 236, 278, 303; *Joseph Smith's "New Translation" of the Bible*, page 8; Sections 45:11b, 73:2a, 76:3c, 87:5a, 90:12, Appendix A, 107:28b. [2]Section 28:2d, 7b; 32:2a.

SECTION 38

The third conference of the church was held in the house of Father Whitmer at Fayette, New York. This revelation was received during the conference, January 2, 1831.

"Thus saith the Lord your God, even Jesus Christ, the great I AM, Alpha and Omega, the beginning and the end" (1a). This and other scriptures have led some to regard the *Father* and the *Son* as being one person. Their oneness

163

is in unity of purpose, however, rather than identity. The splendor of the divine nature may well be studied in the spirit of worship in connection with various sections of the Doctrine and Covenants, e.g. Sections 1:1-3; 17:4-5; 22:2, 22-23; 45:2; 76:1-2; 85:10c, 18b; 90:1-4.

"All things came by me" (1b). There had been doubt in the minds of some regarding the preexistence of Christ, which is here reaffirmed to the church. This doctrine is in complete harmony with the teaching of both Old and New Testaments.[1] Eusebius speaks of the preexistence and divinity of Christ in the following manner:

As no one hath known the Father, but the Son, so no one, on the other hand, can know the Son fully, but the Father alone, by whom he was begotten. For who but the Father hath thoroughly understood that Light which existed before the world was—that intellectual and substantial wisdom, and that living word which in the beginning was with the Father, before all creation and any production visible or invisible, the first and only offspring of God, the prince and leader of the spiritual immortal hosts of heaven, the angel of the mighty council, the agent to execute the Father's secret will, the maker of all things with the Father, the second cause of the universe next to the Father, the true and only Son of the Father, and the Lord and God and King of all created things, who has received power and dominion with divinity itself, and power and honor from the Father.

"The Zion of Enoch" (1b). See Jude 14, Psalm 102:16, Section 36.

"Even as many as have believed on my name" (1c). The punctuation is poor here, but a careful reading shows that the section means that the Zion of Enoch has been taken into the bosom of eternity, and so also have such as have believed on the name of Christ.

"The residue of the wicked have I kept in chains of darkness until the judgment of the great day, which shall come at the end of the earth" (1d). The wicked are "reserved unto judgment" in a condition of conscious existence in the intermediate state between death and the resurrection.[2]

"The day soon cometh that ye shall see me and know that I am" (2b). This was partially fulfilled when the Lord appeared to Joseph and Sidney Rigdon, February 16, 1832,[3]

164

and also at the dedication of the Kirtland Temple. The prophecy has more complete reference, however, to the second coming of the Lord Jesus.

"*All flesh is corruptible before me*" (3a). The revelations speak of the corruption which is in the world[4] and also of the corruptibleness of the world and of the minds and the hearts of men.[5] The relation of the two is important. Every generation is confronted by the fact of corruption. The continuance and expansion of this corruption can be halted only by those who recognize their own involvement and fight it both within and around them in the strength of a power greater than their own.

"*For your salvation I give unto you a commandment*" (4c). This was the commandment to gather at the Ohio. It may well have had immediate rather than permanent significance. But the gathering which is here set forth, is, in its larger sense, a principle of salvation. What is here contemplated is the gathering of the Saints to a specific area in which they will be richly blessed in ways made possible through faithfulness, diligence, and cooperation. It is, of course, a matter of history that many of the Saints did actually gather in this sense, but they were unable to obtain possession of the land which they believed God had designed to be theirs as an "everlasting inheritance." They had much opposition from their "gentile" neighbors, but the essential difficulty was spiritual; "there were jarrings, and contentions, and envyings, and strifes, and lustful and covetous desires among them; therefore by these things they polluted their inheritances."[6]

The failure of this historic attempt to build the kingdom does not invalidate the principles involved. Both the Saints and the world in general are in desperate need of an example of a community of righteousness. Zion cannot be built on the level of customary morality. It can be built only by a sacrificial people who build together in "love unfeigned"[7] such as can be experienced only in its fullness in communities of the faithful.

"*I will be your king and watch over you*" (5a). Some of

165

the enemies of the church have quoted this paragraph as an evidence of the essential disloyalty of Latter Day Saintism. This is not a fair rendition of what is taught here. Obedience to the laws of God is the best kind of obedience to the requirements of the state. Two and a half years after this time, when the Saints were being persecuted unjustly and might have felt that they would be justified in rebellion, they were specifically instructed to support the law of the land.[8]

"Teach one another according to the office wherewith I have appointed you" (5c). Without question members of the priesthood should be the outstanding teachers of the church, every minister seeking to function in harmony with his special calling. It should be remembered, however, that God has also set in the church certain "helps," and while the priesthood should exercise the teaching function, they should not seek to monopolize it.

"Ye hear of wars in far countries" (6c). The year of 1830 was one of widespread upheaval, France, Poland, and Belgium being shaken by revolutions. At the time this revelation was given, an even wider cataclysm seemed probable.

"Ye know not the hearts of men in your own land" (6c). This is possibly a reference to the Civil War which commenced thirty years later. The "Civil War prophecy" was given December 25, 1832. It forms Section 87 of the Mormon Doctrine and Covenants.

"That ye might escape the power of the enemy, and be gathered unto me a righteous people" (7a). The highest type of obedience is that which springs from love. Sometimes men fall short of this high standard of obedience, and become obedient through fear. Here the Lord pleads with his people to prepare for the coming catastrophes that they might have no cause for fear; yet after these many years men are still learning through fear what could have been better learned through love.

"There will I give unto you my law" (7b). This prophecy was remarkably fulfilled when Section 42 was given. In

166

Kirtland, also, the church was fully organized and the small, incomplete, preliminary organization effected at Fayette, New York, was enlarged upon and developed until the church with its quorums and councils provided for in the law became an accomplished reality.

"There you shall be endowed with power from on high" (7c). It is probable that at Kirtland the early church reached the high point of its spiritual development. There priesthood and Saints were endowed with the Spirit of Christ. W. W. Blair wrote many years later regarding this endowment received at Kirtland:

> There were no secrecies in the endowment, no penal oaths and covenants, no secret grips, no secret passwords, no grotesque and mawkish robings, no bewildering scenic exhibitions, no theatrical twaddle, and no promises to follow "file leaders," or to blindly obey the dictates of the priesthood; but all was open, plain, pure, devotional, enlightening, elevating, sanctifying, joyful and spiritual; while the sweet peace of God, and the power of his Holy Spirit manifest in tongues, interpretations, prophecy, visions, healings, and other marvelous things, testified that the endowment was genuine and of heavenly origin.
>
> This endowment was given under the direction of Joseph the Martyr, and there are hundreds of living witnesses who testify to the plain, orderly, and humble manner of preparing for it, and to the loving, peaceful, and Holy Spirit which pervaded all hearts who faithfully received it, and of the mighty power of God which attended it, which was displayed to, and experienced by hundreds, and probably by all whose hearts were right in the sight of God.[9]

In this connection note Section 149A:6.

"From thence, whosoever I will, shall go forth among all nations. . . . I will lead them whithersoever I will" (7c, d). This was fulfilled in a manner beyond any reasonable expectation of the Saints at the time that the revelation was given. From Kirtland went forth the mission to the British Isles in 1837, and the later and larger mission of 1840. On the first mission more than two thousand converts were won in about a year. On the second mission an edition of five thousand copies of the Book of Mormon was published, fifty thousand tracts were distributed, a periodical was

established, and the work of the church was so firmly planted that only internal forces could cause its decay.

"They shall look to the poor and the needy, and administer to their relief" (8b). With such commandments as this written into the basic law of the church from the beginning, Latter Day Saints should be outstanding ministers of hope and courage to those who are in need. This work of relief should not be confined to such immediate help as can be given but should express itself in earnest endeavors to build Zion and thereby eliminate poverty. But, on the other hand, our eagerness for Zion should not blind us to our present duty of relieving the poor.

"This shall be their work, to govern the affairs of the property of this church" (8c). This refers primarily to the work of the Bishopric. Edward Partridge was ordained first bishop of the church about a month after this revelation was received.[10]

THE MOVE TO OHIO

Church Historian Heman C. Smith wrote concerning the move to Ohio:

There is one thing I wish to mention in regard to the revelation to locate at Kirtland, and I will be glad for you to think about it. You are all aware that in the early days of the church, while they were yet at Kirtland, a theory was advanced by the opposition claiming that the Book of Mormon, then attracting so much attention, was but a remodeled romance written by Solomon Spalding. It is said that the romance was written at Conneaut, Ohio; and you who have taken the pains to look this matter up, have doubtless noticed that this place is not more than fifty miles from Kirtland. I want to invite your attention to this consideration. It seems to me improbable, if that theory were true, and that Joseph Smith and Sidney Rigdon, knowing that this romance started there and that they had used it for their purposes, would have transplanted the church from a distant place to the neighborhood where it was most easily detected. If this story had been true, and they had used this manuscript written at Conneaut, they never would have located right where detection was possible. Those who practice fraud do not do such things as that. They evidently would have gone in some other direction, or to a greater distance. The far western country was before them, and they could have located where detection

168

would not have been so easily accomplished. I am satisfied that this is a strong circumstantial evidence that this theory is untrue. It is not at all reasonable that they would go there to locate.[11]

[1]See Genesis 1:26; Colossians 1:16, 17; John 1:10; Hebrews 1:1-6; Ephesians 3:9; John 1:1-5; Hebrews 10:5-9. [2]I Peter 2:4, 9; Jude 6. [3]Section 76:3. [4]Ibid. 3:3a, 105:9a. See also 112:12a. [5]Ibid. 18:6a, 22:1c, e, 98:5b. [6]Ibid. 98:3a. [7]I Peter 1:22, II Corinthians 6:6, I Timothy 1:5. [8]Section 95:2. [9]Journal of History 18:180, 181. [10]Section 41:3. [11]Saints' Herald 48:955.

SECTION 39

Shortly after the third conference of the church, there came to Joseph a man named James Covill, who had been a Baptist minister for about forty years. He seemed to be very interested in the work of the church. At his request Joseph sought the word of the Lord, but when this was received Covill rejected it and returned to his former principles and people. The instruction given him at this time now constitutes Section 39.

"From all eternity to all eternity" (1a). See Psalm 90:2, Section 76:1c.

"He that receiveth my gospel, receiveth me; and he that receiveth not my gospel, receiveth not me" (2a). This is particularly significant in view of Mr. Covill's rejection of the instruction here given. In this connection read II John 9.

"Thine heart is now right before me at this time" (3a). Note the emphasis upon the present time. There is a time in the affairs of every man when it is particularly desirable that he shall make his great decision. If Mr. Covill had taken the advice of this revelation, he would thereby have started on a life of promise in the work of the church. When he failed to take advantage of his opportunity, it became more and more difficult every day for him to beat back to the place of right decision.

"Thou hast rejected me many times because of pride, and the cares of the world" (3b). This was probably what pre-

vented Mr. Covill from joining the church. It has prevented many others. It has also taken out some who have joined the church but who have fallen by the wayside.

"I have prepared thee for a greater work" (3d). It was within the power of James Covill to frustrate the work which God had prepared him to do, and which had possibly been in the divine mind through many generations. God has prepared others, similarly, for a work which the world needs. Such preparation on the part of Divinity does not rob any man of his agency, yet those who exercise their agency to frustrate the work of God thereby incur a great condemnation.

"Thou art called to go to the Ohio" (4c). Here is a further possible reason for Covill's failure. Obedience meant almost immediate migration from New York to Ohio and an abandonment of the interests and friendships which he had built up in the vicinity of Fayette.

SECTION 40

The revelation given Joseph Smith and Sidney Rigdon in Fayette, New York, in January 1831 is the sequel to the revelation preceding it. Its purpose is to explain why James Covill had not fulfilled the covenant he had made with God to join the church and enter into the ministry. Mr. Covill thus touches our history for a moment and then passes beyond our ken. After his rejection of the gospel, we hear no more of him.

It has been suggested by some that this revelation and the preceding one cancel each other out, and that we will be well advised to omit both of them from the Doctrine and Covenants. It should be noted, however, that when the Book of Commandments was printed in 1833 and the Doctrine and Covenants in 1835 the failure of James Covill to join the church was already known. It is an indication of the faith of the early Saints that this and the preceding revelation were included in both books even though the compilers knew that questions would be raised concerning them. They were assured that the teachings of the revelation have value beyond the situation of the man addressed.

SECTION 41

In December 1830 the Lord told the Saints that it was expedient that they should gather together at the Ohio against the time that Oliver Cowdery should return to them there.[1] In addition to this they were promised in January 1831 that in Ohio they would receive the law and be endowed with the power from on high.[2] In harmony with these instructions the exodus from New York began almost immediately. Joseph, Emma, Sidney Rigdon, and Edward Partridge left in the latter part of January and arrived at Kirtland about the first of February. The prophet and his associates were greatly needed, for the converts were new and undisciplined, and in spite of their membership in the church, many strange theories and half truths were held among them.

This revelation, which was the first received in Kirtland, paved the way for the giving of the law five days later. It was given through Joseph Smith, February 4, 1831.

"Ye that hear me not will I curse, that have professed my name, with the heaviest of all cursings" (1a). Here is an early statement of the basic principle that the greater the light the greater the condemnation of those who reject it. The pit pony who has never been above ground does not miss the light as does his brother who remembers earlier days in the sunshine.

"Assemble yourselves together to agree upon my word" (1b). This revelation is addressed to the elders of the church, and they are told to *assemble to agree.* They were not to come together merely for investigation or discussion, but for agreement. For such agreement to be effective and

171

permanent, it must be well founded in revelation and truth, and they must seek harmony and mutual understanding.

"By the prayer of your faith ye shall receive my law" (1b). The Saints in Kirtland were very earnest, but were greatly in need of instruction. Writing of his arrival in Kirtland, Joseph says:

The branch of the church in this part of the Lord's vineyard, which had increased to nearly one hundred members, were striving to do the will of God, so far as they knew it, though some strange notions and false spirits had crept in among them. With a little caution and some wisdom I soon assisted the brethren and proceeded to overcome them. The plan of "common stock" which had existed in what was called "the family," whose members generally had obeyed the everlasting gospel, was readily abandoned for the more perfect law of the Lord: and the false spirits were easily discerned and rejected by the light of revelation.[3]

"He that saith he receiveth it [the law] *and doeth it not, the same is not my disciple, and shall be cast out from among you"* (2b). Even this early in the life of the church, the importance of quality in church membership was recognized. Provision is made here for eliminating from the church those who will not abide by its teachings and purposes. This provision is more clearly stated in subsequent revelations.

"It is not meet that the things which belong to the children of the kingdom, should be given to them that are not worthy" (2c). Commenting on this, Bishop Koehler says:

Why try to build the kingdom of heaven with men who cannot "see"? It is only worth-while to put an egg in the incubator if it has been fertilized. We must build Zion with kingdom-building material.

"It is meet that my servant, Joseph Smith, Jr., should have a house built, in which to live and translate" (3a). At this time Joseph and his wife were living with Newell K. Whitney, from whom they received every kindness and attention which could be expected. The church was now growing so rapidly, however, that it was necessary to supply the temporal needs of the prophet in an orderly way so that he could give his time to the revision of the Scriptures and his other duties as the leader of the church.

"Edward Partridge. . .should be appointed by the voice

*of the church, and ordained a bishop unto the church, to
leave his merchandise and spend all his time in the labors of
the church"* (3c). At this time Joseph Smith was recognized as
the first elder and Oliver Cowdery as the second elder in the
church. There were also other elders, priests, teachers, and
deacons. By the ordination here authorized, Edward
Partridge became one of the leaders of the church and
continued as such until his death in May 1840. The duties of
the Bishopric pertain preeminently to temporal concerns,
the bishop having the duty of gathering, maintaining,
and dispersing the properties of the church subject to the
law and order of the church and as may be directed by
revelation from time to time.

---

[1]Section 37:2. [2]Section 38:7. [3]*Times and Seasons* 4:368.

SECTION 42

Obeying the instruction previously given, twelve of the
elders of the church met in prayer and fasting at Kirtland,
Ohio, and on Wednesday, February 9, 1831, they received
the revelation now printed in its chronological order as
Section 42. In the 1835 edition of the Doctrine and
Covenants, what is now Section 17 was Section 2 and
was called "Articles and Covenants for Church Government." The present Section 42 was Section 13 of this edition
and was called "Laws of the Church." It has frequently
been referred to as the basic constitutional law of the church.
*"Ye have assembled yourselves together. . . and are
agreed"* (1c). In a well researched article in the *Saints'
Herald* Dorothy Moser noted that the twelve elders who met
to agree included several who previously had been members
of the Common Stock Family instituted by Sidney Rigdon
in the Kirtland area.[1] Among them, in addition to Sidney
Rigdon, were probably Lyman Wight, Titus Billings, Isaac

Morley, and Edward Partridge. We do not know how long it took to reach an agreement or whether this agreement was registered by a formal action of some kind, or even whether it had been achieved before the revelation was received. But the agreement seems to have been wholehearted. Joseph Smith wrote: "The plan of Common Stock, which had existed in what was called 'the family' whose members generally had embraced an everlasting gospel, was readily abandoned for the more perfect law of the Lord."

"I give unto you this first commandment, that ye shall go forth in my name, every one of you" (2a). Naturally missionary work must precede any organized pastoral activity, for men have to be won before the kingdom can be built. The obligation to "reap while the day lasts" was therefore laid on every one of the elders. They had had recent experience of the endowment of the Spirit of God, and they were to rely on this Spirit to add power and conviction to their testimony.

"Two by two" (2c). This was the pattern followed by Jesus in sending out the seventy.[2] Its importance has been reiterated to the church on a number of occasions, and as recently as the revelation of 1925.[3]

"Repent ye, repent ye, for the kingdom of heaven is at hand" (2d). This urgent note of repentance should be sounded frequently. A branch which goes from year to year without hearing the stirring call to repentance misses the full message of the gospel. A missionary who presents the doctrinal principles but fails to sound this call has fallen short of his duty.

"The city of the New Jerusalem shall be prepared, that ye may be gathered in one" (3b). The elders already had been told to "seek to bring forth and establish the cause of Zion,"[4] that Joseph Smith had been inspired to move "the cause of Zion in mighty power for good,"[5] and that Zion shall "rejoice upon the hills,"[6] but now the gathering is declared to be the very heart of the church work. It is necessary "that ye may be my people, and I will be your God."[7]

"Ordained by some one who has authority" (4). It is imperative that the representatives of the church shall be properly authorized through call and ordination. The comments of Elder William H. Kelley are noteworthy in this connection:

No church has a just claim upon the conscience of the people. They must know that God authorized and approves their system of worship, in order to inspire within them faith and reverence for it. This was true under the old covenant. God descended upon Mount Sinai in burning fire, and from out of the thick cloud and thunderings and lightnings, the trembling of the earth and sound of the trumpet, the voice of the unseen King was heard uttering the divine mandates. Israel stood still, wrapped in awe and reverence. "Moses spake, and God answered him by a voice." The people heard. Under the superlative grandeur and majesty of this scene every Israelite was made to know that the seal of Jehovah was upon his religion, and that God was with Moses. For the authorization and establishment of the religious services, the Lord said unto Moses, ". . . take thou unto thee Aaron thy brother, and his sons with him, from among the children of Israel, that he may minister unto me in the priest's office, even Aaron, Nadab and Abihu, Eleazer and Ithamar, Aaron's sons." They were consecrated to an "everlasting priesthood throughout their generations." The organization took form in the offices of the priesthood, which was the administrative authority of the constituted service, and a whole tribe was set apart as administrators. The Aaronic or Levitical priesthood was the authority to which every officer was consecrated and by which he was authorized to act in the name of God and the people, without which their acts were mere presumption, to be met with reprimand and rejection. God was the author of the service, and selected men to serve, and authorized them to speak in his name.[8]

"Teach the principles of my gospel" (5a). Whatever other things the ministry may leave undone, its basic teaching task is to explain the principles of the gospel persuasively. No matter who else does or does not do this, the ministry must. It is the primary task of the men of the priesthood, and it is a task which is primarily theirs.

"In the Bible" (5a). The following resolution was adopted September 13, 1878:

That this body representing the Reorganized Church of Jesus Christ of Latter Day Saints, does hereby authoritatively indorse the Holy Scriptures, as revised, corrected and translated by the spirit of revela-

175

tion, by Joseph Smith, Jr., the Seer, and as published by the church we represent.

"And the Book of Mormon" (5a). It will be remembered that the Doctrine and Covenants was not first published until August 1835. That is why it is not mentioned here.

"Observe the covenants and church articles to do them, and these shall be their teachings" (5b). The following General Conference resolution was adopted September 29, 1879:

That the elders should confine their teaching to such doctrines and tenets, church articles and practices, a knowledge of which is necessary to obedience and salvation; and that in all questions upon which there is much controversy, and upon which the church has not clearly declared, and which are not unmistakably essential to salvation, the elders should refrain from teaching; or if called upon, in defense of the church, or when wisdom should dictate, they should so clearly discriminate in their teaching between their own views and opinions, and the affirmations and defined declarations of the church that they shall not be found antagonizing their own and others' views as a conflict in teaching upon the part of the church.

That the advancing of speculative theories upon abstruse questions, a belief or disbelief in which cannot affect the salvation of the hearers, is a reprehensible factor, and should not be indulged in by the elders; especially should not this be done in those branches where personal antagonism must inevitably arise, to the hindering of the work of Grace; and should be reserved for the schools of inquiry amongst the elders themselves.

"If ye receive not the Spirit ye shall not teach" (5b). This is clear and mandatory. The preceding promise should be noted however: "The Spirit shall be given unto you by the prayer of faith." Those who do not receive the Spirit in their ministry should live and pray for its bestowal.

"The fullness of my Scriptures" (5c). This refers to the Holy Scriptures, the inspired correction of which was begun by Joseph in June 1830. At the death of Joseph in 1844 the manuscript was left in the hands of Emma Smith, his widow, by whom it was delivered to William Marks, I. L. Rogers, and W. W. Blair, a committee appointed by the annual conference of 1866. The manuscript was published late in 1867. In connection with its coming forth the following citations may be noted: I Nephi 3:168 to 172; 192-194;

176

II Nephi 2:19-23; Doctrine and Covenants 22, 23.

"I speak unto the church" (6). The preceding instruction had been given to the elders. The law which follows is binding upon all members of the church.

"He that kills shall not have forgiveness in this world, nor in the world to come" (6). Elder John Sheehy comments on this statement:

A man commits a crime. He is arrested, tried, found guilty and sentenced to twenty-five years in the penitentiary. After five or ten years he is pardoned, forgiveness is extended toward him and he is restored to his place in society. He was forgiven, but suppose instead of this he had served his full term of twenty-five years. Then he would be restored to society as before, but this time he would not be pardoned but would be redeemed by paying the price of his sin. One who commits willful murder is not to be forgiven. He must pay the price of his sinning. It is the major crime against the physical life of our fellows.

"He that stealeth and will not repent, shall be cast out" (7b). Repentance, in this case, ought to be much more than willingness to apologize. A person who is guilty of theft does not have the spirit of the gospel. If he deliberately closes his heart and mind to the demands of the gospel, the church cannot help him and he may become a positive hindrance to the building of the kingdom. Of recent years, however, we have become aware that stealing and other offenses against the moral code may have physical, social, or psychological roots. A kleptomaniac may need ministry rather than expulsion. On the other hand, as the spiritual standards of the church become more elevated, many of the forms of dishonesty which are now ignored will be discountenanced by the Saints. Sharp business practice, for example, might well come under the condemnation expressed in this paragraph.

"Thou shalt love thy wife with all thy heart, and shall cleave unto her and none else; and he that looketh after a woman to lust after her, shall deny the faith, and shall not have the Spirit; and if he repents not, he shall be cast out" (7d). There could be no more direct or more specific condemnation of polygamy than this. Any man who fails to cleave

177

unto "his wife and none else" has thereby denied the faith and has lost title to the Spirit of God. When anyone falls into such a sin, it is not to be expected that his ministry will be approved of God, who has said, "If ye receive not the Spirit, ye shall not teach."[9] Any organization entering into such practices has departed from the faith, forfeited the Spirit of God, and lost claim to be truly representative of him. There is no possible reconciliation between this paragraph and the so-called "revelation on the eternity of the marriage covenant."[10]

"He that hath committed adultery and repents with all his heart, and forsaketh it, and doeth it no more, thou shalt forgive; but if he doeth it again, he shall not be forgiven, but shall be cast out" (7b). There is no alternative offered. The church can only forgive the adulterer who repents with all his heart and who manifests his repentance by forsaking his sin.

"Thou shalt not speak evil of thy neighbor" (7f). This is akin to the commandment of the Law of Moses, "Thou shalt not bear false witness against thy neighbor."[11] This commandment is not qualified in any way. It does not say, for example, "Thou shalt not bear witness against your neighbor when you know that witness to be false." Anyone bearing witness against his neighbor is under the solemn obligation of knowing that his witness is true before he bears it. If he reports that which is untrue to the detriment of his neighbor, it is no excuse to say that he thought it was true, for he should have assured himself of its truth before reporting it.

Witness should not be borne against one's neighbor in many of the cases where it might happen to be true, for the instruction goes on "nor do him any harm." Yet there are circumstances in which it is our duty to report facts to the proper officers of the church, e.g., at a court trial.

"Thou knowest my laws concerning these things are given in my Scriptures" (7g). There can be no doubt regarding the specific nature of the laws regarding chastity within the marriage relation as given in the Scriptures prior to this time.

This sentence has a prophetic note which should have warned those who were asked to accept the doctrine of polygamy as of divine origin.

"...*and consecrate*" (8b). In connection with this statement of the law, Bishop J. A. Koehler says:

The test of our regeneration is our willingness to consecrate. "Faith without works is dead." This game of life can be played only with men and means. Both our man power and capital must first of all be flexible; it must be ready for active service. Our willingness to respond to the call of the church and to apply our means to the task of establishing the "cause of Zion" is the first test of our fitness for the kingdom.

"*If thou lovest me... thou wilt remember the poor*" (8a, b). At the opening of his public ministry the Lord Jesus proclaimed, "The Spirit of the Lord is upon me, because he hath anointed me to preach the gospel to the poor."[12] The revelations in the Doctrine and Covenants show that this concern for the poor was characteristic of Zion of Enoch,[13] and a keynote of the Restoration.[14] It is basic to the law of consecration.[15]

"*With a covenant and a deed which can not be broken*" (8b). The procedure followed was for the steward to deed all his property to Bishop Edward Partridge, who then leased back to him the properties which constituted his temporal stewardship and which he was to manage according to his own judgment. The "residue" of his consecration, if any, became part of the common treasury and was available to assist the needy in the establishment of their stewardships.[16] The details of this arrangement proved unworkable. One of the major reasons for this was that it gave the steward no protection in the event that he decided to withdraw from the movement, since what was called his "inheritance" was in fact held on lease from the Presiding Bishop. Later this inequity was adjusted; what was dedicated for the ministry to the poor could not be reclaimed, but the inheritance was held in fee simple.

On June 25, 1833, the presidency of the church gave the bishop in Zion the following items of instruction concerning the consecration of property:

Brother Edward Partridge, Sir, I proceed to answer your questions concerning the consecration of property: First, it is not right to condescend to very great particulars in taking inventories. The fact is this, a man is bound by the law of the church, to consecrate to the bishop, before he can be considered a legal heir to the kingdom of Zion: and this, too, without constraint; and unless he does this, he cannot be acknowledged before the Lord, on the church book: therefore, to condescend to particulars, I will tell you that every man must be his own judge, how much he should receive, and how much he should suffer to remain in the hands of the bishop. I speak to those who consecrate more than they need for the support of themselves and their families.

The matter of consecration must be done by the mutual consent of both parties; for, to give the bishop power to say how much every man shall have, and he be obliged to comply with the bishop's judgment, is giving to the bishop more power than a king has; and, upon the other hand, to let every man say how much he needs, and the bishop be obliged to comply with his judgment, is to throw Zion into confusion, and make a slave of the bishops. The fact is, there must be a balance or equilibrium of power, between the bishop and the people; and thus harmony and good will be preserved among you.

Therefore, those persons consecrating property to the bishop in Zion, and then receiving an inheritance back, must show reasonably to the bishop that he wants as much as he claims. But in case the two parties cannot come to a mutual agreement, the bishop is to have nothing to do about receiving their consecrations; and the case must be laid before a council of twelve high priests; the bishop not being one of the council, but he is to lay the case before them.[17]

"Inasmuch as ye impart of your substance unto the poor, ye will do it unto me" (8c). Here is the essence of the Zionic movement. The redistribution of wealth proposed in this section is not primarily a social affair but a spiritual affair. Its motivation is "if thou lovest me." From such a fundamental dynamic, the social readjustment contemplated will be executed and maintained. If this basic impulsion is removed, we have no guarantee of the effective reorganization of society. This social regeneration will not come out of social experimentation but only as part of a great spiritual enterprise.

"They can not be taken from the church" (9a). Once the title has passed voluntarily from the former owner to the Bishopric, the property consecrated for ministry to the poor

180

cannot be reclaimed. It is obvious that this provision is a requirement of stable administration of the finances of the church. When a transfer of properties has been fully agreed, the Bishopric must know that this action is final. Otherwise, a change of heart or mind on the part of a steward or a group of stewards might easily jeopardize the whole enterprise.

"Residue. . . shall be kept to administer unto those who have not, from time to time" (10a). The initial redistribution of property contemplated under operation of the stewardship law will be the best possible at the time of the redistribution, but changing circumstances will necessarily change the status of individual stewards. Therefore, the provision made is that any "residue" becoming available after the first consecration shall be consecrated for the benefit of those who are lacking. It is most convenient to have this secondary redistribution at annual intervals. This is why the church requests the Saints to file their financial statements annually.

"As shall be appointed by the high council of the church, and the bishop and his council" (10b). In the Book of Commandments, this reads: "as shall be appointed by the elders of the church and the bishop."[18] It will be remembered that at that time there were only elders, priests, teachers, and deacons and one bishop in the church, although Joseph, Oliver, and David had been designated apostles. In the revelation as printed in the Doctrine and Covenants the "elders" are more specifically designated as members of the High Council, which had been organized by the time the section was printed in the Doctrine and Covenants. The phrasing in the Doctrine and Covenants version of this section is an amplification rather than a contradiction. During the early years, prior to the complete organization of the church, many functions which were later assigned to the general quorums had to be discharged by the elders. This is in complete harmony with the law later given that "an elder has a right to officiate in his stead when the high priest is not present"[19] and the law that "the Mel-

181

chisedec priesthood holds the right of presidency, and has power and authority over all the offices in the church, in all ages of the world, to administer in spiritual things."[20] It was natural that at this period bishops and elders should do certain things in the church, even though the more complete organization of the church at the time of the publication of the revelations in 1835 made it possible for the Lord to designate more particularly the quorums and councils that should do this work in the future.

"This I do for the salvation of my people" (10c). Note the repeated insistence that observance of the financial law is basic to "the salvation of my people." This has been emphasized so many times that there is no excuse for members of the church who fail to abide by these laws of spiritual growth. Many who are bewildered by our failure to make reasonable spiritual progress have forgotten this instruction regarding temporalities: "In your temporal things you shall be equal, and this not grudgingly, otherwise the abundance of the manifestation of the Spirit shall be withheld."[21]

"I will consecrate of the riches of those who embrace my gospel, among the Gentiles" (11c). In the Book of Commandments this reads, "I will consecrate the riches of the Gentiles, unto my people which are of the house of Israel."[22] The phrasing in the Doctrine and Covenants appears to be an editorial adjustment of the other statement which does not conflict with it but does make it more specific. It is not unlikely that it was called forth by objection on the part of the "Gentiles" who regarded the original statement as a threat against their property rights.

"Let all thy garments be plain" (12a). The Master delights in a clean and attractive people, but he has warned us against that undue concern with personal adornment which gives rise to pride and arrogance and the beginnings of the caste system.[23] This instruction is still timely.

"Thou shalt not be idle" (12b). This is not only good religion; it is good economics, it is good sociology, it is good

182

ethics. It is evident that only as the ideal of mutual service, of reciprocity concerning mutual benefits, of sharing mutual sacrifices controls men in their relations can there be stable and harmonious living together. A man's right to live among his fellows depends upon his willingness to share in the costs of the joint enterprise. But his contribution does not have to be industrial. It may be artistic.[24]

"Whosoever among you are sick, and have not faith to be healed, but believe, shall be nourished with all tenderness with herbs and mild food" (12c). Here is authority for consultation with those skilled in the use of "herbs and mild food." A fitting sequel to this instruction will be the development of a group of doctors, nurses, and dietitians specializing in the kindly care of the sick. This was envisioned for the Sanitarium.

"If they die, they shall die unto me, and if they live, they shall live unto me" (12d). There is here no promise for healing every time the elders administer. Administration is an aid to faith and an ordinance of the gospel; it is not a guarantee of healing.[25]

"They who have not faith to do these things, but believe in me, have power to become my sons" (13b). Here is the essence of the whole matter, and here is the greatest assurance of all. The blessings of health and physical strength are of secondary importance when compared with the blessings of spiritual life.

"Thou shalt not take. . .; thou shalt pay" (14a). This is a clear indication that private property has place in the Zionic order. President Frederick M. Smith has the following to say in this connection:

The social significance of the Christian religion is crystallized in the doctrine of stewardships, according to which one is held socially responsible for the manner in which he utilizes whatever of property and wealth he may acquire, holding only that which he utilizes, and this determined by his capacity. This envisagement of social responsibility requires that talents as well as property shall be directed toward community welfare, the compulsion being not law but public sentiment. The holding of only what can be utilized (according to capacity or talent) requires that surplus shall revert to the common treasury or to the group. Wealth and property are not for personal pleasure according to caprice, but for service and enlarged contribution to the common weal. Riotous or extravagant living is incongruous with the doctrine of stewardships, while luxury is justified only when common.

"My Scriptures shall be given as I have appointed, and they shall be preserved in safety" (15). This prophetic promise was fulfilled when the Inspired Version of the Holy Scriptures was published in 1867.

The whole of paragraph 16 should be studied in view of the ramifications of this fundamental instruction concerning the importance of the Scriptures. Note how frequently the elders of the church and the church generally are reminded that the teaching and practice of the church must be in harmony with the Scriptures already given. This is a reiteration of the ancient word of Isaiah: "To the law and to the testimony; if they speak not according to this word, it is because there is no light in them."[26]

"He that doeth them not shall be damned, if he continues" (16b). This is not a threat but a statement of the inevitable result of disobedience to fundamental law. Salvation is by way of obedience. Damnation is the necessary sequel to disobedience.

"If thou shalt ask, thou shalt receive revelation upon revelation" (17a). In the preceding paragraph the eyes of the church were turned back to the law already given. Now they are directed forward to the light yet to come. We need to learn to give balanced emphasis to the teachings of the church. Some find it hard to give due weight to present revelations but easy to accept light given many centuries ago. Others find it easier to recognize the "modern" inspiration than ancient light. We need to fuse these two attitudes. "Moderns" should remember that they lose much when they miss the glory of past revelations because these are not clothed in the language of the present age. "Fundamentalists" need to beware of ignoring the revelations of God in this day just because these are not phrased in archaic language or because they come through men like ourselves.

184

"Teach them that shall be converted to flee to the west" (18a). The keynote of missionary preaching in the early years was building the kingdom. The elders are here instructed to urge the Saints to gather, but they must do this in accordance with the directions of the presiding officers of the church. It was a good thing for the Saints to concentrate in the vicinity of Independence, but they could do this effectively only as preparation was made for them or as they could render specific aid in solving the problems of the gathering.

"Or high priests" (19a). This was not included in the earliest transcript of the revelations, but, as stated in the notes on paragraph 8, its later inclusion by the prophet is not a contradiction but an extension and explanation of the earlier version.

"A just remuneration" (19b). Under the operation of the law of stewardships, those working in spiritual or temporal concerns receive their remuneration from the proceeds of the work which they do. This is an anticipation of the principle stated frequently in later revelations that in temporal things the men of the ministry are to be equal. Just remuneration, however, does not mean remuneration based upon the quality of the service rendered but upon the needs and just wants of the contributor as determined both by his situation and the ability of the church to give. When these are supplied, it is just that he shall be expected to give of his best for the furtherance of the Cause.

"Ye shall be watchful and careful, with all inquiry" (20c). The teaching of this paragraph seems to be beyond dispute. No action is to be taken against a church member who puts away his companion because of infidelity. The guilty party, if he does not marry and if he truly repents of his sinning, can be retained or readmitted. But a church member who leaves his companion for the sake of adultery and marries someone else must be expelled from the church. He has undertaken new responsibilities from which he cannot honorably turn away. These are in direct opposition to responsibilities which were undertaken previously and

from which his own sin has not released him. However, after an extended and consistent demonstration of repentance and reformation of character, he can be readmitted by rebaptism. Maintenance of this standard is so important, says the revelation, that it is to be administered with specially watchful care.

"*Every person who belongeth to this church of Christ shall observe to keep all the commandments and covenants of the church*" (21a). Further comment is scarcely necessary other than to underline the word *all*. Anyone who seeks to justify himself in failure to be obedient to any part of the law of the church is in a dangerous position. Such an attitude leads inevitably to disrespect for other commandments of the law and growing areas of disobedience, coupled with growing atrophy of spiritual power.

"*They shall be delivered up and dealt with according to the laws of the land*" (21b). Murder, theft, and lying shall be judged according to the civil law. The church is not authorized to administer civil punishment but is concerned with maintaining the purity and effective righteousness of the body of Christ. As long as sinners show signs of genuine repentance, the church must seek to win them regardless of what the civil law may require. Although murderers are beyond the forgiveness of the church our heavenly Father, whose wisdom is infinitely greater than ours, will, of course, forgive whom he will. In an action which parallels that which permits the rebaptism of adulterers who have demonstrated repentance over a period of years, the Standing High Council authorized the rebaptism of a convicted murderer at the end of his prison sentence and after his repentance indicated that he had undergone a radical change of attitude in the years since his offense.

"*The church shall lift up their hands against him or her, that they may be dealt with according to the law of God*" (22c). The determination of guilt is not a matter for the general membership of the church. This is very properly reserved to the judicial arm. It is the evident desire of

Divinity, however, that the membership shall feel something of the pain of amputating the dead or diseased parts of the body, that they may sense the awfulness of this condition and may profit thereby. Hence the instruction that the church *shall* lift up their hands against the accused after that person has been found guilty before the church courts.

The law on repentance stated in paragraph 23 is clear and constructive. The initial movement toward reconciliation should include only those who are direct parties to the offense. If first efforts fail, then the priesthood may be brought into the situation to attempt a reconciliation, but the general membership must still be excluded lest their inclusion shall lead to the erection of party lines and the creation of a greater fissure than previously existed. If the offense was secret, the offender must be protected from public disfavor "that the church may not speak reproachfully" of him or her. Where such offenses were publicly committed, however, public reconciliation is necessary in order to heal the wounds which have been inflicted.

HISTORICAL NOTE

In his history of the church John Whitmer wrote in this connection:

After the above revelation was received, the elders went forth to proclaim repentance according to commandment, and there were numbers added to the church. The Bishop, Edward Partridge, visited the church and its several branches; and there were some that would not receive the law. The time has not yet come that the law can be fully established, for the disciples live scattered abroad and are not organized; our numbers are small, and the disciples untaught, consequently they understand not the things of the kingdom. There were some of the disciples who were flattered into this church because they thought that all things were to be common, therefore they thought to glut themselves upon the labors of others.[27]

---

[1]*Saints Herald*, March 1, 1964. [2]Luke 10:1. [3]Section 135:4. [4]Section 6:3. [5]Section 19:2. [6]Section 34:6. [7]Section 42:3. [8]*Presidency and Priesthood.* [9]Section 42:5. [10]Utah Doctrine and Covenants 132. [11] Exodus 20:16. [12]Luke 4:18. [13]Section

36:2i. ¹⁴*Ibid.* 34:4d. ¹⁵*Ibid.* 38:8a-b; 42:8, 19b; 44:3; 56:5a; 52:9c; 72:3b; 77:1c; 81:4a; 82:2b; 83:19a, 23a; 101:2g, 102:2b; 122:6d. ¹⁶For a copy of the lease see *Saints' Herald* 110:50; *Journal of History* 16:284-287; *Restoration Scriptures* 252-253. ¹⁷*Journal of History*, Volume 16, page 284. ¹⁸Chapter 44:29. ¹⁹Section 104:6. ²⁰Section 104:3. ²¹Section 70:3. ²²Book of Commandments, page 93:32. ²³In this connection note I Timothy 2:9, 10; I Peter 3:3, 4; Book of Mormon IV Nephi 1:27, 28. ²⁴Sections 60:3e; 68:4; 75:1, 5; 85:19, 38; 87:7; 118:4. ²⁵See Matthew 17:14-20; Philippians 2:25-27; II Corinthians 12:7-12; I Timothy 5:23; II Timothy 4:20. ²⁶Isaiah 8:20. ²⁷*Journal of History* 1:50-51.

SECTION 43

Soon after Joseph received the revelation on the basic law of the church, a certain Mrs. Hubbell came to Kirtland and sought to give revelations and commandments to the church. Since Mrs. Hubbell found some sympathizers, Joseph inquired for light and received this revelation, which reaffirms instruction which had been given previously on this and other subjects. It will be noted that the revelation is addressed to the elders of the church.

"*None other appointed unto you to receive commandments and revelations until he be taken, if he abide in me*" (1b). The provision that instruction for the church shall come through the one person called of God and sustained by the people is undoubtedly a wise one. Under such an arrangement the prophet becomes the personal symbol of divine revelation, and the faithful look to him expectantly and support him with their confidence and prayers. Such a minister knows, moreover, that he will be required to function even under the most difficult circumstances, and he therefore seeks to keep himself in tune with Divinity at all times.

"*Until he be taken*" (1b). There were those in the early church who thought that Joseph was to stand at the head of the church on earth until the coming of the Lord Jesus. This phrase definitely negates such an idea. Joseph would at some time be taken away. The instruction given provides for the selection of his successor.

"None else shall be appointed unto this gift except it be through him" (2a). In accordance with this law, Joseph the Martyr designated his son, Joseph Smith, as his successor. There is abundant evidence confirming this, from which the following quotations are selected:

Sunday, December 8, 1850, bore testimony that Joseph Smith appointed those of his own posterity to be his successor.[1]

I recollect a meeting that was held in the winter of 1843, at Nauvoo, Illinois, prior to Joseph Smith's death, at which the appointment was made by him, Joseph Smith, of his successor. His own Joseph was selected as his successor. Joseph Smith did the talking. There was present Joseph and Hyrum Smith, John Taylor, and some others who also spoke on the subject; there were twenty-five I suppose at the meeting. At that meeting Joseph Smith, the present presiding officer of the complainant church, was selected by his father as his successor. He was ordained and anointed and Joseph, his father, blessed him and ordained him, and Newell K. Whitney poured the oil on his head, and he was set apart to be his father's successor in office, holding all the powers that his father held.[2]

In Liberty jail the promise and blessing of a life of usefulness to the cause of truth was pronounced upon our head, by lips tainted by dungeon damps, and by the Spirit confirmed through attesting witnesses. . . . Subsequent to our baptism in 1843, upon two occasions was the same blessing confirmed by Joseph Smith, once in the council room in the brick store on the banks of the Mississippi, of which we have not a doubt there are witnesses who would confirm the present testimony; once, in the last interview Joseph Smith held with his family before he left Nauvoo to his death. A public attestation of the same blessing was made from the stand in the grove in Nauvoo, sometime prior to the murder in Carthage.[3]

"He that is ordained of me, shall . . . teach those revelations which you have received, and shall receive through him whom I have appointed" (2c). Here is one of the tests of succession in church presidency. Any purported leader of the church who changes the basic law of the church as stated in the revelations is thereby revealed as an impostor. A significant elaboration of this principle was set forth in the revelation of 1894.[4]

"When ye are assembled together, ye shall instruct and edify each other" (3a). This revelation was addressed to the elders of the church, and this specific commandment is a

189

preliminary to the instruction regarding the organization of quorums. It has been restated as recently as 1950.[5]

"*If ye desire the glories of the kingdom, appoint ye my servant Joseph Smith, Jr., and uphold him before me by the prayer of faith*" (3d). Hiram Page and Mrs. Hubbell and others who set themselves up as rival revelators deflected some of the spiritual support which should have upheld the prophet before the Lord. This revelation instructs the elders to support Joseph by their faith and prayers as a condition of receiving the blessings of God through him. This principle is operative in every section of the church structure. Stake presidents, district presidents, and branch presidents should be similarly supported or the Lord cannot use them as outstanding means of blessing.

"*Ye are not sent forth to be taught, but to teach the children of men the things which I have put into your hands by the power of my Spirit*" (4b). The ministry are commissioned especially to teach the truths of the gospel. This does not say that they cannot learn other things from other people but only that they should be preeminent in their special calling as ministers of salvation. In later revelation, the ministry are instructed specifically to seek out of the best books words of wisdom.[6]

"*How oft have I called upon you*" (6c). Note the many ways in which this revelation says that God seeks to reach mankind:

Through the ministry of the priesthood.
Through natural forces.
Through famines and pestilences.
By the voice of judgment.
By the voice of mercy.
By the voice of glory and honor.
By the riches of eternal life.

"*My people shall be redeemed and shall reign with me on earth*" (7b). Here is one of our clearest statements of the sequence of coming events:

The saints will reign with Christ on earth for "a thousand years."

Satan, who has been bound, will be loosed again.

After Satan has reigned for a brief season, the end of the earth will come.

At that time, "he that liveth in righteousness shall be changed in the twinkling of an eye."

The earth will "pass away so as by fire."

The wicked will "go away into unquenchable fire."

"Let the solemnities of eternity rest upon your minds" (8b). An outstanding psychologist, Guy Allen Tawney, says, "Worship is like a breathing spell in a long and arduous foot race, or the hour of roll call in a prolonged and hard fought battle." Another psychologist, Henry L. Wieman, writes: "This art of worship is the only suitable preparation for the greatest creative artistry in all the world, the art of reshaping the total vital process of living."

HISTORICAL NOTE

Concerning Mrs. Hubble and the effect of this revelation, John Whitmer wrote in his history of the church:

About these days there was a woman by the name of Hubble who professed to be a prophetess of the Lord, and professed to have many revelations, and knew that the Book of Mormon was true; and that she should become a teacher in the Church of Christ. She appeared very sanctimonious and deceived some, who were not able to detect her in her hypocrisy. Others, however, had a spirit of discernment; and her follies and abominations were made manifest. The Lord gave revelation that the Saints might not be deceived, which read as follows: [See Doctrine and Covenants, section 43.]

After this commandment was received the Saints came to understanding on this subject, and unity and harmony prevailed throughout the church of God, and the Saints began to learn wisdom, and treasure up knowledge which they learned from the word of God, and by experience as they advanced in the way of eternal life.[7]

---

[1]From the private journal of Lyman Wight. [2]James Whitehead, in the Temple Lot Suit. [3]President Joseph Smith in *Saints' Herald*, Volume 14, page 105. See also Section 152:1a. [4]Section 122:1. [5]*Ibid*. 142:4b. [6]*Ibid*. 85:36. [7]*Journal of History* 1:51.

SECTION 44

Soon after their arrival in Kirtland, it became apparent to Joseph Smith and Sidney Rigdon that the work there would be considerably hampered unless the number of Saints could be increased. They were also greatly troubled regarding the relief of their poor, some of whom had come with the church from New York. In response to their prayers, Section 44 was given at Kirtland in the latter part of February 1831.

"The elders of my church should be called together" (1b). This commandment was fulfilled by calling the fourth conference of the church. It convened June 6, 1831.

"Exercise faith in me" (2a). Evidently faith is not a passive quality. The early Saints were to *exercise* faith as a condition of divine blessing.

"Go forth in the regions round about, and preach repentance....Many shall be converted" (2b, c). Here the elders were called to concentrate their efforts in and around Kirtland until enough converts were won to make the church influential in that region. Joseph was unfamiliar with the people of the surrounding country, for he had arrived from New York just a few weeks before this time. Yet he here gives a definite prophetic promise of great missionary success. This promise was generously fulfilled; hundreds were baptized in the Kirtland region in 1831 and 1832.

"Ye shall obtain power to organize yourselves according to the laws of man" (2c). This, too, was accomplished. Many of the converts from Mentor, Ohio, and other nearby places moved into Kirtland. By taking over their share of the civil offices of the community, they guaranteed the Saints a measure of civil liberty.

The necessity for organizing the Saints "according to the laws of man" in these efforts to build the kingdom arises out of the fact that Zion is to be set up under the overall sovereignty of a national government. Many of the laws of the United States have been designed especially to protect unwary persons who otherwise might be victimized by wicked but plausible men, or even by good but misguided men. Stewardship procedures therefore must be undertaken within the framework of laws and these laws must be enacted to maintain justice, or we must secure the passage of additional just laws adapted to our stewardship purposes.

"Visit the poor and the needy, and administer to their relief, that they may be kept until all things may be done according to my law" (3). Temporary relief measures are only an expedient. The Saints ought to relieve those who are in distress, but such relief ought not to be regarded as a permanent solution to the problem of poverty. The major strength of the Saints should go to building the kingdom of God. The emphasis thus strikes at the cause instead of merely remedying the effect.

SECTION 45

On Monday, March 7, 1831, while Joseph Smith was still in Kirtland, he received a revelation in which the Saints were commanded to gather from the east and the elders were instructed to take the gospel message into the states farther west. One of the factors necessitating this revelation was the circulation of many false reports regarding the belief and purpose of the Saints. The revelation is addressed to the people of the church.

"To whom the kingdom has been given" (1a). The word *kingdom* is evidently used here to mean the gospel and its authority. At that time the church was not fully organized with a First Presidency, Quorum of Twelve, Quorums of Seventy, High Council, etc., nor had much work been done toward the literal building of Zion. Yet the gospel of the kingdom had been committed to the Saints, together with authority to administer its ordinances, and from this seed the kingdom itself was to grow.

Note the reasons urged upon the Saints for their obedience:
They were the custodians and builders of the kingdom (1a).
This was the day of their opportunity (1b).
Jesus had the right to demand their allegiance, since he had suffered so much for them (1d).
Obedience would give them "power to do many miracles," to become the sons of God, and to obtain eternal life (2c).

"The Advocate with the Father" (1c). Read this in connection with I John 2, with particular emphasis on the first verse of the chapter.[1]

"Behold the blood of thy Son which was shed" (1d). Read this in connection with the prayer used in blessing the sacramental wine.[2] Consider also the following scriptures: Acts 20:28; Romans 5:9; Ephesians 1:7; Revelation 1:5; Mark 14:24; I John 1:7; Hebrews 10:29.

"Father, spare these my brethren" (1c). This should be studied in connection with Jesus' prayer for his disciples (John 17).

"Unto as many as received me gave I power to do many miracles and to become the sons of God" (2c). Those who do not receive Jesus can never become the sons of God, but those who do receive him do not thereby finish their work of salvation. Becoming a son of God is the goal, and receiving Jesus is the first step toward that goal.

"A city reserved until a day of righteousness shall come: a day which was sought for by all holy men, and they found it not, because of wickedness and abominations" (2g, h). Holy men of all ages have had concern for and have looked toward the building of the city of God. This building must necessarily be reserved until those who are to be its citizens can be one and together can be strong enough to be at least relatively independent of unbelievers. This was emphasized in a later revelation in which the building of the kingdom is said to require that "the army of the Lord shall become very great" and that it shall be "sanctified

194

before God." In the meantime preparations for the city of God are advanced whenever and wherever the kingdom fellowship grows in unity and truth.

"*Ye have looked upon the long absence of your spirits from your bodies to be a bondage*" (21). This was addressed to the disciples of Jesus. They had been told that the day of their redemption must await the second coming of the Lord,[3] and they were impatient for its coming. They probably had been taught by Jesus that the spirit and the body are the soul of man[4] and that these must be inseparably connected to receive a fullness of joy.[5]

"*This temple which ye now see shall be thrown down, that there shall not be left one stone upon another*" (3c). Herod had endeared himself to the patriotic Jews by enlarging and restoring the temple, which had become the pride of the nation. Already this work had gone on for forty-six years, and the Jews expected that the temple would stand until the great days of their coming power. Yet this temple was torn down in A.D. 70, and not one of the great stones which had composed it remained upon another.

"*This generation of Jews shall not pass away*" (3d). The destruction of Jerusalem occurred while many of those who had crucified Jesus were still alive. Many of the saints, remembering the warning given them by the Master, escaped from the doomed city, but many of the Jews were fanatically sure that they would be saved. More than half a million of them were destroyed in the attack on the city itself, and three times that number perished in the campaigns of Vespasian and Titus.

"*They shall remain until the times of the Gentiles be fulfilled*" (3f). The Inspired Version of the Bible is particularly clear in regard to this phrase.[6]

"*When the time of the Gentiles is come in*" (4b). This seems to indicate a period during which "time of the Gentiles" shall have reached its climax, immediately prior to the completion or fulfillment of the era.

"*A light shall break forth among them that sit in darkness*" (4b). This section is like many others in that its full meaning tends to escape us if we read it too hurriedly. We believe that "a light" did "break forth" in 1820-30 and that this light was, in a sense, the fullness of the gospel. What was given will not be superseded. But the light given at that time was not all that could possibly be given. More light has been given as necessary in succeeding years, and yet more will be given as our progress in spiritual things warrants and demands. In this connection note the words of Peter:

We have therefore a more sure knowledge of the word of prophecy, to which word of prophecy ye do well that ye take heed, as unto a light which shineth in a dark place, until the day-dawn, and the day-star arise in your hearts.

"He that feareth me shall be looking forth for the great day of the Lord to come" (6a). Evidently, expectation of the second coming is to be one of the characteristics of the church in the latter days.

"The remnant shall be gathered unto this place" (6d). This probably refers to the descendants of the children of Israel scattered among all nations (see paragraph 3). Palestine is still a place of gathering for them.

"Your souls shall live, and your redemption shall be perfected" (7b). That is to say, the spirits and the bodies of the saints will be reunited, and the saints themselves will be gathered with the righteous from every generation.

"Upon this mount" (8a). This was the Mount of Olives.

"They that knew no law shall have part in the first resurrection; and it shall be tolerable for them" (10a). For a further exposition of this sentence see Doctrine and Covenants 76:6 and the notes thereon.

"The earth shall be given unto them for an inheritance" (10c). The saints shall inherit the earth, which will fulfill the goal of its creation in becoming a fitting abode for those who inherit celestial glory.[7]

"Not many years hence ye shall hear of wars in your own lands" (11c). Here is another prophetic intimation of the coming Civil War. Note that this is one of the reasons given

196

for the gathering. The next verse starts out "wherefore," or "for this reason."

"That ye may purchase an inheritance which shall hereafter be appointed unto you" (12c). The Saints already were gathering to Kirtland, but the location of the New Jerusalem had not yet been designated. The Saints were promised, however, that it should be a land of peace and of safety for the Saints because the glory of the Lord would be there and because the wicked would find themselves out of place by contrast and would want to leave. In addition to being an actual place of refuge—socially, economically, educationally, spiritually—Zion must be a center from which knowledge of safety and the laws upon which safety is based shall radiate to the ends of the earth. Fulfillment of this promise is yet future.

"Keep these things from going abroad unto the world" (15a). It was necessary that the Saints should receive this instruction in order to encourage them and to broaden their vision, but it was not desirable that they should be boastful. They frequently were warned against such boasting, but the warning was not heeded by some, and this practice did much to fan the flame of resentment against them which their Gentile neighbors felt.

---

[1]See also Acts 2:33; 5:31; 7:55, 56; Romans 8:34-39. [2]Section 17:23. [3]Matthew 23:41 (I.V.). [4]Section 85:4. [5]Section 90:5. [6]See especially Luke 3:8; 21:23, 25, 32; Romans 11:25; Ephesians 1:10. [7]See Section 83:17; 85:4-6.

SECTION 46

This revelation was given at Kirtland, Ohio, March 8, 1831, and was one of five such communications given during that month.

It is easy to fall into a certain routine in our church services. This was as true one hundred years ago as it is today, but the Saints were so conscious of the importance of their work and the routine they followed that they carefully scrutinized every act and sought to make it justify itself according to their new faith. Because of this habit of questioning we find them frequently approaching the Lord for light regarding procedure which is now customary with us. It is against such a background that the revelation given at Kirtland March 8, 1831, must be studied. The major questions at this time were (1) What shall be the order of service in the church? (2) Who shall attend the services of the church? (3) Shall any greater restriction be placed on attendance at Sacrament services than at preaching service? (4) Should confirmation meetings be private? (5) Which of the gifts of the Spirit should we expect to receive? (6) How will the gifts operate? It will be noted that the revelation is addressed to the people of the church.

"Conduct all meetings as they are directed and guided by the Holy Spirit" (1b). This applies to the elders of the church, in whom the right of presidency centers. This is not to say, however, that the elders may conduct the meeting entirely without rule or set purpose. The elders should give careful thought to the structure of each meeting, should study the precedents which have been set and the law which applies to that type of meeting, and then should do their utmost to see that each meeting answers the purpose of its being. At all times, both while preparing for the meeting and while conducting it, the elders should seek to keep in tune with God so they will actually serve as his ministers.

"If any have trespassed, let him not partake until he makes reconciliation" (1d). Here the responsibility of seeing that evildoers shall not partake of the Communion until they have made reconciliation is placed directly on the elders in charge. They should seek to discharge this responsibility quietly and with a view to the total good. Public action is rarely wise or necessary. Nor is remedial action on the part of the elders likely to be effective among any who do not recognize their authority, either members of the church or others.

"That ye may not be seduced by evil spirits, or doctrines of devils, or the commandments of men, for some are of men, and others of devils" (3c). The early Saints had a lively belief in a personal devil served by a host of demonic angels. Because of this there was a tendency among them to overlook the significance of purely human mistakes and misdeeds. It is true, of course, that Satanic influence is constantly seeking to lead the faithful astray and to bring their work to naught, but men are themselves responsible both for yielding to this influence and also for their own mistakes and wickedness.

"Seek ye earnestly the best gifts, always remembering for what they are given" (4a). This is an important extension and explanation of the biblical instruction. According to this paragraph the Lord will not permit the Saints to be deceived if they seek the best gifts in earnestness of purpose, remembering that they are for the benefit of the Saints and purifying themselves of any desire to seek these gifts for the gratification of their own desires such as pride or point of view.

"Retain in your minds what those gifts are. . .; there are many gifts" (5a, b). The gifts of the gospel are so many and so varied that they are beyond our numbering. The best we can do is to learn to appreciate the gifts being manifested among us and to look and live for the further gifts which we need. Even this we frequently fail to do. We often look only for such gifts as prophecy or tongues and so fail to be grateful for the gifts of testimony, or of harmony, or of praise.

"To every man is given a gift by the Spirit of God" (5b). What a source of comfort and strength this should be! Our gifts have been divided among us according to the will of God, and none has been left out. "Now God be thanked, that matched us with this hour." It is unutterably foolish to pine for lack of gifts given to others, and so very wasteful to fail to live for our own gifts and to exercise them under divine guidance.

"That all may be profited thereby" (5c). One of the great

gifts of God to all who will receive it is the gift of membership in his body. Other gifts are to be exercised in harmony with this fundamental one. The members of the body have life in the body, and with the other members of the body, that the body as a whole might be nourished and enabled to accomplish its task. So, also, the gifts given to the several members of the body are not given to honor these members but to enable them to fill their destined places and thus to minister to the total good. Consider two men pictured by Elder Joseph Luff many years ago. The first came to the outer courts of heaven as a beggar, seeking alms to satisfy his own desperate need, and—because he was self-seeking—fearing to be sent away empty. The second came seeking alms also, but he came happy and upright and fearing no refusal because he sought to enlist heaven in a cause which God loved and to which he himself already had given his all.

"*To others it is given to believe on their words*" (5c). The bestowal of the gifts of the Spirit is determined by the wisdom of God and not by the special preparation and sanctity of those who receive the gifts. For example, some are enabled to know by the inspiration of the Holy Ghost that Jesus Christ is the Son of God and that he was crucified for the sins of the world. Others, who have not been given this knowledge by the gift of the Spirit may have the gift of faith in the words of those who do know and whose lives bear witness to the soundness of their testimony. We know of no rule by which knowledge is given to the one group and withheld from the other. What is important, however, is that those who seek earnestly the best gifts for the purpose of blessing the church through the use of those gifts receive whatever the Father sees they can use for the total good.

"*The differences of administration . . . the diversities of operations*" (6). These would seem to be gifts desirable in the presiding officers of the church. By them the elders recognize the working of the Spirit of God, the spirit of evil, and the spirits of men.

"Given unto them to discern all those gifts" (7). From the beginning there always has been a tendency among immature Saints to value the gifts of the Spirit for their own sake rather than for the contribution which can be made to the growth of the church through them. This attitude of eagerness to receive the gifts at times has opened the door to evil spirits or to a loss of self-control, whereby the authority of Divinity is attached to statements of purely human origin. Knowing this, the Lord has provided that presiding officers shall be specially endowed with the gift of discernment to enable them to safeguard the Saints from imposition. This gift is not given without preparation, however, for the rule given to Oliver Cowdery[1] applies everywhere. Those who seek the gifts of the gospel must prepare their hearts and lives so as to become fit channels for divine revelation and guidance.

"Practice virtue and holiness before me continually" (9b). At the inception of the Restoration movement few people believed that the peculiar gifts of the gospel promised in the New Testament could actually be enjoyed among men, but today many Christians recognize that these gifts are promised to all believers, no matter when they live. In earlier paragraphs the Saints were warned that these gifts should be exercised for the good of the body. Here the gifts are associated with the practice of virtue and holiness. This is a renewed emphasis on the earlier statement concerning the gifts: "always remembering for what they are given." Exercise of the gifts is not an end in itself.

---

[1]Section 9:3.

SECTION 47

From the time that he became acquainted with Joseph Smith until his departure for the mission in the West, Oliver Cowdery acted as Joseph's secretary and as unofficial historian of the Restoration movement. After Oliver left Sidney Rigdon was quite closely associated with Joseph, but it soon became apparent that if Sidney gave his time to secretarial work he could not be free for preaching. It was under these circumstances that Section 47 was given at Kirtland, Ohio, March 8, 1831.

It seems that the importance of historical records was not realized fully at this time, for although John Whitmer was sustained as Church Historian until he left the church in 1838, he wrote only eighty-five pages about eight by twelve inches in size, including many of the revelations given during that period. When he ceased to be the official historian, he refused to give up this record, and it did not become available until it was secured from the Whitmer heirs in 1903. It was then published in the *Journal of History*.[1]

There seems to have been no formal appointment of a historian to succeed John Whitmer, but Joseph wrote or dictated his history, which is now in the custody of the Mormon church. In April 1853 the Reorganized Church appointed Elder Jason W. Briggs as historian. However, like John Whitmer, he wrote very little. What he did write was passed on to Elder Heman C. Smith but was destroyed in the Herald Office fire in January 1907.

At the annual conference of 1896 the Board of Publication was authorized to select someone to serve as Church Historian and Frederick M. Smith was appointed. He occupied until the General Conference of 1897 when the body selected Elder Heman C. Smith with Frederick M. Smith as his assistant. Elder Heman C. Smith was historian until his death in 1919. Succeeding Church Historians have been Elders Walter W. Smith (1919), Samuel A. Burgess (1923), A. B. Phillips (1942), John Blackmore (1950), Evan A. Fry (1958), Charles A. Davies (1959), Richard P. Howard (Acting Historian, 1965), and Richard P. Howard (1966).

---

[1] 1:42-63, 135-150, 292-305.

SECTION 48

By the middle of March 1831 a group of Saints from the east were expected in Kirtland and preparation was being made for their reception. Many problems arose, the most pressing being those concerning location, and Section 48 was given on March 8 in reply to the inquiries of the prophet in this regard. It will be noted that this revelation is addressed primarily to the Saints in Kirtland.

"Remain, for the present time, in your places of abode" (1a, c). Kirtland was regarded as a temporary stopping place since it was anticipated that the body of the Saints would move west in the near future. Arrangements in Kirtland were "for a time."

"Purchase lands for an inheritance" (2a). These were to be in Zion. Here an unwarranted suspicion arose that the Saints intended to move into certain areas and there acquire holdings by the force of arms or by some act of divine intervention. It will be seen from reading this and other revelations that the Saints were instructed to purchase their homes.

"Every man according to his family, according to his circumstances" (2d). This is not regimentation. Every family is here recognized as distinct, having its own peculiar problems and therefore needing to be dealt with according to its distinctive wants and opportunities. In satisfying these needs equitably lies one of the major practical problems of kingdom-building. Jealousy and suspicion are fatal. The spiritual factors are therefore preeminently important in the kingdom enterprise.

"Appointed to him by the presidency and the bishop of the church" (2d). Joseph Smith III wrote: "As might be expected, the Bishopric was required to act under the counsel and advice of the Presidency in respect to locating and arranging for the Saints in the gathering . . . and church history records that this order was observed with fidelity, generally, thereafter."[1]

---

[1] *Saints' Herald* 40:146.

SECTION 49

In the early part of March 1831 Lemon Copley joined the church. He had been a member of the society of Shakers and still believed that the Shakers were right in some particulars. At his request Joseph inquired of the Lord and received the instruction contained in Section 49.

"Preach my gospel, which you have received, even as ye have received it, unto the Shakers" (1a). About a dozen persons who came to America in 1780 organized a socioreligious society at New Lebanon, New York, in 1787. While more generally known as "Shakers," they called themselves the United Society of Believers and adopted the following principles:

(1) Innocence and purity, (2) love, (3) peace, (4) justice, (5) holiness, (6) goodness, (7) truth. They taught celibacy and claimed to have divine revelation for the guidance of their society. They practiced dancing and jumping as acts of worship or religious joy. According to one of their own writers, one of their singularities "consists in the manner in which we hold our property, which, perhaps, is well-known to be in common, after the order of the primitive church in the days of the apostles." An account of the society published in 1842 showed fifty societies in the states of New Hampshire, Massachusetts, Connecticut, New York, Ohio, and Kentucky.

"Repent and be baptized in the name of Jesus Christ" (2g). The Shakers did not believe in baptism, nor in the sacrament of the Lord's Supper. It is at such points that the newly converted and ordained Elder Copley is to "reason with them [the Shakers], not according to that which he had received of them, but according to that which shall be taught him by you, my servants."

"Whoso forbiddeth to marry is not ordained of God, for marriage is ordained of God unto man" (3a). In one of his last books, G. Studdert-Kennedy wrote:

We have Christ's authority for believing that the full significance of the sex relationships can only be realized when two free, equal, consecrated personalities enter into a voluntary lifelong, indissoluble union of mutual love and service to God, to one another, and to their children. This is the divine purpose, and the appointed destiny of men and women in time.

"*Whoso forbiddeth to abstain from meats. . is not ordained of God*" (3d). This is in full harmony with the more complete statement of the Word of Wisdom.[1] Evidently a purely vegetarian diet is not contemplated in the law of the church.

"*It is not given that one man should possess that which is above another; wherefore the world lieth in sin*" (3e, f). This goes to the root of our economic difficulties. The Latter Day Saint concept of stewardship includes consecration of the surplus to social ends. The abolition of idleness and unprofitable labor and the equitable distribution of the fruits of toil are essential to the maintenance of equal opportunity for all.

"*Woe be unto man that sheddeth blood or that wasteth flesh and hath no need*" (3f). The spirit and teaching of this paragraph indicates that while killing animals for food is warranted, it should be prompted by necessity and should not be cruelly painful. It is sinful to destroy life needlessly.

Note

John Whitmer, in his Church History, says:

"The above named brethren went and proclaimed according to the revelation given to them, but the Shakers hearkened not to their words, and received not the gospel at that time: for they were bound up in tradition and priestcraft, and thus they are led away in foolish and vain imaginations."[2]

---

[1]Section 86. [2]*Journal of History* 1:55.

SECTION 50

While the prophet was still at Kirtland, in the month of May 1831, the elders began to return from their missions in preparation for the June conference. Some of them reported that they had been embarrassed and troubled by spurious spiritual manifestations, and they therefore joined the local elders in seeking light in this matter. The resultant instruction was addressed to the elders of the church.

"*Satan hath sought to deceive you, that he might over-throw you*" (1b). President Joseph Smith III wrote:

> I never was taken in a trance; but the influence of revelation upon me has always been to quicken, to make vivid and clear. And my understanding of revelation as we have it is that every man stands before God in his individual responsibility, and his individuality never will be taken from him unless he himself consents to it. And if he does, he opens the avenues of his soul for the incoming of a spirit that will ruin him.[1]

"*Woe unto them that are deceivers, and hypocrites, for...I will bring them to judgment*" (2b). There are persons who have a passionate desire for the kind of prominence which comes through exercising the gifts of the gospel. In the absence of genuine gifts, such persons sometimes yield themselves to the domination of evil powers or of their own emotions. According to this statement and according to experience, such persons are their own worst enemies. The ennobling influence of the Spirit of God lifts men to high planes of communion and power, but the presence of this Spirit cannot be artificially induced. Those who willfully or through weakness permit themselves to counterfeit the spiritual gifts soon lose their spiritual effectiveness. Judgment of their weakness or wickedness lies in the act itself, in addition to any further judgments which await them.

"*Let every man beware lest he do that which is not in truth and righteousness before me*" (3c). This statement indicates that some who claim spiritual power which they do not actually possess do this because they are not sufficiently watchful, rather than because of malicious intent. They seek to constrain the Spirit of God and in so doing leave themselves open to the influence of spirits which are not of God. The safeguard against such misrepresentation lies in steady, daily cultivation of vigilant integrity.

"Unto what were ye ordained?" (4b). An infallible test of the spirit moving a man is the work which that spirit prompts him to do. Hyrum Smith had already been instructed: "Put your trust in that spirit which leadeth to do good; yea, to do justly, to walk humbly, to judge righteously, and this is my spirit."[2] But not all the elders had taken this advice to themselves. The spirit under which some of them had labored had brought confusion and lack of understanding.

"You shall proclaim against that spirit in a loud voice, that it is not of God" (7b). The teaching of these paragraphs is that the elders are sent forth to preach the gospel in the power of the Holy Spirit and they are to be subject to this Spirit and to no other. That which is of God is light, and any power or influence which brings darkness or confusion is not of him. Discrimination between the Spirit of light—which is of God—and the spirit of darkness—which is of the devil—is only possible to those who are of God. Elders so living may receive power over the spirit of darkness through prayer, but they are to guard against lack of restraint in proclaiming against this spirit. Those who forget the dignity of their calling and rail against the spirit of darkness are likely to be overcome by the same spirit. Because of this the elders are especially warned to avoid the extremes of accusation. Men who have neglected this instruction and have gone confidently and boastfully into an atmosphere of sin have not infrequently been overtaken by that sin.

"Grow in grace and in the knowledge of the truth" (8d). This is in harmony with the earlier instruction that "he that receiveth light and continueth in God receiveth more light, and that light grows brighter and brighter,

207

until the perfect day."[3] One of the purposes of the gospel is to prepare men for the greater revelations which are to come. We are taught that even the Lord Jesus "received not of the fullness at the first, but received grace for grace; and he received not of the fullness at first, but continued from grace to grace until he received a fullness; and thus he was called the Son of God, because he received not of the fullness at the first."[4]

BIOGRAPHICAL NOTES

Joseph Wakefield made the missionary journey to which he is here appointed with Parley P. Pratt and was subsequently appointed with Solomon Humphrey on a mission to the eastern United States. Very little is known of him in addition to this.

For information on Parley P. Pratt see Section 31.

John Corrill[5] was appointed one of the seven high priests in charge of the church in Zion. On July 23, 1833, when the mob had destroyed the printing press at Independence and was about to demolish the homes and properties of the Saints, John Corrill, John Whitmer, W. W. Phelps, A. S. Gilbert, Edward Partridge, and Isaac Morley offered themselves as a ransom for the church, stating that they were willing to be scourged or to die if that would appease the anger of the mob toward the church. The courage of these men apparently had the desired effect, and violence was halted for the time being on the understanding that the Saints should leave the county by the following April. John Corrill and A. S. Gilbert were allowed to remain as general agents to wind up the business of the church as long as necessity should require. Brother Corrill was prominent also in the affairs of the Saints in the troubles of the following November and was widely regarded as a leader who could be trusted. At the Far West conference held November 7, 1837, Bishop Partridge chose Titus Billings as a counselor in place of John Corrill, but the latter was then chosen to be keeper of the storehouse. The following February Elder Corrill supported David Whitmer, John Whitmer, and W. W. Phelps when the conference in Zion refused to sustain them, and from this time he apparently lost faith in the church. On March 17, 1839, at the conference held at Quincy, Illinois, he was expelled from the church on the charge of having acted against the interests of the body. From this time forward little was known of him, but it should be stated that in those days of persecution feeling ran very high, and men who had made many sacrifices for the church were sometimes expelled for action which now would be considered insufficient to justify such drastic procedure.

---

[1]General Conference Minutes 1906:919. [2]Section 10:6. [3]Section 50:6. [4]Section 90:2. [5]Section 50:8; 52:3.

SECTION 51

By May 1831 the Saints from the East were arriving in Ohio. Church members living in Kirtland had already been instructed to receive and assist them[1] but the problem of locating the newcomers was so important that Bishop Partridge felt justified in asking for more light. The instruction which is given here is directed to him. He was the only bishop in the church at the time. This revelation did not appear in print until 1835, although it was made known to those officials whose duty it was to enforce it.

"I will speak unto my servant, Edward Partridge, and give unto him directions" (1a). The duty of locating the Saints had been laid upon the Presidency and the Bishop and his counselors, Isaac Morley and John Corrill. While many of the details of administration would have to be shared with others as the number of stewards grew, it was vitally important that basic principles be understood

now by those having primary responsibility for setting up and administering stewardships.

"Those whom he has chosen" (1b). This probably refers to Elders Morley and Corrill who had been chosen by Bishop Partridge to be his counselors, but who were not set apart until the next month.

"Let my servant Edward Partridge, when he shall appoint a man his portion, give unto him a writing that shall secure unto him his portion" (1c). It will be noted that every man who received his inheritance was to be made secure in this inheritance as required by the law of the land. This was an amendment of the earlier procedures. As before, however, the surplus consecrated by any steward above his inheritance belonged to the bishop as the representative of the church, and could not be reclaimed.

"Shall only have claim on that portion which is deeded unto him" (1e). Since the steward was to hold his inheritance "until he transgresses" (c), it appears that the steward's right in his inheritance is to be affected, in some manner, by his faithfulness. The problem is to protect every man in his fundamental right to inheritance, a right which persists even after transgression, without giving him power to frustrate group activities in case he should become opposed to the church. Solution of this problem is not easy, but it is clear that the church must be fully just, even to transgressors.

"Let that which belongs to this people be appointed unto this people" (2a). This probably has specific reference to the Saints from Colesville, New York, who were moving to Thompson, Geauga County, Ohio, and for whose special benefit these instructions were given. However, the principles here applied also may be applied to other stewardship communities.

"Let every man deal honestly, and be alike among this people, and receive alike, that ye may be one" (2b). Such an organization as is contemplated here evidently depends on the attitude of the people. No two families or persons have identical needs or circumstances, and equality therefore

210

demands differences. Dishonesty, jealousy, greed, malice, and such spiritual sins make it absolutely impossible for such a society to function.

"Let that which belongeth to this people not be taken and given unto that of another church" (3a). After the stewardship has been established there are two things in which the steward has a vital economic interest—his stewardship and the surplus. If the surplus is handled by anybody other than the stewards of the community concerned, sound economic motives are disregarded. Because of this it is evidently contemplated that each organization shall be distinct, so that the results of its activities can be readily determined, and so that no prosperous stewardship group can be burdened arbitrarily with the great weight of nonprosperous stewards and so be ruined. It is also necessary that there be no merging of surplus in the total fund, except on an agreed and businesslike basis.

"Let all things, both in money and in meat, which is more than is needful for the wants of this people, be kept in the hands of the bishop" (4a). The bishop of each area in which the people are organized according to this pattern is in charge of the storehouse and surplus of that group. For this work he is to be reimbursed from the funds of the local organization.

"I consecrate unto them this land for a little season, until I, the Lord, shall provide for them otherwise, and command them to go hence" (4c). The Colesville Saints did not work out the organization proposed. This was partly because of opposition from without and partly, no doubt, because some of them lacked the necessary spiritual strength. Those who were willing were instructed to move on to Independence, and they thus became the first organized group to settle in Zion.[2]

---

[1]Section 48:1. [2]Section 57:6.

SECTION 52

During the first week of June 1831 the elders who had been laboring in the various parts of the country convened at Kirtland according to an earlier commandment.[1] The Lord displayed his power at this conference in a manner which could not be mistaken, and the first high priests set apart in this dispensation were ordained. The record of John Whitmer indicates that Joseph Smith, Jr., first ordained Lyman Wight and then several of the other elders. Then by commandment, Lyman Wight ordained others, including Joseph Smith, Jr., and his father and Bishop Partridge. About two thousand persons were in attendance.[2] This revelation, given the day after the conference closed, is addressed to the elders of the church.

"The next Conference. . .shall be held in Missouri" (1b). This was nearly a thousand miles away. There a foothold had been established by Elders Parley P. Pratt, Oliver Cowdery, Ziba Peterson, and Peter Whitmer, Jr. Parley had recently returned to report their success. This revelation gives the most definite statement regarding the location of Zion which had been received up to this time.

"Let my servants, Joseph Smith, Jr., and Sidney Rigdon, take their journey as soon as preparations can be made to leave their homes" (2a). Note the continuing close association of Joseph Smith and Sidney Rigdon. Oliver Cowdery, the second elder of the church, was already in Missouri.

"Hyrum Smith. . .by the way of Detroit" (3a). One factor in the assignment of Hyrum to go by way of Detroit may have been that there he could make contact with the family of Stephen Mack, oldest brother of Lucy Mack Smith, and uncle of both Joseph and Hyrum.

Stephen Mack had died prior to this time without hearing the gospel, but Lucy felt that she owed it to his widow, Temperance Mack, and the rest of his family to see that the gospel was explained to them. Lucy went with the missionary team, finding Temperance in Pontiac. Such an

212

interest was raised here that Jared Carter was sent from Kirtland to follow up what had been initiated. He soon baptized seventy people in Pontiac which, says Inez Smith Davis, "may well be known as the cradle of the Latter Day Saint work in Michigan."[3]

"Preaching the word by the way" (3b). The early revelations given to the missionaries emphasize the importance of the fundamentals of the gospel. Many of the men who were sent by various routes to the land of Zion had considerable ministerial experience prior to joining the church, but had been won to the new movement by the appeal of the fundamentals and the testimony of the Holy Spirit.

"Let them go two by two" (3c). It is not now possible to ascertain on what basis the elders were associated with each other in two-by-two evangelism, but it is evident that such association was important both in terms of safety and testimony.

"Laying on of the hands by the water's side" (3c). In an earlier revelation, the church had been told: "The elders or priests are to have a sufficient time to expound all things concerning the church of Christ to their understanding, previous to their partaking of the sacrament, and being confirmed by the laying on of the hands of the elders; so that all things may be done in order."[4] This difference in the instruction given the elders indicates that the procedure may be varied according to circumstances. Under the circumstances of this time a measure of haste was imperative, for the missionaries had to be in Missouri by the end of July. The incidental mention of the Sacrament apparently indicates that it was reserved for those baptized.

"If he obey mine ordinances" (4c). In the preface to the Doctrine and Covenants the rebellious are condemned "for they have strayed from mine ordinances"[5] and the reason for this condemnation is explained in the important revelation to the priesthood. We are told that the "greater priesthood administereth the gospel and holdeth the key of the mysteries of the kingdom, even the key of the knowledge of God. Therefore, in the ordinances thereof

the power of godliness is manifest; and without the ordinances thereof, and the authority of the priesthood, the power of godliness is not manifest unto men in the flesh; for without this, no man can see the face of God, even the Father, and live."[6]

"Let my servants Edward Partridge and Martin Harris take their journey with my servants Sidney Rigdon and Joseph Smith, Jr." (6a). Note the purpose governing the appointment of these men. Bishop Partridge was recognized throughout his life as one of the leaders of the church, and undoubtedly his close association with Joseph and Sidney on this and other occasions helped prepare him for his important work. When Joseph and Sidney and others of the elders returned from Independence, Edward Partridge was left there in charge of both spiritual and temporal concerns.

"Let all these take their journey unto one place, in their several courses" (7a). All of the elders were to go to Independence by different routes. Their work was largely a work of warning and of advertising, and from this point of view it was as important to journey as it was to arrive. The Pratts seem to have sensed this keenly and did not hasten. They were late for the dedication services in Zion, but they won many on the way. Because the journey was undertaken in this spirit there was thereafter widespread interest in the work which was going forward at Independence.

"Let the residue of the elders watch over the churches, and declare the word in the regions among them" (9a). While the important mission to Zion was being carried out, the remainder of the elders were to be concerned with the oversight, strengthening, and encouragement of the local Saints. This, too, is an important missionary task.

"Let my servants Joseph Smith, Jr., and Sidney Rigdon, and Edward Partridge, take with them a recommend from the church" (9d). These three leaders of the church and Oliver Cowdery expected to teach that believers should consecrate their properties to the work of Zion. Good

214

sense required that strangers coming with such a message should be well authenticated so that their converts would know that they were not impostors.

"Which is now the land of your enemies" (9e). Apparently opposition to the Restoration movement dated from the arrival of the first elders in Missouri, for Oliver Cowdery had written to headquarters from Kaw Township, Missouri, under date of May 7, 1831, stating that almost the whole country was united in persecution of the missionaries.

BIOGRAPHICAL NOTES

Lyman Wight was the sixth son of Levi and Sarah (Corbon) Wight, and was born May 7, 1796, at Fairfield, New York. In May 1829 he was baptized by Sidney Rigdon into the Rigdonite or Campbellite faith and was associated with Isaac Morley, Titus Billings, and others in what was called the "Common Stock Family" whose members held their property jointly. On November 14, 1830, he was baptized into the Church of Jesus Christ of Latter Day Saints and ordained an elder a week later. At the June conference of 1831 he was ordained a high priest, and shortly thereafter he moved to Independence. In 1834 he and Parley P. Pratt were sent as messengers to Kirtland and, after they joined Zion's Camp at the Mississippi, on their return journey, Lyman Wight was chosen general of the camp. On July 7, 1834, Elder Wight was ordained a member of the high council of Zion and continued in that position until 1837. On April 8, 1841, he was ordained an apostle to succeed David W. Patten who had been killed. After the death of the Martyr, Elder Wight refused to recognize the usurpation of Brigham Young and in 1845 led a colony to western Texas, where he persistently maintained that the various officers of the church should have remained in the places occupied by them until the son of Joseph Smith should take his father's place. Elder Wight died March 30, 1858, near San Antonio, Texas. Many of his descendants have made distinguished contributions in the Reorganization.

John Murdock was one of the men converted at the opening of the work in Kirtland. He was ordained an elder and soon moved to Missouri where he became a member of the high council. Later he was ordained a bishop and had charge of one of the wards in Nauvoo.

Isaac Morley was born March 11, 1786, in Massachusetts. He was one of the first converts to the missionaries to the West in 1830 and was ordained a high priest June 3, 1831, and first counselor to Bishop Edward Partridge. He was one of the six who offered themselves as hostages to the mob in July 1833. Later he was ordained a bishop. He died June 24, 1865.

Ezra Booth had been a Methodist minister sometime prior to his conversion in the early part of 1831. He performed the mission appointed him in this revelation but soon after apostatized and wrote a series of letters against the church and was later prominently connected with the tarring and feathering of Joseph and Sidney at Hiram on March 25, 1832.

Levi Hancock was born April 7, 1803, at Old Springfield, Massachusetts, and was a cabinetmaker. He was baptized by Parley P. Pratt November 16, 1830, and shortly thereafter was ordained an elder. When the seventies were organized in 1835, he was one of those chosen, and the following day he was selected as a president of seventy and occupied that position at the death of Joseph Smith. He died June 10, 1882.

Zebedee Coltrin was born September 7, 1804, in Seneca County, New York. He was baptized in the early days of the church and ordained an elder sometime prior to June 1831. He was a member of Zion's Camp and was ordained a seventy February 28, 1835, and a president of seventy immediately thereafter. Having been previously ordained a high priest, he vacated his place in the seventies quorum. He died July 21, 1887.

Reynolds Cahoon was chosen counselor to Bishop Newel K. Whitney in September 1837. When the stake at

Adam-ondi-Ahman was organized June 28, 1838, he became first counselor to John Smith as president, and a year later this same presidency was placed over the Saints in Iowa. In 1840 he, with Elias Higbee and Alpheus Cutler, was appointed to the building committee of the Nauvoo Temple.

Wheeler Baldwin united with the church January 8, 1831, in Ohio. He was ordained a high priest June 4, 1831, and fulfilled his mission to Independence. He was present at the dedication of the land of Zion and at the laying of the cornerstone for the Nauvoo Temple. After joining the Reorganization in March 1863 he presided over the Fremont District and performed other effective local labor. He died near Stewartsville, Missouri, May 11, 1887, at the age of 94.

Newel K. Knight was a son of Joseph Knight, Sr., and with his family had been a member of the Universalist Church prior to his baptism in May 1830. He was a member of the Colesville group and was the leader in their journey from the settlement at Thompson, Ohio, to Missouri. He was one of the members of the first high council in Zion.

---

[1]Section 44:1. [2]See *Times and Seasons* 5:416. [3]Inez Davis, *Story of the Church*, pp. 122, 123. [4]Section 17:18. [5]Section 1:3. [6]Section 83:3; John Corrill (see Section 50); Hyrum Smith (see Section 10; Thomas B. Marsh (see Section 30); Ezra Thayre (see Section 32); Edward Partridge (see Section 35); Martin Harris (see Section 2); David Whitmer (see Section 12); Parley P. Pratt (see Section 31); Orson Pratt (see Section 33); Samuel H. Smith (see Section 21).

SECTION 53

Sidney Gilbert was a business associate of Newel K. Whitney in Painesville, Ohio, and there joined the church in the latter part of 1830. He responded to the commission given him in the revelation dated June 1831 and went to Missouri with Joseph Smith and his associates. He became one of the seven high priests in charge of the work in

Missouri, and during the persecution directed against the Saints was one of the six to offer himself as a ransom for his brethren. When the Saints were expelled from Jackson County, he was permitted to remain as their agent. The church lost a valuable minister when he died of cholera June 25, 1834.

SECTION 54

The Colesville, New York, branch of the church moved to Kirtland in a body and members were settled by Bishop Partridge at Thompson, near Kirtland, and organized as stewards under the instruction given in May 1831. Some of the brethren who were living at Thompson, among them Lemon Copley and Ezra Thayre, entered into a stewardship covenant with these Colesville Saints but shortly afterward broke their covenant and withdrew from the organization which had been effected. This endangered the stability of the group, and Newel Knight, who was president of the branch, visited Kirtland to inquire what should be done. The instruction addressed to him in June 1831 was given at this time.

In this revelation Newel Knight is continued in his office as branch president, and the faithful among the Colesville Saints are instructed to go to Missouri and establish themselves there. The Saints followed this instruction, and the company arrived in what is now Kansas City about the end of July. On the second of August, Joseph assisted them to lay the first log for a house and the foundation for Zion in Kaw Township, twelve miles west of Independence. The log was carried and placed by twelve men, in honor of the twelve tribes of Israel. At the same time the land was consecrated and dedicated for the gathering of the Saints through prayer by Sidney Rigdon.

There was sound reason for this movement of the Saints in a body toward the Center Place. They learned much of

218

the importance of mutual helpfulness on the way.

When they arrived in Missouri it was still a frontier area. They could secure land cheaply, but they must work or starve. Again, cooperation was vital as were such personal characteristics as temperance and honesty. In such a community as they began to build farming was necessarily basic, and the majority of those members were farmers.

SECTION 55

While Joseph and those who were to accompany him were preparing for their journey to Missouri, a gentleman by the name of William W. Phelps arrived in Kirtland with his family. He desired to know the will of God concerning him, and in answer to his petition received instruction that he was called to the ministry and was to assist in the literary concerns of the church.[1] This revelation was given about the middle of June 1831 in Kirtland, Ohio.

"Do the work of printing, and of selecting, and writing books for schools, in this church, that little children also may receive instruction before me as is pleasing unto me" (2a). Oliver Cowdery and W. W. Phelps seem to have been too engrossed in other work to fulfill this commandment, but although they failed, the church pioneered in education from the first. Among the earliest buildings erected in Zion was a log schoolhouse, which was the first school in the present limits of Kansas City. Here classes were conducted until the Saints were expelled from Missouri. There was also a school in Independence—a log building which stood, till 1883, at the south side of Lexington a little east of Union.

The first issue of *The Evening and the Morning Star*, June 1832, instructed the Saints:

Those appointed to select and prepare books for the use of schools, will attend to that subject, as soon as more weighty matters are finished. But the parents and guardians in the church of Christ need not wait—it is all important that children, to become good, should be taught so.

In December 1840 the church established a university and complete school system in Nauvoo. The work of education in general was energetically advanced. The children attended the regular services of the church.

BIOGRAPHICAL NOTES

William W. Phelps (see Sections 58, 61, 70) left Kirtland for Missouri on June 19, 1831, and arrived in Independence about the middle of July together with Joseph Smith, Martin Harris, Bishop Partridge, and Joseph Coe. He was present at the dedication of the Temple Lot and later returned to Kirtland with others of the elders. He was then instructed to go back to Missouri by way of Cincinnati, where he was to purchase press and type to publish a monthly newspaper at Independence, Missouri, to be called *The Evening and the Morning Star*. Oliver Cowdery followed him to Missouri with the revelations which were to be printed. The first issue of the *Star* appeared in June 1832, and W. W. Phelps continued to publish it until the press was destroyed in July 1833. After the destruction of the press, Elder Phelps offered himself as a ransom to the mob in an effort to save the other Saints.

When the High Council of Zion was organized July 3, 1834, W. W. Phelps was ordained counselor to David Whitmer in presiding over this body. In May 1835, he became editor of the *Messenger and Advocate* at Kirtland. He also assisted in the compilation of the book of Doctrine and Covenants. In the church difficulties culminating in 1838, he was expelled from the church, but on July 22, 1840, he was again received into fellowship.

Elder W. W. Phelps is probably best known because of the many excellent hymns which came from his pen and which have persisted to this day. These include, "Come All Ye Sons of Zion," "Earth with Her Ten Thousand Flowers,"

"Glorious Things Are Sung of Zion," "Let Us Pray, Gladly Pray," "Now Let Us Rejoice in the Day of Salvation," "O God, the Eternal Father," "O Jesus, the Giver of All We Enjoy," "Redeemer of Israel," and "The Spirit of God Like a Fire is Burning."[2]

---

[1]Church History 1:198. [2]*Journal of History*, Volume 18, pages 276-289.

SECTION 56

Lemon Copley, who resided at Thompson, owned a considerable tract of land which he covenanted to consecrate for locating the Saints from Colesville, New York. Ezra Thayre covenanted to do the same thing with his farm in harmony with instructions previously received.[1] Both men broke their covenants and withdrew from the organization effected by Bishop Partridge in locating the Colesville Branch. Because of their defection, it was impossible to carry through the earlier arrangement, and instruction was given that the faithful among the Colesville group should go on to Missouri.[2]

The defection of Ezra Thayre made it necessary to change the early arrangement by which it had been anticipated that he would accompany Thomas B. Marsh on one of the missionary journeys to the Missouri frontier.[3] The change was made in harmony with this revelation given at Kirtland in June 1831.

"My servant Ezra Thayre must repent" (3a). This repentance was to include completing his contract regarding his property and renewing his fellowship with the church. If he failed to repent he was to receive back certain moneys, vacate his property, and be cut off from the church. There must have been some legal arrangement by which title to the property was to have passed to the church on payment of the money mentioned. However, Ezra Thayre

repented, and it was not necessary to put these penalties into operation. Elder Thayre entered the stewardship organization at Kirtland. He later became a member of Zion's Camp, an organization formed to assist the Saints who had been driven out of Jackson County, Missouri. He was among those who were stricken with cholera on June 21, 1834.

"Your hearts are not satisfied" (4d). Here is the gist of the indictment against Copley and Thayre. They had yet to learn that stewardship is not primarily a device to bring Latter Day Saints financial prosperity or to save them from financial ruin. They were not sufficiently converted and so were constantly measuring the temporal gains or losses under the new arrangement with what they might have been under the old order. Business does not redeem Zion. Zion redeems business; it puts business on a high moral plane.

"Your riches will canker your souls" (5a). Here is the curse of riches, that wealth so frequently controls persons and that persons so infrequently control wealth. The condemnation of such men as Thayre and Copley was not that they were rich but that they loved riches more than they loved the poor. Jesus warned of the "deceitfulness of riches."[4] Paul wrote to Timothy that "the love of money [not money itself] is the root of all evil."[5]

"Woe unto you poor men" (5c). Many poor persons are no more truly converted than their rich brethren. The Lord had shown their true condition to the rich men who had been blinded by their riches. Now he seeks to reveal to themselves the greedy and unsatisfied poor "whose eyes are full of greediness" and who see the kingdom only as a place of security and ease. Note, in contrast, the blessing of the righteous poor as indicated in the next paragraph of this section.

---

[1]Sections 48:1; 51:1, etc. [2]Section 54:2. [3]Section 52:5. [4]Matthew 13:22, Mark 4:19, Luke 8:14. [5]I Timothy 6:10.

SECTION 57

The early members of the church were close students of the Book of Mormon and could not fail to note its prophecies that the New Jerusalem will be built in the New World.[1] One of the first concerns of the church as it grew in numerical strength was to know the location of this western Zion. Oliver Cowdery evidently prayed earnestly in regard to the matter, for in the revelation of September 1830 which appointed him to take a mission to the Lamanites he was told:

It is not revealed, and no man knoweth where the city shall be built, but it shall be given hereafter. Behold I say unto you that it shall be on the borders by the Lamanites.[2]

In the following February, when the great revelation on the law of the church was given, the Saints were promised:

Thou shalt ask, and it shall be revealed unto you in my own due time, where the New Jerusalem shall be built. Ye shall hereafter receive church covenants, such as shall be sufficient to establish you, both here, and in the New Jerusalem.[3]

The Saints were faithful, and on March 7 they were instructed that the preliminary gathering in Kirtland and the mission to the West were initial steps leading to the gathering which should take place in Zion; they were now to gather up their riches that they might purchase "the New Jerusalem, a land of peace, a city of refuge, a place of safety for the Saints of the Most High God . . . and it shall be called Zion."[4]

At the June conference held in Kirtland, Ohio, the elders of the church were directed to assemble in the land of Missouri, where the city of Zion should be pointed out. According to this instruction, the elders designated journeyed to Missouri and began to arrive in Jackson County the latter part of July. Here the revelations known as Sections 57, 58, 59, and 60 were received.

"This is the land of promise, and the place for the city of

Zion" (1b). Joseph Smith writes of the dedication of the land of Zion as follows:

> On the second day of August, I assisted the Colesville Branch of the church to lay the first log, for a house, as a foundation for Zion in Kaw Township, twelve miles west of Independence. The log was carried and placed by twelve men, in honor of the twelve tribes of Israel. At the same time, through prayer, the land of Zion was consecrated and dedicated for the gathering of the Saints by Elder Rigdon; and it was a season of joy to those present, and afforded a glimpse of the future, which time will yet unfold to the satisfaction of the faithful.[5]

Research by Mr. Britton of Kansas City now locates the site of the Colesville Branch near the intersection of the Santa Fe Trail and the trail north and south of the river (now the Paseo). This would place it as near 35th and Paseo, Kansas City, Missouri. The evidence available is not conclusive.

"Independence is the Center Place" (1d). In this connection please note the following:

> Jackson County, in which Independence is situated, lies thirty-four degrees north latitude, and ninety-four degrees west longitude. It is, roughly speaking, almost equally distant from the eastern and western, the northern and southern boundaries of the United States. With Canada on the north, and Mexico on the south, it is centrally located for the whole North American continent. Further, taking into account the direction of flow of the Missouri and Mississippi Rivers, it becomes evident that it would be difficult to find a location of greater centrality or of easier accessibility for the whole western world, including North and South America, than is Independence, Missouri.[6]

"The spot for the temple" (1d). On August 3, 1831, Joseph Smith, in the presence of Sidney Rigdon, Edward Partridge, Oliver Cowdery, Martin Harris, Peter Whitmer, Jr., Frederick G. Williams, W. W. Phelps, and Joseph Coe, dedicated the ground for the building of the temple a little west of the city of Independence. The Eighty-seventh Psalm was read, and the scene was solemn and impressive. The land dedicated did not at that time belong to the church; but on December 19, 1831, Bishop Partridge purchased from J. H. Flournoy and his wife Clara, 63 43/160 acres of land, upon which the lot dedicated for the building

of the temple was located. The purchase price was $130.00. This tract is bounded at present by West Lexington Street on the north and west, Pacific Street on the south, and Union Street on the east. Title was taken by Bishop Partridge in his own name, but the land was purchased with means obtained from members of the church for that purpose and was held in trust for the church. This was done because the Missouri constitution of 1821 prohibited the taking of title in the name of a church.

On March 25, 1839, at which time the church was about to be banished from Missouri by the order of Governor Boggs, Bishop Partridge executed a deed in favor of John Cowdery, Jane Cowdery, and Joseph Smith Cowdery, and this deed included the land purchased in Independence. As a matter of fact, Oliver Cowdery had no son John although his brother Warren did. And apparently Bishop Partridge became confused and included "Joseph Smith Cowdery" when he meant "Josephine." But this is quite readily understandable. The Saints were fleeing for their lives at the time, and the Bishop could not recall the exact names of the Cowdery children. The important thing is that the deed was in reality a declaration of trust entered into to protect the rights of the church. Subsequently all the parties named in this deed died without having made any conveyance of this real estate or of any part thereof. Oliver Cowdery, the father of the grantees, also died in 1850 without making any disposition of the property. On May 25, 1886, Elizabeth Cowdery, mother of the parties named in the deed, executed a deed of conveyance of that part of the original purchase known as the Temple Lot to her daughter, Maria Louise Johnson, the only living child of Oliver Cowdery. In June 1887 Maria Louise Johnson, with her husband, Dr. Charles Johnson, executed and delivered a deed of conveyance to George A. Blakeslee as trustee for the Reorganized Church of Latter Day Saints.

Another chain of title back to Bishop Partridge was found as follows:

May 5, 1848, the heirs of Edward Partridge, consisting of his widow,

Lydia Partridge, and three of his children, viz.; Emily M., Emily D., and Caroline E., made a quitclaim deed to this Temple Lot, to one James Poole. This title was transmitted from one party to another until finally it was transferred to Granville Hedrick for use, in trust, of the Church of Jesus Christ of Latter Day Saints. Granville Hedrick dying, without making any transfer, in an *ex parte* proceeding in the Circuit Court of Jackson County, Missouri, the property was transferred to Richard Hill, as trustee.... Richard Hill, being a member of the organization known as the Church of Christ, claimed the right to execute his trust in the interest of such organization. Bishop George A. Blakeslee, being the trustee in trust for the Reorganized Church of Jesus Christ of Latter Day Saints, claimed that the property should be used or held for the Reorganized Church. The Church of Christ had taken possession of the lots in 1882.... In 1887, the Reorganized Church through its bishop, George A. Blakeslee, took steps to get possession of this property.... The Church of Christ, represented by Elder Hill, failed to give possession according to notice.... The Reorganized Church through Bishop Edwin L. Kelley, filed complaint in equity, setting out its claims as the only true and legal successor to the Church of Latter Day Saints and its right to the Temple Lot property. The case came up for trial in 1892 and 1893.... It was tried upon the validity of the two titles,... and the question of which of the two organizations was the church in succession from the church which originally purchased the land through its bishop.... After an extensive examination (the church in Utah taking an active part in assisting the defendants), a decision was made in favor of the Reorganization.[7]

The defendants appealed from this decision to the U. S. Court of Appeals and... the decision of Judge Phillips was reversed so far as possession is concerned, the decision being undisturbed as far as the principal points were involved but being determined against the Reorganized Church on the ground of laches. This leaves the decision of Judge Phillips unreversed so far as it pertains to the church in legal succession and to the validity of the deed by which the Reorganized Church claims the property, but leaves the Church of Christ in possession on the grounds that the Reorganized Church did not commence suit in time to oust the defendant. Further efforts to open the case have been unavailing.[8]

It should be noted that the decision of Judge Phillips upheld the Reorganized Church as being in legal succession to the church organized April 6, 1830, and exonerated Joseph Smith of any responsibility for polygamy. These important declarations were in no way altered or modified by the appellate decision.[9]

"To be an agent unto the church" (2). This instruction was
226

in fulfillment of the revelation given to Sidney Gilbert, June 1831, in harmony with which he had journeyed to Independence with Joseph Smith and Sidney Rigdon.[10]

"*Let my servant Edward Partridge, stand in the office which I have appointed him*" (3). At this time Edward Partridge was the only bishop in the church, having been appointed in accordance with the revelation received the preceding February.[11] It had been indicated that his work would center for a time in the New Jerusalem[12] and also that he and his counselors should "appoint unto this people their portion, every man equal according to their families, according to their circumstances and their wants and needs."[13] He had been instructed also to "appoint a storehouse unto this church" and that "this shall be an example unto my servant Edward Partridge, in other places, in all churches."[14]

The work of gathering and establishing the Saints progressed under the direction of Bishop Edward Partridge, who, in the absence of President Joseph Smith, Jr., acted as both spiritual and temporal head of the church in Zion. In the year and a half ending July 1833, Bishop Partridge took title to nearly two thousand acres in Independence and west of Independence.

Associated with Edward Partridge in the bishopric of Zion were Isaac Morley and John Corrill. In many respects all three of these men possessed qualifications which fitted them for public responsibility. They were conscientious and honest. Isaac Morley had been formerly connected with Sidney Rigdon's communists at Kirtland, and both of the others had been strongly influenced by him. The conception of sharing alike was therefore not new to them. Such a selection of men appeared from every standpoint to be a wise one.[15]

"*That he may sell goods without fraud*" (4a). In this initial movement to establish Zion the Lord points out that the wealth of the Saints must be made in righteousness before it is dedicated to the purposes of God. The purpose of the store is to "provide for my saints, that my gospel may be preached."

"*Let my servant William W. Phelps be planted in this place, and be established as a printer unto the church*" (5a).

227

This instruction was complied with, and Phelps became the publisher of *The Evening and the Morning Star*, the first periodical in the church.

"Let him obtain whatsoever he can in righteousness, for the good of the Saints" (5a). Evidently Phelps was to make a reasonable profit on his publications and was to secure his livelihood therefrom,[16] but the residue was to be made available "for the good of the Saints" in the same way as that obtained from the store was to be used.

"Let the bishop and the agent make preparations for those families which have been commanded to come to this land" (6a). This refers particularly to the brethren from Colesville who had recently left Thompson, Ohio, under the leadership of Newel Knight.[17] Further directions were promised regarding the residue of both elders and members.

Prior revelation had prepared Cowdery, Partridge, Gilbert, and Phelps for the work which they now were appointed to do in connection with the building up of Independence. Comparison of the preceding revelations with this one shows an interesting and inspiring sequence of preparation.

NOTE

In his excellent study of *Restoration Scriptures*, Church Historian Richard P. Howard comments concerning the situation at Kirtland, as follows:

For reasons not clearly understood many of the key leaders of the church, including Joseph Smith and Sidney Rigdon, chose not to live in Independence but returned to Kirtland in August 1831 and remained there for nearly seven years until the church moved from Kirtland and from Clay County, Missouri, to Far West in 1837 and 1838. In the absence of these key leaders Bishop Partridge, W. W. Phelps, Oliver Cowdery, the Whitmers, and other capable men proceeded to spearhead the gathering to Jackson County in the fall of 1831 until the tragic exodus of the Saints in the winter of 1833-34.[18]

---

[1]Ether 6:4-10; III Nephi 9:57-59. [2]Section 27:3. [3]Section 42:17, 18. [4]Section 45:12. [5]*Times and Seasons* 5:450. [6]Geddes, *The United Order Among the*

Mormons. [7]*Journal of History* 3:55-57. [8]See *Journal* 3:57. [9]Probably the best adverse opinion concerning the foregoing was published by the Church of Christ (Temple Lot) in 1954 under the title "Historical Facts Concerning the Temple Lot." [10]Section 53:2, 3. [11]Section 41:3. [12]Section 42:3. [13]Section 51:1. [14]Section 51:4, 5. [15]Geddes, *The United Order Among the Mormons.* [16]Section 42:19. [17]*Journal of History* 16:264. [18]Pages 250-251.

SECTION 58

Joseph and twenty-one other elders left Kirtland, Ohio, about June 19, 1831, and made their way by different routes to Independence, Missouri. The prophet and his party arrived in Kaw Township, Missouri, about the middle of July, and Section 57, which definitely designated the center place, was received at this time. A week later the branch from Thompson (the Colesville Branch), led by Newel Knight, completed its journey. The dedication of the land of Zion was now uppermost in the minds of the company of Saints, and the revelation dated August 1, 1831, bears directly upon this event and upon the subsequent organization of the work. This revelation is addressed to the elders of the church in Missouri.

"He that is faithful in tribulation" (1b). The Saints had great expectations of prosperity under the divine direction, but they were reminded frequently that the redemption of Zion would come only after great tribulation. In spite of these warnings, however, the early Saints did not think it possible that they could be cast out of the land which was now pointed out by the finger of God.

"For this cause I have sent you" (3b):

That you might be obedient.

That your hearts might be prepared to bear testimony of the things which are to come.

That you might be honored in laying the foundation of Zion.

That you might bear record of the land upon which
Zion shall stand.

That a feast of fat things might be prepared for the
poor.

That the earth may know that the mouths of the
prophets shall not fail.

That a supper in the house of the Lord might be well
prepared and all nations invited unto it.

*"Firstly, the rich and the learned, the wise and the
noble; after that cometh the day of my power; then shall
the poor, the lame, and the blind, and the deaf, come in"*
(3e). The order of the gathering explained here makes no
discrimination between the spiritual standing of the rich and
of the poor. It is concerned with the procedure necessary
to ensure success in the Zionic enterprise. Money was needed
to buy large tracts of land. But these rich pioneers also
must know how to establish and manage large affairs, and,
above all, they must be filled with wisdom and with love
for their fellowmen. If the "rich and the learned, the wise
and the noble" had gathered as they were instructed
to do, there would have been place for their less able brethren
to gather and employment when they arrived. Later Joseph
Smith gave similar instruction for those gathering to Nauvoo,
urging that men of means should establish factories before
the working men of the East came in.

"That the testimony might go forth from Zion" (4a).
Zion has major missionary significances. Stewards do not
live and work for themselves but for the common good
and in the fear of God. And although Zion is to be a place
of safety, yet from it ministers of the church will go out
to the farthermost parts of the earth as long as there
is hope of saving anyone who has not yet responded
to the call of the gospel.

"His mission is given unto him" (4c). The function of
Presiding Bishop Edward Partridge as here indicated is
essentially that of an executive judge in Israel. As such he or
his counselors divide their inheritances equitably among

the Saints and sit in judgment in cases of difficulty between members of the church.

"He that keepeth the laws of God hath no need to break the laws of the land; wherefore be subject to the powers that be" (5b). This instruction was directed to those who were concerned with building the kingdom of God. It would not be supposed that they would enact or utilize laws enabling them to deal unjustly with their brethren. This was illustrated when they revised their earlier stewardship procedures after the courts held that the rights of disaffected members were not sufficiently protected thereby. But beyond the areas of Zionic endeavor there was much legalized injustice, even as there is today. The general import of this instruction would therefore seem to be that the redress of wrongs should be sought within the law rather than by revolt. The Saints followed this procedure when they were the victims of mob violence in Missouri.

"The laws which ye have received from my hands are the laws of the church, and in this light ye shall hold them forth" (5c). This refers specifically to the laws relating to stewardship, including the laws of spiritual preparation which we sometimes know as the fundamental principles of the gospel.

"This land is the land of his residence" (6a). In accordance with this instruction Bishop Partridge, Isaac Morley, John Corrill, and A. G. Gilbert moved their families to Independence and lived there until the expulsion of the Saints.

"It is not meet that I should command in all things" (6c). There had been a tendency among the Saints to inquire of God regarding trivial things. This wore out Joseph, cheapened the idea of revelation, and tended to vitiate the self-reliance of the Saints. The instruction contained in this paragraph was therefore extremely timely. The Saints need to remember that no man is justified in asking for divine guidance until he has made full use of the intelligence which God already has given him.

"He that doeth not anything until he is commanded, and

231

receiveth a commandment with doubtful heart, and keepeth it with slothfulness, the same is damned" (6b). The function of the Spirit of Truth is to *lead* men into all truth, not to carry them. There is no place for the idler in Zion, no matter whether his laziness is physical or mental or spiritual. Failure to meet one's responsibilities with faith and courage brings its own condemnation.

"This is a law unto every man that cometh unto this land, to receive an inheritance, and he shall do with his moneys according as the law directs" (7c). Failure to abide by this instruction was one of the basic causes for the defeat of this first attempt at Zion-building. Martin Harris paid Bishop Partridge the sum of $1,200—a large sum in those days—as his consecration. Others did likewise. But when those who had consecrated their properties saw that others were coming to Independence and there waiting to watch developments before risking anything, they were irritated. In such an enterprise as this, it was essential that every man participating should do so on a similar basis of sacrifice.

"The place of the storehouse" (7d). Bishop Koehler wrote:

The hub of our economic structure is the storehouse.... Through the instrumentality of the storehouse labor becomes its own capitalist. Through it the group controls the flow of capital goods for its own ends. Through it men insure themselves against times of need. The storehouse is both a governmental device and an economic institution which frees both the individual and the community from commercial imperialism. Through the storehouse the functions of finance, insurance, and commerce are socialized. Through the storehouse communities are brought into mutually helpful relations by equitable exchanges of commodities and by reciprocal loans of money and capital goods in times of need. It is an instrument of good will toward men.[1]

A. S. Gilbert managed the storehouse. Serious difficulty arose from giving too much credit to the poor. The Saints learned, and we shall do well to remember, that goodwill is not enough. Goodwill must be reinforced by resources and business judgment. This is no argument against the storehouse principle but for it. It must be a *store*house before it can be a *credit*-house.

232

"*Concerning the residue of the elders of my church, The time has not yet come, for many years, for them to receive their inheritance in this land*" (9e). There could be no effective gathering except as the way was prepared by pioneers who were deeply and courageously committed to the Zionic enterprise. Such pioneers were now in the land of promise. What remained to be done was to implement a permanent program of evangelization in Missouri, pointed toward winning local support and reducing antagonisms, and also more widespread evangelism to proclaim the Restoration message and provide kingdom resources of men and money.

"*A description of the land of Zion*" (11a). See Church History, Volume 1, pages 207-209.

"*Let the work of the gathering be not in haste, nor by flight, but let it be done as shall be counseled by the elders of the church at the conferences*" (12b). The presiding officers of the church sought to carry out this instruction and published such information as the following:

Notwithstanding, the work of the gathering will be accomplished, we believe, in a speedy manner; yet the Lord has commanded that it shall not be done in haste, nor by flight, but that all things shall be prepared before you; and for this purpose he has made it the duty of the bishop or agent in the land of Zion to make known, from time to time, the privileges of the land, to the conferences, which may determine and make known how many can be accommodated.

And the Saints will remember that the bishop in the land of Zion will not receive any, as wise stewards, without they bring a recommend from the bishop in Ohio, or from three elders. The elders, therefore, will be careful not to recommend and send up churches to this place of Zion without first receiving information from the bishop in Ohio, or in the land of Zion, that they can be accommodated when they arrive so as to be settled without confusion, which would produce pestilence. Therefore if a church is desirous to come to the land of Zion, we would recommend that first, by letter or otherwise, they make known their desires and their situation to the bishop in Ohio, or in the land of Zion, and receive information from them before they start. Brethren will perceive as well as we, that where churches of fifty or one hundred souls each are coming to the land of Zion from different parts of the nation and, as may well be the case, from different nations, without a knowledge of each other, they would, when they arrive, be in a state of confusion and labor under many disadvantages, which might be avoided by strictly observing the rules and regulations of the church. Moreover, by being in haste, and forcing the sale of property, unreasonable sacrifices have been made, and although this is a day of sacrifices and tithing, yet to make lavish and unreasonable sacrifices is not well pleasing in the sight of the Lord.[2]

Similar instruction has been issued repeatedly down the years, and it has been ignored again and again by Saints who were quite devoted in other matters. In such situations the emotional factors are overemphasized. Those gathering to Zion without proper consultation feel deeply but do not think clearly. They have every legal right to move to Independence and to regions round about without consultation with the spiritual and temporal authorities involved, but as members of the church they have little moral right to so gather. Their coming rarely betters their situation, and it invariably imposes burdens on the officers of the central stakes. These burdens in turn tend to retard the orderly process of gathering.

"*Let my servant Sidney Rigdon consecrate and dedicate this land*" (13a). The day following the reception of this instruction, the Colesville branch began laying the foundation of Zion, with the elders of the church assisting. The first log was laid for a house in Kaw Township about twelve miles west of Independence, and at the same time the land of Zion was consecrated and dedicated by Elder Sidney Rigdon for the gathering of the Saints.[3] This deference to Sidney, an older and more eloquent fellow minister, was an inspired and heartwarming gesture on the part of Joseph.

"*Let that which has been bestowed on Ziba Peterson be taken from him, and let him stand as a member of the church*" (14b). Ziba Peterson was one of the original missionaries who made the journey from New York to Missouri. This is the first example on record of a minister being silenced.

The procedure recommended for the immediate future was as follows:

234

The land of Zion and the spot for the temple were to be dedicated (13b).

Sidney Rigdon was to write a description of Zion which would be sent to the churches to stimulate contributions for the purchase of the entire region (11a).

An agent was to be appointed especially to receive contributions in Ohio, where the Saints were most numerous. These contributions were for the purchase of lands in Missouri (10).

As land was obtained workmen of all kinds were to be brought in in an orderly way as arranged by Bishop Partridge and his agents (12d).

Those going up to Zion were to consecrate their properties as provided in the law, Martin Harris being a specific example (7).

In this way the rich and the learned, the wise and the noble were to gather first and prepare for the coming of others less able to make a contribution (3e).

Meanwhile, the elders not needed especially in this work of preparation were to be active in missionary testimony both in the regions round about and in more distant fields, building local congregations against the day of greater preparation and opportunity. This was likely to take many years (9e).

The seat of the Presidency was to remain in Kirtland, which was more readily accessible, and to this place Joseph, Sidney, and Oliver were to return (13b).

Bishop Partridge was the ranking officer remaining in Independence. He was to greet elders who were still on the way when they arrived in Independence, and to acquaint them with what had been done so that they could bear effective testimony on their return journey to Ohio.

---

[1]*Problems of Industrial Zion.* [2]*Evening and Morning Star* 1:24. [3]*Journal of History* 16:276.

SECTION 59

On August 4, 1831, the first conference in the land of
Zion, and the fifth of the church, was held at the house
of Brother Joshua Lewis in Kaw Township in the presence
of the Colesville branch of the church. The next day
Sister Polly Knight died. She was the mother of Newel
Knight, the president of the Colesville Saints. This was the
first death in the church in Independence. On Sunday,
August 7, the day of her burial, Joseph received the
revelation bearing that date.

*"Blessed, saith the Lord, are they who have come up unto
this land with an eye single to my glory"* (1a). Note the
beauty of this promise. Picture the reading of the first
passage of this revelation to men who had come up to
Zion at such tremendous cost and had found such a land
as is described by Sidney Rigdon and the prophet Joseph.
Note the triumphant assurances given to the faithful:

> They shall receive for their reward the good things of
> the earth.
> It shall bring forth in its strength.
> They shall also be crowned with blessings from above
> and with commandments not a few, and with revela-
> tions in their time.

"I give unto them a commandment" (2). Here the two
major commandments of the gospel are repeated, and the
basic commandments of the Mosaic Law also are restated.
In addition the Saints are commanded, "Thou shalt thank
the Lord thy God in all things," and this note of gratitude
is reemphasized in paragraph 5. "In nothing doth man
offend God, or against none is his wrath kindled, save
those who confess not his hand in all things, and obey
not his commandments."

*"Verily this is a day appointed unto thee to rest from
thy labors, and to pay thy devotions unto the Most High"*
(2b). The Lord's day is not set apart for idleness, nor is

236

it primarily a day for physical recuperation, although it serves this great purpose. The purpose of the Sabbath among the children of Israel, and of the Lord's day among Christians, is to guarantee that a definite and recurring period of time shall be dedicated to worship and spiritual meditation. Christians should offer their vows of righteousness on all days and at all times, but particularly on the Lord's day. The command to observe the Sabbath was repeated a few months later[1] and renewed in the revelation of 1887.[2]

"Confessing thy sins unto thy brethren, and before the Lord" (2h). James admonishes us, "Confess your faults one to another, and pray one for another, that ye may be healed," and John says that, "If we confess our sins, he is faithful and just to forgive us our sins, and to cleanse us from all unrighteousness."[3]

There are also times in the life of every Saint when he needs to go to the officers of the church and there make a frank statement of his difficulties and seek spiritual counsel. This is not a suggestion that the ministers of the church should profess to forgive sins except through administering the ordinances of the church, but they should be available to help those whose hearts will be relieved of their burdens by confession.

"Let thy food be prepared with singleness of heart, that thy fasting may be perfect" (3a). Fasting is evidently compatible with partaking of food. It is not an emptiness but an attitude. Fasting in the religious sense involves serious purpose, meditation, and prayer. All other things, even eating, should be made secondary to the spiritual purpose of the time.

"Not with much laughter, for this is sin" (4a). This injunction against excessive laughter is not an injunction against quiet happiness but is in its favor, for boisterous merrymaking usually degenerates to a lower level.

"To this end were they made, to be used with judgment, not to excess, neither by extortion" (5a). The Saints are warned here that food and other gifts of God are to be

used with judgment and not to excess. On the other hand, no one is to "corner" the necessities of life to the detriment of his brethren. This is important as a matter of economics, and it is also important as a principle of spiritual life. A man who is prodigal of the gifts of God, or who uses these gifts to the detriment of his fellows, thereby does much to kill the Spirit of God within him.

---

[1]Section 68:4d. [2]*Ibid.* 119:7b. [3]James 5:16; I John 1:9.

SECTION 60

After the land of Zion and the place for the temple had been dedicated and the conference at Independence had been held, the leading elders of the church prepared to return to Kirtland where important matters awaited their attention. The day before they left, Monday, August 8, 1831, a revelation was given instructing them regarding their homeward journey. The revelation is addressed specifically to the elders returning to Kirtland.

"With some I am not well pleased" (1b). The immediate and pressing necessity of the time was for new converts of fundamental spiritual quality, men of integrity who could make a contribution to the building of Zion. A number of the elders, however, were reluctant to preach, and they are chided here for their failure in this regard. Among the ministry were some orators, like Sidney Rigdon, but the times did not demand oratory as much as simple testimony of the things which the Saints most assuredly believed.[1] A tremendous amount of potential missionary power is dissipated today by members of the ministry who are unwilling to testify because they are not able preachers.

"If they are not more faithful unto me, it shall be taken away, even that which they have" (2a). If these elders would enter into the spirit of the new movement, they would

238

become men of power; but if they failed to manifest the characteristic boldness of the Zionic enterprise, this lack of aggressiveness would vitiate their other activities.

"Let there be a craft made, or bought" (2d). Joseph Smith and ten of the elders started for Kirtland on Tuesday, August 9, leaving the Independence landing in canoes. They went as far as Fort Osage (Sibley) the first day.

"Take their journey for Cincinnati" (2e). Joseph and Oliver were the first and second elders of the church, and Sidney Rigdon had acted as the close associate of Joseph while Oliver was in Missouri. Therefore these three may be fairly regarded as the three outstanding leaders of the church. It is highly probable that when in Cincinnati they made the inquiries which resulted in the appointment of W. W. Phelps to go there and purchase the press for *The Evening and the Morning Star.*

"Preach the word, not in haste, among the congregations of the wicked" (3a). On the way to Independence, the elders had to keep up to schedule in order to arrive there about the same time. On the return journey there was no such haste, and all the companies were instructed to take reasonable time to stabilize their missionary gains. The procedure was probably akin to that followed by Oliver Cowdery and his associates on the first missionary journey, and converts were instructed regarding the fundamental doctrines of the church, the building of Zion, and the nature of church administration. Branches raised up were left in the care of local elders, many of whom had previously been ministers of the various denominations.

"Let my servant Edward Partridge impart of the money which I have given him" (3c). The elders were authorized here to call upon the Presiding Bishop for traveling expenses in this emergency, but such as could do so were expected to return this money to the bishop by way of his agent in Kirtland.

"I speak of the residue who are to come unto this land" (3d). This refers to Lyman Wight and others who had not yet arrived. According to this instruction, they were to

239

become acquainted with the situation in Independence and then were to return like those now leaving.

¹Section 58:14.

SECTION 61

Joseph Smith and ten of the elders started for Kirtland, traveling in canoes. On the evening of the third day they camped at McIlwain's Bend on the banks of the Mississippi. Their trip proved hazardous and during the night, W. W. Phelps saw a vision depicting the danger of travel by water. The next morning, Friday, August 12, after prayer, Joseph received the revelation bearing that date. It is addressed to the members of the company.

"Ye elders of my church, who are assembled upon this spot, whose sins are now forgiven you" (1b). A study of this history seems to indicate that the brethren were eager to get back to Kirtland and so had been rather insistent upon traveling to St. Louis by water. Now, after experiencing some of the dangers of river travel, the brethren were in a more chastened frame of mind and were ready to listen to the counsel of God. They then were instructed that six of the eleven were to proceed by land and bear their personal testimony by the way.

"It is expedient that my servant Sidney Gilbert, and my servant William W. Phelps, be in haste upon their errand and mission" (2a). These two brethren were returning to Kirtland to bring their families to Independence. Elder Gilbert was to be keeper of the storehouse, and Elder Phelps was to be printer to the church.

"Let the residue take that which is needful for clothing" (2d). The brethren drew on the common treasury according to their needs, and Sidney Gilbert, the keeper of the Lord's storehouse, retained the remainder.

"The days will come that no flesh shall be safe upon the waters" (3b). This prophecy was made before the days of submarine warfare, but received specific fulfillment through

240

that and similar inventions. Consider the enormous increase in loss of life on the seas and navigable rivers in the past century and a half.

"Whether they go by water or by land; let this be as it is made known unto them according to their judgments hereafter" (3f). Having been warned of the dangers of river travel, the Saints were not to be unduly fearful. They were to give these facts consideration when determining which way to travel and then were to live righteously so that they would merit the special protection of Divinity.

"Let them come not again upon the waters, save it be upon the canal" (4a). There were a number of canals in the East, and especially in Ohio, which served as substitutes for dangerous river courses and as connections between various bodies of water. These could be used with comparative safety, even by inexperienced navigators. Only the more experienced rivermen, however, were to use the river route.

"My servants. . .shall not open their mouths in the congregations of the wicked, until they arrive at Cincinnati" (5c). Joseph, Sidney, and Oliver were to make only one major stop on their journey from Independence to Kirtland. Evidently the missionary task of the church was important, but not sufficiently important to demand the attention of the presiding elders of the church to the exclusion of affairs at headquarters.

Concerning Cincinnati Elder Ralph W. Farrell wrote several years ago:

They must hasten to Cincinnati, one of the modern Babylons, and there lift up a warning voice. The people in this city were well-nigh ripened for destruction. In the "Gazetteer of Ohio" for the early thirties, Cincinnati boasts of her "luxuries of life; the moral and religious character of her population." She styles herself the "Queen City of the West," and boasts of receiving into her borders, "55,000 barrels of whiskey." She laments, however, the fact "that there is no city hall, or other building belonging to the city which can answer the purpose of one." The Lord was right, a place of this kind needed the cry of a prophet.[1]

"Inasmuch as they do this they shall rid their garments, and they shall be spotless before me" (6a). The ministry

241

are responsible for their failure to warn wicked men. This responsibility was reemphasized to the ministry of the Reorganization in the revelation of May 4, 1865, which says, "Many elders have been ordained unto me, and are come under my condemnation, by reason of neglecting to lift up their voices in my cause."

"*Inasmuch as you have humbled yourselves before me, the blessings of the kingdom are yours*" (6c). After their experience of three days on the river and the vision of Elder Phelps, the brethren had been considerably subdued, and the morning prayers had been marked by earnestness and sincerity.

BIOGRAPHICAL NOTES

Reynolds Cahoon had been the companion of Samuel H. Smith on the journey to Independence. While on this journey, they had converted William E. McLellin, who later became one of the first members of the Quorum of Twelve. In 1833 he and Hyrum Smith and Jared Carter were members of the committee which was appointed to raise the money for the school in Kirtland. He held the high priesthood and served in various stake presidencies and also on the Nauvoo Temple committee.

Samuel H. Smith: See notes on Section 21.

---

[1]Senior Religio Quarterly, Vol. 12, p. 13.

SECTION 62

On Saturday, August 13, 1831, Joseph's party met several of the elders on their way to the land of Zion. It was on this occasion that the revelation bearing this date was received. It is addressed to the group of elders bound for Independence.

"Mine eyes are upon those who have not as yet gone up unto the land of Zion" (1a). This probably has dual reference: first, to the missionary party who were on their way, and second, to the unconverted who were yet to be reached by these missionaries. The phrase has a still wider significance today, especially in the distant missions of the church. Zion is the center place for the gathering of the people of God, but our heavenly Father is also mindful of the needs of his people in distant lands.

The six revelations given during the first journey of the prophet to Missouri[1] are of outstanding importance in the development of the stewardship movement. Dr. Geddes has summarized them in his book, *The United Order Among the Mormons*, as follows:

1. The city of Zion is definitely located at Independence, Missouri.
2. The whole of the surrounding country, especially that "to the westward," is to be purchased.
3. Sidney Gilbert is to fill the office of agent, earlier assigned to him, and receive "monies" and "purchase land for the Saints." He is also "to establish a store" and with the profits arising is to assist in "purchasing lands."
4. Edward Partridge is to "stand in his office" and "divide the inheritances."
5. W. W. Phelps and Oliver Cowdery are to be "printers to the church."
6. The bishop and the agent are to make preparation for those who have been "commanded to come to Zion" and for their families. The "residue" of elders and members are to await further instructions.
7. No one is to break the laws of the land.
8. The law of consecration is to apply to all who receive an inheritance in Zion. Martin Harris, a man of some wealth, is asked to set the example.
9. The elders of the church are not, in the main, to receive inheritances for some time to come; but are to

"push the people together from the ends of the earth."
10. An agent also is to be appointed in Ohio "to receive monies to purchase land in Zion."
11. The manner of life the people of Zion are expected to live is enumerated by way of commandment.
12. The route for the "Saints" to take in "journeying to Zion" is to be by land rather than by water.

In connection with the second paragraph of this analysis, it is interesting to note that in 1830 this land sold at $1.00 to $2.50 an acre.

_____
[1]Sections 57-62.

SECTION 63

Joseph Smith, Sidney Rigdon, and Oliver Cowdery reached Kirtland, August 27, 1831, having traveled by stage from St. Louis, Mo. Naturally, great interest was manifest in the story of the land of Zion, and this interest was augmented by the arrival of the other elders. Inquiry was made as to what should be done in relation to the gathering and the purchase of land, and a revelation was received August 30, 1831, in which instruction was given on this important subject. The revelation is addressed to the people of the church.

"There are those among you who seek signs" (3a). Some of the Kirtland Saints were reluctant to practice stewardship without some supernatural assurance that this was the will of God and that they would be safeguarded from loss.

"Faith cometh not by signs, but signs follow those that believe" (3a). One of the earliest and most persistent challenges hurled at our missionaries has been the challenge to work miracles as an evidence of their authority. Such sign-seeking was repeatedly condemned by Jesus.[1] Paul's

244

condemnation of sign-seeking is also clear and definite.[2]

"I gave commandments and many have turned away from my commandments and have not kept them" (4a). This refers specifically to commandments regarding property rights under stewardship which had been violated by Ezra Thayre and Lemon Copley. The faithful from among the Colesville Saints had gone with Newel Knight to Missouri, but the remainder were still nominal members of the church and were in close touch with the Kirtland group.

"They shall not have the Spirit" (5a). (See notes on Section 42:7.)

"Confusion, which bringeth pestilence" (8a). This was a real menace a hundred years ago. Some of the members of Zion's Camp were attacked with cholera and died in June 1834.[3]

"You should purchase the land" (8c). Note the constantly renewed emphasis on purchasing the land in and around Independence and the warning against the dire results of war. The Saints put money into the hands of Bishop Partridge and so enabled him to purchase slightly more than 1,958 acres in Jackson County. More than half of this land lay within the present confines of Kansas City, as follows:

Two tracts on either side of the Paseo, between 27th and 33rd streets and containing Troost Lake.

One tract east of the Paseo between 35th and 39th Streets. The Martha Slavens Memorial Church now is located on this tract.

Sixty acres which now include the Country Club Plaza, Elmsdale, and Bismark Place.

A southwest quarter section, which now includes Westwood Park, Vogel Park, and Waverly Place.

A quarter section located where Ward Parkway now winds through beautiful Sunset Hill.

One half and one quarter section which is now part of the Country Club Golf Links.

The east half of the northwest quarter section which has

become Rockhill and Rockhill Place. Brookside Boulevard winds through this tract and Brookside Hotel is situated thereon.

The west half of the northeast quarter section, including the present Crestwood and Southwood Park.

"The wicked shall slay the wicked, and fear shall come upon every man" (9b). This is not a mere guess at the probability of future wars. Since the times of this prophecy, wars have become more and more menacing to civil populations, and it has been increasingly true that fear has come upon *every* man. The fear of war is one of the most constant and hazardous fears of the present time, and it is admitted on every side that this fear is justifiable because of the greed and hatred among men.

"Declare both by word and by flight, that desolation shall come upon the wicked" (9e). Baptism, confirmation, and the laying on of hands are great dramatic epitomes of spiritual events. The Saints are now called on to make their belief in Zion similarly vivid and appealing in their testimony and their actions.

"Which dwell upon this farm" (9f). This was probably the farm of Isaac Morley, counselor to Bishop Partridge.

"It mattereth not unto me whether it be little or much" (10b). The major necessity was not money but willing compliance with the commands of God. The basic reason for the failure of the efforts of the early church was the lack of sufficient men of spiritual quality. The same lack will be fatal to Zionic endeavor in any age.[4]

"I, the Lord, will give unto my servant Joseph Smith, Jr., power that he shall be enabled to discern" (11). This is an extension of the counsel already given that the Presidency and Bishopric are to determine who shall go to Zion. Joseph was to determine the spiritual readiness of those desiring to go. Bishop Partridge, who was already in Independence, was to send word when opportunity was ripe for the coming of those whom Joseph had chosen. The Presidency, as a quorum, had not yet been organized.

246

"Let him be ordained unto this power; and now speedily visit the churches" (12c). Following this further advice to gather all of the money that could be spared, Newel K. Whitney, as agent of the bishop, visited the churches and gathered funds for the purchase of land in Missouri.

Note the teachings of paragraph 13 of this section concerning the end of the age:

> When the Lord shall come, and old things shall pass away, and all things become new:
>
> The dead that die in the Lord shall rise from the dead and shall not die thereafter, and shall receive an inheritance before the Lord, in the holy city.
>
> He that liveth when the Lord shall come, and has kept the faith, blessed is he. Nevertheless it is appointed to him to die at the age of man.
>
> Children shall grow up until they become old.
>
> Old men shall die.
>
> They shall not sleep in the dust.
>
> They shall be changed in the twinkling of an eye.
>
> For this cause the apostles preached unto the world the resurrection of the dead.
>
> Speaking after the manner of the Lord, these things are now nigh at hand. Yet until that hour there will be foolish virgins among the wise.
>
> The separation between the righteous and the wicked will come at that time.

"Let them be ordained unto this power; for this is a day of warning, and not a day of many words" (15a). The majority of the pioneers had been seeking the gospel for a number of years. Many of them, particularly those who had been associated with Sidney Rigdon in and around Kirtland, Ohio, were well qualified by their training, their willingness to sacrifice, and the witness of the Spirit of God to become his ministers among men. This was particularly true since the basic need of the time was for testimony. Many of the brethren were ordained therefore,

and many of these ministers gave valuable service as missionaries.

"Let all men beware how they take my name in their lips" (15d). This instruction applied to two classes of persons. In one class were those who habitually used the name of Deity in a coarse and boisterous way. In the other group were those who attached the name of Deity to what was really their own opinion. Both groups were under condemnation. For further instruction in this area see Section 119:3b.

BIOGRAPHICAL NOTES

Titus Billings was born March 25, 1793, in Massachusetts. He was one of the first baptized by the missionaries who visited Kirtland in November 1830. Elder Billings was a high priest and served as second counselor to Bishop Partridge until 1840. He died February 6, 1866.

Newel Kimball Whitney (see also Sections 64, 72, 90, 108A) was born February 5, 1795, in Vermont. He was baptized in November 1830 as a result of the missionary work of Parley P. Pratt and his associates. After being associated with Bishop Partridge as agent for the church in Kirtland, he became the bishop of Kirtland. He died September 3, 1850.

---

[1]Matthew 12:39; 16:1-4; Luke 11:30; John 4:46-50. [2]II Thessalonians 2:8-12. [3]Church History 1:476-485. [4]Section 140:5b.

SECTION 64

Joseph Smith spent the early part of September 1831 preparing to move to Hiram in Portage County, about thirty miles southeast of Kirtland, where he and his family were to be guests of John Johnson. Here he and Sidney Rigdon, who was lodged nearby, expected to remain for a time and to be busy in the translation of the Scriptures. In Kirtland those of the elders who were to go to Independence were busy with preparations for their journey. This revelation is directed primarily to them.

It is of interest to remember that this was the last revelation printed in the Book of Commandments. The type had been set as far as "blood of Ephraim" (7b) when the press was destroyed.

"I will that ye should overcome the world" (1a). Note in this connection, "Whatsoever is born of God overcometh the world, and this is the victory that overcometh the world, even our faith. Who is he that overcometh the world, but he that believeth that Jesus is the Son of God?"[1]

"The keys of the mysteries of the kingdom" (2a). In the days when cities were surrounded by walls, the keys of the city were entrusted to men of absolute integrity, and these men were responsible for the lives of the inhabitants. In modern times the custom of giving the key of the city to visiting notables still is practiced. It is in something of this sense that the word *keys* is here used. Joseph held the "keys of the mysteries of the kingdom," which meant that as a man trustworthy in spiritual things, God had bestowed upon him distinctive rights in regard to the kingdom and in making the mysteries of godliness available in the lives of men. Study Matthew 16:19; Revelation 1:18; 9:1, I Corinthians 13:2, 14:2; and Ephesians 1:9, 5:34 in this connection.

"The keys . . . shall not be taken from my servant Joseph Smith, Jr., through the means I have appointed, while he liveth, inasmuch as he obeyeth mine ordinances" (2a). The keys of authority given to Joseph Smith were evidently those pertaining to the presidency of the high priesthood.[2] This authority was shared with Sidney Rigdon and Frederick G. Williams when they became members of the Presidency. The church believes that Joseph retained this authority until his death, and that the Lord who gave it to him passed the same authority to his successors.

"He that forgiveth not his brother his trespasses, standeth

condemned before the Lord, for there remaineth in him the greater sin" (2d). Nothing that my brother may do against me can harm me as much as my own unwillingness to forgive him. No member of the church has the right to hold malice in his heart against anyone. To do so is to forget our own need of forgiveness so clearly set forth in the Lord's prayer. The longer we cherish malice, the bigger it grows.

"He that repenteth not of his sins, and confesseth them not, then ye shall bring him before the church" (2f). This must be done for the good of the brother and the protection of the church; but it must not be done at any time with a feeling of personal grievance against the transgressor.

"They condemned for evil that thing in which there was no evil" (3c). Ezra Booth and Isaac Morley were businessmen who were hesitant in complying fully with the law of stewardship. Booth, who had joined the church because of a miraculous healing and who was interested in the blessings of the gospel rather than in its tasks, soon apostatized and joined the enemies of the church. Isaac Morley, however, saw his error and repented and did effective work as a counselor to Bishop Partridge. The sin of Edward Partridge was apparently his willingness to compromise with these men in a way not contemplated in the law.

"Sidney Gilbert, after a few weeks, should return upon his business" (4a). The presence of Elder Gilbert in Independence was important for two reasons: He could help to maintain the fraternal spirit between Kirtland and Independence, and his wisdom in handling his store and in purchasing lands would be invaluable.

"That my servant Isaac Morley may not be tempted above that which he is able to bear, and counsel wrongfully to your hurt, I gave commandment that this farm should be sold" (4b). Isaac Morley was an associate of Bishop Partridge. He was also the owner of the farm which was under consideration. To relieve him of the responsibility of ordering the farm sold, the Lord gave this command

by revelation. It is probable that in this matter the Lord took into consideration both Isaac Morley's own attitude toward the sale of the farm and the attitude of the people toward Brother Morley.

"Retain a stronghold in the land of Kirtland, for the space of five years" (4c). The clearest evidence of this was probably the building of the temple, which would have been without meaning if the Saints had intended to move away in the immediate future. This revelation was given in September 1831 and the temple was dedicated in March 1836. Those who at first wondered whether the church could stay in Ohio for five years now began to wonder why anyone should leave at the end of five years. But the picture changed again. In the financial panic of 1837 the church underwent the greatest internal upheaval of her early history, while opposition from without waxed stronger and stronger. We were never again as stably planted in the Kirtland area as we were when the temple was being built.

"He that is tithed shall not be burned" (5a). This is the first reference to tithing in the revelations. The word *tithing* is used in reference to the annual payment of one tenth of the increase and also in reference to the financial law as a whole. It is in this latter sense that it is used in this place.

"It is said in my laws, or forbidden, to get in debt to thine enemies" (6a). At almost any point in the history of the early church the work could have been greatly embarrassed if the Saints had been heavily in debt. Joseph already had had some experience in this matter, and he was to have still more. His experience and the revelations of the Lord combined to make the church particularly careful in this regard. The rigors of debt payment in 1930-1945 should warn all future church administrators, general and local, against living in anticipation of future income which may not materialize.

"Ye are agents, and ye are on the Lord's errand; and whatever ye do according to the will of the Lord, is

251

the Lord's business" (6b). It has been charged by some that this paragraph teaches theft. This is not so. A. S. Gilbert and Edward Partridge were accredited agents of the church. In locating the Saints, they found themselves sorely pressed for money, but they hesitated to go into debt. They had been instructed not to do so personally, and it was preferable that they should not do so as agents of the church. But they were here told that if it became imperative, they were to do with care what was necessary and then repay borrowed monies as fast as the Saints made funds available. Any other interpretation is at variance with prior and succeeding instruction.

"Out of small things proceedeth that which is great" (6c). Many of the Saints were very enthusiastic. Some of them expected an immediate and cataclysmic substitution of the kingdom of God for the ways of men. The actual realities were therefore somewhat discouraging, for they had not yet learned that they themselves were not ready for the kingdom, and they were inclined to overlook the importance of laying the foundation for their great work carefully. They needed to be reminded of the greatness of small things well done.

"The Lord requireth the heart and a willing mind" (7a). The business of Zion is an essential part of Zion-building. Zion-building, however, is not just a social or industrial experiment. It is a spiritual enterprise with social and economic resultants. The economics of Zion are grounded in the spiritual quality of the people of Zion, and the economic practices of the Saints are so ordered as to promote that spirituality. It is absolutely basic, then, that "the Lord requireth the heart and a willing mind." Without this there is no possibility of building the kingdom of God.

"The inhabitants of Zion shall judge all things pertaining to Zion" (7c). The destinies of Zion are in the hands of her people. When the moral and spiritual character of the Zionic group rises high above the level of contemporary civilization, then will justice and judgment rule among them, and the very setting up of that standard will tend to eliminate

those who are unwilling to abide by it.

"Even the bishop, who is a judge, and his counselors, if they are not faithful in their stewardships, shall be condemned" (8a). The difficulty with Isaac Morley, who was a member of the Bishopric, made this assurance imperative. The work of the Lord must be conducted in righteousness, and no man's part therein is exempt from investigation by the proper authorities.

BIOGRAPHICAL NOTES

Frederick G. Williams (see Sections 80, 87, 90, 99, 100, 107, 108A) was born October 28, 1787, in Suffield, Hartford County, Connecticut. He was in practice as a doctor in the vicinity of Kirtland, Ohio, when that place was visited by the first missionaries of the church. He accepted their message, left his practice, and accompanied the missionaries, walking most of the way to the western boundaries of the state of Missouri, and was one of the eight men present at the dedication of the temple lot. Elder Williams was designated as counselor to Joseph in March 1832 but the ordination did not take place until March 18, 1833, at Kirtland, Ohio, when the First Presidency was established completely for the first time. About the same time he became the official scribe of Joseph Smith and as such penned many of the important documents of the early church. He served on a committee which arranged the items of doctrine included in the first edition of the book of Doctrine and Covenants and was later a member of the firm which published the *Messenger and Advocate* and *The Evening and the Morning Star* at Kirtland, Ohio. The Saints failed to sustain him as a member of the First Presidency at the conference of September 3, 1837, at Kirtland, Ohio. Joseph again presented his name at the conference held at Far West, November 7, 1837, but he was rejected and left the church. He was rebaptized in 1838, and died at Quincy, Illinois, October 25, 1842.

¹I John 5:4, 5. ²Section 80:1.

SECTION 65

From September 12 until about October 12, 1831, Joseph and Sidney Rigdon lived in the house of John Johnson at Hiram, Portage County, Ohio, while preparing to proceed with their work on the Scriptures. Here, early in October, the revelation on prayer was received. It consists of but one paragraph and may be analyzed as follows:

Listen to the voice of one sent down from on high:
    Who is mighty and powerful.
    Whose going forth is unto the ends of the earth.
    Whose voice is unto men:
    Prepare ye the way of the Lord, make his path straight.

The keys of the kingdom of God are committed unto man on the earth:
    The gospel shall roll forth unto the ends of the earth.

The gospel is as a voice crying:
    Prepare ye the way of the Lord.
    Prepare ye the supper of the Lamb.
    Make ready for the bridegroom.
    Make known his wonderful works among the people.

Pray unto the Lord, call upon his holy name:
    That his kingdom may go forth upon the earth.
    That the inhabitants of the earth may be prepared to receive the gospel.
    That the inhabitants of the earth may be prepared for the second coming of the Son of Man.
The Son of Man shall come down from heaven:
    Clothed in the brightness of his glory.
    To meet the kingdom of God which is set upon earth.

May the kingdom of God go forth:
    That the kingdom of heaven may come.

That God may be glorified in heaven and on earth.
That the enemies of God may be subdued.

Honor, power, and glory be unto God forever and ever.

SECTION 66

The work of translation in progress at Hiram, Ohio, was interrupted by two special conferences. One of these was held October 25, 1831, at the home of Serems Burnett, in Orange, Cuyahoga County. Considerable business was done and four of a committee of six were appointed to instruct the several branches of the church and to present to the Saints the needs of Joseph Smith and Sidney Rigdon, which had to be supplied if these brethren were to continue translating. It was about this time that the revelation to William E. McLellin was given.

"Blessed are you, inasmuch as you have turned away from your iniquities, and have received my truths" (1a). This was Elder McLellin's welcome to the body of the church. He met Joseph for the first time at this conference.

"It is my will that you should proclaim my gospel from land to land, and from city to city; yea, and those regions round about where it has not been proclaimed" (2b). This was not only desirable in itself but was an excellent preparation for the later missionary activities of Elder McLellin, who became one of the first members of the Quorum of Twelve in this dispensation.

"Go not up unto the land of Zion, as yet" (3a). Brother McLellin had been to Independence and had become greatly interested in the work being done there, but there was greater need for his ministry in the East.

"Let my servant Samuel H. Smith go with you" (4). It is interesting to note that Samuel H. Smith here is told to receive the instruction of William McLellin. McLellin

255

had been converted under the ministry of Samuel and of Reynolds Cahoon and had been ordained an elder by them. He was slightly older than Samuel.

BIOGRAPHICAL NOTES

William E. McLellin (see Sections 68:1; 75:2; 87:8) was the seventh of the apostles chosen, but in the arrangement according to age he was the sixth. He was born in Tennessee about the year 1806, and joined the church in June or July 1831. On July 3, 1834, Elder McLellin was chosen a member of the high council of Zion in Clay County, Missouri, but soon afterward returned to Kirtland where he served as teacher in the school of elders. He was ordained an apostle in February 1835 but was expelled from the church in Far West May 11, 1838, for apostasy. After the death of the martyr, Brother McLellin became associated with the Rigdonite movement and later still joined an organization advocating the claims of David Whitmer as president of the church. Elder McLellin finally settled at Independence, Missouri, where he died on Tuesday, March 13, 1883.

SECTION 67

A special conference was held at Hiram, Ohio, on Tuesday, November 1, 1831, because of the anticipated departure of Oliver Cowdery and John Whitmer for Missouri. The proposed publication of the Book of Commandments drew attention to the language in which the revelations were couched, and this apparently became a subject of discussion. This is touched upon in the revelation received during the conference and addressed to the elders of the church.

"There were fears in your hearts; and verily this is the reason that ye did not receive" (1c). The elders were not

condemned for their critical attitude toward the revelations which had been received through the prophet and which were probably before them in manuscript form at this time. They were condemned because they felt it was too much to expect God actually to give them the reassurance which they needed. They hoped, but they did not believe with all their hearts. Such an attitude has made it difficult for God to speak to many who otherwise might have received great light.

"*Appoint him that is the most wise among you. . . that shall make one like unto it*" (2b). It was only natural that the grammatical difficulties of Joseph should disturb some of the educated men of the company. Yet the Lord could make a grammarian in a short time, while he could make a prophet only of such material as yielded itself to his hands. He therefore chose Joseph with prophetic qualifications but lacking in educational equipment in preference to other men who might have had educational equipment but fewer prophetic qualities. In order to impress this on the elders, the challenge contained in this paragraph was issued to them. William E. McLellin made an effort to imitate one of the revelations and failed ignominiously. Joseph says of this effort:

The elders and all present that witnessed this vain attempt of a man to imitate the language of Jesus Christ, renewed their faith in the fullness of the gospel, and in the truth of the commandments and revelations which the Lord had given to the church through my instrumentality; and the elders signified a willingness to bear testimony of their truth to all the world.

"*There is no unrighteousness in them*" (2d). Here is a major test of the revelations purporting to come from God. They are true to our best understanding of the ways of God among men. There' is no unrighteousness in them. They "lead to do good."[1] Their moral tone is high. Their spiritual quality is exalted. They are not the kind of commandments which would be given through an evil and designing man. If Joseph Smith was a hypocrite, then his hypocrisy took the strangest form in history, for the purity of his teaching brought to his side men of independent character who would resent deeply any wickedness of his.

"*You that have been ordained unto this ministry*" (3a). There were present at this conference a considerable number of high priests and elders and some of the Aaronic priesthood. These men were very much in earnest, but they were disturbed by fears and jealousies. Most of all they wanted to be quite sure that they had not been deceived, for the promises of the Lord through Joseph seemed almost too good to be true. Under these circumstances they were not chided but were encouraged to strip themselves of jealousies and fears and to become so humble before the Lord that he could reveal himself to them and work in and through them. They needed to grow in spiritual stature to fit themselves for the richer endowment of spiritual power which should rightfully accompany their ordination. Just as Oliver Cowdery had to learn that the gifts of God depended on his own cooperation,[2] so these men had to learn that the gifts of the priesthood cannot be exercised fully except through faith, righteousness, and expectancy. But if and when they did learn, they were promised that they should see God and enjoy the ministry of his angels.[3]

---

[1]Section 10:6. [2]Section 9:3. [3]See John 1:19 (I.V.); Section 83:3.

SECTION 68

The revelation now Section 68 probably was received during the special conference of November 1, 1831. The first paragraph is concerned with instructions to Orson Hyde, Luke Johnson, Lyman Johnson, and William E. McLellin. The remainder of the revelation concerns itself with an "addition to the covenants and commandments."

Paragraphs 2, 3, and 4 therefore can be rightfully studied in connection with Sections 17 and 42, for these paragraphs deal with the basic law of the church with regard to the calling and ordaining of bishops and teaching of children in Zion.

"*From people to people and from land to land, in the congregations of the wicked, in their synagogues*" (1a). The phrasing of this call is of particular interest. After Elder Hyde's ordination to the apostleship, he ministered in England, Germany, and Egypt, but his best known missionary contribution was his visit to the Mount of Olives and the dedication there of the land of Palestine for the regathering of the Jews.[1]

"*Reasoning with and expounding all Scriptures unto them*" (1a). This is necessary instruction today. The elders of the church should do everything in their power to raise the Scriptures in the estimation of the people. To do this, they should study the Scriptures carefully and be able to expound them with wisdom and understanding. Many unbelievers have much less reason for their unbelief than the Saints have for their belief, and many adverse opinions have been taken secondhand from some aggressive unbeliever. These opinions can be changed by ministers who are informed and patient.

"*Whatsoever they shall speak when moved upon by the Holy Ghost shall be Scripture*" (1c). Spoken truths are just as authoritative as written truths, and inspired preaching is therefore as authoritative as the word in the standard books of the church. But this living word is to be received by both prophet and lesser ministry as they walk in all holiness before the Lord,[2] and it must agree with that which has already been received. This statement gives no sound basis for ministerial authoritarianism. His spoken word must be confirmed by the inner witness of the Spirit before it can be spiritually effective.

"*Ye shall bear record of me, even Jesus Christ, that I am the Son of the living God, that I was, that I am, and that I am to come*" (1d). This word of the Lord is especially

259

addressed to Orson Hyde, Luke Johnson, Lyman Johnson, and William E. McLellin as well as to the faithful elders. It is of interest to note that each of these four men became a member of the Quorum of Twelve when it was organized February 14, 1835. As apostles they became special witnesses of the name of Christ in all the world.[3]

"Go ye into all the world" (1f). Of recent years there has been considerable question regarding the authenticity of Mark 15:18. Here the essence of this teaching is reaffirmed to the elders of the church. This, of course, was long before modern skepticism with regard to this chapter had arisen.

"To you shall be given power to seal them up unto eternal life" (1h). This power is exercised through the proper administration of the ordinances of the gospel.

"Other bishops" (2b). The instructions in this revelation regarding the call and ordination of bishops may be summarized as follows:

Bishops shall be high priests who are worthy.
  They shall be appointed by the First Presidency of the Melchisedec priesthood except that literal descendants of Aaron have a legal right to the bishopric.
The firstborn among the sons of Aaron holds the right of presidency over this (Aaronic) priesthood.
  No man has a legal right to this office, to hold the keys of this priesthood, except he be a literal descendant and the firstborn of Aaron.
A Melchisedec high priest has authority to officiate in all the lesser offices and therefore he may officiate in the office of bishop when no literal descendant of Aaron can be found.
  Provided he is called and set apart and ordained unto this power under the hands of the First Presidency of the Melchisedec priesthood.
A literal descendant of Aaron must be:
Designated by the First Presidency.
Found worthy.

Anointed and ordained under the hands of the Presidency.

Otherwise he is not legally authorized to officiate in this priesthood.

In harmony with the law of lineage, literal descendants of Aaron may claim their anointing:

If they can prove their lineage.

If their lineage is designated in revelation through the Presidency.

Bishops can be brought to trial only before the First Presidency.

"Provided, he is called and set apart, and ordained unto this power under the hands of the First Presidency of the Melchisedec priesthood" (2e). The responsibility for designating bishops inheres in the First Presidency only. Bishops may be set apart, however, by high priests other than members of the Presidency, although such persons must always be acting under the direction of the Presidency. An interesting parallel is suggested in Section 35:1b where the Lord says to Edward Partridge, "I will lay my hand upon you by the hand of my servant Sidney Rigdon." If the Lord can be so represented, it should not be difficult for the Presidency to be represented in similar fashion.

"Children in Zion, or in any of her stakes" (4a). Parents who live in Zion or her stakes should teach their children to understand the principles of the gospel so that they can be baptized when eight years of age and can understand what they are doing. This law applies more particularly to the highly organized centers of church activity where parents have the best opportunity to control the environment of their children and to teach them the principles of the gospel, but it also applies in a lesser degree to other centers.

"They shall also teach their children to pray, and to walk uprightly before the Lord" (4c). This instruction is just as fundamental as the instruction regarding baptism and should be associated with it.

"The inhabitants of Zion shall also observe the sabbath day to keep it holy" (4d). The proper observance of the Sabbath is not a matter of one day only but of the entire week. The peace and quietude which should characterize the Sabbath is possible only against the industry of the other days of the week which is expected of the Saints. The idler is in no position to enter properly into the spirit of the Lord's day.

"He that observeth not his prayers before the Lord in the season thereof, let him be had in remembrance before the judge of my people" (4h). Latter Day Saints should pray at regular and frequent intervals. It has been objected by some that prayer should never be permitted to degenerate into a habit. This is true; but it should also be remembered that the best way to cultivate the spirit of prayer is not to wait until we are in the spirit of prayer but to seek that spirit. Many a man who did not at first "feel right with God" has entered into the heavenly presence while on his knees.

Stakes are first mentioned in the revelations in Section 68:4. In this connection, it is interesting to note that in Isaiah it is written:

> Look upon Zion, the city of our solemnities; thine eyes shall see Jerusalem, a quiet habitation, a tabernacle that shall not be taken down; not one of the stakes thereof shall ever be removed, neither shall any of the cords thereof be broken.[4]

Here Zion is compared to a tabernacle, a tent supported by stakes and cords. In like manner the Zion of our day is supported by her stakes. The figure reappears further on in Isaiah:

> Enlarge the place of thy tent, and let them stretch forth the curtains of thine habitation; spare not, lengthen thy cords, and strengthen thy stakes.[5]

A stake organization consists of a stake presidency, composed of three high priests; a stake high council, composed of twelve high priests; and a stake bishopric, composed of the bishop and two counselors. Kirtland was the first stake to be organized[6] (Section 91:1). After this, other stakes were organized at Far West, Adam-ondi-Ahman, Nauvoo, Ramus, etc.

BIOGRAPHICAL NOTES

Orson Hyde (see also Sections 97:4; 100:7; 107:40) was the fourth man chosen as a member of the first Quorum of Twelve, but when the apostles were arranged according to age, he was the fifth. He was the son of Nathan and Sally Hyde and was born in Oxford, Connecticut, January 8, 1805. Under the preaching of Sidney Rigdon, he became identified with the Disciples and soon afterward founded several churches in Lorain, Ohio. In 1830, he was appointed their pastor. He was converted to the Restoration through reading the Book of Mormon and was baptized by Sidney Rigdon October 31, 1831. Soon he was ordained a high priest and entered actively into missionary labor. On February 17, 1834, he was chosen a member of the high council, and in the same year he made a missionary journey to Missouri. In February 1835 he was ordained an apostle and traveled extensively with his colleagues, setting in order the various churches. In 1837, in company with Heber C. Kimball and others, he assisted in opening the English Mission; but in October 1838 he and Thomas B. Marsh apostatized and joined the opposition to the church. He was suspended from his office May 4, 1839, at Quincy, Illinois. On June 27 of the same year he returned to the church at Commerce, Illinois (Nauvoo), made confession of wrongdoing, and was restored to fellowship and to his standing in the Quorum of Twelve. At the conference of 1840, he and Elder John E. Page were appointed on a mission to Jerusalem and after many hardships he completed this mission. In 1844 Elder Hyde followed the fortunes of the Utah faction. His death occurred at Spring City, Utah, November 28, 1878. He married a sister of Luke and Lyman Johnson.

Luke S. Johnson (see Sections 99:2, 75:2) was born November 3, 1807, in Pomfret, Windsor County, Vermont,

263

and was baptized May 10, 1831. He soon was ordained a priest and later (October 25, 1831) a high priest. In 1834 he was ordained a member of the first high council of the church. He was chosen a member of the Quorum of Twelve on February 14, 1835, and did considerable missionary work in the East and in Canada. At a conference held in Kirtland September 3, 1837, he and his brother Lyman and John F. Boynton were disfellowshiped. He died December 9, 1861.

Lyman E. Johnson (see Section 75:3) was born October 24, 1811, at Pomfret, Windsor County, Vermont, baptized February 1831, ordained an elder the following October and a high priest November 1, 1831. He was called into the active ministry in November 1831 by revelation and performed missionary labor in Ohio, the eastern states, and in eastern Canada. Later he was a member of Zion's Camp and was ordained an apostle February 14, 1835, but was excommunicated for apostasy April 13, 1838. He was drowned in the Mississippi on December 20, 1856.

William C. McLellin (see Section 66).

---

¹Church History, Volume 2, pages 552-556. ²Section 119:2. ³Section 104:11. ⁴Isaiah 33:20. ⁵Isaiah 54:2. ⁶Section 91:1.

SECTION 69

During the conference at Hiram, Ohio, November 1 and 2, Joseph dedicated the Book of Commandments and Revelations, which Oliver Cowdery was to take to Independence for publication. It was after this prayer of dedication had been offered that the revelation which is now Section 69 was received.

"It is not wisdom in me that he [Oliver Cowdery] *should be intrusted with the commandments and the moneys which he shall carry into the land of Zion, except one go*

with him who will be true and faithful" (1a). There have been some comments on this revelation by those who claim that it reflects on the honesty and trustworthiness of Oliver Cowdery; but when we consider that his way lay hundreds of miles through a wild, half-civilized country, often beset with rogues and outlaws, we can see the wisdom of his having his trusted friend and relative with him. There is no intimation in the revelation that the church was in danger of suffering loss because of Cowdery's unfaithfulness; this precaution was for "Oliver Cowdery's sake"—for his protection and help.[1]

"John Whitmer should . . . continue in writing and making a history of all the important things which he shall observe and know concerning my church" (1a, b). If John Whitmer had risen to his great opportunity, his ministry at Kirtland and Independence would have furnished him material for a historical record absolutely invaluable to subsequent church workers. It is one of the tragedies of our early church life that this historical record was so inadequately compiled. It is available to the church in the first volume of the *Journal of History*,[2] and extends to March 1838.

"My servants who are abroad in the earth should send forth the accounts of their stewardships to the land of Zion" (2a). This does not refer to finances only but also to other reports regarding such matters as standards of living and methods of labor which would be of value to the church. The idea of the Saints accounting to the priesthood as the representatives of Divinity and in accordance with their official responsibility is written into the law of the church from the very beginning.

---

[1]Church History, Volume 1, page 229. [2]Pages 45-63, 135-150, 292-305.

SECTION 70

Four special conferences were held between the first and the twelfth of November 1831. At the second of these, the elders requested more information concerning preaching the gospel and the gathering. In answer to their prayers the revelation now known as "the Appendix"[1] was received on Thursday, November 3 (Section 108).

The last of these conferences was held November 12 at the home of Brother Johnson in Hiram, Ohio. Here Oliver Cowdery and John Whitmer were blessed to carry the manuscript of the Book of Commandments to Zion where W. W. Phelps and Company expected to issue it in book form. The work in connection with the Book of Commandments required the time and labor of several of the brethren, and the question of recompense for work done and to be done in preparing and printing the revelations was discussed at the conference. The returns from the sale of the book and the management of the printing establishment which had been provided for by the previous conference also were discussed. In answer to prayer the revelation of November 12, 1831, was received. It will be seen that this revelation not only defines and explains the law of consecration and stewardship but requires every member of the church to be obedient thereto. It makes temporal and spiritual stewards equal, and upon this equality the manifestations of the Spirit are said to depend.

"I, the Lord, have appointed them, and ordained them to be stewards over the revelations and commandments" (1b). This group included Joseph Smith, Jr., through whom the revelations were received and on whom rested the primary responsibility of teaching and interpreting them; Martin Harris, who had given considerable financial and spiritual support from the beginning; Oliver Cowdery, scribe and "second elder," who had done much of the copying and who was to be associated with W. W. Phelps in preparing and printing the manuscript; John Whitmer, church

266

historian, who also had done some of the copying and who was to accompany Oliver Cowdery to Zion; Sidney Rigdon, close associate and secretary of the prophet and later a member of the First Presidency; and William W. Phelps, who was to be responsible for printing the revelations.

"Stewards over the revelations and commandments which I have given unto them, and which I shall hereafter give unto them" (1b). It was evidently contemplated that the committee should publish in the Book of Commandments all the revelations received up to the time of its printing. At the time the mob destroyed the press at Independence, Missouri, in July 1833, only the preface of the Book of Commandments and the revelations up to September 1831 had been published.

"Manage them and the concerns thereof; yea, the benefits thereof" (1c). The elders named are instructed here to take their needs and just wants from the proceeds of selling the Book of Commandments and to place any surplus in the storehouse for the benefit of the inhabitants of Zion. They were partners in a group stewardship.

"This is what the Lord requires of every man in his stewardship" (3a). The stewards were to work diligently in managing the publications of the church. Here it is emphasized that they were to receive according to their necessities and just wants, but the surplus was to become the property of the group. These principles apply to every stewardship no matter how diverse its type might be. In this connection the comment of Harry F. Ward is of considerable interest:

> Christianity demands a fraternal community for the satisfaction of its ideals. It requires that men who call God "Father" should find the way to live as brothers. Now we have rifts and chasms. Our task is to bring the different groups of our community life, the divers nations and races of the world, together in a real brotherhood, until there shall be no handicapped, exploited, dispossessed people. Solidarity is not simply the dream of the workers at the bottom. It is the imperative of the gospel.

"None are exempt from this law who belong to the church of the living God" (3b). This statement is equally

true if it is paraphrased to read "none who exempt themselves from this law fully 'belong' to the church of the living God."

"*Even more abundantly, which abundance is multiplied unto them through the manifestations of the Spirit*" (3c). Stewards in both temporal concerns and spiritual concerns are to be supplied with the necessities of life, but the varying types of stewardship have also their own intrinsic rewards. Spiritual stewards receive the abundance of spiritual blessings, because this is the field in which they labor. Craftsmen have the joy of creative workmanship. Businessmen the joy of business accomplishment. Artists have the joy of creative artistry. Thus it is intended that there shall come to each the joy of his particular service as well as the means to supply his family needs and to maintain himself for continuing his work.

"*In your temporal things you shall be equal, and this not grudgingly*" (3d). The spirit of the Zionic enterprise is all-important. We must not only do good but we must do good ungrudgingly, out of a sincere spirit of mutual concern. What was true of Simeon is true of all: "Thou hast neither part nor lot in this matter: [if] thy heart is not right in the sight of God."[2]

"*For their security for food and for raiment, for an inheritance; for houses and for lands*" (4a, b). As long as the work of the church had not required their full time, these elders had supported themselves. Now that their duties required their full time, it was necessary to arrange for their support. This revelation provided that this support should come from the work they were called to do, which was the publication of the revelations.

---

[1]Section 108. [2]Acts 8:21.

SECTION 71

Following the departure of Oliver Cowdery and John Whitmer for Independence, where the Book of Commandments was to be printed, Joseph continued the translation of the Scriptures with Sidney Rigdon serving as his secretary. During November the attack made on the church by Ezra Booth, who had apostatized, created considerable excitement in the vicinity. This should be kept in mind in considering this revelation given in the closing days of November or the first few days of December 1831 and addressed to Joseph Smith, Jr., and Sidney Rigdon.

"Open your mouths in proclaiming my gospel" (1). In consequence of this revelation, the brethren postponed further translation and went to Kirtland where on Sunday, December 4, 1831, the elders assembled for counsel and instruction.

"Bear record, and prepare the way for the commandments and revelations which are to come" (2c). At this time this instruction had a specific meaning. The elders were to prepare for the publication and sale of the Book of Commandments. For us, however, it has a more general meaning, for the function of the elders of the church is to prepare the world for greater revelations which are to come as men live up to the light which has already been received.

"Confound your enemies; call upon them to meet you, both in public and in private" (2e). Joseph writes that "Ezra Booth...wrote a series of letters which by their coloring, falsity, and vain calculations to overthrow the work of the Lord, exposed his weakness, wickedness, and folly, and left him a monument of his own shame for the world to wonder at."[1]

"Let them bring forth their strong reasons against the Lord" (2f). In addition to slanderous statements regarding the leaders of the work, the points of attack seem to have been the doctrine of current revelation and the method

of promoting the gathering. With regard to the former, Elder R. J. Lambert has written:

It seems to Latter Day Saints that it is a piece of presumption for man to say to God, "We will accept as a revelation of Thy divine will and judgment of what is best for us, the words which you spoke unto Moses, John the Baptist, John the Revelator, and all of the holy prophets and apostles, but we do not believe that any occasion will ever arise when you will again need to speak to us through any servant whom you might commission; and because we believe you have said enough to save us and to give us eternal life, we exonorate you from further responsibility of this nature."

_____

[1]Church History, Volume 1, page 219.

SECTION 72

While the elders were yet assembled at Kirtland, on December 4, 1831, this revelation was given in response to their inquiry regarding temporal and spiritual matters. It is addressed to the high priests who were there, and they were told that it was expedient that a bishop be appointed of their number; that he must be a high priest.

"Verily in this thing ye have done wisely" (1c). Prior to this time, the only bishop in the church had been Edward Partridge, who was in Independence supervising the work of the gathering. In view of the impossibility of maintaining close contact with Bishop Partridge, the high priests at Kirtland had agreed upon the appointment of a bishop for Kirtland also. It is highly probable that this was one of the problems which had been presented to the Lord prior to the receipt of the revelation.

"The elders of the church in this part of my vineyard shall render an account of their stewardship unto the bishop which shall be appointed of me, in this part of my vineyard" (1e). With regard to this arrangement, Bishop Kelley wrote in *The Law of Christ and Its Fulfillment:*

270

There is complete order and harmony of work in the household of faith and no one can properly ignore the office work or administrative authority of another. To do this is to hold lightly, or ignore, the Lord who appoints these messengers, and thus lose the blessings accompanying, as stated by Jesus, "he that heareth you heareth me." No one is so great by birth or calling, as to be exempt from the law of duty or of recognizing and properly answering to the authority and faith of others.

In harmony with the instruction of this paragraph, the members of the Quorum of Twelve in the Reorganization

Resolved that each member of this quorum present to the bishop an inventory of his temporal affairs agreeable to the law of tithing and consecration.[1]

"These things shall be had on record, to be handed over unto the bishop in Zion" (1f). Kirtland was in process of being organized into a stake, and Bishop Whitney became the stake bishop. The elders laboring in this territory are instructed here to render the account of their stewardship to him, and he is in turn to report stewardship matters to the Presiding Bishop in Independence. Bishop Whitney would, of course, be under the direction of the Presidency with regard to his spiritual functions.

"Newel K. Whitney is the man who shall be appointed and ordained unto this power" (2). Bishop Whitney thus became the second bishop of the church in the order of his ordination, and the first bishop appointed specifically for Kirtland.

"The duty of the bishop" (3a). This revelation specifically points out the following duties of Bishop Whitney:

To keep the Lord's storehouse.
To receive the funds of the church in this area.
To take an account of the elders in this area.
To administer to the wants of the ministry.
    They shall pay for what they receive, if they have the money wherewith to pay.
    The bishop of Zion shall pay the accounts of workers who are unable to meet their own obligations.
To issue certificates to the bishop of Zion, rendering

acceptable the elders who have been wise stewards in Kirtland.

"The labors of the faithful who labor in spiritual things . . . shall answer the debt unto the bishop in Zion" (3d). There was some disquietude regarding the idea of supporting spiritual stewards out of the common fund. This is referred to in the revelation, and instruction previously given is confirmed. Those who labor in spiritual stewardships are entitled to a just remuneration for their labors the same as those who labor in temporal stewardships.

"Let my servants who are appointed as stewards over the literary concerns of my church have claim for assistance upon the bishop, or bishops, in all things" (4c). The stewards appointed in the revelation of November 12, 1831,[2] are mentioned here specifically as having claims upon the bishop or bishops so that the publication of the revelations might not be impeded. Under this arrangement Bishop Whitney could supply the needs of those in Kirtland and report his action to the bishop in Independence.

"This shall be an ensample for all the extensive branches of my church, in whatsoever land they shall be established" (4e). The example here set forth evidently is to be followed in the various stakes, districts, and branches of the church. When fully organized, these will include a bishop as part of their official personnel. The duties of this bishop will be similar to those of Bishop Whitney, as outlined in this revelation, and the duties of the Saints to the bishop will be similar to those outlined here.

"Let them carry up unto the bishop a certificate from three elders of the church, or a certificate from the bishop" (5b). It was very difficult to hold back the converts who wanted to move to Zion, and whose coming created problems which the infant church was not yet able to solve. In attempting this, the following instruction was published in *The Evening and the Morning Star:*

To see numbers of disciples come to this land, destitute of means to procure an inheritance, and much less the necessities of life, awakens a sympathy in our bosoms of no ordinary feeling; and we should do injustice to the Saints were we to remain silent, when, perhaps, a few words by way of advice may be the means of instructing them, that hereafter great difficulties may be avoided.

For the disciples to suppose that they can come to this land without aught to eat, or to drink, or to wear, or anything to purchase these necessaries with, is a vain thought. For them to suppose that their clothes and shoes will not wear out upon the journey, when the whole of it lies through a country where there are thousands of sheep from which wool in abundance can be procured to make them garments, and cattle upon a thousand hills, to afford leather for shoes, is just as vain. . . .

Then brethren, we would advise that where there are many poor in a church, that the elders counsel together and make preparations to send a part at one time and a part at another.

---

[1]April 14, 1885. [2]Section 70. [3]Volume 1:219-222.

SECTION 73

From the date of the last revelation until the eighth or tenth of January 1832 Joseph Smith and Sidney Rigdon continued to preach in Shalersville, Ravenna, and other nearby places, declaring the truth of the gospel and seeking to refute the scandalous letters then being published in the *Ohio Star* at Ravenna by Ezra Booth[1] and in counseling the elders of the Kirtland region. The pressure of these duties kept them so busy that the work on the Scriptures was hindered.[2]

On Tuesday, January 10, a revelation was given concerning the work of the elders prior to the forthcoming conference and also concerning the resumption of translation.

"Continue preaching the gospel, and in exhortation to the churches" (1). The obvious and urgent task of the elders was missionary,[3] but exhortation was so important that it was declared to be one of the constant elements of the

ministerial task.[4] Part of Emma Smith's calling was to "exhort the church."[5]

"Continue the work of translation until it be finished" (2a). It was the evident intention and expectation of Joseph and Sidney that the work which they were doing should be brought to completion and made available to the church. Richard Howard has shown that "they were extremely active on the biblical revision, recording perhaps as many as ninety-one pages of manuscript."[6]

---

[1]Church History 1:232. [2]*Restoration Scriptures*, pages 91-92. [3]Section 102:9. [4]*Ibid.* 17:8, 10, 11; 18:5; 21:2-5 123:3. [5]*Ibid.* 24:2c. [6]*Op. cit.*

SECTION 74

Following the instruction to renew translation given in the previous revelation, Joseph Smith and Sidney Rigdon re-entered upon their work and came almost immediately to I Corinthians 7:14. They desired further explanation of the passage. Joseph therefore inquired of the Lord and was led to write the exposition contained in Section 74. It had to do with an ancient problem having modern parallels.

Many of the early Christians believed that it was unnecessary to remain obedient to the rites of Judaism, while others believed that converts ought to become Jews before becoming Christians. If the Judaizing party had won their contention and it had been felt that people *must* be obedient to the laws of Judaism to be real Christians, Christianity would thereafter have been regarded as a mere phase of Judaism instead of a new movement independent of all others. The apostle Paul, who saw the significance of this problem more clearly than any man of his generation, wrote his instructions regarding this matter to the church at Corinth, a Grecian city with a large Jewish population.

"Little children are holy" (3). The thought here is that the Jews believed that little children who were not brought

274

up under the law of Moses were unholy. Paul agreed with this in the sense that when they arrived at maturity those who became Jews rather than Christians were to this degree "unholy." But, from the viewpoint of Christians, children are not made holy or unholy by the actions of their parents but by their own actions after they come to the "years of accountability."[1]

---

[1] Sections 16:d, 17:20.

SECTION 75

Joseph and Sidney were occupied in translating the Inspired Version of the Holy Scriptures during the first three weeks of January 1832. At the end of that time, however, they left Hiram to participate in the conference which was to be held January 25 at Amherst, Lorain County, Ohio. During the conference a revelation was given in response to prayer regarding the work of certain elders who had offered themselves as missionaries. At this conference Joseph Smith was ordained president of the high priesthood of the church.

"Proclaiming the truth according to the revelations and commandments which I have given you" (1b). There is a note of urgency here which we shall do well to heed. The early elders were to "go forth and not tarry," to "be active in the Master's business," to "labor with their might." Moreover, they were to take advantage of the distinctive features of their message. Others were expounding the Scriptures and they also were to do this. In addition to this they were to emphasize the distinctive contribution of the revelations of God, and in so doing they were promised that they would be "laden with many sheaves, and crowned with honor, and glory, and immortality, and eternal life."

"Go ye into the south countries" (2b). William E. Mc-Lellin and Luke Johnson, who were thus associated in the mission to the southern states, were later members of the Quorum of Twelve. Association in this mission undoubtedly helped to prepare them for their service in this quorum.

"Lyman Johnson and . . . Orson Pratt . . . shall also take their journey into the eastern countries" (3b). These two were also later associated in the Quorum of Twelve. They were absent on the mission here assigned them from the beginning of February until the early fall and during this time traveled through Ohio, Pennsylvania, New Jersey, New York, Vermont, New Hampshire, and Connecticut, a total trip of 4,000 miles. They baptized over one hundred persons and organized several branches.

"Going from house to house, and from village to village, and from city to city" (3e). This call to hard missionary work was in full accord with the earlier instruction that the elders should not be idle but should labor with their might. Elders who have followed this instruction, both in local and missionary work, have brought many hundreds of persons into the church. The preaching of the word of God is important, but the intimate contacts of personal evangelism are possibly even more effective in winning people to God and to the church.

"In whatsoever house ye enter, and they receive you, leave your blessings upon that house" (3f). The ministry and the Saints should live so that their very presence becomes a benediction to those who receive them. One of our missionaries makes it a practice to pray every day in the home of at least one friend, and the blessings wrought by the prayers of this good man are innumerable.

"And they receive you not, ye shall depart speedily from that house, and shake off the dust of your feet as a testimony against them" (3f). If the elders are to follow this practice, how particular they ought to be to see that they properly present the word to those whose homes they visit. No sincere servant of God can register the formal protest of such an act as this unless he feels that he has

276

done his best in the Spirit of the Master, and that his Master has been deliberately rejected.

"It is the duty of the church to assist in supporting the families of those... who are called... to proclaim the gospel unto the world" (4b). It has been thought sometimes that the elders under appointment should receive no financial aid from the church for their families but should derive their entire livelihood from their ministry in the field. In this revelation it is clearly stated that the families of the ministry are to be supported by the church. This is in harmony with the instructions previously given.[1]

"Let him provide and he shall in no wise lose his crown" (5a). Paragraph 5 carries forward the thought of the preceding paragraph. Caring for one's family is a Christian obligation. When the church cannot do this, the members of the ministry must shoulder their own responsibilities but also should give such ministerial help as opportunity permits. Even those who cannot accept appointment ought to "labor in the church." Every man is to "be diligent in all things." This includes providing the necessities of life for himself and his family and also proclaiming the gospel according to his opportunities.

BIOGRAPHICAL NOTES

William E. McLellin (see Section 66).
Luke Johnson (see Section 68).
Orson Hyde (see Section 68).
Samuel H. Smith (see Section 21).
Lyman E. Johnson (see Section 68).
Orson Pratt (see Section 33).
Simeon Carter (see Section 52:6).
Elmer Harris—a brother of Martin Harris.
Ezra Thayre (see Section 32).
Thomas B. Marsh (see Section 30).
Reynolds Cahoon (see Section 52:6).
Samuel Stanton became a member of the high council of the stake at Adam-ondi-Ahman June 28, 1838.

Seymour Brunson became a lieutenant in the Nauvoo Legion, a member of the high council at Nauvoo, and an influential high priest in the church. It was he who preferred the charges on which Oliver Cowdery was tried before the Far West High Council in 1838. He died in Nauvoo August 10, 1840.

Sylvester Smith was a member of the high council organized in Kirtland in 1834. The next year he was made one of the presidents of seventy, but having been previously ordained a high priest he was transferred to that quorum and John Gaylord replaced him on the Council of Presidents of Seventy.

Gideon Carter gave some needed ministerial help but met an untimely death in the battle of Crooked River October 24, 1838.

---

[1]Sections 60:3; 72:3.

SECTION 76

After the close of the conference at Amherst, Ohio, where Joseph had been ordained President of the High Priesthood and of the church, he and Sidney Rigdon returned to Hiram. Here the prophet resumed the translation of the Inspired Version of the New Testament with Sidney Rigdon acting as his scribe.[1] On Thursday, February 16, 1832, they came to the fifth chapter and twenty-ninth verse of the gospel according to John and while meditating upon the rendition given them by the spirit of revelation, the glory of the Lord shone round about them and they shared the spiritual vision of which this section is an account. Both of the participants are committed fully to the narrative as contained in the Doctrine and Covenants. The testimony of Joseph Smith is greatly reinforced by the intimate association of another man with him in so rich an experience as this.

"*The Lord is God, and beside him there is no Savior*" (1a). This epoch-marking vision ties up directly with the initial revelation to Joseph Smith, when the young prophet was instructed to "hear him." The revelations of God repeatedly center our attention upon Jesus the Lord. This is one evidence of their divinity.

"*Great is his wisdom*" (1b). Compare this with the words of Paul to the saints in Corinth. "Of him are ye in Christ Jesus, who of God is made unto us wisdom, and righteousness, and sanctification, and redemption,"[2] and "Your faith should not stand in wisdom of men, but in the power of God."[3]

"*Marvelous are his ways*" (1b). The latter-day work has been regarded by its adherents as a direct fulfillment of Isaiah 29:14. "I will proceed to do a marvellous work among the people, even a marvellous work and a wonder." It is well to remember, however, that this marvelous work is possible only through the direct influence of Jesus. It is his wisdom which is great, it is his purposes which fail not, and his power which is vindicated from eternity to eternity.

I . . . delight to honor those who serve me in righteousness and in truth unto the end" (2a). God cannot honor a wicked man, for the honor which comes from God is not something added from without but is an enrichment from within. It is like the beauty of a flower.

"*Great shall be their reward, and eternal shall be their glory*" (2b). This glory is a matter of quality as well as of duration. The faithful will be endowed with light and truth[4] and will know of "all mysteries, yea, all the hidden mysteries of the kingdom." Such a people must necessarily be endowed with such a measure of the Spirit of God as will enable them to view life in terms of the divine purpose in creation.

"*Those things which were from the beginning before the world was, which were ordained of the Father, through his only begotten Son*" (3b). Here is reaffirmed the Christian belief in the pre-mortal life of Jesus. In this connection the

279

following biblical references are important: "Let us make man in our image, after our likeness."[5] "In the beginning was the Word, and the Word was with God, and the Word was God. The same was in the beginning with God. All things were made by him; and without him was not anything made that was made."[6]

"This is the testimony, last of all, which we give of him, that he lives" (3g). It is eminently fitting that Joseph and Sidney, who shared in the apostolic commission to be "special witnesses of the name of Christ to all the world,"[7] should bear this testimony. "Last of all" does not mean that no further testimony could be received after their day but that it was added to the many which had preceded it.

"Rebelled against God, and sought to take the kingdom of our God and his Christ; wherefore he maketh war with the saints of God" (3k, l). Satan makes the kingdom his chief point of attack because it is central to the plan of Divinity.

The first sentence of paragraph 4 is long and involved. The portion beginning with the words, "They are they who are the sons of perdition" and ending with the words, "and put him to an open shame" is really an interpolation intended to explain the term "sons of perdition." The sentence therefore can be better understood if it is first read without this interpolation. Then when the sense of the paragraph is well in mind it can be read through with the interpolation included.

The Sons of Perdition

Know the power of God and have been made partakers thereof.

Suffer themselves, through the power of the Devil, to be overcome.

Deny the truth and defy the power of God.

Deny the Holy Spirit after having received it.

Deny the Only Begotten Son of the Father.

Crucify Jesus unto themselves and put him to an open shame.

The Fate of the Sons of Perdition

It were better for them never to have been born.

They are vessels of wrath, doomed to suffer the wrath of God with the Devil and his angels in eternity.

There is no forgiveness for them in this world nor in the world to come.

They will go away into the lake of fire and brimstone with the Devil and his angels, and this is eternal punishment.

They are the only ones on whom the second death will have any power.

They are the only ones who will not be redeemed in the due time of the Lord, after the sufferings of his wrath.

The end of their torment, its place and its nature are not revealed, nor will be revealed except to those who are made partakers thereof.

Jesus came into the world (4) and (5)

To be crucified for the world.

To bear the sins of the world.

To sanctify the world.

To cleanse the world from all unrighteousness.

That through him all men might be saved, whom the Father has put into his power, and made by him.

To glorify and save all the work of his hands except the sons of perdition.

To work out a perfect atonement through the shedding of his own blood.

Those who come forth in the resurrection of the just (5)

Receive the testimony of Jesus and believe on his name, are baptized and keep the commandments, receive the Holy Spirit by the laying on of hands,

overcome by faith and are sealed by the Holy Spirit
of promise.

These are the church of the Firstborn, unto whose
hands the Father has given all things.

They are priests and kings after the order of Melchisedec.

They are gods, even the sons of God.

Their names are written in heaven, where God and
Christ are the judge of all.

They are just men made perfect through Jesus, the
mediator of the new covenant.

"They are gods, even the sons of God" (5). "They are
gods" must be understood in connection with the succeeding
phrase, "even the sons of God." No interpretation of this
passage must be accepted which ranks the children of
God equally with the Father. The idea is that through
receiving a fullness of Divinity they become akin to Divinity
itself. In this connection it is well to read citations
from the Bible where the term "God" is applied to men.[8]

Those who attain celestial glory (7).

All things are theirs, and they shall overcome all things.

They will dwell in the presence of God and his Christ
forever.

They will accompany Christ when he comes to reign
over his people on earth.

They are come unto Mount Zion, to the city of the
living God, to an innumerable company of angels,
to the general assembly and church of Enoch and of
the Firstborn.

Their bodies are celestial, and their glory is that of
the sun, even the glory of God the highest of all.

The glory of the celestial kingdom excels in all things.
There God the Father reigns upon his throne forever
and before him all things bow and give glory. They
who dwell in his presence see as they are seen

and know as they are known, and have received of the divine fullness and grace, so that they are equal in power and in might and in dominion.

Terrestrial glory: Terrestrial glory is different from celestial glory as the sun differs from the moon (6), but it excels the telestial glory, power, dominion, and might (7). It receives the presence of the Son but not the fullness of the Father (6). Those of the terrestrial world receive the ministrations of those in celestial glory, and they in turn minister to those of the telestial glory (7).

Those assigned to this glory include

Those who die without law.
Those who receive the testimony of Jesus in the "prison house."
Honorable men of the earth blinded by the craftiness of men.
Those who were not valiant in the testimony of Jesus.

Telestial glory (7): This is a lesser glory likened to that of the stars as compared with the moon and the sun. Yet it surpasses all understanding in glory, so that no man knows it except by the revelation of God.

Those assigned to this glory

Receive not the gospel of Christ nor the testimony of Jesus, but deny not the Holy Spirit.
Will not be redeemed from the Devil until the last resurrection.
Will not be gathered with the saints to be caught up unto the church of the Firstborn.

They
Suffer the wrath of God on earth and the vengeance of eternal fire.

Are cast down into hell and suffer the wrath of the
Almighty until the fullness of times.
Finally bow the knee and confess Christ and become
servants of the Most High God.

They
Are as innumerable as the stars or as the sands of the sea.
Will be judged and rewarded according to their works.
Cannot come where God and Christ dwell, worlds without
end.
Will receive the Holy Spirit through the ministration of
the terrestrial order.
"Neither is man capable to make them known" (8b).
Just as the full beauty of a sunset escapes the genius of
the artist, so the fullness of the glory of the kingdom defied
the descriptive abilities of Joseph and Sidney. The richer
glories of the kingdom cannot be expressed in our cumber-
some language, nor can they be understood except by those
whose spiritual vision has been clarified by the ministry of
the Holy Spirit.

---

[1]Church History, Volume 1, page 235. [2]I Corinthians 1:30. [3]I Corinthians 2:5.
[4]Section 90:6. [5]Genesis 1:26. [6]John 1:1-3; see also Colossians 1:16; Ephesians
3:9; Revelation 3:14. [7]Section 104:11. [8]Exodus 7:1; Psalm 82:1; 82:6; John 10:34.

SECTION 77

This revelation is addressed to the high priesthood and was
probably received during the first week of March 1832,
shortly after the vision of Joseph and Sidney noted in the
preceding section. At this time Joseph was living at the
home of John Johnson at Hiram, Portage County, Ohio,
where he was engaged in the work of translating the
Scriptures. The revelation is concerned with the establishing
of the storehouse and the care of the poor in Kirtland and
in Independence.

From the organization of the church, and more particularly since January 18, 1831,[1] the Saints had been concerned greatly regarding the welfare of the poor. From the tenor of this revelation, it is fairly evident that they had prayed for further light in this matter and that the revelation is in answer to their petitions.

"*It must needs be that there be an organization of my people*" (1c). The thought here is that there is no possibility of group salvation without adequate organization, and this fundamental principle is reiterated repeatedly during the revelation. At first glance it might seem that any organization making for efficiency would do, but contemplation will show that the organization of the work of the kingdom ought to breathe the purposes of the kingdom, and any organization which does not actually conserve the kingdom purposes is not of God. Organization is therefore of major importance; it is a vital aspect of the work of the kingdom.

"*The storehouse for the poor of my people*" (1c). The principle of the storehouse is a permanent principle of the Zionic association of the people of God. It is likely to be expressed through varying forms suited to the changing times. But the fundamental principle of the wise conservation of the gains of the rich and learned and wise and noble for the benefit of the needy—the poor, the sick, the young, the unfortunate—is vital to our fellowship under God.

"*If ye are not equal in earthly things, ye can not be equal in obtaining heavenly things*" (1f). This principle, too, is eternal. If we do not have "unfeigned love of the brethren,"[2] then we have no hope of celestial glory, and such unfeigned love is manifested in concern regarding both the spiritual and temporal welfare of our fellows.

"*You must prepare yourselves by doing the things which I have commanded you and required of you*" (1g). There is no provision here for the salvation of men of good intentions. The conditions of celestial glory are clear and specific, and this paragraph shows that they include caring for the poor in the spirit of Christ.

"*It is expedient that all things be done unto my glory*"

285

(2a). These men were engaged in a great spiritual enterprise of which the establishment and maintenance of godly social relationships are a vital part. Whenever social organization is sought as an end in itself it will fail, but as long as all things are done "to the glory of God" they are thereby safeguarded.

"Let my servant Ahashdah, and...Gazelam, or Enoch, and...Pelagoram [Newel K. Whitney, Joseph, and Sidney Rigdon] sit in council with the Saints which are in Zion" (2). N. K. Whitney was the bishop of Kirtland, Joseph was president of the church, and Sidney Rigdon had been closely associated with Joseph in many of the important activities of the church and later became his counselor. This instruction was necessitated by the difficulties in Independence and the friction between the Saints there and at Kirtland. The disguised names were to protect the privacy of those involved.

"Prepare and organize yourselves by a bond or everlasting covenant that can not be broken" (2d). The legal aspects of the association were to be conserved by the execution of a legal document setting forth the rights of the parties thereto. But behind this legal document, and giving it its true weight and significance, must be the kinship of spiritual brotherhood. Love, not law, is the binding force of spiritual union.

"He who breaketh it shall lose his office and standing in the church" (3a). Whoever entered into the contemplated organization and then broke his agreement would, of course, be subject to the legal disabilities connected with the legal instrument. In addition it is here ordained that he shall lose both his office and his membership in the church.

"The church may stand independent above all other creatures beneath the celestial world" (3d). It is to be noted that the church is to be independent rather than its individual members.

At the end of paragraph 3 the specific instruction concerning the organization for the temporal affairs of Zion breaks off suddenly and the prophetic utterance moves

286

from the immediacy of the present to the vast ranges of eternity. Yet the transition is not without significance, for the temporal principles which have been discussed are grounded in the eternal verities now mentioned. Consider the promises made to the faithful:

Revelation—"I will lead you along" (4b).
Achievement—"The kingdom is yours and the blessings thereof" (4b).
Real wealth—"The riches of eternity are yours" (4b). "He that hath eternal life is rich."
Glory—"He who receiveth all things, with thankfulness, shall be made glorious" (4c).
Temporal power—"The things of this earth shall be added unto him, even an hundredfold, yea, more" (4c).

GENERAL NOTES

Adam-ondi-Ahman. This name was given later to a small city located about three miles from Jameson, Missouri, and about sixty miles north of Independence, Missouri. It was first settled by Lyman Wight in 1836 or 1837 and was named by Joseph Smith in the spring of 1838 when the city plat was first selected. Its earlier name had been Spring Hill. A stake was organized at Adam-ondi-Ahman on June 28, 1838, with John Smith, Reynolds Cahoon, and Lyman Wight as the stake presidency and Vinson Knight as the stake bishop. The place was destroyed by an armed mob in October of the same year, and the settlers suffered untold hardships. The location of Adam-ondi-Ahman now has a historical marker.[3]

Michael. The name "Michael" means "like unto God." In an earlier revelation, Michael is identified as "Adam, the father of all, the prince of all, the ancient of days,"[4] and again as the archangel who will sound his trump to call forth the dead before the earth shall pass away.[5] It is presumed that these are the same person. In this revelation we are told that God "hath appointed Michael,

287

and established his feet, and set him up on high; and given unto him the keys of salvation, under the counsel and direction of the Holy One."[6] A letter from Joseph Smith indicates that Michael conferred the keys of his dispensation on the prophet of these last days.[7] Michael, the archangel, is also to lead the hosts of heaven to victory in the final conflict with the Devil.[8]

In connection with these statements of the revelations concerning Michael, we shall do well to consider also the references in Jude 9 and Revelation 12:7 and possibly Daniel 12:1, although this latter reference may be modified by the earlier references to Michael in Daniel 10:13, 21. But we should remember that the name "Michael" also is applied to an Asherite,[9] two Gadites,[10] a Gershonite Levite,[11] a descendant of Issachar,[12] a captain of Manasseh,[13] the father of Omni,[14] the son of Jehoshaphat,[15] and the father of Zebadiah.[16]

It would appear that Michael, the prince and the archangel, is a person of great spiritual stature who has played and is to play a major part in the drama of human destiny. A shadow of doubt exists as to whether all the statements in the Doctrine and Covenants and those in Jude and Revelation refer to the same person, some students holding that Michael means any person who is "like unto God" and that Adam was only one such person. This doubt is strengthened somewhat by the wide use of the name "Michael" in other scripture connections and by the use of the name "Elias" to refer to several persons.[17]

---

[1]Section 38:4. [2]I Peter 1:22. [3]Church History 2:153, 154, 156. [4]Section 26:2. [5]Section 28:7. [6]Section 77:3. [7]Appendix C(110):20:21, see also Section 104:28. [8]Section 85:35, [9]Numbers 13:13. [10]I Chronicles 5:13, 14. [11]I Chronicles 6:40. [12]I Chronicles 7:3. [13]I Chronicles 12:20. [14]I Chronicles 27:18. [15]II Chronicles 21:2-4. [16]Ezra 8:8. [17]Malachi 4:5; Matthew 11:14; Romans 11:2, etc.

SECTION 78

The revelation was given at Hiram, Portage County, Ohio, in March 1832 nearly three years before the organization of the distinctively missionary quorums of the church. It provides that Jared Carter shall be directed in missionary work by the Comforter. This instruction is similar to that given in Section 75:4. Today, with the Church more fully organized, similar direction usually comes through the administrative officers of the church. But this does not eliminate the need for the ministry of the Holy Spirit.[1]

Prior to this time, Jared Carter had been ordained a priest in accordance with instructions received June 7, 1831,[2] and had done some missionary work in the East. He accepted the appointment made in this revelation and discharged the mission effectively. Later he was associated with Hyrum Smith and Reynolds Cahoon on the Kirtland Temple building committee. He became a member of the first Standing High Council of the church at its organization February 17, 1834, and after the exodus from Kirtland became a member of the high council at Far West, April 7, 1838.

---

[1]Section 104:12, 13, 16. [2]Section 52:9.

SECTION 79

This revelation was received at Hiram, Portage County, Ohio, March 1832, where the prophet was engaged in the revision of the Holy Scriptures.

Stephen Burnett and Eden Smith, who are mentioned here, also are mentioned in Section 75:5, although their ministerial companions were then Ruggles Eames and Micah B. Welton respectively.

With Kirtland as the headquarters of church activities, it was desirable that the gospel be preached throughout the surrounding country. Others of the ministry who had contacts in specific places were sent to these places, but these two men, not having any such specific contacts, were left free to travel as wisdom and revelation should direct. We have no record of their subsequent activities, but it is probable that they went from village to village within a comparatively short distance of Kirtland. Note that the essence of their ministry was to be testimony. They were witnesses and must speak what they knew.

SECTION 80

The revelation in this section is the last of the four received by Joseph during March 1832 while he was staying at the home of John Johnson at Hiram, Portage County, Ohio.

Joseph Smith, Jr., had been ordained president of the high priesthood at the conference held at Amherst, Lorain County, Ohio, January 25, 1832, and the further organization of the Presidency is projected in this revelation. Elder Williams was ordained a high priest at this time, but for some reason his ordination as counselor in the Presidency was delayed until March 18, 1833, ten days after the revelation of March 8, 1833.

The president of the church is president of the high priesthood and of the quorum of the First Presidency. His counselors are joined with him in the work of presiding and are members of the quorum of the First Presidency. As such they "are equal with him in holding the keys of this last kingdom."[1]

The instructions to F. G. Williams in this section are essentially those which pertain to him as a counselor, that is, as a support and adviser to Joseph, although his ministry as a member of the Presidency is given passing notice. This latter phase of his work is more fully covered in the revelation calling him to active and immediate participation in the work of the Presidency.

¹Section 87:3.

SECTION 81

In accordance with the instruction previously given,¹ Joseph Smith, Jr., Newel K. Whitney, and others left Hiram, Ohio, on April 1, 1832, for Missouri. They were joined on the way by Sidney Rigdon and later by Titus Billings and a company of Saints journeying to Independence. Here a general council of the church convened April 26, 1832, and important business matters were transacted. Among other things Joseph was acknowledged president of the high priesthood according to the ordination received at the Amherst, Ohio, conference January 25, 1832.² This revelation was given about this time.

"Inasmuch as you have forgiven one another your trespasses" (1a). This initial statement evidently alludes to the hard feelings which had existed between Bishop Edward Partridge, who was in charge at Independence, and Sidney Rigdon, scribe and close associate of Joseph Smith. But it is extended immediately to include other matters which had hampered the development of the work in Zion.

"Refrain from sin lest sore judgments fall upon your heads" (1c). It is significant that in this revelation, given a full year before the expulsion of the Saints from Jackson County, the Saints are enjoined specifically to "refrain from sin lest sore judgments fall." This harmonizes well with Section 98:1-3, given after the expulsion. Both revelations state that the basic reason for the non-success of Zion was not persecution from without but failure of those within.

One of the outstanding sins of this period was failing to abide by the specific instruction of the Lord regarding the order of gathering. This had been stated clearly in the

291

preceding August,[3] "Firstly, the rich and the learned, the wise and the noble." This instruction had been reinforced by the specific injunctions of the Presidency and Bishopric.

"Go your ways and sin no more; but unto that soul who sinneth shall the former sins return" (2). By failing to repent, or by returning to their sins after a brief period of repentance, the Saints not only became liable for their new disobedience to the law but also fell into the way of destruction because of the renewed strength of their earlier sins. The instruction in this paragraph is fundamentally important. It applies in every field of life, today as well as when this revelation was given.[4]

"I, the Lord, am bound when ye do what I say, but when ye do not what I say, ye have no promise" (3b). This applies directly to the concerns of Zion, but it also applies to every other field. The priesthood, for example, have many wonderful promises of divine benediction and protection, but these promises are conditional and will be vindicated only when the priesthood observe the commands of God in all things.

This was a period of intense persecution. Joseph wrote that the pioneers were "settling among a ferocious set of mobbers, like lions among wolves"; it is highly probable, therefore, that the names (4a) were used to avoid informing their enemies of their plans.

"You are to have equal claims on the properties" (4e). In harmony with the pattern here set forth, Oliver Cowdery and Martin Harris, who lived in Independence, and Joseph Smith, Sidney Rigdon, and N. K. Whitney, who were located at Kirtland, entered into a joint stewardship agreement, looking toward the relief of the poor at both centers. They were not to draw identical amounts from the treasury but to have equal claims on their joint properties for the discharge of the responsibilities over which they severally presided and for their individual needs. The surplus gained through their joint functioning was to be placed in the Lord's storehouse.

"This order I have appointed to be an everlasting order

292

unto you... as you sin not" (5a). This does not mean necessarily that the local details of this organization must be observed without change. But the fundamental principles of joint legal and spiritual responsibility, of stewardship practice, and of consecration of the surplus, are permanent and will be operative whenever the people of God are living the celestial law.

The Saints evidently took quite seriously the instruction that those who transgressed this covenant should be dealt with according to the laws of the church and delivered over to the buffetings of Satan until the day of redemption (5). Part of the charge against Oliver Cowdery was that he had sold his lands in Missouri in contravention of the commandments of God. On being found guilty, he was excommunicated from the church.

"Leave judgment alone with me, for it is mine and I will repay" (6a). Some of the Saints were indignant and resentful because of the persecutions heaped on them in Missouri. And truly, if ever they were likely to have just cause for resentment, this was the time. Against such a background, the inspired wisdom of the instruction here given is clearly apparent. Vengeance has nothing constructive to offer any of us.

"The kingdom is yours... if you fall not from your steadfastness" (6c). The early Saints were warned repeatedly of the sins which would destroy them and were promised as repeatedly that the kingdom would be given to them in spite of all outside opposition if they would but do the will of God. The same assurance has come to the people of God in every age.

NOTES ON THE GATHERING

The gathering continued as reported in the November issue of *The Evening and the Morning Star:*

There is a great anxiety manifested to learn how the church of Christ prospers, since it commenced settling in the western part of the state of Missouri. To satisfy this inquiry, and more especially to

publish the truth upon the great subject, that none may be deceived by flying reports, we shall endeavor to give all the information in our possession. Since the gathering commenced, which is a little over a year, the number of the disciples who have come from the East and who have been baptized in this region is 465
Children and those not members, about 345
Total 810

By March 1833 five hundred and thirty-four Saints had "covenanted to keep the commandments of the Lord and walk in his statutes blameless with thanksgiving forever." The revelations of God and directions of the officials intrusted with the application of the law of consecration and stewardship were accepted and complied with by many of those who came to Zion. However, some persisted in purchasing land for themselves and conducting their temporal affairs without regard to the Order of Enoch over which Bishop Partridge presided, which by revelation was organized to regulate and establish the temporal affairs of the Saints in Zion.[5]

---

[1]Section 77:2. [2]Church History 1:249. [3]Section 58:3. [4]See Ezekiel 18:24. [5]*Journal of History*, Volume 16, pages 278-280.

SECTION 82

The council in Zion continued several days. During this time the brethren were organized according to the instruction in the revelation of April 26, and arrangements were made for supplying the Saints with stores in Missouri and Ohio. Plans also were perfected for printing the revelations, a hymnbook, and a monthly paper (*The Evening and the Morning Star*). The revelation which is now Doctrine and Covenants 82 was given April 30, 1832.

As the work of organizing stewardships continued, many practical problems arose, and Joseph remained in Independence listening to questions and complaints and endeavoring to lay the foundation for what was yet to be done. Naturally in those pioneer times, when the loss of a husband and father meant that women and children must face hardships alone, the question of the security of widows and orphans under stewardship conditions soon came to the fore.

"The laws of the church concerning women and children" (1a). These include the following:

The law of marital affection.[1]
The law relating to wives who are not members of the church.[2]
The law on the blessing of children.[3]
The law on the teaching of children.[4]
The law on the salvation of children.[5]
The law on the baptism of children.[6]
Note that Paul teaches that any man who "provideth not for his own. . .he hath denied the faith, and is worse than an infidel."[7]

Widows, if faithful, have the same standing under the law of stewardships that they would have if their husbands were alive, except that their contributions and needs are necessarily different. The basic rule of contribution according to ability and support according to need applies here as elsewhere.

Women not members of the church are safeguarded in their inheritance by their legal title in that inheritance, for the property which legally belonged to their husbands is legally transmitted to them regardless of church affiliation. If they do not belong to the church and prefer not to come under the stewardship law, their rights are therefore conserved under the law of the land rather than under the law of stewardship.

The needs of children whose parents are members of the church are part of the needs of their respective families and should be supplied on the usual stewardship basis until they become of age. After they become of age such young people can enter upon independent stewardship activities according to their desires and abilities. If they do not become stewards, they should be self-sustaining, not being a charge on the stewardship of their parents if they are not in sympathy with the stewardship purpose.

Children under age, whose parents are dead, become the wards of the church. If their parents lived the stewardship law, the children have rightful claim upon the church. If their parents were not stewards, then such help as is given them pending their maturity is aid.

There is one limitation which necessarily applies in all stewardship concerns. The security of individual stewards is related directly to the stability of the total stewardship group. Lack of integrity or skill or foresight on the part of some stewards may seriously handicap other stewards, no matter how faithful these others may have been. The organization of stewardships is important; but the integrity, skill, and foresight available to the whole group is even more important. Names are not enough; Zion can be built only by men who are "stewards indeed."

---

¹Sections 42:7; 49:3. ²Section 74:1. ³Section 17:19. ⁴Sections 55:2; 68:4. ⁵Sections 28:13; 63:13; 74:3. ⁶Section 68:4. ⁷I Timothy 5:8.

SECTION 83

In August and September the elders returned to Kirtland from their several missions in the East, and on Saturday and Sunday, September 22 and 23, 1832, this revelation was received in the presence of six of them. It is now put in chronological sequence with the other revelations, but in the 1835 edition it was placed near the beginning—Section 4—because of its importance in connection with priesthood organization and government.

"The city New Jerusalem...shall be built, beginning at

the Temple Lot" (1c). The location of the "New Jerusalem" is here definitely established at Independence, Missouri, and it is said that the gathering will begin at "this place, where a temple is to be built within one generation." "This place" may be either the place just spoken of (Independence) or the place where the revelation was being received (Kirtland), although the consensus has been that Independence was the place intended.[1]

A person who attempts to translate from English into a less exact language comes sooner or later to a word for which there is no single word in the other tongue. He then has to stop and explain his meaning in some detail. Something akin to this apparently happened to Joseph when he was receiving and recording this revelation. After stating that the glory of the Lord should rest upon his house, he wished to continue that the "sons of Moses and also the sons of Aaron shall offer an acceptable offering and sacrifice in the house of the Lord." But the nature of the priesthood held by these sons of Moses and Aaron became so apparent to him that it seemed to crowd him into speech. The revelation, therefore, breaks off at this point and endeavors to give the significance of the priesthood held by Moses and Aaron before proceeding with the discussion of the priesthood in the temple. The student should note the interpolation which begins in paragraph 2 with the words, "according to the holy priesthood," and ends in paragraph 6 with the words, "upon the consecrated spot, as I have appointed." This interpolation can be studied by itself, and the forepart of paragraph 2 then can be regarded as joining the latter part of paragraph 6.

"The sons of Moses, according to the holy priesthood" (2c) are evidently those holding the Melchisedec priesthood. This priesthood was transmitted from Abel to Noah through those denominated "sons of God."[2] By him it was brought across the flood,[3] and it remained with his descendants as long as they continued in the true order of worship. It belonged of right to Abraham, who was a descendant of Noah through Shem.[4] Abraham received the priesthood

from Melchisedec, and in his day Esaias also was set apart to this priesthood. From Esaias the spiritual authority descended in regular order to Jethro and from him to Moses.[5]

"The Lord confirmed a priesthood also upon Aaron" (3a). Note "confirmed." The Aaronic priesthood did not originate with Aaron, nor in his day, neither was it prepared for him, but he for it.[6] The Lord said unto Moses: "Take Aaron, thy brother, and his sons with him, from among the children of Israel that he may minister unto me in the priest's office." The office was all ready and was waiting for an occupant.[7]

Moses "sought diligently" to persuade the children of Israel to respond to the authority and the opportunities of the Melchisedec ministry (4a) but they hardened their hearts, and it was therefore impossible for them to enter into the fullness of divine glory. Since they would not respond, the Lord took the holy priesthood from their midst.* The Aaronic priesthood, holding authority of great but secondary importance, still remained with them, but now the emphasis was on "carnal commandments" rather than upon the higher law of the Melchisedec priesthood. The situation would be roughly parallel if in our own time the high priesthood should be removed from the church and the Bishopric should direct the affairs of the church by right of their Aaronic presidency.

The lesser, or Aaronic, priesthood administers the gospel of preparation: repentance, baptism for remission of sins, and tithing. These are all important, but their purpose is to prepare the way for a richer life properly administered by the Melchisedec priesthood. If we confine ourselves to these things, we are living on the plane of the Aaronic

---

*I have found it difficult to understand the full meaning of this statement, although its general intent is clear enough. Is the "holy priesthood" referred to in Section 83:4c the high priesthood only, or did it include the eldership? Seeming exceptions to the most inclusive interpretations of the statement have been noted from time to time, but have little importance for today. The basic principle of the interdependency of priesthood and the Saints is, of course, always operative.

priesthood. We are in tune only with the opportunities of the present dispensation when we use these "carnal commandments" as a means of preparation for the fuller and richer life which the Melchisedec authority makes possible. The children of Israel were required to live under this Aaronic priesthood ministry "until John, whom God raised up" to prepare the way for the coming of the Lord. It was a "schoolmaster" to prepare them for greater things.

"John, whom God raised up" (4d). Apostle Heman C. Smith made the following comments on the work of John the Baptist:

The events to attend the mission of this forerunner were not fulfilled when John and Christ were upon earth; so we must look for a second appearing of John to prepare the way before him, ere Christ "shall suddenly come to his temple," "sit as a refiner and purifier of silver," purifying "the sons of Levi [the priesthood] and purge them as gold and silver, that they may offer unto the Lord an offering in righteousness" ere the "offering of Judah and Jerusalem be pleasant unto the Lord, as in the days of old, and as in former years"; and ere the Lord "come near to you to judgment." As he mingled with the fathers in turning their hearts to the children, so in some way must the influence of his ministry be felt among the children in turning their hearts to the fathers; and no system of religion having for its object the restoration of gospel peace, power, and love is the proper one unless the personal ministry of John the Baptist is connected therewith. . . .

Thus John came in the spirit and power of Elias (Elijah) who holds the keys, to point our fathers to our day; and then, after the darkness of the past, came again to ordain these men, Joseph and Oliver, to the power of priesthood, that in the spirit of Elias they could call our minds back to the pure gospel principles received and enjoyed by our fathers. Thus the prophecies are fulfilled, and the hopes of the fathers realized in our day, as thousands have testified and can testify, to their great satisfaction and joy. It is marvelous in our eyes, yet true.[8]

While *"the offices of elder and bishop are necessary appendages belonging unto the high priesthood"* (5a), the bishop stands at the head of the Aaronic priesthood.[9] At the present time the bishops of the church are high priests acting in the office of bishop by virtue of the provision that a high priest can act in any office in the church in cases of emergency.[10] Their calling is explained more fully in Sections 128:2, 3, 129:8, 149:3, and 149A:1-4.

"The sons of Moses and of Aaron . . . whose sons are ye" (6b). According to this paragraph, the sons of Moses are men who hold the Melchisedec priesthood, and the sons of Aaron are those who officiate in the Aaronic priesthood.

"Sanctified by the Spirit unto the renewing of their bodies" (6c). As the members of these two priesthoods enter fully into their ministry, so this ministry shapes their lives and they become the children of Abraham (the "father of the faithful") and the spiritual successors of Moses and Aaron. In them the church and the kingdom become as one, for the church is living up to its highest privileges, and they are "elect of God" since he chooses them as his ministers in accomplishing his great purposes. This paragraph should be compared with paragraph 3 of the following section. From the two paragraphs together, it appears that the lineage of the priesthood is recognized in their calling. If this is so, "the renewing of their bodies" seems to indicate a quickening of inherited attitudes and abilities.

"All they who receive this priesthood receiveth me" (6e). The blessings of the priesthood are not confined to those who officiate in the ministry, but are extended to those who accept and respond to the ministrations of the priesthood. These become heirs of God's promise to the faithful, the "oath and covenant of my Father." The revelation affirms that God will never break the promises which he has made to the righteous, but whoever breaks his part of a covenant made with God, after having properly received this covenant, will not have forgiveness in this world nor in the world to come.[11]

"Everyone that hearkeneth to the voice of the Spirit, cometh unto God" (7d). Our heavenly Father has many forces at work in the world, many of which we do not readily recognize. But one purpose dominates all his work, and one call sounds through all his messages to mankind. Everything which is of God leads men back to him, not merely to find him but to love and serve him.

300

"Your minds in times past have been darkened because of unbelief" (8a). Unbelief works that way. In the ordinary associations of life, we impose sufficient confidence and trust in our friends to accept their testimony at its face value and act as though this testimony were true. We do not think of asking our friends to show their credentials every time they tell us anything. This does not mean that we are uncritical but that we are affirmatively interested. We expect the things that they tell us to be true and helpful, and because of this attitude, we receive a great deal of help from them. Our spiritual attitude, on the contrary, is frequently negatively critical. Our minds are not open to the revelations of God. The door to our understanding has to be forced. Openmindedness is not blind credulity but it involves readiness to be taught, and this is a basic requirement for spiritual light and growth.

"You have treated lightly the things you have received" (8a). This was addressed to a group of elders who had just returned from a mission requiring great sacrifices of them, but was immediately broadened to include the whole church. And, of course, the principle is valid today. Treating lightly the things of God is as destructive as unbelief. The businessman grows because he treats seriously any opportunity to make a profit. Men grow in the same way in spiritual things because they recognize the primary importance of spiritual facts and influences. The Jews became one of the outstanding nations of antiquity because they regarded spiritual realities as much too serious to be treated lightly. The condemnation which neglect entails includes, at the least, the loss of the guidance of the Spirit which accompanies devout study of the word of God.

"The works" (11) enumerated here are not to be boasted of before the world. They are signs *"following,"* and are for the church rather than for nonbelievers. They are resultants of righteousness and should not be sought as ends in themselves. No one should be encouraged to join the church for the sake of these gifts but in order to do the works of righteousness.

301

"They who believe not. . . shall be damned" (12a). In every field of activity, power comes through obedience to law. This is true in the spiritual realm as well as in all others. God has therefore revealed the laws of his kingdom for our guidance, and those who will not obey these laws are damned by their own willfulness. Those who do not come into the light, stumble and are hurt in the darkness where they have chosen to remain. That is what damnation is.

"Your brethren in Zion (are to be upbraided] *for their rebellion against you at the time I sent you"* (12d). The difficulties were not all on one side, however, as the following quotation will show:

> On March 26, 1833, a council of high priests convened at Kirtland to consider the welfare of the church in Zion. The revelation, letter and epistle had awakened a satisfactory response from the brethren in Zion, but a new disturbance had arisen. Some of the traveling high priests and elders went up to Zion, claiming for themselves as much power and authority to set in order and regulate the branches as those set apart and appointed to preside over the branches. The council discussed this matter and it was decided that it was according to the revelations already given that the elders when they arrived in Zion were to be submissive to those appointed to preside in Zion. Those appointed to build up Zion were, Oliver Cowdery, W. W. Phelps, John Whitmer, Algernon S. Gilbert, Bishop Edward Partridge, and his two counselors, Isaac Morley and John Corrill. This decision gave general satisfaction and the elders soon saw the beauty of every man standing in his place.

Note the promises to the faithful missionaries contained in paragraphs 13, 14, 15, and 16.

"Take no thought for the morrow" (14a). The primary task of the missionary is to preach the gospel of salvation in the kingdom of God. He must let nothing else interfere with this. His major concern must not be to accumulate the things of this world in which there is no final security but, rather, he must believe in his message enough to trust his own life and livelihood to it. This does not mean improvidence. It means hard work in line with his ministry, and then faith in God and the people to provide what is necessary.

302

"Treasure up in your mind continually the words of life" (14d). This statement modifies very definitely the following sentence: "It shall be given unto you in the very hour that portion that shall be meted unto every man." Men who are under the responsibility of preaching should be constant and inquiring students of the word of God and the needs of men. The Lord promises to quicken the understanding gained in such studies. He does not promise to supply that which the ministry can get for themselves by active sharing in the responsibilities of their ministry.

"He that receiveth you not, go away from him alone by yourself, and cleanse your feet. . .and bear testimony of it" (16c). It is unthinkable that the Lord wants his ministers to be a vengeful people. If, however, a minister follows this instruction scrupulously, and cleanses his feet as a ceremonial indication that he has gone as far as he can and yet has been unsuccessful, he will do this only when he has made the most diligent effort to succeed in his mission. If he will enter into his ministry with an earnestness such as is implied in this instruction, many a conversion which now is dying stillborn will come to full life and power.

"The Lord hath brought again Zion" (17a). Note the frequent references to the songs of Zion in the various revelations.[13] Note, also, Isaiah 11:9, 12:1-6.

"The earth has travailed and brought forth her strength" (17b). Dean Inge of London, England, a distinguished philosopher and theologian, wrote:

The doctrine that the heavenly bodies have an endowment of soul life does not seem to me to be ridiculous or improbable. Each of our bodies is a world populated by millions of minute living beings. We are not conscious of them, nor are they conscious of the unitary life of the organism to which they belong. Why should not our planet have a life of its own, thinking thoughts of which we know nothing?[14]

"Take with you those who are ordained unto the lesser priesthood" (20a). This principle was followed in the New Testament, and we note such young ministers as Timothy, Titus, John, and Mark.

303

"The deacons and teachers should be appointed to watch over the church, to be standing ministers unto the church" (22). Standing ministers should note the following:

We cannot always live in great moments. In ministerial life—you had better face it—you will be nearly always overtired; yet when people come to you you must have good news for them, whether you "feel like it" at the time or not. It will often happen that people want us most when we are least fit for their demands. All this means that we cannot live on emotion. We must try to work through to that sheer certainty of moral and intellectual conviction which will keep us going in the dark days. "They shall not be confounded in the perilous time, and in the days of dearth they shall have enough."[15]

"The bishop, Newel K. Whitney, also, should travel round about and among all the churches, searching after the poor" (23a). Newel K. Whitney was bishop of Kirtland. In accordance with this instruction, he and Joseph visited New York, Albany, and Boston. The close relation between missionary activity and Zion-building, as expressed in this paragraph, is noteworthy.

"Verily I say unto you, the rest of my servants, Go ye forth as your circumstances shall permit" (24a). Evidently in 1832 no members of the priesthood were exempt from missionary duty. All were called to minister and bear testimony in accordance with their calling and opportunities.

---

[1]For a discussion of this point see Heman C. Smith: *Journal of History,* Volume 11, pages 150-153. [2]Genesis 6:2; Job 1:6. [3]Genesis 8:20. [4]Genesis 11:1. [5]Section 83:2. [6]Exodus 28:1. [7]Exodus 19:20-24. [8]*Autumn Leaves,* April 1891. [9]Section 104:8. [10]Section 104:7, 8. [11]Section 76:4. [12]Isaiah 29:9, 10. [13]Sections 24:3; 45:14; 66:5; 98:4. [14]Quoted in the *Christian Century,* Oct. 27, 1927, p. 1260. [15]*Theology and Life,* by F. R. Barry.

SECTION 84

Joseph Smith spent the late summer of 1832 in translating and in ministering to the church in Ohio, and in the early fall he made a hurried trip to Boston and Albany with Bishop

Whitney. He returned home to Kirtland Tuesday, November 6, 1832, the day young Joseph was born, exactly a month prior to the receipt of this revelation.

The first child of Joseph Smith had been born in Harmony, Pennsylvania, July 1828, and had died at birth. Early in 1831 twin children of Joseph died at birth in Kirtland. Joseph Smith III was therefore the fourth child of the prophet and of his only wife, Emma, but was the oldest to grow to maturity. After the twins died at Kirtland, Joseph and Emma adopted the twin children of Elder John Murdock, and one of these, Julia, grew to womanhood. The other died in infancy.

Note the parallel between this exposition of the parable of the wheat and the tares and the exposition in Matthew 13:24-30, 37-43. Matthew says that the Sower is the Son of Man, and this will be reconciled with the revelation when we realize that he works through the apostles who are sowing the seed under his direction.

While Section 83:6 speaks of those who become the sons of Moses and of Aaron through obedience, this section speaks of those in whom the priesthood has *"continued through the lineage of your* [their] *fathers"* and who *"are lawful heirs, according to the flesh."* Here is a definite statement of the law of lineage which applies to the priesthood in general and not necessarily to any particular office.[1] It seems, according to this, that lineage is twofold, both spiritual and physical, and that frequently, if not always, in effective priesthood the two lines of lineage are conjoined, i.e., that effective ministers for God are "heirs according to the flesh. . . hid from the world with God in Christ" who are also sons of the priesthood through their active functioning therein. It is because of this necessity for combining lineal right with actual functioning that paragraph 4 goes on to state, "blessed are ye *if* ye continue in my goodness."

---

[1]Discussed in *True Succession in Church Presidency,* Heman C. Smith, pages 51-52.

SECTION 85

The revelation given at Kirtland, Ohio, and dated December 27, 1832, is known, at times, as "The Olive Leaf." This is probably because the prophet referred to it in this way in a letter to Elder William W. Phelps dated January 14, 1833. The revelation was given a few days after the prophecy on the Civil War, and the seriousness of that earlier revelation probably accounts in part for the earnest petitions of the Saints at this time and for their readiness to receive the word which was communicated to them.

The opening sentence of this revelation shows that this is one of the many given in response to specific petitions and needs. The basic conditions of revelation include the eagerness of the people for light and their urgent need for it. Both of these conditions were present at this time, and this remarkable revelation is the result.

"You, who have assembled yourselves together to receive his will concerning you" (1a). There is an interesting difference between the attitudes implied in Section 41:1b where the elders were instructed to "assemble yourselves together to agree upon my word" and this revelation which indicates that they were assembled to receive the divine word. There were a number of reasons for this change. Perhaps the most important was that in the intervening months the prophetic calling of Joseph had been vindicated upon many occasions. Note, in this connection, the attempt of William E. McLellin to duplicate a revelation at the time when the Book of Commandments was presented for publication.[1]

"The Lord of Sabaoth" (1b). This term is used many times in the Old Testament and twice in the New Testament.[2] It is possibly best understood as "the Lord of Hosts" or, more familiarly, as "the Almighty."

"The Holy Spirit of promise" (1c). This Spirit is to the disciples of all ages what the Lord Jesus was to the

306

disciples who were with him. The Spirit gives a foretaste of eternal life in the life that now is. It is the power which gives us

all things that pertain unto life and godliness, through the knowledge of him that hath called us unto glory and virtue; whereby are given unto us exceeding great and precious promises; that by these ye [we] might be partakers of the divine nature, having escaped the corruption that is in the world through lust.[3]

"*Eternal life, even the glory of the celestial kingdom*" (2a). Celestial glory is the fullness of eternal life. As we respond to the leadings of the Spirit, we come to know truly our heavenly Father and his Son, Jesus Christ, and not just to know about them. So we take on the nature of God, who is eternal. We become, in truth, members of the church of the Firstborn. We are so prepared for the life which lies beyond mortality that the change occurring at death becomes an incident rather than a crisis. In its most significant aspects, therefore, we can enter into eternal life now, and can receive a foretaste of celestial glory even while we await the fullness of our coming rapture.

The wonderful insight of paragraphs 2 and 3 ties up directly with that of Section 83, paragraph 7, "The word of the Lord is truth, and whatsoever is truth is light, and whatsoever is light is Spirit, even the Spirit of Jesus Christ." Christ the Creator is manifest in the sun, the moon, the stars, the earth, and all the other creations of Divinity.

"*God . . . is in the bosom of eternity*" (3b). This sublime truth has been recognized by the servants of God all down the ages and in many lands. One of our modern poets has written:

This universe
Exists, and by that impossible fact
Declares itself a miracle; postulates
An infinite Power within itself, a Whole
Greater than any part, a Unity,
Implying every attribute of God.[4]

"*Through the redemption which is made for you, is*

brought to pass the resurrection from the dead" (4a). The teaching of the Book of Mormon is particularly important in this connection:

> "The death of Christ bringeth to pass the resurrection."[5]
> "The resurrection of Christ redeemeth mankind, yea, even all mankind, and bringeth them back into the presence of the Lord."[6]
> "The bodies and the spirits of men will be restored one to the other; and it is by the power of the resurrection of the Holy One of Israel."[7]

One of the most beautiful biblical statements in this field occurs in Paul's letter to the saints in Corinth:

Now is Christ risen from the dead, and become the firstfruits of them that slept. For since by man came death, by man came also the resurrection of the dead. For as in Adam all die, even so in Christ shall all be made alive.[8]

"The spirit and the body is the soul of man" (4a). Neither is complete without the other. They belong together, and "the resurrection from the dead is the redemption of the soul"—both body and spirit. This is true of the soul of man, and it is also true of the soul of Zion. The spirit of Zion is the Spirit of God at work in the lives of men, filling them with discontent with all that is less than the best and spurring them onward to build a worldwide brotherhood under the reign of Christ. This spirit of Zion needs to be clothed with a living body. It must be given actual visible form among men, that Zion may become a living soul.

It is unchristian to belittle the physical aspects of life. Our bodies are extremely important, for they may become the temples of the living God. Similarly no one should belittle the temporal organizations which are established among men in the process of building Zion. It is only through such organizations that we can give body and significance to our ideals of freedom and justice and brotherhood and godliness.

"It [the earth] *must needs be sanctified from all unrigh-*

teousness" (4c). It is a stimulating thought that the earth was made as a habitation for the righteous, and that the blights upon nature which make it seem "red in tooth and claw" are the results of lack of light and understanding brought about by our disobedience. This section teaches that the earth will yet fulfill its purpose, and that when it is "crowned with glory, even with the presence of God the Father" it will become in every way fitted for the habitation of those who are enlightened by the glory of his presence. When men are sanctified by the fullness of the celestial glory, then will the earth be ready for their habitation: "for this intent was it made and created; and for this intent are they sanctified."

"*They who are not sanctified through the law which I have given you . . . must inherit another kingdom*" (5a). If we abide the laws of the celestial kingdom, we can attain and enjoy the glory of that kingdom. If we shape our lives by the laws of a lesser kingdom, then this makes us fit subjects for that lesser kingdom. We can find no satisfaction in the kingdom whose laws we have not followed. If we have trained ourselves to enjoy cheap literature, then we cannot enjoy good literature. As ignorant men are out of place in the company of learned men, so are worldly men unable to enjoy the blessings of a spiritual environment.

"*The earth abideth the law of a celestial kingdom, for it filleth the measure of its creation*" (6a). Here is the basic law of the celestial kingdom, for us as well as for the earth. It is that we shall fill the measure of our creation. "God so loved the world that he gave his only begotten Son, that whosoever believeth in him should not perish but should have everlasting life."[9] We abide the law of the celestial kingdom, fill the measure of our creation, and fit ourselves to enjoy the presence of God and of the church of the Firstborn when we become willing that God shall spend our lives with that of his dear Son for the salvation of humanity.

Paragraphs 4 to 7

This part of the revelation contains a discussion of the

relation between law and achievement. Both in the natural world and in the spiritual world the great glory of any created thing is that it shall fully serve the purpose for which it was created. Thus there is a point of view from which it may be said the glory of a table is that it shall be an outstandingly good table, or the glory of a ship that it shall weather wind and tide. Similarly, the glory of the earth is that having been created for men, at their best, it shall bring forth rich life and shall prove a fitting habitation for the people of God.

Similarly, also, men who are created for the glory of God receive that glory in the measure that they are obedient to the laws of celestial life. If they fail to be thus obedient, they cannot enjoy celestial life nor bear its fruit. If they live up to the laws of the celestial kingdom, then their bodies partake of the quality of their lives and are quickened thereby. Those who live the telestial law are fitted only for the enjoyment of a telestial life, and any higher glory is beyond their comprehension and enjoyment.

This may be illustrated by saying that a man who has lived for his business, has learned the laws of industrial life and has found his delight there and nowhere else, comes to a place where he can find happiness only in business success and where his capacity for enjoyment of politics and music and pictures and the beauty of nature and of spiritual life is entirely atrophied. It is useless to bestow on him the gifts and opportunities in which an artist would be delighted. The artist, similarly, may become immersed in the beauties of physical life, but may have neither eye nor ear for the spiritual realities which lie behind these physical things. Such a man cannot be benefited by any offer of the joys of celestial glory, for he has fitted himself only for the joys of earthly beauty. But the man who has lived the celestial law can be quickened to enjoy a fullness of the glory which he has already begun to enjoy in part. Men of celestial quality inherit a world of celestial opportunity.

"That which is governed by law, is also preserved by

310

law, and perfected and sanctified by the same" (8a). In every field of life, the best comes through obedience to law. The orderly sequence of cause and event is at the basis of modern progress. It is of the very nature of God. But law should not be regarded as legal requirement. Law, as used here, refers to the true nature of the thing or situation involved. Without obedience to law, progress is impossible. Every man who is true to the purpose of his being will blossom into spiritual life and power. No man can secure such spiritual life and power by being untrue to the fundamental purposes of his creation.

"That which breaketh a law,...can not be sanctified by law, neither by mercy, justice, or judgment" (8b). Nothing will secure to us the results of abiding by the laws of life other than actually abiding by these laws. The function of justice and mercy and judgment is to inspire us to do this, for law is not hard and cold but is God's own means of guaranteeing power to men. Nothing makes anything right other than actual rightness. Obey the laws of life, and success will crown your efforts; ignore them, and you are doomed to fail.

"Unto every kingdom is given a law; and unto every law there are certain bounds also, and conditions" (9b). Success in any kingdom is achieved by obedience to the laws of that kingdom and in no other way. Thus intelligence is promoted through intelligence and wisdom through acting wisely; truth is akin to truth, and virtue has fellowship only with that which is virtuous; light seeks other light while the merciful have fellowship with those who are merciful; justice proceeds from one just act to another and promotes its own ends, while judgment is executed out of the laws of life. God is represented in the laws of the universe. When the observance of these laws brings celestial power and glory, God who set these laws in motion is thereby glorified.

"Any man who hath seen any or the least of these, hath seen God moving in his majesty and power" (12c). Indeed, no man has truly seen these heavenly bodies until he has seen God as the creator of their wonderful

life. In the same way, no man sees the true beauty of a garden who becomes so immersed in the glory of the flowers that he ignores the loving care of the Gardener who made them possible. Alfred Noyes writes in "Watchers of the Sky":

> What is all science then
> But pure religion, seeking everywhere
> The true commandments, and through many forms
> The eternal Power that binds all worlds in one?
> It is man's age-long struggle to draw near
> His Maker, learn his thoughts, discern his law—
> A boundless task, in whose infinitude,
> As in the unfolding light and law of love,
> Abides our hope, and our eternal joy.

"Seek me diligently and ye shall find me" (16c). In the light of the preceding instuction of this revelation, it is reasonable to suppose that one of the ways in which we can seek God is to study his handiwork. Our heavenly Father surely loves those who delight in his creation. It is a pity that some forget the Creator while they are studying the creation.

"If ye ask anything that is not expedient for you, it shall turn unto your condemnation" (16f). The point here is that prayer is a responsible spiritual exercise. If we pray thoughtlessly this turns to our condemnation in that we tend to think that our petitions have somehow committed God to something that we would not have asked for if we had been more aware of our situation before him. Thoughtless prayer becomes a sedative and an opiate, not a spiritual force. In this connection Paul wrote the saints in Rome:

The Spirit also helpeth our infirmities; for we know not what we should pray for as we ought; but the Spirit itself maketh intercession for us.[10]

"Sanctify yourselves that your minds become single to God" (18b). No one can become a great artist, no matter what his personal endowment might be, unless he dedicates himself to his art. He must hunger and thirst after beauty. So, also, no one can become a great spiritual artist overnight.

312

God may speak to us as he did Paul, but we can only become artists in the things of the kingdom as we constantly hunger and thirst after righteousness. Among other things, this requires those who wish to serve God acceptably to develop occasions for worship. Many spend more time on the daily news than on the Good News of the kingdom. This proportion is not conducive to sanctification.

"You who are the first laborers in this last kingdom . . . assemble yourselves together, and organize yourselves" (20a). In harmony with this instruction the school of the prophets was organized at Kirtland, Ohio, about two months later. Although the church was not yet three years old, those who assembled for instruction in the things of their ministry formed a notable company. They included Joseph, Hyrum, Samuel, and William Smith, Oliver Cowdery, David Whitmer, Sidney Rigdon, Parley P. Pratt, Orson Pratt, and Orson Hyde.

"Teach one another" (21). The following are suggested topics for study by the ministry:

> "The doctrine of the kingdom"—theology, the promises of the gospel.
> "The laws of the gospel"—church procedure.
> "Things in heaven"—spiritual realities and/or astronomy, meteorology, etc.
> "Things in earth"—biology, agriculture, botany, etc.
> "Things under the earth"—geology, mining, etc.
> "Things which have been"—history, philosophy.
> "Things which are"—current events.
> "Things which must shortly come to pass"—prophecy.
> "Things which are at home"—sociology, politics.
> "Things which are abroad"—international law, industry, travel, world affairs, race relations.
> "The wars and the perplexities of the nations"—international law, international peace.
> "The judgments which are on the land"—drought, cyclones, labor disputes, with their correctives.
> "Countries and kingdoms"—physical and political geography, languages, etc.

"It becometh every man who hath been warned, to warn his neighbor" (22a). Occasionally it is thought that we cannot reasonably expect men and women of education and culture to be active missionaries. This is a serious mistake induced by our own unwillingness to testify. These early church leaders of outstanding intelligence were instructed to "teach diligently" and to become "instructed more perfectly in theory, in principle, in doctrine" in order that they might become effective missionaries.

"Let those who are not the first elders continue in the vineyard" (23c). The school of the prophets was designed for the instruction of the leading elders of the church. This was not because the Lord wished to reserve the opportunities of education to a small group but because the circumstances of the times made it particularly important that the leaders of the church should be men of broad understanding combined with consuming missionary passion.

"Not many days hence" (24b). The paragraphs which follow chronicle the events of the last days (24-35).

> Physical phenomena.
>> The earth shall tremble and the moon be darkened; there will be earthquakes, thunder, lightning, tempests, tidal waves (25).
>
> Men's hearts shall fail them, for fear shall come upon all people (25).
>> The first trump (25).
>
> A great sign shall appear in heaven, and all people shall see it together (26).
>
> "The mother of abominations" shall be denounced (26).
>
> The curtain of heaven shall be unfolded, and the face of the Lord shall be unveiled (27).
>
> Saints who are alive will be quickened and caught up to meet the Lord.
>
> The righteous dead will also be caught up to meet him (27).

The second trump (28).

Announcing the redemption of those converted in the prison house.

The third trump (29).

Announcing "the judgment of those found under condemnation."

"These will not live again until the thousand years are ended."

The fourth trump (30).

Indicating these are to remain until the end, who remain filthy still.

The fifth trump (31).

Sounded by the angel "who committeth the everlasting gospel," announcing glory to God for ever and ever, and the coming of the hour of his judgment.

The sixth trump (32).

Announcing the fall of "the mother of abominations."

The seventh trump (33).

The triumphal announcement of the victory of the lamb of God, the crowning of his saints, and the dividing of their celestial inheritances among the people of God (33).

The end of time:

Satan shall be bound (35).

He shall not be loosed for a space of a thousand years.

Then, being loosed for a season, the Devil and his armies will be defeated and cast away to their own place.

"Seek learning even by study, and also by faith" (36a). Understanding is not a matter of the mind only but also of the heart; not just of intelligence but also of character. Those men can best understand the purposes of God who have faith in him and through faith come to share his way of life.

It is probable that there are more students in today's world than in any other time in history. There are more people, and there are more incentives to study. The admonition to "seek learning by study, and also by faith" is therefore particularly pertinent.

What we get out of our study depends on what we bring to it. So students are advised to read with questions in mind, approaching each paragraph as though it is one side of a conversation and asking "Why?" and "How?" and "Is that really so?"

What we learn from our study depends, also, on our faith—our basic response to the love of our heavenly Father who wants us to know him and the beauty and truth and goodness which he has to share with us. This attitude of faith is not something we put on in times of special need, such as our need to know or to be healed or to find comfort. Rather, it is our attitude toward life itself. It is life in the light of God. It is fundamental to our work and play and study and to everything we do and are.

Our heavenly Father has admonished us to seek learning. He has also called us to be men of faith. These are not two callings. They belong together.

"Cease from all your light speeches" (37a). In this connection study also Section 119:9.

"The ordinance of washing feet is to be administered by the president, or presiding elder of the church" (46a). In this connection Joseph Smith wrote:

On the twenty-third [February 1833], we again assembled in conference; when, after much speaking, singing, praying and praising God, all in tongues, we proceeded to the washing of feet (according to the practice recorded in the thirteenth chapter of John's Gospel), as commanded of the Lord. Each Elder washed his own feet first, after which I girded myself with a towel, and washed the feet of them all, wiping them with the towel with which I was girded.

THE SCHOOL OF THE PROPHETS

This school was opened in temporary quarters early in 1833 and was continued until the month of April, when it was closed until the fall. Frederick G. Williams, M.D., William E. McLellin, M.D., Sidney Rigdon, Orson Hyde, and Joseph Smith taught the common academic subjects.

The disruption of church affairs incident to the expulsion of the church from Jackson County, Missouri, made it impossible to hold the school during the winter of 1833-34. However, during the latter part of November 1834, the school opened its second session which continued until March 1835. Joseph Smith, Sidney Rigdon, and others delivered lectures, and study of the doctrine of the church occupied much of the time, although the elders also gave attention to history, geography, literature, and philosophy. It was during this winter that Joseph Smith and Sidney Rigdon delivered lectures on theology (The "Lectures on Faith") which subsequently were revised and published in the forepart of the book of Doctrine and Covenants.

The third winter session of the school was opened on Monday, November 2, 1835, and before the semester closed Hebrew, Greek, and singing had been added to the curriculum. Classes closed about the third week in March 1836, and the unsettled conditions of church affairs made it impossible for the work of this school to be resumed at this place. However, the church had scarcely become settled at Nauvoo, Illinois, following the expulsion from Missouri when steps were taken to secure a charter for the University of Nauvoo.

[1]Church History 1:224. [2]Romans 9:29, James 5:4. [3]II Peter 1:3, 4. [4]Alfred Noyes in "Watchers of the Sky." [5]Mormon 4:72. [6]Helaman 5:71. [7]II Nephi 6:29, 30. [8]I Corinthians 15:20-23. [9]John 3:16. [10]Romans 8:26.

SECTION 86

The revelation familiarly known as the "Word of Wisdom" was given to a council of twelve high priests at Kirtland on Wednesday, February 27, 1833. This inspired instruction is addressed primarily to the council to whom it was given and to the remaining Saints in Kirtland, but it also is addressed to the Saints in Zion. Careful study of the available

317

literature indicates quite clearly that the introduction is not intended to weaken the teaching of this revelation but to incline the Saints in Zion to give heed to it. They might not have done this without such an approach.[1]

"In consequence of evils and designs which do and will exist in the hearts of conspiring men in the last days" (1a). Pure food laws which have been passed in almost all civilized countries since this guidance was given indicate the justice of this indictment.

"And will exist" (1a). At times it has been suggested that the counsel given here is not needed in view of pure food laws subsequently adopted. This phrasing anticipates the continuance of "evils and designs" leading to food adulteration.

"Wine or strong drink. . . is not good" (1b). The church was many years ahead of the times in making this prohibition. It is interesting to note that a general assembly of the church held at Far West, Missouri, November 7, 1838, after an address by President Sidney Rigdon, voted unanimously not to support stores or shops selling spirituous liquors, tea, coffee, or tobacco. Joseph Smith was present and voted in support of the resolution.[2]

"Hot drinks are not for the body or belly" (1e). Hot drinks are here differentiated from wine and strong drinks. It is not likely that the early Saints interpreted "hot drinks" as meaning only tea and coffee, but it is practically certain that tea and coffee were specifically included under this heading. Hyrum Smith so stated in 1842. A work printed by John Corrill in 1839 states:

> For a general rule they (the Saints) exclude the use of ardent spirits, tobacco, tea, and coffee, in accordance with the revelation called the Word of Wisdom.

It should be noted that these prohibitions are not only desirable from a dietary point of view but also from an economic point of view. The expenditure of money for foods which do not nourish the body is a double waste.

"All wholesome herbs God hath ordained for the constitution, nature, and use of man, every herb in the season

318

thereof, and every fruit in the season thereof" (2a). The revelation does not say that fruits and herbs should not be used out of season. It is the wise provision of nature, however, that fruits and herbs are particularly beneficial and are most easily obtainable when they are in season in the various localities.

Meat: A number of the brethren had come into the church from the Shakers and had continued to urge that Christian people should abstain from the use of meat. Because of this, the Saints had been instructed as early as March, that "whoso forbiddeth to abstain from meat, that man should not eat the same, is not ordained of God."[3] Less than a week after the dedication of the land of Zion, and before the elders began their return journey, this instruction was repeated.[4] Now, once again, the Saints are told that "flesh, also" is "ordained for the use of man, with thanksgiving." A great many food specialists have found that large quantities of meat are not good for the human body. Some have therefore jumped to the conclusion that all flesh food, at all times, is injurious. The Word of Wisdom does not teach this, but, on the contrary, says that meat, in common with other foods, has been "ordained for the use of man." The extreme of urging that no meat be eaten at any time is no doubt preferable to the other extreme of overindulgence, but neither extreme is wise or necessary.

In warm weather fresh meats putrify rapidly unless kept under refrigeration. The eating of tainted meats often results in ptomaine poisoning. The wisdom of the warning is especially clear when we look back to conditions in 1833.

---

[1]Church History, Volume 1, pages 264-279. [2]Church History, Volume 2, page 120. [3]Section 49:3. [4]Section 59:4.

SECTION 87

The revelation to Joseph Smith, Jr., bearing the date of Friday, March 8, 1833, was received at Kirtland, Ohio.

"Thou art blessed from henceforth that bear the keys of the kingdom given unto thee" (1b). The word *keys* as used here, evidently has the significance of "authority" or "power to unlock." In this connection read Matthew 16:19.

"Through you shall the oracles be given to another; yea, even unto the church" (2a). The "oracles" here mean the communications, revelations, or messages delivered by Divinity to inspired men.[1] The meaning of the passage in question is that through Joseph, who held the authority of the prophetic office, the revelations and commandments of God would be given to the church. The word *oracles* may refer also to the persons through whom such inspired messages are received. If the word is used in this sense, the sentence would appear to mean that through Joseph shall other ministers (oracles) of God be given to the church. The remainder of the paragraph seems to indicate that the word is used with the former meaning, but the passage is true in both senses. Not only was the basic law of the church made clear through Joseph but he also called the men who occupied ministerial positions close to him, and in addition named his son as his own successor in the prophetic office.

"They are accounted as equal with thee in holding the keys of this last kingdom" (3a). In accordance with this instruction, the quorum of the First Presidency was organized on March 18, 1833. Joseph describes the ordination as follows:

On the eighteenth of March the high priests assembled in the school-room of the prophets and were organized according to revelation, in prayer by S. Rigdon. Doctor Hurlbut was ordained an elder; after which Elder Rigdon expressed a desire that himself and Brother F. G. Williams should be ordained to the office, to which they had

320

been called; viz., that of presidents of the high priesthood, and to be equal in holding the keys of the kingdom with Brother Joseph Smith, Junior, according to the revelation given on the eighth of March, 1833.

Accordingly I laid my hands on Brothers Sidney and Frederick and ordained them to take part with me in holding the keys of this last kingdom, and to assist in the presidency of the high priesthood, as my counselors; after which I exhorted the brethren to faithfulness, and diligence in keeping the commandments of God, and gave much instruction for the benefit of the Saints, with a promise that the pure in heart would see a heavenly vision; and after remaining a short time in secret prayer, the promise was verified; for many present had the eyes of their understandings opened by the Spirit of God so as to behold many things.[2]

The calling of Elders Rigdon and Williams (3a) completed the organization of the First Presidency in this dispensation. Among the children of Israel a similar organization was set up "according to the pattern shown to him in the mount,"[3] and had as its head a presidency of three—Moses, Aaron, and Hur.[4] So in the New Testament church we catch glimpses of a presiding group.[5]

While the revelation provides that the counselors in the First Presidency are to be equal with the president in holding the keys, the presiding elder nevertheless has prerogatives or duties which do not belong to his counselors, but which he exercises as Prophet, Seer, and Revelator.

"The keys of the school of the prophets" (3b). It is eminently fitting that the presidency of the high priesthood should preside over the preparatory activities of the priesthood, especially since these are of a spiritual as well as an intellectual nature. The Presidency are here confirmed in this important work.

"Every man shall hear the fullness of the gospel in his own tongue, and in his own language, through those who are ordained unto this power" (4). This worldwide preaching of the gospel of Christ can be accomplished only by the sacrificial ministry of an increasing number of men and women from every walk of life. Even if every person baptized into the church should become an ardent missionary, there would still be a stupendous work to be done. It cannot be done if the missionary task is restricted to the priesthood alone or to any group of the priesthood alone.

The principle here set forth is elaborated in Section 116:1b-c. Obviously the peoples of the various nations can hear the gospel message most clearly and persuasively when presented by those who talk their language and are acquainted with their customs and traditions.

"Continue in the ministry and presidency" (5a). Church Historian Heman C. Smith commented on this:

It appears from this revelation that the primary right of presiding over the church and of regulating and setting in order all the affairs of the same is resident in the First Presidency; and that the true philosophy of the organization is, that if others shall be appointed to those duties, these rights and prerogatives inhere in them in a secondary sense to be exercised under the direction and control of the First Presidency.[6]

"When you have finished the translation of the prophets" (5a). The Inspired Version of the New Testament had been finished February 2, 1833, but the Old Testament was not completed until July 2, 1833. It was not published in the lifetime of Joseph Smith. One reason may have been his desire to do further revision.

"Study and learn, and become acquainted with all good books" (5b). The church was growing rapidly, and it was important that its presiding officers should be familiar with the best thought of the day on a wide variety of subjects. It may be objected that the Lord could have directed Joseph so as to save him the hours of arduous study which are here commanded. The Lord prefers, however, to have his people grow through actual sharing in the work of Divinity. It is not the province of inspiration to save men from hard work but only to guide and supplement their efforts. Joseph did not merely need new ideas; he needed the growth which should come through studying these ideas against the background of his experiences in the gospel.

"And with languages, tongues, and people" (5b). The

322

following report of the signing of the Locarno Peace Pact is of interest here:

> Sir Austen [Chamberlain] signed the document with a pen of gold presented to him by his staff at Locarno. How much he owes to his perfect French and German is not easy to measure. I am inclined to suspect that a statesman who can speak these languages perfectly starts with a great advantage in such a conference. A very little experience of a polyglot assembly shows how much influence comes through the gift of tongues. Such a man, for example, as the archbishop of Sweden can speak with equal ease in at least four languages, and in any international assembly he starts with a handicap in his favor. If we want to seek peace in this modern world we shall have to learn each other's languages.

"Let your families be small" (6f). With many visitors coming and going in order to learn of the church, there was a tendency for the leading men to keep open house at all times. In some ways this was eminently desirable, but the privilege was likely to be abused by some who were either thoughtless or lazy. Since the leading ministers were depending on the church for support, the Lord counseled them in this matter, so that the money of the church would not be wasted.

"Vienna Jacques, should receive money to bear her expenses, and to go up unto the land of Zion" (7a). Sister Jacques was a widow of some means. In accordance with this instruction she went to Independence and there received an inheritance from Bishop Partridge. In June 1834 she was at Liberty, Missouri, and helped to care for the brethren who had been attacked by cholera.

"Your brethren in Zion begin to repent" (8b). A letter of conciliation had been written by the brethren in Independence under date of February 26, 1833, but this letter had not yet been received in Kirtland.

"I am not well pleased with my servant" (8c). The brethren mentioned here had been disturbed over precedence in authority and over the question of Joseph's relation to the work in Independence while he lived in Kirtland. These are apparently the things for which they are required to repent.

323

¹See *Webster's International Dictionary.* ²*Times and Seasons* 5:738; Church History 1:283. ³Hebrews 8:5. ⁴Exodus 24:14. ⁵Matthew 17:1-3; 26:37; Luke 8:51; Acts 12:17, 15:13. ⁶Church History 1:281.

SECTION 88

In the course of their work on the Holy Scriptures, Joseph and Sidney came to the Apocrypha and inquired whether this was to be incorporated in the revision. The revelation of March 9, 1833, given at Kirtland, Ohio, is the reply to this inquiry.

The word *apocrypha* in its wider application denotes spurious Hebrew literature, but technically it means books which were included in the Septuagint and Vulgate versions of the Bible but were not included in the Hebrew canon.

The Apocrypha of the Old Testament, as used by Protestants, includes the following books: First Esdras, Second Esdras, Tobit, Judith, Additions to Esther, Wisdom of Solomon, Ecclesiasticus, Baruch, the Song of the Three Holy Children, the History of Susannah and the Dragon, the Prayer of Manasses, 1 Maccabees, 2 Maccabees. Most of the books date from the first or second century B.C.

The New Testament Apocrypha refers to deliberate attempts to fill in the gaps of the New Testament story. There are gospels such as "The Gospel According to the Hebrews" and "The Gospel According to the Egyptians." Among extensions of the "Acts of the Apostles," we have "The Acts of Paul" and "The Acts of Thomas." Among the apocryphal epistles are "The Epistles of Paul to the Laodiceans and Alexandrians." And prominent among the early apocalyptic books ("Revelations") is "The Apocalypse of Peter."

The Apocrypha, while not of the same value as the Bible, nevertheless gives us a glimpse into the religious life and ideals of the Jewish people. Luther denied that the books of the Apocrypha were as sacred as the scripture but

deemed them valuable because of their good moral teachings. This latter attitude seems to be the one more closely
adopted by the Protestants. The sixth article of the Church
of England states that other books of the church may be
read for the sake of example and teaching but not for
the establishment of doctrine.

SECTION 89

As early as March 1832 the Lord had given direction
authorizing the organization of the Order of Enoch[1] for
the management of the affairs of the Bishopric both in Zion
and in Kirtland. At that time Newel K. Whitney, Joseph
Smith, Sidney Rigdon, Oliver Cowdery, and Martin Harris
had become members of the order. In this revelation,
given March 15, 1833, at Kirtland, Ohio, they are instructed
to admit to membership Frederick G. Williams who had
just been made a member of the First Presidency. It is
highly probable that Edward Partridge and Isaac Morley
were also members of the order.

---

[1]Section 77.

SECTION 90

On May 4, 1833, a conference of high priests assembled
in Kirtland to consider building a schoolhouse for the accom-
modation of the elders, who were to come together to
receive instruction regarding their ministry according to a
revelation given December 27, 1832.[1] By unanimous voice of
the conference, Hyrum Smith, Jared Carter, and Reynolds
Cahoon were appointed to obtain subscriptions for the
purpose of erecting such a building. Two days later,
Tuesday, May 6, 1833, the revelation bearing that date
was received at Kirtland, Ohio.

In connection with this section an early *Religio* quarterly written, I believe, by Elder Ralph Farrell, contained the following:

At this time slavery in two forms existed in the United States— spiritual and physical. Joseph Smith and his associates, under the direction of God, were struggling to arouse men and women from spiritual lethargy and Wendell Phillips, Garrison, Lovejoy, Whittier and other great men, also under the direction of God, were struggling to bring mental and physical freedom to thousands of slaves. Of these two men, Smith and Lovejoy would soon be called upon to give life itself as a sacrifice to the cause that they had espoused. The spirit of lawlessness, unrest, revolution was in the lives of men. At the time (May 6) the Prophet was receiving the revelations in sections 90 and 91, the President of the United States was being assaulted by Lt. Randolph. In the same month Texas began a war of independence from Mexico. At this time also William Gladstone made his maiden speech in Parliament, against slavery: and Daniel O'Connell was pleading most eloquently the cause of injured innocence in Ireland.[2]

"Shall see my face, and know that I am" (1a). This promise, we believe, will be vindicated fully at the second coming of Christ, but it has been partially fulfilled in the revelation of Jesus Christ to a number of his disciples since the date of this revelation. One such notable occasion was shortly after the dedication of the Kirtland Temple when on Sunday, April 3, 1836, Joseph Smith and Oliver Cowdery retired to the pulpit in the Kirtland Temple and had the experience which is described by Joseph in the following words:

The veil was taken from our minds, and the eyes of our understanding were opened. We saw the Lord standing upon the breastwork of the pulpit before us, and under his feet was a paved work of pure gold in color like amber. His eyes were as a flame of fire, the hair of his head was white like pure snow, his countenance shone above the brightness of the sun, and his voice was as the sound of the rushing of great waters, even the voice of Jehovah, saying: "I am the first and the last; I am he who liveth; I am he who was slain; I am your advocate with the Father. Behold, your sins are forgiven you, you are clean before me, therefore lift up your heads and rejoice, let the hearts of your brethren rejoice, and let the hearts of all my people rejoice who have, with their might, built this house to my name, for behold, I have accepted this house, and my name shall be here, and I will manifest myself to my people in mercy in this house;

yea, I will appear unto my servants, and speak unto them with mine own voice, if my people will keep my commandments, and do not pollute his holy house; yea, the hearts of thousands and tens of thousands shall greatly rejoice in consequence of the blessings which shall be poured out, and the endowment with which my servants have been endowed in this house; and the fame of this house shall spread to foreign lands; and this is the beginning of the blessing which shall be poured out upon the heads of my people. Even so. Amen."

"I am in the Father and the Father in me, and the Father and I are one" (1b). This is closely akin to the words of John in the Inspired Version:

> "I and my Father are one."—John 10:30.
> "No man cometh unto the Father but by me."—John 14:6.
> "He that hath seen me hath seen the Father."—John 14:9.
> "I am in the Father and the Father in me."—John 14:11.

The Book of Mormon teaches us:

> "Jesus is the Christ, the Eternal God."—II Nephi 11:78.
> "Redemption cometh through Christ the Lord, who is the very eternal Father."—Mosiah 8:91.
> "I am Jesus Christ, the Son of God. . . . I was with the Father from the beginning."—III Nephi 4:44, 45.
> "They did pray unto Jesus, calling him their Lord and their God."—III Nephi 9:19.
> "I am Jesus Christ. I am the Father and the Son."—Ether 1:77.

Concerning the Lord Jesus, this revelation also says:

> The Son was in the beginning before the world was.
> He is the creator of all things.
> He is God manifest in the flesh.
> He is the Word, the messenger of salvation, the light and the Redeemer of the world.

He is the Spirit of truth.

He is the light that lighteth every man that cometh into the world.

In him was the life of man and the light of man.

He received not the fullness of God at first and for this reason he is called the Son of God.

He received all power both in heaven and in earth.

The glory of the Father was with him, for he dwelt in him.

The Father and the Son shared the work of creation. They are one in the work of redemption and are united in every purpose. Yet the Son is the active agent in the work of redemption, and while the Father participated in this work, it was the Son who divested himself of the garments of Infinity and, by accepting the limitations of humanity, growing from grace to grace, and condemning sin in the flesh, wrought the salvation of those who put their trust in him. In spite of all our attempts at explanation, these great truths will continue to be mysterious for they partake of Infinity; but we catch here and there a glimpse of the majesty and glory and infinite love of the Father and the Son who were so essentially united that Jesus could say to the people of one continent, "I and the Father are one," and to those of another, "I am the Father and the Son."

"The Spirit of truth" (1e). Keep this phrase in mind and then read the paragraph through again from the beginning. Note, for example, that the Son, who is the very spirit of truth, lighteth every man that cometh into the world and in him is the life of men and the light of men. It is true that our physical bodies are allied closely to animals. But it is also true, and infinitely more important, that the life and light of the Son of God dwells in us, and in us the spirit of truth is constantly seeking expression. We are made for him and, as Augustine affirmed, we are "restless until we find our rest in him."

"He received not of the fullness at the first, . . . but con-

328

*tinued from grace to grace, until he received a fullness;
and thus he was called the Son of God"* (2a, b). When
Jesus took upon himself the form of man he divested
himself of all things which would make it impossible
for him to become our example and our savior and our redeemer. Then, by the very fact of growing in grace, he
revealed to men the wonderful possibilities of their own
nature.[3]

*"I give unto you these sayings that you may understand
and know how to worship, and know what you worship"*
(3b). At the present time there is pronounced emphasis
upon worship, yet much of this is shallow and pretentious.
Worship is of importance in the lives of the Saints, for in
the act of worship our understanding is enriched, our affec-
tions are ennobled, and our purpose is steadied. But worship
demands earnest and dignified consideration of the nature
and purpose of God and of what he rightfully demands
of his people. It is not receptive only; it is also responsive.

"The church of the Firstborn" (4a). The Lord Jesus is
the Firstborn in the sense that he is the first and preeminent
Son of God. His disciples who partake of his spirit and
share his work share also in his glory, and are in
this sense the church of Jesus Christ the Firstborn.

*"He that keepeth his commandments, receiveth truth and
light, until he is glorified in truth, and knoweth all things"*
(4e). There is a difference between knowing facts and knowing the truth. Facts are true, but they are dead. Truth is
living. Men are not glorified by the facts which they recognize but by the truth which they live. Thus they are glorified
in truth and grow in light and understanding.

*"Intelligence, or the light of truth, was not created or
made, neither indeed can be"* (5a). Here is a wonderful
definition of intelligence. It is "the light of truth." Intelligence takes the facts of life and uses them creatively.
Such intelligence is shared by men but it is not their
private possession. It centers in God, and is necessarily
coexistent with him. All life and truth come from him,
and all enlightenment and power are borrowed from his

store. We light our little candles and walk by them, but when we pass on to the next room, others light their candles from the same undiminished source. There is no understanding which men can achieve that does not already exist in Him. He has thought our greatest thoughts before us; he has felt our deepest longings; he has surpassed our most wonderful creations. Yet something of the wonder of his divine nature is revealed in the fact that he never treats us with contempt or even with condescension but always shares with us the glory of his divinity in the full measure that we are willing to partake of it.

"Here is the agency of man" (5c). Every man possesses something of the light of truth. By this intelligence men are able to discern between right and wrong. If they could not discern this difference, they would have no actual choice, for one way would seem as good as another. Since men know the difference between right and wrong they become responsible for their choice of one or the other, and herein is their agency manifest. The condemnation which rests upon the world is that men, knowing the light, so frequently choose darkness.

"The elements are eternal" (5e). This can hardly mean that the elements coexist with God from eternity to eternity. If this was so, then they are not created and are to that degree independent of God. The sentence is better understood in light of Section 18:2d by which we can understand that the elements are *of* God, who is eternal. This is consistent with the remainder of the paragraph.

"Light and truth forsaketh that evil one" (6a). Wicked persons lose their perspective. Their cleverness in this life is of very little profit because their present purpose is not geared to the larger objectives which reach beyond the present. But truly intelligent men make every effort count toward a life purpose which envisions both time and eternity. Those who lose the larger perspective through evil living work in the small areas of the present while all around them is darkness.

"Bring up your children in light and truth" (6d). In

330

this and the following paragraphs of this revelation, the three members of the First Presidency and the bishop in Kirtland are all reminded of the imperative need for giving time and care to the spiritual development of their children. Unquestionably there was need for this instruction in their particular cases, but it is probable that they were used also as examples for the other Saints of Kirtland and of the church.

"Or be removed out of their place" (8c). Evidently the families of Joseph Smith and Bishop Whitney had a definite place and work in the church. The operation of the law of lineage is here taken for granted, but it involves grave responsibility. God can use the gifts he has entrusted to men only when these gifts are dedicated to him through personal devotion. Members of the priesthood who believe that they have been called according to the foreknowledge of God, and that the gifts which made their call possible should be passed on to their posterity, need to give special attention to the spiritual development of their children in order that this work might go forward from generation to generation.

"It is my will that you should hasten to translate my Scriptures" (12). The work on the Old Testament was still in progress, the New Testament having been completed already.

"Obtain a knowledge of history" (12). The concern here is hardly with the events of the past as such, for a knowledge of history in this sense has no moral or spiritual value. Concern is, rather, with factors which have been significant in man's continuing struggle toward achievement with and among his fellows—factors which have forwarded or retarded the coming of the kingdom of God.

---

[1]Section 85:36. [2]Senior Religio Quarterly, Vol. 12, No. 4, p. 18. [3]See Philippians 2:5-8.

SECTION 91

A second revelation was given through Joseph the Seer at Kirtland, Ohio, on May 6, 1833. Considerable land had been purchased in Kirtland. This included the French farm on which was a stone quarry and the basic materials for brickmaking. Instruction was given for building Kirtland as the central city of the Kirtland Stake of Zion. Specifically, instructions were given concerning a house for the work of the Presidency and a further building which was to become the literary headquarters of the church. Locations were indicated for the houses of Hyrum Smith, Reynolds Cahoon, and Jared Carter, who constituted the building committee, but the houses were not to be built at this time.

Kirtland, Ohio, is here referred to as a stake of Zion. Evidently it is not essential that stakes shall be contiguous to each other or to the Center Place, although it is to be expected that near the center there will be a steadily growing nucleus of stakes.

SECTION 92

Two days after Christmas 1832 the church had been instructed to "prepare every needful thing, and establish a house, even a house of prayer, a house of fasting, a house of faith, a house of learning, a house of glory, a house of order, a house of God."[1] In harmony with this instruction, a building committee was appointed consisting of Hyrum Smith, Jared Carter, and Reynolds Cahoon. These brethren made plans to erect a building to serve as a schoolhouse. Further instruction was given on May 6[2] and on June 1, 1833, the revelation bearing that date was received. This revelation retained the same committee but enlarged its scope. It now became the building committee for the temple.

"Ye have not considered the great commandment in all things. . .concerning the building of mine house" (1b). In extenuation of the failure of the Saints to build, it may be

urged that their number were few, they were poor, they were harassed by persecution, and they were attempting to build the city of Zion a thousand miles away. Yet these reasons evidently were not sufficient to justify them in failing to obey the command of God.

"*I design to prepare mine apostles*" (1c). There was no Quorum of Twelve at this time. It is quite probable that the word *apostles* is used here with the significance of "those sent." It is used elsewhere in this sense.[3]

"*But few of them were chosen*" (1d). Some of the elders had been properly ordained, but they had not magnified their calling. God chooses to use those who choose to do his will, but these men were "walking in darkness at noonday." No man's work is acceptable to the Lord merely because he "holds" the priesthood. Every member of the priesthood must actually discharge his ministerial responsibilities if he is to be accepted as a worthy servant.

"*In the which house I design to endow those whom I have chosen with power from on high*" (2a). The spiritual benedictions poured out on the Saints in the Kirtland Temple in fulfillment of this promise were not accompanied by secret oaths and grips and penalties.[4] They were given in response to careful and prayerful preparation which included physical, mental, and spiritual activity. The Saints who participated in these endowments kept the Word of Wisdom, attended the school of the prophets, and were active in the spiritual concerns of their calling.

"*It is my will that you should build an house*" (3a). At a conference of high priests held in the translating room in Kirtland on June 3, 1833, the First Presidency were appointed to obtain a draft for construction of the inner court of the House of the Lord. On July 23 of the same year, the cornerstones were laid, and from that time until the dedication in 1836, the members of the church exerted every effort to complete the work on the temple. While Joseph Smith and other elders of the church went to Missouri with Zion's Camp in 1834, Sidney Rigdon was left in charge of the work in Kirtland; it is to his strength

333

and confidence that we owe the success of the temple project. When Joseph was in Kirtland he acted as the foreman in the temple stone quarry, and when other duties would permit he labored there with the other brethren.

The Kirtland Temple stands on elevated grounds south of the east fork of the Chagrin River, about three miles southeast of Willoughby, Ohio, nine miles southwest of Painesville, and about six miles in direct line from Lake Erie. The building is of stone, plastered within and without. It is three stories high, exclusive of the basement. The first and second stories are auditoriums, each sixty-five by fifty-five feet on the inside, exclusive of the vestibule on the east end, through which the building is entered and in which are the stairways. The lower room is dedicated for sacrament offerings, for preaching, for fasting and praying, and for offering up the most holy desires unto the Lord. The second floor is dedicated for the school of the prophets. In each of these rooms are eight pulpits, four in each end, one above the other. Those in the west end are intended for the Melchisedec priesthood and those in the east end for the Aaronic priesthood. The third story is divided into four rooms. The outside walls are about two feet thick. The outside of the building is fifty-nine by seventy-nine feet.

The temple was occupied by the church as long as the Saints remained in Kirtland and was left in a good state of preservation when the Saints left for Missouri. Since the property came into possession of the Reorganized Church under the findings of the Court of Common Pleas in the famous Kirtland Temple suit, five General Conferences have been held in the temple, vis.: 1883, 1887, 1891, 1896, and 1904. The first conference of the high priesthood was held here in 1950. The temple is kept in good repair by the World Church. Many thousands of people inspect it every year.

---

[1]Section 85:36. [2]Section 91. [3]Sections 64:7; 83:10, etc. [4]Section 149A:6.

SECTION 93

On Tuesday, June 4, 1833, a conference of high priests met in the translating room to discuss the use of the French farm, which had been purchased nearly three months earlier for $5,000.00 They could not agree on procedure or on a manager, and in response to their request for divine guidance, they received the revelation of June 4, 1833.

According to this instruction, Bishop Newel K. Whitney was appointed to take charge of the farm with directions to divide it into lots for inheritances as should be determined in council among them. They were to take special care, however, that the portion necessary for the benefit of "mine order" (the United Order of Enoch) should be reserved for the use of the order.

They were instructed further to accept and ordain John Johnson as a member of the order.

BIOGRAPHICAL NOTES

John Johnson was born in 1779 and was the father of Luke S. and Lyman E. Johnson who were members of the first Quorum of Twelve. He opened his home at Hiram, Ohio, to Joseph and Sidney Rigdon as a retreat from the pressure of work in Kirtland, and some of the revision of the Holy Scriptures took place there. He showed his devotion to the work in many such ways. He and his son, Luke, became members of the first standing high council of the church on February 14, 1834. He served here until September 3, 1837, when he was rejected as a high counselor because of difficulties connected with the failure of the Kirtland Bank. He died in Kirtland July 13, 1843.

SECTION 94

During the summer of 1833, the Saints at Kirtland were concerned greatly regarding the welfare of their brethren in Zion who were suffering severe persecution at that time. Despite differences which had arisen between the Saints in the two places, those living at Kirtland prayed earnestly for the Saints of the West and kept in as close communication with them as the times and means of transportation would permit. It is worthy of mention that on July 20, 1833, the very day when the cornerstones of the temple were laid at Kirtland, the troubles in Missouri reached a crucial point, and an agreement was made that the leaders and one half of the body of Saints should move out of Jackson County by the first of January, 1834, and the remainder by the first of April, 1834, and that no others should move into the county. As soon as this agreement was reached, Oliver Cowdery was sent to Kirtland to report the matter to the First Presidency. He did not arrive until early in September 1833.

"Concerning the school in Zion" (2a). From the autobiography of Elder Parley P. Pratt we quote the following regarding the school of elders which had been organized in Zion some time prior to this date:

A school of elders was also organized, over which I was called to preside. This class, to the number of about sixty, met for instruction once a week. The place of meeting was in the open air under some tall trees, in the retired place in the wilderness where we prayed, preached and prophesied, and exercised ourselves in the gifts of the Holy Spirit. Here great blessings were poured out and many great and marvelous things were manifested and sought. The Lord gave me great wisdom, and enabled me to teach and edify the elders, and comfort and encourage them in their preparation for the great work which lay before us. I was also much edified and strengthened. To attend this school I had to travel on foot, and sometimes with bare feet at that, about six miles. This I did once a week besides visiting and preaching in five or six branches a week.

"There are those that must needs be chastened, and their works shall be made known" (2d). As has been previously

noted, some of those who went up to Zion were unwilling to obey the laws of stewardship until the enterprise proved successful. This gave rise to envying and jealousy, and the spiritual condition of some of the members of the church was consequently impaired. Read Section 83:8 in this connection.

"It is my will that an house should be built unto me in the land of Zion" (3a). Undoubtedly the phrase "in the land of Zion" was interpreted by the Saints at Kirtland to mean in or near Independence. The persecution of the Missourians made it impossible to fulfill this command, however, and the temple was never built, although a temple was projected at Far West, Missouri, and another was partially completed at Nauvoo, Illinois.

"Let it be built speedily by the tithing of my people" (3a). The word *tithing* is used here in its larger sense and includes surplus and offerings.

"An house built unto me for the salvation of Zion" (3b). The purpose of this temple is indicated in this and the preceding paragraph:

> It was a place of thanksgiving for all Saints.
> It was a place of instruction for the ministry in their several callings.
> It was a place of worship.
> It must be kept undefiled.
> The presence of God would then rest upon it.
> The pure in heart should see God.

It is to be expected that the purpose of any future temple in Zion will be the same as is here indicated.

"If Zion do these things, she shall prosper" (5a). The Saints were expelled from Jackson County before they had opportunity to build this temple. In the first paragraph of this revelation some of these are highly commended. However, the revelations show quite plainly that if the Saints had "observed to do all things whatsoever they had been commanded," no persecution directed against them would have destroyed their work. To say this is not an

attempt to minimize the responsibility of the people of Missouri at this time. Without doubt they treated the Saints in a cruel and inhuman fashion. But the fact remains that the major reason for the failure of this first attempt to build a literal Zion centering in Independence, Missouri, was the unwillingness of many of the Saints to pay the price of that great work. This was so in spite of the fact that there were many truly saintly persons among them.

"Zion can not fall, neither be moved out of her place, for God is there" (5b). Despite what happened in Missouri at this time, and the expulsion of the Saints from the lands they had purchased for their everlasting inheritance, there is a sense in which Zion has never been moved out of her place in the hearts of the people of God. It has been the faith of all succeeding generations of Latter Day Saints that they and their children would return "with songs of everlasting joy."

"Let Zion rejoice, for this is Zion, the pure in heart" (5c). Zion is expected to be a place of gathering for the people of God. The place is important, and this has been stated again and again in the revelations. But the spirit of the Saints who occupy the land of Zion, the spirit of purity and love, must precede the gathering and continue among those gathered.

SECTION 95

On August 6, 1833, before news of the culmination of the Missouri troubles had yet reached the Saints in Kirtland, this further revelation was received through the prophet.

"All things wherewith you have been afflicted, shall work together for your good, and to my name's glory saith the Lord" (1c). This is a reiteration of the affirmation of the apostle Paul in his letter to the Romans.[1] It was particularly pertinent in view of the situation of the Saints,

and when understood in light of the conditions accompanying the admonition that the Saints must be faithful even in tribulation it will be recognized as a universal principle.[2] Ella Wheeler Wilcox had this in mind when she wrote:

> One ship drives east, another drives west
> With the selfsame winds that flow.
> 'Tis the set of the sails
> And not the gales
> Which tells us the way to go.
>
> Like the winds of the sea are the ways of fate,
> As we voyage along through life:
> 'Tis the set of a soul
> That decides its goal,
> and not the calm or the strife.[3]

"*It is my will that my people should observe to do all things whatsoever I command them*" (2a). The gospel of Jesus Christ constitutes the "perfect law of liberty." Therein is true freedom to be found. Freedom found outside the law of righteousness is only partial and illusory. Only the truth in action can make men free among each other and as the sons of God.

"*That law of the land, which is constitutional, supporting that principle of freedom . . . is justifiable before me*" (2a). The purpose of the law of the land is to support the principle of freedom. The Constitution is the bulwark of American political liberties, and laws which are in harmony therewith minister to the political freedom of the people of the United States and should be supported by those who believe that it is the will of God that men should be free.

"*Whatsoever is more or less than these, cometh of evil*" (2b). Laws which are not in harmony with the spirit of the Constitution and which do not support the spirit of freedom do not merit the support of free men.

"*When the wicked rule the people mourn*" (2c). Even though the laws of the land are designed to promote justice and freedom, they will serve this end only as they are administered by men of righteous purpose. Latter Day Saints therefore should use their influence to ensure that wise

339

and just legislation is enacted and men of integrity selected to carry these wise laws into effect. This puts legislators under a multiple obligation. Both integrity and skill are needed. Integrity, though of major importance, is no substitute for political and administrative insight and skill.

"Whoso layeth down his life in my cause, for my name's sake, shall find it again; even life eternal" (3b). This will be recognized as reflecting the statement of the Master to his disciples: "Whosoever will save his life shall lose it: and whosoever will lose his life for my sake shall find it. For what is a man profited, if he shall gain the whole world, and lose his own soul? or what shall a man give in exchange for his soul?"[4] Throughout this revelation, as is true of others, there is clear evidence that the mind of the prophet was informed by the statements of the Bible which became luminous as current situations called attention to them.

"I will prove you in all things, whether you will abide in my covenant, even unto death" (3c). As was forecast here, it was to be many years from the time that the Saints were driven from Jackson County until the first of them returned there, and these years were years of persecution and bitter disappointment.

"If ye will not abide in my covenant, ye are not worthy of me; therefore, renounce war and proclaim peace" (3d). This advice given at such a time, marks Joseph Smith as one of the long succession of prophets of God who have raised an ensign of peace before the Saints and before the world. Forty years after this date Joseph Smith, the son of the Martyr, commented as follows regarding the military organizations of the Nauvoo period of our history:

> The raising of a standard of peace was one of the duties devolving upon the Saints. Military organizations among them should have been the result of state law direct, not the result of domestic primary action. The military organizations of the state were sufficient for the practical purposes of defense against invasion from without; but would have been powerless against dissension from within.
>
> There were three evils connected with the existence of military organizations among the Saints. One of these evils was the appear-

ance of hostility which it gave to the Saints, as a religious body, crying peace unto all people. Another was, that there was an unnecessary expenditure of time and money in keeping up drill, parade, dress, equipage, and arms. But the worst evil of the three, as it appears to us, looking at it from our chosen standpoint, was the dependence upon the arm of flesh in warlike demonstration, rather than in God and the practice of holiness; and we may add another, closely connected with the last, military titles and appellations usurped the place of the plainer callings, and the higher dignities of "elders in Israel," "ministers of the gospel." Some of the publications of the church show an unmistakable tendency to foster the love of distinctive titles, and "Captain," "Colonel," and "General," are prefixes; where to our democratic taste, "Mr." and "Elder," would have looked far better, and would have served more palpably to enhance the value of church distinctive titles.

We blame no one for this,—we cannot say where it first began, nor that any absolute wickedness was wrought; but we regard it as an error.[5]

"I, the Lord, am not well pleased with many who are in the church at Kirtland" (4a). The people of Kirtland are here warned in terms similar to those which had been addressed to the people of Zion, for unrighteousness menaced the success of the work in Kirtland just as it did in Jackson County. The Saints were not wicked people when measured by the standards of the world. Indeed, in many things their righteousness exceeded the righteousness of the religious people of the time. But while some of them lived lives of sacrificial devotion, others were unwilling to live according to the high standard required of Saints, and their influence within the church lowered the spiritual level of the group. Nothing their enemies could do hurt them as much as their own grudging spirit in regard to the things of the kingdom.

"If thou wilt spare him thou shalt be rewarded for thy righteousness" (5e). The counsel of this paragraph is not a counsel for weaklings. The Lord is not here urging his children to live as cowards. He is urging a policy of self-restraint which recognizes that speedy resentment and retaliation frequently bring greater injustice and misery than are occasioned by the original wrongs. Anyone who permits injustice to make him bitter and resentful has done

341

himself greater harm than the person who dealt unjustly with him.

First lift a standard of peace unto that people, nation, or tongue" (6c). If it is thought that this counsel of peace is impractical, consider the following facts of World War I which was made and run by "practical" men:

> If those killed in the World War could march past a reviewing stand ten in a row and the rows two seconds apart, it would take forty-six days for the army of the dead to pass that stand.
>
> If every day for seventy years we should lose as many persons as were lost with the "Lusitania," that would about equal the number of dead and missing soldiers and dead civilians in the World War.
>
> During the World War enough money was spent every four days to finance all the hospitals in America for a year.

As we all know, the figures for the second world conflict are many times greater than these.

"If. . . he repent and come unto thee praying thy forgiveness thou shalt forgive him" (7a). This instruction on forgiveness was particularly timely during these years when the Saints felt that their neighbors were persecuting them without excuse, but it is still valid, even though those causes of irritation have been removed. According to this teaching, Latter Day Saints have no justification for holding resentment against repentant transgressors.

---

[1]Romans 8:25. [2]Matthew 5:12. [3]"The Winds of Fate." [4]Matthew 16:25, 26, K.J. [5]Church History 3:676.

SECTION 96

During the month of August 1833 Elder John Murdock was called by this revelation to do missionary work in the East. Brother Murdock already had done some missionary work, for he and Hyrum Smith had made a missionary trip from Kirtland to Independence by way of Detroit in June 1831.[1]

Brother Murdock was a widower. His twin children had been adopted by Joseph and Emma Smith, but the boy had died because of exposure. His daughter Julia grew up in the household of the prophet. After Elder Murdock finished this mission, he went to Missouri with Zion's Camp in 1834, and after serving on the high council in Clay County, Far West, and Nauvoo, he was ordained a bishop.

---

[1]Section 52:3.

SECTION 97

Joseph Smith, Sidney Rigdon, and Freeman Nickerson left Kirtland, October 5, 1833, on a mission to Canada, traveling in a vehicle belonging to Brother Nickerson. While at Perrysburg, New York, they stopped at the Nickerson home and there preached to a large congregation. Here, on October 12, 1833, the prophet received a revelation bearing that date. It is addressed to Joseph and Sidney.

"An effectual door shall be opened in the regions round about in this eastern land" (1b). This phrase "regions round about" is applied elsewhere in a rather technical sense to the territory in the vicinity of Independence, Missouri. Here it apparently applies to the regions near Perrysburg, New York, where the revelation was given.

"Speak the thoughts that I shall put into your hearts, and ye shall not be confounded before men" (1d). Joseph and Sidney were going into new territory, and were instructed not to strive for polished oratory but to bear testimony of the wonderful experiences they had shared and to expound the scriptures. They did this with telling effect, and their mission became noteworthy as the first

mission to Canada in this dispensation.

"Sidney should be a spokesman unto this people; yea, verily, . . . a spokesman unto my servant Joseph" (3a). At the organization of the church, Oliver Cowdery was designated as "second elder," Joseph being the "first elder." Since that time the First Presidency had been more completely organized with Joseph Smith as president of the church and Sidney Rigdon and Frederick G. Williams as his counselors. It is not surprising, therefore, to find that the words addressed to Sidney Rigdon in this revelation are closely akin to those addressed to Oliver about three years earlier.[1]

"Orson Hyde and John Gould are in my hands" (4b). Soon after Oliver Cowdery arrived in Kirtland with information regarding the expulsion of the Saints from Jackson County, arrangements were made to dispatch Elders Orson Hyde and John Gould to the Saints of Zion, bearing the advice of the leaders of the church regarding their unfortunate situation. Naturally the welfare of these messengers and the situation in Missouri were matters of great concern to Joseph and Sidney and the words of this revelation therefore comforted them considerably. The elders reached their destination toward the end of September 1833. John Gould became one of the Presidents of Seventy during the year 1837. Later in the same year he was ordained a high priest.

---

[1]Section 27:2.

SECTION 98

In April 1833 there commenced a series of persecutions of the Latter Day Saints which all good people must condemn. We are not willing to say that the Latter Day Saints always acted wisely or that they were right in every particular. Joseph Smith acknowledged this at the time, in the *Messenger and Advocate*,[1] where he says:

The sound of the gathering, and of the doctrine, went abroad into the world.

Many, we have reason to fear, having a zeal not according to knowledge, not understanding the pure principles of the doctrine of the church, have no doubt, in the heat of enthusiasm, taught and said many things that were derogatory to the genuine character and principles of the church.

For these things we are heartily sorry, and would apologize if any apology would do any good.

While it is unwise and untrue to the facts of history to exonerate the Saints of all blame in connection with the Missouri trouble, careful students of the situation will agree that the standard of morals and general character of the Saints were above the level of the time and place, and that they were the victims of misunderstanding and cruelty on the part of their neighbors. Those were days of deep feeling regarding doctrinal issues, and many of the clergy and those acting as missionaries to the Indians or to the frontier citizens were among the most prominent persons active in despoiling the Saints.

The first notable gathering of the mob was in April 1833 when about three hundred men came together to force the Saints to leave Jackson County. This gathering broke up in a drunken row, but in the following July, the mob renewed their hostilities. On July 18, 1833, a document was circulated among those hostile to the Saints.[2] This document may be analyzed as follows:

Believing, as we do, that the arm of the civil law does not afford us a guarantee...against evils which are now inflicted upon us...we deem it expedient...to form ourselves into a company for the better and easier accomplishment of our purpose.

This purpose is justified by the law of nature as well as by the law of self-preservation.

It is more than two years since the first of these fanatics or knaves...made their first appearance among us pretending:

To hold personal communications and converse face to face with the Most High God.

> To receive communications and revelations direct from
> heaven.
> To heal the sick by laying on hands.
> With very few exceptions they were of the very dregs of
> the society from which they came; lazy, idle, and vicious.
> They brought little or no property into our county.
> They have been tampering with our slaves.
> They invite free Negroes and mulattoes from other states
> to become Mormons and remove and settle among us.
> They declare openly that their God has given them this
> county of land, and that sooner or later they must and
> will have the possession of our land for an inheritance.
> We therefore agree, that after timely warning, and receiving
> an adequate compensation for what little property they
> cannot take with them, if they refuse to leave us in
> peace, as they found us, we agree to use such means
> as may be sufficient to remove them, and to that end
> we each pledge to each other our bodily powers, our
> lives, fortunes, and sacred honor.

In accordance with the foregoing document, between four and five hundred persons assembled in Independence on July 20, 1833, and sent thirteen of their number to meet six representatives of the Saints, demanding that they should immediately cease publication of *The Evening and the Morning Star* and that the elders should agree to remove out of the county forthwith. The elders requested three months for consideration. This was refused. They asked for ten days. They were told that fifteen minutes was the longest time they would be allowed.

Following this conversation, the mob demolished the printing office and dwelling house of W. W. Phelps and Company and broke the press, pied the type, and destroyed the book work, furniture, apparatus, and office property with an immediate cash damage of $6,000. The mob then started to demolish the storehouse and to destroy the goods of Gilbert and Whitney, but after a time they turned from this and tarred and feathered Bishop Partridge and Brother Allen in the public square of Independence.

The mob reassembled three days later, but on that occasion John Corrill, John Whitmer, W. W. Phelps, A. S. Gilbert, Edward Partridge, and Isaac Morley offered themselves
346

as ransom for the Saints, expressing themselves as being willing to be scourged or to die if that would appease the anger of the mob toward the church.

Under these circumstances the church representatives entered into an agreement that ten of the leaders and their families should remove from the county on or before the first of January 1834 and should use all their influence to induce all the brethren at that time in Independence to remove as soon as possible—one half by January 1, 1834, and the remainder by April 1, 1834; and to use all means in their power to prevent further immigration. John Corrill and A. S. Gilbert were permitted to remain as general agents to wind up the business of the church.

The Saints appealed to the governor, Daniel Dunklin, for aid. He replied that their memorial had been duly considered, and he would advise them to obtain a warrant and place it in the hands of the proper officers to see if the law could be peaceably executed. If not, and the Saints would notify him, Governor Dunklin promised to take such steps as would be required to secure favorable execution of these legal documents. The difficulty was, however, that the mob included the very officers who should have put the law into execution.

Following this, the leaders of the mob broke their pledge, and between October 31 and November 7 the Saints were driven from Jackson County with great loss of property and great danger to their health. They took refuge, chiefly, in Clay County, and engaged Attorneys Wood, Reese, and Doniphan to bring suit against their persecutors. When the appeal of the Saints came up on February 24, 1834, the mob collected and so intimidated the court that no trial was had. Convinced that no recourse to the courts of Jackson County would be availing, the Saints appealed to President Jackson April 10, 1834. At the same time they asked Governor Dunklin, who had shown a disposition to be fair to them, to assist them in their appeal to the President. The governor felt that this was a purely state affair, and this opinion was borne out in the reply received from Lewis Taft, Secretary of War, on behalf of the President. No recourse was therefore possible, and the injustice done the Saints remained unrequited.

It was against this background, although some of these events had not yet transpired, that Joseph received the revelation of December 16, 1833, at Kirtland, Ohio. The revelation was addressed to the Saints in Ohio but had major reference to those in Missouri "who had been afflicted, and persecuted, and run out from the land of their inheritance."

"*I . . . have suffered the affliction to come upon them, wherewith they have been afflicted in consequence of their transgressions*" (1a). This does not deny the culpability of the mob in Missouri, but it does emphasize the fundamental principle which the Saints of every age need to keep in mind: that the redemption of Zion depends, primarily, on spiritual forces. It is our faith and expectation that Zion will be built when the children of the kingdom are in fact obedient to the commands of God.

"*There were jarrings, and contentions, and envyings, and strifes, and lustful and covetous desires among men*" (3a). These difficulties centered in the application of the doctrine of stewardship. There were some splendid Saints who were dedicating their all, but others were still tinctured with the spirit of the world and wanted "to play safe." These demanded the full rights of membership but were unwilling to make the sacrifices and to cultivate the spirit required of Zion builders. Their presence and influence disrupted the affairs of the church.

"*Mine indignation is soon to be poured without measure upon all nations*" (4c). The prophecy on the Civil War had been delivered about a year prior to this time. This is possibly another reference to the calamities which have come upon the nations of the earth since the Civil War. The remainder of the paragraph, however, seems to indicate that still greater catastrophes lie ahead, for in the day of their occurrence those "that have been scattered shall be gathered," etc.

"*Zion shall not be moved out of her place, notwithstanding her children are scattered*" (4g). Independence has been indicated as the center place for the gathering of the Saints, and in spite of the persecution and scattering of the people, it is still so designated. All other gatherings must be secondary to the one centering in Independence.

"*They that remain and are pure in heart shall return and come to their inheritances*" (4g). This promise is now being literally fulfilled for more than 25,000 members of the Reorganization live in Independence, Missouri, and the contiguous stakes, and their number is increasing every year.

"*Gather together and stand in holy places*" (5a). The term "holy places," as used here, has two possible meanings. It applies to Zion and her stakes, places which have been especially pointed out for the gathering of the Saints. It also applies to the places made holy by the presence of the righteous. Even the stakes of Zion are not holy places unless they are made holy by the righteousness of the people of God.

Characteristics of the millennium (5).

> Every corruptible thing shall be consumed.
> All things shall become new, that the knowledge and glory of God may dwell upon all the earth.
> The enemy of all flesh shall cease from before the face of the Almighty.
> The prayers of the righteous shall be abundantly answered.
> Satan shall not have power to tempt any man.
> There shall be no sorrow, because there is no death.
> An infant shall not die until he is old, but when he dies he will not sleep in the earth but will be changed in the twinkling of an eye.
> The Lord shall reveal all things:
> > Things which are past.
> > Hidden things which no man knew.
> > The manner and purpose of the creation of the earth.

Things most precious in the earth and on the earth and in heaven.

Those who suffer persecution for the name of Christ, and endure in faith, shall partake of all his glory.

The parable continued in paragraphs 6 to 8 of this section has been summarized as follows by Elder Heman C. Smith:

1. The subject of the parable is the redemption of Zion.
2. The servants of the nobleman (the people of God) were to be directed to occupy a choice piece of land.
3. They were to do as they were commanded.
4. While they were yet laying the foundation they were to get at variance one with another and become slothful.
5. As a result of this unfaithfulness their enemies were to come upon them and destroy their works.
6. They were to become affrighted and flee.
7. The nobleman (God) was to remonstrate with them for their unfaithfulness and to hold them responsible for allowing his vineyard to be destroyed.
8. Then he was to call upon one of his servants to gather together the residue of his servants (not the body which had fled).
9. This servant at the head of this residue was to go straightway into the vineyard and redeem it, break down the walls of the enemy, throw down their tower, scatter their watchmen, etc.
10. This servant was to inquire when these things should be, but was simply to be told, "When I will."
11. He was told that if he performed his part he should be a faithful and wise steward and a ruler in the kingdom.
12. He was to do whatsoever he was commanded and after many days all things (concerning the redemption of Zion) were to be fulfilled.

This prophecy has been most remarkably fulfilled. To quote Elder Heman C. Smith further:

When the church became slothful and failed to do the work commanded within the time appointed; their enemies came upon them and they became affrighted and fled, not simply to another part of the choice vineyard, as in the case of former moves, but entirely outside of the appointed Zion. Since the body had fled, one of God's servants has been sent to gather the "residue," or remnants left behind; and they have gone straightway into the waste places of Zion and are redeeming them; are breaking down the wall, throwing down the tower, and scattering the watchmen of the enemy; not by use of carnal weapons, but by fearlessly defending the faith against opposition; by consistent honorable lives, and square dealing; and by adhering to "the code of good morals," taught in the Bible, the Book of Mormon, and the Doctrine and Covenants, and to which President Smith pledged himself on that memorable day of 1860.

This has disarmed the enemy, and the Reorganization is realizing, in a measure, the fulfillment of the promise that the church should find "favor and grace" in the eyes of the people.

Mark it well, this servant who was to be sent to lead this movement was not only to be "a faithful and wise steward" in the midst of God's house, but he was to be "a ruler in my [God's] kingdom!"

"That the work of the gathering of my Saints may continue" (9a). Even though Jackson County now was closed to the Saints, they were instructed to continue the work of gathering. Throughout the lifetime of the founder of the church, the Saints endeavored to gather, and such places as Far West and Nauvoo became temporary centers of these endeavors. However, it was never expected that these places would supplant Independence. The Saints hoped to go back to the center place as soon as possible.

"Let not your gathering be in haste, nor by flight; but let all things be prepared before you" (9e). Much of the difficulty in Independence had arisen because members of the church were so eager to rush into Zion and partake of her benefits that they did not make the necessary spiritual and material preparation. This was in spite of the repeated pleadings of the Presidency and Bishopric that only those who could make a definite contribution to her upbuilding should move to Zion.

"In the region round about the land which I have appointed to be the land of Zion" (9f).

Jackson County included the present counties of Jackson, Cass, and Bates. The adjacent counties included the territory beginning on the eastern boundary of Caldwell County, north to the nothern line of the state; then west to the Missouri River, and down the Missouri River. South of the Missouri River Lafayette County included its present dimensions on the Missouri River, extending directly south of the Osage River. Crawford County extended south for one and one-half counties, and crossed the state from the west to Washington and Franklin Counties. West of the State of Missouri was the unorganized territory.

The "adjacent counties" would evidently have included the Far West Stake, Lamoni Stake, Central Missouri and Kansas City Stakes, the Rich Hill, Missouri, District, and possibly a large part of the Spring River District, as well as territory in Kansas.

How far the "regions round about" may have extended is a matter of opinion. But Zion evidently included a large part, if, not all, of Missouri, probably southern Iowa and Eastern Nebraska, Kansas, and a corner of Oklahoma.[3]

"Let all the churches gather together all their monies; let these things be done in their time" (10a). Only two courses remained open to the Saints at this time. They must either relinquish all idea of building Zion in that generation, or they must go steadily forward, learning the lessons of their past mistakes and trying through sacrifice and devotion to accomplish the work entrusted to them. They were instructed to choose the latter course.

"There is even now already in store...abundance to redeem Zion" (10c). It took courage for the prophet to bring such a message as this to the Saints in Missouri. They thought that they had been wickedly treated. Some of them were very bitter. Many, having felt the hatred of their oppressors, were almost without hope. Yet, though they needed protection from their enemies, their greatest need was for spiritual strength among themselves.

Some misunderstanding has occurred with reference to the word "redeem" used here, it being thought by some that if sufficient money had been consecrated by Saints in the East Zion could have been established without delay.

352

This is not what the revelation intimates. It was the land which was to be redeemed. If this had been done it would have given the Saints a legal and political foothold which would have greatly strengthened their enterprise. The purchase of the land was evidently desirable to the end that it should be occupied in peace by the people of the Zionic community. But while kingdom-building involves land purchase it also involves spiritual growth. As a later prophet was to write: "Zionic conditions are no further away nor any closer than the spiritual condition of my people justifies."[4]

"*According to the laws and constitution of the people*" (10e). This emphasis upon the importance of seeking redress through constitutional procedure is akin to the earlier instruction commanding the Saints to "renounce war and proclaim peace."[5] Respect for law is basic in organized society, but it is not to be expected that this respect can be long maintained except as the law ministers to freedom and justice and as it is administered fearlessly and impartially.

"*It is not right that any man should be in bondage one to another*" (10g). This possibly refers to the spiritual bondage in which the Missourians sought to hold the Saints. The sentence also refers to the question of slavery, which had been one of the issues between the Saints and their neighbors. In view of this revelation, no petition for redress could include a promise to compromise on the Negro question. In the very paragraph instructing the Saints to apply for redress, they are reminded that slavery is not of God.

"*Let them importune*" (12a). The Saints appealed to Governor Daniel Dunklin on February 4, 1834. The governor replied, offering the Saints an escort and protection at the trial of Colonel Thomas Pitcher and urging them to put their trust in the operation of the law. He could not guarantee them protection if they remained in Independence after the trial was over. At the time set for the trial, the mob again collected and so intimidated the court that no trial was had. Thereupon, being convinced that recourse to the courts of Jackson County would be unavailing, the Saints petitioned President Andrew Jackson (April 10, 1834). The President referred this matter to the War Department, but the matter was dropped because the President refused to interfere in a matter which primarily concerned the state. In this view, the President was probably quite correct.

"It is contrary to my commandment, and my will, that my servant Sidney Gilbert should sell my storehouse" (13a). The principle here, involved is that it was better for the Saints to retain legal title to their holdings in Missouri than to give up this title for the pittance they would be paid under the circumstances. The storehouse accordingly was retained, but Brother Gilbert died shortly afterward, and the Saints never had opportunity to regain possession. It is of interest to note that title to what is here called "my storehouse" (the Lord's) was held in fee simple by Elder Gilbert.[6]

---

[1]*Messenger and Advocate,* Volume 1, page 180. [2]Church History, Volume 1, pages 312-315. [3]*Journal of History,* Volume 17, pages 307, 308. [4]Section 140:5c. [5]Section 95:3. [6]*Saints' Herald* 67:429.

SECTION 99

On February 17, 1834, the Standing High Council of the church was organized by President Joseph Smith at his home in Kirtland, Ohio. The next day President Smith reviewed and corrected the minutes of this organization. On February 19, the council reassembled, the minutes were read three times, and then unanimously adopted and received for a form and constitution of the high council of the church. The counselors then were set apart to their several offices.

The minutes of this council now form Section 99. This section is not a revelation.

"Appointed by revelation for the purpose of settling important difficulties" (1). This is the highest court of the church. After the council has acted, the matter at issue "shall be had in remembrance no more before the Lord; for this is the highest council of the church of God, and a final decision upon controversies in spiritual matters."[1]

"The number composing the council" (3). Church Historian Charles A. Davies wrote the author February 15, 1960, as follows:

> There were 24 High Priests in the original Council and they nominated men to occupy and there were 3 presidents, which makes 15 people of the 24 up for consideration. This leaves 9 High Priests only who would be free to give a legitimate vote on the Council as a whole. It appears in the third paragraph that the action was presented before what we could call a general conference of those available at this place at the time, and therefore only 9 High Priests could vote. The number composing the council who voted in the name of the church were 43 - 9 High Priests, 17 elders, 4 priests, 13 members. There would be probably 58 people present at that meeting if the members of the council that were being appointed were there and abstained from voting. Perhaps the words "the members of the council who voted" should have been "the members of the conference who voted." The word "council" seems to have been a misnomer here.

"Whenever any vacancy shall occur" (5a). Our present procedure is in harmony with this requirement. High priests are approved for ordination by a General Conference or by a general or stake high council. High counselors are set apart from among the high priests on nomination of the presidencies of the church or of the stakes and approval by the appropriate conferences.

The president shall give a decision" (9b). The members of the Presidency submit their decision to the council. If it is approved it stands, but if not there is further discussion. While the law permits majority approval, high council decisions are almost always unanimous.

"The president may inquire and obtain the mind of the Lord by revelation" (10). Divine instruction for the guidance of the church may be approved in either of two ways:

355

after consideration by the quorums and the church, or by its influence on high council decisions in matters which properly come before the high council, and from which there is therefore no appeal. There is no record of the formal presentation of a revelation to the high council, but divine guidance frequently has been evidenced in the interpretation of the law in the council by the Presidency and with the approval of the high councilors.

"*The council of high priests abroad*" (12a). This is a temporary council which may be called by presiding officers of distant territories for advice in difficult situations, but it ceases to exist after the passing of the specific purpose for which the council is called together. The decision of such a council may be appealed to the Standing High Council of the church.

"*The latter* [Quorum of Twelve] *can only be called in question by the general authorities of the church in case of transgression*" (13b). This is a reference to the functioning of the quorums on concurrent jurisdiction.[2]

The work of the high council. The following comments on the work of the high council are from the pen of Frederick M. Smith, and may well be studied here:

Let it be understood that all the courts of the church, from Elders' courts to the Standing High Council, are church courts, and represent and speak for the general church. Elders' courts are temporary in appointment; Bishop's courts and the Standing High Councils are permanent. Other temporary courts would be such high councils as may be called into existence to meet any emergency or exigency. This view makes it clear that the judicial voice of the church may be expressed anywhere, with respect to geographical locality, where a necessity exists for such judicial expression. This safeguards the question of expediency and justice considered from the standpoint of availability of witnesses, testimony, local coloring, and the matter of reputation and character of witnesses or accused.

The functions of the Standing High Council of the church, under the provisions of the law are widespread and far-reaching, and its sittings may well be considered a general court in "equity and justice," not limited by the rigid and sometimes narrow provisions of mere technicalities. It has original as well as appellate functions and jurisdictions.

In all cases where charges are brought against general officers of

356

the church, such charges when properly formulated should be lodged promptly with the First Presidency, except where the charges are against a member of the First Presidency when they should be lodged with the Presiding Bishopric. From the degree of importance of the charges, the Presidency shall determine whether the Standing High Council shall examine the charges, and the High Council shall from its examination of the charges determine the judicial course of the case, and may hear the case in all its details, or pass it to an inferior court for hearing and finding subject always to the appeal provided in the law without prejudice from the preliminary examination of the charges.[3]

In 1903 a question arose concerning the authority of the member of the First Presidency under paragraph 14 of this section.

President Joseph Smith stated he had placed a paper containing some of his views thereon before the Twelve and Seventy, wherein he took position substantially as in an editorial in a recent number of the *Saints' Herald.*

Resolution was then passed expressing it as our opinion that Section 99, paragraph 14, confers authority directly upon the [Presidency and Twelve] Presidency, one or all, to determine whether appeals made to the High Council are of sufficient importance to be heard by the High Council, the determination to be made before bringing it to the attention of the Council.[4]

The Seventy reported that they had

Resolved that it is the opinion of this quorum that under the provisions of the law found in paragraph 14 of section 99 of the Doctrine and Covenants the president or presidents of the church are empowered to determine *all* cases of appeal from whatever source as to whether they are entitled to rehearing or not before the High Council.[5]

---

[1]Section 104:35. [2]Section 104:11, last sentence. [3]*One*, January, 1919. [4]First Presidency Minutes, March 26, 1903, p. 55. [5]*Ibid.*, April 13, 1903, p. 68.

SECTION 100

A conference was held at the house of Elder Parley P. Pratt in Clay County, Missouri, January 1, 1834. Bishop

Edward Partridge presiding. In addition to other business, it was decided to send Lyman Wight and Parley P. Pratt to Kirtland, Ohio, to inform the Presidency regarding the situation in Zion and to ask their advice. The messengers were destitute of proper clothing for the journey and had to leave their families in the care of the impoverished Saints. Nevertheless, they left on January 12, 1834, and reached Kirtland, February 22. This revelation was received two days later.

"They shall...begin to prevail against mine enemies from this very hour" (2b). This promise, made in the face of the terrible tidings brought by the messengers from Zion, is a renewal of the earlier promises of triumph which had been given to the Saints but like those earlier promises, it was contingent on their obedience. That they were not fully obedient is evident from the history of the times and is reflected in the revelation.[1] However, despite the seeming success of their enemies, the expulsion of the Saints from Missouri, and the hardships this entailed, they did "begin to prevail." A nucleus maintained their faith, learned by the things they suffered, and laid the foundation for the acceptance and growth which came with later years.

"Inasmuch as they keep not my commandments, and hearken not to observe all my words, the kingdoms of the world shall prevail against them" (2c). The fact that the Saints were not reinstated in their inheritances at this time does not mean that all of them fell short of their Zionic possibilities. Some, undoubtedly, were people of God and worthy of a place in Zion.

"The redemption of Zion must needs come by power" (3d). The redemption of Zion is essentially a spiritual enterprise. As the Saints have been told many times, it was not to be accomplished by the shedding of blood but by demonstration of the power of God. All kinds of power are involved—the wisdom and skills and strength of people with infinitely diverse talents—but these must be directed by the Spirit of God.

"My servant Baurak Ale" (4). This title is generally

358

held to refer to Joseph Smith who did in fact take the lead in gathering the men who became the members of Zion's Camp. Baurak Ale are Hebrew words meaning "the Lord blesseth."

"Let all the churches send up wise men, with their monies, and purchase lands even as I have commanded them" (5b). Those who were to be gathered for this enterprise must be young and middle-aged men who could stand the rigors of the journey to Independence and who could defend themselves if necessary. However, the emphasis on the wisdom and financial standing of those who were to go up, together with the prior teaching against the shedding of blood, indicate that the purpose of the journey to Zion was not primarily military, but the wise, peaceful, and legal reestablishment of the Saints in their homes in Jackson County.

"Inasmuch as mine enemies come against you to drive you from my goodly land, which I have consecrated to be the land of Zion; even from your own lands after these testimonies, which ye have brought before me, against them, ye shall curse them; and whomsoever ye curse, I will curse" (5b). It is altogether probable that some of the company who went up to Zion at this time regarded this as a guarantee of divine favor if they attacked the unrepentant mobbers who had despoiled their brethren. The more sober among them, however, related this paragraph to Section 95:6, 7, and recognized that they were to present the "testimony" of the continued ill will of the Missourians before the Lord, and were to leave vengeance in his hands. This is borne out in the fact that the effect of the "curse" or presentation of "testimonies" before the Lord was to reach to the third and fourth generation of those persecuting the Saints. No one had any idea that the members of Zion's Camp or their successors would use military force against the Missourians for that long a period.

In this connection, the following excerpts from an article by Elder Heman C. Smith are of particular interest:

It is too well known to require comment that Jackson and other counties on the borders were for many years infested with bands of guerillas and jayhawkers who filled the inhabitants with terror and fear. The climax came, however, during the Civil War, when on August 23, 1863, General Thomas Dewey issued his Order Number 11.

This desolation [which followed this infamous order] was more far reaching and fully as heart-rending as that which many of these despoiled people had visited upon the Saints in this territory thirty years before. Both of these outrages were committed under the color of military law. In 1833 the state militia was called out and the Latter Day Saints were treated as public enemies. In 1863 a brigadier-general [General Ewing] of the Union Army called out the force under his command to despoil the very people of the very homes and farms that had been taken from the Saints. but of course, as has always been true, many innocent ones suffered with the guilty.

Latter Day Saints are not alone in the conviction that in the events of the Civil War and other calamities which followed, the displeasure of God was made manifest. When in 1878 the scourge of yellow fever was desolating the Southern States some prominent citizens of Philadelphia, Pennsylvania, wrote to President Hayes that the conviction was growing deeper with thoughtful men that "the Lord has had a controversy with the inhabitants of the land" and that the fact of the many calamities which had visited the country since the Civil War attested the displeasure of the Supreme Ruler over the world against this nation.[2]

The men named in this revelation left immediately to visit among the churches and to secure volunteers to go to Missouri in a body later known as "Zion's Camp." At a conference held at Avon, Livingston County, New York, March 17, 1834, for example, Joseph stated that the object of their gathering was

To obtain young and middle-aged men to assist in the redemption of Zion.

To encourage the churches to gather up their riches to purchase land.

To obtain means for the relief of the brethren in Kirtland, for Kirtland was in debt about $2,000.

To determine the course which the company should pursue after leaving that place.

President Smith wrote in his journal under date of May 5, 1834:

Having gathered and prepared clothing and other necessaries to carry to our brethren and sisters who had been robbed and plundered of nearly all their effects; and having provided for ourselves horses and wagons, and firearms and all sorts of munitions of war of the most portable kind for self-defense, as our enemies were thick on every hand, I started with the remainder of the company, from Kirtland for Missouri.

This group joined those who had started earlier, and after crossing the Mississippi River they were joined by a smaller company which had been recruited in Michigan and nearby regions, bringing the number of the whole company to two hundred and five men and twenty-five baggage wagons. While en route the organization was very strict, each man having definite responsibility and work to do.

Approaching the scene of trouble, the expedition was met by Colonel Sconce and other leading men of Ray County, who came to learn the intentions of the leaders. To their inquiries, Joseph Smith related

the suffering of the Saints of Jackson County and also of our persecution generally, and what we had suffered by our enemies for our religion, and that we had come a thousand miles to assist our brethren, to bring them clothing, etc., and to reinstate them upon their land; and that we had no intention to molest or injure any people, but only to administer to the wants of our afflicted friends.[3]

As they neared their destination in Missouri and learned that their coming in a body had caused misgivings in the minds of their enemies and tended to increase the excitement, the expedition immediately disbanded, the provisions were distributed to the needy, and such help was offered as was in the power of the individual members to give.

From time to time persons not familiarly acquainted with the history of Zion's Camp have regarded it as a purely military expedition which ended in a dismal failure. This is not true. The revelation called for a band of five hundred young and middle-aged men. If this number had responded and had made the journey to Jackson County in the same way the camp actually did and had arrived there united and peaceably inclined but determined to secure their rights by legal procedure, there is no doubt that this accession of strength to the settlement of the Saints

361

would have made it politic for the governor to give them the protection and support to which they were entitled. Even when only two hundred men made the journey, their coming made such a difference to the situation in Missouri that the mobbers were disturbed greatly.

When the quorums of Twelve and Seventy were first organized on February 28, 1835, the seventies were selected from those who had been members of Zion's Camp and who had proved themselves on the journey.

---

[1]Section 102:2a. [2]*Journal of History*, Volume 5, page 198. [3]*Church History*, Volume 1, page 466.

SECTION 101

In March 1832 the Saints had been instructed to organize in Kirtland and in Zion and to bind themselves by a covenant of stewardship that could not be broken, i.e. by a legal agreement. Newel K. Whitney, Sidney Rigdon, Joseph Smith, Oliver Cowdery, and Martin Harris were named members of the organization.[1] On April 26 of that year, further instruction was received regarding the manner of this organization and the permanence of the order in the church.[2] Accordingly the brethren were organized into the "United Order of Enoch" and arrangements were made for supplying the Saints with stores in Missouri and Ohio.

By that time 534 Saints had "covenanted to keep the commandments of the Lord and walk in his statutes blameless with thanksgiving forever," but some persisted in purchasing land for themselves and conducted their temporal affairs without regard to the Order of Enoch.

In March 1833 Frederick G. Williams had been added to the order[3] to strengthen its personnel in Kirtland, and later still Bishop Newel K. Whitney was put in charge of the French farm in Kirtland.[4]

The gathering in Zion was brought to an end by the

work of the mob on July 20, 1833, when the printing establishment and storehouse were wrecked and Bishop Partridge and Charles Allen were tarred and feathered on the public square. About 1,200 Saints were driven out by the fury of the mobbers that fall and early winter and 203 dwelling houses and one gristmill were burned.

The beginning of 1834 found the Saints in Kirtland, as well as those in Missouri, in dire straits. The Order of Enoch at Kirtland was in debt, and the church was beset by persecution and mob violence so that the greatest courage was required to forward the work on the temple, to publish the papers, and to carry on the general work of the order. On January 11 Joseph Smith, Jr., Frederick G. Williams, Newel K. Whitney, John Johnson, Oliver Cowdery, and Orson Hyde united in prayer concerning the work of the order. On April 10 a council of the order agreed that it should be dissolved and that each member should have his stewardship appointed to him.

It was with this background that a revelation was received April 23, 1834 (Section 101), before the members of Zion's Camp left for Missouri, directing what should be done with the property of the order. When the revelation was received there were 1,000 to 2,000 Saints in and around Kirtland and a similar number in Clay County, Missouri. The temple was in process of building but was not yet completed.

"*Which I commanded to be organized and established, to be an united order*" (1a). This refers to the instruction given in March 1832.[5]

"*Some of my servants have not kept the commandment, but have broken the covenant, by covetousness and with feigned words*" (1c). This, it will be seen, was an infraction of the fundamental nature of the order. The stewards were bound together to manage their properties for spiritual purposes, and the introduction of covetousness and strife made it impossible for them to continue.

"*All this that the innocent among you, may not be con-*

demned with the unjust" (1e). Not all the members of the United Order had broken the spirit of the covenant. Some of them had done so, and this had given the enemy power so that the remainder could not carry on their work effectively.

"A commandment I give unto you, that ye shall organize yourselves, and appoint every man his stewardship" (2b). The property of the order now was divided among the worthy stewards, who were made accountable as stewards over the property thus committed to their management as well as over that which they had previously held as individuals. The principle of consecration of the surplus still applied.

In accordance with the instruction of paragraphs 3 to 8, the following division of property was made:

Sidney Rigdon retained his home and the tannery.

Martin Harris received the farm formerly owned by John Johnson.

Frederick G. Williams received his home.

Oliver Cowdery was granted the land upon which his father resided and also the lot next to the printing house.

Frederick G. Williams and Oliver Cowdery were assigned to manage the printing house and all things pertaining to it.

John Johnson received his home with the exception of the land reserved for the building of the temple and the printing house.

Newell K. Whitney retained his home and the store and two other lots including the ashery.

Joseph Smith received the temple lot and the home of his father.

All these arrangements were made according to the council of the order in Kirtland. The property of the order in Jackson County had been confiscated by the mob.

"You shall no longer be bound as an united order to your brethren of Zion" (9a). The association between the

Kirtland and the Jackson County groups had been dissolved by the expulsion of the Jackson County Saints and the loss of their properties. The brethren in Kirtland were now to compose the united order of the stake of Zion, the city of Shinehah (Kirtland), and those in Missouri were to be organized as the united order of the city of Zion.

"Ye shall prepare for yourselves a place for a treasury" (11a). The proceeds of printing the revelations were to be put into this treasury known as "the sacred treasury of the Lord." Withdrawals from this treasury were to be by the voice of the order or by revelation and were to be for sacred purposes only.

"There shall be another treasury prepared" (12a). Each man was to pay into this treasury the proceeds of his business, and to draw thereon according to his needs as long as he was a wise and faithful steward. The net result of this procedure was that the stewards managed the various properties assigned to them, subject to general review by the order to determine whether they were "wise and faithful stewards." In return they had access to the common treasury. The surplus created was disbursed in accordance with the will of the order.

Bishop Koehler commented on the principle of socializing the surplus as follows:

> The wisdom of God directs that the surplus be owned and controlled by the group. It is wise not only from an economic standpoint, but from a social, a moral, a biological, and a cultural standpoint. The consecration of the surplus breaks down class interests based on private possession, and therefore class distinctions based on property; and the conflicts, and the hatreds growing out of the inequalities arising from a diversion of the products of the labors of many hands into the hands of a few. The consecration of the surplus gives society power over its own resources and leaves society free purposively to direct the course of its own civilization. It gives control in society to the "human welfare type" and not to the "money-getting type." "Human" values, not property values, is the goal of advancing civilization. The consecration of the surplus is a corollary of the doctrine that each and every individual should take his place and do his part to help win the game of life. Society is the umpire in this game, and it is the right of society, and not of any particular

individual privately in society, to dispose the resources of society in the interests of the group.[6]

"It is my will that you should pay all your debts" (13b). At this time, the order in Kirtland owed considerable money. They were instructed to write to New York and borrow the money needed on the security of the properties held by the stewards. They were told, however, that this practice must not be continued. They must keep out of debt as fully as possible.

With regard to the names used in this and other revelations, President Joseph Smith III has written:

In the Book of Covenants there are several revelations, which are given to the church as examples for their guidance. These revelations are professedly the commandments given to Enoch, and the names which are there given, with few exceptions, are evidently the names of men living in Enoch's time. Orson Pratt, and perhaps some others, in teaching these revelations, in order more fully to illustrate the principles, used the names as types, which was perhaps permissible. A difficulty has grown out of it, which has resulted in embarrassing the brethren in certain localities when defending the faith. This difficulty is, that the rumor that there was a secret organization in the church to which these names answered, has color from the interpretations. What we wish to state then is this, that when the order which is contemplated in these revelations is fully established, the persons holding the various positions therein provided, will fill the types given in those names; not that they shall of necessity be called by those names, but simply to correspond with the example.[7]

---

[1]Section 77. [2]Section 81. [3]Section 89. [4]Section 93. [5]Section 77:1. [6]*Problems of Industrial Zion.* [7]*The True Latter Day Saints' Herald*, April 15, 1870.

SECTION 102

On the night of June 19, 1834, the brethren of Zion's Camp reached an elevated piece of land between two branches of Fishing River and were obliged to stay there because of a heavy rain and hailstorm. About five miles from here on the prairie, the Fishing River revelation was received on June 22.

"Were it not for the transgression of my people, speaking concerning the church and not individuals, they might have been redeemed even now" (2a). The men of the camp who had come on a peaceful mission were indignant at the hostile reception which they received on every hand. They needed to be reminded once again, therefore, that while their enemies must bear the responsibility for their treatment of the Saints, the basic reason for the expulsion of the Saints from Jackson County was the lack of consecration and spiritual unity among their own numbers.

"Do not impart of their substance, as becometh Saints, to the poor and afflicted among them" (2b). This was a major criticism, for the Saints had been repeatedly instructed that they must care for those of their number who were in need. Indeed, this duty is mentioned almost as frequently as the duty of carrying the gospel to the world.

"Are not united according to the union required by the law of the celestial kingdom" (2b). The union thus required was not merely the union of common membership in the church. It was a spiritual union made evident through obedience to the law of consecration and stewardship. Zionic living is much more than obedience to the temporal law, but it does not exist without such obedience.

The society of spiritually developing men and women, bound together by their devotion to the higher aims of life—this is the enduring empire of God. The hate and war and fear and selfishness and cruelty and greed and injustice that divide and destroy society today have only one remedy. We must gain a new estimate of human worth. It is not the zoological esteem of men that will make us love one another, but the spiritual estimate. It is not the economic civilization that will endure nor the well-governed nation. It is the society built upon foundations of ethically vitalized persons.[1]

"Zion can not be built up unless it is by the principles of the law of the celestial kingdom" (2c). Zion is an ideal and a goal, but it is also a working program. Zion will not be built by good intentions but by practical righteousness along the lines laid down in the revelations of God.

"I speak concerning my churches abroad" (3a). The leaders of the church had called on the branches in the

East to furnish money for the purchase of lands and equipment in Missouri. Some had responded, but others had refused to invest further monies until the success of the enterprise had been guaranteed. While this is understandable from the viewpoint of economic security, this endeavor to retain investments in both the kingdom of God and the kingdoms of this world was at the root of many of their problems.

"*It is expedient in me that mine elders should wait for a little season for the redemption of Zion*" (3c). At first the Saints thought that this "little season" would be a matter of a very few years. Subsequent experience and later revelation have shown that these years are just as few or as many as we make them. It is useless to move to Zion with the expectation of building the kingdom of God unless we discipline ourselves to live according to the law of the celestial kingdom. Moreover, this self-discipline must be a stable reference, and not just an intention before the move to Zion is made. In this connection note Section 140:5c.

"*This can not be brought to pass until mine elders are endowed with power from on high*" (3d). This is but another way of saying what had already been told the Saints many times. The building of Zion is a spiritual achievement. For this achievement, the builders need to be endowed with spiritual power. Such power comes only to those who have faith in God and who practice the principles of righteousness. It is not primarily power to defeat enemies without, but rather to overcome fears and doubts and impurities within.

"*The destroyer I have sent forth to destroy and lay waste mine enemies*" (4a). The doctrine of "cursing" and "avenging enemies" we accept only as explained in paragraphs 3 and 4 of Section 102. Here the Lord is made the sole executor in behalf of the children of Zion.[2]

"*The strength of mine house have not hearkened unto my words*" (5b). This refers to the failure of the eastern churches to support the movement for the relief of Zion. A much larger force of men and a greater amount of money could have been gatherered and made available if the churches had supported the movement as they should have done.

"*I have prepared a blessing and an endowment for them, if they continue faithful*" (5b). This referred to the members of Zion's Camp. From their number, the members of the first Quorum of Twelve and the first seventies were subsequently chosen.

"*Talk not judgment, neither boast of faith, nor of mighty works*" (7b). This counsel had been given before, but it is here repeated because of the difficulties which had arisen out of the overconfidence of the Saints. If they had been content to purchase the land and to worship humbly and quietly, bearing testimony to their neighbors but avoiding all threatening, their way would have been much smoother.

"*Until my servant Baurak Ale* [Joseph Smith], *and Baneemy* [other leading elders], *whom I have appointed, shall have time to gather up the strength of my houses*" (8b). Before the expedition left Kirtland, the elders went out to the various branches to gather young men and means for the support of the Saints in Zion. Those who had come up to Missouri now were commanded to locate there, if possible, while the leaders resumed their efforts to gather more men and money.

"*I will hold the armies of Israel guiltless in taking possession of their own lands*" (8c). The Saints had bought considerable property in and around Independence, Missouri. It belonged to them. They had every right to possess it. They therefore were instructed not to relinquish these holdings, but to make the most peaceable settlement possible. This course had already been urged by the leaders, who had recommended that twelve disinterested men should be chosen, six from each side, and that these men should assess the value of the possessions of those who were unwilling to live in the same county with the Saints. If this was agreed to, the Saints promised that they would pay the purchase price within one year and that none of them would enter Jackson County to reside until the money was paid. They also agreed that the damages sustained by the Saints should be assessed by these twelve men. On the other hand, they agreed that persons who owned property in Jackson County could continue to live there without molestation from the Saints no matter how numerous the Saints might become. This document containing these proposals concluded:

If the above proposals are complied with, we are willing to give security on our part; and we shall want the same of the people of Jackson County for the performance of this agreement. We do not wish to settle down in a body, except where we can purchase the land with money; for to take possession by conquest or the shedding of blood, is entirely foreign to our feeling. The shedding of blood we shall not be guilty of, until all just and honorable means among men prove insufficient to restore peace.[3]

"Firstly, let my army become very great, and let it be sanctified before me" (9a). Here again is emphasized the importance of a sufficient number of citizens to command respect, but with it the demand for sanctification—dedication in holiness—is renewed. The best possible solution for difficulties in Missouri would be the conversion of the Saints' neighbors and their subsequent help in the Zionic enterprise. This was not to be accomplished by merely adding to their numbers but by elevating the quality of their lives.

"The first elders of my church should receive their endowment from on high, in my house, which I have commanded to be built unto my name in the land of Kirtland" (10a). As far back as January 1831[4] the Saints had been promised that in Ohio they should be "endowed with power from on high." Such an endowment was received at Kirtland Temple in 1836. It was prepared for in an orderly and humble manner and was realized in the marked presence of the Holy Spirit, which pervaded the hearts of the faithful and was manifest in a moving display of the power of God. There was no secrecy in the endowment, no fealty oaths and covenants, no secret grips or passwords, no grotesque and mawkish gownings, no

370

bewildering scenic exhibitions, no theatrical twaddle, and no promises to follow "file leaders" or to obey blindly the dictates of the priesthood; but all was open, plain, devotional, elevating, sanctifying, joyful, and spiritual; while the sweet peace of God, and the power of his Holy Spirit manifest in tongues, interpretations, prophecies, visions, healings, and other marvelous things testified that the endowment was genuine and of heavenly origin.[5]

"*They shall have power after many days to accomplish all things pertaining to Zion*" (10d). Here is an intimation of the long time which should elapse before the completion of the work of building Zion. The same phrase occurs at the end of the parable contained in Section 98 (verse 8).

---

[1]Herbert Alden Youtz in *Affirmations of Christian Belief.* [2]Resolution adopted by the General Conference, April 9, 1886. [3]*The Evening and Morning Star,* Volume 2, page 351. [4]Section 38. [5]W. W. Blair—see *Journal of History,* Volume 18, page 180.

SECTION 103

A small branch was organized at Freedom, New York, early in 1834. By May it numbered twenty-six members, and about this time Warren A. Cowdery was put in charge of the work there. Within a short time the branch reported sixty-five members, and on November 25, 1834, a revelation was given providing that Warren A. Cowdery should be ordained a high priest and outlining some of his duties. It will be noted that although Warren Cowdery thus became one of the standing ministers of the church, he had definite missionary responsibilities and was instructed clearly to preach the "everlasting gospel, and lift up his voice and warn the people, not only in his own place, but in the adjoining countries."

SECTION 104

A special meeting was called at Kirtland February 14, 1835, for all those who were members of Zion's Camp. Others who wished to attend were invited also. President Joseph Smith presided and announced the purpose of the meeting. After a brief adjournment the meeting reassembled and the three witnesses of the Book of Mormon proceeded to select the first members of the Quorum of Twelve in this dispensation in accordance with the commission given them in June 1829.[1] The following were chosen in this order.

1. Lyman E. Johnson, born October 24, 1811.
2. Brigham Young, born June 1, 1801.
3. Heber C. Kimball, born June 14, 1801.
4. Orson Hyde, born January 8, 1805.
5. David W. Patten, born 1800.
6. Luke S. Johnson, born November 3, 1807.
7. William E. McLellin, born 1806.
8. John S. Boynton, born September 11, 1811.
9. Orson Pratt, born September 19, 1811.
10. William B. Smith, born March 13, 1811.
11. Thomas B. Marsh, born November 1, 1799.
12. Parley P. Pratt, born April 12, 1807.

These were not all ordained immediately, for several were away on missions, but the ordinations were all held at Kirtland and took place as soon as the brethren were available. The oldest of them was thirty-five. The youngest, and first chosen, was twenty-three. The average age of the group was less than thirty.

On February 27, 1835, a council of nine of the newly ordained members of the Twelve was held at the house of President Joseph Smith, Jr.; Frederick G. Williams, Sidney Rigdon, and three elders were present also. President Smith proposed the following question:

"What importance is there attached to the calling of these Twelve Apostles different from the other callings or offices of the church?"

After the question had been discussed by Apostles Patten, Young, Smith, and McLellin, President Joseph Smith, Jr., gave the following decision:

"They are the Twelve Apostles, who are called to the office of Traveling High Council, who are to preside over all the churches of the saints, among the Gentiles, where there is a Presidency established; and they are to travel and preach among the Gentiles, until the Lord shall command them to go to the Jews. They are to hold the keys of this ministry, to unlock the door of the kingdom of heaven unto all nations, and to preach the gospel to every creature. This is the power, authority, and virtue of their apostleships."[2]

The day after this council, the first members of the Quorums of Seventy were selected from the remainder of those who participated in Zion's Camp. This was the beginning of the organization of the seventies in this dispensation, and about one and one-half quorums of the seven quorums possible were filled.

There was some difficulty in selecting the Presidents of Seventy, since the inexperience of the elders led them to select some of the high priests as presidents of these quorums. This was declared to be wrong, and new Presidents of Seventy accordingly were ordained. President Joseph Smith explained the distinction between high priests and seventies as follows:

A high priest is a member of the same Melchisedec priesthood with the presidency, but not of the same power or authority in the church. The seventies are also members of the same priesthood, but are a sort of traveling council or priesthood and may preside over a church or churches until a high priest can be had. The seventies are to be taken from the quorum of elders and are not to be high priests. They are subject to the direction and dictation of the Twelve, who have the keys of the ministry. All are to preach the gospel by the power and influence of the Holy Ghost; and no man can preach the gospel without the Holy Ghost.[3]

During the next month a number of councils were held, and at the suggestion of President Joseph Smith, the Twelve arranged to take their first quorum mission through the eastern states to the Atlantic Ocean. On March 28, 1835, the Twelve met for their final assembly prior to leaving

373

on this mission, and at this time they petitioned the president of the church to seek light for their instruction and guidance while they should be away. The minutes of the meeting contained the following:

> The time when we are about to separate is near; and when we shall meet again, God only knows; we therefore feel to ask of him whom we have acknowledged to be our Prophet and Seer, that he inquire of God for us, and obtain a revelation (if consistent), that we may look upon it when we are separated, that our hearts may be comforted. Our worthiness has not inspired us to make this request, but our unworthiness. We have unitedly asked God our Heavenly Father to grant unto us through his Seer, a revelation of his mind and will concerning our duty the coming season, even a great revelation, that will enlarge our hearts, comfort us in adversity, and brighten our hopes amidst the power of darkness.

In compliance with this request, President Smith inquired of the Lord, and Section 104 is the result.

"There are, in the church, two priesthoods" (1a). Alma the Younger has an informative comment concerning the Melchisedec priesthood.[4] Note, also, the following from *Presidency and Priesthood:*

> The Melchisedec priesthood administered a higher code, a more perfect system than did that of Aaron. Priests of this order were made "like unto the Son of God; abideth a priest continually" (Hebrews 7:3). Made "after the power of an endless life."[5] What was this higher and more perfect code or system that required the authority of the Melchisedec priesthood for its administration? It was evidently the gospel: for James presents the gospel as "the perfect law of liberty" (1:25). Again, a "royal law" (2:8). This is the system through which perfection may be secured to the believers, "as pertaining to the conscience." It converts the soul, makes wise the simple (Psalm 19:7). In short, "It is the power of God unto salvation to every one that believeth."
>
> There is a distinction in the two priesthoods, the Melchisedec being the greater. The "law of carnal ordinances" was administered by the Aaronic priesthood. It did not "make the comers thereunto perfect." Priests of that order were made "after the law of a carnal commandment,"—this phrase expresses simply the rites and ceremonies of the Mosaic institutions that were "added because of transgressions," and which were not a necessary part of the gospels[6],—and "were not suffered to continue by reason of death."[7]

"The Aaronic, including the Levitical priesthood" (1a). The Aaronic priesthood administers the "law of carnal

374

commandments" and was conferred upon Aaron, the brother of Moses, and upon his seed. The Levitical priesthood takes its name from the tribe of Levi, who were set apart to this authority and responsibility. The Levites under the Mosaic dispensation were employed in the lower services of the tabernacle and temple, and as special servants of the Lord.

"*The Melchisedec priesthood holds the right of presidency*" (3b). If this is kept in mind, it will explain many of the questions that arise regarding the respective authority of the Melchisedec and Aaronic priesthoods.

"*The presidency of the high priesthood...have a right to officiate in all the offices in the church*" (4).[8] This follows from the law laid down in paragraph 5, for the Presidency preside over the high priests and the high priests can act in any office in the church in case of necessity.

"*The high priest and elder are to administer in spiritual things, agreeably to the covenants and commandments of the church*" (7). This is in accord with Section 17:9, which states that the elders are to conduct the meetings as they are led by the Holy Ghost, according to the commandments and revelations of God. The high priests and elders administer within the boundaries clearly defined in the law, but within these limits they have freedom to function according to their personal qualifications and inspiration.

"*It was conferred upon Aaron and his seed, throughout all their generations*" (8a).[9]

"*The lesser priesthood*" (8b). The Aaronic priesthood is authorized to administer "outward ordinances" or "the law of carnal commandments." These ordinances minister to the spiritual life of the individual and of the church. Baptism and tithe-paying, for example, are very important, but they must lead to something even greater, the spiritual endowment which comes through the Melchisedec priesthood.

"*The bishopric is the presidency of this priesthood*"

(8c). This is a reiteration of the law found in Section 68:2. In the church today, the Presiding Bishopric constitutes the presidency of the Aaronic priesthood in much the same way as the First Presidency constitutes the presidency of the Melchisedec priesthood. Their major concern is in setting standards and instructing the Aaronic priesthood. In the duties of their several offices, the members of the Aaronic priesthood are, of course, under the direction of the local administrative officers.

"Legal right to this office" (8c). The legal right here referred to pertains to the law of lineage in this office, for the presidency of the Aaronic priesthood rightly belongs with the seed of Aaron. The presidencies of both the Melchisedec priesthood and the Aaronic priesthood descend in accordance with the law of worthiness, the law of revelation, and the law of lineage. But since no known descendant of Aaron is now available, the members of the Presiding Bishopric are chosen with regard to the first two of these three principles as indicated in the next paragraph.

"A high priest. . . may officiate in the office of bishop" (8d). At the present time no descendant of Aaron having been designated to occupy in the Bishopric, the present bishops of the church are high priests, holding office in the Melchisedec priesthood. They are functioning in the lesser, Aaronic, priesthood by virtue of having been specially set apart to this responsibility.

Paragraph 8 of this section should be read in connection with Section 68:2 and also with 129:8.

"The power and authority of the higher, or Melchisedec, priesthood is to hold the keys of all the spiritual blessings of the church" (9a). In the Mosaic dispensation, blessings came through obedience to the law of carnal commandments. In the gospel dispensation, the greater spiritual blessings of the church are administered through a priesthood who are "made, not after the law of a carnal commandment, but after the power of an endless life."[10]

"The mysteries of the kingdom of heaven" (9a). The mysteries of science are amazing to the man of uncultivated

376

mind. In a similar way the "mysteries of godliness" and the "mysteries of the kingdom of heaven" are beyond the understanding of the man who is unacquainted with spiritual realities.

"*The general assembly and church of the Firstborn*" (9b). (See Hebrews 12:22-24; Doctrine and Covenants 90:4.)

"*The power and authority of the lesser, or Aaronic, priesthood is, to hold the keys of the ministering of angels*" (10). Many questions have been raised concerning the meaning of this statement, but as far as I know no official interpretation has been made.

In the first paragraph of this revelation it is stated that the Aaronic priesthood is included with the Levitical priesthood (1a). In the next paragraph of the revelation the Aaronic priesthood almost seems to be identified with the Levitical priesthood. But in view of the statement in paragraph 1a, and of the biblical reference, any exact consideration seems to apply the title "Aaronic priesthood" to those holding the office of bishop or priest.[11] The Levitical priesthood is then regarded as including teachers and deacons and to be an appendage to the Aaronic priesthood.

Along this line of argument it has been held that the provision concerning holding the keys of the ministry of angels applied primarily to the presidents of the Aaronic priesthood—bishops—and most particularly to the Presiding Bishopric. It has been widely held, however, that all who hold the office of priest come under this provision in a lesser degree.

"*Of necessity*" (11a). The various officers of the church are set in their respective places because of the necessities of orderly procedure. The necessity for presiding officers is particularly apparent when we contemplate the endeavor of some groups to conduct their work without such presidents. The greater the work, the greater the necessity for unified supervision and direction of that work.

The First Presidency consists of "three presiding high priests properly called of God. . . chosen by the body. . .

appointed and ordained to the presidency. . . upheld by the confidence, faith, and prayer of the church." If any of these essentials is lacking, the effective power of the Presidency is limited to that extent. In this connection note, "If my people will respect the officers whom I have called and set in the church, I will respect these officers; and if they do not, they can not expect the riches of gifts and the blessings of direction."[12]

"The Presidency of the church" (11b). A presidency akin to this existed in the time of Moses.[13] The early apostles were evidently well aware of the importance and the prerogatives of the Presidency, for they debated among themselves "which of them should be accounted the greatest."[14] The men who engaged in this strife already filled the twelve apostolic seats. If the apostolic office was the highest office known, the strife as to who should be the greatest had no purpose.

In this connection, note that James, the Lord's brother, Cephas (Peter), and John occupied a special position in the church by virtue of which they directed the apostle Paul in his work. [15]

The following quotation from an article on "James, the Lord's Brother" in the *Encyclopedia of Religion and Ethics,* Volume 8, is of interest here:

Christian antiquity agrees in giving St. James a local ministry at Jerusalem, and yet in making him, in a real sense, equal to the Twelve, and in ascribing to him rule or presidency over the presbyters, though nothing is said of any autocratic powers possessed by him. This account of his position is borne out by the N. T. writers. In Acts 12:17 Peter bids those who are assembled in Mary's house to tell of his escape "unto James and to the brethren." In 15:13ff James presides over, or at least takes leading part in, the apostolic council, and gives the decision, i.e., interprets the evident sense of the assembly. In 21:18 Paul and his companions visit him assembled with presbyters in a formal meeting. In Galatians 1:19 he is, perhaps, called an apostle (see paragraph 2); he and Cephas are visited by Paul at Jerusalem. In 2:9 he is named before Cephas and John, and the three are "reputed to be pillars." In 2:12 the Jewish Christians who come from Jerusalem to Antioch are said to have come "from James."

"The twelve traveling councilors are. . . special witnesses

of the name of Christ, in all the world" (11c). The members of the chief missionary quorum of the church are charged with the distinctive duty of bearing witness for Jesus. To an earlier Quorum of Twelve, the Master himself said,

Ye shall receive power, after that the Holy Ghost is come upon you; and ye shall be witnesses unto me both in Jerusalem, and in all Judea, and Samaria, and unto the uttermost part of the earth.[16]

The Lord Jesus is himself the "chief cornerstone" on which the church is built. But the apostolic testimony is a major part of the foundation. A large part of the New Testament is concerned with apostolic testimony. Furthermore, when the term "apostle" is applied in its broader sense so as to include all who are sent of God, it will be seen that apostolic testimony in every generation is fundamental to conversion and discipleship.

"They form a quorum equal in authority and power to the three presidents previously mentioned" (11d). This, of course, applies to the quorum as a quorum and not to the individual members of the quorum. The individual apostles are under the direction of the Presidency of the church (paragraph 12).

"The seventy are also called to preach the gospel" (11e).

Luke is the only writer who mentions the sending of the seventy; and he does not say that they were ordained to positions in the priesthood, but there is every reason to believe that they were ordained, and that, too, to the Melchisedec order; for there was no such office as that of seventy in the Levitical priesthood. Then, again, the seventy possessed about as much power and right as did the apostles. They went forth two and two and preached the gospel, healed the sick, cast out devils, and were given authority over all the power of the enemy.[17]

"The decisions of these quorums" (11i). The blessings of direction promised through the presiding quorums are based upon the worthiness of their individual members, and upon their right attitudes in their relations with each other. The decisions must be quorum decisions, that is, the results of a patient investigation, a sharing of understanding, and a maturing of judgment. In this process such qualities

379

as temperance, patience, godliness, brotherly kindness, and charity are of vital importance.

"The Twelve are a traveling, presiding high council" (12). This statement of the function of the apostolic quorum is elaborated in Appendix E, Section 123. It should be noted that the latter is not a revelation but an opinion of the First Presidency communicated to the council of Presidency and Twelve and unanimously adopted by them.

"The Seventy are to act in the name of the Lord, under the direction of the Twelve" (13a). The duties of the seventy are closely akin to those of the apostles, except that the field of the individual seventies is restricted more than that of the individual apostles, and the work of the seventy is more exclusively missionary than that of the apostles.

"The standing high councils, at the stakes of Zion" (14). These high councils are patterned after the Standing High Council of the church, but their jurisdiction is restricted to the stakes of which they form a part. Each stake high council is presided over by the stake presidency.

"Evangelical ministers" (17). This is the first mention of evangelical ministers in the book of Doctrine and Covenants. The duties of evangelical ministers were not explained at length until 1901.[18]

At this point in the revelation (paragraphs 18 to 30) occurs an interpolation explaining the succession of patriarchal ministry. The revelation states, *"The order of this priesthood was confirmed to be handed down from father to son, and rightly belongs to the literal descendants of the chosen seed, to whom the promises were made"* (18). The intention here appears to be to reveal and emphasize the lineal roots of the high priestly calling. Underlying this is the affirmation that the purpose of God from the beginning has not been one of general goodwill but of specific preparation and calling. This is directly related to the doctrine of election which was devoutly believed by the children of Israel but was restated by the writers of the gospels and by Peter and Paul.[19]

"Adam-ondi-Ahman" (28a). See general notes on Section 77.

"Michael, the Prince" (28b). See general notes on Section 77.

"Thou art a prince over them for ever" (28c).

The priesthood was first given to Adam; he obtained the first presidency, and held the keys of it from generation to generation. He obtained it in the creation, before the world was formed, as in Genesis 1:20, 26, 28. He had dominion given him over every living creature. He is Michael, the arch-angel, spoken of in the Scriptures. Then to Noah, who is Gabriel, and who stands next in authority to Adam in the priesthood; he was called of God to this office and was the father of all living in his day, and to him was given the dominion. These men held keys first on earth, and then in heaven. The priesthood is an everlasting principle, and existed with God from eternity, and will to eternity, without the beginning of days or the end of years. The keys had to be brought from heaven whenever the gospel is sent. When they are revealed it is by Adam's authority.

Daniel speaks of the Ancient of Days; he means the oldest man, our father Adam, Michael. He will call his children together and hold a council with them to prepare them for the coming of the Son of Man. He (Adam) is the father of the human family, and presides over the spirits of all men, and all that have had the keys must stand before him in this grand council.[20]

"It is the duty of the Twelve, also, to ordain and set in order all the other officers of the church" (30). This does not mean that the members of the Twelve are to do all the ordaining to be done, but that they supervise the work of organization in the various branches and districts and see that the necessary priesthood members are set in their places. This paragraph must be read in connection with the following paragraph and with Doctrine and Covenants 120:1; 122:8.

"There must needs be presiding elders" (31b). See paragraphs 38 to 41. Evidently the Twelve are to be especially concerned in quorum organization. There is good reason for this. Apostolic supervision of the work in the field is not through detached instruction to specific individuals but through priesthood training and direction through the proper local officers.

"*It must needs be that one be appointed, of the high priesthood, to preside over the priesthood*" (31e). The president of the church is ordained as well as appointed.[21]

"*A bishop must be chosen from the high priesthood, unless he is a literal descendant of Aaron*" (32b). See notes on paragraph 8.

"*A common judge among the inhabitants of Zion*" (33a). The lowest court of the church is the elders' court, consisting of one or more elders. This court is temporary, and when bishops are appointed in stakes, districts, and large branches, the elders' court is superseded by the bishop's court, consisting of the bishop and his two counselors. Appeal may be had from the bishop's court to the high council of the stake or church.[22]

"*Act in the office of bishop independently, without counselors*" (34a). Jesus, the rightful head of the Melchisedec priesthood, probably presided in the early church without counselors. The literal descendant of Aaron, when properly designated by revelation through the Presidency (paragraph 8), presides over the Aaronic priesthood in a similar way.

"*After this decision it shall be had in remembrance no more before the Lord*" (35c). There must be some end to matters of controversy. The Lord says that the end comes when the high council has spoken. Many members of the church who insist on pushing trivial cases through the various courts until they have been heard by the high council will be well advised to end the case before that time. It is as hard to feel satisfied with an adverse decision rendered by the high council as with one rendered by the bishop's court.

"*Inasmuch as a president of the high priesthood shall transgress, he shall be had in remembrance before the common council of the church*" (37a). This means before the bishop's court. The bishop in this case, however, is to be assisted by twelve high priests. The fact that the bishop is to be assisted by members of the high priesthood in a trial of this kind seems to indicate that even though the bishop might be a descendant of Aaron he also should

382

hold the high priesthood. Note the importance of "transgress." The members of the First Presidency are not amenable to a bishop's court for their administrative actions. For these they may be called in question by a World Conference or by "a general assembly of the several quorums which constitute the spiritual authorities of the church."[23]

"*To sit in council with them, and to teach them their duty*" (38). This is a major purpose of quorum organization.

"*A seer*" (42b). Essentially this term applies to one gifted with supernatural powers of discernment. It has been applied specifically to the prophets using the Urim and Thummim to obtain revelation from God, including Samuel, Iddo, Amos, and others. Amos was mentioned as a seer as late as 787 B.C.

"*A prophet*" (42b). Literally this word signifies "one who speaks for another," but it has special reference to one who speaks for God in interpreting the divine mind and will to men. A prophet is generally regarded as one who foretells events yet future. This is part of the prophetic function, but not all. An important prophetic task is to interpret current trends and events in the light of the nature and purpose of Divinity. Such prophets are great moral leaders of their own and succeeding generations.

"*It is according to the vision*" (43a). While no revelation in this connection received prior to March 28, 1835, has been included in the book of Doctrine and Covenants, some such instruction must have been given, for some of the Presidents of Seventy were ordained a month before that time.

"*Are not under the responsibility to travel among all nations*" (43c). This responsibility rests primarily on the Twelve and Seventy. As far as possible, local presiding officers should be chosen from the people over whom they are to preside, so that the people of every nation will be enabled to make the best contribution of which they are peculiarly capable under their own leadership, and yet all of them will be welded together by the direction and guidance of the general officers of the church.

"He that is slothful. . . learns not his duty. . . shows himself not approved" (44b). These are some of the conditions under which men of the priesthood can be placed under silence. Moral delinquency is of course a further condition.

JOSEPH SMITH III ON THE TWELVE AND SEVENTY

The duties of the Twelve, as a quorum, are to sit in council upon matters appertaining to the spread of the work abroad, and the firm continuation of it in the land of Zion; and upon this is based the recognition of their right to ordain and set in order all other officers in the church.. . . .

Their decisions (if unanimous) are of high importance, equal in authority to those of the First Presidency and are to be made in righteousness; how carefully then ought this band of special witnesses to walk as a quorum and as individuals.

At our April conference, just passed, the Spirit seemed to indicate that the establishment of lines and boundaries, over which the Twelve as integral parts were set to preside, was a contraction of duty inconsistent with the character of the work, and an effort was made to place them more immediately under the impulses of the Spirit of God and the direction of the Presidency of the church. We can all see that this accords with our understanding of the law; and no fears ought to be entertained that the Spirit will direct to be done that which is not in keeping with the law and the revelations heretofore received.. . . .

The seventy are a body of elders set apart for the work of the ministry as a traveling quorum, working under the more immediate call of the Twelve, to preach the word, build up churches, officiate in the various directions necessary in the spreading the gospel, and all acts that an elder may do by virtue of his office as such elder, a seventy may do. But there are certain conditions which require a seventy to travel, as especial witnesses, that are not binding upon the body of the elders.

There can be by the law seven quorums of seventy, seemingly too small a number for evangelization purposes; and yet when we consider the number of elders there may be in the church, we are forced to acknowledge that God is wiser than man, and does not wish to cumber the legislative bodies of the church with too great numbers.

The seventy then are to be men of action; ready to go and to come, full of energy and zeal, prepared at a moment's warning to follow the lead of the Spirit, to the north, east, south, or west; proclaiming the gospel as they go, baptizing all who come unto them, laying their hands upon the sick in common with their brethren of the Twelve; under no responsibility of presiding, but when the Spirit so directs, or exigency requires, they may preside by virtue of their right to officiate as elders in the church.

The law also contemplates the Seventy as a legislative body, and a decision made by these quorums (if unanimous) is of like importance as a decision of the Twelve.

It may also be concluded that any act which an high priest might do, while abroad as a minister of the gospel building up the church, might be legitimately done by one of the Seventy; for in speaking of the difference between the two quorums, the law says: that those who belong not unto this quorum, neither unto the twelve, are not under the responsibility to travel, nevertheless they may hold as high and responsible offices in the church; evidently carrying the inference that this was an office in authority greater than an elder, and if an elder may, why may not a Seventy, or an apostle preside?[24]

---

[1]Section 16:6. [2]Church History 1:549. [3]*Millennial Star* 15:849. [4]Alma 10:1-15. [5]Hebrews 7:16. [6]Galatians 3:19. [7]Hebrews 7:16, 18, 19, 23; 10:9, 10, 11, 12; Galatians 2:16; Acts 13:39. [8]Section 104:8. [9]Leviticus 8; Numbers 3:3, 10. [10]Hebrews 7:16. [11]Section 104:8c. [12]Section 125:14c. [13]Exodus 24:14, 15. [14]Luke 22:22-24, 9:46; Mark 9:34. [15]Galatians 2:9. [16]Acts 1:8. [17]Luke 10:1-19; W. H. Kelley, *Presidency and Priesthood.* [18]Section 125:3. [19]Matthew 24:22, 24, 31; Mark 13:20, 22, 27; Luke 18:7; Romans 8:33; 9:11, 5, 7, 28; Colossians 3:12; I Timothy 5:21; II Timothy 2:10; I Thessalonians 1:4; Titus 1:1; I Peter 1:2, 2:6; II Peter 1:10. [20]*Millennial Star*, 1855, pp. 310, 311. [21]Section 117:3. [22]Sections 99:1; 104:35. [23]Section 104:11j. [24]Joseph Smith III, *Saints' Herald*, May 1, 1866.

SECTION 105

The spring and summer of 1837 was a time of great public unrest, and this was paralleled by disunity within the church. Some of the members of the leading quorums were found in opposition to Joseph Smith and his supporters. These difficulties culminated in the apostasy of some, the rejection of some by the church, and the reconciling of still others, until the personnel of the presiding quorums was greatly changed.

Joseph wrote of the situation a few months prior to the September conference, at which these difficulties came to a head:

A few weeks before the twelve were expected to meet in full quorum (some of them having been absent for some time), God revealed to me that something new must be done for the salvation of his church. On or about the first of June, 1837, Heber C. Kimball, one of the Twelve, was set apart by the spirit of prophecy and revelation, prayer and the laying on of hands by the First Presidency, to preside over a mission to England, to be the first foreign mission of the church of Christ in the last days. While we were about ordaining him, Orson Hyde, another of the Twelve, came in, and upon listening to what was passing his heart melted within him (for he had begun to drink of the cup filled with the overflowings of speculation). He acknowledged all his faults, asked forgiveness, and offered to accompany President Kimball on his mission to England. His offer was accepted, and he was set apart for that purpose.[1]

The missionaries sailed from New York on the *Garrick*, July 1, 1837, their company including Heber C. Kimball, Orson Hyde, Willard Richards, John Goodson, Isaac Russell, Joseph Fielding, and John Snyder. They landed in Liverpool July 18, 1837; five days later, Heber C. Kimball preached the first Latter Day Saint sermon in Europe at Preston, England. On the same day, Sunday, July 23, this revelation to Thomas B. Marsh, president of the Quorum of Twelve, was received by the prophet Joseph at Kirtland, Ohio.

"Thy brethren who were chosen to bear testimony of my name" (1). At this time the members of the Quorum of Twelve were as follows: Thomas B. Marsh, David W. Patten, Brigham Young, Heber C. Kimball, Orson Hyde, William E. McLellin, Parley P. Pratt, Luke S. Johnson, William Smith, Orson Pratt, John F. Boynton, and Lyman E. Johnson. Of these, Luke S. Johnson, John F. Boynton, Lyman E. Johnson, William E. McLellin, Orson Hyde, Orson Pratt, and Parley P. Pratt had been involved to some degree in the disturbances of the period. The first three of these were not sustained by the General Conference of September 1837 and were expelled in 1838. Brother McLellin left the church in 1838. Orson Hyde fulfilled his mission to Europe but after his return was out of harmony with the church and was not sustained for a time. He was later restored. The Pratt brothers continued in their ministry and apparently recovered themselves.

"Thou shalt send forth my word unto the ends of the earth" (2b). This was in harmony with the calling of Thomas B. Marsh, who was president of the chief missionary quorum of the church. The word *send* indicates that his missionary task is administrative as well as personal. This is emphasized as the revelation continues.

"Let thy habitation be known in Zion, and remove not thy house" (4a). Brother Marsh had changed his location several times in the course of a few years, living successively in Jackson County, Lafayette County, and Clay County, Missouri; in Kirtland, Ohio; in Clay County and in Far West, Missouri; and then again in Kirtland. It was necessary that he should locate himself definitely with one of the groups of the Saints, so that they would know where to look to him for the guidance rightfully expected from a leading minister.

"Thy path lieth among the mountains, and among many nations" (4b). Four days after this revelation was given Thomas B. Marsh started with Joseph Smith and Sidney Rigdon on a mission to Canada.

"At thy rebuke let the tongue of the slanderer cease its perverseness" (4c). Elder Marsh was in a key position and his support of the Presidency of the church was likely to be particularly effective, especially among his brethren of the Twelve.

"The keys which I have given unto him, and also to you-ward, shall not be taken from him until I come" (6b). The presiding authority over the whole church rested in Joseph and his counselors. The calling of the Presidency included the responsibility of directing the Twelve. It was this that some of the apostles resented, but Elder Marsh here was reminded that the keys "to youward," or "toward you" as we would say it now, were still held by Joseph.

"My servant Joseph, and my servant Sidney, and my servant Hyrum" (7a). Frederick G. Williams was still nominally a member of the First Presidency of the church, but he was aligned with the opposition to Joseph. Even after this revelation Joseph presented the name of Frederick G.

Williams as one of his counselors, but the church refused to sustain him and at a conference held at Far West, Missouri, November 7, 1837, he was rejected as a member of the Presidency, and Hyrum Smith was sustained in his place.

"Whosoever ye shall send in my name, by the voice of your brethren, the Twelve, duly recommended and authorized by you, shall have power" (8a). This should be read in connection with Sections 104:13 and 120:3.

"See to it that ye trouble not yourselves concerning the affairs of my church in this place" (11a). The members of the Presidency were in charge in Kirtland and were available. There was therefore no specific need for the work of the Twelve in that place, and the apostles were urged to be busy in their missionary activities instead of becoming embroiled in the difficulties of the Kirtland situation.

"The power of this priesthood" (12a). This is evidently the apostolic authority, for the Presidency, as well as the Twelve, are apostles.

---

[1]*Millennial Star*, Volume 16, page 11.

SECTION 106

After being expelled from Jackson County, Missouri, most of the Saints settled in Clay County and remained there in comparative peace until the summer of 1836. At that time a committee of the Clay County citizens suggested that the Saints should move to another location because of their different customs and beliefs. Accordingly, part of Ray County was settled by the Saints and was named Caldwell County, legislative approval being given December 29, 1836.

The settlement of the Saints centered in Far West, where the townsite was entered August 8, 1836, and a number of log and frame houses were built. The north half of the original townsite was entered in the name of W. W. Phelps and the south half in the name of John Whitmer, both men holding as trustees in trust for the church. Later the townsite was extended, and it was decided that Bishop Partridge and his counselors should act as trustees for the entire area in harmony with the law of the church. During 1837, many Saints gathered from various parts of the state of Missouri and from the East and built up the Far West settlement.

With this background, certain of the elders met July 8, 1838, and petitioned the Lord for an answer to the question, "O Lord, show unto thy servants, how much thou requirest of the properties of thy people for a tithing."

"*I require all their surplus property*" (1a). This consecration of the surplus was to be put into the hands of Bishop Partridge for the building of the temple,[1] for the purchasing of lands, in harmony with prior commandments, and for payment of the debts which the Presidency had incurred on behalf of the church.

"*Those who have thus been tithed, shall pay one tenth of all their interest annually*" (1b). In February 1831 the ministry of the church had been instructed to "teach the principles of my gospel which are in the Bible and the Book of Mormon."[2] This included the payment of one tenth of the increase, as here commanded.[3]

In a "Memorandum Interpreting Section 106" prepared while he was Presiding Bishop, Elder L. F. P. Curry wrote:

From the beginning, the payment of the tithe, the tenth, as a part of the tithing law, has been based upon the net increase after the deduction of necessary living expenses. Genesis 14:20 (see also Hebrews 7:2, 4) recites that Abram gave "tithes of all" to Melchisedec. The Inspired Version of the Bible reads, "tithes of all he had taken," and refers to the goods recovered from the marauding kings. This view is verified by the thirty-ninth verse (Inspired Version) which points out the habit of Abram to pay "unto him [Melchisedec] tithes of all that he had, of all the riches which he possessed, which God had given him more than that which he had need."

This was the practice restored in 1831, and that under which the people of Far West lived in 1838. They had not, however, consecrated their surplus, and section 106:1 specifically calls this to their attention. Hitherto they had been partially obedient. Now, upon payment of the surplus they would become wholly obedient, and thus for them it was the "beginning" of complete observance of the law. Thereafter, they were to pay the tenth of their annual increase, which here is referred to as "interest," and which usage must not be confused with that meaning the payment made for the use of borrowed money. The "standing law" is (1) the payment of the tenth of the net worth at the outset, (2) the consecration of any surplus remaining, and (3) thereafter, payment of the tenth of the annual net increase.[4]

"This shall be an ensample unto all the stakes of Zion" (2c). Because of this sentence, it has been urged that tithing applies only in Zion and her stakes, but our heavenly Father enjoined the administration of the law when there was no membership in Zion or in any stake.[5]

An editorial supporting the statement quoted from Bishop Curry appeared in the same issue of the *Saints' Herald*. It was signed by President Frederick M. Smith and said, in part:

There is one aspect of section 106 which should not be overlooked, as it goes far in clarifying the subject. Let me suggest to our readers that this be kept in view while studying the section in relation to the subject of tithing. It is the historical setting of the time in which the matter came to the church. It must be remembered that in 1838 the church was attempting to establish new headquarters, after having made trying journeys from western New York, Kirtland, Ohio, and Independence, Missouri. These journeys, made under most unfavorable conditions, especially at times, had made heavy inroads on their resources; and further, all their economic and financial resources were needed, individually as well as collectively, to re-establish themselves in the newly selected region for gathering, needed for building of dwellings, schools, store buildings, the temple, for equipping farms with agricultural implements, establishing stores of goods, and founding substantial businesses. In fact, there was pressing need for much greater financial resources than they actually had. Their money and possessions had undergone depletion through adverse circumstances and experiences. But they had deep religious convictions, and knew the social and spiritual security which lay in full compliance with divine law and mandates. The financial law of the church was as close to their hearts as any other part of the whole. They knew a tithe was a tenth, and that that was required of them. But they also knew their straightened circumstances. Pressed as they were for means to establish their new community and to get their lands into a state of needed productivity, and realizing their need for every dollar at their command, they still have a deep-seated and religiously foundationed desire to yield full compliance with the temporal law; they desired to "Keep the Law." To keep it they must *begin* compliance therewith. They knew also the mercy and justice of the Being in whom they placed their trust. It was quite logical for them in their anxiety to inquire how they might, under the strain and stress of pioneer work and demands, start to keep the law in a way which would conserve their own resources needed in developments and yet in spirit make a righteous beginning. Their inquiry was answered in a way indicating the mercy and understanding of Divinity. They were told that their desire to keep the law was pleasing, and that the real spirit of the law of tithing should not work a hardship on those desiring to keep the law. So let them take careful survey of their resources, determine just what they had and what was needed for their social and religious expenditures, and from their surplus pay into the church treasury. And this would be accounted unto them as a tithing. It is not at all unlikely that in most cases the surplus had, or that above needs, was much less than a tithe of their wealth; but this cheerfully given in the real spirit of the financial law would be counted as a tithe; and after that, a tenth of the increase would be the rule. The instructions given viewed in this light are quite harmonious with the instructions elsewhere given on the temporal law. The beginning of compliance therewith is a tenth. And the Lord has good enough business judgment to know that the income from the contributions of the Saints will, in the long run, be more substantial if the rendition of the law does not cramp the tithe payer. Paid thus out of surplus it becomes harmonious with that part of the law which requires all surplus to be consecrated, as will be required in Zion and her stakes, when the law is fully observed.

This envisagement of section 106 has always afforded me pleasure in contemplation, as it sees the equitable application of the law under all circumstances, and bespeaks the mercy and magnanimity of the Master in leading his people towards higher and better things. He wants obedience to the law and his commands; but he is concerned with the welfare and frugality and security of the people. Willingness and desire to comply with the law is recognized by Divinity, and the righteous desire of the Saints means more to him than extorting the pound of flesh.

---

[1]Church History 2:151-2. [2]Section 42:5a. [3]Matthew 23:23; Hebrews 7:2; Genesis 28:22; Malachi 3:10; Alma 10:8. [4]*Saints' Herald* 87:804. [5]Section 114.

SECTION 107

See Appendix A, pages 564-575

SECTION 108

The revelation known as "The Preface" was given November 1, 1831, at Hiram, Ohio. Two days later the brethren came to Joseph and asked for information concerning the preaching of the gospel and the gathering. In answer to their importunities, Joseph received a revelation on Thursday, November 3, which has since been known as "The Appendix." The probable explanation for this designation is that it is a valuable supplement to the earlier revelations, and since the elders expected to print the Book of Commandments immediately they decided that it would make a good conclusion to that book. Although the Book of Commandments was never completed, so that the appendix does not occur therein, it was printed at the end of the revelations received by Joseph Smith included in the edition of 1835.

It has been suggested that Section 108 might well be placed in its natural order between the sections at present numbered 70 and 71. If this were done it would make the allusions in paragraphs 2 and 12 more clear than they now are.

"The Lord who shall suddenly come to his temple" (1a). This phrase and the remainder of the paragraph are closely akin to Malachi 3. This reference was particularly appropriate at the time that the revelation was given, for the gathering to Jackson County was just beginning, and the problems which later developed had not yet arisen.

"Prepare ye, prepare ye, O my people; sanctify yourselves" (2a). The Lord who thus called upon his people to sanctify

392

themselves in preparation for the gathering to Zion is still calling. This is one of the "principles of the law of the celestial kingdom,"[1] without which Zion cannot be built. All things must be done decently and in order; we must have all things prepared before us, but the major preparation is a preparation of heart and mind which will make the Saints willing to obey the laws and demands of Zionic living. It is, furthermore, a preparation which must be made continuous as the righteous grow from grace to grace.

"Go ye out from Babylon" (2b). In an earlier revelation,[2] Babylon is referred to as "the same which has made all nations drink of the wine of the wrath of her fornications." This has been held by many to mean the Roman Catholic Church which has usurped the place of the pure bride of Christ.[3] It is also more widely applied, however, as a personification of the sinful world. It will be remembered that the angel who was to fly in the midst of heaven bearing the everlasting gospel was to be succeeded by another angel, saying,

Babylon is fallen, is fallen, that great city, because she made all nations drink of the wine of the wrath of her fornications.[4]

In the preface which was given immediately before the appendix there occurs the following:

Every man walketh in his own way, and after the image of his own god, whose image is in the likeness of the world, and whose substance is that of an idol, which waxeth old and shall perish in Babylon, even Babylon the great, which shall fall.[5]

Later in the same revelation (paragraph 4) occurs the sentence, "Go ye out from among the nations even from Babylon, from the midst of *wickedness* which *is spiritual Babylon.*"

"Send forth the elders of my church unto the nations which are afar off" (3a). The foreign missionary work of the church began July 1, 1837, when the *Garrick* sailed from New York with seven missionaries who were to establish the work in England. From that time it has continued with varying success, and many of our members are either converts gained in these foreign missions or the

children of such converts. Persons later converted in these missions include F. Henry Edwards (who served as an apostle and as a member of the First Presidency), Peter Andersen, John W. Rushton, George G. Lewis, C. George Mesley, A. A. Oakman, and W. E. Timms of the Quorum of Twelve; Presiding Bishop Walter N. Johnson; and many other general church officers. A steady stream of Zion builders has migrated to Zion since the missions to Europe and Australia were opened.

"Prepare yourselves for the great day of the Lord" (3d). The building of Zion is a work of preparation for the coming of the Lord Jesus. These two great dreams of the Latter Day Saints are inseparably connected. We look forward confidently to the time when "he shall reign whose right it is to reign" in the assembly of his Saints.

"Let them, therefore, who are among the Gentiles, flee unto Zion. And let them who be of Judah, flee unto Jerusalem" (4a, b). The Lord will return to the Mount of Olives, from which he ascended into heaven;[6] but he will come also to the land of Zion.[7] In preparation for this, the Gentile Saints are instructed to flee to Zion and the converted Jews to Jerusalem, where they may be prepared for his return.

"He calleth upon all men and he commandeth all men everywhere to repent" (5b). The doctrine of repentance is a keynote of the gospel, and it was never more appropriate than at the present time. It is the purpose of God that the good news of repentance shall be sounded to the ends of the earth and that men shall be attracted by the love of God to seek and find forgiveness and to join with him in building his kingdom.

"The hour of his coming is nigh" (5c). The *Indexed Bible* states: "The second coming of Christ is a fundamental doctrine of the Christian religion, and the coming of Jesus Christ so frequently mentioned in the New Testament[8] as a great hope of the church is still in the future. It is mentioned 318 times in the New Testament. Christ is coming again to receive his own and will come in the

394

glory of the Father with the holy angels. At this coming the Saints will be caught up with his angels in the clouds and meet the Lord in the air, to be with him for ever."

"They who are in the north countries shall come in remembrance before the Lord, and their prophets shall hear his voice" (6a). In this connection read III Nephi 7:13-26 and 9:46 to 10:30.

"The children of Ephraim" (6c). Ephraim was the younger son of Joseph, but Reuben, oldest son of Israel, lost his birthright through transgression, and Ephraim succeeded him. Thus Jeremiah wrote: "I am the father of Israel, and Ephraim is my firstborn."[9] In the children of Ephraim resides the lineal right to the Melchisedec priesthood and the primary responsibility of gathering the children of Israel from among the nations in these last days. It is because of this that one revelation states:

The Lord requireth the heart and a willing mind; and the willing and obedient shall eat the good of the land of Zion in these last days; and the rebellious shall be cut off out of the land of Zion, and shall be set away, and shall not inherit the land; for, verily, I say that the rebellious are not of the blood of Ephraim, wherefore they shall be plucked out.[10]

"They also of the tribe of Judah" (6f). In this connection consider Isaiah 11:12, 13:

He shall set up an ensign for the nations, and shall assemble the outcasts of Israel, and gather together the dispersed of Judah, from the four corners of the earth. The envy also of Ephraim shall depart, and the adversaries of Judah shall be cut off. Ephraim shall not envy Judah, and Judah shall not vex Ephraim.

"And the servants of God shall go forth" (7b). The message of these servants is to be the same as the one brought by the angel flying in the midst of heaven, for the words here attributed to the ministry are the ones attributed to this angel in Revelation 14:6, 7.

"Who is this that cometh down from God in heaven with dyed garments" (9a). This paragraph is a close paraphrase of Isaiah 63:1-6.

"Who were with Christ in his resurrection" (10c). Matthew tells us: "Many bodies of the saints which slept

395

arose, and came out of their graves after his resurrection, and went into the holy city, and appeared unto many."[11]

"*They shall come forth and stand on the right hand of the Lamb*" (10d). We believe that the righteous are waiting in conscious anticipation of this great day of resurrection and reunion. In this connection read Doctrine and Covenants 76, particularly paragraph 5. The righteous, being clothed with the glory of the Son of God, will share his presence and join with him in the administration of justice and judgment and in the continuing work of creation.

"*For this cause*" (11a). It is the will of God that as many of his children as will be obedient to the requirements of celestial glory shall share that glory with him. To this end the gospel has been revealed in these last days, and for this purpose it must be carried to the ends of the earth. With such a mission, it is hardly surprising that the elders moved out from Kirtland with an all-pervading sense of the importance of their work.

---

[1]Section 102:2. [2]Section 34:3. [3]See Revelation 17:5; 17; 18. [4]Revelation 14:8. [5]Section 1:3. [6]Acts 1:11. [7]Section 108:5. [8]Hebrews 9:28; II Peter 3:3, 4, 11, 14; I John 2:28; 3:2; Jude 14:15; Revelation 1:7; 20:11, 12. [9]Jeremiah 31:9; see also Zechariah 10:8-10. [10]Section 64:7. [11]Matthew 27:52, 53.

SECTION 108A

See concluding paragraphs of the Introduction to the edition of 1970.

SECTION 109

See Appendix B, pages 575–576

SECTION 110

See Appendix C, pages 576–578

SECTION 111

This section on marriage is not a revelation. It was prepared while the book of Doctrine and Covenants was being compiled, was read by W. W. Phelps at the general assembly of August 17, 1835, was adopted unanimously by that assembly, and was ordered to be printed in the 1835 edition of the Doctrine and Covenants. It has been retained in every edition of the book published by the Reorganization, and the church knows no other law of marriage than that here set forth.

"Marriage is regulated by laws and ceremonies" (1a). Among the most important of these laws are those safeguarding the institution of monogamy. These laws include the laws of the various states, but underlying them all is the divine principle, "Therefore shall a man leave his father and his mother, and shall cleave unto his wife; and they shall be one flesh."[1]

It should not be done covertly nor clandestinely. Even though it be a "private home wedding," it is in a sense "public" in that it is not secret but is known to the neighborhood. Society has a stake in every marriage and has a perfect right to take cognizance of marriages and legislate to govern them in ways beneficial to society, since the family thus established is an integral part of society, and further because the offspring of the union may become a burden or a menace to society on the one hand or pillars of the church and state on the other hand.[2]

"The solemnization should be performed by a presiding high priest, high priest, bishop, elder, or priest" (1c). For many reasons it is desirable that a person of experience and dignified approach shall perform the marriage ceremony. It is unwise to have these ceremonies performed by persons lacking experience. . . and whose well-intentioned experimentation with the order of service may easily rob the ceremony of its dignity and its significance as an act of worship.

"It is not right to prohibit members of this church from marrying out of the church" (1d). The safeguards against

397

marriage between church members and others are much more fundamental than those likely to be adduced in an argument after marriage is contemplated. Quite possibly the first safeguard is to build sufficiently large branches so that persons of marriageable age may have opportunities to meet church members of the opposite sex. Another safeguard lies in the provision of ample opportunities for young people to meet in college, reunions, and similar gatherings. A young man or young woman living in a small branch and isolated from other church contacts can hardly be expected to refuse all attentions from those who are not church members.

"Such persons will be considered weak in the faith" (1d). Members of the church approaching marriageable age are well advised to give full weight to the importance of harmony in matters of religion between husband and wife. If they think that such harmony is important but fail to safeguard their own religious rights, this can be only because they are "weak in the faith."

"For each other, and from all others" (2b). There is both a positive and a negative aspect of this promise. First, the husband and wife must keep themselves for each other. Then, also, they must keep themselves from all others in all matters which should be rightfully shared between them and them alone. Not infrequently the negative side of the foregoing is the only part of the contract to be emphasized. But sustained attention should be given, also, to the constructive aspect of the marriage covenant which requires the parties thereto to give their best intelligence and ripest understanding to the problems of happy mutual adjustment. "This requires the exercise of patience and mutual confidence and fidelity, and each must so live as to merit the respect of the other, for respect must underlie love. It is a task to be worked at, thought about, stayed with, and it is the most worthwhile task in life."[3]

---

[1]Genesis 2:24; see also Malachi 2:15; Matthew 19:5, 6; I Corinthians 7:2, 5 (I.V.); Jacob 2:23-36; Sections 42:7; 49:3, etc. [2]Elbert A. Smith in *Marriage and the Home.* [3]Elbert A. Smith in *Marriage and the Home.*

SECTION 112

This section, dealing with governments and laws in general, is not a revelation. The article was prepared at the same time as the article on marriage and was read by Oliver Cowdery at the general assembly of August 17, 1835. It was adopted unanimously and ordered to be printed in the first edition of the Doctrine and Covenants. It has been retained in all subsequent editions.

During the Civil War this remarkably able document was published as the political sentiment of the church by authority of the conference of 1863.

Every paragraph of the section will repay careful study, particularly when this study is made against the background of social and spiritual conditions over one hundred years ago, and with the recent persecution of the Saints well in mind.

SECTION 113

See Appendix D, pages 578–579

On June 27, 1844, Joseph Smith and his brother, Hyrum— the president and the patriarch of the church—were assassinated. Following this catastrophe, and with persecution continuing, the church split into many factions. The largest and best known of these soon migrated beyond United States territory and founded Salt Lake City and the territory of Utah. In effect, this group organized a new church, for Brigham Young, one-time president of the Quorum of Twelve, and two of his associates were elevated to the First Presidency without divine authorization, and a number of changes in doctrine and practice were introduced.

Among the other leaders of factions the most noteworthy were William Smith, Sidney Rigdon, James J. Strang, Charles B. Thompson, James C. Brewster, William Bickerton, and Alpheus Cutler.

Unsatisfied with the leadership available, Jason W. Briggs sought divine guidance, as did many others. They were not disappointed. On November 18, 1851, Elder Briggs received instruction which led him and others to gather those who were to form the nucleus of the Reorganization. These people were familiar with the teachings of the revelations in regard to succession in church presidency, and many of them knew of the occasion when Joseph Smith, Jr., blessed his son, Joseph Smith III, to be his successor. They anticipated that the leaders of the various factions would give way to "young Joseph" when he should reach the years of maturity and show readiness and ability to take his father's place.[1]

The group under Elder Briggs held a conference at Beloit, Wisconsin, in June 1852 and adopted a series of resolutions, as follows:

Resolved, that the conference regard the pretensions of Brigham Young, James J. Strang, James Colin Brewster, and William Smith and Joseph Wood's joint claim to the leadership of the Church of Jesus Christ of Latter Day Saints as an assumption of power, in violation of the law of God, and consequently we disclaim all connection and fellowship with them.

Resolved, that the successor of Joseph Smith, junior, as the Presiding High Priest in the Melchisedec Priesthood, must of necessity be the seed of Joseph Smith, junior, in fulfillment of the law and promises of God.

Resolved, that as the office of the First President of the church grows out of the authority of the Presiding High Priest, in the High Priesthood, no person can legally lay claim to the office of First President of the church without a previous ordination, to the Presidency of the High Priesthood.

Resolved, that we recognize the validity of all legal ordinations in this church, and will fellowship all such as have been ordained while acting within the purview of such authority.

Resolved, that we believe that the Church of Christ, organized on the 6th day of April, A.D., 1830, exists as on that day wherever six or more Saints are organized according to the pattern in the Doctrine and Covenants.

Resolved, that the whole law of the Church of Jesus Christ is contained in the Bible, Book of Mormon, and Book of Doctrine and Covenants. . . .

Resolved, that this conference believes it is the duty of the elders of the church, who have been legally ordained, to cry repentance and remission of sins to this generation, through obedience to the gospel as revealed in the record of the Jews, the Book of Mormon, and Book of Doctrine and Covenants, and not to faint in the discharge of duty.

Another conference of this group assembled at Zarahemla, Wisconsin, April 6, 1853, and, acting under divine instruction, Zenos H. Gurley, Sr., Henry H. Deam, Jason W. Briggs, Daniel B. Rasey, John Cunningham, George White, and Reuben Newkirk were ordained apostles to form a majority of the Quorum of Twelve. A number of seventies also were ordained and Jason W. Briggs, who had been chosen to be the president of the Quorum of Twelve, was recognized as representing the presidency of the church, pending the anticipated ordination of members of the First Presidency. The organization thus effected continued in preaching the gospel and warning the scattered Saints, and in looking forward to the time when Joseph, the son of the martyr, would be ordained and recognized as president of the high priesthood and of the church. A number of stalwart elders were added to their ranks from time to time, and their anticipations were fulfilled when young Joseph came to the conference at Amboy, Illinois, April 6, 1860, and was there recognized and ordained as president of the high priesthood and of the church.

Looking back a few weeks prior to his death in 1914 Joseph wrote:

In accepting the office of President of the High Priesthood, as I did on April 6, 1860, I knew that one consequence of my ordination to that office would be an assumption of one of the most responsible duties—and perhaps the most gravely important—that could be placed upon a human being. That was that I was being inducted into the position of "Prophet, Seer, and Revelator," understood by those with whom I was associating myself as being the instrument through whom questions of grave importance to the body could be presented to the divine director of the faithful and through whom the church should receive whatever that beneficent power might deem wise to give for its guidance. I was not blind to the fact that the position I was to occupy would place me under obligation to hold myself in readiness, as far as was possible for me, to ask the great Teacher for instruction of value to the people, and that—what was perhaps more important—it would be expected that I would at all times be worthy to receive and transmit to the body that which would be acceptable as the word of the Lord, or the voice of the Spirit.

Those who will read these memoirs may have some conception of what this responsibility meant to me, but it is doubtful, unless they have a sufficiently large degree of imagination and the ability of thorough self-analysis, if they can, by simply reading what I have written, feel the gravity and seriousness of this obligation as deeply as did I. There would be, I definitely anticipated, a constant demand and eagerness for revelation; and my experiences from the very beginning of my labors have confirmed this expectation.

I have noted, too, that whenever differences of opinion occurred among the brethren there was a disposition on the part of many of them to shun the important duty of conferring together as counseled in the Word and to prefer to seek for a decision to be given through inspiration or revelation.

Thus it was with a recognition of these factors and a deep consciousness of the gravity of my situation that I began my service as President of the High Priesthood of the church.[2]

---

[1]Sections 27:2; 43:2; 107:18. [2]*Joseph Smith III and the Reorganization.*

SECTION 114

This section is an "appendix" added by Joseph Smith III to the First General Epistle of the Council of Twelve to all the Saints. The "appendix" was in the nature of a revelation from God, given through the Prophet and Seer of the church October 7, 1861. The semiannual conference of 1878 authorized its inclusion in future editions of the Doctrine and Covenants. This is the first revelation given to the church through Joseph Smith III.

This section should be read in connection with the above mentioned "Epistle of the Council of Twelve"[1] and Sections 122:5 and 123 (Appendix E):24.

Concerning this revelation, President Smith wrote in his memoirs:

The first revelation I received for the church as incorporated in the Doctrine and Covenants is dated October 7, 1861, and was given at the fall conference. The question as to the rights, privileges, and duties resting upon the church by virtue of what is known as the law of tithing had been brought into prominence and seriously and earnestly discussed. Since opinion about its administration and operation varied, it seemed that an opportune time had come for asking for a directing word from the Lord, and upon me was laid the burden of making the inquiry needed in the case.

Accordingly I placed the matter before the Lord in humble and sincere prayer, doing all that lay within my power to put myself in a proper condition before him that I might receive the answer desired.

While pondering over the matter after an earnest engagement in such prayer, I became aware of a power being exercised over me such as I had never before experienced.[2] That which is embodied in the revelation mentioned was vividly impressed upon my consciousness and was presented in words to the church, as stated, on the seventh day of October, 1861. By this voice of the Spirit, or Word of the Lord, the burden of presenting and executing the law of tithing was, for the time being, placed upon the Quorum of Twelve.[3]

"In order to place the church in a position to carry on the promulgation of the gospel" (1a). The first sentence of the first revelation given through President Joseph Smith III is concerned with the promulgation of the gospel. In the Reorganization, as in the entire Restoration movement, missionary work is basic. Prior to this time, the missionary work of the Reorganization had been carried on by the local ministry laboring as circumstances permitted. E. C. Briggs, Samuel Gurley, and others had taken brief missions and had been supported by the contributions of the Saints rather than through the operation of the law of tithing.

"The Twelve will take measures in connection with the Bishop to execute the law of tithing" (1a). In deference to the law on the call of bishops[4] no bishop had been ordained prior to the ordination of President Joseph

Smith III. Elder Edwin Caldwell was church treasurer from June 11, 1859, until Israel Rogers was ordained the day after Joseph was set apart. The record says: "On the 7th Israel Rogers was ordained Bishop of the Church under the hands of Elders Blair, Gurley, and Powers, as directed by President Joseph Smith."[5]

The primary task of teaching the law of tithing rests upon the Bishopric. In this work they should be supported by the various quorums, but particularly by the Presidency and the Twelve. At this time Joseph was presiding over the church without counselors, and since he had not yet fully proved himself to the Saints, and the Twelve were widely known for the work which they had done in bringing the Reorganization into being, the Lord gave instructions that the Twelve should teach the law of tithing as one of their special duties. Some misunderstanding arose because of this,[6] and the Lord made the matter clear in a subsequent revelation. If this revelation and the later one are studied together, several principles become apparent, e.g., the association of the presiding quorums with the Bishopric, protection of the Presidency by use of the Twelve, and the adoption of the most expedient lawful means to gain the desired ends. This is a classic example of the expedient use of the Twelve because of the temporary and unavoidable limitations of the Presidency.

"See to it, that the temporal means so obtained is truly used for the purposes of the church" (1b). This instruction did not require the Twelve to subject the work of the Bishopric to detailed scrutiny, but it did call for an agreement as to principles. For a time this was not understood, and considerable difficulty ensued and became apparent in the conferences. This was allayed partially by the agreements reached between the Twelve and Bishopric and adopted by the conferences in 1881 and 1888, but the difficulties were not finally cleared up until the conference of 1894 and the adoption of the revelation already referred to.

GENERAL NOTES

Note the difference in style between the revelations received prior to this time and those received after this time. When this instruction was given to the church, the prophet was not yet twenty-nine years of age. His style was youthful and vigorous and free from theological phraseology. One of the minor difficulties of the time was the dissatisfaction of some of the Saints that this revelation was not couched in language similar to that used by the martyr.

At this time Joseph Smith was the only member of the Presidency. The members of the Quorum of Twelve were Jason W. Briggs, W. W. Blair, Z. H. Gurley, Samuel Powers, John Shippy, James Blakeslee, and E. C. Briggs. Israel L. Rogers was Presiding Bishop.

---

¹*True Latter Day Saints' Herald*, 2:155-157; Church History 3:298. ²See Section 139, Introduction. ³*Joseph Smith III*, pp. 602-603. ⁴G.C.R. 216. ⁵These were members of the Twelve: Church History 3:252. ⁶Church History 4:222-6.

SECTION 115

This revelation was addressed to the elders of the church. The 1863 annual conference was held at Amboy, Lee County, Illinois. Elder J. W. Briggs, president of the Quorum of Twelve, made some remarks concerning a revelation given in March 1863 about the appointment of Elder William Marks as counselor to the president of the church. Following this, Elder W. W. Blair of the Quorum of Twelve stated that at the June conference of 1859 it had been prophesied that Brother Marks would be called to this position. Brother Blair then read the revelation referred to, following which it was resolved that Elder William Marks be ordained counselor to the president of the church.

"*I have seen your efforts in my cause, and they are pleasing unto me*" (1a). The work of the ministry was very difficult in those days, and results materialized slowly. The older men could remember the wonderful experiences of thirty years earlier when it had seemed that no one could be indifferent to the gospel message. Now they confronted an entirely different situation, and the elders needed encouragement in their work.

"Ordain and set apart my servant William Marks to be a counselor to my servant Joseph" (1b). There seems to have been general approval of this ordination. Joseph at this time was thirty years of age and William Marks was seventy. Together they formed the First Presidency until the death of William Marks in May 1872.

In 1914 President Smith wrote in his memoirs,

I will confess it was with a definite sense of relief and gratitude that I welcomed the assistance of even one Counselor, as permitted in this second revelation, and thus stand on a partial equality, at least, with the existent Quorums of Twelve and Seventy as represented at the Conference. William Marks had been President of the Nauvoo Stake and President of the High Council of the church under the presidency of Joseph Smith the Prophet. Having felt the call of the Spirit of the Reorganization he had given credence to and united with it, which gave a prestige to the church of no small importance, and I counted it fortunate for me that the Lord recognized his worth and ordered his ordination to the co-ordinate position in the First Presidency.[1]

This ordination was regarded by many as a fulfillment of the vision concerning William Marks given to Joseph the Martyr in 1838. In this vision it was plainly revealed that after severe trials "the Lord would raise him up for a blessing unto many people, and cause him to triumph over his enemies."[2]

"Two by two let them be sent" (1d). In response to a question by the Quorum of Twelve the Presidency later wrote them:

In the matter of question touching the revelation of 1863, in which it is stated that in sending the gospel to the nations it is expedient that the elders be sent "two by two" it is our understanding that it refers to missions taken into foreign lands, or into fields not previously occupied, or organized into districts or missionary fields; and it does not necessarily apply to the mission fields now organized in the United States and territory, except it might be in entirely new and large districts.

406

The two-by-two principle was reiterated in Section 135:4.

BIOGRAPHICAL NOTES

William Marks was born at Brooklyn, Vermont, November 15, 1792. He joined the church soon after its organization and chosen a member of the High Council in Kirtland, September 3, 1837. Two weeks later he was appointed agent for Bishop N. K. Whitney, to transact the business of the bishop in Kirtland so as to liberate him that he might travel as provided for in Section 83:23. When the stake of Zion was organized at Commerce (afterward Nauvoo), Illinois, October 3, 1839, William Marks was chosen president of the stake. He held this position until after the death of Joseph Smith in 1844. However, in October 1844, he was not sustained as president of the stake because he failed to acknowledge the authority of the Twelve under Brigham Young. Following this period, he successively investigated the claims of Sidney Rigdon, James J. Strang, Charles B. Thompson, John E. Page, and others. These investigations proved unsatisfactory until he became acquainted with the Reorganization; he was received into the church June 11, 1859, on his original baptism, his ordination as a high priest being recognized. From this time forward he was prominently identified with the work of the church. President Marks was a man of sterling integrity, true to his convictions, faithful and courageous in the discharge of duty. He died at Plano, Illinois, May 22, 1872.

---

[1]*Joseph Smith III*, p. 606. [2]Church History 2:147.

SECTION 116

A council of the First Presidency and Quorum of Twelve was held at the residence of Bishop I. L. Rogers, near

Sandwich, Illinois, May 1-5, 1865, at the close of the Civil War. At this council, considerable time was given to discussion of missionary work among the Negroes, and it was then:

Resolved, that we refer the above matter to the Lord and that we come together fasting and praying to God that he will reveal his will on this point unto his servant Joseph Smith.

The revelation of May 4, 1865, was received in response to these petitions. The revelation is addressed to the elders of the church. It is included in the Doctrine and Covenants by authority of General Conference of 1878. Joseph wrote:

At the Conference of 1865, considerable discussion was had upon the proposition of ordaining Negroes. I was considerably surprised to find that a number of our ministers held opinions adverse to our having much dealings with the people of that race. The discussion was not finished at the Conference, but at a meeting held in the month of May following, at the home of Brother Israel L. Rogers, near Sandwich, there came the Word of the Lord on the matter.[1]

"It is my will that my gospel shall be preached to all nations in every land" (1b). As early as the conference of 1862 missionaries had been appointed to Canada and to England as well as to various states. The work in Utah had been opened two years prior to the time this revelation was given.

"It is expedient in me that you ordain priests unto me, of every race who receive the teachings of my law" (1c). The comments of President Smith at this point are very illuminating. He wrote:

I was of the opinion at the time that the term "priests" occurring in the opening portion of the revelation covered the authority to preach and administer in the gospel ordinances, as such authority was ordinarily represented by anyone properly ordained according to the New Testament plan. This opinion, however, did not prevail with a majority of the members of the Council, who believed that the word "priests" should be controlled by the subsequent clause which counseled great care in ordaining members of the Negro race, claiming, by such interpretation, that such ordinations should be restricted to the office of priest, only. I did not contend for my own understanding very strongly, as at the time there was no apparent necessity for making any such serious discrimination; since the office of priest would permit the preaching of the Word, I felt that time would either soften asperities or the Lord would make the matter still plainer by further direction.

It would seem that since Joseph phrased the revelation his statement concerning the meaning he intended to convey when he used the term "priests" should have been accepted or the document should have been rejected. The difficulty was more superficial than deep-rooted, however. The ordination of Negro ministers was approved. It was procedure that was in doubt, and Joseph rightly saw that time would tend to take care of this. Later ministers of that race were ordained to the eldership and gave good service. Elder William Blue, a Negro, served for many years as a local elder. He was a member of the Kansas City High Council before being called to the patriarchate.

Modern missionary methods are in accord with this principle of developing local ministry in every community into which the gospel is taken. In this way, these centers become self-supporting in the matter of leadership, and leaders are available who know local customs and prejudices and therefore can avoid the difficulties which beset the pathway of leaders trained elsewhere.

"They themselves may be saved (if doing no evil) though their glory, which is given for their works, be withheld" (2b). In this connection, note the following:

Every man's work shall be made manifest: for the day shall declare it, because it shall be revealed by fire; and the fire shall try every man's work of what sort it is. If any man's work abide which he has built thereupon, he shall receive a reward. If any man's work shall be burned, he shall suffer loss; but he himself shall be saved; yet so as by fire.[2]

"The time is soon when others shall be added to your number till the quorum be full, even twelve" (3b). This was fulfilled in 1897, when the Presidency and Twelve were filled for the first time in the Reorganization.[3]

"Be not hasty in ordaining men of the Negro race" (4a). The problem was many-sided. There was, of course, a great deal of racial prejudice. And beyond this there were few Negroes who had had such opportunities for leadership

experience, for education, or for the accumulation of resources as would qualify them for ministerial tasks. There can be little doubt of the ultimate intention of our heavenly Father, but the time factor was important. Despite their sporadic idealism, there were few people who welcomed the erstwhile slaves to brotherhood and leadership.

---

[1]*Joseph Smith III*, p. 606. [2]I Corinthians 3:13-15. [3]Section 124:2-4.

SECTION 117

At the Conference of 1873, the Reorganization had been functioning for twenty years, and many of the leaders who had been chosen in 1860 and before had been removed by death and other factors. The need for new material in the presiding quorums had been made clearly apparent by the death of William Marks of the First Presidency in May 1872 and the reduction of the apostolic council to five members by the death of Apostle Samuel Powers in February 1873. Everywhere the prayers of the Saints were being offered for light in this crucial situation. President Smith wrote:

For some time I had been seriously engaged in thought and meditation over these conditions, and as conference time approached I had become more and more engrossed in prayer and concern over them. As far as my human wisdom was involved I realized I was at a standstill; I had no opinions of my own as to what changes might or should be made, nor had I the least intimation of what possible answer might be given to the prayers of the church that I knew were ascending in connection with my own. . . .

The answer to our necessity and these specific appeals is to be found in the revelation that came to me [in Plano, Illinois] on March 3, 1873. . . . In the days following its reception I was permitted to enjoy the presence of the Spirit in a remarkable degree.[1]

The document was approved by the remaining members of the Twelve and on April 9 was presented to the body.

On the tenth it was acted upon by sections and the several ordinations were provided for. The Conference minutes say that

...At the ordination meeting...the Holy Ghost like a mantle rested upon the assembly, and every heart was moved with joy and gladness, in that the Dayspring from on high had visited them, and that the Lord had again manifested himself to his people. The hardest heart was melted to tenderness, and all were made to feel that this was indeed the house of God, the very gate of heaven.

"*Let them be set apart to this office by the laying on of hands*" (3b). The highest ranking church officers available, other than President Smith himself, were the members of the Twelve. Under the law these were authorized to "ordain and set in order all the other officers of the church,"[2] so that there was no surprise when they were designated to function in these ordinations. The addition of the president of the Quorum of High Priests and the Presiding Bishop to serve with them was largely symbolic, indicating the scope of the presidential responsibility being conferred; this appears to have been appreciated.

Those officiating at the ordination of David H. Smith were Jason W. Briggs, spokesman, and E. C. Briggs and Josiah Ells of the Twelve; Isaac Sheen of the Quorum of High Priests; and Bishop Israel L. Rogers. The same ministers officiated at the ordination of W. W. Blair, except that in this case Apostle E. C. Briggs was spokesman. The precedent set at this time has been followed in most of the ordinations to the Presidency but not in all of them.[3]

"*They shall become men of power and excellent wisdom in the assemblies of my people*" (5). This prophetic promise was abundantly fulfilled, most notably, perhaps, in the case of Joseph R. Lambert. Brother Lambert's health was so poor in 1873 that no one expected he would survive for lengthy service with the apostolic quorum; yet he was actually the last survivor of the large group of men named in this revelation, and he gave excellent service to the church throughout this long ministry.

"*The record of the Quorum of the Twelve*" (6). Prior

411

to this time members of the Twelve had been chosen by committees of the General Conferences. Since 1873 all have been called through the president of the church.

"It is expedient for the good of my cause that my servant Jason take the active oversight of his quorum" (7e). Brother Briggs had been president of the Quorum of Twelve for twenty years. He was the senior member of the quorum in point of ordination, and one of the three continuing members. Evidently his position involved some significant responsibility, or his selection would have been taken for granted under the circumstances instead of being confirmed specifically in this revelation. It is to be noted, too, that he was instructed to take "active" oversight of the quorum. Of the other men who have occupied as presidents of the Quorum of Twelve in the Reorganization, Alexander H. Smith (1890-1897),[4] William H. Kelley (1897-1913),[5] and J. A. Gillen (1922-1934)[6] were designated by revelation through the president of the church; Gomer T. Griffiths (1913-1922),[7] Paul M. Hanson (1934-1958), Charles R. Hield (1958-1964), and Clifford A. Cole (1964-—) were chosen by nomination and vote within the quorum, approved by the General Conference.

"Special witnesses of the Seventy" (8b). At the opening of the conference of 1873 there were four Presidents of Seventy, all of whom had been ordained in 1860. Of these elders Wilsey, Morton, and Rarick were now to be ordained high priests. Only Crowell G. Lanphear continued in the council. He was now joined by Charles Wandell and Duncan Campbell who were ordained in 1873 and E. C. Bland who was ordained in 1875. These were designated "witnesses of the Seventy." Of the other four, who were called "witnesses of the Seventy" Glaud Rodger became a member of the Presidents of Seventy in 1880 and John T. Davies and John S. Patterson in 1885.

"Their decision, if unanimous and agreeing with that of the quorum of Twelve, shall be considered the same as if the quorum were filled" (9b). Section 104:11g indicates that "a majority may form a quorum, when circumstances

412

render it impossible to do otherwise." The provision now made that the unanimous decision of the Seventy must agree with that of the Twelve in order for it to be effective merely emphasizes the requirement. A unanimous decision of the Presidency and Seventy would naturally override any opposing decision of the Twelve.

"*Ordained to their office as my law directs*" (10a). Bishop Israel L. Rogers chose Elijah Banta and David Dancer to be his counselors and they were ordained by Presidents Joseph Smith and W. W. Blair.

"*It is not expedient in me that there shall be any stakes appointed until I command my people*" (11a). A stake had been organized at Zarahemla in 1853 but had been discontinued sometime prior to this conference. There were not enough men of high priesthood caliber available to provide the necessary leadership. No further stakes were organized until the conference of 1901. After that time, however, it was understood that the ban on stake organization had been removed. New stakes were now made on recommendation of the First Presidency to the Presidency, Twelve, and Presiding Bishopric and favorable action by the World Conference.

"*The different organizations for good among my people*" (12). Soon after Joseph Smith became president of the church, he organized a Sunday school in Nauvoo. This was quite possibly the first such organization in the church. At the council of May 1865 the Twelve gave approval to such organizations. In April 1864, the Zion's Hope Sunday School was organized in St. Louis. Other Sunday schools were organized, and by 1869 the movement had grown sufficiently for the General Conference to approve a resolution recommending the issuance of a monthly or semi-monthly Sunday school paper. It was thus that *Zion's Hope* was brought into being, with the president of the church acting as its editor for several years. In 1871 the Presidency and Quorum of Twelve joined in recommending to all the branches of the church the establishment of Sunday schools wherever practicable.

"Let contentions and quarreling among you cease" (13). Many of the members of the church in the early decades of the Reorganization came to the church after careful consideration and rejection of the claims of the various factions. In the spirit of the times a high proportion of the ministers among them became skillful debaters. Those who came into positions of responsibility with any extended background of leadership, and while the various functions of the quorums were not yet clear, tended to bring their debating habits with them. Criticism is not decried in this instruction, but contentions and quarrelings are denounced. Unfortunately the contentions of these years were not easily eradicated and the warning against contention was repeated in later revelations.[8]

GENERAL NOTES

It will be noted that when the provisions of this revelation had been carried out, the First Presidency was complete for the first time in the history of the Reorganization, and there were ten active members in the Quorum of Twelve. Two members of the Twelve had been released for inactivity in spite of the fact that there was room for them in the quorum. Members of the council of Presidents of Seventy who had grown old in service were ordained high priests and their places filled by able young men. The Bishopric had been strengthened by the addition of two counselors, and undue haste in rushing into local organizations without proper preparation had been countermanded. This is one of the most important revelations of the Reorganization.

BIOGRAPHICAL NOTES

William Wallace Blair (see also Sections 123:1, 2; 124:2, 7; 125:1) was born in New York, October 11, 1828, and baptized by William Smith, brother of the martyr, October 8, 1851. In 1857 Brother Blair attended the annual conference at Zarahemla, Wisconsin, and, since he had previously been a member of a faction rather than of the parent body, he was baptized April 7, 1857, by Elder Z. H. Gurley. The next day he was ordained a high priest. On October 7, 1858, at the semiannual conference at Zarahemla, Wisconsin, Elder Blair was ordained an apostle. He remained in the Quorum of Twelve until 1873, when he was called to be a counselor to the president of the church. After this he spent more of his time at headquarters, yet he was still an ardent missionary. Elder Blair died suddenly while returning to Lamoni from the General Conference at Kirtland April 18, 1896.

David Hyrum Smith (see also Sections 121:1; 122:4) was born November 17, 1844, at Nauvoo, Illinois, nearly five months after the death of his father Joseph Smith the Martyr. He was baptized October 27, 1861, ordained a priest in March 1863, and an elder the following October. Brother Smith did missionary work in Michigan and Utah and on the Pacific Slope, besides acting as assistant editor of the *Herald*, after being ordained counselor to his brother Joseph on April 10, 1873. He continued in the Presidency until incapacitated for all church labor and was released at the General Conference of April 1885. He died August 29, 1904.

William H. Kelley (see also Sections 124, 130) was born April 1, 1841, in Johnson County, Illinois, and was a brother of Bishop E. L. Kelley. He joined the church at an early age, entered the mission field when nineteen, and rapidly became one of the most able defenders of the faith. He served as a seventy from 1860 to 1873 and as an apostle from 1873 to 1913, being president of the quorum during the last sixteen years of this time. In 1913 he retired from active service in the Quorum of Twelve but continued in ministerial work as far as his strength and opportunity permitted. Elder Kelley died August 14, 1915.

Thomas Wood Smith (see also Section 122:15). was born March 7, 1838, in Philadelphia, Pennsylvania, and baptized

415

March 14, 1866. He was ordained an elder immediately and a seventy at the succeeding General Conference. After his ordination to the Twelve on April 10, 1873, his labors were widely scattered in this country and extended to the Society Islands and Australia. He served for many years as secretary of the Quorum of Twelve. His death occurred May 27, 1894.

James Caffall (see also Sections 123:27; 126:7) was born July 14, 1825, in England and joined the church in December 1845. He united with the Reorganization in 1864 in Salt Lake City and later settled in Council Bluffs, Iowa, where he labored as a local elder. After being called to the Twelve, Brother Caffall's missionary work was principally in the Midwest and in the European field. In 1902 he was released from the Quorum of Twelve in harmony with the revelation of that year, but he preferred not to accept ordination to the office of patriarch. He labored locally until his death, which occurred February 7, 1906.

John H. Lake (see also Section 126) was born December 4, 1829, in Yates County, New York, and was a carpenter when a young man. Brother Lake was baptized December 13, 1860. He was ordained a deacon the next day and an elder on June 21, 1863, and labored locally until his ordination to the office of seventy on April 10, 1871. He was ordained to the Twelve at Plano, Illinois, during the conference of 1873, released from the Quorum of Twelve in 1902 by revelation, and on April 12 was ordained an evangelical minister. He died at Kirtland, Ohio, March 6, 1914, leaving a record of able service.

Alexander Hale Smith (see also Sections 120:8; 124:2) was born at Far West on June 2, 1838, and was baptized May 25, 1862. He was ordained a teacher the following September, an elder at the April conference the following year, and a high priest April 12, 1866. He did considerable and effective missionary work in many fields but particularly in Utah and on the Pacific Slope, both before and after being ordained an apostle April 10, 1873. Brother Smith

416

labored in this quorum until the General Conference of 1897, being president of the quorum from 1890 till that time. At the conference of 1897, he was called to be counselor to the president of the church and patriarch and evangelical minister to the church. He was released from responsibility in the Presidency by the revelation of 1902, but continued as Presiding Patriarch until his death which occurred August 12, 1908.

Joseph R. Lambert (see also Section 126:7) was born October 4, 1845. Baptized in Nauvoo November 5, 1863, he was ordained a teacher three years later, a priest at the beginning of 1870, and an elder in September of that year. He was ordained an apostle April 10, 1873, and continued in this office in spite of ill health until his release by the General Conference of 1902. At this time he was ordained a patriarch. He served as acting Presiding Patriarch between the death of Alexander H. Smith and the ordination of Alexander's son, Frederick A. Smith. Elder Lambert died in Independence, Missouri, February 17, 1932.

Daniel B. Rasey, who was born November 27, 1814, in Washington County, New York, was baptized in June 1851, in Wisconsin. He was ordained an elder a year later and became one of the seven original apostles of the Reorganization in April 1853. He was not very active in his apostleship and was released by the revelation of 1873.

Reuben Newkirk was born October 29, 1822, in Ohio, was baptized in 1850 or 1851, becoming a member of the Yellowstone Branch. He was chosen one of the first apostles of the Reorganization and ordained to that office April 8, 1853. He retained his position in the Quorum of Twelve until 1873, although he did not give himself entirely to the ministry. After his release he labored in a local capacity in western Iowa and maintained an excellent character until his death.

Jason W. Briggs (see also Section 121:2) was born June 25, 1821, at Pompey, Onondaga County, New York; joined the church, June 6, 1841, in Wisconsin; and was ordained an elder the next year. In 1845 he recognized that the faction under Brigham Young was in error and consequently renounced it. Subsequently he worshiped temporarily with J. J. Strang and with William Smith. Finding that they were teaching error, he renounced them also. He was the leader in the initial stages of the Reorganization and was ordained an apostle on April 8, 1853. He was subsequently chosen as president of the Quorum of Twelve and as representative president of the church, relinquishing the latter position to President Joseph Smith in April 1860. In the early and middle eighties, Apostle Briggs became involved in controversies over the interpretation of certain lines of policy and doctrine; when he considered that he was unjustly discriminated against, he withdrew from the church. However, he retained his friendship for the church and at no time entered into opposition thereto. He died January 11, 1899, at Harris, Colorado.

Josiah Ells was born March 4, 1806, in Essex County, England. He was baptized October 1, 1838, and ordained an elder and selected as branch president the following December. After the assassination of the prophet, he remained with Sidney Rigdon for a time, regarding him as the "guardian" of Young Joseph. When he discovered his error, he left the Rigdonite movement, and in 1860 he joined the Reorganized Church and was instrumental in establishing the work in Pittsburgh and vicinity. At the annual conference in 1865, he and Charles Derry were chosen to fill the vacancies in the Quorum of Twelve occasioned by the rejection of Daniel B. Rasey and Reuben Newkirk. He occupied in this office faithfully the remainder of his life, doing missionary work in various parts of the United States and Europe, and died at Wheeling, West Virginia, October 15, 1885.

Edmund C. Briggs (see also Sections 121:2; 126:7) was born February 20, 1835, in Wheeler, Steuben County, New York. He joined the church in July 1852 and was ordained an elder the same day. For a time he was the only missionary of the church in the field. In April 1860 he was ordained one of the seven presidents of the seventies,

418

and at the semi-annual conference of the same year he was selected as a member of the Quorum of Twelve. Here he served until 1902, when he was ordained an evangelical minister, in which office he continued until his death at Independence, Missouri, July 4, 1913.

---

¹*Joseph Smith III*, pp. 610-611. ²Section 104:30. ³In 1922, for example, Floyd M. McDowell was set apart to be a counselor in the First Presidency under the hands of Elders F. M. Smith and T. W. Williams. ⁴Section 120:8. ⁵Section 124:3. ⁶Section 134:4. ⁷Section 130:4. ⁸Sections 119:5, 134:7, 136:3.

SECTION 118

For a number of years prior to the semiannual conference of 1882 there had been differences of opinion regarding the status of the work in Chicago, some contending that it should be prosecuted as a distinct mission and others maintaining that it should be attached to the Northern Illinois District and made subject to local authority. This was made an item of special prayer before the conference.¹

In the Quorum of Twelve and in the church generally there was deep concern over the illness of David H. Smith of the presidency and the two vacancies in the Quorum of Twelve. Against this background the Twelve adopted the following resolution:

Whereas the ministry of the church in the several quorums seems to be in a measure inadequate to the present demands made upon them and believing this quorum should by virtue of their calling take the lead in establishing the work in the regulating of its affairs in general, therefore be it

Resolved we hereby ask the church to engage in solemn, earnest prayer, asking the Lord to reveal his will concerning the various quorums that they may be properly filled, and that in so doing we act agreeably to that will.

The revelation received in response to these petitions was presented to the quorums and to the body and was then adopted by them. It is addressed to the elders of the church and is dated September 28, 1882. It was the first revelation received at Lamoni, Iowa.

"*I will hasten my work in its time*" (1a). Personal and group insights, skills, and unity are basic to any effective extension of the work of the church. As the remainder of the revelation shows, these had not yet been achieved to the necessary degree. Stable missionary success awaited the development of internal order and unity.

"*We cannot now prosecute missions in many foreign lands*" (1b). The membership of the church at this time was about 15,000, including small nuclei in Great Britain, Scandinavia, the Society Islands, and Australia.

"*Nor is it expedient that the elders of the first quorums be sent out of the land of America until the work of the reorganization of my church be more fully established*" (1b). There was wisdom in this instruction, for the effective administration of the church in later years depended directly on the foundation laid by the members of the presiding quorums at this time. The instruction was modified in 1887.[2]

"*It is my will that ye more fully honor and pay heed to the voice and counsel of the traveling ministry in spiritual things*" (3). The revolt from the priestcraft which had wrecked the church in "the dark and cloudy day" had resulted in too much emphasis on democratic rights in contrast to the proper spiritual leadership which the priesthood should exercise. The Saints were here warned that their belief in priesthood should be made evident in practice, and that they should give due heed to the admonitions of the general officers of the church. There was sound reason for this. Branches and districts were small and widely scattered and were presided over by such ministers as were available locally. The general officers, and particularly the seventy, were the only ministers likely to be available who had fairly wide experience and the benefit of quorum and council discussions.[3]

"*Be not hasty in withdrawing your support from them, peradventure ye shall injure my work*" (4b). This had specific reference to certain leading officers of the church who were in difficulties regarding the question of tithing, the gathering, etc. The situation culminated in the withdrawal of Jason W. Briggs and Zenas H. Gurley and their families from the church.

"Space is granted for repentance and a renewal of diligence" (4c). Note the kindliness of Divinity is expressed in this sentence. Joseph was also extremely patient, even though he stood firmly for what he believed to be right. His wise administration at this time certainly saved the church from disastrous losses in manpower and led toward a clearer understanding of the principles of effective church organization and administration.

GENERAL NOTES

This revelation was given while Joseph was in his fiftieth year. It carried a note of conservatism which contrasted strongly with the impetuous eagerness of many of the younger ministry. The instruction of Divinity as expressed here is toward the stabilization of the church through a conservative program of care in the selection of general representatives, and of respect due to those appointed to spiritual leadership. The emphasis, moreover, is on stabilization as a basis for extension of the work, and the church would have done well if greater heed had been given to the fundamental principles here emphasized. One of our major difficulties from a missionary point of view has been that we have neglected to apply the principle of the gathering in our missionary work. We have been told that we should build strongly around carefully selected centers from which the work can be extended to nearby regions.[4] This is one of the purposes of stake organization.[5]

---

[1]Section 121:4. [2]*Ibid.* 119:8a. [3]*Ibid.* 120:4; 125:14. [4]*Ibid.* 141:6. [5]*Ibid.* 125:10.

SECTION 119

The General Conference of 1887 met at Kirtland, Ohio. On April 7 a communication from the Quorum of Twelve was read as follows:

We, of the Quorum of Twelve, report to your honorable body, that we have but seven members, one of whom [T. W. Smith] is in a distant land [Australia]. Thus you will see that the second quorum of the church, as a quorum, does not exist in the land of America. Will your honorable body adopt such measures as you may deem proper, with a view to bettering our condition. We deem this as important a matter as can engage the attention of the conference; and we believe that God is willing to hear our prayer, and relieve us from this embarrassment.[1]

On April 8 the following preambles and resolutions were adopted upon the basis of this report:

Whereas, The depleted condition of the Quorum of the Twelve, and the important character of work needing to be done by it, has led the present members thereof to request this body to take some action regarding it, and

Whereas, They have expressed a belief that God is willing to hear and answer our prayers at this time regarding the matter, and

Whereas, The Quorum of Seventy have expressed anxiety in the same direction; therefore, be it

Resolved, That we unitedly ask the President of the church to present the case again before the Lord, and that we, also, go before the Lord in earnest humble prayer and fasting, that he may give instruction regarding this matter, and all other matters representing present need for further revelation to his church.[2]

Subsequently a resolution was passed setting apart Saturday, April 9, as a day of fasting and prayer for the purposes named. This day was so observed, and in answer to prayers offered a revelation was given on April 11. The revelation was presented to the several quorums, and each reported that it had received the revelation by unanimous vote. The document was read before the General Conference on April 12, and adopted by unanimous vote of the body, all members voting.

The revelation is addressed to the elders of the church.

"It is not yet expedient that the Quorum of the Twelve shall be filled" (1a). Since 1873, when the most recent additions to the Quorum of Twelve had been made, the following losses had taken place:

Jason W. Briggs, released April 1886.
Josiah Ells, died 1885.
Zenas H. Gurley, Jr., released April 1886.

Now James W. Gillen, Heman C. Smith, Joseph Luff, and Gomer T. Griffiths were added, and the quorum had eleven members. It was a day of very strong opinions. If the quorum had been full, conflict with the Presidency (which had but two members) would have been quite serious. Such a conflict could have developed over the 1887 Epistle of the Twelve in which the Presidency did not concur.

Instructions to the elders (2, 3): These two paragraphs are of outstanding beauty and spiritual value. They should be studied carefully by all men of the ministry, and their precepts followed. The following quotation from *Theology and Life*, by R. W. Selbie, is of interest at this point:

The modern idea that a minister of God is just the same as other men, while a healthy reaction against the old aloofness and priestly arrogance, may easily be carried too far. A minister is not a man on an unapproachable pedestal, nor does he wield any magic powers. But he is a man set apart, and consecrated to very definite task. Therefore, while all things are lawful for the minister, all things are not expedient. He has to deny himself many things for the sake of his message and of his flock and often to say, "I am doing a great work, I cannot come down." Men will listen to him and accept his message in proportion as they realize that he is an expert in the things of God, and speaks because he knows. He can only win the privilege of this confidence at a great cost, but when he has won it he verily has his reward. His life will then speak even more powerfully than his words.

"Avoid the use of tobacco and be not addicted to strong drink in any form" (3d). The Saints were pioneers in the cause of temperance. In a letter to the church Joseph Smith gave this advice on the subject:

Brethren, from henceforth let truth and righteousness prevail and abound in you, and in all things be temperate, abstain from drunkenness, profane language, and from everything which is unrighteous and unholy, and from the very appearance of evil: be honest one with another; for it seemeth some have come short in this thing, and some have been uncharitable toward their brethren who were indebted to them; while they have been dragged about in chains and cast into dungeons: such persons will have their turn and sorrow in the rolling of the great wheel; for it rolleth and none can hinder: remember whatsoever measure you mete it shall be measured to you again.[3]

Pursuant to the instruction of this paragraph, the following was adopted April 16, 1898:

Whereas, The Lord has spoken against the use of tobacco and strong drink on different occasions; and whereas, in all our appointments we ought to show respect unto said counsel. Therefore, resolved, That henceforth we recommend no man for General Conference appointment whom we know to be addicted to either of the above evils and that this decision take effect one year from date.

"Cease to be overcareful concerning the return of those who were once of the faith but were overcome in the dark and cloudy day" (4a). Much of the missionary work of the Reorganization up to this date had been done among members of the various factions. The following instruction given by President Joseph Smith at a special conference held in Lee County, Iowa, June 20-22, 1863, has a bearing on the teaching of this paragraph:

Another thing should be avoided by the elders; and that is, preaching so hard against the various denominations, or otherwise pulling down the doctrine of the various sects, instead of building up our own. We should preach the peaceable things of the kingdom. There should be no malice, anger, or hatred; all should be kind and affectionate one to another, exercising love and charity to all. There should be no talebearing and if we are injured, say nothing at the time, but think of it and consider whether it is worthy of our notice, and let us try and forgive them; and let us examine ourselves and see if we have done altogether right. Perhaps we also may need forgiveness ourselves, and by doing so we will not be so easily injured, but will be able to go through the world smoothly.[4]

"Cease to contend respecting the sacrament and the time of administering it" (5a). The present practice of the church is to administer the sacrament the first Sunday of every month. Some have thought that this custom should not be

departed from under any circumstances, but this section teaches otherwise. Of course the sacrament should be surrounded with every safeguard, and it should not be used on special occasions unless these occasions are sufficiently distinctive to warrant the changed procedure.

Paragraph 5 of this section is the basic statement of recent revelation regarding the sacrament of the Lord's Supper. Fundamental requirements for the proper service of the sacrament are (a) that it shall be administered by the officers of the church with sincerity of heart and in purity of purpose, and (b) that it shall be partaken of in remembrance of Jesus Christ and in willingness to take his name upon them. The following are advised as matters of expediency:

The emblems shall be properly prepared prior to the meeting.

Both bread and wine should be uncovered when presented for the blessing.

The emblems should be administered in the early part of the meeting, before weariness and confusion ensue.

"The service of song in the house of the Lord" (6a). The Saints have always been a singing people, continuing the Protestant emphasis set by Martin Luther and the influence of the Wesleyan revival. In the late nineteenth century, however, there were areas of uncertainty concerning the place of music in worship, and some members of the Reorganization had trouble in this regard. The encouragement given in this paragraph of the revelation led to the enlistment of many dedicated and talented music lovers in service which has enriched worship and become a vehicle of revelation in the succeeding years. By the end of the century most branches had choirs. The important contribution of music, however, is still in the congregational singing which draws on minds and hearts in the thanksgiving and praise which are at the center of true worship.

"Let the organ and the stringed instrument, and the instrument of brass be silent when the Saints assemble for prayer and testimony" (6e). This statement is quite clear, and as long as it is not amplified by further revelation

the instruments named should not be used in prayer and testimony meetings. The reason for this prohibition seems to be that some who objected to the use of the instruments in an earlier day might have been denied the benefits of prayer and testimony if the organ and other instruments had been used. Nowadays, when objection to the use of instruments has almost entirely passed away, it is conceivable that this prohibition might be removed. We sometimes combine prayer and testimony meetings with Sacrament services and when this is done, the instruments should remain silent, but they may be used in Sacrament services which do not merge into prayer and testimony meetings.

"Concerning the Sabbath of the Lord" (7a). The principle of Sabbath observance is that this day is sacred to the Lord and is intended as a day of rest and worship.[5] During the Babylonian captivity it was regarded as a mark of distinction between the faithful Jews and their heathen neighbors.[6] Later prophets regarded its observance as an important religious duty.[7]

The gospels show that Jesus went to the synagogue on the Sabbath[8] but he did not give to the rules for Sabbath keeping which had been developed by the scribes the primacy which the Jewish leaders desired.[9] Later, the early Christians found the Sabbath rules burdensome and began to keep the first day as the special day of worship and rest, calling it "The Lord's Day."

Despite the weight of evidence favoring celebration of the Lord's day there have been many arguments among devout Christians about reverting to the seventh day sabbath. A hundred years ago it was debated in many quarters, including gatherings of the elders, and tended to provoke disunity. It was not likely that any statement authorizing conformity to either interpretation would have met with ready approval throughout the church. Nor was it imperative that such authorization be given. In view of these considerations the wisdom of the counsel given becomes quite clear. The end designed has been achieved by it.

"Prosecute the missionary work in this land and abroad so far and so widely as you may" (8a). Hitherto the elders of the Reorganization had been instructed not to extend their work too widely.[10] Now the church has grown in numbers and in understanding and the emphasis is slightly changed. The Saints are still to be careful but now are encouraged to do their best with the resources at their command.

"Let him that laboreth in the ministry and him that toileth in the affairs of the men of business and of work labor together with God for the accomplishment of the work instrusted to all" (8b). Prior to this time there had been a tendency to regard the ministry of the word as uniquely holy. Here the voice of instruction points out that all are called, and that the sincere and honest endeavor of all who seek to labor in harmony with their divinely given powers is equally acceptable in the sight of God and equally necessary to the building of the kingdom.

"Cease to complain of pain and sickness and distress of body" (9a). The prophet here is concerned not only to comfort those who are not relieved of pain by the use of the means set in the church but also to eliminate the additional harm which comes from worrying and complaining. Subsequent scientific investigation has abundantly confirmed the wisdom of this instruction.

"Take sleep in the hours set apart by God for the rebuilding and strengthening of the body and mind" (9a). The prophetic emphasis upon this important physical instruction should serve to remind us of the importance of our bodies in the divine economy. Many times in modern revelation our Father has condescended to warn and instruct us regarding the proper care of our physical equipment in order that it may be available to further his spiritual purposes.

GENERAL NOTES

Note some of the principles which are enunciated in this very important revelation. Among them are the following:

427

Power lies in the quiet exercise of spiritual strength (2a).

The reasonable expectations of the people regarding ministerial demeanor should be respected by the ministry (2 and 3).

Cleanliness of mind and body is important in relation to the indwelling of the Spirit (3c).

Unworthy suspicion is unbecoming ministers for Christ (4a).

Contention, even regarding desirable things, is to be avoided (5a).

Every service should be conducted in the full light of the purpose for which it was instituted (6).

The Sabbath was made for man and not man for the Sabbath (7).

Learning how to bear burdens in a Christlike spirit may be a greater boon than having these burdens removed.

BIOGRAPHICAL NOTES

James W. Gillen was born in Ireland March 18, 1836, came to the United States when quite young, and was baptized December 3, 1861. He labored as an elder for a brief period before being ordained a seventy on April 8, 1863; after twenty years in the mission field he became a President of Seventy in April 1885 and an apostle in April 1887. Elder Gillen was one of the pioneers of the Reorganization in the West and performed effective ministerial labor in Australia, in addition to being in joint charge of the European Mission for one year. He resigned from the Quorum of Twelve in November 1899.

Heman C. Smith (see also Section 129:3), a grandson of Lyman Wight, was born September 27, 1850, and baptized October 7, 1862. Brother Smith was ordained an elder March 14, 1874, after which he immediately entered the field. He was ordained a seventy at the semi-annual conference of 1876, and at the annual conference of 1885 was ordained one of the Presidents of Seventy. He continued in his office until his ordination to the Twelve. His assignment to the Pacific Slope Mission delayed

428

this until March 1888. At the annual conference of 1897, he was appointed church historian and the increasing burden of this work made necessary his release from the Quorum of Twelve in 1909. Brother Smith was one of the key men of the second generation of the Reorganization and left an indelible impression on our church life. He died April 17, 1919, at the Independence Sanitarium.

Joseph Luff (see also Sections 127:2, 129:2) was born October 31, 1852, baptized May 27, 1876, ordained an elder the following August, and immediately entered the ministry. Brother Luff was ordained an apostle April 13, 1887, and served as church physician also from 1906 till the double burden became too heavy, and he was released as a member of the Quorum of Twelve by the revelation of 1909. He was greatly blessed with the spirit of prophecy and is specially remembered in connection with his hymn "Admonition." He died in Independence, Missouri, January 6, 1948.

Gomer T. Griffiths (see Section 125:13), was born at Minersville, Pennsylvania, June 2, 1856. He was baptized April 22, 1877, and ordained a priest on the same day and an elder in January 1878, beginning his missionary work shortly thereafter. At the conference of 1879, he was ordained a seventy and in April 1887 became an apostle and succeeded Elder William H. Kelley as president of the quorum in 1913. As president of the Twelve, he was spokesman at the ordination of Frederick M. Smith to the office of president, prophet, seer, and revelator of the church. He was released by revelation in October 1922 and was ordained a patriarch a year later. He officiated in this office until his health failed shortly before his death May 24, 1950.

---

[1]*Saints' Herald*, Volume 34, page 293; [2]*Ibid.*, page 294. [3]*Times and Seasons*, Volume 1, page 86. [4]Church History, Volume 3, pages 325, 326. [5]Exodus 20:8-11, 23:12, 34:21. [6]Nehemiah 10:31, 13:15 ff. [7]Isaiah 56:2 ff., 58:13 f., 66:23; Jeremiah 17:19 ff. [8]Mark 2:25 f. [9]Acts 20:7, I Corinthians 16:2. [10]Section 118:1.

SECTION 120

Those of the Twelve who had been present at the General Conference of 1887 remained in Kirtland after adjournment. On April 21 of that year they issued an epistle which was published in the *Herald* for May 7, 1887, which set forth the duties of presidents of districts and branches and gave information in regard to other matters of importance. This epistle was widely discussed in the years following and met with considerable opposition. In 1888 the Twelve made a few corrections and then unanimously endorsed it. It was afterwards unanimously approved by the Seventy. In 1889 this matter was discussed again. The Presidency and the small group of high priests were against the Epistle and the Twelve and Seventy were practically unanimous in support of it.

The Quorum of Twelve minutes for April 4, 1890, contain the following:

Whereas, after much deliberation and debate this Joint Council of the First Presidency and Quorum of Twelve has failed to reach an agreement regarding the subjects under consideration and whereas, there is no apparent likelihood of an agreement being reached in the near future by means of either argument or study and whereas, it is highly important that unanimity of understanding, and practice should characterize all general church officers, that the work throughout the world may be made effective for good in the fullest sense and whereas, the Lord has encouraged us to hope and look for light from Him upon some of the matters involved, therefore,

Resolved: That we humble ourselves before the Lord and ask him to give us such light upon the matter as He may deem necessary to help us to the desired unity; also that we earnestly petition Him to provide for the filling of the First Presidency and Quorum of Twelve and for the Presidency of the Quorum of the Twelve if it be in accordance with His will; and enlighten us upon all matters upon which action is pending and whereon more light is now needed.

Resolved: That we ask the President of the church to present the above request before our Heavenly Father and that we sustain him in so doing by prayer and fasting in order to receive through him the intelligence asked for and the help required.

Upon motion it was resolved that tomorrow be appointed as a day of fasting and prayer for the objects named in the resolutions.

It was in response to this action that the revelation of April 8, 1890, was received at Lamoni, Iowa, the revelation being addressed to the First Presidency and the traveling high council of the church (the Quorum of Twelve).

"The epistle is to be left. . . as the judgment of the Quorum of Twelve" (1a). The Quorum of Twelve subsequently amended their epistle to harmonize with this revelation.

"Branches and their officers, and districts and their officers are to be considered as provided for by my law" (1b). Districts were originally associations of branches, missions, and scattered members banded together for mutual aid. There were similar associations in the days of Joseph Smith, Jr., usually called "conferences." They were associations of convenience and there was no specific delineation of their function or authority in the law.

The members of the missionary quorums had been disturbed at two points in particular; (a) The creation of districts seemed likely to interpose a local minister between them and branches which might be the most promising centers for missionary endeavor, and (b) districts tended to be thought of in terms of the areas occupied; if these areas were considered the primary responsibility of the district officers the missionaries could be shut out from points within districts which the local officers could not reach but the seventy might have developed. The inclusion of districts and branches within the structure of church organization laid the foundation for future growth, but every local situation was unique and it took many years to work out a generally accepted and observed procedure.

"Branches and districts are organized. . . by direction of the conferences, or by personal presence and direction of the Twelve" (1c). This provision was made to guard against premature organization by members of the church able to meet together but lacking adequate experience. It brought to the question of organization either the experience of the missionaries or that of the conferences. The conferences were particularly concerned since the organization

431

of a new branch might draw membership away from branches already organized but struggling to come into a position of strength.

"*A branch may be presided over by a high priest, an elder, priest, teacher, or deacon*" (2a). At this time a branch could be organized with six members of the church who lived near a central point if one of them held the priesthood. This instruction permitted preliminary organization with Aaronic priesthood in charge pending the development of greater ministerial experience or the coming of new ministerial strength from elsewhere. The branch president directed the affairs of the group. All lines of activity in the branch were gathered up and centered in his hands as the coordinating officer, so that he could balance the group endeavors toward their common objectives.

"*Chosen and sustained by the vote of the branch*" (2a). While the general officers had important influence in the organization of branches, when branches were organized they were to be free to choose their own officers.

"*Districts may be presided over by a high priest, or an elder*" (2b). A district may not be presided over by a member of the Aaronic priesthood. It will be noted, furthermore, that the procedure in district organization differs from that in branch organization. The district president is to be "received" rather than chosen. As matter of practice this difference was generally ignored, the district president being chosen in the various conferences by nomination and vote. However, this provision did permit nominations by general officers in circumstances that warranted such action. When this occurred the person chosen was to be "sustained" by the vote of the conference.

"*If an elder be chosen who may by experience be found qualified to preside, as soon as practicable thereafter he should be ordained an high priest by the spirit of wisdom and revelation in the one ordaining*" (2d). This frequently has been interpreted to mean that an elder chosen to preside over a district or large branch and sustained in that office should for this reason be ordained to the high priesthood.

Another possible interpretation, and one more consistent with our history and practice, is that one chosen to preside over a district or large branch should by this fact be commended to the attention of the general church officers having to do with the calling of high priests, and these officers should then seek light in regard to the possible ordination of the one so presiding.

Nominations for ordination to the high priesthood must be submitted to the First Presidency, who are presidents of the high priesthood, before being presented to a general conference or high council. There is sound reason for this. If necessary, it may provide a means for requiring a nominating officer to justify his nomination, and this is frequently helpful to all concerned. Indeed, as a matter of experience, those recommending generally submit the reasons with their recommendations. The Presidency also have access to records and to needs which may have a bearing on the recommendation.

"The Twelve and Seventy are traveling ministers and preachers of the gospel, to persuade men to obey the truth" (3b). The word *persuade* is stronger than the word *invite*. It is not enough that the missionaries of the church shall state the purpose and ideals of the church. Men and women must be persuaded to join the church and to become active in its work. The fact that some have been over-persuaded is no legitimate argument against the fulfillment of this divine instruction.

Abraham Lincoln has this to say regarding the art of persuasion:

When the conduct of men is designed to be influenced, persuasion, kind, unassuming persuasion, should ever be adopted. It is an old and true maxim that "a drop of honey catches more flies than a gallon of gall." So with men. If you would win a man to your cause, first convince him that you are his sincere friend. Therein is a drop of honey that catches his heart, which say what he will, when once gained, you will find but little trouble in convincing his judgment of the justice of your cause. On the contrary, assume to dictate to his judgment, or to command his action, or mark him as one to be shunned or despised, and he will retreat within himself, close all the avenues to his head and heart; and though you throw with more than Herculean force and precision, you will be no more able to pierce him than to penetrate the hard shell of the tortoise with a rye straw. Such is man, and so must he be understood by those who would lead him, even in his own best interests.

"*The traveling presiding councils of the church*" (4b). This refers to the Twelve and the Seventy.

"*Representing it abroad*" (4b). This does not refer to labor in foreign fields but to work in any field and particularly in unorganized areas (see Section 123:23).

"*Where cases of difficulty are of long standing*" (7c). The principle underlying the law stated in this paragraph is that local authorities shall be fully respected in their offices, and that representatives of the traveling councils of the church shall concern themselves only with matters of personal importance and conduct arising in branches and districts when local authorities fail to adjust these through neglect or incompetence and so hamper the missionary work, which is the primary concern of the Twelve and Seventy.

"*Those who were presented by the high priests for ordination to their number, if approved by the council of the high priests now present, and the conference, may be ordained*" (9a). High priests ordained in the interim between General Conferences are so ordained by authority of a high council. High priests ordained by authority of General Conference generally are presented to that body by the Presidency after their names have been approved by the quorum of high priests. This practice has its rise in the instruction of this paragraph.

After consultation, the committee provided for in the revelation recommended that the following men compose the high council: W. H. Blair, F. G. Pitt, J. C. Crabb, A. S. Cochran, William Anderson, David Chambers, J. H. Peters, R. M. Elvin, David Dancer, Charles Derry, J. A. Robinson, C. A. Beebe. These were all approved by the conference.

"*Provide that such council* [the high council] *may be convened at any General Conference when emergency may demand, by reason of their residing at or near to places where conferences may be held"* (9d). At that time the church was sufficiently small, and cases of grave importance sufficiently infrequent, for the Standing High Council to care for these needs at the annual conferences. Now, however, the church has grown to such proportions that the high council meets much more frequently, generally at least once a month. Because of this the high councilors must reside in or near Independence, Missouri. This same principle of selecting the majority of the high councilors so that they can meet frequently without inconvenience was applied to the stake organizations in the revelation of 1901.[1]

"Presidents of Seventy should confer with the several quorums" (10b). The seventy are chosen by the Presidents of Seventy in joint council. The council is instructed here to confer with "the several quorums" in doing their work. These quorums include the Presidency and Twelve, under whose direction the seventies are appointed to missionary labor.

---

[1]Section 125:10.

SECTION 121

This section includes instructions given in April, 1885. This was during the first conference held in Independence, Missouri, by the Reorganization. In studying this section paragraph 6 should be read first. The following comment, written by President Joseph Smith nearly thirty years later, may also be found helpful.[1]

It seems sufficient for me to state, in addition to the explanations set forth in the section itself, that the consideration of the question involved was pressed upon me by conditions which apparently demanded and justified an open presentation to the body of the dictations of the Spirit in regard to them instead of submitting the communication first to the various quorums, as had been customary. This was all that was claimed for it, and my heart has ever been grateful for the fact that, involving references to persons as the section does, taken as a whole it was effective in settling vexatious questions. It established positions in church procedure and government sufficiently ample to govern, under similar circumstances thereafter, the entire history of the church and its work.

Prior to the conference considerable disquietude had been occasioned in the church by controversial discussions carried in the *Herald*. The Twelve had also reported that they had censured Elders Jason W. Briggs, E. C. Briggs, and Z. H. Gurley, of their number. Such matters, and the church-wide concern over the physical condition of Elder David H. Smith and his retention in the Presidency, clouded the background of the conference gathering and led the Saints to present the condition of the first quorums of the church before the Lord in special prayer.

"David H. Smith" (1b). In accordance with the instruction recorded here, Elder Smith was released from the First Presidency. That quorum then continued without further change until after the death of William Wallace Blair in 1896.

"The voice of the Spirit is that E. C. Briggs be sustained for the present. J. W. Briggs, and Z. H. Gurley are in your hands" (2b). After the instruction of this paragraph had been considered by the conference, Elders Jason W. Briggs and Z. H. Gurley were not sustained. Thereupon the conference requested the Presidency to rule on the status of the two brethren, and in reply the Presidency stated the following:

They [Briggs and Gurley] are still members of their quorum and hold priesthood; but by reason of the vote not to sustain, are not authorized to act as members for the church, until such time as the disability imposed by the vote of conference is removed.[2]

Elders John F. Patterson, John T. Davies, James W. Gillen, Heman C. Smith, and Columbus Scott were selected as Presidents of Seventy in harmony with paragraph 5 of this revelation. These, with Elders E. C. Brand and Duncan Campbell, completed the council of Presidents of Seventy.

---

[1]*Joseph Smith III*, p. 620. [2]*Saints' Herald*, May 16, 1885.

SECTION 122

The First Presidency, Quorum of Twelve, and Quorum of High Priests held a joint session during the conference of 1894, and after considerable discussion, a report was presented to the conference on their respective callings, duties, and prerogatives.

This report did not cover all of the ground which had been discussed, and the next day the following resolutions were adopted by the Quorum of Twelve:

Resolved that we request President Joseph Smith to present the matter before the Lord and ask for further revelation in explanation of the authorities and duties of the several quorums and their members, also for instructions providing for the filling of vacancies in the leading quorums, including also a designation of the Patriarch if it shall be the pleasure of our Heavenly Father to so enlighten us.

Resolved further, that we humble ourselves before the Lord and unitedly engage in fasting and prayer, on such day as the President shall advise, for the purpose of making earnest supplication that God will favor his church with the revelation necessary.

Resolved further, that we invite the quorums of Seventy and the Bishopric to join with the Quorums of the Joint Council in this service of sacrifice and devotion.[1]

The revelation known as Section 122 was received in response to this request. It is dated April 15, 1894, was received at Lamoni, Iowa, and is addressed to the elders and the church. Concerning it President Smith wrote:

The revelation, Section 122, Doctrine and Covenants, was asked for and given at a time when there was considerable controversy in regard to church procedure and the inactivity of certain persons holding leading office in the body. Bishop George A. Blakeslee had died; Bishop Edmund L. Kelley had been recognized as Acting Presiding Bishop, and Edwin A. Blakeslee, son of the former officer, had been chosen and ordained as his counselor. The Presidency, once composed of Brother Blair, my brother David, and myself, was held by some to be objectionable for the reason that my brother, through illness incapacitated for acting in his office, had been released, giving rise again to the question whether or not that quorum could be considered as functioning properly—a question that disturbed the minds of many. When the message came, it again announced that my afflicted brother

437

was in the hands of the Lord and should there remain until his Will was wrought in that matter.

For similar reasons some had considered that since Brother Thomas W. Smith had suffered a stroke of paralysis and was incapable of acting with his quorum, that body was also crippled in its work. The same Wisdom that decided in regard to David was manifest in his case, the statement being that Brother T. W. was in the hands of the Lord and if he recovered sufficiently would again take his position in the quorum, his bishopric to be continued for a season.[2]

"Those whose duty it is to teach the revelations which my church has already received" (1a). Saints who truly believe in the gift of revelation will seek to carry into practice those things which the revelations enjoin. In doing this, they are to be led by the priesthood, and particularly by the First Presidency whose specific task it is to teach the revelations. One of the conditions of further revelation is that the Saints shall give proper heed to revelations already received.

"It is not yet expedient in me that the Quorum of the Presidency and the Quorum of the Twelve Apostles shall be filled, for reasons which shall be seen and known unto you in due time" (4a). In light of subsequent events it appears that the basic reason for this was that the Presidency and Twelve had failed as yet to reach the unity of understanding which was necessary if they were to work together, particularly with the understanding then current of the functions of the Presidency, Twelve, and Seventy. Another factor may have been that the ministers needed were not yet readily available. This is hinted in paragraph 14 of this revelation which says that "it is not expedient that a patriarch for the church should be indicated and appointed." At that time Alexander H. Smith was president of the Twelve. It was three more years before he became Presiding Patriarch of the church.

"The Twelve will take measures in connection with the bishop" (5a). In 1861 the Twelve, rather than the Presidency, had been associated with the Bishopric in executing the law of tithing. This was because Joseph, the sole member of the Presidency, had not yet proved himself to the Saints. While Joseph was thus incapacitated, the Lord turned to the Twelve

438

as the quorum next in authority in spiritual things. They were not at any time expected to exercise detailed supervision of financial matters but to teach the financial law by precept and example.

Since the revelation of 1861 had been given a third of a century had passed, and Joseph had commended himself to the Saints throughout the world. The major reason for laying this burden on the Twelve therefore had ceased to exist, and the burden was rightfully transferred back to the Presidency. The Quorum of Twelve, however, in common with the other presiding quorums, is still under the necessity of protecting the interests of the church wherever "abuse in the administration of the temporal affairs" of the church becomes apparent.

"The high council. . .advisory" (6d, e). The first high council was organized in 1834, before either the Twelve or the Seventy had taken their places in the church structure. For this reason, the high council at first discharged functions which were later transferred to other bodies, and there was no clear understanding of the exact duties of the council or of the limits of its authority. Among other things, the relation of the high council to the Bishopric was not clear. The emphasis on the advisory function of the high council given in this revelation was therefore quite timely.

"Purchasing lands" (6f). The activities enumerated here have such wide missionary and Zionic significance that they are rightfully administered after the most careful consultation among general and local authorities.

The early attempts at stake organization in the Reorganization were not very effective, and these were later abandoned by the instruction of the Lord through revelation. Thereafter, there was for a time no intermediate organization between the local branch and the general church. The growth of adjacent branches, however, and the need for conferences for settling their common problems, led to the formation of loose confederacies of branches into districts. As experience proved the wisdom of this procedure, districts came to have a more definite part in the organic structure of the church, although they had no place in the law until recognized by the revelation of 1890.[3] Even after the conference of 1890 there was some feeling on the part of the Twelve and Seventy that these local organizations impeded their work. This was one of the particular points on which the Twelve wished for light at this time.

"Leaving the branches and districts" (7b). It is eminently desirable that branches and districts shall not be organized until adequate local leadership is available. It is equally desirable that when such organization is effected, the distinctively missionary authorities shall not continue in local affairs, but shall push out into new fields and leave the local work to the standing ministry. These principles are as important today as they were then. It should be remembered, however, that many ailing branches and districts need missionary work more than they need anything else, and that even the "standing ministry" have definite missionary responsibilities.

"Set high priests or elders to preside" (8e). The word *set* as used here must be understood in connection with other scriptures. It cannot mean that the standing ministry can be put in their respective places without the consent of the body, for "common consent" is specifically provided for in the law. On the other hand, the word cannot be ignored. It implies action by general authorities. Reconciliation of the two points of view seems to be in the fact that men are called to the higher ranks of the priesthood through the general authorities, and that those thus called should be given prior consideration for positions of presiding responsibility; e.g., a high priest should always be chosen to preside rather than an elder unless specific reasons advise to the contrary.

"Evangelical ministers" (8e). No ministers of this order had been ordained in the Reorganization up to this time. The law provides for these officers to be called through the Twelve[4] but lack of clear vision in the matter had made the apostles hesitate to function. At the Kirtland conference

440

of 1890, the Twelve had adopted the following resolution:

Resolved that it is our opinion that the time is near at hand, if it has not already come, when that part of the law providing for the ordination of evangelical ministers should be carried into effect.

The instruction now received encouraged them to proceed, and after Alexander H. Smith became the first Presiding Patriarch at the conference of 1897 and the law was further clarified in 1901, the members of the Evangelical Order gradually were set in their places and began to function as revivalists and as fathers of the flock. A comparatively recent and important development has been the selection of local evangelists for service in their own communities. The ministry of such local evangelists is likely to be increased.

"Precedence in office" (9a). The president of the church and his counselors are presidents over the entire church. The Twelve form a "second presidency," by which it is meant that as a quorum they are "next in authority in spiritual things" (5b) and that individually they serve as representatives of the Presidency and as ranking officers where no member of the Presidency is present. In unorganized territory the Presidency, Twelve, and Seventy take precedence in that order. In organized branches and districts the high priests, elders, priests, teachers, and deacons take precedence in that order. In missionary work the Twelve are first and the Seventy second, although the Twelve are, of course, under the direction of the First Presidency.

"It is wisdom that the Presidency and Twelve in council together make such appointments as may be necessary" (11). These two quorums are the appointing authorities of the church. It is the practice, however, for the Bishopric to meet with them so they can advise on financial matters bearing on appointments.

"The seat of the Presidency of the church" (12a). Previous headquarters of the church had been as follows:

Fayette, Seneca County, New York, April 6, 1830, to February 1831.

Kirtland, Cayuga County, Ohio, February 18, 1831, to

January 12, 1838.

Far West, Caldwell County, Missouri, March 14, 1838, to January 29, 1839.

Quincy, Adams County, Illinois, March 17, 1839, to May 4, 1839.

Nauvoo, Hancock County, Illinois, May 9, 1839, till the rejection and disorganization which followed the assassination of Joseph and Hyrum Smith in 1844, and from the ordination of "Young Joseph" until January 1866.

Plano, Kendall County, Illinois, January 1866 to April 19, 1881.

The publishing house was transferred to Lamoni, Iowa, November 3, 1881, and President Joseph Smith moved there at the same time; thereafter Lamoni was considered the seat of the Presidency. Subsequently Graceland College, the Saints' Home, Liberty Home, and the Children's Home were located in Lamoni.

Independence was declared to be headquarters of the church by action of the General Conference of 1920, and the Herald Publishing House was transferred to Independence in 1921.

"It is not expedient to fill the quorums" (14). The basic reason for this, judged in the light of subsequent experience, seems to have been that the Presidency and Twelve had failed as yet to reach unanimity of opinion on matters of importance. It was this lack of common understanding which made necessary the Joint Council reported in Section 123.

"His bishopric shall be continued for a season" (15). The word *bishop* is not always used with the same significance. Thus Acts 1:22 reads: "His bishopric let another take," evidently referring to the apostolic office held by Judas. The word *bishop* means an overseer.

---

[1]April 13, 1894. [2]*Joseph Smith III*, p. 621. [3]Section 120:1. [4]Section 104:17.

SECTION 123

See Appendix E, pages 579–582

SECTION 124

Elder W. W. Blair, counselor to President Joseph Smith, died on the train April 18, 1896, while returning from the General Conference at Kirtland, Ohio, to his home at Lamoni, Iowa. Joseph Smith thus once more became the sole member of the First Presidency of the church. Because of this, he met with the available members of the Quorum of Twelve and with Bishop E. L. Kelley, and it was arranged that Elder Alexander H. Smith, president of the Twelve, act as counselor to the president during the conference year. The church was notified of this action in the Conference Minutes of 1896, and it was approved by the General Conference of 1897.

The following action also was taken by the Quorum of Twelve and reported to President Smith prior to the conference of 1897:

Whereas the First Presidency notified this quorum two years ago that we should consider the matter of ordaining Evangelical Ministers in all large branches of the church, and whereas, we have had but little information as to what is meant by Evangelical Ministers, and whereas, we believe that if those ministers were declared to be Patriarchs the movement toward their selection and ordination should be preceded by the ordination of one who shall be known as the Patriarch of the church, and whereas, said officers are to be selected by revelation, and whereas, we desire to perform in proper season all the duties connected with the office held by us, and are of the opinion that the patriarchs of the church should now be appointed.

Resolved that we ask President Joseph Smith to present the subject before our Heavenly Father, and seek a revelation for our enlightenment as to the character and duties of the office named, also designating who shall hold the office of Patriarch to the church.

443

The condition of the presiding quorums and the need for further light regarding the ordination of patriarchs or evangelical ministers were therefore prominent in the prayers of the church prior to the conference and during its continuance, and the revelation, now Section 124, was given in answer to those prayers. It is dated April 7 and 8, but was adopted by the church on April 9, 1897.[1]

"I was in the Spirit and was commanded to write." Joseph later wrote,

It will be noticed that in the reception and embodiment of the revelation found in Doctrine and Covenants as Section 124, there was a marked change in the method employed. That I was directed to write gives the communication the characteristic of apparent dictation. I seemed to feel and recognize the presence of an Administrator by whom the counsel was delivered to me, and I was more sensibly impressed by the personification of the Spirit in form than I had ever been before—if that were possible.

Upon two or three occasions in my life, when occupying in the pulpit I had been permitted to preach as if consciously aware of the nearness of some Divine Personage. This Personage at one of these times placed his hand upon my shoulder with a sufficient degree of pressure as to make me sensibly aware of his presence. So it was in the ministration of the dictation received in this revelation of 1897.[2]

"Separate and set apart my servant Alexander Hale Smith . . . to be patriarch to the church, and an evangelical minister to the whole church" (2a). The first patriarch of the church was Joseph Smith, Sr., father of the martyr (January 21, 1836, to September 14, 1840). He was succeeded by his oldest living son, Hyrum Smith (January 24, 1841, to June 27, 1844). After the death of Hyrum Smith, William, his younger brother, was ordained patriarch under the administration of Brigham Young and the Twelve. The Reorganization did not recognize this ordination, and when he was received into the church in 1878 on his original baptism, William Smith was enrolled with the high priests' quorum. There was no patriarch in the Reorganization until the ordination of Alexander H. Smith on April 12, 1897.

"Appoint my servant E. L. Kelley, Bishop of the church, to act as counselor to the President of the church" (2b).

444

Bishop Kelley acted with the Presidency for five years and in this capacity went to England in 1901. He continued to function as Presiding Bishop during the entire period. Students of history will remember that Presiding Bishop Edward Partridge was in charge of both spiritual and financial concerns in Zion for a time.

"The Quorum of Twelve. . . may choose" (3). Note how carefully the right of the Quorum of Twelve to choose their own president is conserved here. William H. Kelley was chosen and ordained, and continued to function until his release from the Quorum of Twelve by the revelation of 1913.

"That the quorum [Twelve] *may be filled"* (4a). In the ten years which had elapsed since new members were ordained into the Quorum of Twelve, Thomas W. Smith had died (1894), and now Alexander H. Smith was to be ordained to the Presidency. The ordination of Elders White, Wight, and Evans filled the quorum for the first time in the history of the Reorganization.

"In like manner they [the Presidents of Seventy] *may fill any other vacancy"* (5b). Elder I. N. White had been one of the Presidents of Seventy and his ordination to the Twelve left a vacancy in that council. The procedure indicated here has been followed in the selection of Presidents of Seventy since that time. The present members of the council are A. Alex Kahtava (Senior President), Kenneth E. Stobaugh, Clayton H. Condit, Victor B. Hatch, Jr., Richard W. Hawks, Joe B. Bayless, Ray J. Burdekin.

BIOGRAPHICAL NOTES

Edmund Levi Kelley was born near Vienna, Illinois, November 17, 1844, and was baptized May 23, 1864. He taught school and studied law. In 1871 he attended General Conference and was ordained a priest and appointed to do missionary work. In 1872, with the consent of the general church, he left the field to further study law. At the General Conference of 1882, Brother Kelley was ordained an elder and counselor to Presiding Bishop George A. Blakeslee and continued in this position until the death of Bishop Blakeslee September 20, 1890. He then became Presiding Bishop, being ordained April 10, 1891. Bishop Kelley was selected as second counselor to President Joseph Smith by the revelation of 1897 and so served for the succeeding five years, after which his entire time again was given to the work of the Presiding Bishopric. He was released by the revelation of 1916 and died May 10, 1930. Bishop Kelley was one of the most able men that the Reorganization has produced, and his name is directly connected with most of the outstanding achievements of the period during which he occupied in the presiding quorums.

Isaac N. White was born December 27, 1841, in Ohio, and baptized March 2, 1868. He was ordained a priest the following August; elder, October 23, 1870; seventy, April 14, 1886; president of seventy, April 1888, and apostle, April 1897. After his release from the Quorum of Twelve in 1913, he was ordained a patriarch and evangelical minister in which office he continued active until his death December 3, 1925.

John W. Wight, son of Apostle Lyman Wight, was born August 8, 1856, at Manton Valley, Texas, and was baptized October 8, 1864, at Gallands Grove, Iowa. Ordained an elder in 1880 and a seventy in 1888, he served with distinction in Australia from 1888 to 1894. Brother Wight was ordained to the apostleship April 12, 1897, at Lamoni, and returned to Australia, 1902-1903, after which he had charge of important missions in the United States. Released from activity in the Quorum of Twelve by the revelation of April 14, 1913, he was ordained a patriarch April 20, 1913. He died May 14, 1921, while in active service at Council Bluffs, Iowa.

R. C. Evans was born in Canada October 30, 1861, and joined the church November 5, 1876. He was ordained a priest July 3, 1882; elder May 26, 1884; seventy, May 12, 1886; apostle, April 12, 1897, and counselor in the Presidency April 20, 1902. Elder Evans was released from service in the Presidency by the revelation of 1909 and ordained a bishop at the conference of that year. When certain difficulties developed in Toronto in 1919, Brother Evans seceded from the church and was expelled by the action of the Standing High Council on March 26, 1919. In the days of his power, Elder Evans was one of the most able preachers of the Reorganization.

---

[1]Subsequent Presiding Evangelists have been Joseph R. Lambert (Acting, 1910-1913), Frederick A. Smith (1913-1938), Elbert A. Smith (1938-1958), Roy A. Cheville (1958-1974), and Reed M. Holmes (1974 -). [2]*Joseph Smith III*, pp. 622, 623.

SECTION 125

The introduction printed with this revelation explains something of the conditions under which it was given. It will be noted that the revelation was presented to the conference at the session of April 15, 1901, before being presented to the quorums. After President Smith had made his statement, it was prepared in written form, presented to the quorums as inspired instruction for the guidance of the church, and adopted by the body.

"The successor of my servant W. W. Blair" (1). For eleven years following the release of David H. Smith, W. W. Blair was the sole counselor of President Joseph Smith. He died in April 1896. The next year Alexander H. Smith, the presiding patriarch of the church, and E. L. Kelley, presiding bishop of the church, were associated with President Smith as counselors, although they also retained their responsibilities as patriarch and bishop, respectively. This arrangement was recognized as temporary. Now, after four years, the ministry and the Saints were anxious for a more permanent organization of the presiding quorums of the church. But conditions were not yet ripe for the desired reorganization.

"The vacancy in the twelve" (2). This vacancy was occasioned by the resignation of J. W. Gillen.

"The patriarch is an evangelical minister" (3a). There had been some doubt prior to this time regarding the relation between the patriarchal and evangelical functions. They were shown now to be two phases of the work of the same office.

"The duties of this office" (3a). Some of the duties of the evangelists are common to the various offices of the priesthood. The distinctive duties mentioned in this paragraph are as follows:

To be a revivalist.

To comfort the Saints.

To be a father to the church.

To be a spiritual counselor.

To lay on hands for conferring spiritual blessings.

If so led the patriarch may indicate the lineage of the one who is blessed.

"The privileges which attach to the office of patriarch and evangelical minister" (4e).

He is to be free from local responsibility.

He is to labor in connection with branch and district officers.

He is not subject to the control of the missionary in charge unless he teaches false doctrines or is found in transgression.

He is not to meddle with local affairs.

He is not to listen to cases of difficulty.

Such as are insistently reported to him he must secure in writing and pass to the local officers.

He is not to be put in charge of branches or districts.

"The Presiding Patriarch" (5):

Is to be considered the first of the patriarchs of the church.

When the patriarchs meet in council he is to preside.

He may meet with other quorums in their quorum meetings.

Here he may be asked for counsel.

He will have neither voice nor vote except by courtesy.

He has no direct control of quorums.

"Other evangelical ministers" (6a):
Have duties similar to the presiding patriarch but are limited to the districts where they are appointed.

"Those upon whom this burden has lain" (6b). This refers to the members of the Quorum of Twelve.

"Let my servants take heed and hesitate no longer" (6b). The Twelve followed this instruction, and several patriarchs were ordained, as is indicated in the following quotation from the revelation received a year later:

> On that platform I saw the quorum of the Presidency, the Bishopric, the Twelve, and a line above the Twelve on the seat behind them, a number of the brethren, including four of the present members of the Twelve and *the patriarchs* now ordained and recognized in the church.[1]

"My servant was directed to present to the church rules of representation" (7a). This took place in 1881. The Rules of Representation operative at present (1977) provide for the following ex officio members of the World Conference: all high priests, the seventy, World Church department heads, the church secretary, superannuated ministers, district presidents, branch presidents, congregational presiding elders in stakes, and World Conference appointees not included in the foregoing.[2] Delegates to the World Conference are chosen from the stakes and districts and from branches in unorganized territory on the basis of one delegate for districts or branches of less than one hundred members and one further delegate for each additional one hundred members.

In his memoirs President Smith, writing of Section 126 which reports an open vision, said:

> Certain rules for representation by delegates to Conference were also given me in open vision, but the church seemed not then to be ready for it. At the following Conference their adoption was still opposed, and the scope as to those who were ex officio members was made wider, and subsequently still wider. I have not felt it advisable for me to press the validity nor the sacredness of the revelation I received about them, preferring to allow the church to reach the matter in its own due time.[3]

The basic concern of President Smith appears to have been

to strengthen the delegate representation in Conference by relating the ex officio vote to the necessities of the Conference rather than to priesthood standing as such. I have found no clear evidence at this point and my opinion has no official weight, but it seems to me that he would have preferred to limit ex officio rights to the Presidency, Twelve, Presiding Bishopric, the Standing High Council, and a comparatively small number of others who must be members of the Conference if it is to function soundly. In parallel fashion, in local conferences the official participation of the appropriate local officers is vital to sound conference action.

"*Membership and good standing*" (9). It is not quite clear what is meant by "membership" in this case, whether it is membership in the branch or district or membership in the church. The latter interpretation is followed more generally, particularly in places distant from Independence. Foreign missions, for example, frequently are represented by missionaries who have labored there and who subsequently have returned to headquarters.

"*My people are directed to establish two stakes; one at Independence, one at Lamoni, Iowa*" (10a). The General Conference referred the organization of stakes to the Presidency and the Twelve, authorizing them to proceed. Procedure was as follows:

After consultation with the other members of his quorum and with the Twelve, President Joseph Smith presented a nomination for stake president, stating that "if the nomination was rejected he was authorized to present another."

President Smith then stated that when the stake president was chosen and ordained, seven of the high council were to be chosen and ordained. The president would choose his two counselors, and if these were chosen from the seven to be nominated for the high council, he (President Smith) was authorized by the Joint Council to present the names of two others to complete the majority of seven of the high council. President

Smith presented seven nominations. These nominations were confirmed.

President Smith, on behalf of the council, presented nominations for the stake bishopric. These nominations were confirmed.

President Smith then stated that the president of the stake, his counselors, and the seven members of the high council now chosen would be ordained. These brethren would then retire to choose five others to complete the membership of the high council.

President Joseph Smith, on behalf of the Joint Council of the Presidency and the Twelve, turned over to the authorities appointed the affairs of the stake as now organized.

It is well to note here that in organizing these stakes, which are the highest form of local organization within the church, nominations for the stake presidency and stake bishopric and for a majority of the stake high council were made by the presiding authorities of the general church. These recommendations had to be approved by the membership before they became effective. From this procedure, and from a careful study of the law, it seems that the more stable the organization the more necessary it is that its affairs shall be "regulated and set in order" by those having official jurisdiction. Presiding officers of branches rarely are nominated by the general church officers unless these branch presidents are General Conference appointees. Presiding officers of districts are nominated more frequently by the general officers. Presiding officers of stakes invariably are nominated by the general officers. In branches and districts the right to make other nominations is with the body. In stakes the sole right of nomination is with the presiding authorities of the church, but even here a nomination may be rejected. In this event the general authorities may present other nominations.

"A bishop and his counselors" (10). A few local bishops were set apart in the early days of the Reorganization, but the growth of the work did not warrant many such ordinations. By 1900 the only active bishop in the church was the Presiding Bishop. At the conference of that year, however, the following report of the First Presidency was adopted and its provisions carried out:

Having been led thereto by the leadings of the Spirit, as we understand them, we feel assured that the time for the beginning of the appointment of bishops, as seems suggested by the revelation of 1873, has come; we present for consideration the following names to be set apart for ordination as bishops: C. A. Parkin, San Francisco, California; C. J. Hunt, Deloit, Iowa; Ellis Short, Independence, Missouri; R. May, Independence, Missouri; William Anderson, Lamoni, Iowa; John Zimmermann, Philadelphia; R. Bullard, Boston, Massachusetts; William Leeka, Thurman, Iowa; George P. Lambert, Rock Creek, Illinois; Thomas Taylor, Birmingham, England.

If approved, we request that such ordinations be provided for and attended to upon their acceptance of the appointment as named.

"It is the duty of the church to provide tracts in the Scandinavian, German, Chinese, Japanese, and Portuguese languages" (11a). In this connection this excerpt from a letter of Gilbert J. Waller of Hawaii to President Smith is of interest:[4]

I hope you will take some action in regard to the translation and printing of tracts for distribution among the Japanese and Chinese peoples of the city of Honolulu. It seems to me that the church ought to try to bring our work to the notice of these nations, of which there are many here.[4]

The letter was dated April 3, 1901.

"The missions abroad other than those of the land of Joseph which were opened officially during the lifetime of the martyrs" (12a). Missions outside of the United States and Canada opened during the lifetime of the Martyr included the following: England, Scotland, Wales, Ireland, Palestine, Germany, South Australia, the West Indies, South Sea Islands. Undoubtedly missionary work also was done in the Scandinavian countries.

In the Reorganization the foreign missions were reopened as fast as possible. Jason W. Briggs was requested to go to England by the semiannual conference of 1860, but Elder Charles Derry was actually the first to arrive there. Elders Mangus Fyrando and H. N. Hanson opened the work

452

in Denmark in 1875. Elder E. Jasper went to Holland in 1869, John Avondet to Switzerland in 1872, Glaud Rodger and Charles W. Wandell to the Society Islands and Australia in 1873, Albert Haws to Hawaii in 1890, G. T. Griffiths, F. G. Pitt, and Reese Jenkins to Palestine in 1911, W. D. Tordoff to the Isle of Pines in 1920, and Hinman W. Savage to the Maoris of New Zealand in the same year. Some of these missions lapsed but before World War II we were preaching the gospel in England, Scotland, Wales, Norway, Sweden, Denmark, Germany, Poland, Holland, Australia, New Zealand, Hawaii, and the Society Islands, in addition to the United States and Canada.[5]

"A high priest to officiate in the office of bishop in England" (13c). When Bishop Kelley, representing the First Presidency, arrived in England with Apostle Griffiths they organized the work locally and ordained Elder Thomas Taylor to act as first bishop in England in the Reorganization. This ordination had been approved at the General Conference of 1900.[6] Elder Taylor chose as his counselors Elders Charles H. Caton and Joseph Dewsnup and the bishopric as thus constituted continued until interrupted by the death of all three parties in 1908. After a lapse of about three years Bishop Roderick May became bishop of the British Isles Mission under appointment from headquarters and continued until 1921. He was succeeded in that year by Bishop Charles Fry who served until 1925. The work was carried on by Bishop Fry's counselors until Bishop A. T. Trapp was ordained at the mission conference of 1930.

"Authorize the patriarch as one of the Presidency to visit Australia and the islands of the sea, the Society Islands" (13d). Patriarch Alexander H. Smith left the United States in the fall of 1901 for the South Sea Islands and Australia. On this trip he ordained Elder Metuaore bishop for the South Sea Islands (November 26, 1901) and Elder George Lewis bishop for Australia. Bishop Metuaore, a native of the South Sea Islands, died April 19, 1909. Bishop A. V. Karlstrom served as bishop of the islands under

appointment from headquarters from 1919 to 1923. Bishop George Lewis served in Australia from 1902 until his death in 1930.

"These affairs are not to be conducted by manifestations of the Spirit unless these directions and manifestations come through the regularly authorized officers of the branch or district" (14b). This extremely important instruction was commented on by President Elbert A. Smith as follows:

District and branch officers are to be honored in their respective places, and are responsible presidents of their respective organizations; no irresponsible person (even though acting professedly under the impulses of inspiration) is to set them aside and attempt to regulate.

Note the following in this connection:

President Joseph Smith then gave an explanation of the gift of tongues; that it was particularly instituted for the preaching of the gospel to other nations and languages, but it was not given for the government of the church.[7]

"The college debt" (16a). At this time Graceland owed $24,000 on bills payable and $1,000 on a real estate contract. Before the conference closed, $11,000 had been subscribed toward this indebtedness.

"Their right to free speech. . .does not permit them as individuals to frustrate the commands of the body in conference assembly" (16b). This principle, while enunciated primarily in regard to General Conference, applies also in regard to district conferences and local branch business meetings. Incalculable harm has been done by earnest members of the church who have not been content to determine matters of policy in the proper business sessions but have felt called upon to discuss matters at issue in the interim between these meetings. Very frequently the passage of time reveals that the things which once seemed so urgent are not nearly so urgent as they appeared to be under the pressure of the moment.

BIOGRAPHICAL NOTES

Peter Andersen was born on the island of Moen, Denmark, April 1, 1860, and was converted in Denmark. Finding no opportunity to be baptized there, he migrated to the United States, where he joined the church December 9, 1880, and was ordained a priest the following year. In 1882 he was appointed by General Conference on a mission to Denmark. Since funds were not available, he labored among the Scandinavian people in western Iowa. Brother Andersen was ordained an elder in 1883 and a seventy in 1888, during which latter year he labored in the Utah Mission. He went to Scandinavia in 1893 and worked in that field for many years with sober but significant success. Brother Andersen served in the Quorum of Twelve from his ordination in 1901 until his release because of ill health in 1920. He was the founder of *Sandheden's Banner* and edited it until his death June 1, 1920. He and Elder Peter Muceus translated the Book of Mormon into the Dano-Norse language during the year 1903. Among his other translations was a selection of 108 hymns for use among the Scandinavian Saints.

---

[1]Section 126:2. [2]*Rules and Resolutions* IV:22. [3]*Joseph Smith III*, p. 625. [4]*Saints' Herald* 48:261. [5]Missions have been opened recently in Japan, Korea, the Ryukyu Islands (1960); Nigeria (1965); India, Peru, Brazil, and the Philippine Islands (1966); Argentina, Fiji Islands, French Polynesia, Haiti, Honduras, and New Caledonia. [6]General Conference Minutes 1900:293; Church History 5:498. [7]*Millennial Star* 15:182; see *Saints' Herald* 37:627.

SECTION 126

The revelation dated Lamoni, Iowa, April 18, 1902, and addressed to the officers and members of the conference was received on the night of April 16 of that year. Paragraph 1 of the revelation is a partial explanation of the circumstances under which it was given. Some of the members of the conference felt that nothing in the experience narrated by the prophet indicated that the time had come for action based upon it to be taken. This is reflected in the action of the Quorum of Twelve, taken when the document was presented to them for approval.

Resolved that as a quorum we view the vision granted to President Joseph Smith on the night of the 16th of this month as being prophetic, and that should the conference accept this as authority for immediate action in changing present conditions to conform to this revealment, we are willing to concur in such action and operate in harmony therewith.

On the day following its presentation the document was accepted and made a rule of action in connection with the laws and usages already adopted by the body.

A few days before his death President Smith wrote of this revelation:

The communication of 1902, Section 126, as far as the method of receiving direction for the action of the church was concerned, was most remarkable, for again there was an entire change of procedure. Direction as to the calling of persons to office and position came as a result of a vision clearly reflecting in their arrangement and relations the gradations in authority as referred to in the revelation, Section 104.

The individuals mentioned were clearly seen by me in vision in their different positions, and I so stated to the body. The instructions I received by word came as if from One who stood by me, answering my questions and giving direction. Thus by combined sight and hearing a wide range of the method of receiving and transmitting divine direction was covered. I have felt that the most satisfactory method was that in which, being in the Spirit, I received verbal direction and precise statement as to what was to be given to the church.[1]

"The Bishopric as at present constituted" (5a). The term "Bishopric" is generally used to indicate the Presiding Bishop and his counselors. The term, "Order of Bishops," is used to include all those holding the office of bishop.

"The bishop should not be burdened with the spiritual care of the church" (5b). This had particular reference to Bishop E. L. Kelley, who had been acting as a member of the First Presidency for the preceding five years. He was released from that responsibility by this revelation.

"These younger men should be prepared by association to be of assistance to whosoever should be chosen as the President upon the emergency which should occur" (6). Elder R. C. Evans, who was ordained to the Presidency at this time and who might conceivably have been as-

456

sociated with Frederick M. Smith when the latter became president of the church, was removed from the Presidency in 1909 after he had failed to approve himself to the Quorum of Twelve and other leading officers of the church. The purpose designed in this paragraph therefore was frustrated in part, but his successor, President Elbert A. Smith, was a member of the First Presidency for five years before the death of President Joseph Smith. He thus was prepared to fulfill the provisions of this paragraph and did in fact continue as counselor to President Frederick M. Smith after the latter was ordained. President Israel A. Smith had similar training before succeeding his brother as president of the church, as did President W. Wallace Smith, who was counselor to President Israel A. Smith. Elder Wallace B. Smith has been designated to become president and is preparing for his coming responsibility.

"*Sitting with the Quorum of the Twelve*" (7b). This was a most significant development. For the first time some of the older brethren were honorably released from responsibility as apostles, and their places were taken by younger men. For the first time, also, the foreign missions were strongly represented; Peter Andersen (Denmark), J. W. Rushton (England), and C. A. Butterworth (Australia) had places in the Quorum of Twelve.

"*The application of the law as stated by the bishopric should be acceded to*" (10c). During the conference there had been considerable discussion of the means to be adopted looking toward the establishment of Zion, and leadership in connection therewith. In this connection President Smith wrote:

"The application of the law as stated by the Bishopric should be acceded to." If in this application wrong should be the result, there is a remedy which may be applied, and should be. No one is necessarily free to disregard the proper application of remedial procedure against wrong-doing. Unfair and unjust criticism and opposition to the ministration of the Bishopric can never remedy any wrong which may exist, and it certainly should have been found out by this time that continued and caviling attacks upon the Bishop in an endeavor to force him and his associates to follow the interpretation of extremists is productive of

457

nothing but a preventing of carrying out the law in any form. Too many minds are busy, each striving to enforce his own application and understanding of the law, resulting in the confusing of those who are willing to become subject to the law as interpreted by the Bishop, and to be helpful in the financial affairs of the church. The conservative element among the members can not justly be made to accede to the conclusions of the extreme and violent element.[2]

"In case of transgression in his office the Bishop should be called in question before the council which is provided for in the law" (11). The bishop and all other general officers of the church are subject to trial before the High Council. They are not subject to trial before elders' courts or bishop's courts.

"The rule which has been supposed to govern the selection of evangelical ministers" (13). This rule provides that the Twelve shall call "evangelical ministers, as they shall be designated unto them by revelation." A parallel case occurred in 1938 when J. F. Curtis was called to the Order of Evangelists by revelation. Others called in like manner since that time have been M. A. McConley, (1948), E. J. Gleazer and D. T. Williams (1958), Roscoe E. Davey and Arthur A. Oakman (1964), Henry L. Livingston (1966), and D. O. Chesworth (1972).

BIOGRAPHICAL NOTES

Frederick A. Smith, son of Elder Alexander H. Smith, and Elizabeth Agnes (Kendall) Smith was born in Sonora Township, Hancock County, Illinois, January 19, 1862, and baptized June 24, 1877. He served successively in the following offices: deacon (July 9, 1882), priest (June 3, 1890), elder (April 14, 1891), seventy (April 15, 1894), high priest (April 19, 1900), apostle (April 19, 1902), presiding patriarch of the church (April 20, 1913). Brother Smith became Presiding Patriarch Emeritus at the conference of 1938.

Francis M. Sheehy was born June 1, 1851, and baptized January 29, 1871. He was ordained a deacon September 1872; a teacher April 1873; a priest May 1874; an elder April 1876; a seventy April 1886; President of the Seventy

April 1897; a high priest April 1900; and an apostle April 1902. Honorably released from active service in the apostolic quorum in April 1920, he died October 17, 1923. Most of Brother Sheehy's missionary work was in the eastern states, although he also saw service in the western and central territories. Elder Sheehy was one of the first members of the church to achieve an informed interest in American archaeology in relation to the Book of Mormon.

U. W. Green was born June 16, 1865, in Massachusetts and baptized August 10, 1882, entering into the ministry soon after his baptism. Brother Greene served in the following offices in the priesthood: deacon (September 15, 1882), priest (December 14, 1884), elder (January 15, 1888), seventy (April 8, 1890), apostle (April 20, 1902), evangelist (March 26, 1922). He died in Independence, Missouri, in 1938.

C. A. Butterworth was born in Iowa in 1864. He was ordained an elder in 1888 and appointed to Australia at the April conference of 1889. Ordained a seventy in 1890, he did outstanding work in that office and was called to the Twelve by the revelation of 1902, and ordained to that office by Alexander H. Smith who was in Australia at that time. He devoted himself to the interests of the work in Australia, keeping in touch with the general interests of the church by occasional visits. Released by the revelation of 1922 because of ill health, he continued to serve as his strength permitted until his death September 1, 1928.

John W. Rushton was born at Leeds, England, February 12, 1874, and joined the church there September 15, 1888. He served as priest, elder, and seventy in England, and after his ordination to the apostolic quorum was in charge or joint charge of the mission until 1911, when he located in the United States. Thereafter he served in all of the major geographic areas of the church. Elder Rushton died May 8, 1950.

Frederick Madison Smith was a son of Joseph and Bertha (Madison) Smith, and was born January 21, 1874, at Plano, Illinois. He married Ruth Lyman Cobb August 3,

1897. Ordained to the eldership in 1897, he served for a time as church librarian, assistant church historian, and as counselor to William Anderson, bishop of Lamoni Stake. He was ordained counselor to his father, the president of the church, in April 1902, and became president of the church May 5, 1915. President Smith made many major and permanent contributions to the growth of the church, notably in the field of education and in the refinement of worship. He died at the Independence Sanitarium on March 20, 1946.

R. C. Evans (see notes on Section 124).

---

¹*Joseph Smith III*, p. 625. ²*Saints' Herald* 55:409.

SECTION 127

At the pre-conference sessions held in April 1906, the Presidency presented a recommendation to the Quorum of Twelve concerning the establishment of a sanitarium and the appointment of Dr. Joseph Luff of the Twelve as its presiding officer. On this recommendation the Quorum took the following action:

Resolved, that while we favor the general sentiment of the document presented by the First Presidency relating to the medical work of Brother Joseph Luff and the establishment of a hospital, we are, nevertheless, uncertain as to whether such work is consistent with said brother's calling as a member of this quorum.

Believing, as we do, that Brother Luff was called of God to be an apostle, we would much prefer to know what is the will of God in this matter before we express ourselves upon it, lest we move unwisely. We would therefore, gladly engage in an effort to learn the Master's will concerning it and other matters should you approve of it.

The inquiries resulting from this action led to the revelation addressed to the church presented to the conference April 14, 1906, at Independence, Missouri.

In connection with the Sanitarium, President Joseph Smith wrote in 1914:

The directions given in 1906 concerning the establishing of the Sanitarium were clearly presented to me, and came as the result of several years of prayer and consideration of the question as to how we were to place ourselves before the world as advocating the healing art. Since these directions have been acted upon by the church I am content to leave them as they are, for I have been vouchsafed no further information concerning them.[1]

"It is the will of the Lord that a sanitarium, a place of refuge and health for the sick and afflicted, be established by the church, at Independence, Missouri" (1a). In accord with this instruction, Bishop E. L. Kelley purchased a tract of land in Independence which came to be known as the "Kensington Addition," and on a part of this the Sanitarium was located. Excavation for the building began in August 1907, and it was formally opened December 15, 1909, entirely free from debt. A new, modern hospital was completed in 1958, and subsequent additions have been built as funds have been made available.

"The Presiding Bishopric and his counselors and the Bishopric of the Independence Stake should take counsel together in locating and establishing this sanitarium" (1c). Note the principle involved here. The matter of locating and establishing the Sanitarium had to do with the physical properties of the church. It was therefore properly referred to the Bishopric. However, the matter was both a general and a local concern, and so the general and local bishopric was associated in the enterprise. Elder Roderick May was at this time bishop of Independence Stake.

"It is also expedient that these should be assisted by the advice and counsel of one of my servants who is acquainted with the laws of health and the practice of medicine" (2a). This reasonable provision for the advice of an expert was fulfilled by the appointment of Apostle Joseph Luff, M.D.

"That he may be an assistant to those who seek the aid of this institution of the church, in his spiritual office and his calling as a physician" (2c). This intelligent association of faith and specialized training in ministering to the sick is in entire harmony with the early practice

461

of the church.[2] In this connection we call attention to the following quotation from the writings of John Wesley:

> I earnestly advise every one, together with all other medicines, to use that medicine of medicines—prayer. Where is the cure for either lingering or impetuous passions that either furiously overturn this house of earth, or sap the foundations of health and life by sure approaches? The whole *materia Medica* is of no avail in this case. What can cure it but the peace of God? No other medicine under heaven. What but the love of God, that sovereign balm for the body as well as the mind. The passions have a greater influence on health than most people are aware of. All violent and sudden passions dispose to, or actually throw people into acute diseases. The slow and lasting passions, such as grief or hopeless love, bring on chronic diseases. Till the passion which caused the disease is calmed, medicine is applied in vain. The love of God, as it is the sovereign remedy of all miseries, so in particular it effectually prevents all the bodily disorders the passions introduce, by keeping the passions themselves within due bounds. And by the unspeakable joy, and perfect calm, serenity and tranquillity it gives the mind, it becomes the most powerful of all the means of health and long life.

"There should also be a home for children established"(3). The Daughters of Zion, an organization among the women of the church, raised a fund for the erection of this home and requested the conference of 1907 to authorize them to appoint a committee to act with the Bishopric in completing this work when such completion should be deemed advisable. The conference concurred, and the women appointed Sisters B. C. Smith, Callie B. Stebbins, Ruth L. Smith, Eveline Burgess, and Emma Hougas. The home was located at Lamoni, Iowa, and was formally opened August 15, 1907.

"Debt should not be contracted nor too large nor expensive buildings be built at the outset" (4a). In this connection Bishop Kelley reported to the conference of 1909 as follows:

> The Sanitarium was built with funds raised especially for that purpose, and from church tithes and offerings also. We need not have sent out and asked a single special contribution for the Sanitarium, if we had not wished to do so. The authority is with the Bishopric to have built it from the tithe and offering fund. But since we did not have sufficient of the tithe and offering fund, we made special collections for that, and it has been builded, and not one cent against it, nor has the church been involved in debt by reason of building it.[3]

"It is necessary that some one or more be sent to the South Sea Islands" (5a). During February 7 and 8, 1906, a tidal wave and devastating hurricane swept across the Society Islands. The Saints suffered severe losses. Joseph F. Burton who is here designated to comfort and encourage them was in his sixty-ninth year, but accepted the assignment and gave excellent service to the mission. He and his wife, Emma, were accompanied by Charles and Alberta Lake. Charles, a son of Apostle John H. Lake, succeeded Brother Burton as minister in charge and served until his death in June 1913.

"The mission to Utah and the west should be continued" (6). One of the difficulties of missionary work in Utah was that conditions in that region were made so unfavorable for persons joining the Reorganization that the majority of those converted moved out within a short time and located on the coast or nearer the center place. Although many have joined the church in Utah it has always been difficult to maintain a working nucleus in this area.

"The gathering" (7). During the early years of his administration considerable pressure was brought to bear on President Joseph Smith, urging him to sound the call to gather to Zion. With a wisdom which was in advance of his experience, he resisted this pressure until the years solved problems which would have brought division if the Saints had gathered earlier. In the late eighties and nineties, however, many of these difficulties had been overcome, and at the turn of the century, the ordination of local bishops marked a definite state in emphasis upon the gathering. When the enthusiasm and energetic leadership of President Frederick M. Smith was added to the statesmanship of his venerable father, interest in the necessity and value of the gathering grew apace. It was necessary, however, that the errors of an earlier generation should not be repeated, and the revelation of 1906 therefore gave some fundamental and timely instruction regarding the gathering. Note the following principles:

The gathering must not be in haste.

It must be in harmony with the revelation on Fishing River.[4]

The Saints must learn to be obedient to the things which the Lord requires at their hands.

Zion cannot be built up unless it is by the principles of the law of the celestial kingdom.

The full preparation of the priesthood must await their more complete endowment.[5]

The Saints should gather only after consultation with the Presidency and Bishopric, as provided in the law.

The spirit of speculation and of greed for gain should be avoided.

Those preaching and writing upon the gathering should be careful to remove the principle of selfishness from their appeal.

President Smith evidently had been concerned for several years about the spirit of speculation. In a *Herald* editorial written in 1894 he commented:

> Speculation, in proper directions, may be right; but the spirit of speculation does not always nicely discriminate between the legitimate in trade and the illegitimate—if there be money to come out of the transaction. We shall be sorry, indeed, if there be in Lamoni cause to believe that dishonest practices obtain among her promoters and forwarders in business affairs.[6]

"My servant Frederick M. Smith, if he remain faithful and steadfast, should be chosen" (8b). It may be noted that President Joseph Smith was in his seventy-fourth year at this time, and that there was widespread concern regarding the manner of choosing his successor. Undoubtedly, therefore, this matter also had been frequently mentioned in the prayers of the Saints.

Frederick Madison Smith was more fully designated in the "Letter of Instruction" issued by President Joseph Smith, March 4, 1912. .He was ordained President of the High Priesthood, and prophet, seer, and revelator of the church May 5, 1915, by Gomer T. Griffiths, president of the Quorum of Twelve, assisted by Apostle Peter Andersen; Bishop E. L. Kelley, president of the Aaronic priesthood; and Elder Joseph A. Tanner, president of the Quorum of High Priests.

---

¹*Joseph Smith III*, p. 626. ²Section 42:12, 13. ³General Conference Minutes 1909:1211. ⁴Section 102. ⁵Section 102:3. ⁶*Saints' Herald*, December 19, 1894.

SECTION 128

In his report to the General Conference of 1909, Presiding Bishop E. L. Kelley included the following paragraph:

The church in its work of preparation and arrangement has arrived at the place where in the opinion of the Bishopric we must consider the question of carrying into effect the law relating to the purchase of land for the good of the work and the settlement properly, of the Saints.

There is another matter, however, that should in the opinion of the Bishop, be taken up and passed upon before largely entering upon this work, that it presents the conditions so special to the business interests of the church, that it would be preferable to first present the same before a special meeting of the elders, under the supervision of the Presidency, or present to the Joint Council; but since the action of the body will be required subsequently, it would save time by going before the eldership, where it could be heard and first passed on.

On Tuesday, April 20, the Joint Council of the Melchisedec priesthood presented the following report:

To the General Conference: At a meeting of the eldership of the church called by the Bishop April 9, he requested that the organizations be formed to hold properties for the benefit of the poor of the church. A motion prevailed to refer this request to the Presidency of the church for instruction.

April 17, the Presidency called another meeting of the eldership, at which time the President requested the support and prayers of the ministry present. In accord with this request a day of fasting and prayer was held by them on the 18th instant.

On April 19, another meeting was called by the Presidency, and there was presented an answer to the request for instruction upon the subject under consideration purporting to be from the Lord.

The document was presented to the several quorums of the eldership for consideration and action, and favorable reports were received by all, when a motion prevailed, "That this council report its action to the General Conference;" which action was, "That the document be adopted as a whole."

The revelation referred to in the report is addressed to the eldership and dated Lamoni, Iowa, April 18, 1909.

"The conditions surrounding the work" (1a). This seems to be a prophetic reference to the coming of the recent years of economic unrest. A major tragedy of the war years and the intervening period has been the absence of any Zionic area in which the Saints could work out their spiritual purposes for their own salvation and the enlightenment of humanity.

"The increase of the membership of the church" (1a). In 1909 the church numbered almost sixty thousand members.

"Under the existing laws" (1b). The laws of the state and nation are properly designed to protect the interests of the individual against possible predatory purposes on the part of other persons or organizations. This is as it should be; and the gathering of the Saints must be in harmony with these laws, or other laws must be enacted which recognize the spiritual purposes of our association.

"The custodians of the properties of the church" (2a). This phrase is explained more fully in the succeeding paragraphs and refers to "the Bishop and his counselors, together with the other bishops of the church." In "the work of caring for and using" properties in any particular locality, the Presiding Bishopric and the local bishopric will be directly associated. This is in harmony with the principles followed in the location and establishment of the Sanitarium.[1]

"Consult with the elders and the bishops before removing" (4a). This frequently repeated counsel must be observed if the gathering is to proceed in an orderly way and without disrupting the work of the church in more distant fields. It is not enough that a family wishing to move to Independence or the regions round about shall be spiritually and financially able. It is necessary that their removal shall not create too great a hardship in the branch

466

or district from which they are transferred.

"*Regions round about*" (5). This area would certainly include the territory covered by the central stakes plus land as near to Independence but lying to the south and west.

"*They can not withdraw themselves*" (8a). The associations of the Saints are designed for purposes of mutual helpfulness. These associations cannot be independent but must have some contacts with the surrounding world. Yet these contacts should be of a high ethical and spiritual order and so should quicken the admiration of our neighbors and bear testimony to them of the high quality of our endeavors. The Saints cannot descend to some of the business practices current in the world. The revelation of 1906[2] is particularly significant in this connection.

"*The general authorities of the church who are made the proper counselors in spiritual and temporal things*" (9). It will be noted that this entire revelation carefully safeguards the prerogatives of the Bishopric as those "made the custodians of the properties of the church." Before its conclusion, however, it requires these financial leaders to consult with the general authorities of the church in matters of major importance. This is in harmony with the general principle of the subordination of temporalities to the achievement of spiritual purposes and with earlier revelation.[3] The principle is discussed more fully in the revelations of 1968.[4]

---

[1]Section 127:1. [2]Section 127:7. [3]Section 122:6. [4]Sections 149, 149A.

SECTION 129

Wednesday, April 14, 1909, while the problems introduced by the Presiding Bishop were still under consideration by the Joint Council of the Melchisedec priesthood, the following resolution was adopted by the General Conference:

Desiring to place ourselves in such attitude as an assembly before our heavenly Father, such as to especially commend ourselves to him, and thereby invite his special blessing and immediate divine direction to be given to us in his wisdom and pleasure.

Resolved, that tomorrow be set apart as a day of fasting and prayer, to be so observed as far as practicable by the assembly and the Saints.

Five days later, at the business session of April 19, 1909, President F. M. Smith stated that by instruction of President Joseph Smith, he presented to the body a document containing a communication to the church, with the recommendation that it be referred to the various quorums for consideration and action. At the business session of April 20, after reports had been received indicating that the quorums accepted the revelation as of divine origin, it was moved "that we accept the document as a revelation from God and pledge ourselves to be governed by it." The motion was adopted by unanimous vote.

This revelation is dated April 18, 1909, at Lamoni, Iowa, and is addressed to the church.

"*It is no longer wise that my servant R. C. Evans be continued as counselor in the Presidency*" (1a). By reason of certain administrative difficulties, the members of the Quorum of Twelve already had notified the First Presidency of their inability to sustain Elder Evans as a member of the First Presidency. Brother Evans was released from the Presidency in harmony with the instruction of this revelation and later in the conference was ordained a bishop.

"*Release him* [Joseph Luff] *from the responsibilities of the active apostleship as a member of the quorum, that he may act unreservedly in his calling*" (2b). At the time of Dr. Luff's selection as church physician, the members of the Quorum of Twelve had been doubtful whether he could carry that responsibility in addition to his apostolic duties. In reply the Lord had stated that Brother Luff could function in both capacities.[1] The growth of his responsibilities at the Sanitarium, however, now made necessary the change recommended in this paragraph. Dr. Luff continued as church physician until 1918. He died January 6, 1948.

"*The historian of the church*" (3a). Elder Heman C.

Smith had already completed his work on the first four volumes of Church History (1903) but was doing important work on the *Journal of History* and by lectures and correspondence. He continued to be active until his death in 1919.

The releases of Elders Luff and Smith had been anticipated by them. In the 1908 minutes of the First Presidency are the following statements:

Brother Joseph Luff has been released from duty as a missionary in charge that he might give attention to his special duties as physician to the church, which have increased to the extent that he cannot give time to the active oversight of a missionary field. . . .

The appointment of Bro. H. C. Smith is with the understanding that he will give necessary attention to his special duties as Church Historian.[2]

"Holding the high priesthood" (4). Members of the Presidency, Twelve, Order of Bishops, and Order of Evangelists are all high priests set apart to a special work. When they are relieved from responsibility connected with these special callings, the members of these groups continue to serve as high priests.

Enrolled with the high priests" (7a). Although bishops and evangelists have place in any general assemblies of the high priesthood which may be called, they meet most frequently in their several orders to consider matters which are the distinctive concern of these orders.

"The attention of the church is called to the consideration of the revelation, given in answer to earnest supplication, with regard to temporal things" (8a). This revelation[3] was given at the same conference but addressed to the eldership.

"The Bishopric, men holding office of bishop under a presiding head" (8b). In stakes, districts, and large branches, where bishops are appointed and ordained, they rightfully take charge of the temporal concerns of these groups. The Presiding Bishopric preside over the bishops of the church in temporal things and also appoint agents in those branches and districts where no bishops are ordained and set in their places. Thus the Bishopric—men holding the office of bishop under a presiding head—gather, care

for, and disburse the monies and temporal properties of the entire church.

"The church has been directed to accede to the rendition of the Bishopric with respect to the temporal law" (8f). Read Sections 126:10, 149, and 149A in this connection.

"Until such heed is paid to the word which has been given. . . the church can not receive and enjoy the blessings which have been looked for when Zion should be fully redeemed" (8g). The basic principle underlying this instruction is found in Section 125:14c:

> If my people will respect the officers whom I have called and set in the church, I will respect these officers; and if they do not, they can not expect the riches of gifts and the blessings of direction.

This applies to the Presidency, whose duty it is to teach the revelations and to coordinate the activities of the various departments of church work. It applies to the Twelve, who are "the chief missionaries of the church."[4] It applies to the Bishopric who are in charge of "the temporalities of the church." It applies also to the other officers and ministers of the church in their several callings. Due care should, of course, be taken to see that the rights of the church are properly safeguarded, and there is ample provision in the law for this safeguarding. If the priesthood is to be effective in the life of the church, then the ministry must be supported in discharging their duty.

"The Lord is well pleased" (9a). It will be noted that this commendation is received despite the differences of opinion which had been held during the preceding conference year, because these differences had been "held in unity of purpose and desire for the good of my people" and would therefore "result in bringing to pass a unity of understanding." It was on this background that the elders and the Saints generally were told "so be ye encouraged and press on to the consummation designed of God for his people—unity, honor, sanctification, and glory."

BIOGRAPHICAL NOTES

Elbert A. Smith, son of David Hyrum and Clara Charlotte

Hartshorn Smith, was born March 8, 1871, at Nauvoo, Illinois. In 1876 he moved with his mother to a farm in western Iowa, and in 1892 to Lamoni, where he was a printer and bookbinder in the Herald Publishing House. He married Clara, daughter of Asa Cochran, in Lamoni, September 4, 1895. Entering the ministry in early manhood, Brother Smith served as pastor of the congregation at Burlington, Iowa, assistant and associate editor of the *Saints' Herald* for over twenty years, and editor of *Autumn Leaves* for a similarly long period. He was ordained counselor to President Joseph Smith, his uncle, in 1909; counselor to President Frederick Madison Smith on May 5, 1915; and Presiding Patriarch of the church April 10, 1938. Elder Smith resigned as Presiding Patriarch in 1958 and died in 1959. He and Sister Smith left two sons, Ronald Gibson and Lynn Elbert.

J. Frank Curtis was born January 26, 1875, in Livingston County, Missouri. He was baptized June 10, 1883. In July 1899 Brother Curtis was ordained an elder and in April 1903, a seventy. Six years later he was called to the apostolic office and served as a member of the Quorum of Twelve until his ordination to the evangelical order April 10, 1938. He was an outstanding missionary. He died in December 1966.

Robert Clark Russell was born August 23, 1867, in Dundalk, Ontario, Canada. On September 16, 1894, he became a member of the church and on December 3 of the same year was ordained a teacher. June 21, 1897, he was ordained a priest and in June 1901 an elder. Four years later he was set apart as a seventy, and in April 1909 as an apostle. In October 1922 he became an evangelist. He died February 5, 1929.

---

[1]Section 127:2. [2]Minutes of First Presidency, April 18, 1908, page 46. [3]Section 138. [4]Section 122:5.

SECTION 130

By 1913 it was apparent that President Joseph Smith III and several of his closest official associates were finding their responsibilities arduous. Provision had already been made for succession in the office of president of the church, but the Presiding Bishop was in his sixty-ninth year and Apostles W. H. Kelley and Isaac N. White were in their seventies. Personnel needs were undoubtedly part of the concern of Joseph as he "made supplication to the One whom we serve" and, at the time of the conference, renewed his "supplication in the spirit of the desire of the church." It was in response to this prayer and concern of the prophet and the people that President Smith was able to present "the voice of the Spirit."

The revelation of April 14, 1913, was received at Lamoni, Iowa, and is addressed to the elders and the members of the conference assembled there.

"*Stand with their associates among the high priests and patriarchs of the church*" (2c). Elder W. H. Kelley continued to serve as a high priest until his death. Elders I. N. White and J. W. Wight were ordained patriarchs and served in this office with distinction.

"*It is also expedient that Elder Frederick A. Smith be released . . . that he may take the place of his father*" (3a). Elder Joseph R. Lambert had acted as Presiding Patriarch since the death of Alexander H. Smith in August 1909. Frederick A. Smith, who was now ordained, served until succeeded by his cousin, Elbert A. Smith in 1938. Subsequently Elders Roy A. Cheville (1958-1974) and Reed M. Holmes (1974-) have served as Presiding Evangelists.

"*The Twelve in its reorganization for its work may choose its own officers*" (4d). The presidents of the Quorum of Twelve have been designated on several occasions.[1] At this time Elder Gomer T. Griffiths was chosen to succeed Elder William H. Kelley as president of the quorum,

472

and Elder John W. Rushton was chosen to succeed Elder Frederick A. Smith, as secretary of the quorum. Later presidents of the Twelve have been Elders J. Arthur Gillen (1922-1934), Paul M. Hanson (1934-1958), Charles R. Hield (1958-1964), and Clifford A. Cole (1964 -).

"That he may serve as did his father" (5c). Elder George A. Blakeslee was presiding Bishop from 1882 to 1890.

Note the instruction regarding temporalities in paragraph 7. It applies both to individuals and to the body at large:

Avoid the unnecessary building of houses of worship or places of entertainment.

Avoid expending tithes and offerings in that which may not be essential to the continued onward progress of the general work.

Carry into active exercise the principle of sacrifice and the repression of unnecessary wants. This instruction was renewed in 1964.[2]

Permit the accumulation of tithes and offerings to discharge the indebtedness of the body.

In view of subsequent developments no comment is needed on the prophetic nature of this instruction.

"The sons of the leading officers of the church are called and may be chosen to the respective offices to which the Spirit may direct" (9a). This revelation contains four illustrations of the application of this law of lineage. Frederick A. Smith succeeded his father, Alexander H. Smith, as presiding patriarch; James E. Kelley succeeded his father, Elder William H. Kelley, in the Quorum of Twelve; James A. Gillen succeeded his father, Elder James W. Gillen, in the Quorum of Twelve; and Elder E. A. Blakeslee succeeded his father, Elder George A. Blakeslee, in the Presiding Bishopric. In 1974 William T. Higdon succeeded his father, Elder Earl T. Higdon, in the Quorum of Twelve. In 1976 Wallace B. Smith was designated to succeed his father as president of the church.

BIOGRAPHICAL NOTES

James E. Kelley was born June 11, 1879, at Madison,

Indiana, and baptized April 13, 1896, at Kirtland. He was ordained an elder July 7, 1901; a seventy April 16, 1908; and an apostle April 19, 1913. He occupied here until his death June 4, 1917. Elder Kelley's health was poor for several years, but he served ably according to his strength.

William M. Aylor, who was born January 9, 1864, and baptized December 1, 1891, was ordained an elder April 13, 1898, a seventy three years later, and an apostle at the conference of 1913. He served until his resignation from the Quorum of Twelve in April 1920 and died March 28, 1928.

Paul M. Hanson, born January 8, 1878, at Crescent, Iowa, became a member of the church October 15, 1893. Three years later he was ordained a priest. In 1902 he was called to the eldership and in less than a month to the seventies. On April 19, 1913, Brother Hanson was ordained an apostle. He was ordained president of the Quorum of Twelve at the General Conference of 1934 and served with distinction until his release in 1958. He died June 17, 1972.

James Arthur Gillen was born May 24, 1868, at Malad, Idaho. On May 21, 1876, he became a member of the church. In September 1900, he was ordained an elder, in April 1909 a high priest, and in April 1913 an apostle. He was selected as president of the Quorum of Twelve October 19, 1922, and served in that capacity until his resignation from the Twelve in April 1934. Brother Gillen died February 11, 1946, at Independence, Missouri, after a long illness.

E. A. Blakeslee, see notes on Section 123.

---

[1]Sections 117:7; 120:8; 124:3; 134. [2]Section 147:5b.

SECTION 131

The revelation of April 5, 1914, the last received by the church through President Joseph Smith III, was addressed to the officers, delegates, and members of the Reorganized Church of Jesus Christ of Latter Day Saints in conference assembled. The conference for this year was held at Independence, Missouri.

The revelation was presented to the conference Wednesday, April 15, with the endorsement of the various quorums of the church. After it had been approved by them and the conference, President Joseph Smith made a statement, from which the following is cited:

Brother President: It would have been manifestly improper for me to have spoken to the adoption or rejection of this document, for no one knows better than I, who stand in the presence of God today, I shall have to answer for the genuine character of that which was presented, and shall be judged as one who stands upon the honesty of purpose and the integrity of duty to be performed. Called, as has been acknowledged by the church, by divine authority, under which the church originated, and under which it has always existed, and that call and the investiture of the right to act having been received from the people of the church in solemn assembly and acquiesced in for fifty-three years, I have a right to believe that as I stand to answer before God for my honesty and uprightness of intent and purpose and for the integrity of duty which I may have performed under this calling, knowing full well that I stand nearer to the answering of my duty before God than perhaps any other man in this assembly (with perhaps two or three exceptions); hence I may say with confidence that I feel very grateful indeed to God and very grateful to the people composing the church and its representatives here for the kindness of their treatment to me in the discharge of this duty of answering to the call of the people in imploring divine direction and in transmitting what I received through the Spirit which directs the work unto those who represent the body at large.

The difficulties rise up before me, and it is necessary, and it always has been for me to take a careful survey of the whole field, so far as my ability enables me to do, and when that is done, to transmit faithfully, the intent and purpose and the will of the Master, who has so far carried the work, in his wisdom, and has not as yet permitted it to meet with defeat or disaster. Hence, I would, if I could, put within the mind,—and I may add, the soul—of everyone present today, what I have felt of the difficulty of the situation under which I was called to act, and of that which I have felt in discharging that duty. For the wisdom of it, I do not answer; for the reason of it, any portion of it, I do not answer; I know not, beyond what is given, what may have been in the divine mind, and should any one of you ask me about this or that in any of the revelations which I have been permitted to give to the church, I must answer, inevitably, unless the revelation itself contains a reason, or reasons for them, I am not able to answer. I am but an humble instrument in the hands of God, as are all of you; I claim no higher tribute, no higher characteristic or qualification of honesty, or intent or purpose, than each one of you may claim. I am not to be considered as within the counsel of the Almighty, only so far as that counsel is transmitted by the voice of inspiration to me, when action on my part is required. I dare not listen to the cries of disaster, of loss or damage. I dare not lift up my heart in triumph at apparent conquest over enemies that oppose the church. I can only, as the rest of you, do that duty that lies nearest to me, and which I am expected to perform, and leave the result in the hands of God; and brethren, before him, if he does not know his duty, and has not had the ability to perform it, I am sure, so far as I am concerned, he has chosen weak instrumentality. Whether or not, individuals called thus, choose to serve the church or refuse, it lies with them; if they refuse to receive the word of God, that which must ensue, lies with us; if we do, and we are blessed as we have been hitherto in many instances by following the divine mind, we surely are justified in a large degree for still making appeal to him, and trusting to that which he may give us.

"Bishops Edwin A. Blakeslee and Edmund L. Kelley should be more closely associated in the carrying on of the financial affairs of the church" (2a). At this time Bishop Kelley was in his seventieth year. Bishop Blakeslee was the first counselor to the Presiding Bishopric of the Reorganization to hold the office of bishop, having been ordained in harmony with Section 130:5. The evident intention was that Bishop Blakeslee should succeed Bishop Kelley as Presiding Bishop of the church. After the release of Bishop Kelley in 1916 however, Bishop Blakeslee preferred not to accept this responsibility, and Elder Benjamin R. McGuire therefore was named in his stead.[1] He served until 1925. Other Presiding Bishops have been Elders Albert Carmichael (1925-1932), L. F. P. Curry (1932-1940), G. Leslie DeLapp

(1940-1966), Walter N. Johnson (1966-1972), and Francis E. Hansen (1972-   ). The closing paragraph of the statement just quoted is significant in this connection.

The intention of paragraph 3 of this revelation seems to have been that Richard C. Kelley should be associated with his father and Bishop Blakeslee as the remaining member of the Presiding Bishopric. After consideration Brother Kelley thought it wise to refuse to accept ordination at this time.

"The spirit of distrust and want of confidence. . .is unbecoming" (4a). In this connection please note the following from a communication given through President Elbert A. Smith at the Stone Church, Independence, Missouri, April 4, 1920:

You have been told in the past that in your public and private ministrations you should avoid sowing the seeds of distrust and division. That which a man sows, that shall he also reap. If any man shall sow discontent he shall reap discontent and be unhappy. If any man shall sow doubt he shall reap doubt in his own heart, and shall be fortunate if he shall not actually deny the faith. But he who sows the seeds of faith shall reap faith, and it shall cause his soul to enlarge and expand. He who gives forth love—love shall come back to him. He who is very tender and merciful, to him will I be tender and merciful, but *if any man will betray my cause, him will* I judge. He who puts the trust of my people in jeopardy for a little thing he himself will be in jeopardy.

"The church has been admonished heretofore in this respect" (4c). The last word of revelation coming to the church through Joseph Smith, its president and prophet for more than fifty-four years, pleads with the church to cast out the spirit of distrust and want of confidence, and to support those who have been chosen as leaders.[2]

---

[1]Section 132:1, 2. [2]Sections 116:3; 117:13; 118:3, 4; 122:16, 17; 125:14; 130:8.

SECTION 132

President Joseph Smith died at Independence December 10, 1914. His oldest living son, Frederick Madison Smith, had been designated as his successor in the revelation of 1906 (Section 127:8) and again in the Letter of Instruction issued March 4, 1912. The church happily concurred and he was set apart as President of the Church and of the High Priesthood at Stone Church in Independence on May 5, 1915. At that time he was in his forty-second year. He had been a member of the First Presidency for thirteen years. Elbert A. Smith was continued as counselor in the First Presidency, being set apart at the same service as President Frederick M. Smith.

The introduction to the revelation begins, "The matter of selecting one to succeed Bishop E. L. Kelley in the office of Presiding Bishop. . . " This somewhat abrupt introduction is explained by the fact that the revelation formed part of a document presented by the president of the church to the Joint Council of the First Presidency, Quorum of Twelve, and Presiding Bishopric. This, in turn, is explained by the fact that the honorable release of Presiding Bishop Edmund L. Kelley had been under consideration at the Conference of 1915 and had been referred to the First Presidency and Council of Twelve by that body.[1] The refusal of Bishop Blakeslee to accept this responsibility cleared the way for the designation of Bishop McGuire.[2]

"The matter. . . has received by me careful and prayerful consideration" (Introduction). This statement is characteristic of President Smith's approach to his prophetic function. Apparently the light which he received corrected and enriched the results of his own careful and prayerful thought.

"He may act as traveling bishop" (1). This seems to be the first specific designation of a "traveling bishop" in the Reorganization, although there are references to traveling

478

bishops in the early church. G. Leslie DeLapp was given a similar assignment on his release as Presiding Bishop in 1966.[3]

"*Counseling and advising on the law of temporalities in harmony with his successor and the Presidency*" (1). This indicates the basic importance or harmony between the Presidency and the Presiding Bishopric in relation to the law of temporalities. There have been differences of opinion between these groups on matters of administration, but no significant difference at any time as to the basic "law of temporalities."

"*Set apart and ordained*" (2). The expression "set apart" is usually used in relation to the rite by which a minister is authorized to act in one of the orders of the high priesthood. "Ordained" usually has reference to basic ministerial authority. It is quite probable that the terms are not used here with any attempt at technical exactitude. It is interesting to note that Brother McGuire was a high priest but not a bishop prior to this time, so that he was "set apart and ordained" both as bishop and Presiding Bishop.

"*One to be selected by him and supported by the conference*" (2). Elder Israel A. Smith, next younger brother of President Frederick Madison Smith, was ordained counselor in the Presiding Bishopric at the Conference of 1920. He had been a high priest since 1915. He was ordained a bishop on authorization of the Standing High Council, concurred in by the Joint Council of First Presidency, Council of Twelve, and Presiding Bishopric on July 4, 1920.

The other to be Bishop James F. Keir" (2). Bishop McGuire was new to the Presiding Bishopric. Bishop Keir had been working with Bishop Kelley since his ordination to the Bishopric in June 1915. His selection provided an important connection with the preceding administration. The Presiding Bishopric consisted of Bishops McGuire and Keir until the ordination of Elder Israel A. Smith in 1920.

"*The hastening time*" (3a). This phrase has been used prophetically by both Joseph Smith, Jr., and Joseph

479

Smith III.[4] Here the phrasing indicates that the hastening time is "upon us" and this was repeated in 1948.[5] The revelation of 1925, however, says that "the hastening time is here."[6] More recently it is stated that "the hastening time is at hand."[7] Of further interest in this connection are the revelations of 1950 and 1968.[8]

"Confidence in the men of the church chosen for positions of great responsibility" (3a). This instruction was particularly apropos since Bishop McGuire was comparatively unknown to the church. But the principle is not related to him exclusively. The necessity for such confidence is general, with regard to local leaders as well as general leaders.

"All should consecrate" (3b). This is a restatement of Section 119:8b and other important scriptures. The emphasis was continued in later years.[9]

"Everywhere the demand for great activity exists" (4). This was a keynote of the early years of the administration of Frederick M. Smith. The emphasis can be traced in his conference messages and his preaching as well as in his inspirational communications to the church. In the church there was unprecedented broadening of the areas of activity, as world mission and Zionic calling were emphasized.

CALLS TO THE PRESIDING BISHOPRIC

Edward Partridge, the Presiding Bishop of the church, was called to that office by revelation,[10] and Church History says that George Miller had "by revelation been appointed bishop" to succeed Elder Partridge.[11] Neither Israel L. Rogers, George H. Blakesley, nor E. L. Kelley, the Presiding Bishop who served during the administration of Joseph Smith III, was called by revelation approved as such by the church, although divine guidance in their selection was indicated.[12] Since the call of Bishop McGuire, all the presiding bishops of the Reorganization have been called by revelation through the prophet and approved by General Conference.[13]

480

One counselor under Bishop McGuire was named in the revelation of 1916 and the bishop chose the other counselor four years later. Bishop DeLapp was named as one counselor to Bishop Curry in 1932 and Bishop N. Ray Carmichael was chosen by Bishop Curry in 1934. Presiding Bishops Albert Carmichael and G. Leslie DeLapp were authorized to choose their counselors, but counselors to Bishops Walter N. Johnson and Francis E. Hansen were named in the revelations designating their call.

Among others, two major factors may be noted in connection with the selection of counselors in the Presiding Bishopric. Obviously those chosen must be acceptable to the Presiding Bishop whose counselors they are. But it is also highly desirable that when a change in the Presiding Bishopric occurs the new Presiding Bishop shall have had experience under his predecessor. This makes the choice of counselors in the Presiding Bishopric of major concern to the president of the church through whom succeeding Presiding Bishops are called.

It is also worthy of note that although the counselors in the First Presidency are "accounted as equal with" the president of the church in the quorum of the First Presidency,[14] there is no such provision with regard to the Presiding Bishopric.

---

[1]General Conference Minutes 1915:2056. [2]*Ibid.* 2182. [3]Sections 17:16; 83:20a; 148:5. [4]*Ibid.* 85:20a, 118:1a. [5]*Ibid.* 141:5. [6]*Ibid.* 135:2b. [7]*Ibid.* 148:9a. [8]*Ibid.* 142:5, 149:6a. [9]*Ibid.* 141:8, 142:5. [10]*Ibid.* 41:3. [11]Church History 2:513, 797. [12]Ibid. 3:252, 4:389, 5:96-97. [13]Sections 135:1, 136:1d, 138:2, 148:8, 150:4a. [14]*Ibid.* 87:3a.

BIOGRAPHICAL NOTES

Edmund L. Kelley (see notes on Section 124).

Benjamin R. McGuire was born May 18, 1877, at Allentown, New Jersey. He was baptized August 21, 1899, and ordained an elder in 1905 and a high priest in 1910. Responding to the call of the church, he was ordained to the office of bishop and Presiding Bishop on April 16, 1916. Brother McGuire had a master's degree in law, and this was especially useful in the transition from the administration of Bishop E. L. Kelley when the growth of the church demanded that our financial affairs should be put on a sound legal basis. His service as Presiding Bishop was comparatively brief but was of great importance. After leaving the Presiding Bishopric he practiced law in Independence. He died in the Independence Sanitarium April 14, 1944.

James F. Keir was born February 7, 1876, in Braidwood, Illinois. He was baptized July 19, 1887, and ordained a priest in 1889, an elder in 1908, a high priest in 1914, and a bishop in June 1915, at which time he accepted church appointment (see notes on Section 135).

SECTION 133

The second revelation presented to the church by President Frederick M. Smith is dated April 6, 1920, at Independence, Missouri. It was submitted first to the general conference and then to the various quorums. Only six members of the Twelve were in attendance since there was one vacancy, occasioned by the death of Apostle Kelley, and Apostles Butterworth, Rushton, and Hanson were in Australia. Apostles Andersen and Sheehy were involved. The remaining members of the Twelve voted as members of the Quorum of High Priests. Unanimous approval was given by all the other quorums except the Seventy. This quorum reported that those who approved the document were unanimous; it was supported by 54 of those present but 21 of the Seventy refused to vote for or against.

There was some disquietude because this message was presented to the conference before going to the quorums, as had been traditional. This may have been the reason for the refusal of some members of the Seventy to vote. However, the action submitting such documents to the church before taking them to the quorums was not without precedent. The revelations of 1901[1] and 1909[2] were presented to the conference and afterward received quorum consideration before conference action was had.

Prior to presenting this revelatory document President Frederick M. Smith said:

I have still one other matter to present to the church, but I wish to presage it by saying that as much as I should have desired, and as badly as is needed a third member in the Presidency, I am not yet permitted to suggest a name.

I have been admonished that a number of changes will eventually be made in the Quorum of Twelve. Some I present today. Others will be presented in due time, contingent upon the development of conditions.[3]

"Having given to the general missionary needs of the church" (Introduction). As the revelation of 1916 was concerned with the work of the Presiding Bishopric, so the revelation now under consideration is almost exclusively concerned with the work of the Twelve and the missionary forces under their direction. One factor calling for "much thought and prayer" in this connection was the vacancy in the Quorum of Twelve which had existed since the death of James E. Kelley of June 4, 1917. Another was the intense desire of president Smith that the work of the church should be pushed into distant fields. This is made apparent in the assignments of the Twelve and Seventy at this Conference. The work in all the missions abroad was strengthened and President Smith accompanied by Apostle T. W. Williams went to Europe where they were joined later by Apostle James A. Gillen.

"I am permitted to say to the church" (Introduction). President Smith did not present the recommendations contained in this document as his own recommendations, although he was fully identified with them. The procedure indicated here and in the introduction of the revelation of 1938 seems to indicate that "much thought and prayer"

led to the clarification of the understanding of the prophet under the ministry of the Spirit resulting in a sense of freedom and divinely attested authority in presenting the message.

"To fill the vacancies created by these releases" (1). The vacancy created by the death of Elder J. E. Kelley was not filled at this time. After the ordinations here authorized, the members of the Quorum of Twelve were Elders Gomer T. Griffiths, John W. Rushton, C. A. Butterworth, U. W. Greene, R. C. Russell, J. F. Curtis, William M. Aylor, Paul M. Hanson, James A. Gillen, M. A. McConley, and T. W. Williams.

"The burden of the missionary work upon them" (2a). The members of the Twelve are elsewhere called "the chief missionaries of the church."[4]

"The work in this line must be hastened" (2a). In the preceding revelation it had been stated that "Everywhere the demand for great activity exists."[5] Basic to all the work of the church is effective missionary endeavor. Looking back from the vantage point of the years we can see how urgent it was, and still is, that missionary work be given persistent, urgent, and expanding consideration. "I give unto you this first commandment, that ye shall go forth in my name, every one of you;"[6] "It becometh every man who hath been warned, to warn his neighbor;"[7] "Firstly, let my army become very great, and let it be sanctified before me."[8]

The scope of the apostolic assignments made at this conference was the most ambitious in the history of the Reorganization. These assignments were as follows:

Gomer T. Griffiths: The American Indians.

J. W. Rushton and Paul M. Hanson: To join Apostle Butterworth in Australasia.

J. F. Curtis and J. Arthur Gillen: Minutemen available for later assignment (Elder Gillen went to Europe in 1921).

R. C. Russell: Ottawa and Quebec, Canada.

William Aylor: South Africa.

T. W. Williams: Europe with President Smith.

Apostles U. W. Greene and M. A. McConley were given assignments in the domestic field and were to represent the Twelve at headquarters. Apostle Greene was considerably handicapped by ill health.

"*Let them* [the Twelve] *not be unduly concerned with the work of the standing ministry, only as they shall be directed by the Presidency therein*" (2b). This is an amplification of similar instruction given in 1890 and 1894[9] and on other occasions. It should be noted that it does not contemplate the complete exclusion of the Twelve from direction of the standing ministry, but, rather, from the details of local administration. Perhaps the clearest prior statement of the revelation in this connection is in 122:7. While the provisions of 125:14c are shown by the context to have prior reference to "the regularly authorized officers of branch or district" (14b) and to be directed primarily to the people of the church in the several branches, nevertheless the principle applies as from the general authorities of the church to local presiding officers.

"*Let contention cease concerning the prerogatives of the leading quorums*" (2b). This was not a new note in the revelations. It evidently indicates a deep prophetic concern which was justified by subsequent events.[10] Nevertheless, this statement must not be interpreted as authority to prohibit or limit the expression of differences of opinion. It is concerned with the spirit of contention.

"*Taking to the peoples of the world the message of peace*" (2d). This reaffirmation of the world mission of the church was characteristic of the early days of the Restoration and Reorganization, but somewhat dimmed during the struggle to perfect the organization and strengthen the resources of the church. This is a reversal justified by circumstances, of the instruction given in 1882.[11]

"*They shall find comfort and satisfaction in their labors*" (2d). This is a reaffirmation of the promise made in connection with similar prior instruction.[12]

485

BIOGRAPHICAL NOTES

Francis M. Sheehy (see notes on Section 126).

Peter Andersen (see notes on Section 125).

Myron A. McConley was born at Sterling, Colorado, September 17, 1885, and baptized May 27, 1894. Brother McConley was ordained a priest in June 1907 and an elder in April 1910 at which time he was appointed and assigned to Hawaii. After his return from that mission he was ordained a seventy in 1914 and in 1916 was reassigned to Hawaii. After his call to the apostleship he served in Hawaii, Tahiti, Australasia, Europe, and the domestic fields. He was released from the Council of Twelve in the revelation of October 1948 but served as an evangelist from 1948 until his death in 1964.

Thomas W. Williams was born August 23, 1866, in Sanpete County, Utah. Baptized when nine years of age, he was ordained a priest in 1887 and went under appointment in 1889. He was ordained an elder in 1890, a seventy in 1892, a high priest in 1900, and counselor in the Presidency of the Quorum of High Priests in 1901. He was absent from appointment between 1911 and 1916. After his reappointment he served as president of the Religio Department (1920-1925) and as an apostle. He was not sustained by the Conference of 1925 and thereafter became a member of the City Council of Los Angeles, California. He died in Los Angeles April 11, 1931.

---

¹Section 125. ²*Ibid.* 128. ³Church History 7:387. ⁴Section 122:5c. See also 104:12, 105:7-8, 122:9, 125:12. ⁵*Ibid.* 132:4-6. ⁶*Ibid.* 42:2a. ⁷*Ibid.* 84:22a. ⁸*Ibid.* 102:9a. ⁹*Ibid.* 120, 122. ¹⁰*Ibid.* 117:13, 119:5, 121:4, 122:16, 132:4. ¹¹*Ibid.* 118:1. ¹²See particularly Section 122:7d and 8f.

SECTION 134

At the General Conference of 1920 the system of biennial conferences was approved. However, the absence of President Frederick M. Smith in Europe, and other factors,

486

delayed the next Conference until October 1, 1922. The assembly met in a large canvas tent where the Auditorium now stands. It had a seating capacity of about three thousand.

This was the longest conference interim in the history of the Reorganization. There were both annual and semi-annual conferences until 1883.[1] There was no General Conference at all in the year 1900.

At the first business session of the Conference President Frederick M. Smith presented the revelation of that year to the body and stated: "I suggest the Conference disassemble and that this be further considered in committee capacity, as our quorums really constitute."[2] This procedure was followed. The Quorum of Twelve and the Presiding Bishopric joined in recommending to the quorums that "action be deferred pending the settlement of important matters pending before the Joint Council of the Presidency, Twelve, and Presiding Bishopric, in which the. . . personnel of the Twelve are vitally interested,. . . and yet undecided and unsettled. . . believing it to be an error to remove those men from the Quorum before these matters are properly adjudicated."[3] Thereafter debate continued in some of the quorums until the Conference set four o'clock Thursday, October 12, as time for the vote. This vote was taken and resulted in a total of 656 for the document and 452 against.[4] Specific points at issue were the presentation of the document to the Conference without prior consideration by the general quorums, and the release of some of the apostles while differences between the Presidency and Twelve were undecided. Debate soon broadened, however, to include discussion of the entire administration of President Smith.

"Filling the leading quorums of the church in which vacancies now exist" (Introduction). The quorum of the First Presidency had not been filled since the death of President Joseph Smith III. There were vacancies in the Twelve due to the death of Elder J. E. Kelley and the resignation of Elder William Aylor.

"Ordained counselor to the president as a member of the First Presidency" (1). Note that this phrasing parallels that in 129:5 and is further elaborated in 139:1a and 142:1b. This is in line with the basic statements of the law in this connection.[5]

"Local work or as evangelical ministers" (2). Those released from the Twelve would serve as high priests unless they were set apart to some other responsibility within the high priesthood. Elders Griffiths, Greene, and Russell were subsequently ordained to the Evangelical Order. Elder Butterworth served as a high priest and continued to reside in Australia. For the duties of members of the Evangelical Order see comments on Section 125:3.

"Ordained president of the Quorum of Twelve" (4). Jason W. Briggs was chosen as president of the Twelve in 1853 in harmony with the rule of seniority, the two senior to him having previously declined. The choice of Elders Alexander H. Smith (1890-1897) and William H. Kelley (1897-1913) was in harmony with the voice of revelation.[6] Gomer T. Griffiths (1913-1922) was chosen by the Quorum of Twelve as provided for in the revelation of 1913. Apostle Paul M. Hanson (1934-1958), who was to succeed Elder J. Arthur Gillen in 1934, was selected by quorum action, as were Charles R. Hield (1958-1964) and Clifford A. Cole (1964-   ).

Paragraphs 5, 6, and 7 constitute a reiteration of 133:2, which itself reaffirms principles stated in 120:4-7; 122:7, 8.

BIOGRAPHICAL NOTES

Floyd Marion McDowell was born at Excelsior, Wisconsin, March 26, 1889, and baptized October 1, 1899. Prior to his ordination to the First Presidency Brother McDowell was nationally recognized as an authority in the junior college field. He was ordained an elder January 10, 1915, a high priest August 6, 1916, and a member of the Lamoni Stake High Council October 15, 1916. He served in the Presidency for almost exactly sixteen years, making a major contribution in the fields of religious education and priesthood education. After his resignation in October 1938, he continued to direct these departments. Elder McDowell was ordained an evangelist in 1954 and served in many fields before his death in 1964.

Gomer T. Griffiths (see notes on Section 119).

Ulysses W. Greene (see notes on Section 126).

Cornelius A. Butterworth (see notes on Section 126).

Robert C. Russell (see notes on Section 129).

Clyde F. Ellis was born at Chase, Michigan, December 19, 1891, and baptized in June 1900. He was ordained a priest in September 1909, and accepted General Conference appointment in 1910. His first assignment to the Society Islands Mission was in 1914. He was ordained an elder in 1912, a seventy in 1913, and an apostle after his return from the Islands at the October Conference of 1923. He was an excellent Polynesian linguist and had deep love for the people of the Society Islands Mission. Apostle Ellis died June 21, 1945.

John Franklin Garver was born at Bristol, Indiana, January 28, 1878, and baptized September 26, 1897. He was ordained a priest in November 1901, and soon thereafter went to Graceland College. He became a counselor to Elder John Smith, president of Lamoni Stake, in October 1907, and suceeded him as president of the stake in June 1916. Brother Garver was a member of the Board of Trustees of Graceland College from 1910 until his death, serving as president of the board from 1932 onward. He was assistant editor of the *Saints' Herald* from 1913 to 1916 and an editor of *Zion's Ensign* from 1922 to 1932. He was a member of the Standing High Council from February 1922 to March 1924 and served as an apostle from 1922 to 1946. In April 1946 he was ordained a member of the First Presidency and was serving in this office at the time of his death March 3, 1949.

Daniel T. Williams was born December 13, 1888, and baptized in February 1898. He was ordained a deacon in 1904, a priest in 1912, an elder in February 1913,

489

and a high priest in April 1917. From 1918 until he was called to the apostleship he served as counselor to Elder John F. Garver, president of Lamoni Stake. He served as an evangelist between his release from the Twelve in 1958 and his death in 1975.

F. Henry Edwards was born in Birmingham, England, August 4, 1897, and baptized in November 1905. He was ordained a priest in 1916 and an elder in 1920, at which time he accepted General Conference appointment. He served as secretary of the Council of Twelve from 1922 to 1945. Elder Edwards served as counselor in the First Presidency from April 1946 until April 1966. He has written extensively, chiefly on doctrinal themes, and since his release from the Presidency in 1966 has compiled Volumes 5, 6, 7, and 8 of *The History of the Church of Jesus Christ of Latter Day Saints.*

Edmund John Gleazer was born in Belfast, Ireland, March 23, 1895, and after the death of his parents came to the United States where he was baptized in February 1912. He was ordained an elder in 1917 and a seventy in August 1918, having accepted appointment at the General Conference of 1916. He became an apostle in 1922 and an evangelist in April 1958. He died on September 13, 1980.

Roy Sparks Budd was born May 3, 1890, at Schell City, Missouri, and baptized in May 1898. He was ordained to the office of priest in 1911, elder in 1916, and high priest in 1920. He accepted General Conference appointment in 1914 and was serving as pastor at Cameron, Missouri, when called to the apostleship. Brother Budd resigned from the Twelve in October 1936. He died as a result of an accident June 5, 1956.

James Arthur Gillen (see notes on Section 130).

---

[1]Semiannual conferences were discontinued after October 1882; see *Saints' Herald* 29:318. [2]G.C.M. 1922:3200. [3]Report of the Seventy, G.C.M. 1922:3207-8. [4]*Ibid.* 3240-44. [5]Sections 104:11b; 87:3. [6]Sections 120:8, 124:3.

SECTION 135

Early in 1924 the church was experiencing financial difficulties and there were serious differences between the First Presidency and the Presiding Bishopric. After consultation with the Standing High Council of the church, the First Presidency called a council of the First Presidency, Council of Twelve, and Order of Bishops. This council met in April 1924. During the sessions of this council the right and duty of the Presiding Bishop to veto expenditures approved by the Presidency was debated, and the Presidency was asked to submit a statement on authority in church government. This was done and the statement was approved as were documents on the building of the Auditorium and the establishment of Zion. Of these the two latter provoked little comment. The document on church government, however, seriously disturbed some of the senior members of the Twelve and the members of the Presiding Bishopric, and their point of view was later shared with others who were not present at the April council. The matter was widely discussed prior to the opening of the Conference of 1925. In a few districts delegates were chosen with specific relation to their stand on the issue. When the document on church government came before the Conference it was approved on a yea and nay vote by 919 to 405.[1] The whole experience was divisive and frustrating. Looking back, it is impossible to assess responsibility with any degree of exactitude, and unwise to attempt to do so. But the fact that so many good and devoted leaders and members of the church were so deeply hurt shows with what great care problems like this should be approached even though at times the responsibility for defining procedures may be urgently necessary.

After the document on church government had been approved, the Order of Bishops took action stating that: "A continuance of the ministrations of the Presiding Bishopric is incompatible with the action of the present Conference."

This action of the order paid high tribute to the ability and integrity of the brethren of the Presiding Bishopric, but recommended that they be honorably released from their positions. This recommendation came before the General Conference and after some discussion a motion was adopted providing: "That further consideration of this matter be deferred and that we seek the Lord through the Prophet, in fasting and prayer, for direction."[2] It was against this background that the communication dated April 18, 1925, was received. The Conference adopted "The document coming from the President of the Church for what it purports to be, a revelation from God."[3]

"Ordained to act in the office of Presiding Bishop for a time" (1). Bishop Carmichael served until the Conference of 1932.

"The documents from the joint council of April 1924" (2a). The document on church government was adopted by the General Conference April 11, 1925, and is now General Conference Resolution 849. The document on the establishment of Zion was adopted April 13, 1925, and is now General Conference Resolution 851. The document on the building of the Auditorium was adopted April 13, 1925, and may be found in General Conference Minutes 1925:3832. It is excluded from the compilation of Conference resolutions because its provisions had been fulfilled.

"To missionary tasks. . . send out by twos" (4). This principle was followed in the early Restoration.[4] It was reaffirmed in the early days of the Reorganization.[5] In 1925 the church had recently been shocked by the loss through transgression of a promising missionary who had worked in comparative isolation. This principle is particularly emphasized in missions abroad, and in many domestic fields it is achieved by the closest possible association between the district president and the missionary.

BIOGRAPHICAL NOTES

Benjamin R. McGuire (see notes on Section 132).

492

James F. Keir (see notes on Section 132).

Israel Alexander Smith (see notes on Section 138).

Albert Carmichael was born September 14, 1863. He was baptized December 18, 1873, and was ordained an elder in 1893, a high priest in 1899, a bishop in 1908, bishop of Lamoni Stake in 1916, Presiding Bishop in 1925, and patriarch in 1932. He served as a patriarch in California and Independence until his superannuation at the Conference of 1938. Brother Carmichael died May 4, 1956, at Independence, Missouri. He was a man of deep faith and devotion, an outstanding teacher of the financial law.

GENERAL NOTES

After Section 135 was approved, Bishop Carmichael nominated Bishop Mark H. Siegfried to be one of his counselors, and this received the approval of the General Conference. In a document dated April 12, 1926, Bishop Carmichael nominated Bishop John A. Becker to be the other member of the Presiding Bishopric, and this was approved by the General Conference.

At the General Conference of 1926, after the sharp feelings of the 1925 period had subsided somewhat, a proposed amendment to the document on church government was presented to the General Conference for consideration. After some discussion this was referred to the First Presidency, the Council of Twelve, and Presiding Bishopric. This council recommended adoption of the explanatory statement which now constitutes General Conference Resolution 861. This report was adopted by a vote of 463 to 28.[6]

---

[1]G.C.M. 1925:3827-31. [2]*Ibid.* 3855, 3858. [3]*Ibid.* 3863, 3865. [4]Sections 42:2; 52:3; 60:3; 61:6; 62:2. [5]Section 115:1. [6]G.C.M. 1926:40, 71.

SECTION 136

The financial depression which swept the United States in the thirties required drastic curtailment of the activities of the church. The number of General Conference appointees was sharply cut and work on the Auditorium and Sanitarium was brought to a standstill. In February 1931 the counselors to Presiding Bishop Albert Carmichael (Elders M. H. Siegfried and J. A. Becker) resigned from the Presiding Bishopric. Bishops L. F. P. Curry and G. Leslie DeLapp were selected as their successors by arrangement between the Presidency and Brother Carmichael, concurred in by the Twelve. Retrenchments initiated at this time were augmented by still further adjustments agreed to in a September council.

The document now forming Section 136 of the Doctrine and Covenants was presented to the Conference on Thursday, April 14, 1932. It was immediately referred to the quorums for consideration, and the next day all the quorums reported their approval. The Conference received it "as a revelation from God" by unanimous standing vote.[1]

"Believing that such wisdom and inspiration have been given me" (Introduction). Note the inevitable implication of the prophet himself in the message. Revelation does not make him an automaton but treats him as a responsible person even though greater light than he can command is given him.

"Under conditions existing" (1a). Bishop Carmichael was primarily a teacher of the financial law. In this area he had done outstandingly good work, and for this contribution the church is greatly indebted to him, as is recognized in the revelation. But the financial situation called for the leadership of a man of such special training as Bishop Curry had.

"A vacancy existing in the number of the Twelve" (2). This had been occasioned by the loss of Elder T. W. Williams from the quorum in 1925. Elder John W. Rushton,

494

who had resigned during the difficulties of 1925, had resumed his place in the Twelve immediately prior to receipt of this revelation.

"The active work of the apostolic quorum and as representatives of the church" (2). The members of the Council of Twelve have dual functions. As members of their quorum they have joint responsibility in directing missionary affairs and as individual ministers they are "directing, regulating, and advising authorities of the church" and are among its leading representatives.[2]

"The movements toward better understanding" (3a). These had been gathered up into specific statements of objectives and procedures and were adopted by the General Conference. They included "Procedure in Ordinations,"[3] "Procedure and Objectives in Zion and Her Stakes,"[4] "Teaching Objectives,"[5] and "Next Steps in Religious Education."[6]

BIOGRAPHICAL NOTES

Albert Carmichael (see notes on Section 135).

L. F. P. Curry was born July 22, 1887, and baptized January 21, 1906. He had extensive experience in the local ministry as a teacher (1907), an elder (1908), a high priest (1923), and a bishop (1926). He came to the Presiding Bishopric with long experience in the fields of finance, business supervision, and reorganization, and served as the chief financial minister of the church between 1932 and 1940. Brother Curry was a member of the First Presidency from 1940 until the Conference of 1946. Thereafter he served locally in Center Stake as associate pastor of the Stone Church and member of the Stake High Council. He was mayor of Independence 1962-1966. He died January 23, 1977.

George Leslie DeLapp was born November 4, 1895, at East Delavan, Wisconsin, and baptized on June 7, 1909. Brother DeLapp was ordained a priest in 1925, an elder in the same year, and a high priest and bishop at the General Conference of 1926. His first appointment was as bishop of the Lamoni Stake in February 1928. His experience in finance and farm management was excellent preparation for his work in the Presiding Bishopric. He succeeded Bishop L. F. P. Curry in 1940 and served with marked distinction until his release from the Presiding Bishopric in 1966. He died December 1, 1981.

George Gregory Lewis was born November 17, 1901, at Wallsend, New South Wales, Australia. He was baptized there in 1909 and ordained a deacon in 1917. He attended Graceland College, and after graduation took his master's degree from the University of Chicago. He was ordained an elder in 1927 and went under appointment shortly thereafter. He was secretary to the Council of Twelve for the three years preceding his death in an automobile accident in September 1948.

---

¹G.C.M. 1932:132. ²Section 120:4b. ³G.C.R. 1932:916. ⁴*Ibid.* 917. ⁵*Ibid.* 918. ⁶*Ibid.* 919.

SECTION 137

The Conference of 1938 met in a mood of renewed optimism. The worst rigors of the depression were past. The debt reduction program was going forward rapidly. The time was near when we could begin making further General Conference appointments. The Saints were justifiably proud of the way they had responded to a major challenge.

At the business session of Thursday, April 7, President Smith read the communication he had been led to present to the church, and announced that copies would be distributed to the various quorums "for consideration and action, in harmony with our established procedure."¹ The next day the quorums reported unanimous approval, and the Conference then adopted "this communication with its provisions as the voice of divine inspiration to the church."[2]

"Two vacancies in the Quorum of Twelve" (Introduction). Apostle J. Arthur Gillen had resigned at the Conference of 1934 and Apostle Roy S. Budd had resigned in 1936. Elder Paul M. Hanson had succeeded Brother Gillen as president of the Quorum of Twelve.

"The functioning and work of this order is of great importance" (4b). The patriarchs and evangelists (the two terms are used interchangeably although they emphasize different aspects of the joint ministry[3]) are selected through members of the Quorum of Twelve and are high priests. Their ordination is approved by the quorum and by world or local conference action. Their duties are outlined in Sections 125:3-6 and 145:6.[4] The work of the Evangelical Order calls for an affectionate concern in the welfare of individual Saints, for wisdom, sound judgment, and a high degree of prophetic insight. Note the new emphases on the work of this order in this revelation. The evangelists are "to build up faith in the gospel and the church and its work," laboring with "vigor, deep faith, and unreserved consecration." The evangelists are greatly aided in their ministry if they have such prior administrative experience as will enable them to sense the problems of administrative officers and to cooperate with them.

"The vacancy in the First Presidency" (5). This was now being created by the release of President Elbert A. Smith for his work as Presiding Evangelist. The situation was to be made more difficult six months later by the resignation of President Floyd M. McDowell.

BIOGRAPHICAL NOTES

J. Frank Curtis (see notes on Section 139).

C. George Mesley was born October 15, 1900, at Bairnsdale, Victoria, and baptized April 7, 1918. He was ordained a priest March 31, 1920, and elder April 1, 1923.

He accepted General Church appointment in October 1928 soon after his graduation from Graceland College, and was assigned to Kansas City Stake. Ordained a high priest on April 20, 1930, he became president of Kansas City Stake November 25, 1934, and was serving in this office when called to the apostleship. He resigned from the apostolic quorum March 31, 1954.

Arthur Alma Oakman was born March 30, 1905, in Ponder's End, London, England, and baptized there September 5, 1915. He was ordained a priest in 1928 immediately prior to leaving England for Graceland College. Soon after taking the field in 1930 he was ordained to the eldership. He became a seventy in April 1934 and a high priest in April 1936. He was serving as pastor at Stone Church in Independence, Missouri, when called to the Twelve. He was ordained an evangelist in 1964. He died at Independence, Missouri, December 26, 1975.

Charles R. Hield was born August 11, 1896, at Janesville, Wisconsin, and baptized September 3, 1905. He was ordained to the eldership September 3, 1922, and to the high priesthood in February 1938. His work in the University of New York made it impossible for him to be at the General Conference and he was ordained to the apostleship in the year 1938 in his home branch of Brooklyn, New York. Brother Hield served as president of the Council of Twelve from 1958 to 1964, when he was released from the quorum to concentrate on research and translation. He has made a distinctive contribution in the field of Spanish literature and, particularly, in supervising the production of the Spanish edition of the Book of Mormon.

Frederick A. Smith (see notes on Section 126). Brother Smith died June 25, 1954.

Elbert A. Smith (see notes on Section 129).

---

[1]G.C.M. 1938:93. [2]*Ibid.* 101. [3]Section 145:6. [4]See also Section 147:3.

SECTION 138

The historical background of this revelation is explained in the introductory paragraph (1).

"This left the President without Counselors" (1b). This situation was discussed between President Smith and the Council of Twelve at the October 1938 council referred to. The Twelve advised President Smith to seek light looking to the filling of the Quorum of the First Presidency. Those selected under inspirational guidance by President Smith were already high priests. They served by consent of the general officers most directly involved pending action by the Conference of 1940.

It was at this council that President Smith indicated his brother, Israel, as his successor. The record says: "Citing the letter of instruction issued by his father, he [President Smith] called attention to the fact that in the event of himself passing, Israel would be in line for the office of President, and would have the advantage of the additional experience which this appointment would give."[1]

"He being left free to nominate his counselors in due time" (2). Bishop DeLapp had served as a counselor in the Presiding Bishopric since 1931. He was intimately acquainted with the problems to be confronted in his enlarged responsibility, and was in close touch with every member of the Order of Bishops. The day after the revelation was approved Bishop DeLapp nominated Bishop C. A. Skinner of Kansas City Stake and Bishop Henry L. Livingston of Far West Stake to serve as his counselors, and these were unanimously approved. Bishop Walter N. Johnson was chosen a member of the Presiding Bishopric when Bishop Skinner resigned because of ill health at the Conference of 1946 and succeeded Brother DeLapp as Presiding Bishop in 1966.

"The task of establishing Zion... unity should prevail" (3a, c). It was fitting that these two emphases, so dear to

499

the heart of President Frederick Madison Smith, should be the dominant notes sounded in the last paragraph of his last inspirational communication to the church. President Smith died in Independence March 20, 1946.

BIOGRAPHICAL NOTES

Floyd M. McDowell (see notes on Section 134).

Israel Alexander Smith, (see notes on Section 132:2) son of President Joseph Smith and Bertha Madison Smith, was born at Plano, Illinois, February 2, 1876. He was baptized June 25, 1886. He was active in church work in various connections from his early youth. He was associate editor of the *Saints' Herald* from 1908 to 1914 and assistant editor in 1914. He was ordained to the high priesthood April 11, 1915, and served as a member of the Stake High Council in Independence 1915-1917 and as a member of the Center Stake Presidency from 1917 to 1920. Brother Smith was a counselor in the Presiding Bishopric from 1920 to 1925. After leaving the Presiding Bishopric he was secretary of the church until his call to the First Presidency. During this period he also served as a member of the Standing High Council of the church. He was admitted to the Iowa bar in 1912 and the Missouri bar in 1913, and served in the Iowa Legislature from 1911 to 1913. He was a member of the Missouri Constitutional Convention 1943-1944. President Smith succeeded his brother as president of the church in 1946 and served until his death on June 14, 1958.

L. F. P. Curry (see notes on Section 136). Brother Curry served as a member of the Presidency until the Conference of 1946. Thereafter he served locally in Center Stake as associate pastor of the Stone Church and member of the Stake High Council.

G. Leslie DeLapp (see notes on Section 136).

SECTION 139

At a meeting with the Council of Twelve held October 20, 1938, and acting under "such inspirational impulsions" as were given him at the time, President Frederick M. Smith chose Elder Israel A. Smith to serve as one of his counselors (D. and C. 138:1b). At this time he indicated that the experience gained in the Presidency would be of value in preparing his brother in the event that Israel should be called to be president of the church.

When President Frederick M. Smith died March 20, 1946, the Council of Twelve took note of his prior designation of Elder Israel A. Smith to be his successor, but thought it wise to ask the Presiding Patriarch of the church, Elbert A. Smith, to seek such further light as the Lord might be pleased to give.

When General Conference of 1946 convened the remaining members of the First Presidency presided until the Conference was fully organized. They then made an offical report of the death of President Frederick M. Smith and turned the chair over to Elder Paul M. Hanson, president of the Council of Twelve. Elder Hanson narrated the facts already set forth and then called on the Presiding Evangelist for any statement which he might feel was pertinent to the existing situation. In a somewhat lengthy recital of events connected with the death of President Frederick M. Smith, Brother Elbert included the following:

> To this matter [succession in the Presidency] I have given earnest prayer and thought, with an increasing conviction that it is in harmony with the spirit of wisdom and revelation that the choice indicated by the late president should be approved and that without unnecessary delay Israel A. Smith should be ordained president of the high priesthood and the church and prophet, seer, and revelator to the church. I am persuaded that this also will find confirming witness of the Spirit in the minds of numerous people.[1]

In light of the evidence presented, the Conference endorsed the call of Israel A. Smith and he was ordained prophet,

501

seer, and revelator, and president of the church on April 7, 1946. The revelation dated April 9, 1946, is the first of the six presented to the church by him during his prophetic ministry.

"That the quorums might be filled" (Introduction). This had primary reference to the Quorum of the First Presidency and the Quorum of Twelve. President Smith could have presided without counselors, as his father had done in 1860-1863, or with one counselor as Joseph Smith III did from 1885 to 1896, and as Frederick M. Smith did from 1915 to 1922. Nevertheless at least one addition to his quorum was eminently desirable.

The Twelve had nine members. Additional apostles were especially important, since council activity is severely handicapped whenever distant places make it difficult for a majority to meet on call at Independence.

"The burden of the church was laid upon me" (Introduction). This is a reference to a statement found in Doctrine and Covenants 122:2a, "The burden of the care of the church is laid on him who is called to preside over the high priesthood of the church. . . ."

"The mind of the Lord was manifested to me, and in the order named my brethren have been presented to me" (Introduction) President Smith later stated to his counselors that he became clear concerning the call of John F. Garver during the experience of Monday, April 8, and of the call of F. Henry Edwards during the continuing experience on Tuesday, April 9.

"To be counselors to my servant, the president of the church" (1a). The brethren named were now to share "the burden of the care of the church" and the presidency of the high priesthood.[2]

"To be presidents in the Quorum of the First Presidency" (1a). The counselors to the president of the church "are accounted as equal" with him "in holding the keys of this last kingdom."[3] Together they form a quorum of the Presidency of the church.[4] In the actual functioning of the Quorum of the First Presidency decisions are reached in

502

mutual consultation and agreement, deference being paid to the president of the church as the prophetic leader of the quorum as well as of the high priesthood and of the church. The quorum is then represented before the church and the world by any of its members as may be agreed among them, and as circumstances may indicate to be wise.

"*Their apostleship is extended in presidency*" (1b).[5] Those chosen were no longer members of the Quorum of the First Presidency. Yet they continued to function as apostles, as their predecessors had done.[6] Their apostleship was extended in that they were now members of the First Presidency rather than of the second presidency and exercised functions specifically reserved to the Presidency and exercised by the apostles only under special circumstances, e.g., in bearing the burden of the care of the work of the church in all its departments in all the world.

"*D. Blair Jensen . . . who is called and chosen to this office, and should be ordained*" (2a). It should be noted that Elder Jensen was already called of God. He was to be ordained if the church recognized this call and consented to it.

"*The quorums and the body*" (conclusion). In effect, the various general quorums of the church act as special committees of the General Conference. Their several responsibilities give them diverse points of view from which to scrutinize and react to the revelations presented to the prophet. The body acts in light of this diverse scrutiny and approval.

BIOGRAPHICAL NOTES

John F. Garver (see notes on Section 134).

F. Henry Edwards (see notes on Section 134).

Dorman Blair Jensen was born April 21, 1901, at Moorhead, Iowa. He was ordained a priest in September 1926 and an elder in February 1928, and accepted general church appointment at the conference of that year. Ordained a high priest in 1930, he became a counselor

503

to the president of that quorum in 1932 and served until his ordination as a member of the Twelve. His field assignment included pastorates in Minneapolis, Omaha, and Detroit, and the presidencies of the Lamoni and Kansas City Stakes.

After serving as an apostle in the domestic field and in Europe, he was ordained a patriarch-evangelist at the General Conference of 1966. He was superannuated in 1972. Apostle Jensen was regarded as an unusually able administrator. His wife, the former Delia Schieuer, has given quiet but understanding support throughout his ministry. He died March 17, 1984.

----

[1]G.C.M. 1946:3. [2]Section 122:2a. [3]*Ibid.* 87:3a. [4]*Ibid.* 104:11b. [5]This phrase was used in a similar connection in Sections 145:3 and 148:2. [6]Section 19:1a.

SECTION 140

This revelation was presented to the quorums and councils of the church and then to the Conference on Monday, April 7, 1947. Here it was approved and its inclusion in the Doctrine and Covenants was ordered.

"The unity among my people and in the councils of the church" (1a). The instruction that the priesthood are to "perform their responsibilities in good fellowship, and sustain each other" (1b) is closely akin to that given more than eighty years before to President Joseph Smith III[1] and repeated positively or negatively in many of the subsequent revelations. It was a major concern of President Israel A. Smith.[2]

"Vacancies already existing" (2). In 1946 the vacancy in the Twelve left by the death on June 21, 1945, of Apostle Clyde F. Ellis was filled by the ordination of Apostle D. Blair Jensen. The vacancies existing at the beginning of the 1947 Conference were those occasioned by the ordinations of John F. Garver and F. Henry Edwards to the Presidency at that time.

"His works are with me and his reward is sure" (3). In this connection note Doctrine and Covenants 116:2b, 129:1b, etc.

"This call was made known before" (4b). This was in 1946 when the call of W. Wallace Smith to the apostleship was shared by President Smith with his counselors. President Smith was not entirely clear as to whether this was a time for the call to be consummated and so delayed bringing it to the attention of the body.

"The gathering and temporalities connected therewith are within my law" (5a). They were not to be conducted in haphazard fashion, but after proper consultation with the administrative authorities most directly concerned and with the bishopric.[3]

"Zionic conditions are no further away nor any closer than the spiritual condition of my people justifies" (5c). A very timely and significant reminder. Temporalities are of great importance in the Zionic enterprise, but what makes the enterprise Zionic is the spiritual purpose to which temporal means are consecrated. The fruits of the Spirit are always the major characteristics of Zionic achievement.

BIOGRAPHICAL NOTES

Roscoe E. Davey was born in Butte, Montana, February 11, 1896, and baptized July 6, 1909. He served successively as priest (1916), elder (1920), seventy (1922), and President of Seventy (1926) before being called to the apostleship. He married Mabel M. Johnson in 1919 and went under appointment in 1920, at which time he was assigned to the Religious Education course at Graceland. Thereafter he served widely and was an able missionary. Brother Davey held a number of important assignments as a member of the Twelve, the most notable of these as apostle in charge of the Australasian Field. He was ordained an evangelist April 7, 1964. He died November 7, 1983.

Maurice Lee Draper was born August 24, 1918, at

505

Arma, Kansas. He was baptized June 10, 1928, and served successively as deacon (1935), priest (1937), elder (1937), seventy (1940), and President of Seventy (1946). He is married to the former Olive Ruth Willis and together they have formed a distinguished ministerial team. They have three children: David, Edward, and Janette. Appointed in April 1937 toward the close of the Depression, he was one of the youngest missionaries in the field and served with distinction wherever his calling took him. After his ordination to the apostleship he served in Australasia and in the domestic missions before being called to the First Presidency in October 1958. He has published books on doctrinal themes and made many contributions to the *Saints Herald*. He was ordained to the office of evangelist-patriarch April 9, 1980.

John W. Rushton (see notes on Section 126).

William Wallace Smith was born at Lamoni, Iowa, November 18, 1900, and is the son of Joseph and Ada Clark Smith. He was baptized June 6, 1909, and served as an elder from September 1928. At the time of his call to the apostleship he was pastor of the First Church in Portland, Oregon. He and his wife, the former Rosamond Bunnell, have two children, Wallace B., and Rosalee (Mrs. Otto Elser). After serving in the Twelve for three years, President Smith was named a counselor to his brother Israel A. Smith at the Conference of 1950 and succeeded Israel as president of the church on October 6, 1958.

---

[1]Section 116:3. [2]*Ibid.* 141:7a, 142:3. [3]*Ibid.* 58:12, 127:7.

SECTION 141

The Conference of 1946 adjourned for one year instead of the usual two-year period in order to enable the new Presidency and the general administration of the affairs of the church to adjust to the changed situation occasioned by the death of President Frederick M. Smith. In order that the succeeding conference would return to the pattern previously established, the conference of 1947 adjourned for a year and one-half. This 1948 conference therefore met in October.

"I have been led. . . I am permitted" (salutation). From the verbiage used in introducing the revelation it is quite clear that the prophet of the church felt that whatever human understanding and insight he brought to his task had been augmented and enriched to such a degree that he became, in fact, the servant of the Lord in bringing to the church the instructions he transmitted.

"My servant Myron A. McConley is honorably released from further duty as an Apostle" (2). Apostle McConley had served in the apostolic quorum since 1920. His health failed while on a mission to Europe in 1947. At the time of his release he was sufficiently recovered to engage in some ministerial labor but not to carry heavy administrative burdens. He died at Independence, Missouri, July 2, 1964.

"The Seventies under appointment" (6a). For many years the ideal was for all seventies to be under appointment so that they would be free to travel at the call of the church under the direction of the Council of Twelve.[1] This statement is, perhaps, a slight intimation of the coming change in this mode of operation, a change more fully authorized after the revelation of 1954.

"Let the Twelve seek to perfect the work in regions closer to the Center" (6a). In evangelism near to the Center Place considerable resources of personnel, equipment, etc., are available. Further from the Center Place these resources are not so readily available and the work to be done is more characteristic of the calling of the seventy who are to "open up the work in new places."[2]

"The standing ministers, and especially district and stake authorities, are called to assist" (6b). This anticipates organized missionary endeavor as already intimated. While the standing ministry have primary responsibility for the nurture and care of the Saints, they also have continuing missionary responsibility.[3]

"Many of the elders not under appointment have a desire and will labor in new places" (6c). In the early days of the church the frontier communities were sufficiently widely separated to require considerable travel in going from one to the other. Now, with the increasing urbanization of the United States, new openings could be made without a great deal of travel, and could be initiated by elders having missionary interest and capacity but unable for various reasons to serve under General Conference appointment.

"Joint responsibility is laid on all" (8a). This, along with the admonition to be united, is a constantly recurring theme of the revelations.[4]

BIOGRAPHICAL NOTES

Percy Elgin Farrow was born at Derby, Ontario, Canada, July 16, 1902. He was baptized October 13, 1912, and has served the church as a priest (1921), elder (1922), seventy (1926), and President of Seventy (1942). He married Clara Thompson in 1929. Brother Farrow was first appointed in November 1923, but was released in 1931 because of the depression of that time. Reappointed in December 1939, he served widely in both the United States and in his native Canada. While a member of the Council of Twelve he presided in several domestic fields and in the Australasian Mission. He was ordained an evangelist at the Conference of 1966.

Reed M. Holmes was born at Mansfield, Washington, June 17, 1917, and baptized four days after his eighth birthday. He served as a priest (1934), an elder (1941), and a high priest (1946). He has been an appointee since December 1940 and was set apart as presiding patriarch of the church in 1974.[5] His wife is the former Dorothy Carter to whom he was married in 1943.

---

[1]Section 104:13, 16, 41b. [2]*Ibid.* 120:3, 122:7. [3]*Ibid.* 103. [4]*Ibid.* 119:8a, 120:3, 122:16b. [5]*Ibid.* 151:2.

SECTION 142

The revelation received through President Israel A. Smith on April 2, 1950, is addressed to the elders and to the church. There appears to be no significance in this form of address as distinguished from that of the other recent revelations.

"Counselor to the president of the high priesthood and as a member of the Quorum of the First Presidency" (1b). Although this is not specifically stated, W. Wallace Smith became one of the three presidents who together compose the First Presidency of the church.[1]

"The Joint Council" (3). There are many joint councils held in the church as circumstances may demand. These include joint councils of the Presidency and Twelve; the Presidency and Presiding Bishopric; the Presidency, Twelve, and Seventy; the Presidency, Twelve, and Order of Bishops; etc. In such joint gatherings decisions are usually arrived at by majority vote, but any of the component councils can at any time withdraw and function separately. The joint meeting is for joint information and joint determination of related responsibilities, but it does not rob any of the component councils of their basic functions and responsibilities and prerogatives. The definite article (the Joint Council) is usually applied to a council consisting of the Presidency, Council of Twelve, and Presiding Bishopric. This may be because such a council was authorized by the revelation of 1894.[2]

"Meet often for study" (4b). This is a continuation of the introduction to study repeated from time to time since the beginning of the Restoration.[3]

BIOGRAPHICAL NOTES

John Franklin Garver. See notes on Section 134.
William Wallace Smith. See notes on Section 140.
Donald O. Chesworth was born in Fall River, Massa-

509

chusetts, September 21, 1910, and baptized in June 1922. He served as a deacon (1928), priest (1934), elder (1938), and high priest (1941). He was a member of the Kansas City Stake High Council from 1941 until his appointment in 1942, and a bishop in the Atlantic States from 1946 until his ordination to the apostleship. In June 1935 he was married to Alice Kathryn Lane. He was ordained an evangelist in 1972. He died October 17, 1981.

---

[1]Section 139:1a. [2]*Ibid.* 122:13a, 123. [3]*Ibid.* 85:36, 141:5b.

SECTION 143

A revelation given to the church through President Israel A. Smith, dated April 7, 1954, was presented to the Conference on April 10. Elder Lents was called to fill the vacancy in the Twelve occasioned by the resignation of Elder C. G. Mesley.

"Accept the direction of the Council of the Presidents of Seventy" (3a). Elder Harry L. Doty was called to fill one of the vacancies in the council early in the Conference. Before the Conference was concluded Elder Sylvester R. Coleman was called, and his ordination completed the membership of the council.

"Should not be overcareful" (3a). The concern of President Smith with the work of the seventy had extended over a period of years and may be noted in the revelation of 1948.

The tendency to be "overcareful" as it is used here may have reference to the practice of selecting for ordination as seventies only those free to accept appointment and thus able to travel far and near at the call of the church. The expression is used in Section 119:4a with reference to overcarefulness in receiving those who had been affiliated with the Mormon church.

510

"For them to be given missionary assignment" (3b). When this instruction was considered by the Presidents of Seventy they were concerned lest it blur the distinction between missionary elders and the seventy. In practice the only distinction between the seventies under appointment and those who serve on a self-sustaining basis has been that the former are more free to travel to more distant places.

There was considerable soul-searching among responsible officers of the church concerning this matter. The report of the Council of Twelve stated that that council

endorses the first two paragraphs of the document submitted by the President of the Church as the word of the Lord, leaving the balance of the document without approval or disapproval by the Council of Twelve.

The Quorum of Seventy reported:

We approve the document insofar as it pertains to the call and ordination of Donald V. Lents and we request that the remainder of this document be referred to the Councils of Presidency, Twelve, and Seventy for consideration during the period before the Conference of 1956.

The other quorums and orders of the priesthood expressed approval of the document as presented to them.

After the revelation had been approved by the World Conference Elder Z. Z. Renfroe, Senior President of Seventy, stated:

Since the Conference has voted to accept this document as the mind and the will of the Lord, we wish to say that we are with you and pledge our support to the fulfilling of the intent and purpose to the best of our ability. We also desire to pledge our allegiance anew, to the support of the Prophet of the Church as the prophet, seer, and revelator, and we will do all in our power to the furthering of the cause of the building of the kingdom of God here below.[1]

Since it was agreed that the call of seventies is a function of the Council of Presidents of Seventy, no seventies were designated until the Council was satisfied. This was ten years later.

BIOGRAPHICAL NOTES

Donald V. Lents was born at Rhodes, Iowa, July 30, 1917,

and baptized August 2, 1925. He studied at Graceland College, Lamoni, Iowa, Ohio State University, and at Brown University, Providence, Rhode Island. He was ordained an elder in June 1939, and began almost immediately to serve the church under appointment. He was later ordained a high priest (1945) and a member of the Center Stake High Council (1950). He was assigned to the British Isles Mission as minister in charge at the Conference of 1952 and was still serving there when called to the apostleship. He was ordained August 29, 1954, and served in the Twelve until 1980, when he was ordained an evangelist-patriarch. His apostolic assignments included Europe, the Caribbean, Australia, Canada, and many states in the United States. He established the Independence Sanitarium and Hospital chaplain program which remains a valuable community service. Don and Helen (Draper) Lents have three children: Pamela, Don G., and John R.

¹G.C.M. 1954:115, 116.

SECTION 144

On May 28, 1952, President Israel A. Smith informed his counselor, Elder F. Henry Edwards, that he had clear light that W. W. Smith should in time succeed him as president of the church. On this date President Smith also prepared the statement addressed to the church and the Council of Twelve Apostles which now constitutes Section 144 of the Doctrine and Covenants. At the request of President Smith this was witnessed by F. Henry Edwards and, a short time later, by Bishop G. Leslie DeLapp in the presence of President Smith and Elder Edwards. It was then committed to the custody of President Edwards who attached to it, in a separate document, a statement giving instructions that in the event of his own death prior to that of President Smith the document should be handed to President Smith or in the event of his death at the same time as that of President Smith it should be handed to the other witness, Bishop DeLapp, or to the president of the Council of Twelve. From this time forward the document was never mentioned between President Smith and either of the witnesses or between the witnesses themselves, nor were its contents communicated to President W. Wallace Smith by the witnesses.

After the death of President Smith on June 14, 1958, and prior to the funeral President Edwards handed the letter to President W. Wallace Smith for his information. By agreement between them the letter was then brought to the attention of Elder Paul M. Hanson of the Twelve and, in due time, to that of the Council of Twelve, the Presidents of Seventy, and the Presiding Evangelist. It was then returned to the safekeeping of President Edwards.

This document was considered by the Council of Twelve, and then by agreement between the Presidency and Twelve was submitted to the various quorums, orders, and councils of the church and, later, to the General Conference of 1958. In harmony with its provisions Elder William Wallace Smith was ordained as President of the High Priesthood and prophet, seer, and revelator to the church at the Auditorium, Independence, Missouri, October 6, 1958. The document itself is clear and forthright and is self-explanatory.

SECTION 145

While at his desk in the Auditorium on August 21, 1958, President W. W. Smith gave sustained consideration to many needs confronting the church. He continued this consideration at his home that evening and after sleeping for several hours he awoke and resumed his thinking and his prayer for guidance. After narrating the foregoing in a message to the elders and the General Conference, President Smith continued: "I bring this word to the Saints as being the mind and the will of God unto his people."

"I have taken unto myself my own" (1). In the revelations there are many references to the situation of those who die in the Lord.[1] Most of these are quite general. It is therefore of interest to note some of the more specific references to the faithful dead. In Appendix A[2] it is stated that David Patten and Edward Partridge are with the Lord and "my aged servant Joseph Smith, Sr.,... sitteth with Abraham, at the right hand, and blessed and holy is he, for he is mine."[3] W. W. Blair was referred to in 1897 as "my servant W. W. Blair, whom I have taken unto myself."[4] When Elbert A. Smith was called into the Presidency he was referred to as "the son of my servant David H. Smith, who was taken and who awaits his reward."[5] With reference to Apostle George G. Lewis the revelation of 1938 says that he "has been taken for mine own purposes."[6] Of John F. Garver the revelation of 1950 says his "sacrifices and labor were acceptable to me."[7] Of Israel A. Smith this revelation says, in the name of the Lord, "I have taken unto myself my own. It was wisdom that my servant Israel A. Smith be released from his onerous duties. He has found his reward with the faithful."[8]

While the existing situations made these comments timely, the absence of such comments after the death of Apostle Ellis in 1945 and President Frederick M. Smith in 1946 does not mean that their labors were any less acceptable than the labors of those who were named. Nor should the mention of general officials be thought to imply that they are especially cherished by the Lord. All the faithful in Christ share the reassuring affirmation that "blessed are the dead that die in the Lord from henceforth."[9]

"Sustained as a counselor" (2). There have been times when a counselor in the Presidency has not been continued in the quorum after the death of the president of the church. This adjustment does not carry with it any adverse

reflection on the one who relinquishes the place he has held in the Presidency. In 1946, for example, Elder L. F. P. Curry, who had served the church with ability and devotion, was not continued in the Presidency when President Israel A. Smith succeeded his brother, President Fred M. Smith. But President Israel gave early recognition to the service President Curry had given.[10]

There was one occasion when a counselor was continued in the Presidency although no specific revelation authorizing this had been approved by the quorums or by the World Conference. President Elbert A. Smith had served as a counselor to President Joseph Smith III and as a member of the First Presidency from 1909 until 1914. When President Fred M. Smith was notified of the conference action on his call to be president of the church he was ill at Worchester, Massachusetts. He wired the conference: "I greatly appreciate your expression of confidence and accept the responsibility with a full realization of its arduousness. I unhesitatingly nominate Elbert A. Smith as a counselor, but am not prepared at the present to nominate the other."[11] The only question raised was concerning the need for specific revelation. Approval of the selection of Brother Elbert was by vote of 254 to 43.

The advantage of continuity in administration is also important in relation to membership in the presiding councils. In this connection see Sections 126:6 and 150:5a.

"Should be ordained for the strength and support he can give" (2). Members of the general quorums serve as presidents, apostles, high priests, or seventies, and also as members of the quorums or orders to which they are set apart. This dual responsibility had been mentioned in earlier revelations but is now restated. This restatement has additional importance in that it calls attention to the principle involved. As early as 1865 when it was difficult to find financial support for the families of the Twelve, the members of that quorum were admonished:

Loosen ye one another's hands and uphold one another, that ye who are of the Quorum of Twelve may all labor in the vineyard, for upon you rests much responsibility; and if ye labor diligently the time is soon when others will be added to your number till the quorum be full, even twelve.[12]

"His apostleship is extended in presidency" (3). This phrase was first used in connection with the call of apostles J. F. Garver and F. Henry Edwards to be counselors in the First Presidency.[13] Later it was also used when Duane E. Couey[14] was called from the Twelve to become a member of the First Presidency. The phrase expresses an aspect of a call which was involved when others became members of the Presidency but it was not used in connection with their designation.[15] Other counselors were called who had not previously been members of the Twelve. These included William Marks, Elbert A. Smith, and Floyd M. McDowell who were called from among the high priests;[16] E. L. Kelley, L. F. P. Curry, and Israel A. Smith who were called from among the bishops;[17] and David H. Smith and Frederick M. Smith who were called from the eldership.[18] All members of the Presidency exercise apostolic ministry no matter what their prior responsibilities may have been.

The revelation of 1972 provides that the high priestly ministry of Elder John C. Stuart shall be "extended *into* apostleship.[19] Here the meaning seems clear enough: new responsibilities are being undertaken while existing responsibilities are also continued. In a later revelation, however, it is stated that the "apostolic witness [of Cecil R. Ettinger] is to be extended as a high priest."[20] This seems to indicate that the apostolic witness of Elder Ettinger is to continue but is to be exercised within the general ranks of the high priesthood rather than as a member of the Council of Twelve.

"This is in harmony with my instructions to the Saints at an early date" (4b). This instruction is clear in as far as it pertains to the call of Evangelist Roy A. Cheville to preside over the Order of Evangelists of which he was

already a member. But the phrase "at an early date" appears to direct attention to Appendix A which was listed as Section 107 prior to 1970. There is no other Doctrine and Covenants reference to the Presiding Patriarch prior to the call of Alexander H. Smith in 1897 and the expansion of the instruction concerning his functions which came four years later.[21]

BIOGRAPHICAL NOTES

F. Henry Edwards (see notes on Section 134).

Maurice L. Draper (see notes on Section 140).

Roy Arthur Cheville was born at Maxwell, Iowa, October 2, 1897, and became a member of the church on January 14, 1914. He was ordained a deacon in 1916, a priest in 1917, an elder in 1919, a high priest in 1925, and a patriarch-evangelist in 1950.

He served under appointment to the Des Moines, Iowa, District in 1918-19 after which he attended Graceland as a member of the first class in religious education. The University of Chicago awarded him four degrees (Ph.B., M.A., B.D., and Ph.D.). In 1968 Graceland College granted him an honorary D.D. He joined the faculty at Graceland College in 1923 and taught sociology, philosophy, and religion and was a leader among students until 1968 when he was designated as professor emeritus. During these years he was closely associated with leadership in various areas of stake endeavor and served for a time as a member of the Stake Presidency. His major concern was in the field of religious education and his influence in this field was church-wide through his association with the Department of Religious Education. He has been one of the most prolific writers the church has produced and has added to his other ministries through his hymns and his leadership in worship. He served as Presiding Patriarch of the church until April 1974 when he was designated "Presiding Patriarch Emeritus."

Elder Cheville was married to Nell Weldon in 1929 and is the father of Richard Cheville and Mrs. Charlotte Farrand. His wife died in December 1957.

Edmund J. Gleazer (see Section 124).

Daniel T. Williams (see Section 134).

Charles D. Neff was born at Hardin, Missouri, March 24, 1922. He holds a degree in economics from Central Missouri State University and has done considerable postgraduate work as opportunity has afforded. During World War II he spent two years in the Pacific area as a naval officer.

Charles Neff was baptized in 1946 in St. Louis and shortly thereafter was ordained a priest. He accepted General Church appointment in 1948 and was ordained to the eldership. His first assignment was to Omaha as pastor and while here he was called to the high priesthood in 1951. Thereafter he served as an assistant to the First Presidency and, briefly, as General Church secretary. He and his wife, the former Frances Dillon, have four children—Robert, Nancy, Susan, and John. Since being ordained to the apostleship he has specialized in evangelism in the Orient and recently completed the first million miles of travel undertaken in this connection. He was president of the Twelve from 1980 until his release in 1985.

Clifford Adair Cole was born in Lamoni, Iowa, November 16, 1915, and was baptized in Wyoming October 5, 1924. After graduating from Graceland College he secured an M.A. in Education at the University of Missouri in Kansas City and has done graduate work at the Universities of Iowa, Chicago, and Missouri. In 1936 he married Lucille Hartshorn. They have three children—Althea Rae, Beverly Sue, and Lawrence Dean.

Ordained a priest in 1935, an elder in 1939, and a high priest in 1950, Elder Cole became a General Church appointee in 1947. While serving as president of the Northwest Iowa District he was granted a leave of absence at the request of Graceland College and served as Dean of Students 1951-1954. Returning to appointment Brother Cole served in the Department of Religious Education as director of children's work, and later as director of the department. Apostle Cole became a member of the Basic Beliefs Committee of the church when the committee was organized in 1960 and served as chairman of the committee from 1966 to 1970. He had been closely associated with the educational work of the church as Commissioner of Education (1963-1966) and in General Church relations with Graceland and with the School of the Restoration. He has traveled widely, especially since becoming president of the Quorum of Twelve in 1964. As president of his quorum he is director of Field Ministries. Among his books have been *The Prophets Speak, Faith for New Frontiers, The Revelation in Christ, Modern Women in a Modern World,* and *The Mighty Act of God.* Elder Cole was president of the Twelve from 1964 till 1980. Since 1982 he has been an evangelist-patriarch.

---

[1]Sections 28:3c; 42:12b; 58:1b; 59:1; 63:13c; 85:35f; 95:3b, c; 98:5. [2]Appendix A 107:7. [3]Galatians 3:9. [4]Section 124:2b. [5]*Ibid.* 129:5. [6]*Ibid.* 141:1. [7]*Ibid.* 142:1a. [8]*Ibid.* 145:1. [9]*Ibid.* 63:13c. [10]*Saints' Herald* 93:479. [11]G.C.M. 1915:2070. [12]Section 116:3. [13]*Ibid.* 139:1b. [14]*Ibid.* 148:2. [15]W. W. Blair, 117:3a; A. H. Smith, 124:2a; R. C. Evans, 126:8; and W. Wallace Smith, 140:4a. [16]Sections 115:1b; 129:5; 134:1. [17]*Ibid.* 124:2b; 138:1e. [18]*Ibid.* 117:3a; 126:8. [19]*Ibid.* 150:2a. [20]*Ibid.* 151:3b. [21]*Ibid.* 124:2a, 125:5.

SECTION 146

The revelation which now constitutes Section 146 was presented to the councils, quorums, and orders of the church prior to the first business session of the General Conference of 1960. It was read to the conference immediately after the organization was completed together with the reports of the ministerial groups who had already considered it. Every group reported unanimous approval, as did the conference and the visitors.[1]

"Follow the leadership which I have provided" (2b). This was in harmony with instructions given from time to time but also envisions the necessary concentration of direction in general authorities as the church grew into constantly widening areas. While the instruction here given is directed toward the ministry of the general authorities, the administrative decentralization which has also become necessary for the growth of the church makes it important that the principles shall be applied in areas of local administration and spiritual guidance.

"Contention over minutiae" (3). The existence of contention in the church has been a matter of major concern for church leaders from the beginning. It was named as one of the reasons for the problems encountered in the early 1830s.[2] The admonition to "let contention cease" was renewed by President Joseph Smith III.[3] It was mentioned specifically in the revelations through Frederick M. Smith[4] and was described by him as "unseemly."[5] On the other hand the "unity and spirit of tolerance" is commended many times.[6]

BIOGRAPHICAL NOTES

Cecil Ray Ettinger was born in Taylorville, Illinois, July 26, 1922, and baptized there in 1930. He holds degrees from Graceland College, the State University of Iowa, and the American Divinity School. A pilot during World War II, he flew 72 combat missions in the European theater and received the Distinguished Flying Cross, ETO Ribbon with four stars, the Air Medal with nine clusters, and the Presidential Citation with one cluster. He returned to Graceland briefly after his war service and there met Betty Jean Russell whom he later married. They have three children—Cecil Ray III, Stephanie Lynn Kelley, and David Alexander. He was ordained a priest in 1945, an elder in 1947, a seventy in 1950, and a high priest in 1955. After his appointment in 1948 he was in charge of the church historical properties at Nauvoo, Illinois, was radio minister for two years, and pastor at Des Moines. As a member of the Twelve he was in charge of missionary and administrative work in eight states and eight regions. He was Commissioner of Congregational Life 1968-1970. He was the first minister of the church assigned to Africa. He was relieved of responsibility in the Twelve at the World Conference of 1974 and has since served as Executive Assistant to the First Presidency.

Duane E. Couey was born September 13, 1924, at Milwaukee, Wisconsin, and was baptized there in September 1932. He was active in church work as a young man and was ordained a priest in 1948 and an elder in 1952, serving pastorates in Wisconsin. In June 1954 he accepted World Church appointment and was assigned to the Kentucky-Tennessee District. In 1956 he was ordained a high priest and two years later briefly served as an assistant to the First Presidency prior to his assignment as president of Los Angeles Stake. As an apostle he was minister in charge in the Pacific Southwest, Hawaii, and California and was director of administrative and missionary work in eleven areas in 1964. He has traveled widely both as a member of the Twelve and after his appointment as counselor to President W. Wallace Smith in April 1966.

President Couey was married to the former Edith Griswold who died September 2, 1982. Their children are Patricia and Ralph.

---

¹*Conference Bulletin* 1960:84, 85. ²Section 98:3a. ³*Ibid.* 117:13; 119:5g, 6b. ⁴*Ibid.* 133:2b; 134:7; 135:2a. ⁵*Ibid.* 136:3b. ⁶*Ibid.* 141:7; 142:3; 142:2a.

SECTION 147

The instruction contained in the revelation of 1964 was received and confirmed to President Smith in a manner which later communications have shown to be characteristic: after thought, prayer, and rest and a specific experience of divine guidance. The document was committed to writing on March 11, 1964, and presented to the World Conference at the opening business session. It received unanimous approval.

"*Apostolic witness is to be extended*" (1). Members of the Twelve are high priests set apart for special ministries. There was a sense in which the field of Elder Hield's ministry was narrowed by his release from the Twelve, but it was also broadened in that he was now to have more time and opportunity to serve in high priestly areas for which he was especially qualified. It is in this sense that his witness has been "extended" and has become a valuable tool in carrying the gospel to Spanish speaking peoples.

"*Witnessing ministry in the Order of Evangelists*" (2, 3). One of the important duties of the evangelical minister is "to be a revivalist."[1] The members of the order have special responsibilities for reviving and maintaining the faith of the Saints. There is no better approach to this than through sharing the testimony of Jesus. For this work Elder Davey was especially qualified by virtue of his twenty-five years as a seventy and seventeen years as an apostle. This was also true of Elder Oakman, who had served for two years as a seventy and for twenty-six years as a member of the Twelve.

"*Stewardship is the response of my people to the ministry of my Son*" (5a). This basic principle has been recognized among the disciples down the generations,[2] but this clear and concise statement of the principle has made a deep impression on the church. It has been recognized, also, that such other aspects of sound discipleship as testimony and sacrifice and thanksgiving are also responses to the ministry of the Son of God, initiated and blessed by the Spirit of the Father and the Son.

"*Repression of unnecessary wants*" (5b). This reminder goes back to the revelation of 1913,[3] and should be studied in connection with the more extended instruction given at that time. When this is done it will be noted that "sacrifice and the repression of unnecessary wants is a principle." It was therefore fundamental in 1913. It is fundamental today. It will be fundamental on all the tomorrows. It applies to the body as well as to individuals, to the councils and conferences and local administrators and assemblies. Catering to unnecessary wants is both wasteful and destructive of character, individual and corporate.

The revelation of 1913 was pointed toward the elimination of the church debt. During the depression of the 1930s the wisdom of the repeated admonitions to stay out of debt was made clear and impressive.[4] But the principle of sacrifice and the repression of unnecessary wants goes much deeper than is generally recognized. Its obligations are the obligations of love. The Saints are called to sacrifice and to exercise self-discipline so as to free themselves and the church for the ministries of outgoing love to which all are called.

"*Nothing which has been given hitherto by way of instruction should be so interpreted as to restrict the right of the General Conference to determine its own membership or to exercise its best judgment on legislative matters*" (6b). The general officers are, first of all, servants of God.[5] This means, among many other things, that they are under obligation to seek divine guidance and to lead the Saints in harmony with that guidance and in love and the spirit of humility. They are also the servants of the body.[6] They are "overseers," not "overlords,"[7] and are required to recognize the inherent rights of the body. These rights are manifest in diverse ways, but are most evident in the conferences which are provided for in the law. Conferences meet, for example, as they may determine, and are authorized to do whatever church business is necessary to be done at the time.[8] Conferences operate on the principle of "common consent." This "consent" is more than "assent," and this fact places obligations on both leaders and the body. Leaders are called to guide the body to understanding, not merely to acquiescence, and they should await that understanding and not coerce it.[9] The members of the conferences have much to contribute out of their varied and diverse experiences as these are illumined by their prayers and their knowledge of the laws and the covenants of the gospel. At its best consent is informed, honest, and open. It is often very desirable that conference concerns be discussed by the Saints in their local gatherings, but local conferences should exercise great care in the matter of "instructing" their delegates to world conferences. Delegates should be free to seek enlightenment by giving attention to views expressed at the world gatherings even when these views are different from those prevalent in their home congregations.

"Principles shall be evaluated and subjected to further interpretation" (7). Principles abide but the circumstances in which they are applied may vary. Methods which were wisely conceived may be outmoded by these changing circumstances. In 1890, for example, the church was instructed that when the representative authorities of the church were present in a branch or district "their counsel and advice should be sought and respected when given."[10] At that time branches and districts were small and there were few high priests other than the members of the general councils. The seventies were included among the representative authorities[11] and were much more likely to have broad experience than the presidents of small groups. This situation has now changed. Many who are now high priests were once seventies and to require them to seek and respect the advice of ministers with much less experience than their own would hamper rather than expedite the work. In unorganized fields, where the seventies are especially called to serve, the instruction to seek their counsel and advice is still sound.

Keeping principles in mind while adjusting to new situations and opportunities is attended by many difficulties.

Nevertheless, it makes for stability of administration. Both the activist and the conservative play important parts. Neither is wise to say to the other, "I have no need of thee."

BIOGRAPHICAL NOTES

Charles R. Hield (see Section 137).
Roscoe E. Davey (see Section 140).
Arthur A. Oakman (see Section 137).
Russell F. Ralston was born May 20, 1913 in McClave, Colorado, and was baptized in 1921. After graduating from Graceland he taught music until his induction into the United States Army. He accepted World Church appointment in 1946. Brother Ralston was ordained a priest in 1933 and an elder in 1937. After accepting appointment he became one of the Seventy in 1948, a member of the Council of Presidents of Seventy in 1950, and Senior President in 1960. As a member of the Twelve he directed the work of the church in many of the domestic fields. He is the author of *Succession in Presidency, Fundamental Differences Between the Reorganized Church and the Church in Utah*, and coauthor (with Charles R. Hield) of *Baptism for the Dead*. Elder Ralston and Miss Florence Mae Gamet were married in 1936. They have three children—Allan, David, and Jon.

After serving in the Apostolic Quorum for twelve years Elder Ralston was relieved of further responsibility in that council and now serves under the direction of the president of the Council of Twelve.

William E. Timms was born in Stratford on Avon, England, September 23, 1912, and baptized in November 1923 at Clay Cross, England. He attended Chesterfield Technical College 1930-1933 and, later, the British College of Secretaries. Before coming to the United States in July 1951 he held important positions in the colliery industry and was a self-sustaining pastor of the Clay Cross Branch and a counselor in the presidency of the Midland and ·Southern

England District. He was ordained a priest in 1941, an elder in 1942, and a high priest in 1955. He was a member of the Order of Bishops from 1958 to 1964 and served as an assistant to the Presiding Bishopric for ten years. His apostolic service has been almost entirely in connection with the stakes. Between 1968 and 1970 he headed the Commission on Zionic Development. Elder Timms was released from the Quorum of Twelve in 1978 and called to serve as a member of the Evangelical Order.

Apostle Timms and Nancy Hicken were married in England in 1939. Their two grown children, Patricia Ethel and Lloyd William, came with them to the United States and have made their home in this country since that time.

---

[1]Section 125:3, 4. [2]I Corinthians 4:1, 2; Titus 1:7. [3]Section 130:7. [4]See Sections 87:6d, 101:17, 125:16, 127:4. [5]Section 117:3-5. [6]*Ibid.* 90:8b, 131:5. [7]Acts 20:28. [8]Section 117:13. [9]See comments on Section 27:4. Note Section 125. [10]Section 120:4b. [11]Appendix E, 123:13.

SECTION 148

This revelation, dated April 18, 1966, received the unanimous approval of the quorums, councils, and orders of the church and of the World Conference; and the ordinations provided for took place without delay.

"Relieved of presiding" (1). This is more inclusive than "released from further responsibility in the First Presidency." It is without qualification. While it is not often recognized, relief from presiding also occurs when those who have served in the presiding quorums are designated to serve as evangelical ministers.[1] General officers who are released generally serve thereafter as evangelists or high priests. At times, but not always, specific areas of service are indicated for them, as was the case with Elders Joseph Luff and Heman C. Smith who served as church physician and church historian respectively.[2]

526

"In the capacity of Presiding Bishop" (5). Elder DeLapp served as a counselor in the Presiding Bishopric for nine years before becoming Presiding Bishop in 1940. Like Bishop E. L. Kelley he became a traveling bishop on his release from presiding responsibility, but he was also called to serve "in other capacities."

"If willing" (6). Elder Livingston accepted this call to be an evangelist and was ordained during the conference, as were elders Jensen and Farrow.

"Others. . . are also to be enlisted" (9b). This principle had been established in earlier revelations.[3] Its reiteration at this time was of great importance because of the growth of the church in both numbers and resources, the increased number of business and professional men of experience, the academic preparation of many young people, the improved means of transportation, the emergence of the "one world" concept, and many other related factors.

"The second presidency" (10b). This is a term used in the revelation of 1894.[4] The pattern of instruction given there is akin to what is here stated somewhat more broadly. In earlier days the Twelve spent most of their time in their several fields, meeting at conference time and only occasionally between conferences. Today changed circumstances and the availability of more and better prepared field officers make it possible for them to meet frequently to confer concerning the needs of the new fields "widening before them."[5]

"The burden of the care of the church" (10b). This, too, is an extension of what had been stated in 1894.[6] In this connection see the notes on Section 104:11. With the continuing growth of the church the close association of the Presidency and Twelve is likely to become constantly more necessary, but the distinctive responsibilities of their callings must be maintained. The primacy of the First Presidency is "of necessity."[7]

"Withdraw from detailed administration in organized areas" (10c). For many years members of the Twelve were assigned to geographic areas and administered the work in

these fields according to their several skills. While this was the best that could be done at the time, the only way in which the diverse needs of the fields could be fully cared for was to move the Twelve around with some frequency. Even this was not entirely satisfactory. The revelation of 1894 pointed toward the remedy when the organization of Lamoni into a stake was forecast, and its administration was placed under the district officers and the First Presidency, no member of the Twelve being assigned to the area.[8] This arrangement was not acceptable to the Twelve and others and was allowed to lapse. Gradually, however, the necessity for such organizations as the stakes became apparent and the withdrawal of the Twelve from local to general responsibilities has gone forward at an increasing tempo.

"Principles and procedures in spiritual and temporal realms" (10e). While the temporal affairs of the church are the special concern of the Order of Bishops[9] it is inevitable that those responsible for opening new fields and administering them shall be concerned both with the financing of their expanding enterprises and the spiritual values involved in this financing (see notes on Section 122:5). Although further instruction received in the World Conference of 1968 may have been influenced by discussions in the Board of Appropriations meetings during the preceding week, this paragraph indicates that relations between the spiritual and temporal authorities of the church were in the heart and mind of President Smith at least two years prior to 1968.

BIOGRAPHICAL NOTES

F. Henry Edwards (see Section 134).

Duane E. Couey (see Section 146).

D. Blair Jensen (see Section 139).

Percy E. Farrow (see Section 141).

Earl T. Higdon was born at Ft. Scott, Kansas, July 9, 1907. After graduating from Graceland he went to Northwestern University and the State University of Iowa and has a master's degree in economics. In 1928 he married Faith L. McCall. Their children are William T., Winifred Piepergerdes, Betty Graeff, and Mary F. Seely. Mrs. Higdon died in February 1972. In 1973 he married Lucille M. Garrett who died March 7, 1982. Earl and his third wife, the former Cleda Garrett Grier, who were married May 15, 1983, were killed in an automobile accident on September 15, 1983.

Prior to entering full-time ministerial work Elder Higdon was an accountant for two oil companies, taught school for one year, and was an instructor in accounting and economics at Graceland College for five years. He has been a full-time appointee since 1940 serving as bishop of Far West Stake, bishop of Lamoni Stake, and assistant to the Presiding Bishopric. For twelve years he was a member of the Graceland College Board of Trustees, and from June 1964 until mid-1966 he was the acting president of Graceland College. Following his ordination to the apostleship he was for four years Commissioner of Education. Later he directed the work of the church in the Texas-Oklahoma Region, in the New Mexico Missionary District, in Unorganized Texas, and in the Latin American field. After leaving the apostolic council he served under the First Presidency until his superannuation in 1976.

Alan D. Tyree was born at Kansas City, Missouri, December 14, 1929. He holds a B.A. degree in Music and has taken postgraduate work at the University of Missouri and the University of Iowa. His wife was formerly Gladys Louise Omohundro. They have three children: Lawrence Wayne, Jonathan Tama, and Sharon Avis. Elder Tyree's great-grandfather, grandfather, and father all served in the Melchisedec priesthood. He was ordained a priest in 1947 and an elder in 1950. Shortly after his appointment in that year he was assigned to French Polynesia, where he remained for four years. After becoming a member of the Council of Twelve he served on the Commission on Field Organization. He also served briefly in the areas of Haiti and Michigan and more recently has been in charge of the Australia-New Zealand Region, the Caribbean Region, the French Polynesia Region, the Hawaii Region, and the South Pacific Region.

Aleah G. Koury was born in Toronto, Ontario, Canada, September 26, 1925. He was baptized in 1934 and ordained a priest in 1946, an elder in 1950, and has been under appointment since 1949. Elder Koury earned a B.A. degree from the University of Toronto. He received a master's in divinity from Midwestern Baptist Theological Seminary, Kansas City, Missouri, in 1982. He and his wife, the former Patricia Lee Reynolds, have five children—Patricia Lynn, Aleah G. W., Gregory Scott, Rebecca Jane, and Cynthia Ann.

Elder Koury gained prior to his appointment was of value to him in his editorial relationships to the *Restoration Witness*. He became an evangelist-patriarch in 1980, and served as secretary of that order until June 1985 when he became chaplain of the Independence Sanitarium and Hospital.

G. Leslie DeLapp (see notes on Section 136).

Henry L. Livingston was born at Condon, Oregon, April 30, 1902. He has been active in the work of the church throughout his life. He was ordained a priest in 1920, an elder in 1928, a high priest in 1932, and a bishop in 1934. He and Eunice O. Smith were married October 17, 1925. They have two grown sons, David and Richard.

Brother Livingston became a General Church appointee in 1928 and was pastor in Philadelphia from that time until his ordination to the Bishopric and his designation as bishop of Far West Stake in 1934. He was still serving in that capacity when chosen by Bishop DeLapp to be his counselor in the Presiding Bishopric. After he was released from this responsibility he fitted well into the work of the Patriarchal Order.

Walter N. Johnson was born in New South Wales, Australia, May 4, 1905, and became a member of the church in 1916. He received his early education in Australia and in 1930 enrolled at Graceland College. From here he went on to the University of Chicago School of Business where he received his bachelor's degree. In June 1940 he was married to Bertha Garver, a daughter of the late President John F. Garver. Their grown children are Lois Kay and Garver William.

Elder Johnson entered the full-time ministry in 1938 and for the next two years served as pastor in Boston, Massachusetts. Ordained to the Bishopric in 1940, he served as bishop of Kansas City Stake until 1944 and then became an assistant to the Presiding Bishopric. Two years later he was called to serve as a counselor to Bishop DeLapp. For twenty-four years he served as chairman of the church's Board of Publication. As a counselor in the Presiding Bishopric and, later, as Presiding Bishop, Elder Johnson has traveled throughout the church, making contact with every mission and all parts of the domestic field. He was released from further responsibility as the chief financial officer of the church in 1972 but continues to advise and minister as time and circumstances permit.

Francis E. Hansen was born at Underwood, Iowa, October 30, 1925. After his graduation from Graceland College he took a Bachelor's degree in Business Administration from the University of Kansas. He and his wife, the former Wanda Ann Hoss, have two children, Blair and Cheryl Fae. Active in the work of the church from boyhood he was ordained a deacon in 1943, a priest in 1948, an elder in 1951, a high priest in 1955, and a bishop in 1956. Prior to his appointment he was a counselor in the Southwestern Iowa District Presidency and district bishop's agent. His assignments include two years in the Office of the Presiding Bishopric as their assistant and as bishop of Los Angeles Stake from 1956 to 1966. As Presiding Bishop Elder Hansen has traveled throughout the church in addition to his responsibilities at headquarters. He is a member of the Independence Sanitarium and Hospital Board, the Board of Publication, the Central Development Association, and other important church organizations.

Harold W. Cackler was born September 30, 1912, in Lucas, Iowa. He was baptized in 1923 and was ordained a teacher in 1933, an elder in 1935, a high priest in 1942, and a bishop in 1947. It was that year that he accepted General Church appointment and was assigned as an assistant to the Presiding Bishopric. From 1949 until 1966 he was bishop of Center Stake. As a member of the Presiding Bishopric he has served as president of the Central Development Association Board, president of the Central Professional Building, Inc., and as a member of the Board of Trustees of the School of the Restoration and the Independence Sanitarium and Hospital, and has ministered in all the major centers of church activity.

Elder Cackler and Arline Fowler were married in 1941. They have made their home in Independence since 1947. Their only child, John, was killed in an accident in February 1982.

---

[1]Section 125:4. [2]*Ibid.* 129:2, 3. [3]*Ibid.* 119:8b; 122:16b. [4]*Ibid.* 122:9c. [5]*Ibid.* 122:7c. [6]*Ibid.* 122:2. [7]*Ibid.* 104:11. [8]*Ibid.* 122:12a. [9]*Ibid.* 129:8b.

SECTION 149

The revelation dated April 1, 1968, was presented to the priesthood quorums and councils and to the World Conference in the usual order. At first it was not accepted with the readiness experienced in many parallel situations. Some of the difficulties were adjusted when President Smith was available to talk to those who had been disturbed. More generally, a supplemental document, which later became 149A, did much to remove the uncertainty which had prevailed. When Section 149 was approved the associated statement (149A) had already been presented to the conference and made possible the almost unanimous approval of the document of April 1.

At the request of President Smith the close association of these two documents was indicated by numbering the explanatory statement as Section 149A.

"Prophetic utterance" (Introduction). In bringing this inspired word to the church the prophet does not function in a vacuum, but is "appointed by revelation, and acknowledged...by the voice of the church"[1] and, with his associates in the First Presidency, should be "upheld by the confidence, faith, and prayer of the church."[2] That such support is of great importance is clear from the introductions to many of the sections of the Doctrine and Covenants.[3] It should not be reserved for the approach of the World Conference, but should be maintained at all times.[4]

"The confirmation of the Spirit so necessary" (1). This phrasing has parallels in many of the introductions to the sections of the Doctrine and Covenants, but here the process of revelation is perhaps made clearer than it is elsewhere by the use of the word "confirmation."[5] It is in the nature of his calling that the president of the church shall give constantly renewed thought to the basic needs of the church. But in giving instruction which is to guide the trend of the faith and procedures of the body the prophet needs more than human judgment. The prophet and the church need "the confirmation of the Spirit of God."

"The office of bishop is a 'necessary appendage' to the high priesthood" (3). This is a restatement of the word of the Lord given in 1832. A further revelation given in March 1835 says that "as a high priest of the Melchisedec priesthood has authority to officiate in all the lesser offices, he may officiate in the office of bishop."[6] All the current members of the Order of Bishops are high priests who have been set apart to

have "charge and care... under a presiding head" of the temporal affairs of the church.[7] Their effectiveness in teaching the temporal law and in administering the temporal resources of the church is vital to the effectiveness of the spiritual authorities in other realms. But to achieve the maximum contribution in their special field high priests serving as bishops must direct their services away from other areas of high priestly ministry. In parallel fashion, high priests serving as evangelists avoid involvement in administrative affairs in order to concentrate on their specific patriarchal ministries.[8]

"Since... members of the Order of Bishops are charged with the ministry of temporalities, they will act in support of leadership given by the spiritual authorities for the achievement of the purposes of my church" (3). Many of the bishops and others found this instruction difficult to accept as it stood. To them it appeared to so emphasize the calling of bishops to be "appendages" that they might well be excluded from any significant place in policy-making. No one thought that they should have such authority in temporal matters as would enable them to defeat the policy of the spiritual officers, but many felt that both the law[9] and the history of the church[10] indicated the right of bishops to have a more significant voice in matters of policy than was here envisioned.

The disquiet expressed in the Order of Bishops and summarized in a conciliatory but deeply serious statement of the Presiding Bishop (Elder Walter N. Johnson) on the floor of the conference was evident from the reports of the Order of Evangelists, the First Quorum of Seventy, and elsewhere. The evangelists voted to accept the document presented by President Smith only after hearing an explanatory statement by him. The First Quorum of Seventy voted approval, but added "cognizant of the possible differences of interpretation which have arisen and may arise, we respectfully suggest that some clarifying statement be made to the Conference, that unity of fellowship might prevail."[11]

During the discussion of the revelatory document (149) President Couey read a statement prepared by President Smith which sought to answer some of the major concerns expressed on the conference floor. There were a number of attempts on the part of members of the conference to authorize inclusion of this statement by President Smith as a preface or attachment to the document under consideration. While it was evident that some action was desired so as to preserve the explanations now offered, the Chair ruled that this could not be done in the forms suggested. The conference thereupon ordered that the explanatory document be referred to President W. W. Smith and that the conference await his further instructions. This led to the presentation of Section 149A in revelatory form and its submission to the quorums, orders, and councils of the church and to the conference body.

"By study and by faith" (5). This phrase occurs in one of the most important revelations given through Joseph Smith, Jr.[12] The promise that those who follow this counsel shall be rewarded in the life to come is an addition to the earlier counsel, and probably applies to the Christlike character which is to be sought through faith and study and obedience.

"The time has come for a start to be made toward building my temple in the Center Place" (6a). This is not a command to build a temple without delay but, rather, to prepare for the building. Four fundamental areas of concern to temple builders are set forth.

The location of the temple is made known: "it shall stand on a portion of the plot of ground set apart for this purpose many years ago by my servant Joseph Smith, Jr."

The shape and character of the temple will be determined by the ministries to be carried out within its walls.

The nature of these ministries will be made known to the Presidency.

The temple is to be financed from the consecration of surplus.

Blessings are promised those "who are diligent in moving to effect this project."

Members of the Reorganization have taken great satisfaction in the ownership of the Kirtland Temple but for various reasons its use has been greatly limited. The building of a temple at the Center Place has been anticipated throughout the history of the Reorganization. Part of the preparation for the building which is now brought into focus will center in the study of such instructions in the Doctrine and Covenants as can be found in the various revelations.[13]

BIOGRAPHICAL NOTES

Howard Sherman Sheehy, Jr., was born at Denver, Colorado, March 19, 1934, and baptized in June of 1942. He and his wife, the former Florine Cline, have three children: John Robert, Lisa Florine, and Michael Howard.

Elder Sheehy attended Graceland College and Central Missouri State College, where he received his Bachelor's degree in Education. The next 3½ years were spent as an officer of the United States Navy, his service taking him to the Southeast with the Seventh Fleet. After leaving the Navy he continued his college work at the University of Kansas and has a Master's degree in Education followed by additional work toward his doctorate.

Elder Sheehy was ordained a priest in 1950 and an elder in 1954. After his appointment in 1960 he served as Center Stake youth director and as a member of the stake presidency until his assignment to Des Moines Stake in 1964. He was ordained a high priest in 1962.

Since his ordination to the Twelve Apostle Sheehy has served in Canada, India, New Zealand, and in the North Atlantic States. In June 1975 he was appointed to represent the interests of the church in the World Scouting movement, with which he has been associated since his boyhood.

[1]Section 99:6a. [2]*Ibid.* 104:11b. [3]*Ibid.* 117:1, 121:6b, 130:1. [4]*Ibid.* 59:2g. [5]See also the introductions to Sections 134 and 145. [6]Sections 83:5a, 104:8d; see also 104:32. [7]Section 129:8b, f, g. [8]Section 125:4. [9]*Ibid.* 126:10, 128:1, 2, 3; 129:8. [10]For example, the depression of the 1930s. [11]*World Conference Bulletin,* 1968:265. [12]Section 85:36. [13]*Ibid.* 59:1; 58:3; 83:1; 91; 92:2-3; 94:3-4. See also *Journal of History* 11:149 and Church History 1:265, 294.

SECTION 149A

"A 'necessary appendage'" (1-3). This explanatory statement emphasizes the necessity of the contribution of the bishops to the effective functioning of the church. It provides for consultation and, where necessary, for initiation. It was directed to the local members of the Order of Bishops as well as to the Presiding Bishopric. It was, in effect, a reaffirmation of the instruction given in 1909 with regard to consultation between the Presiding Bishop and "the general authorities of the church who are made the proper counselors in spiritual and temporal things to carry out the provisions of the law of organization which are by the law made the duty of the Bishop."[1]

"The rightful line of appeal" (4). Where general church finances are involved local members of the Order of Bishops serve as agents of the Presiding Bishopric and are responsible to them. In the past there has been some tendency to include in this responsibility matters of local church concern. This important statement of the supplementary document makes the line of appeal clear. It says, in effect, that local affairs are under the direction of the local officers with appeals to the First Presidency as the chief administrative quorum of the church. There is, of course, no reason why the First Presidency cannot consult with members of the Presiding Bishopric or other general officers concerning matters appealed to them.

"Surplus shall be construed in its wider meaning" (5). This instruction was given in response to questions which had been raised on the conference floor.

"There is no provision for secret ordinances" (6). Although the importance of the temple in the education of the priesthood has been emphasized from time to time in the revelations given to the church, it should be remembered that the setting in which this training is to be carried forth must be one of faith and worship.

From the earliest days of the Restoration the elders have been told of their need for "a great endowment and blessing" to equip them to fulfill their several ministries.[2] In the "Fishing River" revelation they were told specifically:

It is expedient in me that the first elders of my church should receive their endowment from on high, in my house, which I have commanded to be built unto my name in the land of Kirtland.[3]

After this, the special endowments of the Spirit of God were widely anticipated in connection with temple exercises, although it is obvious that there are also other times and places of great endowment. Nevertheless, no celebrations in the temple, or elsewhere, will guarantee a great endowment of spiritual power to faithless or disobedient persons. As important as these functions are, no temple and no special rites can serve as substitutes for the faith, repentance, and dedication of the priesthood or of the Saints in general.

[1]Section 128:9. [2]*Ibid.* 38:7, 8; 43:4d; 102:3d, e. [3]*Ibid* 102:10a.

SECTION 150

The section dated April 11, 1972, was not presented to the World Conference until two days later. It was delayed while quorum reports were awaited. These reports, when received, indicated ready approval of the paragraphs having to do with changes in official personnel but also the desire of the Quorum of Seventy and the Order of Patriarchs for deferment of action on the later paragraphs in order to permit further consideration. During the presentation of the reports, the Chair stated that President Smith objected to the document being divided for deferral or referral, but that the conference might take such action if it desired.[1]

After the reading of the report of the First Quorum of Seventy the following statement from President Smith was read relative to the contents of the document:

This in no way invades the rights of the Presidency as the chief administrative officers of the church and interpreters of the doctrines and ordinances of the gospel as already provided for in the law of the church.[2]

Consideration was given to the document paragraph by paragraph. On the suggestion of the Chair it was understood that the first two paragraphs, which are the preamble, were subject to such editorial treatment as President Smith desired.

The remaining paragraphs of the document were numbered and paragraphs 1 through 9 were approved. During consideration of paragraph 10 it was moved that this paragraph "be left without approval or disapproval by the conference until further experience shall have tested the matters therein stated." The motion to defer lost and the paragraph was approved by a substantial majority.

During the consideration of paragraph 11 it was moved that this be referred to "a general assembly of the high priesthood and its orders and the Quorums of Seventy to report back to the 1974 World Conference." During the debate President Couey read the following statement by President Smith:

I offer the following sentence, not to be included in the document but by way of clarification: They will do that within the framework of the existing church law as then constituted.[3]

There was extended discussion on paragraph 12 but it was thereafter approved.

When the Chair called for the vote on the document as a whole this carried, but President Draper indicated for the record that there was a substantial negative vote.

"To my servant, Donald O. Chesworth" (1a). This direct personal approach, unusual in recent revelations, is reminiscent of some of the revelations given to leaders of the church in an earlier time.[4]

"Into apostleship" (2a). Comparison between the statements that apostleship may be "extended in Presidency"[5] comes to mind when consideration is given to

the instruction that the ministry of Elder John C. Stuart "as a high priest can be extended *into* apostleship." The apostleship exercised by the First Presidency and shared by the second presidency is something other than the apostleship which an earlier revelation said is shared by high priests.[6]

"*President of the Aaronic priesthood in matters of teaching and training*" (4b). This is a reiteration of the law concerning the Bishopric and the Aaronic priesthood.[7] Reference to the comments on these sections may be helpful.

"*Continue your study toward defining the purpose and selecting a place for erecting a temple*" (8). In an earlier revelation determination of the character and function of the temple was made the special responsibility of the First Presidency.[8] Here, apparently, the instruction to study the purpose of the temple is somewhat broadened, although it is to be conditioned by the responsibility already given to the Presidency. The selection of the site of the temple had also been indicated.[9] Further studies, and possibly some acquisition of land within the original temple area, is to be pursued.

"*Support your officers. . . that I may honor them*" (9). This principle had been set forth in the revelation of 1901:

> If my people will respect the officers whom I have called and set in the church, I will respect these officers; and if they do not, they can not expect the riches of gifts and the blessings of direction.[10]

"*Monogamy is the basic principle on which Christian married life is built*" (10a). This statement is directed toward the problems confronted by the Twelve and their associate missionary officers in seeking to establish the work of the church in areas where polygamy is permitted and where it often has important economic significance. Approached from a different angle, it could be said in light of the Scriptures that mutual love under God is the basic principle on which Christian married life is built.

"*The church must be willing to bear the burden of their sins*" (10b). Hitherto the church had regarded the abandonment of plural wives as a necessary precondition of baptism, no matter what the attendant circumstances might be. In the instruction now received the Twelve are reminded that the basic principle on which Christian married life can be built is that of monogamy, but the Twelve are also admonished to administer the law with proper regard to the circumstances of those involved.

"Put aside petty differences" (12b). We tend to be concerned about what others may regard as petty because we think that they are of great importance. What is needed is not a momentary resolve that we will not entertain petty differences but an enlargement of understanding, a maturing of self-discipline, and—above all—a continuing and shared endeavor to learn the will of God that we may do his will rather than our own. A key guide in this connection is contained in Section 129:9b:

> Though there may have been differences of opinion, these differences have been held in unity of purpose and desire for the good of my people, and will result in helping to bring to pass a unity of understanding.

Of great importance also is the admonition through President Joseph Smith III:

> Let nothing separate you from each other and the work whereunto you have been called; and I will be with you by my Spirit and presence of power unto the end.[11]

BIOGRAPHICAL NOTES

Donald O. Chesworth, see Section 142:2.

John Cameron Stuart was born in Cashion, Oklahoma, August 6, 1915, and has been a member of the church since 1924. After leaving Graceland he earned his B.A. at the University of California and has done considerable postgraduate work, when possible, in connection with his various assignments. He was ordained a priest in 1933 and an elder in 1937, at which time he accepted appointment. He has been a high priest since 1945. His assignments have taken him to Cameron, Missouri; St. Louis; Central Kansas City;

the Chicago District; and London, Ontario, in all of which places he served as pastor. For six years he was Campus Minister at Graceland College and thereafter was Director of Administrative Services and Commissioner of Ministerial Personnel. Since his ordination as an apostle he has been minister in charge in Canada, the British Isles, Europe, and the Israel Region.

Elder Stuart was married in 1941 to Eleanor Ruth Fairbanks. Their children, now grown, are Linda Jane and John Cameron, Jr. Elder Stuart was released from the Quorum of Twelve in 1982. Since that time he has served widely as an evangelical minister.

Walter N. Johnson, see Section 148:7.

Francis E. Hansen, see Section 148:7.

Harold W. Cackler, see Section 148:7.

Gene M. Hummel was born at Lancaster, Ohio, November 12, 1926. He became a member of the church May 11, 1958. He has degrees in Agriculture and Agricultural Engineering from Ohio State University. He served in the United States Naval Aviation program during World War II. Before taking up full-time ministry Brother Hummel was, for eleven years, in various managerial positions while serving locally in his home branch and as a member of the Central Florida District Presidency. He went under appointment in December 1961. He was ordained an elder in 1958, a high priest in 1962, and a bishop in 1964. He travels extensively representing the Presiding Bishopric, in addition to his work at headquarters. His responsibilities have taken him throughout the domestic field and to Mexico, Europe, and the Far East.

Sister Hummel is the former Jeannine Lane. The Hummels have two grown sons, Gregory L. and G. Michael.

[1]*Conference Bulletin* 1972:267. [2]*Ibid.* 266. [3]*Ibid.* 268. [4]See Section 8:1. [5]*Ibid.* 139:1b. [6]*Ibid.* 83:10. [7]*Ibid.* 104:8; 68:2. [8]*Ibid.* 149:6a. [9]*Ibid.* 149:6a. [10]*Ibid.* 125:14c. [11]*Ibid.* 122:17b.

SECTION 151

The revelation dated April 1, 1974, was considered by the various groups of the priesthood in the usual manner and was brought before the World Conference at the session of Thursday, April 4, 1974. Elders Draper and Couey of the First Presidency reported their approval in considerable detail, as did the Order of Bishops. The approval of the Twelve and Seventy, high priests and evangelists, was apparently unanimous. The approval of the elders was by a "sizable majority" and that of the Aaronic priesthood was by an "overwhelming affirmative vote."[1] Abstentions and negative votes among the elders and Aaronic priesthood were not numerous but reflected uncertainty concerning the application of the principle of lineage to the Presiding Patriarchate. No objections were voiced concerning the elders involved.

"The title of Presiding Patriarch Emeritus to the church" (1a). The phrasing here is slightly different from that used in reference to Elder Frederick A. Smith. Elder Smith was given the honor of being President Emeritus of the Order of Evangelists.[2] Elder Cheville was given the title of "Presiding Patriarch Emeritus to the church." The only other occasion for the term "emeritus" is mentioned in the revelation of 1976 where it is stated that after his retirement President W. Wallace Smith shall "be given the title president emeritus."[3]

"Under what I interpret as the direction of the Holy Spirit." The prophet does not lose his agency when he functions under the direction of the Holy Spirit. Indeed, it is impossible for him to avoid the responsibility of determining whether that which he experiences is truly of God. This applies to everyone who so functions, not only in the specific office but in the evaluation of and response to any spiritual experiences. Apparently the terms "especial" and "special" are used interchangeably in the revelation. When Joseph Smith and Oliver Cowdery were the first and second elders of the church[4] they were also designated as "special

543

witnesses."[5] Joseph, of course, became president of the church, but Oliver was never a member of the First Presidency or Twelve or Seventy. For a brief time he served as "assistant president."[6] All other references to special or especial witnesses referred to the Twelve or Seventy.

"The call was made known at a previous time" (5b). There are other examples of a call being made known before it was expedient that it be announced. In this connection note Sections 130:9c, 140:12b, 143:1a.

"Seek to be reconciled one with another" (8b). A major emphasis is on the word "seek." This part of the revelation is addressed to the Saints everywhere, but particularly to those whose concern over changing procedures had tended to breed division. All who have felt alienated are here admonished to take the initiative toward reconciliation and the mutual respect and understanding which make reconciliation possible. This is an application of the principle set forth by the Master in the Sermon on the Mount.[7]

BIOGRAPHICAL NOTES

Roy A. Cheville (see notes on Section 145).

Reed M. Holmes (see notes on Section 141).

Cecil R. Ettinger (see notes on Section 146).

Earl T. Higdon (see notes on Section 148).

William T. Higdon was born January 4, 1930, and baptized June 12, 1938. He was ordained a priest in 1946, an elder in 1952, and a high priest in 1960. He became a full-time minister in 1974. A Graceland graduate (1949), he received his baccalaureate degree from the University of Missouri and this was followed by an M.A. and a Ph.D. After his selection as president of Graceland in 1966, but before he entered into his duties, he spent a year of further preparation at the University of Michigan.

Sister Higdon is the former Barbara McFarlane of Independence, Missouri. She too holds a doctorate from the University of Missouri. They have three children—Beth, Ruth, and Dick.

Since his ordination to the Council of Twelve Elder Higdon has been president of the Temple School of Zion. He has also had charge of missionary and administrative work in the Alaska, North Atlantic States, Upper Ohio Valley, and East Central States regions and has given special attention to ministry among the American Indians.

Lloyd Bernard Hurshman, born in Independence, Missouri, May 20, 1930, was baptized in June 1938. He holds a B.A. degree from Graceland College and has done postgraduate work where his assignments have permitted. Prior to entering full-time church appointment in 1961 he was physical education instructor and director of activities at Colegia Americano, Guatemala. He was ordained a priest in 1951 and an elder in 1957. After his appointment he was assigned to the Pacific Northwest and, in 1964, was ordained a seventy. He became a high priest while serving in Alaska in 1967. He was regional administrator of the Upper Ohio Valley Region between 1967 and 1972. Thereafter, until called to the Twelve, he was director of the Division of Administrative Services.

Brother Hurshman married Jean Amsberry the day they were graduated from Graceland—June 1, 1951. They have three daughters—Becky (Mrs. Gregory Savage), Linda (Mrs. John Thatcher), and René (Mrs. Lawrence Tyree)—and one son, Alma.

Paul W. Booth was born at Caraway, Arkansas, July 30, 1929. He was ordained a priest in 1952, an elder in 1953, and a high priest in 1966. He has been an appointee minister since 1967. He has an M.A. in Sociology from the University of Louisville and has done postgraduate work at St. Paul School of Theology and the University of Missouri at Kansas City.

The assignments of Elder Booth prior to his ordination as an apostle have been to the Southern Indiana District and the East Central States and West Central States regions. As an apostle he has continued his work as director of the Division

545

of Program Planning and has also been in charge of missionary and administrative work in the Michigan and North Central regions. Elder Booth is married to the former Lavanda Joan Colbert. Their children are Dennis Paul, Donald Wayne, and Karen Sue.

---

[1]*World Conference Bulletin* 1974:247-249. [2]Section 137:3. [3]*Ibid.* 152:1c. [4]*Ibid.* 17:1b. [5]*Ibid.* 26:3a. [6]Church History 2:101. [7]Matthew 5:23-24, Section 42:23.

SECTION 152

The revelation dated March 29, 1976, is of great importance in relation to the presidency of the high priesthood and of the church. The principle of lineal succession had been recognized in the days of Joseph Smith, Jr., and throughout the history of the Reorganization.[1] The statement in this revelation, however, is the most specific in this connection in the Doctrine and Covenants.

The councils, quorums, and orders of the church reported approval of the document and after consideration, the World Conference also voiced approval and authorized its inclusion in future editions of the Doctrine and Covenants.

Approval of this document and its implementation created an entirely unprecedented situation within the First Presidency. Anticipating this, Elders Draper and Couey, counselors to the First Presidency, introduced their report to the General Conference as follows:

By its nature the matter of succession in the prophetic office identifies the counselors to the President of the Church as parties in interest due to the fact that the Reorganization of the Quorum is involved. For this reason our comments in regard to paragraphs one and two are limited to the following statement of principle:

1. The provision of a period of preparation and experience seems to be appropriate and desirable.
2. The church is thereby given an opportunity to observe and evaluate the provisions for succession under the guidance of the Holy Spirit prior to

the time of final decision "through the process of common consent of the body" as provided for in the document.

3. We shall be as helpful as we know how to be in making this period fruitful for all concerned.

"Elder Wallace Bunnell Smith is called" (1a). In view of the history already mentioned the selection of Elder Wallace Bunnell Smith was anticipated in many quarters, but his specific designation was accepted throughout the church with marked satisfaction. It should be noted that the prophet and president designate was to serve as assistant both to his father and to the Quorum of the Presidency as a whole.

"A period of spiritual preparation and study" (1b). The younger Elder Smith had gained considerable experience in positions of leadership in the Center Stake and during his eight years of service on the Standing High Council of the church.

Paragraphs 4a-c are an almost verbatim reiteration of part of the statement made by Presiding Evangelist Elbert A. Smith in validation of the call of President Israel A. Smith to be the prophet and president of the church.[2]

BIOGRAPHICAL NOTES

President Wallace Bunnell Smith, was in practice as an ophthalmologist in Independence, Missouri, when he was called to make special preparation to succeed his father after approximately two years for study and travel. He would be an assistant to his father, President W. Wallace Smith, and to the First Presidency, and would be known as the president-designate of the church. He had already had considerable experience as a member of the priesthood, having been ordained a priest in 1945, an elder in 1964, and a high priest in 1965. He had also served as a member of the Center Stake bishopric and of the Center Stake presidency before becoming a member of the Standing High Council of the church in 1968.

President Smith's wife, Ann McCullough Smith, is a registered nurse. They have three daughters: Carolyn, Julia, and Laura.

Clair Eugene Austin was born in Wagner, South Dakota, March 15, 1929, and was baptized June 13, 1937. His college major was in music. He served in the United States Army from 1951 to 1954 and was decorated for meritorious service. Prior to accepting appointment in 1969 he had been engaged over a fifteen-year period in fund raising, public relations, and professional counseling. His only assignment between his appointment and his call to the apostleship was as president of Detroit International Stake. Since his ordination to the Twelve he has been in charge of the work of the church in the stakes.

Sister Austin is the former Madge Gravenmier. They have two children: Clair Eugene, Jr., and Nina Renee.

[1]Sections 127:8, 144; *Saints' Herald* March 12, 1912; Church History 6:560-578 (567-575); 8:226, 354. [2]Church History 8:358.

Statements of Resignation and Acceptance are found in Appendix F

SECTION 153

The new president of the church had a period of two years for preparation for the position he was called to assume,[1] and when the time came for him to serve he accepted humbly, but without hesitation. The first revelation presented by him was available the day after his ordination. It was received and approved in good spirit.

President W. Wallace Smith[2] was the first president of the church to retire from office and to name his successor. This revelation was therefore the first occasion for the use of the term "president emeritus." However, when Presiding Patriarch Frederick A. Smith was released in 1938 the revelation of that year provided that "he be given the honor of being president emeritus of that order."[3] In 1974 Presiding Evangelist Roy A. Cheville was similarly honored by the adoption of the revelation of that year.[4]

Elder Duane E. Couey had served as a member of the Council of Twelve since 1960 and of the First Presidency since 1966. His continuance in the presidency was not automatic but was stated to be because of his loyalty, his experience in the Presidency, and his "deep devotion to the cause of the kingdom."[5]

Maurice L. Draper has been a high priest since his ordination to the Twelve in 1947. On his release from the Presidency he reverted to this basic calling, as have others in like situations (for example, L. F. P. Curry, F. Henry Edwards, Charles R. Hield, Russell F. Ralston). After his release from the Presidency he completed work on a doctorate in sociology while continuing to serve at Graceland and in the domestic and European fields.

Since becoming a member of the Presidency, Elder Sheehy has traveled widely throughout the church. He is an able speaker and presiding officer.

The passage of time requires that there shall be changes in the personnel of the presiding quorums, and the changes initiated in this revelatory document were of great importance. But the reaffirmation of fundamental needs and the duties arising out of them is also deeply important. I found myself remembering past inspired instruction when I read, "Let my word be preached to the bruised and the brokenhearted" (9a). And I thought of the patriarchs called from the Twelve. They would have no further administrative responsibilities in order that they might give needed evangelical service. They were to become fathers to the church, comforting the distressed and, undoubtedly, the bruised and brokenhearted. Alexander H. Smith had been called from the presidency of the Twelve to be a counselor to his brother in the Presidency and Presiding Patriarch, but very few others had been called to evangelical ministries. It did not appear to be a very important development, but down the years patriarchal ministry has become a major source of spiritual power in the church.

BIOGRAPHICAL NOTES

Duane E. Couey (See notes on Section 146).
Maurice L. Draper (See notes on Section 140).
Howard S. Sheehy, Jr. (See notes on Section 149).
Harold W. Cackler (See notes on Section 148).

William E. Timms, served in the Twelve for fourteen years, and was released for service as an evangelist. He had worked in the office of the Presiding Bishopric and was well known among the appointees. In the Twelve his practical kingdom concerns were evident in his administration. His first assignment as an evangelist was to the British Isles Mission. (See notes on Section 147).

Roy H. Schaefer, one of the two new members of the twelve, was in practice as a dentist in Independence, Missouri, prior to his acceptance of World Church appointment in September 1968. He has B.A. and D.D.S. degrees from the University of Missouri, Kansas City, and a M.P.H. from John Hopkins University School of Hygiene where he specialized in international health. He served for two years as captain in the U.S. Air Force Dental Corps.

For four years Elder Schaefer was an assistant to the Council of Twelve, with primary emphasis on health outreach, and was commissioner of Health Ministries from January 1974 to April 1978. He has traveled widely on health missions.

Mrs. Schaefer, the former Marilyn Keiper, is a registered nurse. She and Roy are the parents of two children, David Alan and Nan Leslie.

Phillip M. Caswell was born in Knoxville, Iowa. He holds an M.S. degree in sociology from the University of Missouri in Kansas City, and a B.S. from Drake University in Des

550

Moines. He has also studied at Graceland College, Lamoni, Iowa, the University of Iowa, Iowa City, Iowa, and the University of Hawaii in Honolulu.

He was ordained an elder in 1962, high priest in 1967, and apostle in 1978. A full-time appointee since April 1966, he has served in Australia, New Zealand, Bangladesh, French Polynesia, Indonesia, Sri Lanka, and the South Pacific region. He was president of the Korean Mission from 1967 to 1978. He was ordained an apostle in 1978. Prior to accepting full-time church appointment he was assistant executive secretary to the First Presidency for four years.

Mrs. Caswell (Darlene Oetting) of Mansfield, Missouri, was World Church director of Girls' Work from June 1960 till September 1964. She and Phillip have two sons: Brent Alan and Gregory Mark.

Ray E. McClaran, a native of Independence, Missouri, was graduated from William Chrisman High School and received his B.S. degree from Northwest Missouri State University. He is a certified public accountant. For the four years immediately preceding his appointment in 1975 he was financial vice president and comptroller of a Kansas City-based oil company. He is a retired captain in the Missouri National Guard.

He was ordained a priest in 1964, elder in 1968, high priest in 1972, and bishop in 1976. Previous assignments have included counselor to the Center Stake bishop 1975–1976, bishop of the St. Louis pre-stake district, and later of the St. Louis Stake, 1976–1978. He became counselor to Presiding Bishop F. E. Hansen in 1978.

Mrs. McClaran is the former Katie Lou Cooper. They are the parents of three children: Brenda, Sheryl, and Dale.

---

[1]Introduction to Section 152:1. [2]Section 506. [3]Section 137:3. [4]Section 151:1a. [5]Section 153:2.

SECTION 154

The important revelation of 1980, calling to the Twelve three elders having experience in distant missions was akin in this respect to the revelation of 1902, when Elders C. A. Butterworth of Australia and John W. Rushton of England were called.[1] Elder Peter Andersen, who had been born in Norway, had been called a year before.[2]

The revelation renews the emphasis on the world mission of the church. This outreach was now more fully possible than before because of changing political, economic, and social aspects of the dawning "One World," the growth in church membership in the domestic fields and available leadership in these fields, and the emergence of capable leadership in the newer fields. One of the rarely noticed additional gains comes from the participation within the leading councils of persons of world vision. Apostles Tyree and Graffeo, both accomplished linguists, have had extended experience in French Polynesia. Facility with languages other than English was increasingly important.

The counsel given the Bishopric reflects parallel needs in the realm of finances. We tend to think of the law of tithing as "the financial law." But this is only partially true. The law of stewardship goes much deeper.[3] And the world expansion of the church calls for clearer interpretation of Doctrine and Covenants 119:8b:

All are called according to the gifts of God unto them; and to the intent that all may labor together, let him that laboreth in the ministry and him that toileth in the affairs of the men of business and of work labor together with God for the accomplishment of the work intrusted to all.

When we have been a world church in name rather than in outreach the call to pursue our world mission more fully calls for adjustments in our point of view which can be difficult and, sometimes, painful. Down the years the church has struggled with such adjustments. The revelation of 1882, for example, was crucial in this connection[4] and may well be studied in connection with the revelations of the remainder of the century.[5]

The problem was how to relieve the Twelve of detailed concern for branches and districts so that they could push the work "into . . . new fields."[6] This is our problem now, but the scale of our operations becomes steadily more far-reaching and more demanding.

The gospel is intended for all people everywhere, and the basic principle of expansion has been the testimony of the truly converted. But in the great ages of expansion this outreach has rarely been haphazard. Paul, for example, did much to plant the work in the major centers of the Roman Empire: Ephesus, Thessalonica, Corinth, Antioch, Philippi. Then, after he had pushed on into new regions awaiting the Good News his converts spread the word into the regions round about (Acts 19:10).

Early in the Restoration the Saints were instructed, "I sent you out to testify and warn the people, and it becometh every man who hath been warned, to warn his neighbor" (Doctrine and Covenants 85:22a). But before this, even before the church was organized, and before many of those who were to become the first apostles of the Restoration had joined, the church was told that "the twelve . . . are called to go into all the world to preach my gospel to every creature" (Doctrine and Covenants 16:5b). The first apostles and seventies were ordained in February 1835, and the first mission abroad (to the British Isles) left in July of the same year. Its success was phenomenal.

Although the early Reorganization was hampered by lack of money and personnel, the sense of world mission continued. Indeed the church was promised that if local affairs were left to the standing ministry, while the Twelve and Seventy gave themselves to the work of preaching with the warning voice, "good will and peace [will] come to the people as a cherishing fountain" (Doctrine and Covenants 122:8f).

While the personal outreach of faithful members of the

church will always be important in the spread of the gospel, the planned strategy of evangelism is becoming more and more important as we merge into the "one world" of the future. It must be concerned with available and prospective leadership, language and literature, educational needs and opportunities, health ministries, etc. A world church must be in time, a church which derives strength from all its parts. While this is the primary concern of the Presidency, Twelve, and Seventy, it opens doors of opportunity for all who love the kingdom.

The light of the Spirit comes as a gift of God to those whom God chooses to enlighten and empower. The Lord Jesus affirmed this when acknowledging the confession of his messiahship by Peter. Peter had said, "Thou art the Christ, the Son of the living God. And Jesus answered. . . Blessed art thou, Simon Bar-Jona; for flesh and blood hath not revealed this unto thee, but my Father who is in heaven" (Matthew 16:17–18). This is true in the all-inclusive sense which distinguishes the people of God. It is also uniquely true of those called to special ministries, as are the prophets.

The prophets serve as they are called and sent to serve. But within the church as an institution the prophetic ministry tends to be expressed in two major areas of need: in the designation of those called to be leaders in extending the gospel, and in bringing specially pertinent counsel in things spiritual. Of these the former tends to attract more attention, but is of secondary importance. Leaders pass with the passage of time, but the faith of the Saints calls for unceasing exploration in time and in eternity. Where the pursuit of righteousness is concerned, as in the old hymn, "There shall be no furloughs granted in the army of the Lord."

Considerations such as these call for careful and devout study of such admonitions as the following:

Continue always to be aware of the need to render unreserved and fully accountable service (6).

If you will move out in faith and confidence to proclaim my gospel my Spirit will empower you and there will be many who respond (7a).

BIOGRAPHICAL NOTES

Clifford A. Cole (See notes on Section 145).
Donald V. Lents (See notes on Section 143).
Aleah G. Koury (See notes on Section 148).

Kisuki Sekine was born in Saitama-ken, Japan, and attended Graceland College, Lamoni, Iowa, from 1951 to 1953 and 1955 to 1957, and the University of Ryukyus, Naha, Okinawa, Japan, from 1965 to 1967. He was self-employed in the export and import business and was a language teacher for two years in Tokyo.

Brother Sekine was ordained an elder in 1957 and became a World Church appointee minister in April 1963, serving in the Ryukyu Islands until 1970 when he became a national minister and president of the Japan Mission. He was ordained a member of the Quorums of Seventy (1964) a high priest (1977) and a bishop (1978). He was regional bishop of the Orient and the Southeast Asia Region (1978–1980).

Elder Sekine is a member of the Okinawa Prefectural Board of Education and International Training Team of World Bureau, Council Commissioner of the Okinawa Prefectural Council of Boy Scouts of Nippon, and Vice-chairman of the Okinawa Marine Activity Center for Youth.

Mrs. Sekine is the former Saku Nishizawa. She attended Tokyo Women's College, Tokyo, Japan, and Graceland College, Lamoni, Iowa. They have a son, Yiyoshi, and a daughter, Michiyo.

Everett S. Graffeo was born in Mapleton, Iowa. He received a B.A. in religion from Graceland College, Iowa, and a M.A. degree in recreation administration from the University of Indiana. He was an administrative intern with the city of Philadelphia, Pennsylvania, from 1959 to 1961.

He became an appointee minister for the church in 1961 and has held the priesthood offices of priest (1957), elder (1960), seventy (1962), high priest (1972), and apostle (1980). He was campus minister at Graceland from May 1978 to May 1980. He was president of the Honolulu Metropole

(1973–1977), and administrator of the Hawaiian Region (1977–1978). For his outstanding work with the youth of the islands he holds the Medal of Honor of Youth and Sports from the French government which he received in 1969.

Mrs. Graffeo was formerly Judy Yarrington. They have three children: Steven, Angela, and Juli Ann.

Kenneth N. Robinson, who was born in Perth, Western Australia, received his bachelor's and master's of psychology degrees from the University of Western Australia. He served as a clinical psychologist for the Western Australia Mental Health Services and Child Welfare Services in Perth, as head of student counseling at Canberra College of Advanced Education, and from August 1972 to January 1977 was director of the Counseling Center of Australian National University in Canberra.

Brother Robinson was ordained a deacon (1961), a priest (1963), an elder (1967), and a high priest (1972).

An appointee minister from 1977, he became president of the Blue Valley Stake in 1978, and was ordained an apostle in 1980. His current assignment is as apostle in charge of missionary and administrative work in the Pacific Field, which includes the Australia-New Zealand, French Polynesia, and South Pacific regions.

Mrs. Robinson is the former Patricia Anne Moxham. They have three children: Jennifer Anne, Gail Annette, and Anthony Neal.

---

[1]Section 126:7b. [2]Section 125:2. [3]Section 147:5a. [4]Section 118. [5]Sections 120 to 125; Appendix E. [6]Section 122:7c.

SECTION 155

The revelation of 1982 is primarily concerned with changes in the personnel of the presiding quorums. Elder

Reed M. Holmes, who had served as presiding patriarch since the World Confernce of 1974, was relieved of further responsibility as presiding patriarch of the church although he remained as a member of the Order of Evangelists. He had shown concern for the developing of the work in the Holy Land, and his superannuation at this time gave him opportunity to pursue this interest more specifically.

The ministry of Elder Duane E. Couey had been of special value during the transition from the administration of President W. Wallace Smith to that of President Wallace B. Smith. As presiding patriarch he was relieved of the burden of presidential responsibility, except as this might develop from the spiritual needs which now became his special concern.

The first presiding evangelist of the church had been Joseph Smith, Sr., the father of the martyr. Hyrum, the older brother of Joseph, succeeded their father and was a close associate of Joseph for the remainder of their lives. He was killed at Carthage, Illinois, a few minutes before Joseph. Although William, the next surviving brother, was ordained to this office under the administration of Brigham Young, this ordination was never recognized by the Reorganization.

The call of evangelical ministers is the special responsibility of the Twelve, but uncertainty about the nature of the evangelical calling and the absence of men of stature who could be spared from the pressing missionary needs of the time (which were also their concern) delayed the filling of this office. A specific problem had to do with the importance of choosing a presiding officer so that the work of the evangelists could be rightly coordinated. The Twelve asked for guidance, but were told that the selection of a presiding patriarch was not yet "expedient" (Doctrine and Covenants 122:14). In 1897, however, after a renewed expression of need, Elder Alexander H. Smith, president of the Twelve, was called to be "patriarch to the church, and evangelical minister to the whole church" (Doctrine and Covenants 124:2a). Alexander also served as a counselor to his brother, Joseph, until the Presidency was reorganized in harmony with the revelation of 1902 (126:8). At first the growth of the order was quite slow, but it quickened after Elbert A. Smith became its presiding officer in 1938. The membership of the order when Elder Duane E. Couey became president was approximately 315.

"Test my words" (7). This invitation is not new. It has been extended to saints and inquirers in every dispensation (John 7:16–17). One of the best known references among Latter Day Saints is in Alma, where he likened minimal faith to a seed which is planted to test its vitality. Such planting accompanied by reasonable nurture makes for conviction.

"Be not overly concerned with methods" (7). The method of heartfelt personal testimony is basic. It can be augmented by appropriate aids, but these should not supersede personal element in witness. The prophetic word given to Martin Harris is of value here. Martin was one of the three witnesses of the Book of Mormon. He financed its publication, and loved to bear his testimony. But he was no theologian. So long as he testified of what he knew he was on solid ground. But when he was distracted and discussed "tenets" about which he was not informed he could be confused. When this happened it tended to cast discredit of his basic witness. So he was told, "Of tenets thou shalt not talk, but thou shalt declare repentance and faith on the Savior, and remission of sins by baptism and by fire; yea, even the Holy Ghost" (Doctrine and Covenants 18:4d). Martin Harris was not the first believer to be distracted by matters of secondary importance.

BIOGRAPHICAL NOTES

Reed M. Holmes (See notes on Section 141).
Duane E. Couey (See notes on Section 146).
Alan D. Tyree (See notes on Section 148).
John Cameron Stuart (See notes on Section 150).
Elder Joe A. Serig was born in Wheeling, West Virginia. He worked as a school administrator in San Jose, California, and graduated from the San Jose State College with an M.A. in

secondary education with "great distinction" and "departmental honors." His Ph.D. in higher education is from the University of Missouri in Kansas City, Missouri.

Elder Serig has been a full-time appointee minister of the church since 1971. Since then he has served as director of the Christian Education Department (1971–1973), Pastoral Services Commissioner (1973–1975), director of the Division of Program Services (1975–1978), director of the Division of Program Planning (1978–1982). He was ordained a deacon in 1953, an elder in 1956, and a high priest in 1964. An apostle since 1982, his current assignment is to the Europe-Africa field which includes the Europe Region, the British Isles Region, the Africa Region, and the American Indian Region.

Mrs. Serig is the former Beverly Jean Wilson. They have four children: Deborah, Marjorie, Craig, and Daniel.

James C. Cable, a graduate of the University of Kansas at Lawrence, Kansas, earned a master's degree in public administration from the University of Missouri–Kansas City. Later he was employed as editor of *Building Magazine*, a national real estate management journal. He served locally in the ministry as a priest (1967), elder (1972), and high priest (1975), and accepted appointment in May 1976. He was director of the Leadership Office 1969 to 1976. His current assignment is the Asia Field: Orient Region, India Region, and Southeast Asia Region. He is also the associate apostle in the North Central Field.

Elder Cable is married to the former Marlene Deaver. They have two daughters: Susan and Karen.

SECTION 156

The revelation dated April 3, 1984, called for the release from the Council of Twelve of Apostle Charles D. Neff and the ordination to membership in the apostolic council of Elder Geoffrey F. Spencer, for the acceleration of the work on the temple at Independence, for the enrichment of the quality of priesthood, and for the ordination of women properly called to the priesthood. The tone of the revelation is quietly persuasive and unhurried. It fits well into the mood of expansion being felt throughout the church. (See "Answers to Questions We've Heard," *Saints Herald,* June 1, 1984, pp. 3–6. In this article representative questions are answered in a nonargumentative manner. It is recommended as enlightening background material for those desiring to study the revelation further.)

"*Let this work* [on the building of the temple in the Center Place] *continue at an accelerated rate. . .for there is great need of the spiritual awakening that will be engendered by the ministries experienced within its walls*" (3).

The principle of building "temples" for the worship of God and the instruction of the priesthood and the Saints had been affirmed in the erection of the Kirtland (Ohio) temple (centennial March .27–29, 1936). Instruction concerning the building of another temple was given in April 1968 (Doctrine and Covenants 149:6; 149A 5–6) and in 1972 (150:8). It should be noted, however, that it is the principle of temple building and worship which is affirmed: The ordinances of the Hebrew temples belonged to a pre-Christian dispensation. The temple which is now proposed to be built is to be "dedicated to the pursuit of peace" (Doctrine and Covenants 156:5a). In this connection it is of interest to note that David, who had hoped to build the temple at Jerusalem, was not allowed to do this because he had been "a man of war" (I Chronicles 28:3; see also I Kings 5:3–5).

It is in the nature of our spiritual situation that the call to build the temple shall presuppose a spiritual awakening among the Saints. Worship in the temple will be distinctive, and preparation for that worship also must be uniquely suited to the worship which it anticipates. The spirit of such preparation and experience was a major emphasis in the work of the great Old Testament prophets (Amos 5:21; Hosea 6:6; Isaiah 1:11–15). The temple worship of our time is to be made known to the First Presidency (Doctrine and Covenants 149:6a).

"The church has experienced a loss of spiritual power" (7d). This occurs whenever members, priesthood or not, "stray" from the ordinances (Doctrine and Covenants 1:3d). Not a high proportion of those who are lost to the cause leave deliberately, intending to sever the ties in which they once delighted. Some drift away because no one goes after them, despite the clear duty of the elders and the Aaronic priesthood to "watch over" them (Doctrine and Covenants 17:8–10) and to "visit the house of each member, and exhort them to pray vocally and in secret" (Doctrine and Covenants 17:10b).

"I say to you now, as I have said in the past, that all are called according to the gifts which have been given them. This applies to priesthood as well as to any other aspects of the work" (9b).

To accept membership in the church of Jesus Christ is to respond to the call of Christ to be Saints (Romans 1:7; I Corinthians 1:2, etc). This response is not a single act, but a lifetime commitment calling for the dedication of heart, might, mind, and strength (Matthew 22:27–33; I Corinthians 1:23–31). There are distinctive areas of special calling within the calling to membership but they are not substitutes for it. Members of the priesthood, for example, are first of all members of the church, and within their general calling to active membership all are equal in the sight of God. Similarly, all members of the priesthood are equal in the sight of God. Perhaps the best known example of this equality occurs in Paul's letter to the saints in Corinth (I Corinthians 1:9–10, 3:2–11). But the principle has been restated in our generation: "There should be no conflict or jealousy of authority between the quorums of the church; all are necessary and equally honorable, each in its place" (Doctrine and Covenants 120:3a).

The members of the church together form the body of Christ. The priesthood are called of God, set apart to discharge certain functions within the body, and sustained by the church in these several callings. Without them the church would not survive. But the mutual dependence of both ministers and members is such that neither can rightly say to the other, "I have no need of thee" (I Corinthians 12:21. Read I Corinthians 12:12–27).

Down the generations, for a complexity of reasons, leaders in such areas as government, economics, and religion have said to women who have shown interest in these and related fields, "We have no need of thee." But in recent decades women have found places in many fields hitherto closed to them, and many have distinguished themselves. This has created pressures and expectations in all fields, including the Restoration. Evidence of this is available in a fifty-two-page booklet, *Resources for Women's Ministries*, issued in 1975 by the Women's Ministries Commission. It was able, affirmative, and challenging. Though not particularly argumentative, it called attention to so many things which need to be done, and to ways in which the women of the church can be organized to cooperate in getting them done, that opposition seemed unwarranted and wasteful. It discussed Women and the Leadership, Creative Organizational Possibilities, Delegation through Assistant Presiding Elders, The Conventional Women's Department (and variations), Tools for Ministry, Community Outreach, Strategies for Study, and related topics.

The foregoing is but an illustration of the many indicators pointing toward opportunities for augmenting the kingdom forces. The step toward the ordination of women to priesthood ministries, however, was not one to be taken lightly. A mere Conference resolution would not be enough. Surely, it seemed, this was a situation calling for recognition of the principle which Amos had set forth long ago and to which the church had turned from time to time: "Surely the Lord God will do nothing, until he revealeth the secret unto his servants the prophets" (Amos 3:7). Evidently the prophet himself, as well as many of the Saints, thought that this was an area of concern to which he should dedicate his fasting and his prayers (Doctrine and Covenants 156: Introduction and 9 and 10). And both the instruction received and the kindliness with which it was to be implemented made for its acceptance in freedom and unity.

There are references in the Old Testament to prophetesses: Miriam, Exodus 15:20-21; Deborah, Judges 4:4f; Huldah, II Kings 22:14. There are also references in the New Testament to prophetesses (Acts 21:8-9), although Anna is the only one whose name is mentioned (Luke 2:36). These were evidently persons of note, but their function is not clear, although it has been widely understood that they "gave inspired instruction in moral and religious truth" (Driver, Cambridge Bible).

On another level the term *deacon* occurs in the New Testament, but here, too, its precise meaning is not fully understood. Its primary meaning is "servant," but it is not clear as to whether this always refers to the service of an office in the church, although Romans 16:1 seems to point that way. The implication in I Timothy 3:2, 4, seems to be that the deacon is a man since his wife and family are mentioned. But by the time the local churches were well established and numerically strong, deacons and deaconesses were widely accepted as discharging important functions in the churches.

Analytical study of scriptural and historical records is fascinating and often enlightening. Where the need is urgent and the evidence uncertain, however, those who believe in divine guidance in situations of difficulty look for that guidance, and in it find wisdom and peace.

In the present situation of the church and of the world we can find no satisfaction in mere unwillingness to deviate from the practices of the past. The problems of our times are greater than ever before, and at the same time our resources are greater than ever before.

BIOGRAPHICAL NOTES

Charles D. Neff will be remembered for his leadership in the breaking down of racial prejudices, the opening of new fields, and his insistence on health and educational ministries among the underprivileged. He was president of Outreach International, and succeeded his friend Clifford A. Cole as president of the Twelve and director of Field Ministries in 1980. (See notes on Section 145).

Geoffrey F. Spencer, a native of Teralba, New South Wales, graduated from Newington College, New South Wales, in 1944, and holds a B.A. degree with a major in psychology from Sydney University, an M.A. in American History from the University of Missouri in Kansas City, Missouri, and an M.A. in divinity from the St. Paul School of Theology in Kansas City, Missouri, where he is currently a candidate for the degree of doctor of divinity. He has held the priesthood offices of deacon (1941), priest (1945), elder (1949), and high priest (1958). He was ordained an apostle in 1984.

Accepting church appointment in 1954, Elder Spencer was a missionary in South and West Australia for four years and president of the Hunter-Manning District and coordinator of departments and priesthood education for six years. The Spencer family came to the United States from Drummoyne, New South Wales, in 1966 when Elder Spencer was assigned to the Department of Religious Education where he was director of the Church School Division. He was commissioner of Religious Education (1970–1971) and president of the Quorum of High Priests and of the Temple School of Zion (1974–1982).

Mrs. Spencer is the former Jill Marcia Godwin. Their children are Paul, Mark, and Shelly.

APPENDIX A (107)

The introduction to the 1970 edition of the Doctrine and Covenants states:

This present edition is so arranged that the items of uncertain authority are included in a historical appendix and prefaced with introductions explaining circumstances of publication and the reasons for placement in the appendix.

Comments which appeared in earlier editions of the *Commentary* are included here for their historical value but should be read in connection with the introduction to Appendix A provided by the First Presidency.

Troubles between the Saints and their Gentile neighbors culminated finally in the infamous "extermination order" of Governor L. W. Boggs, October 27, 1838. This order stated that "the Mormons must be treated as enemies and must be exterminated or driven from the state if necessary for the public good." In pursuance of this order, Joseph and Hyrum Smith, Lyman Wight, Sidney Rigdon, Caleb Baldwin, and Alexander McRae were lodged in Liberty jail to await trial for treason and murder, and the Saints were required to make the following additional concessions:

Deliver up all arms in their possession.

Sign over their properties to defray the expenses of the "Mormon War."

Concentrate in Caldwell County for the winter and then leave the state.

With the other leaders of the church in prison, the exodus was conducted under the general supervision of the Twelve with Brigham Young at their head. Joseph and his companions escaped and traveled toward Illinois, arriving at Quincy, Illinois, April 22, 1839, about the time that the Saints were beginning to congregate in that vicinity. Quincy, Illinois, is about 200 miles from Far West, and there the Saints were received very hospitably. On the first of the next month land was purchased at Commerce, Illinois, and this became the center of the new settlement by the Saints. One year later, April 21, 1840, the name of the post office there was changed officially from Commerce to Nauvoo.

The following events witness to the fact that the church was again busy with constructive work:

July 7, 1839, the Twelve made their farewell address, and left for a mission to England.

October 5, 1839, the new location was organized into a stake by General Conference, William Marks being the first president.

November 1839 the first issue of *Times and Seasons* was published. At first it was a monthly paper; later it was issued twice monthly.

April 6, 1840, Orson Hyde was appointed on a mission to Palestine.

June 1, 1840, about 250 houses and many more buildings had been erected.

December 16, 1840, charters were granted for the city of Nauvoo, the Nauvoo Legion, and the University of the City of Nauvoo.

The year of 1841 opened in Nauvoo with fair prospects. The revelation now Section 107 was received there by the prophet Joseph, January 19, 1841.

"This stake. . . shall be polished with that refinement which is after the similitude of a palace" (1b). This was in part fulfilled, for Nauvoo grew rapidly and was soon the largest city in the state, a center of frontier culture, and a city of considerable commercial promise. Complete fulfillment of this prophecy is yet future.

"Call ye, therefore, upon them with loud proclamation, and with your testimony, fearing them not" (2a). The principle involved here is extremely important and deserves the careful thought of the Saints. The instruction to call upon the prominent people of the earth is not a prohibition from doing missionary work among less prominent people. It is a reminder, however, that the work of the church must be conducted on a plane which will commend it to honest men and women of good position. These have a right to hear the gospel in their own tongue, which may be the language of culture and of refinement just as other people of lesser culture have a right to hear the gospel presented in a way which will appeal to them. From some points of view, the Moravians have been the most active missionary denomination in Europe. Their success has been extremely limited, however,

since their work has been conducted almost exclusively among people who needed their help but were not qualified to furnish their part of the leadership needed to carry the movement forward.

"David Patten, who is with me at this time" (7b). Elder Patten had been killed in an engagement with the mob in Caldwell County, October 25, 1838.

"My servant, Edward Partridge" (7c). Bishop Partridge had died May 27, 1840, at Nauvoo, Illinois.

"My aged servant, Joseph Smith, Sr." (7c). Presiding Patriarch Joseph Smith had died September 14, 1840, from tuberculosis brought on by exposure.

"I seal upon his head the office of a bishop, like unto my servant Edward Partridge" (8b). There were other bishops in the church at this time, the best known probably being Bishop Newel K. Whitney, who had been bishop of Kirtland. Elder Miller, however, was set apart to be the presiding bishop of the church and continued in this office until superseded therein after the death of the Martyr.

"Build a house unto my name. . . a house for boarding, a house that strangers may come from afar to lodge therein" (9a, b). Those named in this communication to take stock in the boardinghouse immediately commenced their efforts to carry this instruction into effect. They applied to the legislature of Illinois for a charter, and the Nauvoo House Association was incorporated by act of the Legislature on February 23, 1841. The site, consisting of the south half of lot 156 of the city of Nauvoo, was procured from Joseph Smith, in consideration of which provision was made that his family should have place therein from generation to generation. The cornerstone was laid October 2, 1841, with imposing ceremonies, but since the temple was under construction at the same time and was considered of greater importance than the boardinghouse, the building of the hotel was retarded. At the time of the assassination of Joseph and Hyrum, the building was completed to the top of the windows of the second story. When Nauvoo was abandoned, the house was left in its uncompleted state.

After the Saints left Nauvoo, the title to the Nauvoo House passed into other hands, and Major Lewis Bidamon, the second husband of Emma Smith, later became the owner of the property. He built a substantial residence on the southwest corner by tearing down the wing and building up the corner to three stories. Title passed from Mr. Bidamon's son to Bishop E. L. Kelley, trustee in trust for the Reorganized Church of Jesus Christ of Latter Day Saints, October 13, 1909, for a consideration of $3,000.

"Build a house to my name, for the Most High to dwell therein" (10c). The church, having been reproved for attempting to build a temple at Far West before receiving a command to do so, had not undertaken to build at Nauvoo until after this command was given. Immediately after this revelation was received, however, plans were made and on April 6, 1841, the cornerstones were laid. The building of the temple was kept prominently before the Saints until the death of Joseph Smith in June 1844, but it would appear that the people were not as diligent or as sacrificing as they should have been, for the calamities predicted by Joseph Smith if the church should fail in this important work came upon the church, and the Saints were driven from Nauvoo.

It has been claimed by some that the temple was finished, but the evidence does not support this contention.[1] The temple stood in its uncompleted state until about the year 1848, when it was burned down.

The Nauvoo Temple was built of gray limestone and was 128 feet long, 88 feet wide, 60 feet high. It was 200 feet to the dome of the tower. The total cost of the building was about one million dollars.

"A baptismal font there is not upon the earth; that they, my saints, may be baptized for those who are dead; for this ordinance belongeth to my house" (10e). A temporary baptismal font was dedicated in the still uncompleted Nauvoo Temple November 8, 1841, and the first baptisms for the dead in the font were administered Sunday, November 21, 1841, by Elders Brigham Young, Heber C. Kimball, and John Taylor.

568

"Ye shall be rejected as a church with your dead" (11a). The history of the church during these difficult years indicates that the Saints became enamored of other things and put them before the building of the temple of the Lord. Because of this, the rejection here foreshadowed overtook them, and the reorganization of the church in 1852 and 1853 became necessary. Attention is invited to the following quotation from *One*, January, 1920:

> As in the case of the church when it was driven out of Jackson County, the rejection here spoken of was not the rejection of any one man; but the failure of the church as a whole to live up to the requirements that God had placed upon them. . . . Any man, either ordained or not, who lived up to the requirements of God, would not be rejected, but evidently the failure to build the temple at Nauvoo, under the circumstances, constituted an offense by the church, sufficient for its rejection.
>
> This temple was not finished; it was burned in 1848 and every stone thrown down, since which time the various fragments of the church, rejected by the Lord, have sought to reorganize. This was undoubtedly the right and prerogative of any man holding the priesthood, and the only means of telling who was right and where the truth was being honored was the observance of the acts of those seeking to reorganize. If they conformed to the constitutional and organic law of the church, contained in the revelations of God, they would be acceptable to him; otherwise they would not.

"My holy house, which my people are always commanded to build unto my holy name" (12c).

You will note that it does not state that my people are commanded to always build temples, but that my people are always commanded. This is not a general blanket command, which instructs the church to proceed with the building of temples, but just the opposite—a restriction, denying the church the right to build any temples without a command from God. Every temple built by the church of Christ before its rejection—or even started—was begun at the command of God. Once, at Far West, in 1838, the church appointed a committee to locate a building lot, and commence a temple; but when Joseph Smith came, he asked them to discontinue the work and abide the command of God; and it was not commenced until a revelation was given, directing such building.

Since 1968 the Reorganized Church has anticipated the building of a temple at Independence in the near future.[2]

"If you build a house unto my name, and do not do the things that I say, I will not perform the oath which I make unto you, neither fulfill the promises which ye expect at my hands" (14a). The position of the Reorganized Church in this matter is quite clear. The Saints in Nauvoo had been persecuted and driven from place to place. Now they found themselves in a position of political strength with excellent prospects for temporal prosperity. This seems to have been too much for them, and, like the Nephites, they became lifted up in pride and lost their zeal in performing the commands of the Lord. The prophet and patriarch were taken from among them, the temple and Nauvoo House remained uncompleted, and Nauvoo was left desolate. The church as an institution was rejected for failing to give heed to the commands of God, and it remained for those who were faithful and humble to submit themselves to the direction of Divinity for the rebuilding of his church and people.

"It behooveth me to require that work no more at the hands of those sons of men, but to accept of their offerings" (15b). Representatives of the dominant church in Utah have claimed that this paragraph specifically vindicates the Saints in Nauvoo who did not have opportunity to complete the temple. The position of the Reorganization, however, is that the facts of history show that if the Saints had been as diligent in building the temple as they were in their other activities, they could have completed it. Many other buildings were erected, and much work was done which could have waited until this primary task had been accomplished.

"Let my servant Joseph and his house have place therein, from generation to generation; for this anointing have I put upon his head, that his blessing shall also be put upon the head of his posterity after him" (18b). In consideration of the statements of this paragraph, Elder Heman C. Smith writes as follows:

The boardinghouse is the subject under consideration.

The family of Joseph Smith was to have place in that house from generation to generation forever and ever.

The reason for this is that they were to inherit the blessing of their father.

This blessing entitles them to hold the keys of the mysteries of the kingdom of heaven.

These keys belong always to the Presidency of the High Priesthood.

Hence the Presidency should be held by the posterity of Joseph.

It is quite fitting, therefore, that this revelation shall affirm that in Joseph Smith and his seed "shall the kindred of the earth be blessed."[3]

"Let it be a delightful habitation for man, and a resting place for the weary traveler, that he may contemplate the glory of Zion, and the glory of this the corner stone thereof; that he may receive also the counsel from those whom I have set to be as plants of renown, and as watchmen upon her walls" (18d, e).

Here we have the purpose of the house described as being a resting place for the "weary traveler, that he may contemplate the glory of Zion, and the glory of this the cornerstone thereof; that he may receive also the counsel from those whom I have set to be as plants of renown, and as watchmen upon her walls." This being the purpose of the house, does it not follow that those whom God decreed should remain in the house, notwithstanding their property rights were no better than others, were "set to be as plants of renown and as watchmen" upon the walls of Zion? Someone may ask, Could they not "be as plants of renown, and as watchmen" without being in the Presidency? In a general sense they might be; but this indicates that their counsel was to be in a special manner sought by the investigator. Why should they be thus specially pointed out and located where their counsel could be had unless their position was to be a special one? Had Nauvoo been built up according to the command of God, this provision would doubtless now be in force.[4]

"Publish the new translation of my holy word unto the inhabitants of the earth" (28b). William Law was a well-to-do young man of great ability. He here is called to be counselor to Joseph Smith in place of Hyrum, who is

designated as successor to his father as presiding patriarch of the church. It is therefore quite appropriate that the task of publishing the Inspired Version of the Holy Scriptures should be given to William Law. This assignment was never fulfilled, and the Inspired Version of the Holy Scriptures was not published until issued by the Reorganized Church in 1867.

"Crowned with the same blessing, and glory, and honor, and priesthood, and gifts of the priesthood, that once were put upon him that was my servant Oliver Cowdery" (29e). Oliver, who had once been known as the second elder of the church, had been disassociated from his former companions for about two years. He was missed greatly, yet Hyrum Smith had proved to be such a tower of strength that his commendation in this revelation is not at all surprising. In later years his nephew, Alexander H. Smith, who had succeeded him in the office of presiding patriarch of the church, also was officially associated with the president of the church (1897-1902).

"If my servant Sidney will serve me, and be counselor unto my servant Joseph, let him arise and come up and stand in the office of his calling and humble himself before me" (32a). For some time Sidney Rigdon had been in ill health brought on in part by the privations which he had suffered. In harmony with this exhortation Elder Rigdon again became active in the Presidency, even though his popularity had waned somewhat. In 1843 he was suspected of treasonable correspondence with ex-Governor Carlin and others but at the conference of that year he was exonerated completely.

"First, I give unto you Hyrum Smith to be a patriarch unto you, to hold the sealing blessings of my church" (38). Some query has arisen because Hyrum, who was presiding patriarch, here is mentioned before Joseph, who was president of the church. The exact reason for this is not apparent from the revelation. It is nevertheless noteworthy that Hyrum is designated "a prophet, and a seer and a

revelator" to the church and instructed to "act in concert" with Joseph.[5] His work is likened to that of Oliver Cowdery, who was the "second elder" of the church. As presiding patriarch, Hyrum held a position of major spiritual significance, akin to that of Joseph but without administrative duties. This near equality with Joseph, coupled with freedom from the vexatious problems of Presidency, made Hyrum an important factor in the subsequent life of the church.

"The twelve traveling council" (40a). Only six of the apostles chosen in 1835 now remained in the Quorum of Twelve (Brigham Young, Heber C. Kimball, Parley P. Pratt, Orson Pratt, Orson Hyde, and William Smith). William E. McLellin, Luke S. Johnson, John F. Boynton, and Lyman E. Johnson had been expelled in the troubles of 1837-1838. Thomas B. Marsh, first president of the quorum, was expelled March 15, 1839, because of his association with the enemies of the Saints. David W. Patten had been killed October 25, 1838, in the Missouri troubles. John Taylor and John E. Page had been ordained apostles December 19, 1838; Wilford Woodruff and George A. Smith, April 26, 1839; and Willard Richards in England April 14, 1840. Lyman Wight was ordained an apostle April 8, 1841, to fill the vacancy occasioned by the death of Apostle Patten.

"Standing presidents or servants over different stakes scattered abroad" (42a). This seems to indicate that stakes are not necessarily contiguous. The stakes at one time formed a continuous area, but other stakes have since been organized at greater distances from the center place and without all the intervening distances being organized into stakes.

"The one has the responsibility of presiding from time to time, and the other has no responsibility of presiding" (44c). It is in harmony with their calling that the seventies shall work under the direction of the Twelve in extending the gospel into new territory. In so doing they have no need of presiding authority in the local sense. They are elders, however, and when not acting as missionaries can, of course, function as local presiding officers in harmony with their

573

Melchisedec priesthood. Sometimes both missionary and local functions are combined. This is desirable only in preeminently missionary situations.

BIOGRAPHICAL NOTES

Robert B. Thompson was born October 1, 1811, in England, and joined the church in Canada in May 1836. Elder Thompson was general church recorder from 1840 to 1841, was a colonel in the Nauvoo Legion, and in May 1841 was associated with Don Carlos Smith as editor of the *Times and Seasons*. He died August 27, 1841.

John C. Bennett was born in Massachusetts in 1804. He joined the church soon after the Saints moved to Nauvoo. He was a man of many gifts, and it seemed that he would be a valuable addition to the organization. After a time, however, it became apparent that he had not entirely forsaken his earlier impure way of life, and he was excommunicated from the church in May 1843 and thereafter became one of its most bitter enemies. He was at one time mayor of Nauvoo and brigadier-general of the Nauvoo Legion.

Lyman Wight (see notes on Section 52).

George Miller, who was baptized in July 1839, was called to the Presiding Bishopric in this revelation and ordained in February 1841. He was ordained by the First Presidency "under the hands of Elder William Marks." He succeeded Don Carlos Smith as president of the Quorum of High Priests on August 7, 1841, and after the assassination of Joseph was relegated to the position of "second bishop." Newel K. Whitney became Presiding Bishop in his place when Bishop Miller was discovered to be unwilling to recognize the authority of Brigham Young.

William Law was born September 8, 1809, and converted at Toronto, Canada, when he was about thirty years of age. He joined the Saints at Nauvoo in the latter part of 1839. He was called to succeed Hyrum Smith as counselor to the President of the church January 19, 1841, but after a few years partook of the spirit of apostasy and was excommunicated in 1844. He is generally credited with being sympathetic to the movement which resulted in the martyrdom of Joseph and Hyrum.

---

[1]*Journal of History*, Volume 3, pages 149-163. [2]Section 149:6. [3]Heman C. Smith, *True Succession in Church Presidency*, page 45. [4]*Ibid.* pages 42, 43. [5]Section 107:29.

APPENDIX B (Section 109)

A letter addressed to the Saints in Nauvoo and dated September 1, 1842, was published in the *Times and Seasons* shortly thereafter.[1] This letter was included in the second edition of the Doctrine and Covenants, issued about September 1844 from Nauvoo, Illinois, by John Taylor of the Quorum of Twelve and editor of the *Times and Seasons*. We do not know by what authority it was inserted among the revelations. It was nevertheless retained in subsequent editions of the Doctrine and Covenants published by the Utah church and in those published by the Reorganization prior to 1970. Its publication as an appendix, for its historical value, was authorized by the World Conference of that year.

On Monday, August 8, 1842, Joseph Smith was arrested by the deputy sheriff of Adams County and two assistants on a warrant issued by Governor Carlin of Illinois, founded on a requisition from Governor Reynolds of Missouri, on the charge of "being an accessory before the fact, to an assault with an intent to kill, made by one O. P. Rockwell, on Lilburn W. Boggs (ex-governor of Missouri) on the night of May 6, 1842." O. P. Rockwell was arrested at the same time. After the formalities of the arrest had been gone through, the officers returned to Governor Carlin for further instructions, taking with them the original writ. Without this writ it was illegal for the marshall to hold the two brethren, and so they went about their business. When it was later desired to apprehend him, Joseph Smith felt that public sentiment was so strong that he should stay in hiding until the excitement had died down. He accordingly lived at various places in Nauvoo for the next several months, and it was during this period that he wrote the letters contained in Sections 109 and 110. Joseph continued to avoid arrest until January 1, 1843, when Governor Carlin was succeeded by Governor Thomas Ford. Joseph and his friends were anxious to test the legality of his arrest as soon as the way was clear, and they therefore requested Governor Ford to issue a duplicate warrant. Upon receiving this, Joseph went to Springfield, Illinois, and surrendered. He was discharged by the circuit court of the United States for the district of Illinois on the ground that his arrest was illegal.[2]

"The work of my temple" (4a). This was the temple at Nauvoo. Work on this temple continued intermittently, but the structure was not finished at the death of Joseph nor was it ever fully completed.

"A word in relation to the baptism for your dead" (5a). This doctrine had been mentioned as early as the revelation of January 19, 1841 (Section 107:19-12), and had been practiced to some degree following that time, but no baptisms for the dead were performed in the temple until the temporary baptismal font was first used Sunday, November 21, 1841, by Elders Brigham Young, Heber C. Kimball, and John Taylor.[3]

---

[1]*Times and Seasons* 3:919. [2]Church History, Volume 2, pages 621-637. [3]Note the comments concerning baptism for the dead in Appendix A (1970).

APPENDIX C (Section 110)

The letter of Joseph Smith written September 1, 1842, was followed by a second letter dated September 6, 1842.[1] It was written and became part of the book of Doctrine and Covenants under the same conditions as the earlier letter.

The first paragraphs of the letter are concerned with recording the baptisms of the dead, and Joseph quotes Revelation 20:12 as scriptural authority for his great concern in this matter.

Paragraphs 8 to 11 are concerned with the authority for baptism for the dead and with vindicating the rights of the priesthood as indicated in Matthew 16:18-20.

Paragraphs 12 to 16 discuss the importance of the symbolism of baptism, both for the living and for the dead.

Paragraphs 17 and 18 discuss the importance of baptism for the dead in relating "the hearts of the fathers to the children and the hearts of the children to their fathers" (Malachi 4:4, 5).

The remainder of the letter seeks to encourage the Saints by reminding them of the great blessings they had received. The following are mentioned specifically: Moroni and the coming forth of the Book of Mormon; the vision of the three witnesses of the Book of Mormon; Joseph's vision of Michael (Adam) on the banks of the Susquehanna River; the vision of Peter, James, and John, who held the keys of authority of the dispensation of the fullness of time; the revelation of the voice of God in the home of Father Whitmer, where the church was organized.

BAPTISM FOR THE DEAD[2]

The Quorum of Twelve presented a series of preambles and resolutions to the General Conference of 1884, and among others the following was adopted by the conference:

Resolved that it is the sense of this quorum that the commandments of a local character, given to the first organization of the church, are binding on the Reorganization, only so far as they are either reiterated or referred to as binding by commandment to this church.

When Jason W. Briggs, Zenos H. Gurley, and four others withdrew from the church at the conference of 1886, they stated among their reasons for so doing their inability to believe in the doctrine of baptism for the dead. The

577

document of withdrawal was referred to a committee consisting of E. L. Kelley, I. L. Rogers, and Heman C. Smith, who, in their reply, pointed out that baptism for the dead is one of the local questions referred to in the resolution of 1884. This report was adopted by the body.[3]

---

[1]*Times and Seasons* 3:934. [2]See Introduction to   Appendixes A and C. [3]Church History 4:524-528.

APPENDIX D (Section 113)

This report of the assassination of Joseph and Hyrum Smith was probably written by John Taylor, editor of *Times and Seasons* and member of the Twelve. He had been with Joseph and Hyrum at Carthage and was wounded in the attack in which they were killed. This statement was placed at the end of the Nauvoo edition of the Doctrine and Covenants and retained the same relative position until the General Conference of 1970. At that time it was ordered transferred to its present place among the appendixes.

The appendix is particularly important in that it gives a contemporary picture of the attitude of the church toward Joseph and Hyrum Smith at the time of their death and advances the Book of Mormon and the book of Doctrine and Covenants as worthy contributions to the religious literature of the world.

The General Conference of 1896 gave serious consideration to the question whether this section should be continued in the Doctrine and Covenants. After debate, a resolution was adopted providing for its continued publication with an appended explanation by the president of the church and the Board of Publication.

Section 113 is not a revelation, nor is there in it any statement of faith, doctrine, or belief which by its publication is made part of the church articles and covenants. It was published in the editions of 1845, in England and America,

578

and all subsequent editions. The Reorganized Church has deemed it better to leave it in than to invent excuses for not publishing. So far as the facts are stated they are a part of the history of that event. (Also see commentary on pp. 399-402.)

APPENDIX E (Section 123)

Section 123 is not a revelation but is a report of the Joint Council of Presidency, Twelve, and Presiding Bishopric authorized in Section 122:13. Its publication in the Doctrine and Covenants was ordered by the General Conference of 1895 and its transfer became Appendix E by the Conference of 1970.

"Lamoni College" (4, 5, 6). After considerable pioneer work had been done by President Joseph Smith and others, the General Conference of 1890 authorized a committee to take steps to establish a college under church auspices. The 1894 Joint Council approved the work done to that date and gave impetus to the project. At the succeeding conference, the committee reported that forty acres of land had been donated for college grounds at Lamoni by Brother W. A. Hopkins, Sisters Marietta Walker, and M. A. Wickes, and that these together with twenty-six acres which the committee had purchased from Brother Hopkins would be devoted immediately to college purposes.

On September 17, 1895, Graceland College opened its doors in the "France Block" downtown in Lamoni, as the college building was not yet erected. The faculty consisted of Thomas J. Fitzpatrick, M.S.; Joseph T. Pence, A.B.; Jeremiah A. Gunsolley, B.S.; and Nellie Davis. The total enrollment was thirty-five students.

The cornerstone of the new college building was laid November 12, 1895, with Bishop E. L. Kelley presiding and President Joseph Smith officially laying the stone.

Joseph T. Pence, the first president of the college, served

579

until 1898, when he was succeeded by Ernest R. Dewsnup who served one year. He was succeeded by R. A. Harkness who served until 1901, when he was succeeded by H. S. Salisbury. Brother Salisbury was followed by C. C. Taylor and Charles M. Barber, acting presidents. In 1901 Ernest R. Dewsnup resumed the presidency of the college and continued until 1905. He was followed by Rolland Stewart, who served until 1908 when David A. Anderson came to the president's chair for one year. He was succeeded by J. A. Gunsolley as acting president. In 1913 Samuel A. Burgess came to the college as president for two years. George N. Briggs succeeded Brother Burgess and gave outstanding service until his retirement in 1944.[1] Later Graceland presidents have been E. J. Gleazer, Jr. (1946); Harvey Grice (1958); Earl T. Higdon (acting: 1964); William T. Higdon (1966); Velma Ruch (acting: 1974); Gerald Knutson (1975); and Franklin Hough (1977).

"*Write tracts. . .all of which shall be placed in the hands of the Presidency for examination*" (14). This is in harmony with the basic law of the church which makes the Presidency the primary teachers of the revelations and doctrines of the church.

"*Whether or not under certain circumstances the President would not be privileged to call others to assist him, is a query*" (21b). Since that time there have been occasions on which presidents of the high council have called special assistants to their aid. In so doing these members of the First Presidency do not vacate any of their rights as presiding officers of the council, but they seek expert assistance in matters requiring specialized knowledge.

"*The following opinion of the First Presidency, as communicated to the Quorum of the Twelve, in 1890, was adopted as the opinion of this joint council*" (23a). It should be noted that this "opinion" was communicated to the Twelve in an attempt to compromise differences prior to the revelations of 1890 and 1894. The "opinion" therefore has historical significance but lacks the authority of the revelations included in the Doctrine and Covenants.

"The committee as heretofore named" (25). This was the First Presidency (paragraph 14).

"The Herald" (25). The *Saints' Herald*, a twenty-page, octavo, monthly journal was first published in January 1860 in Cincinnati, Ohio, by Isaac Sheen, editor and manager. It continued to be published from Cincinnati until March 1863. The April issue of that year was printed and distributed from Plano, Illinois. President Joseph Smith succeeded Elder Isaac Sheen as editor of the *Herald* on May 1, 1865, and continued as senior editor until his death December 10, 1914, when editorial responsibility was assumed by Elbert A. Smith, who served as senior editor until July 11, 1915. At that time Frederick M. Smith and Elbert A. Smith were chosen joint editors. At the present date the members of the First Presidency are joint editors.

The *Herald* was published at Plano, Illinois, until October 1881. The November 1 issue of that year was published at Lamoni, Iowa, where it continued to be published until May 1921. The issues since May 24, 1921, have been published at Independence, Missouri. It was a weekly from January 1883, until January 1962, when it became a twice-monthly publication. Since January 1969 it has been a monthly.

BIOGRAPHICAL NOTES

George H. Hilliard was born at Senecaville, Guernsey County, Ohio, November 7, 1838. He joined the Reorganization July 3, 1867, and was ordained an elder February 9, 1868, and a seventy in January 1887. In April 1891 he became counselor to Presiding Bishop E. L. Kelley, and served here with distinction until his death October 8, 1912. Unlike later counselors in the Presiding Bishopric, he himself did not hold the office of bishop, although he was ordained to the high priesthood in April 1894.

Edwin A. Blakeslee (see also Sections 123, 130, 131), was a son of Presiding Bishop George A. Blakeslee and grandson of Apostle James Blakeslee. He was born at Galien, Michigan, July 18, 1865; baptized June 27, 1875; ordained an elder at Kirtland, Ohio, April 14, 1891, and counselor to Presiding

Bishop E. L. Kelley at the same time, serving in the Presiding Bishopric until the release of Bishop Kelley in April 1916. He was ordained high priest and bishop in Lamoni, April 19, 1913. He became the first general superintendent of the Sunday School Association at the time of its organization at Kirtland, April 4, 1891. He did not continue in the Presiding Bishopric after the release of Bishop Kelley.

---

[1]*Journal of History*, Volume 15, page 385.

APPENDIX F

Statements of Resignation and Acceptance

Approval of the revelation of 1976 (Doctrine and Covenants 152) opened the way for the orderly transition of the prophetic leadership of the church from the administration of W. Wallace Smith to that of his son, Wallace B. Smith.

On Monday, April 3, 1978, President W. Wallace Smith read a statement of resignation and instruction for the ordination of his successor. The Conference approved the recommended procedure. The statement of President W. Wallace Smith was as follows:

To the World Conference:

It was my happy privilege to respond to the leadings of the Spirit which prompted me to bring the document to the church at the World Conference held here in the Auditorium during March and April of 1976, which is now included in the Doctrine and Covenants as Section 152.

In that document Elder Wallace Bunnell Smith was named as Prophet and President-Designate and the one to succeed me in the office of Prophet, Seer, and Revelator and President of the High Priesthood and of the church.

Also, there were certain other provisions in the document, i.e., "...during a period of spiritual preparation and study approximating two years," and "...if he remain faithful...." Two years have passed since this document was presented to and acted on by the Conference for the church. It is my considered judgment, now sincerely expressed, that these two requirements have been met in a most admirable manner by the diligent application to duty of the Prophet-Designate.

Another provision in the document calls for this matter to be considered by the delegates to the World Conference and "...through the process of common consent of the body of my church, he is to be chosen as president...."

In conformity with the foregoing I hereby tender my resignation as prophet-president to become effective at the completion of the ordination of my successor. I now ask you to accept my resignation and to move as expeditiously as possible to implement the provisions contained in the 1976 document which was accepted as a revelation of the mind and will of God covering this very significant matter.

Further, in recognition of their responsibility in former situations pertaining to the setting apart of the President of the High Priesthood, members of the Council of Twelve will preside, with the President of the Council in the chair, during the consideration of the content of this letter of resignation.

If affirmative action is taken there will be an ordination service on Wednesday evening, April 5, to set apart Wallace B. Smith as the Prophet, Seer, and Revelator to succeed me in office. In the meantime and until the ordination has been completed, the Quorum of the Presidency under the direction of President W. Wallace Smith will continue to preside over the Conference.

After reading this statement President W. Wallace Smith left the Conference Chamber. Elder Clifford A. Cole, president of the Council of Twelve, who had been left in charge, asked that Elders D. V. Lents and C. D. Neff of the Twelve be associated with him in presiding. A motion was made by W. E. Timms and H. W. Black approving the ordination of Wallace B. Smith as president of the church. Elder Cole then asked President-Designate Wallace B. Smith to address the Conference.

ACCEPTANCE STATEMENT

I have read what some of the other men who have come to this moment in the life of the church have said, and I have been deeply moved by those statements. I sense now something of what they felt as they spoke to a Conference assembled to consider taking action to approve their ordination to the Presidency of the High Priesthood and of the Church.

I have stood in similar ways before to express my willingness to serve in particular priesthood offices or in specific assignments. In so doing I have always felt that, even though I might not feel adequate for the particular responsibility to which I was being called, I would go forward in faith, trusting my heavenly Father to use me in my weakness and sustain me for his purposes. The teachings of my father and mother, the great faith and wonderful examples which they set for me, have ever sustained me in that belief; and I thank my heavenly Father for such goodly parents.

I have never aspired to this particular office; and, as I have said on various occasions, there might be those who would say I have seemed at times to be running in the other direction. From the time I was a small boy, however, I have heard it said at various times and in various ways that some day I might be President of the Church. When I was very young that made me uncomfortable; as an adolescent, rebellious; and as an adult, with an active career in another profession, incredulous. Nevertheless, as I moved to Independence and found myself and my family being drawn more closely into the work of the church I found myself wondering from time to time if such a call

When my father did finally come to me over two years ago and affirm to me that he had received the indication that I should prepare for such a responsibility, my immediate reaction was to resist such a call. I felt that in my medical profession I was making a contribution, that I was ministering in a very real way to the needs of people, and I felt that such activity ought to be my reasonable service. But as I thought further about it and prayed for guidance the impression became stronger and stronger that such a call did indeed represent the will of my heavenly Father. And, believing that furthering the success of God's church here on earth is the most important and challenging work in which anyone could be engaged, I agreed to become President-Designate in April of 1976. Many times in the past two years the affirmation of that choice has been borne to me by the Spirit, and I rejoice that I am privileged to be a part of this great work.

As I come before you now to say that I will accept the will of the Conference in the matter of succeeding to the office of President and Prophet of the Church, however, I do so with no feeling of worthiness. In no sense do I feel deserving of such office. As I look back over the events of my life and perceive the pain that some of my choices have brought to other persons, as I review the many ways in which I have failed not only those who loved me or looked up to me but more importantly the ways I have often let sin separate me from my heavenly Father, I realize just how unworthy I am. Many times and in many ways I have separated myself from his love by my thoughts or actions, and for those things I am truly sorry. For those of you who have been offended at any time because of my actions, I hope that the sincerity of my repentance will be perceived by you, and I pray that the loving grace of Christ Jesus will cleanse my soul in such a way that I can be your servant through him to the edification of the church.

I would be remiss if I were not to mention my wife and family as I accept this responsibility. Anne has always been completely supportive of that which I have chosen to do. She was a great help in the early years of our marriage in sustaining us through the lean times of resident medical training, and she has always been the best example for me of a true Christian witness in her quiet but efficient and loving way. I appreciate that support more, perhaps, than I can ever express to her and pray that the affirming witness of the Spirit will minister to her and my three lovely daughters as together we seek to serve our heavenly Father.

If it be the will of the Conference I will strive to the best of my ability to bring a prophetic voice to the church. I deeply appreciate your prayers in my behalf up until now and earnestly solicit them for the days ahead as we move forward together in the cause of the kingdom.

After making his statement of acceptance Wallace B. Smith left the chamber.[1] Following his departure the Conference voted to "accept the resignation of W. Wallace Smith as president of the church as requested"[2] and to approve the ordination of Wallace B. Smith.

Elder Wallace B. Smith was ordained prophet, seer, and revelator to the church and the president of the High Priesthood of the church on April 5, 1978. Elders Duane E. Couey and Howard S. Sheehy, Jr., were set apart as counselors in the First Presidency and High Priesthood.[3]

At the afternoon session of the Conference on April 6, Wallace B. Smith was in the chair. He made a brief statement to the Conference, and then he and W. Wallace Smith withdrew. Apostles Lents and Neff were again associated with Apostle Cole in the chair. Apostle Neff read a revelatory document submitted by President Wallace B. Smith and dated April 6, 1978.[4]

Bishop F. E. Hanson and Ronald Van Fleet moved that the Conference accept the document from President Wallace B. Smith, dated April 6, 1978, as inspired counsel and direction to the church and authorize that it be included in the Doctrine and Covenants.[5] The elders mentioned in the document were called upon and addressed the Conference. Statements from the councils, quorums, and orders of the church and from the mass meeting of the elders and priests were read. The document had already been approved by these groups and it was approved section by section and then as a whole.

APPENDIX G

ORDINATION OF WALLACE B. SMITH

By Apostle Clifford A. Cole

O God, our heavenly Father, with profound awe we stand as thy servants in this sacred moment. We have placed our hands on the head of thy servant, Wallace Bunnell Smith, to ordain him a prophet and to set him in the midst of thy people to be the prophet, seer, and revelator and the President of the High Priesthood and of the Church. In days past we have

585

recognized thy Spirit moving to call him to this sacred service. Thy people gathered here in this Conference have expressed their approval. We ask thee now to bestow on him the mantle of this holy calling to which thou hast called him.

We pray, our Father, that thou wilt create in him a sense and an awareness of that living history that has brought us to this day, that thou wilt help him to see the power of thy hand across the broad sweep of time that has led us to this moment. Grant him the insight to see those directions of history pulling us into the tomorrows that he may prophetically understand and speak thy will for today. Assist him now to take his place among those great men and women of all ages in thy work which was and is and is to come.

We do not ask that thou wilt separate him from the struggles of this world. Indeed, let him share both the tears and the laughter, and wrestle with the perplexities that he may lead the church to be thy healing, reconciling, and saving power in the world. Give to him the capacity to understand that he may lead, and the power of presidency that he may preside over thy church. Let him have the wisdom to join structure and organization and facilities with spirit and divine purpose, that the church may be released from indecision and bondage. Let him walk among all people with a power to call them to repentance and to inspire them to preside over their own lives in the attitude of stewardship and responsibiity to each other and to thee.

Bless him, we ask, with a spirit of peace and serenity when tumult abounds. Give to him clarity of perception in the time when confusion reigns in the hearts of the multitude. And grant him vision when despair darkens the future. Give to him that physical and mental and emotional reserve of strength which is so important to meet the pressures of leadership. And bless the members of his family that they may share and understand his calling so they can sustain him in that sensitive, intimate way in which loved ones make each other strong. And, in the larger sense, O God, let us unite together behind this thy son in support of him as he takes his

place now at the head of thy church, We ask it in Jesus'
name. Amen.

---

¹*Saints Herald* 1978, p. 264. ²Official Minutes of the World Conference, April 3, 1978, p. 244. ³Doctrine and Covenants 153:2, 4. ⁴Doctrine and Covenants 153. ⁵World Conference Minutes 1978, p. 264.

ABOUT THE AUTHOR

F. Henry Edwards has served in General Church ministry since 1920. He was born in Birmingham, England, just before the turn of the century, and was first called to serve the church as a priest at the age of nineteen. In 1921 he came to the United States and entered Graceland College preparatory to more effective ministry. At the 1922 Conference he was ordained an apostle and served in the Council of Twelve for twenty-four years. In 1946 he was ordained counselor to President Israel A. Smith. He continued in the counselor position under President W. Wallace Smith until his release in April 1966. Since then he has served as a contributing editor to the *Saints Herald*, traveled extensively as a lecturer, and compiled four volumes of church history.

A prolific author, he has written many magazine articles, a number of study courses for church school, plus several books. Among his books are *Fundamentals*, *The Life and Ministry of Jesus*, *Missionary Sermon Studies*, *God Our Help*, *Authority and Spiritual Power*, *The Whole Wide World*, *All Thy Mercies*, *For Such a Time*, and *The Joy of Creation and Judgment*. He has also recently written a church history course for the Temple School.

Brother Edwards was married to Alice M. Smith in 1924. She died July 7, 1973. They had three children: Lyman F. and Paul M. (both appointee ministers) and the late Ruth Ellen (Mrs. L. D. Fairbanks).

Biographical Index

590